Presented by;

The Rotary Club
of **North Berwick**

to;

Grace McCallum

Oxford Mini School Dictionary

Chief Editor: Andrew Delahunty

OXFORD
UNIVERSITY PRESS

OXFORD
UNIVERSITY PRESS

Great Clarendon Street, Oxford OX2 6DP

Oxford University Press is a department of the University of Oxford.
It furthers the University's objective of excellence in research,
scholarship, and education by publishing worldwide in

Oxford   New York

Auckland Cape Town Dar es Salaam Hong Kong Karachi
Kuala Lumpur Madrid Melbourne Mexico City Nairobi
New Delhi Shanghai Taipei Toronto

With offices in

Argentina Austria Brazil Chile Czech Republic France Greece
Guatemala Hungary Italy Japan Poland Portugal Singapore
South Korea Switzerland Thailand Turkey Ukraine Vietnam

Oxford is a registered trade mark of Oxford University Press
in the UK and in certain other countries

© Oxford University Press 2016

Database right Oxford University Press (maker)

• First published 1998 • Revised first edition 2002 • Second edition 2007
• Third edition 2012 • This edition 2016

All rights reserved. No part of this publication may be reproduced,
stored in a retrieval system, or transmitted, in any form or by any means,
without the prior permission in writing of Oxford University Press, or as
expressly permitted by law, or under terms agreed with the appropriate
reprographics rights organization. Enquiries concerning reproduction
outside the scope of the above should be sent to the Rights Department,
Oxford University Press, at the address above

You must not circulate this book in any other binding or cover
and you must impose this same condition on any acquirer

British Library Cataloguing in Publication Data
Data available

ISBN: 978-0-19-274708-2

10 9 8 7

Printed in Italy

Paper used in the production of this book is a natural, recyclable product
made from wood grown in sustainable forests. The manufacturing process
conforms to the environmental regulations of the country of origin.

Contents

Preface

The *Oxford Mini School Dictionary* has been specially written for students aged 10 and above. It is particularly useful for students who are about to start secondary school and who need an up-to-date, student-friendly, quick-reference dictionary that they can use at home or at school. The dictionary is specially designed for students and includes a range of curriculum vocabulary, covering subjects such as Science, Information and Communication Technology, and Geography.

The *Vocabulary Toolkit* section offers guidance on such topics as prefixes and suffixes, confusable words and phrases, phrases from different languages, and idioms and proverbs.

The *Oxford Mini School Dictionary* can also be used very effectively in conjunction with the *Oxford Mini School Thesaurus* which offers further support in creative writing and vocabulary building.

The *Oxford Mini School Dictionary* gives all the information students need for exams in an accessible and portable format. Use of the dictionary will help students to develop the best English language skills and equip them with the best reading, writing and speaking skills for years to come.

The publishers and editors are indebted to all the advisors, consultants and teachers who were involved in the planning of this dictionary. Special thanks go to Andrew Delahunty, Chief Editor.

How to use this dictionary

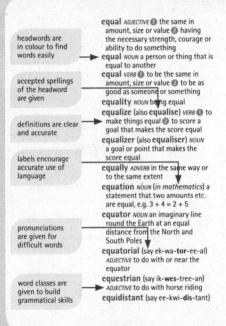

headwords are in colour to find words easily

→ **equal** ADJECTIVE ❶ the same in amount, size or value ❷ having the necessary strength, courage or ability to do something

equal NOUN a person or thing that is equal to another

accepted spellings of the headword are given

→ **equal** VERB ❶ to be the same in amount, size or value ❷ to be as good as someone or something

equality NOUN being equal

definitions are clear and accurate

→ **equalize** (also **equalise**) VERB ❶ to make things equal ❷ to score a goal that makes the score equal

equalizer (also **equaliser**) NOUN a goal or point that makes the score equal

labels encourage accurate use of language

equally ADVERB in the same way or to the same extent

equation NOUN (in mathematics) a statement that two amounts etc. are equal, e.g. $3 + 4 = 2 + 5$

pronunciations are given for difficult words

equator NOUN an imaginary line round the Earth at an equal distance from the North and South Poles

equatorial (say ek-wa-**tor**-ee-al) ADJECTIVE to do with or near the equator

word classes are given to build grammatical skills

equestrian (say ik-**wes**-tree-an) ADJECTIVE to do with horse riding

equidistant (say ee-kwi-**dis**-tant)

vi

Aa

a *DETERMINER* (called the *indefinite article* and changing to an before most vowel sounds) ❶ one (but not any special one) ❷ each; per

aback *ADVERB* ➤ **taken aback** surprised and slightly shocked

abacus (say ab-a-kus) *NOUN* a frame with rows of beads that slide on wires, used for counting and adding

abandon *VERB* ❶ to stop doing something when it becomes impossible ❷ to leave someone or something without intending to return

abandon *NOUN* a careless and uncontrolled manner

abashed *ADJECTIVE* feeling guilty and embarrassed

abate *VERB* to become less or die down

abattoir (say ab-at-wahr) *NOUN* (*British*) a place where animals are killed for food; a slaughterhouse

abbess *NOUN* the head of a convent

abbey *NOUN* ❶ a monastery or convent ❷ a church that was once part of a monastery

abbot *NOUN* the head of an abbey of monks

abbreviate *VERB* to shorten a word or phrase

abbreviation *NOUN* a shortened form of a word or words, especially one using the initial letters, such as St. or USA

abdicate *VERB* a queen or king abdicates if they give up the throne

abdomen (say ab-dom-en) *NOUN* ❶ the lower front part of a person's or animal's body, containing the stomach, intestines and other digestive organs ❷ the rear section of an insect's body

abduct *VERB* to take a person away by force and against their will; to kidnap someone

abet *VERB* to help or encourage someone to commit a crime

abhor *VERB* (*formal*) to hate or dislike something very much

abhorrence *NOUN* hatred or strong dislike

abide *VERB* abides, abiding, abided ❶ you can't abide something when you detest it or can't bear it ❷ to abide by a promise or agreement is to keep it and do what you said you would

abiding *ADJECTIVE* lasting or permanent

ability *NOUN* ❶ ability is being able to do something ❷ an ability is a special skill or talent

abject (say ab-jekt) *ADJECTIVE* ❶ hopeless or pitiful ❷ grovelling or humiliating

ablaze *ADJECTIVE* ❶ on fire and burning fiercely ❷ full of bright light or colours

able *ADJECTIVE* ❶ having the power or skill or opportunity to do something ❷ skilful or clever

able-bodied *ADJECTIVE* fit and healthy; not disabled

abnormal *ADJECTIVE* not normal; unusual

aboard *ADVERB & PREPOSITION* on or

into a ship or aircraft or train

abode NOUN (formal) the place where someone lives

abolish VERB to put an end to a law or custom

abolition (say ab-ol-**ish**-on) NOUN getting rid of a law or custom

abominable ADJECTIVE very bad or unpleasant

abomination NOUN something that disgusts you

aborigine (say ab-er-**ij**-in-ee) NOUN one of the original inhabitants of a country

abort VERB to put an end to something before it has been completed

abortion NOUN an operation to remove an unborn child from the womb before it has developed enough to survive

abound VERB ❶ things abound when there are a lot of them ❷ a place abounds in things when there are a lot of them there

about PREPOSITION ❶ near in amount or size or time; approximately ❷ on the subject of; in connection with ❸ all round; in various parts of

about ADVERB ❶ in various directions ❷ not far away

above PREPOSITION ❶ higher than ❷ more than

above ADVERB at or to a higher place or point

above board ADJECTIVE & ADVERB honest; without deception

abrasion NOUN an area of skin that has been scraped

abrasive ADJECTIVE ❶ something

abrasive rubs or scrapes things ❷ a person is abrasive when they are harsh or hurtful in what they say

abreast ADVERB ❶ side by side ❷ to keep abreast of a situation is to have all the most recent information about it

abroad ADVERB (British) in or to another country

abrupt ADJECTIVE ❶ sudden and unexpected ❷ rather rude and unfriendly

abscess (say **ab**-sis) NOUN an inflamed place where pus has formed in the body

abseil VERB (British) to lower yourself down a steep cliff or rock by sliding down a rope

absence NOUN not being in the place where you are expected

absent (say **ab**-sent) ADJECTIVE not in the place you should be; not present

absent (say ab-**sent**) VERB ➤ absent yourself to stay away from somewhere you should be

absentee NOUN a person who is not present when they are expected to be

absent-minded ADJECTIVE having your mind on other things; forgetful

absolute ADJECTIVE complete; not restricted

absolutely ADVERB ❶ completely ❷ (informal) yes, I agree

absolute zero NOUN the lowest possible temperature, calculated as -273.15°C

absolve VERB ❶ to clear a person of blame or guilt ❷ to release

a person from a promise or
obligation

absorb VERB ❶ to soak up a liquid
or gas ❷ to receive something and
reduce its effects ❸ to take up a
person's attention or time

absorbent ADJECTIVE able to soak up
liquids easily

abstain VERB ❶ to keep yourself
from doing something you enjoy
❷ to choose not to use your vote

abstinence NOUN going without
something, especially from alcohol

abstract (say **ab**-strakt) ADJECTIVE
❶ to do with ideas and not with
physical things ❷ an abstract
painting or sculpture shows the
artist's ideas or feelings rather
than showing a recognizable
person or thing

abstract (say **ab**-strakt) NOUN
❶ a summary of a longer piece of
writing ❷ an abstract painting or
sculpture

abstract (say ab-**strakt**) VERB
(*formal*) to take something out or
remove it

absurd ADJECTIVE ridiculous or
foolish

absurdity NOUN something that is
ridiculous or foolish

abundance NOUN a large amount
of something, often more than
you need

abundant ADJECTIVE things are
abundant when there are plenty
of them

abuse (say ab-**yooz**) VERB ❶ to
use something badly or wrongly;
to misuse something ❷ to hurt
someone or treat them cruelly

❸ to say unpleasant things about
a person or thing

abuse (say ab-**yooss**) NOUN ❶ a
misuse of something ❷ physical
harm or cruelty done to someone
❸ words that offend or insult a
person

abusive ADJECTIVE rude and insulting

abysmal (say ab-**iz**-mal) ADJECTIVE
extremely bad

abyss (say ab-**iss**) NOUN a deep
dark hole or pit that seems to go
on for ever

academic ADJECTIVE ❶ to do with
education or studying, especially
at a school or college or university
❷ theoretical; having no practical
use

academic NOUN a university or
college teacher

academy NOUN ❶ a school
or college, especially one for
specialized training ❷ a society of
scholars or artists

accede (say ak-**seed**) VERB ❶ to
accede to a request or suggestion
is to agree to it ❷ to accede to the
throne is to become queen or king

accelerate VERB to become
quicker; to increase speed

acceleration NOUN ❶ the rate
at which the speed of something
increases ❷ the rate of change
of velocity

accelerator NOUN the pedal that
a driver presses to make a motor
vehicle go faster

accent (say **ak**-sent) NOUN ❶ the
way a person pronounces the
words of a language ❷ the
emphasis or stress used in

a b c d e f g h i j k l m n o p q r s t u v w x y z

3

pronouncing a word **❸** a mark placed over a letter to show how it is pronounced, e.g. in *résumé*

accentuate (say ak-**sent**-yoo-ayt) *VERB* to make something more obvious

accept *VERB* **❶** to take a thing that is offered or presented to you **❷** to say yes to an invitation or offer

acceptable *ADJECTIVE* good enough to accept; satisfactory

acceptance *NOUN* **❶** accepting something, such as an invitation or offer **❷** agreeing with something and approving of it

access (say **ak**-sess) *NOUN* **❶** a way to enter or reach something **❷** the right to use or look at something

access *VERB* to read and use the information that has been stored in a computer

accessible *ADJECTIVE* able to be reached or understood easily

accession *NOUN* reaching a rank or position; becoming king or queen

accessory (say ak-**sess**-er-ee) *NOUN* **❶** an extra thing that goes with something **❷** a person who helps someone else to commit a crime

accident *NOUN* something unexpected that happens, especially when something is broken or someone is hurt or killed

accidental *ADJECTIVE* happening or done by accident

accidentally *ADVERB* to do something accidentally is to do it by mistake or without meaning to

acclaim *VERB* to praise someone or something enthusiastically

acclaim *NOUN* enthusiastic praise

acclimatize (also **acclimatise**) *VERB* to become used to a new climate or new surroundings

accolade (say ak-ol-**ayd**) *NOUN* praise or a prize given to someone for something they have done

accommodate *VERB* **❶** to provide someone with a place to live, work or sleep overnight **❷** to help someone by providing what they need

accommodation *NOUN* somewhere to live, work or sleep overnight

accompany *VERB* **❶** to go somewhere with somebody **❷** to happen or appear with something else **❸** to play music, especially on a piano, that supports a singer or another musician

accomplice (say a-**kum**-pliss) *NOUN* a person who helps another in a crime or bad act

accomplish *VERB* to do something successfully

accomplished *ADJECTIVE* skilled or talented

accomplishment *NOUN* something you have achieved or are good at

accord *NOUN* agreement or consent

accord *VERB* **❶** to be consistent with something **❷** (*formal*) to give or grant something

accordance *NOUN* ➤ in accordance with in agreement with

accordingly *ADVERB* **❶** in the way that is suitable **❷** because of what has just been said; therefore

according to *PREPOSITION* **❶** used to show where a piece of

4

information comes from ❷ used to show how one thing relates to another

accordion NOUN a portable musical instrument like a large concertina with a set of piano-type keys at one end, played by squeezing it in and out and pressing the keys

accost VERB to go up to a person and speak to them, especially in an annoying way

account NOUN ❶ a description or story about something that has happened ❷ a statement of the money someone owes or has received; a bill ❸ an arrangement to keep money in a bank or building society ❹ an arrangement to use a computing or social media service

account VERB ➤ account for to explain why something happens

accountable ADJECTIVE responsible for something and having to explain why you have done it

accountant NOUN a person whose job is to record and organize the money a person or organization spends and receives

accounting NOUN the business of keeping financial accounts

accredited ADJECTIVE officially recognized

accumulate VERB ❶ to collect things or pile them up ❷ to increase in quantity

accumulator NOUN a large battery that can be recharged

accuracy NOUN being exactly right or correct

accurate ADJECTIVE correct or exact

accurately ADVERB correctly or exactly

accusation NOUN a statement accusing a person of a crime or doing something wrong

accuse VERB to say that a person has committed a crime or done something wrong

accustom VERB to be accustomed to something is to be used to it

ace NOUN ❶ a playing card with one spot ❷ (in tennis) a serve that is too good for the other player to reach ❸ a very skilful person

acetylene (say a-**set**-il-een) NOUN a gas that burns with a bright flame, used in cutting and welding metal

ache NOUN a dull continuous pain

ache VERB to have an ache

achieve VERB to succeed in doing or producing something

achievement NOUN something good or worthwhile that you have succeeded in doing

acid NOUN a chemical substance that contains hydrogen and neutralizes alkalis. The hydrogen can be replaced by a metal to form a salt.

acid ADJECTIVE ❶ sharp-tasting; sour ❷ looking or sounding bitter

acidic ADJECTIVE ❶ very sour ❷ containing acid

acknowledge VERB ❶ to admit that something is true ❷ to let someone know that you have received or noticed something ❸ to express thanks or appreciation for something

acne (say **ak**-nee) NOUN inflamed

a b c d e f g h i j k l m n o p q r s t u v w x y z

red pimples on the face and neck

acorn NOUN the seed of the oak tree

acoustic (say a-**koo**-stik) ADJECTIVE ❶ to do with sound or hearing ❷ an acoustic guitar or other musical instrument does not use an electric amplifier

acoustics (say a-**koo**-stiks) PLURAL NOUN ❶ the qualities of a hall or room that make it good or bad for carrying sound ❷ the properties of sound

acquaint VERB to tell somebody about something

acquaintance NOUN ❶ a person you know slightly ❷ getting to know someone

acquiesce (say ak-wee-**ess**) VERB to agree to something, even though you might not like it completely

acquire VERB to get or be given something

acquisition NOUN ❶ something you have got or been given recently ❷ the process of acquiring something

acquit VERB to decide that somebody is not guilty of a crime

acre (say **ay**-ker) NOUN an area of land measuring 4,840 square yards or 0.405 hectares

acrid ADJECTIVE having a strong bitter smell or taste

acrobat NOUN a person who performs spectacular gymnastic feats for entertainment

acronym (say **ak**-ron-im) NOUN a word or name that is formed from the initial letters of other words and pronounced as a word in its own right

across PREPOSITION & ADVERB ❶ from one side to the other ❷ on the opposite side

acrostic NOUN a word puzzle or poem in which the first or last letters of each line form a word or words

acrylic (say a-**kril**-ik) NOUN a kind of fibre, plastic or resin made from an organic acid

acrylics PLURAL NOUN a type of paint used by artists

act NOUN ❶ something someone does ❷ a pretence ❸ one of the main divisions of a play or opera ❹ each of a series of short performances in a programme of entertainment ❺ a law passed by a parliament

act VERB ❶ to do something; to behave in a certain way ❷ to perform a part in a play or film etc. ❸ to function or have an effect

action NOUN ❶ doing something ❷ something you do ❸ a battle; fighting ❹ a lawsuit

action replay NOUN (British) playing back a piece of sports action on television, especially in slow motion

activate VERB to activate a machine or process is to start it working

active ADJECTIVE ❶ taking part in many activities; energetic ❷ functioning or working; in operation ❸ (in grammar) describing the form of a verb when the subject of the verb is performing the action. In 'The shop *sells* DVDs' the verb is active; in 'DVDs *are sold* by the shop' the verb is passive.

activist *NOUN* a person who takes action to try to bring about change, especially in politics

activity *NOUN* ❶ an activity is an action or occupation ❷ activity is doing things or being busy

actor *NOUN* a person who acts a part in a play or film etc.

actress *NOUN* a woman who acts a part in a play or film etc.

actual *ADJECTIVE* really happening or existing

actually *ADVERB* really; in fact

acupuncture (say ak-yoo-punk-cher) *NOUN* pricking parts of the body with needles to relieve pain or cure disease

acute *ADJECTIVE* ❶ sharp or strong ❷ having a sharp mind

acute accent *NOUN* a mark over a vowel, as over é in *résumé*

acute angle *NOUN* an angle of less than 90°

AD *ABBREVIATION* Anno Domini (Latin = in the year of Our Lord), used in dates counted from the birth of Jesus Christ

adamant (say ad-am-ant) *ADJECTIVE* determined not to change your mind

Adam's apple *NOUN* the lump at the front of a man's neck

adapt *VERB* ❶ to change something so that it is suitable for a new purpose ❷ to become used to a new situation

adaptation *NOUN* ❶ a play or film that is based on a novel etc. ❷ changing to suit a new situation

adaptor *NOUN* a device that

connects pieces of electrical or other equipment

add *VERB* ❶ to put one thing with another ❷ to make another remark

addenda *PLURAL NOUN* things added at the end of a book

adder *NOUN* a small poisonous snake

addict *NOUN* a person who does or uses something that they cannot give up

addicted *ADJECTIVE* not able to give up a habit or drug

addictive *ADJECTIVE* causing a habit that people cannot give up

addition *NOUN* ❶ the process of adding ❷ something added

additional *ADJECTIVE* extra; as an extra thing

additive *NOUN* a substance added to another in small amounts for a special purpose, e.g. as a flavouring

addled *ADJECTIVE* muddled or confused

address *NOUN* ❶ the details of the place where someone lives or of where letters or parcels should be delivered to a person or firm ❷ (*in computing*) a string of characters which shows a destination for email messages or the location of a website ❸ a speech to an audience

address *VERB* ❶ to write an address on a letter or parcel ❷ to make a remark or speech to somebody

adenoids *PLURAL NOUN* thick spongy flesh at the back of the nose and throat, which can make breathing difficult

adept (say a-dept) *ADJECTIVE* very good or skilful at something

adequate *ADJECTIVE* enough or

7

good enough

adhere VERB ❶ to stick to something ❷ to adhere to a belief or rule is to keep to it

adherent (say ad-**heer**-ent) NOUN a person who supports a certain group or theory etc.

adhesive ADJECTIVE sticky; causing things to stick together

adhesive NOUN a substance used to stick things together; glue

Adi Granth (say ah-di-**grunt**) NOUN the holy book of the Sikhs

adjacent ADJECTIVE near or next to

adjective NOUN a word that describes a noun or adds to its meaning, e.g. *big, honest, strange*

adjourn (say a-**jern**) VERB ❶ to break off a meeting until a later time ❷ to break off and go somewhere else

adjust VERB ❶ to change something slightly, especially because it is not in the right position ❷ to adjust to something new is to get used to it

adjustment NOUN a small change that you make to something

ad-lib VERB to say or do something without any rehearsal or preparation

administer VERB ❶ to give or provide something ❷ to make sure that something is carried out properly ❸ to control or manage the affairs of a business, organization or country

administration NOUN ❶ the work of running a business or governing a country ❷ the group of people who run an organization; the government of a country

❸ administering something

administrative ADJECTIVE to do with running a business or country

administrator NOUN a person who helps to run a business or organization

admirable ADJECTIVE worth admiring; excellent

admiral NOUN a naval officer of high rank

admiration NOUN a feeling of thinking that someone or something is very good

admire VERB ❶ to think that someone or something is very good ❷ to look at something and enjoy it

admission NOUN ❶ permission to go in ❷ the charge for being allowed to go in ❸ a statement admitting something; a confession

admit VERB ❶ to allow someone or something to come in ❷ to say reluctantly that something is true; to confess something

admittance NOUN permission to go in, especially to a private place

admittedly ADVERB as an agreed fact; without denying it

admonish VERB to tell someone that you do not approve of what they have done or to warn them

ado NOUN ➤ **without more or further ado** without wasting any more time

adolescence (say ad-ol-**ess**-ens) NOUN the time between being a child and being an adult

adolescent NOUN a young person at the age between being a child and being an adult

adolescent *ADJECTIVE* at the age between being a child and being an adult

adopt *VERB* ① to take a child into your family as your own child ② to accept something; to take something up and use it

adorable *ADJECTIVE* lovely; sweet and attractive

adore *VERB* to love a person or thing very much

adorn *VERB* to decorate something or make it pretty

adrenalin (say a-**dren**-al-in) *NOUN* a hormone produced when you are afraid or excited. It stimulates the nervous system, making your heart beat faster and increasing your energy and your ability to move quickly.

adrift *ADJECTIVE & ADVERB* a boat is adrift when it is drifting and out of control

adult (say **ad**-ult) *NOUN* a fully grown person or animal

adultery *NOUN* a sexual relationship between a married person and someone who is not their husband or wife

advance *NOUN* ① a forward movement ② a development or improvement ③ a loan of money or a payment made before it is due

advance *ADJECTIVE* given or arranged beforehand

advance *VERB* ① to move forward ② to make progress

advanced *ADJECTIVE* at a high level; highly developed

advantage *NOUN* ① something useful or helpful ② (in tennis) the

next point won after deuce

advantageous (say ad-van-**tay**-jus) *ADJECTIVE* giving an advantage; beneficial

Advent *NOUN* the period just before Christmas, when Christians celebrate the coming of Christ

advent *NOUN* the arrival of a new person or thing

adventure *NOUN* ① an exciting or dangerous experience ② doing exciting and daring things

adventurous *ADJECTIVE* liking to do exciting and daring things

adverb *NOUN* a word that adds to the meaning of a verb or adjective or another adverb and tells how, when or where something happens, e.g. *gently, soon* and *upstairs*

adverbial *NOUN* a group of words that functions as an adverb. Examples of adverbials are *last night* in the sentence *We saw him last night* and *more or less* in the sentence *She had more or less finished.*

adversary (say **ad**-ver-ser-ee) *NOUN* an opponent or enemy

adverse (say **ad**-vers) *ADJECTIVE* bad or harmful

adversity *NOUN* trouble or misfortune

advert *NOUN* (*British*) (*informal*) an advertisement

advertise *VERB* ① to give out information about the good features of a product or service in order to get people to buy it or use it ② to make something publicly known ③ to give information

9

about someone you need for a job

advertisement NOUN a public notice or announcement, especially one advertising goods or services in newspapers, on posters or in broadcasts

advice NOUN ① telling someone what you think they should do ② a piece of information

advisable ADJECTIVE that is the wise or sensible thing to do

advise VERB ① to tell someone what you think they should do ② to inform someone about something

advocate (say **ad**-vok-ayt) VERB to speak in favour of something; to recommend something

advocate (say **ad**-vok-at) NOUN ① a person who recommends or publicly supports something ② a lawyer presenting someone's case in a law court

aerial NOUN a wire or rod for receiving or transmitting radio or television signals

aerial ADJECTIVE from or in the air or from an aircraft

aerobatics PLURAL NOUN a spectacular display by flying aircraft

aerobics PLURAL NOUN exercises to improve your breathing and strengthen the heart and lungs

aerodynamic ADJECTIVE designed to move through the air quickly and easily

aeronautics NOUN the study of aircraft and flying

aeroplane NOUN (British) a flying vehicle with wings and at least one engine

aerosol NOUN a container that holds a liquid under pressure and can let it out in a fine spray

aerospace NOUN the industry of building aircraft, vehicles and equipment to be sent into space

aesthetic (say iss-**thet**-ik) ADJECTIVE to do with beauty or art

afar ADVERB far away

affable ADJECTIVE polite and friendly

affair NOUN ① an event or matter ② a brief romantic relationship between two people who are not married to each other

affairs PLURAL NOUN the business and activities that are part of private or public life

affect VERB ① to have an effect on someone or something; to influence them ② to pretend to have or feel something

affectation NOUN unnatural behaviour that is intended to impress other people

affected ADJECTIVE unnatural and meant to impress other people

affection NOUN a strong liking for a person

affectionate ADJECTIVE showing affection; loving

affidavit (say af-id-**ay**-vit) NOUN a statement that someone has written down and sworn to be true, for use as legal evidence

affinity NOUN a close similarity, relationship or understanding between two things or people

affirm VERB to state something definitely or firmly

affirmative ADJECTIVE that says

'yes' Compare with **negative**.

affix (say a-**fiks**) VERB to affix something is to stick it on to something else

affix (say **aff**-iks) NOUN a prefix or suffix

afflict VERB to be afflicted with something unpleasant, such as a disease or problem, is to suffer from it

affluent (say **af**-loo-ent) ADJECTIVE having a lot of money; wealthy

afford VERB ❶ to have enough money to pay for something ❷ to be able to do something without suffering bad consequences ❸ to have enough time to do something

affront VERB to insult or offend someone

affront NOUN an insult

afield ADVERB at or to a distance; away from home

aflame ADJECTIVE & ADVERB in flames; glowing

afloat ADJECTIVE & ADVERB floating; on the sea

afoot ADJECTIVE happening or likely to happen

afraid ADJECTIVE frightened or alarmed

afresh ADVERB again; in a new way

African ADJECTIVE to do with Africa or its people

African NOUN an African person

African Caribbean NOUN a person of African descent living in or coming from the Caribbean

Afrikaans (say af-rik-**ahns**) NOUN a language developed from Dutch, used in South Africa

Afrikaner (say af-rik-**ah**-ner) NOUN a white person in South Africa whose language is Afrikaans

Afro-Caribbean NOUN & ADJECTIVE African Caribbean

aft ADVERB at or towards the back of a ship or aircraft

after PREPOSITION ❶ later than ❷ next in position or order ❸ trying to catch; following ❹ as a result of ❺ in imitation or honour of ❻ about or concerning

after ADVERB later

afterbirth NOUN the placenta and other membranes that come out of the mother's womb after she has given birth

aftermath NOUN events or circumstances that come after something bad or unpleasant

afternoon NOUN the time from noon or lunchtime to evening

aftershave NOUN a pleasant-smelling lotion that men put on their skin after shaving

afterthought NOUN something you think of or add later

afterwards ADVERB after that; at a later time

again ADVERB ❶ another time; once more ❷ as before

against PREPOSITION ❶ touching or hitting ❷ opposed to; not in favour of ❸ in order to protect you from

age NOUN ❶ how old you are; the length of time a person has lived or a thing has existed ❷ a special period of history or geology

age VERB to become old or to make someone old

aged ADJECTIVE ❶ (say ayjd) having the age of ❷ (say **ay**-jid) very old

agency NOUN an office or business that provides a special service

agenda (say a-**jen**-da) NOUN a list of things that people have to do or talk about at a meeting

agent NOUN ❶ a person or business that organizes things for other people ❷ a spy

aggravate VERB ❶ to make a thing worse or more serious ❷ (informal) to annoy someone

aggregate (say **ag**-rig-at) ADJECTIVE combined or total

aggregate NOUN a total amount or score

aggression NOUN starting an attack or war; aggressive behaviour

aggressive ADJECTIVE likely to attack people; forceful

aggressor NOUN the person or nation that started an attack or war

aggrieved (say a-**greevd**) ADJECTIVE resentful because you think you have been treated unfairly

aghast ADJECTIVE shocked and horrified

agile ADJECTIVE moving quickly or easily

agility NOUN the ability to move quickly or easily

agitate VERB ❶ to make someone feel upset or anxious ❷ to shake something about

aglow ADJECTIVE glowing

agnostic (say ag-**nost**-ik) NOUN a person who believes that it is

impossible to know whether God exists

ago ADVERB in the past

agog ADJECTIVE eager and excited

agonizing (also **agonising**) ADJECTIVE ❶ causing great pain or suffering ❷ an agonizing choice or decision is one that you find very difficult to make

agony NOUN very great pain or suffering

agree VERB ❶ to agree with someone is to think or say the same as they do ❷ to agree to do something is to say that you are willing to ❸ to suit a person's health or digestion ❹ to correspond in grammatical number, gender or person. In 'They were good teachers' they agrees with teachers (both are plural forms) and were agrees with they; was would be incorrect because it is singular.

agreeable ADJECTIVE ❶ willing to agree to something ❷ pleasant or enjoyable

agreement NOUN ❶ having the same opinion ❷ an arrangement that people have agreed on

agriculture NOUN cultivating land on a large scale and rearing livestock; farming

aground ADVERB & ADJECTIVE stuck on the bottom in shallow water

ah EXCLAMATION a cry of surprise, pity, admiration, etc.

ahead ADVERB ❶ further forward; in front ❷ before; more advanced ❸ winning

ahoy EXCLAMATION a shout used by

sailors to attract attention

aid NOUN ❶ help ❷ something that helps someone to do something more easily ❸ money, food, etc. sent to another country to help it

aid VERB to help someone

aide NOUN an assistant

Aids NOUN a disease caused by the HIV virus, which greatly weakens a person's ability to resist infections

ail VERB (old use) to make a person ill or troubled

ailing ADJECTIVE ❶ ill; in poor health ❷ in difficulties; not successful

ailment NOUN a slight illness

aim VERB ❶ to point a gun or other weapon at a target ❷ to throw or kick a ball etc. in a particular direction ❸ to try or intend to do something

aim NOUN ❶ aiming a gun or other weapon ❷ a purpose or intention

aimless ADJECTIVE without a definite aim or purpose

air NOUN ❶ the mixture of gases that surrounds the earth and which everyone breathes ❷ the space around and above things ❸ an appearance or impression of something ❹ a grand or haughty manner

air VERB ❶ to put clothes etc. in a warm place to finish drying ❷ to allow air to circulate round a room ❸ to express an opinion or complaint

airborne ADJECTIVE ❶ an aircraft is airborne when it has taken off and is in flight ❷ carried by the air

air-conditioning NOUN a system for controlling the temperature,

purity, etc. of the air in a room or building

aircraft NOUN an aeroplane, glider or helicopter etc.

aircraft carrier NOUN a large ship with a long deck where aircraft can take off and land

airfield NOUN an area equipped with runways etc. where aircraft can take off and land

air force NOUN the part of a country's armed forces that is equipped with aircraft

airgun NOUN a gun in which compressed air shoots a pellet or dart

airily ADVERB in a casual way that shows you are not treating something as serious

airline NOUN a company that provides a regular service of transport by aircraft

airliner NOUN a large aircraft for carrying passengers

airlock NOUN ❶ a compartment with an airtight door at each end, through which people can go in and out of a pressurized chamber ❷ a bubble of air that stops liquid flowing through a pipe

airmail NOUN letters and parcels carried by air

airman NOUN a man who is a member of an air force or of the crew of an aircraft

airport NOUN a place where aircraft land and take off, with passenger terminals and other buildings

air raid NOUN an attack by aircraft, in which bombs are dropped

airship NOUN a large balloon

13

with engines, designed to carry passengers or goods

airstrip NOUN a strip of ground prepared for aircraft to land and take off

airtight ADJECTIVE not letting air in or out

airy ADJECTIVE ❶ with plenty of fresh air ❷ casual and not treating something as serious

aisle (rhymes with *mile*) NOUN ❶ a passage between rows of seats, pews in a church or shelves in a supermarket ❷ a side part of a church

ajar ADVERB & ADJECTIVE slightly open

akimbo ADVERB ► arms akimbo with hands on hips and elbows out

akin ADJECTIVE related or similar to

alabaster (say al-a-bast-er) NOUN a kind of hard white stone

à la carte ADJECTIVE & ADVERB ordered and paid for as separate items from a menu

alacrity NOUN speed and willingness

alarm NOUN ❶ a warning sound or signal; a piece of equipment for giving this ❷ a feeling of fear or worry ❸ an alarm clock

alarm VERB to make someone frightened or anxious

alarm clock NOUN a clock that can be set to ring or bleep at a fixed time to wake someone who is asleep

alas EXCLAMATION a cry of sorrow

albatross NOUN a large seabird with very long wings

albino (say al-been-oh) NOUN a

person or animal with no colouring pigment in the skin and hair (which are white)

album NOUN ❶ a book with blank pages in which you keep a collection of photographs, stamps, autographs, etc. ❷ a collection of songs on a CD, record or other medium

albumen (say al-bew-min) NOUN the white of an egg

alchemy (say al-kim-ee) NOUN an early form of chemistry, the chief aim of which was to turn ordinary metals into gold

alcohol NOUN ❶ a colourless liquid made by fermenting sugar or starch ❷ drinks containing this liquid (e.g. wine, beer, whisky), that can make people drunk

alcoholic ADJECTIVE containing alcohol

alcoholic NOUN a person who is seriously addicted to alcohol

alcove NOUN a section of a room that is set back from the main part

alder NOUN a kind of tree, often growing in marshy places

alderman (say awl-der-man) NOUN a senior member of an English county or borough council

ale NOUN a type of beer

alert ADJECTIVE watching for something; ready to act

alert NOUN a warning or alarm

alert VERB to warn someone of danger etc.; to make someone aware of something

A level NOUN (in the UK except Scotland) an exam in a subject taken by school students aged

14

16–18, or the course leading up to it; short for Advanced Level

alfresco ADJECTIVE & ADVERB in the open air

algae (say al-jee) PLURAL NOUN plants that grow in water, with no true stems or leaves

algebra (say al-jib-ra) NOUN mathematics in which letters and symbols are used to represent quantities

algorithm NOUN a process or set of rules a computer uses to make calculations or to solve a problem

alias (say ay-lee-as) NOUN a false or different name

alias ADVERB also named

alibi (say al-i-by) NOUN evidence that a person accused of a crime was somewhere else when it was committed

alien (say ay-lee-en) NOUN ❶ in stories, a being from another world ❷ a person who is not a citizen of the country where he or she is living; a foreigner

alien ADJECTIVE ❶ foreign ❷ not natural or familiar

alienate (say ay-lee-en-ayt) VERB to make someone less friendly or sympathetic towards you

alight ADJECTIVE ❶ on fire ❷ bright or shining

alight VERB ❶ to get out of a vehicle or down from a horse etc. ❷ to fly down and settle

align (say a-lyn) VERB to arrange things so they are in the correct position or form a straight line

alike ADJECTIVE like one another

alike ADVERB in the same way

alimentary canal NOUN the tube along which food passes through the body

alive ADJECTIVE ❶ living ❷ you are alive to something if you are well aware of it

alkali (say alk-al-y) NOUN a chemical substance that neutralizes an acid to form a salt

all DETERMINER the whole number or amount of

all PRONOUN ❶ everything ❷ everybody

all ADVERB ❶ completely ❷ to each team or competitor

Allah NOUN the Muslim name of God

allay (say a-lay) VERB to calm or relieve an unpleasant feeling

all-clear NOUN a signal that a danger has passed

allegation (say al-ig-ay-shon) NOUN a statement accusing someone of doing something wrong, made without proof

allege (say a-lej) VERB to accuse someone of doing something wrong without being able to prove it

allegiance (say a-lee-jans) NOUN loyal support

allegory (say al-ig-er-ee) NOUN a story in which the characters and events represent or symbolize a deeper meaning, e.g. to teach a moral lesson

alleluia EXCLAMATION praise to God

allergic ADJECTIVE you are allergic to something that is normally safe when it makes you feel ill or unwell

allergy (say al-er-jee) NOUN a

condition of the body that makes you react badly to something that is normally safe

alleviate (say a-**lee**-vee-ayt) VERB to alleviate a pain or difficulty is to make it less severe

alley NOUN ❶ a narrow street or passage ❷ a place where you can play skittles or tenpin bowling

alliance (say a-**leye**-ans) NOUN an agreement between countries or groups who wish to support each other and work together

allied ADJECTIVE ❶ joined as allies; on the same side ❷ of the same kind; closely connected

alligator NOUN a large reptile of the crocodile family

alliteration NOUN the repetition of the same letter or sound at the beginning of several words, e.g. in *whisper words of wisdom*

allocate VERB to give things to a number of people

allot VERB to give a number of things to different people

allotment NOUN a small rented piece of public land used for growing vegetables, fruit or flowers

allow VERB ❶ to let someone do something ❷ to decide on a certain amount for a particular purpose

allowance NOUN an amount of money that is given regularly for a particular purpose

alloy NOUN a metal formed by mixing two or more metals etc.

all right ADJECTIVE & ADVERB ❶ satisfactory ❷ in good

condition ❸ yes, I agree

all-round ADJECTIVE (British) able to do many different things well; general

allude VERB to mention something briefly or indirectly

allure VERB to attract or fascinate someone

allusion NOUN a reference made to something without actually naming it

ally (say **al**-eye) NOUN ❶ a country that has agreed to support another country ❷ a person who cooperates with another person

ally VERB to form an alliance

almanac NOUN an annual publication containing a calendar and other information

almighty ADJECTIVE ❶ having complete power ❷ (informal) very great

almond (say **ah**-mond) NOUN an oval edible nut

almost ADVERB near to being something but not quite

alms (say ahmz) PLURAL NOUN (old use) money and gifts given to the poor

almshouse NOUN a house founded by charity for poor people

aloft ADVERB high up; up in the air

alone ADJECTIVE & ADVERB without any other people or things; without help

along PREPOSITION following the length of something

along ADVERB ❶ on or onwards ❷ accompanying somebody

alongside PREPOSITION & ADVERB next

16

to something; beside

aloof ADVERB apart; not taking part

aloof ADJECTIVE distant and not friendly in manner

aloud ADVERB in a voice that can be heard

alpha NOUN the first letter of the Greek alphabet, equivalent to Roman *A*, *α*

alphabet NOUN the letters used in a language, arranged in a set order

alphabetical ADJECTIVE to do with the alphabet

alpine ADJECTIVE to do with high mountains

already ADVERB by now; before now

Alsatian (say al-**say**-shan) NOUN a German shepherd dog

also ADVERB in addition; besides

altar NOUN a table or similar structure used in religious ceremonies

alter VERB to make something different in some way; to become different

alteration NOUN a change you make to something

alternate (say ol-**tern**-at) ADJECTIVE ❶ coming in turns, one after the other ❷ one in every two

alternate (say **ol**-tern-ayt) VERB to use or come in turns, one after the other

alternating current NOUN electric current that keeps reversing its direction at regular intervals

alternative ADJECTIVE for you to choose instead of something else

alternative NOUN one of two or more things that you can choose between

alternative medicine NOUN types of medical treatment that are not part of ordinary medicine. Acupuncture, homeopathy and osteopathy are all forms of alternative medicine

although CONJUNCTION though; in spite of the fact that

altimeter NOUN an instrument used in aircraft etc. for showing the height above sea level

altitude NOUN the height of something, especially above sea level

alto NOUN ❶ an adult male singer with a very high voice ❷ a female singer with a low voice

altogether ADVERB ❶ with all included; in total ❷ completely ❸ on the whole

aluminium NOUN a lightweight silver-coloured metal

always ADVERB ❶ at all times ❷ often or constantly ❸ whatever happens

Alzheimer's disease NOUN a serious disease of the brain which affects mainly older people and makes them confused and forgetful

a.m. ABBREVIATION before 12 o'clock midday

amalgam NOUN ❶ an alloy of mercury ❷ a mixture or combination

amass VERB to heap up or collect something

amateur (say **am**-at-er) NOUN a

person who does something for pleasure, not for money as a job

amateurish ADJECTIVE not done or made very well; not skilful

amaze VERB to surprise somebody greatly; to be difficult for somebody to believe

amazement NOUN a feeling of great surprise

amazing ADJECTIVE very surprising or remarkable; difficult to believe

ambassador NOUN a person sent to a foreign country to represent his or her own government

amber NOUN ① a hard clear yellowish substance used for making jewellery and ornaments ② a yellow traffic light shown as a signal for caution, placed between red for 'stop' and green for 'go'

ambiguous ADJECTIVE having more than one possible meaning; unclear

ambition NOUN ① a strong desire to do well and be successful ② something you want to do very much

ambitious ADJECTIVE ① wanting very much to do well and be successful ② difficult or challenging

amble VERB to walk at a slow easy pace

ambrosia (say am-**broh**-zee-a) NOUN something delicious

ambulance NOUN a vehicle equipped to take sick or injured people to hospital

ambush NOUN a surprise attack from a hidden place

ambush VERB to attack someone after lying in wait for them

amen EXCLAMATION a word used at the end of a prayer or hymn, meaning 'may it be so'

amenable (say a-**meen**-a-bul) ADJECTIVE willing to accept or try out a suggestion or idea

amend VERB to change something slightly in order to improve it

amend NOUN ➤ make amends to make up for having done something wrong

amendment NOUN a change that is made to a piece of writing, especially to a law

amenity (say a-**men**-it-ee or a-**meen**-it-ee) NOUN a pleasant or useful feature of a place

American ADJECTIVE ① to do with the continent of America ② to do with the United States of America

amethyst NOUN a purple precious stone

amiable ADJECTIVE friendly and good-tempered

amicable ADJECTIVE done in a friendly way, without argument

amid, amidst PREPOSITION in the middle of; among

amino acid (say a-**meen**-oh) NOUN an acid found in proteins

amiss ADJECTIVE wrong or faulty

ammonia NOUN a colourless gas or liquid with a strong smell

ammunition NOUN a supply of bullets, shells, grenades, etc. for use in fighting

amnesia (say am-**nee**-zee-a) NOUN loss of memory

amnesty NOUN a general pardon for people who have committed

18

a crime

amoeba (say a-**mee**-ba) NOUN a microscopic creature consisting of a single cell which constantly changes shape and can split itself in two

amok ADVERB ➤ **run amok** to rush about wildly in a violent rage

among, amongst PREPOSITION ❶ surrounded by; in the middle of ❷ between

amorous ADJECTIVE showing or feeling love or passion

amount NOUN ❶ a quantity ❷ a total

amount VERB ➤ **amount to** ❶ to add up to ❷ to be equivalent to

amp NOUN ❶ an ampere ❷ (informal) an amplifier

ampere (say **am**-pair) NOUN a unit for measuring electric current

ampersand NOUN the symbol &, which means 'and'

amphetamine NOUN a drug used as a stimulant

amphibian NOUN ❶ an animal able to live both on land and in water, such as a frog, toad, newt and salamander ❷ a vehicle that can move on both land and water

amphibious ADJECTIVE able to live or move both on land and in water

amphitheatre NOUN an oval or circular building without a roof and with rows of seats round a central arena

ample ADJECTIVE ❶ quite enough ❷ large

amplifier NOUN a piece of equipment for making a sound or electrical signal louder or stronger

amplify VERB ❶ to make a sound or electrical signal louder or stronger ❷ to give more details about something

amplitude NOUN (in science) the greatest distance that a wave, especially a sound wave, vibrates

amply ADVERB generously; with as much as you need or even more

amputate VERB to cut off an arm or leg by a surgical operation

amuse VERB ❶ to make a person laugh or smile ❷ to amuse yourself is to find pleasant things to do

amusement NOUN ❶ a game or activity that makes time pass pleasantly ❷ being amused

amusement park NOUN a large outdoor area with fairground rides and other amusements

amusing ADJECTIVE making you laugh or smile

an DETERMINER see **a**

anachronism (say an-**ak**-ron-izm) NOUN something wrongly placed in a particular historical period or regarded as out of date

anaemia (say a-**nee**-mee-a) NOUN a lack of red cells or iron in the blood, that makes a person pale and tired

anaesthetic (say an-iss-**thet**-ik) NOUN a substance or gas that makes you unable to feel pain

anaesthetist (say an-**ees**-thet-ist) NOUN a person trained to give anaesthetics

anagram NOUN a word or phrase made by rearranging the letters of another

anal (say **ay**-nal) ADJECTIVE to do

19

with the anus

analgesic (say an-al-**jee**-sik) NOUN a substance that relieves pain

analogous (say a-**nal**-o-gus) ADJECTIVE similar in some ways to something else and so able to be compared with it

analogy (say a-**nal**-oj-ee) NOUN a comparison or similarity between two things that are alike in some ways

analyse VERB ❶ to examine and interpret something ❷ to separate something into its parts

analysis NOUN analyses ❶ a detailed examination of something ❷ a separation of something into its parts

analyst NOUN a person who analyses things

anarchist (say **an**-er-kist) NOUN a person who believes that all forms of government are bad and should be abolished

anarchy (say **an**-er-kee) NOUN ❶ lack of government or control, leading to a breakdown in law and order ❷ complete disorder

anatomy (say an-**at**-om-ee) NOUN ❶ the study of the structure of the bodies of humans or animals ❷ the structure of an animal's body

ancestor NOUN anyone from whom a person is descended

anchor NOUN a heavy object joined to a ship by a chain or rope and dropped to the bottom of the sea to stop the ship from moving

anchor VERB ❶ to fix or be fixed by an anchor ❷ to fix something firmly

anchovy NOUN a small fish with a strong flavour

ancient ADJECTIVE ❶ very old ❷ belonging to the distant past

and CONJUNCTION ❶ together with; in addition to ❷ so that; with this result ❸ to

android NOUN (in science fiction) a robot that looks like a human being

anecdote NOUN a short amusing or interesting story about a real person or thing

anemone (say a-**nem**-on-ee) NOUN a plant with cup-shaped red, purple or white flowers

anew ADVERB again; in a new or different way

angel NOUN ❶ an attendant or messenger of God ❷ a very kind or beautiful person

angelic (say an-**jel**-ik) ADJECTIVE kind or beautiful; like an angel

angelica NOUN a sweet-smelling plant whose crystallized stalks are used in cookery as a decoration

anger NOUN a strong feeling that you want to quarrel or fight with someone

anger VERB to make a person angry

angle NOUN ❶ the space between two lines or surfaces that meet; the amount by which a line or surface must be turned to make it lie along another ❷ a point of view

angle VERB ❶ to put something in a slanting position ❷ to present news or a story from one point of view

angler NOUN a person who fishes with a fishing rod and line

20

Anglican ADJECTIVE to do with the Church of England

Anglo-Saxon NOUN ❶ an English person, especially at the time before the Norman conquest in 1066 ❷ the form of English spoken from about 700 to 1150; Old English

angry ADJECTIVE feeling that you want to quarrel or fight with someone

anguish NOUN severe suffering or misery

angular ADJECTIVE ❶ an angular person is bony and not plump ❷ having angles or sharp corners

animal NOUN ❶ a living thing that can feel and usually move about ❷ a cruel or uncivilized person

animate VERB ❶ to make a thing lively ❷ to produce something as an animated film

animated ADJECTIVE ❶ lively and excited ❷ an animated film is one made by photographing a series of still pictures and showing them rapidly one after another, so they appear to move

animation NOUN ❶ being lively or excited ❷ the technique of making a film by photographing a series of still pictures

animosity (say an-im-**oss**-it-ee) NOUN a feeling of strong dislike and anger towards someone

aniseed NOUN a sweet-smelling seed used for flavouring things

ankle NOUN the part of the leg where it joins the foot

annals PLURAL NOUN a history of events, especially when written

year by year

annex VERB ❶ to take control of another country or region by force ❷ to add or join a thing to something else

annexe NOUN a building added to a larger or more important building

annihilate (say an-y-il-ayt) VERB to destroy something completely

anniversary NOUN a day when you remember something special that happened on the same day in a previous year

annotate (say **an**-oh-tayt) VERB to add notes of explanation to something written or printed

announce VERB to make something known, especially by saying it publicly or to an audience

announcement NOUN a statement that tells people about something publicly or officially

announcer NOUN a person who announces items in a radio or television broadcast

annoy VERB ❶ to make a person slightly angry ❷ to be troublesome to someone

annoyance NOUN ❶ the feeling of being annoyed ❷ something that annoys you

annual ADJECTIVE ❶ happening or done once a year ❷ calculated over one year ❸ living for one year or one season

annual NOUN ❶ a book that comes out once a year ❷ a plant that lives for one year or one season

annul VERB to cancel a law or contract; to end something legally

anode NOUN the electrode by which

electric current enters a device. Compare with **cathode**.

anoint *VERB* to put oil or ointment on someone or something, especially in a religious ceremony

anomaly (say an-**om**-al-ee) *NOUN* something that does not follow the general rule or that is unlike the usual or normal kind

anon *ADVERB* (*old use*) soon

anon. *ABBREVIATION* anonymous

anonymous (say an-**on**-im-us) *ADJECTIVE* without the name of the person responsible being known or made public

anorak *NOUN* a thick warm jacket with a hood

anorexia (say an-er-**eks**-ee-a) *NOUN* an illness that makes a person so anxious to lose weight that he or she refuses to eat

anorexic *ADJECTIVE* suffering from anorexia

another *DETERMINER & PRONOUN* a different or extra person or thing

answer *NOUN* ❶ a reply ❷ the solution to a problem

answer *VERB* ❶ to give or find an answer to a question or for a person asking it ❷ to respond to a signal

ant *NOUN* a very small insect that lives as one of an organized group

antagonism (say an-**tag**-on-izm) *NOUN* an unfriendly feeling; hostility

antagonize (also **antagonise**) *VERB* to do something to make someone angry with you

anteater *NOUN* an animal that feeds on ants and termites

antelope *NOUN* a fast-running animal like a deer, found in Africa and parts of Asia

antenna *NOUN* ❶ a feeler on the head of an insect or crustacean ❷ an aerial

ante-room *NOUN* a room leading to a more important room

anthem *NOUN* a religious or patriotic song, usually sung by a choir or group of people

anther *NOUN* the part of a flower's stamen that contains pollen

anthill *NOUN* a mound of earth over an ants' nest

anthology *NOUN* a collection of poems, stories, songs, etc. in one book

anthrax *NOUN* a very serious disease of sheep and cattle that can also infect people

anthropoid *ADJECTIVE* looking like a human being

anthropology *NOUN* the study of human beings and their customs

anti- *PREFIX* against or preventing something (as in *antifreeze*)

anti-aircraft *ADJECTIVE* used against enemy aircraft

antibiotic *NOUN* a substance (e.g. penicillin) that destroys bacteria or prevents them from growing

antibody *NOUN* a protein that forms in the blood as a defence against certain substances which it then attacks and destroys

anticipate *VERB* ❶ to expect something to happen and be ready for it ❷ to look forward to something

anticipation NOUN looking forward to something

anticlimax NOUN a disappointing ending or result where something exciting had been expected

anticlockwise ADVERB & ADJECTIVE (British) moving in the opposite direction to the hands of a clock

antics PLURAL NOUN funny or foolish actions

anticyclone NOUN an area where air pressure is high, usually producing fine settled weather

antidote NOUN something that takes away the bad effects of a poison or disease

antifreeze NOUN a liquid added to water to make it less likely to freeze

antihistamine NOUN a drug that protects people against unpleasant effects when they are allergic to something

antimony NOUN a brittle silvery metal

antipathy (say an-tip-ath-ee) NOUN a strong dislike

antipodes (say an-tip-od-eez) PLURAL NOUN ► the Antipodes Australia, New Zealand and the areas near them, in relation to Europe ► Antipodean ADJECTIVE

antiquarian (say anti-kwair-ee-an) ADJECTIVE to do with the study of antiques

antiquated ADJECTIVE old-fashioned or out of date

antique (say an-teek) NOUN something that is valuable because it is very old

antique ADJECTIVE very old; belonging to the distant past

antiquity (say an-tik-wit-ee) NOUN ancient times

anti-Semitic (say anti-sim-it-ik) ADJECTIVE hostile or prejudiced towards Jews

antiseptic ADJECTIVE ❶ able to destroy bacteria, especially those that cause things to become septic or to decay ❷ thoroughly clean and free from germs

antiseptic NOUN a substance with an antiseptic effect

antisocial ADJECTIVE unfriendly or inconsiderate towards other people

antithesis (say an-tith-iss-iss) NOUN the antithesis of something is the exact opposite

antivirus ADJECTIVE designed to find and destroy computer viruses

antler NOUN the horn of a deer, which divides into several branches

antonym (say ant-on-im) NOUN a word that is opposite in meaning to another

anus (say ay-nus) NOUN the opening at the lower end of the alimentary canal, through which solid waste matter leaves the body

anvil NOUN a large block of iron on which a blacksmith hammers metal into shape

anxiety NOUN ❶ anxiety is a feeling of being worried ❷ an anxiety is something that you are worried about

anxious ADJECTIVE ❶ worried and slightly afraid ❷ wanting to do something very much

any DETERMINER & PRONOUN ❶ one or

any ADVERB at all; in some degree

some ❷ no matter which ❸ every

anybody PRONOUN any person

anyhow ADVERB ❶ anyway; in any case ❷ (*informal*) carelessly; in no special way

anyone PRONOUN anybody

anything PRONOUN any thing

anyway ADVERB whatever happens; whatever the situation may be

anywhere ADVERB in or to any place

anywhere PRONOUN any place

aorta (say ay-**or**-ta) NOUN the main artery that carries blood away from the left side of the heart

apart ADVERB ❶ away from each other; separately ❷ into pieces ❸ excluded

apartheid (say a-**part**-hayt) NOUN the political policy that used to be practised in South Africa, of keeping people of different races apart

apartment NOUN ❶ a set of rooms ❷ (*North American*) a flat

apathy (say **ap**-ath-ee) NOUN not having much interest in or caring about something

ape NOUN any of the four kinds of monkey (gorillas, chimpanzees, orangutans, gibbons) that do not have a tail

ape VERB to copy or imitate something, often in a ridiculous way

aperture NOUN an opening

apex (say **ay**-peks) NOUN the tip or highest point

aphid (say **ay**-fid) NOUN a tiny insect (e.g. a greenfly) that sucks the juices from plants

aphis (say ay-fiss) NOUN an aphid

apiece ADVERB to, for or by each

apologetic ADJECTIVE showing or saying that you are sorry

apologize (also **apologise**) VERB to tell someone that you are sorry for something you have done

apology NOUN ❶ a statement saying that you are sorry for doing something wrong or badly ❷ something very poor

Apostle NOUN in Christianity, any of the twelve men sent out by Christ to preach the Gospel

apostrophe (say a-**poss**-trof-ee) NOUN the punctuation mark (') used to show that letters have been missed out (as in *I can't* = I cannot) or to show that something belongs to someone (as in *the boy's book*; *the boys' books*)

app NOUN a computer program designed to do a particular job, especially one you use on a smartphone

appal VERB to shock somebody very much

apparatus NOUN the equipment for a particular experiment or task

apparel NOUN (*formal*) a person's clothes

apparent ADJECTIVE ❶ clear or obvious ❷ seeming; appearing to be true but not really so

apparently ADVERB as it seems; so it appears

apparition NOUN something that you imagine you can see, especially a ghost

appeal VERB ❶ to ask for something that you badly need ❷ to ask for a decision to be changed ❸ to seem attractive or interesting

appeal NOUN ❶ asking for something you badly need ❷ asking for a decision to be changed ❸ attraction or interest

appear VERB ❶ to come into sight; to begin to exist ❷ to seem ❸ to take part in a play, film or show etc.

appearance NOUN ❶ coming into sight ❷ taking part in a play, film or show etc. ❸ what somebody looks like; what something appears to be

appease VERB to calm someone down, often by giving them what they want

appendage NOUN something added or attached; a thing that forms a natural part of something larger

appendicitis NOUN inflammation of the appendix

appendix NOUN ❶ a small tube leading off from the intestine ❷ a section added at the end of a book

appetite NOUN ❶ desire for food ❷ an enthusiasm for something

appetizer (also **appetiser**) NOUN a small amount of food eaten before the main meal

appetizing (also **appetising**) ADJECTIVE appetizing food looks and smells good to eat

applaud VERB to show that you like something, especially by clapping your hands

applause NOUN clapping by the audience at the end of a performance

apple NOUN a round fruit with a red, yellow or green skin

appliance NOUN a device or piece of equipment

applicable (say **ap-lik-a-bul**) ADJECTIVE suitable or relevant

applicant NOUN a person who applies for a job or position

application NOUN ❶ a formal written request for something, such as a job ❷ a computer program or piece of software designed for a particular purpose ❸ the practical use of something ❹ hard work or effort

applied ADJECTIVE put to practical use

apply VERB ❶ to put or spread one thing on another ❷ to start using something ❸ to ask for something in writing ❹ something applies to a person or thing when it concerns them and they are affected by it

appoint VERB ❶ to choose a person for a job ❷ an appointed time is one officially decided on for a meeting or deadline

appointment NOUN ❶ an arrangement to meet or visit somebody at a particular time ❷ choosing somebody for a job ❸ a job or position

apportion VERB to divide something among people; to give someone a share of something

appraise VERB to judge the value or quality of a person or thing

appreciable ADJECTIVE large enough to be noticed or felt

appreciate VERB ❶ to enjoy or

25

value something ❷ to be grateful for something ❸ to understand something ❹ to increase in value

appreciation NOUN ❶ showing that you enjoy or value something ❷ the feeling of being grateful for something ❸ understanding of a situation or problem

appreciative ADJECTIVE ❶ showing pleasure or admiration ❷ grateful for something

apprehend VERB ❶ to seize or arrest someone ❷ to understand something

apprehension NOUN ❶ fear or worry ❷ the arrest of a person

apprehensive ADJECTIVE anxious or worried

apprentice NOUN a person who is learning a trade or craft by a legal agreement with an employer

apprentice VERB to give someone a position as an apprentice

apprenticeship NOUN the time when someone is an apprentice

approach VERB ❶ to come near ❷ to go to someone with a request or offer ❸ to set about doing something or tackling a problem

approach NOUN ❶ a way of dealing with something ❷ coming near ❸ a way or road leading up to something

approachable ADJECTIVE friendly and easy to talk to

appropriate (say a-**proh**-pree-at) ADJECTIVE suitable or right for a particular situation

appropriate (say a-**proh**-pree-ayt) VERB to take something, usually

without permission and use it as your own

approval NOUN ❶ thinking well of someone or something ❷ agreeing to a plan or request

approve VERB ❶ to say or think that a person or thing is good or suitable ❷ to agree formally to something

approximate (say a-**proks**-im-at) ADJECTIVE almost exact or correct but not completely so

approximate (say a-**proks**-im-ayt) VERB to be almost the same as something

approximately ADVERB roughly; almost exactly

approximation NOUN a number or amount that is a rough estimate and not exact

apricot NOUN a juicy orange-coloured fruit with a stone in it

April NOUN the fourth month of the year

apron NOUN ❶ a piece of clothing worn over the front of the body, especially to protect other clothes ❷ a hard-surfaced area on an airfield where aircraft are loaded and unloaded

apt ADJECTIVE ❶ to be apt to do something is to be likely to do it or to do it a lot ❷ appropriate or suitable

aptitude NOUN to have an aptitude for something is to be naturally good at it

aqualung NOUN a diver's portable breathing apparatus, with cylinders of compressed air connected to a face mask

aquamarine *NOUN* a bluish-green precious stone

aquarium *NOUN* a tank or building in which live fish and other water animals are displayed

aquatic *ADJECTIVE* to do with water or living in water

aquatint *NOUN* an etching made on copper by using nitric acid

aqueduct *NOUN* a bridge carrying a water channel across low ground or a valley

Arab *NOUN* a member of a Semitic people living in parts of the Middle East and North Africa

Arabic *ADJECTIVE* to do with the Arabs or their language

Arabic *NOUN* the language of the Arabs

Arabic numerals *PLURAL NOUN* the figures 1, 2, 3, 4, etc. Compare with Roman numerals.

arable *ADJECTIVE* arable land is suitable for ploughing or growing crops on

arachnid (say a-**rak**-nid) *NOUN* a member of the group of animals that includes spiders and scorpions

arbitrary (say **ar**-bit-ree-ee) *ADJECTIVE* chosen or done on an impulse, not according to a rule or law

arbour (say **ar**-ber) *NOUN* a shady place among trees

arc *NOUN* ① a curve; part of the circumference of a circle ② a luminous electric current passing between two electrodes

arcade *NOUN* a covered passage or area, especially for shopping

arcane *ADJECTIVE* secret or mysterious

arch *NOUN* ① a curved structure that helps to support a bridge or other building etc. ② something shaped like this

arch *VERB* to form something into an arch; to curve

arch *ADJECTIVE* pretending to be playful; mischievous

archaeology (say ar-kee-**ol**-oj-ee) *NOUN* the study of ancient civilizations by digging for the remains of their buildings, tools, etc. and examining them

archaic (say ar-**kay**-ik) *ADJECTIVE* belonging to former or ancient times

archangel *NOUN* an angel of the highest rank

archbishop *NOUN* the chief bishop of a region

arch-enemy *NOUN* a person's chief enemy

archer *NOUN* a person who shoots with a bow and arrows

archery *NOUN* the sport of shooting at a target with a bow and arrows

archipelago (say ark-i-**pel**-ag-oh) *NOUN* a large group of islands or the sea containing these

architect (say **ark**-i-tekt) *NOUN* a person who designs buildings

architecture *NOUN* ① the work of designing buildings ② a particular style of building

archive (say **ark**-yv) *NOUN* ① (also **archives**) a collection of old documents and records that show the history of an organization or community ② (*in computing*) a set of computer files that are stored and no longer in active use

archivist (say **ar**-kiv-ist) NOUN a person trained to deal with archives

archway NOUN an arched passage or entrance

arc lamp, arc light NOUN a light using an electric arc

arctic ADJECTIVE very cold

arduous ADJECTIVE needing much effort; difficult and tiring

area NOUN ❶ the extent or measurement of a surface; the amount of space a surface covers ❷ a particular region or piece of land ❸ a subject or activity

arena (say a-**reen**-a) NOUN an area with seats around it where sports events or concerts are held

argue VERB ❶ to say that you disagree; to exchange angry comments ❷ to state that something is true and give reasons

argument NOUN ❶ a disagreement or quarrel ❷ a reason or series of reasons someone puts forward

argumentative ADJECTIVE fond of arguing

aria (say **ar**-ee-a) NOUN a solo in an opera or oratorio

arid ADJECTIVE having little or no rain; dry and barren

arise VERB arises, arising, arose, arisen ❶ to come into existence; to come to people's notice ❷ (old use) to rise; to stand up

aristocracy (say a-ris-**tok**-ra-see) NOUN people of the highest social rank; members of the nobility

aristocrat (say **a**-ris-tok-rat) NOUN

a member of the aristocracy

arithmetic NOUN the science or study of numbers; calculating with numbers

ark NOUN ❶ (in the Bible) the ship in which Noah and his family escaped the Flood ❷ a wooden box in which the writings of the Jewish Law were kept

arm NOUN ❶ either of the two upper limbs of the body, between the shoulder and the hand ❷ a sleeve ❸ something shaped like an arm or jutting out from a main part ❹ the raised side part of a chair, on which you can rest your arm

arm VERB to prepare someone to fight by supplying them with weapons

armada (say ar-**mah**-da) NOUN a fleet of warships

armadillo NOUN a small burrowing South American animal whose body is covered with a shell of bony plates

armaments PLURAL NOUN the weapons of an army etc.

armature NOUN the part of a dynamo or electric motor that carries the current

armchair NOUN a large comfortable chair with arms

armed ADJECTIVE ❶ carrying a weapon, especially a gun ❷ involving weapons

armed forces, armed services PLURAL NOUN a country's army, navy and air force

armful NOUN the amount you can carry in your arms

armistice *NOUN* an agreement to stop fighting in a war or battle

armour *NOUN* ❶ metal clothing worn in the past to protect soldiers in battle ❷ a metal covering on a warship, tank or car to protect it from missiles

armoury *NOUN* a place where weapons and ammunition are stored

armpit *NOUN* the hollow underneath the top of the arm, below the shoulder

arms *PLURAL NOUN* ❶ weapons ❷ a coat of arms

arms race *NOUN* competition between nations in building up supplies of weapons, especially nuclear weapons

army *NOUN* ❶ a large number of people trained to fight on land ❷ a large group of people doing something together

aroma (say a-**roh**-ma) *NOUN* a smell, especially a pleasant one

aromatic (say a-ro-**mat**-ik) *ADJECTIVE* having a pleasant smell

around *ADVERB & PREPOSITION* all round; about

arouse *VERB* ❶ to stir up a feeling in someone ❷ to wake someone up

arpeggio (say ar-**pej**-ee-oh) *NOUN* (*in music*) the notes of a chord played one after the other instead of together

arrange *VERB* ❶ to make plans and preparations for something ❷ to put things into a certain order ❸ to prepare music for a particular purpose

arrangement *NOUN*

❶ arrangement is how you arrange or display something ❷ an arrangement is something you agree with someone else

array *NOUN* a large display or choice of things

array *VERB* ❶ to be arrayed in fine or special clothes is to be wearing them noticeably ❷ to arrange things in a special order

arrears *PLURAL NOUN* ❶ money that is owing and ought to have been paid earlier ❷ a backlog of work etc.

arrest *VERB* to seize a person by authority of the law

arrest *NOUN* arresting somebody

arrival *NOUN* ❶ reaching the place to which you were travelling ❷ a person or thing that has just arrived

arrive *VERB* ❶ to reach the end of a journey or a point on it ❷ to come to a decision or agreement ❸ to come or happen

arrogant *ADJECTIVE* behaving in an unpleasantly proud way because you think you are better than other people

arrow *NOUN* ❶ a pointed stick to be shot from a bow ❷ a sign with an outward-pointing V at the end, used to show direction or position

arsenal *NOUN* a place where weapons and ammunition are stored or manufactured

arsenic *NOUN* a strong poison made from a metallic element

arson *NOUN* the crime of deliberately setting fire to a house or building

art NOUN ❶ producing something beautiful, especially by painting, drawing or sculpture; things produced in this way ❷ a skill

artefact NOUN an object made by humans, especially one from the past that is studied by archaeologists

artery NOUN ❶ one of the tubes that carry blood away from the heart to all parts of the body. Compare with **vein**. ❷ an important road or route

artesian well NOUN a well that is dug straight down into a place where water will rise easily to the surface

artful ADJECTIVE crafty or cunning

arthritis (say arth-**ry**-tiss) NOUN a disease that makes joints in the body stiff and painful

arthropod NOUN an animal of the group that includes insects, spiders, crabs and centipedes

artichoke NOUN a kind of plant with a flower head used as a vegetable

article NOUN ❶ a piece of writing published in a newspaper or magazine ❷ an object or item

articulate (say ar-**tik**-yoo-lat) ADJECTIVE able to express things clearly and fluently

articulate (say ar-**tik**-yoo-layt) VERB to say or speak clearly

articulated ADJECTIVE (*British*) an articulated vehicle is one in two sections that are connected by a flexible joint

artifice NOUN a piece of clever trickery

artificial ADJECTIVE not natural; made by human beings in imitation of a natural thing

artificial intelligence NOUN the use of computers to perform tasks normally requiring human intelligence, e.g. decision-making

artificial respiration NOUN helping someone to start breathing again after their breathing has stopped

artillery NOUN ❶ large guns ❷ the part of the army that uses large guns

artisan (say art-iz-**an**) NOUN a skilled worker

artist NOUN ❶ a person who produces works of art, especially a painter ❷ an entertainer

artistic ADJECTIVE ❶ to do with art or artists ❷ having or showing a talent for art

artless ADJECTIVE simple and natural

arts PLURAL NOUN subjects (e.g. languages, literature, history) in which opinion and interpretation are very important, as opposed to sciences where measurements and calculations are used

as ADVERB used in making a comparison

as PREPOSITION in the function or role of

as CONJUNCTION ❶ when or while ❷ because ❸ in a way that

asbestos NOUN a fireproof material made up of fine soft fibres

ascend VERB to go up to a higher point

ascendancy NOUN being in control over other people

ascension NOUN the process of going up

ascent NOUN ❶ the process of going up; a climb ❷ a way up; an upward path or slope

ascertain (say as-er-**tayn**) VERB to find something out

ascetic (say a-**set**-ik) ADJECTIVE not allowing yourself pleasure and luxuries

ascetic NOUN a person who leads an ascetic life, often for religious reasons

ascribe VERB to ascribe an event or situation to something is to regard that thing as the cause or source

asexual ADJECTIVE (in biology) by other than sexual methods

ash NOUN ❶ the powder that is left after something has been burned ❷ a tree with silver-grey bark

ashamed ADJECTIVE feeling shame

ashen ADJECTIVE grey or pale

ashore ADVERB to or on the shore

ashtray NOUN a small bowl for putting cigarette ash in

Asian ADJECTIVE to do with Asia or its people

Asian NOUN an Asian person

Asiatic ADJECTIVE to do with Asia

aside ADVERB ❶ to or at one side ❷ to put something aside is to keep it in case you need it later

aside NOUN words spoken so that only certain people will hear

ask VERB ❶ to speak so as to find out or get something ❷ to ask for something is to say that you want it ❸ to ask someone to something is to invite them

askance (say a-**skanss**) ADVERB
➤ look askance at to regard a person or situation with distrust or disapproval

askew ADVERB & ADJECTIVE crooked; not straight or level

asleep ADVERB & ADJECTIVE sleeping

AS level NOUN (in the UK except Scotland) an exam in a subject that represents the first part of an A level qualification; short for Advanced Subsidiary Level

asp NOUN a small poisonous snake

asparagus NOUN a plant whose young shoots are eaten as a vegetable

aspect NOUN ❶ one part of a problem or situation ❷ a person's or thing's appearance

aspen NOUN a tree with leaves that move in the slightest wind

asphalt (say **ass**-falt) NOUN a sticky black substance like tar, often mixed with gravel to make a surface for roads, etc.

aspidistra NOUN a house plant with broad leaves

aspirant (say **asp**-er-ant) NOUN a person who tries to achieve something

aspiration NOUN ambition; strong desire

aspire VERB to have an ambition to achieve something

aspirin NOUN a medicinal drug used to relieve pain or reduce fever

ass NOUN ❶ a donkey ❷ (informal) a stupid person

assailant NOUN a person who attacks someone

assassin NOUN a person who assassinates someone

assassinate VERB to kill an important person deliberately and violently, especially for political reasons

assault NOUN a violent or illegal attack

assault VERB to assault someone is to attack them violently

assegai (say **ass**-ig-y) NOUN an iron-tipped spear used by South African peoples

assemble VERB ❶ to assemble something is to fit the separate parts of it together ❷ to assemble is to come together in one place ❸ to assemble people or things is to bring them together in one place

assembly NOUN ❶ an assembly is a regular meeting, such as when everyone in a school meets together ❷ an assembly is also a group of people who regularly meet for a special purpose; a parliament ❸ assembly is putting the parts of something together to make it

assent NOUN assent is agreement or permission to do something

assent VERB If you assent to something, you say you agree or give your permission.

assert VERB to state something firmly

assertion NOUN a statement that you make confidently

assertive ADJECTIVE acting forcefully and with confidence

assess VERB to decide or estimate the value or quality of a person or thing

assessment NOUN an opinion about the value or quality of a person or thing

asset NOUN something useful or valuable to someone

assets PLURAL NOUN a person's or company's property that they could sell to pay debts or raise money

assign VERB ❶ to give a task or duty to someone ❷ to appoint a person to perform a task

assignment NOUN a piece of work or task given to someone

assimilate VERB to take in and absorb something, e.g. nourishment into the body or knowledge into the mind

assist VERB to help someone, usually in a practical way

assistance NOUN help someone gets when they need information or support

assistant NOUN ❶ a person whose job is to help another person in their work ❷ a person who serves customers in a shop

assistant ADJECTIVE helping a person and ranking next below him or her

associate (say a-**soh**-si-ayt) VERB ❶ to associate one thing with another is to connect them in your mind ❷ to associate with a group of people is to spend time or have dealings with them

associate (say a-**soh**-si-at) NOUN a colleague or companion

association NOUN ❶ an organization for people sharing an

interest or doing the same work
❷ a connection or link in your
mind ❸ being friendly with or
working with someone

Association football NOUN
(British) the game usually known
as football, which uses a round ball
that may not be handled during
play except by the goalkeeper

assonance (say **ass**-on-ans) NOUN
a close similarity of the vowel
sounds in two or more words, e.g.
in sonnet and porridge

assorted ADJECTIVE of various kinds
put together; mixed and different

assortment NOUN a mixed
collection of things

assume VERB ❶ to accept without
proof that something is true or
sure to happen ❷ to assume a
particular manner or expression is
to show it or put it on ❸ to assume
a burden or responsibility is to
agree to take it on

assumption NOUN something that
you accept without proof that it is
true or sure to happen

assurance NOUN ❶ a promise or
guarantee that something is true
or will happen ❷ confidence in
yourself

assure VERB ❶ to tell someone
something confidently ❷ to make
something certain to happen

aster NOUN a garden plant with
daisy-like flowers in various
colours

asterisk NOUN a star-shaped
sign * used to draw attention to
something

astern ADVERB ❶ at the back of a
ship or aircraft

asteroid NOUN one of the small
planets found mainly between the
orbits of Mars and Jupiter

asthma (say **ass**-ma) NOUN a
disease that makes breathing
difficult

asthmatic ADJECTIVE suffering from
asthma

asthmatic NOUN a person who
suffers from asthma

astonish VERB to surprise somebody
greatly

astonishment NOUN a feeling of
great surprise

astound VERB to astonish or shock
someone greatly

astray ADVERB & ADJECTIVE ➤ go
astray to be lost or mislaid ➤ lead
someone astray to make someone
do something wrong

astride ADVERB & PREPOSITION with
one leg on each side of something

astrology NOUN the study of the
position and movements of stars
and planets in the belief that they
influence people's lives

astronaut NOUN a person who
travels in a spacecraft

astronomical ADJECTIVE ❶ to do
with astronomy ❷ extremely large

astronomy NOUN the study of
the stars and planets and their
movements

astute ADJECTIVE clever and good at
understanding situations quickly;
shrewd

asunder ADVERB (literary) apart;
into pieces

asylum NOUN ❶ refuge and safety

33

offered by one country to political refugees from another ❷ (old use) an institution for the care of mentally ill people

at PREPOSITION This word is used to show ❶ position or location (*I was at the hospital.*), ❷ time (*at midnight*), ❸ direction towards something (*Aim at the target.*), ❹ cost or level (*Water boils at 100°C.*), ❺ cause (*We were annoyed at the delay.*)

atheist (say ayth-ee-ist) NOUN a person who believes that there is no God

athlete NOUN a person who is good at sport, especially athletics

athletic ADJECTIVE ❶ physically fit and active; good at sports ❷ to do with athletics

athletics PLURAL NOUN physical exercises and sports, e.g. running, jumping and throwing

atlas NOUN a book of maps

atmosphere NOUN ❶ the air around the earth ❷ a feeling or mood given by surroundings ❸ a unit of pressure, equal to the pressure of the atmosphere at sea level

atmospheric ADJECTIVE ❶ to do with the earth's atmosphere ❷ having a strong atmosphere

atoll NOUN a ring-shaped coral reef

atom NOUN the smallest particle of a chemical element

atom bomb, atomic bomb NOUN a bomb using atomic energy

atomic ADJECTIVE ❶ to do with an atom or atoms ❷ to do with atomic energy or atom bombs

atomic energy NOUN energy created by splitting the nuclei of certain atoms

atomic number NOUN (*in science*) the number of protons in the nucleus of the atom of a chemical element

atone VERB to make amends; to make up for having done something wrong

atrocious (say a-**troh**-shus) ADJECTIVE extremely bad or wicked

atrocity (say a-**tross**-it-ee) NOUN an extremely bad or wicked thing that someone does, such as killing a large number of people

attach VERB ❶ to fix or join one thing to something else ❷ to attach importance or significance to something is to believe that it is important or worth thinking about

attaché (say a-**tash**-ay) NOUN a special assistant to an ambassador

attaché case NOUN a small case in which documents etc. may be carried

attachment NOUN ❶ an extra part to add to a piece if equipment for a special purpose ❷ a file or piece of software sent with an email ❸ fondness or friendship

attack NOUN ❶ a violent attempt to hurt or overcome someone ❷ a piece of strong criticism ❸ a sudden illness or pain ❹ the players in a team whose job is to score goals; an attempt to score a goal

attack VERB to act violently against someone or to start a fight with them

attain *VERB* to succeed in doing or getting something

attempt *VERB* to make an effort to do something

attempt *NOUN* an effort to do something; a try

attend *VERB* ① to attend something like a meeting or a wedding is to be there ② to attend school or college is to be a pupil or student there ③ to attend to someone is to look after them ④ to attend to something is to spend time dealing with it

attendance *NOUN* ① attendance is being present at a place ② the number of people present at an event

attendant *NOUN* a person who helps or goes with someone else

attention *NOUN* ① watching, listening to or thinking about someone or something carefully ② a position in which a soldier stands with feet together and arms straight downwards

attentive *ADJECTIVE* giving your attention to something

attest *VERB* to declare or prove that something is true or genuine

attic *NOUN* a room in the roof of a house

attire *NOUN* (*formal*) a person's clothes

attire *VERB* (*formal*) to be attired in particular clothes is to be wearing them

attitude *NOUN* ① the way you think or feel about something and the way you behave ② the position of the body or its parts; posture

attorney *NOUN* ① a person who is appointed to act on behalf of another in business matters ② (*North American*) a lawyer

attract *VERB* ① to get someone's attention or interest; to seem pleasant to someone ② to make something come ③ to pull something by means of a physical force

attraction *NOUN* ① the process of attracting or the ability to attract ② something that attracts visitors

attractive *ADJECTIVE* ① pleasant or good-looking ② interesting or appealing

attribute (say a-**trib**-yoot) *VERB* to believe that something belongs to or is caused by a particular person or thing

attribute (say **at**-rib-yoot) *NOUN* a quality or characteristic

attrition (say a-**trish**-on) *NOUN* gradually wearing down an enemy by repeatedly attacking them

attuned *ADJECTIVE* familiar with and used to something

aubergine (say **oh**-ber-zheen) *NOUN* (*British*) a deep-purple vegetable with thick flesh

auburn *ADJECTIVE* auburn hair is reddish-brown

auction *NOUN* a public sale where things are sold to the person who offers the most money for them

auction *VERB* to sell something in an auction

auctioneer *NOUN* an official in charge of an auction

audacious (say aw-**day**-shus) *ADJECTIVE* bold or daring

35

audacity NOUN the confidence to do something daring or shocking

audible ADJECTIVE loud enough to be heard

audience NOUN ❶ the people who have come to hear or watch a performance ❷ a formal interview with an important person

audio NOUN reproduced sounds

audio-visual ADJECTIVE using both sound and pictures to give information

audition NOUN a test to see if an actor or musician is suitable for a job

audition VERB to have or give someone an audition

auditorium NOUN the part of a theatre or hall where the audience sits

augment VERB to increase or add to something

augur (say **awg**-er) VERB to augur well or augur badly is to be a good sign or a bad sign

August NOUN the eighth month of the year

august (say aw-**gust**) ADJECTIVE majestic or impressive

auk NOUN a kind of seabird

aunt NOUN the sister of your father or mother or your uncle's wife

auntie, aunty NOUN (informal) aunt

au pair (say oh **pair**) NOUN a person from abroad, usually a young woman, who works for a time in a family's home, helping to look after the children

aura (say **or**-a) NOUN a general feeling surrounding a person or thing

aural (say **or**-al) ADJECTIVE to do with the ear or hearing

au revoir (say oh rev-**wahr**) EXCLAMATION goodbye for the moment

aurora (say aw-**raw**-ra) NOUN bands of coloured light appearing in the sky at night, the **aurora borealis** (say bor-ee-**ay**-liss) in the northern hemisphere and the **aurora australis** (say aw-**stray**-liss) in the southern hemisphere

auspices (say **aw**-spiss-eez) PLURAL NOUN ➤ under the auspices of someone with the help, support or protection of an organization

auspicious (say aw-**spish**-us) ADJECTIVE showing signs that something is likely to be successful in the future

austere (say aw-**steer**) ADJECTIVE ❶ very simple and plain; without luxuries ❷ an austere person is very strict and serious

austerity NOUN ❶ a plain or simple way of living, without much comfort or luxury ❷ a time when people do not have much money to spend because there are bad economic conditions

authentic ADJECTIVE genuine or true

authenticate VERB to confirm something as being authentic

authenticity NOUN authenticity is being genuine or true

author NOUN the writer of a book, play, poem, etc.

authoritarian ADJECTIVE believing that people should be completely obedient to those in authority

authoritative ADJECTIVE having proper authority or expert knowledge

authority NOUN ❶ authority is the right or power to give orders to other people ❷ an authority is a person or organization with the right to give orders ❸ an authority on a subject is a person or book that gives reliable information about it

authorize (also **authorise**) VERB to give official permission for something

autistic (say aw-**tist**-ik) ADJECTIVE having a mental condition that makes it difficult for someone to communicate with other people

auto NOUN (informal esp. North American) a car

autobiography NOUN the story of a person's life written by himself or herself

autocrat NOUN a ruler with total and unlimited power

autocue NOUN (trade mark) (British) a device that displays the script for a television presenter or public speaker to read

autograph NOUN the signature of a famous person

automate VERB to make something work by an automatic process

automatic ADJECTIVE ❶ working on its own without continuous attention or control by people ❷ done without thinking

automatically ADVERB ❶ by automatic means; without having to use controls all the time

❷ without thinking

automation NOUN making processes automatic; using machines instead of people to do jobs

automaton (say aw-**tom**-at-on) NOUN ❶ a robot ❷ a person who seems to act mechanically without thinking

automobile NOUN (North American) a car

autonomy (say aw-**ton**-om-ee) NOUN ❶ self-government ❷ the right to act independently without being told what to do

autopsy (say **aw**-top-see) NOUN an examination of a dead body to find out the cause of death; a post-mortem

autumn NOUN the season between summer and winter

auxiliary ADJECTIVE giving help and support

auxiliary NOUN a person who gives help and support

auxiliary verb NOUN a verb such as do, have and will, which is used to form parts of other verbs, e.g. have in I have finished.

avail NOUN ➤ to or of no avail of no use; without success

avail VERB ➤ avail yourself of to make use of something

available ADJECTIVE able to be found or used

avalanche NOUN a mass of snow or rock falling down the side of a mountain

avant-garde (say av-ahn-**gard**) NOUN people who use a very modern style in art or literature etc.

avarice (say av-er-iss) *NOUN* greed for money or possessions

avenge *VERB* to punish someone for something they have done to harm you or your family

avenue *NOUN* ❶ a wide street ❷ a road with trees along both sides

average *NOUN* ❶ the value obtained by adding several quantities together and dividing by the number of quantities ❷ the usual or ordinary standard

average *ADJECTIVE* ❶ worked out as an average ❷ of the usual or ordinary standard

average *VERB* to work out, produce or amount to as an average

averse (say a-vers) *ADJECTIVE* unwilling to do something or opposed to something

aversion *NOUN* a strong dislike

avert *VERB* ❶ to turn something away ❷ to prevent something

aviary *NOUN* a large cage or building for keeping birds

aviation *NOUN* the flying of aircraft

avid (say av-id) *ADJECTIVE* keen or eager

avocado (say av-ok-ah-doh) *NOUN* a pear-shaped tropical fruit

avoid *VERB* ❶ to avoid a person or place is to stay away from them ❷ to avoid doing something is to make sure you do not do it

await *VERB* to wait for someone to come or something to happen

awake *ADJECTIVE* not asleep

awake *VERB* awakes, awaking, awoke, awoken to wake up

awaken *VERB* ❶ to wake up or to make someone wake up ❷ to produce a feeling in someone

award *VERB* to give something officially as a prize, payment or penalty

award *NOUN* something awarded, such as a prize or a sum of money

aware *ADJECTIVE* knowing or realizing something

awash *ADJECTIVE* with waves or water flooding over it

away *ADVERB* ❶ to or at a distance; not at the usual place ❷ until disappearing completely ❸ continuously or persistently

away *ADJECTIVE* played on an opponent's ground

awe *NOUN* ❶ a feeling of great wonder and perhaps slight fear ❷ to be in awe of someone is to respect and admire them a lot

awesome *ADJECTIVE* ❶ very impressive and perhaps slightly frightening ❷ (*informal*) excellent

awful *ADJECTIVE* ❶ very bad ❷ (*informal*) very great

awfully *ADVERB* (*informal*) very, extremely

awhile *ADVERB* for a short time

awkward *ADJECTIVE* ❶ difficult to use or deal with; not convenient ❷ embarrassed and not at ease ❸ clumsy or uncomfortable

awl *NOUN* a small pointed tool for making holes in leather, wood, etc.

awning *NOUN* a roof-like shelter made of canvas etc.

awry *ADVERB & ADJECTIVE* ❶ twisted to one side; crooked ❷ wrong; not according to plan,

axe NOUN ❶ a tool for chopping things ❷ (*informal*) a person or organization faces the axe when they are about to be made redundant or closed

axe VERB to cancel or abolish something

axiom NOUN an established general truth or principle

axis NOUN **axes** ❶ a line through the centre of a spinning object ❷ a line dividing a thing in half ❸ the horizontal or vertical line on a graph

axle NOUN the rod through the centre of a wheel, on which the wheel turns

ayatollah (say eye-a-**tol**-a) NOUN a Muslim religious leader in Iran

aye (rhymes with *by*) ADVERB (*dialect or old use*) yes

azalea (say a-**zay**-lee-a) NOUN a kind of flowering shrub

Bb

baa NOUN the cry of a sheep or lamb

babble VERB ❶ to talk very quickly without making sense ❷ to make a gentle bubbling sound

baboon NOUN a kind of large monkey from Africa and Asia, with a long muzzle and short tail

baby NOUN a very young child or animal

babyish ADJECTIVE like a baby or suitable for a baby

babysit VERB to look after a child while its parents are out

babysitter NOUN someone who looks after a child while its parents are out

bachelor NOUN a man who has not married

back NOUN ❶ the part that is furthest from the front ❷ the back part of a person's or animal's body, from the shoulders to the base of the spine ❸ the part of a chair etc. that your back rests against ❹ a defending player near the goal in football, hockey, etc.

back ADJECTIVE ❶ placed at or near the back ❷ to do with the back

back ADVERB ❶ to or towards the back ❷ to the place you have come from ❸ to an earlier time or position

back VERB ❶ to move backwards or drive a vehicle backwards ❷ to give someone support or help ❸ to bet on something ❹ to cover the back of something

backbencher NOUN a Member of Parliament who does not hold an important position

backbiting NOUN unkind or nasty things said about someone who is not there

backbone NOUN ❶ the column of small bones down the centre of the back; the spine ❷ strength of character; courage

backdrop NOUN a large painted cloth that is hung across the back of a stage

backfire VERB ❶ if a car backfires, it makes a loud noise, caused by an explosion in the exhaust pipe ❷ if a plan backfires, it goes wrong

backgammon NOUN a game played on a board with draughts and dice

background NOUN **1** the back part of a picture, scene or view **2** all the things that help to explain why an event or situation happened **3** a person's family, upbringing and education

backhand NOUN a stroke made in tennis etc. with the back of the hand turned outwards

backing NOUN **1** support or help **2** material that is used to line the back of something **3** music that is played or sung to support the main singer or tune

backlash NOUN a strong and angry reaction to an event

backlog NOUN an amount of work that should have been finished but is still waiting to be done

backpack NOUN a bag with straps for carrying on your back; a rucksack

backpacking NOUN travelling or hiking with your belongings in a rucksack

backside NOUN (informal) your backside is your bottom

backstage ADVERB in or towards the parts of a theatre behind the stage

backstroke NOUN a way of swimming lying on your back

back-up NOUN (in computing) a spare copy of a file, disk, etc. stored in safety separately from the original

backward ADJECTIVE **1** facing or moving towards the back **2** having not developed at the expected rate

backward ADVERB backwards

backwards ADVERB **1** to or towards the back **2** with the back end going first **3** in reverse order

backwater NOUN **1** a branch of a river that comes to a dead end with stagnant water **2** a quiet place that is not affected by progress or new ideas

backyard NOUN **1** an open area with a hard surface behind a house **2** (North American) a back garden

bacon NOUN smoked or salted meat from the back or sides of a pig

bacterium NOUN bacteria a microscopic organism that can cause disease

bad ADJECTIVE worse, worst **1** of poor quality; not good **2** not able to do something very well **3** serious or unpleasant **4** ill or unhealthy **5** harmful **6** decayed or rotten **7** wicked or evil

baddy NOUN (informal) an evil or wicked character in a story

bade old past tense of bid

badge NOUN a button or sign that you wear to show people who you are, what school or club you belong to or what kind of thing you like

badger NOUN a grey animal with a black and white head, which lives underground and is active at night

badger VERB to keep asking someone to do something; to pester someone about something

badly ADVERB **1** in a bad way; not well **2** severely; causing serious injury **3** very much

badminton NOUN a game in which players use rackets to hit a light object called a shuttlecock across a high net

bad-tempered *ADJECTIVE* always angry and in a bad mood

baffle *VERB* to puzzle or confuse someone

bag *NOUN* a container made of a soft material, for holding or carrying things

bag *VERB* ❶ (*informal*) to catch or claim something ❷ to put something into bags

bagatelle *NOUN* a game played on a board in which small balls are struck into holes

bagel *NOUN* a ring-shaped bread roll

baggage *NOUN* luggage

baggy *ADJECTIVE* baggy clothes hang loosely from your body

bagpipes *PLURAL NOUN* a musical instrument in which air is squeezed out of a bag into pipes. Bagpipes are played especially in Scotland.

bail *NOUN* ❶ money that is paid or promised as a guarantee that a person who is accused of a crime will return for trial if he or she is released in the meantime ❷ one of the two small pieces of wood placed on top of the stumps in cricket

bail *VERB* ❶ to provide bail for a person ❷ to scoop out water that has got into a boat

bailey *NOUN* the courtyard of a castle; the wall round this courtyard

bailiff *NOUN* ❶ an official who takes people's property when they owe money ❷ a law officer who helps a sheriff by serving writs and

carrying out arrests

Bairam (say by-**rahm**) *NOUN* either of two Muslim festivals, one in the tenth month and one in the twelfth month of the Islamic year

Baisakhi *NOUN* a Sikh festival held in April to commemorate the founding of the Khalsa

bait *NOUN* ❶ food that is put on a hook or in a trap to catch fish or animals ❷ something that is meant to tempt someone

bait *VERB* ❶ to put bait on a hook or in a trap ❷ to try to make someone angry by teasing them

baize *NOUN* the thick green cloth that is used for covering snooker tables

bake *VERB* ❶ to cook food in an oven with dry heat; to make bread or cakes ❷ to become very hot, especially in the sun ❸ to make clay hard by heating it

baked beans *PLURAL NOUN* cooked white beans, usually tinned with tomato sauce

baker *NOUN* a person who bakes or sells bread or cakes

bakery *NOUN* a place where bread and cakes are baked or a shop where they are sold

baking soda *NOUN* sodium bicarbonate

balaclava, balaclava helmet *NOUN* (*chiefly British*) a hood covering the head and neck and part of the face

balance *NOUN* ❶ a steady position, with the weight or amount evenly distributed ❷ a person's feeling of being steady ❸ a device for weighing things, with two containers hanging from a bar ❹ the difference between money paid into an account and money taken out of it ❺ the amount of money that someone owes

balance VERB ❶ to balance on something is to make yourself steady on it ❷ something is balanced when it is steady with its weight evenly distributed

balcony NOUN ❶ a platform that sticks out from an outside wall of a building ❷ the upstairs part of a theatre or cinema

bald ADJECTIVE ❶ without hair on the top of the head ❷ a bald statement or description is one without any details or explanation

bale NOUN a large bundle of hay, straw or cotton, usually tied up tightly

bale VERB ➤ **bale out** (British) to jump out of an aircraft with a parachute in an emergency

ball NOUN ❶ a round object used in many games ❷ anything that has a round shape ❸ a formal party where people dance

ballad NOUN ❶ a traditional song or poem that tells a story ❷ a slow romantic pop song

ballast (say **bal**-ast) NOUN heavy material that is carried in a ship or hot-air balloon to keep it steady

ball bearings PLURAL NOUN small steel balls rolling in a groove on which machine parts can move easily

ballerina (say bal-er-**een**-a) NOUN a female ballet dancer

ballet (say **bal**-ay) NOUN a style

of dancing in which a group of dancers perform precise steps and movements to tell a story to music

ballistic (say bal-**ist**-ik) ADJECTIVE to do with objects that are fired through the air, especially bullets and missiles

ballistic missile NOUN a missile that is powered and guided when it is launched and then falls under gravity on its target

balloon NOUN ❶ a bag made of thin rubber that can be inflated and used as a toy or decoration ❷ a large round bag inflated with hot air or light gases to make it rise in the air, often carrying a basket in which passengers may ride ❸ an outline round spoken words in a cartoon

ballot NOUN ❶ a secret method of voting, usually by making a mark on a piece of paper and putting it in a box ❷ a piece of paper on which a vote is made

ballpoint pen NOUN a pen with a tiny ball round which the ink flows

ballroom NOUN a large room where dances are held

balm NOUN ❶ a sweet-scented ointment or cream that soothes you

balmy ADJECTIVE ❶ balmy weather is gentle and warm ❷ sweet-scented like balm

balsa NOUN a kind of very lightweight wood

balsam NOUN ❶ a kind of sweet-smelling oily resin produced by certain trees, used to make perfumes and medicines ❷ a tree

42

producing balsam

balti NOUN a type of Pakistani curry, cooked in a bowl-shaped pan

balustrade NOUN a row of short posts or pillars that supports a rail or strip of stonework round a balcony or staircase

bamboo NOUN ❶ a tall plant with hard hollow stems ❷ a stem of the bamboo plant

bamboozle VERB (informal) to puzzle or trick someone

ban VERB to officially forbid someone from doing something

ban NOUN an order that bans something

banana NOUN a long curved fruit with a yellow or green skin

band NOUN ❶ an organized group of people doing something together ❷ a group of people playing music together ❸ a strip or loop of something ❹ a range of values, wavelengths, etc.

band VERB to band together is to form an organized group

bandage NOUN a strip of material for tying round a wound

bandage VERB to tie a bandage round a wound

bandit NOUN a member of a gang of robbers who attack travellers

bandstand NOUN a platform for a band playing music outdoors, usually in a park

bandwagon NOUN ➤ jump on the bandwagon to join other people in something that has become successful or popular

bandy ADJECTIVE bandy legs curve outwards at the knees

bandy VERB if a name, word or story is bandied about, it is mentioned or told by a lot of different people

bane NOUN if something is the bane of your life, it causes you a lot of trouble or worry

bang NOUN ❶ a sudden loud noise like that of an explosion ❷ a sharp blow or knock

bang VERB ❶ to hit or shut something noisily ❷ to make a sudden loud noise ❸ to bump part of your body against something

bang ADVERB (informal) exactly

bangle NOUN a stiff bracelet

banish VERB ❶ to punish a person by ordering them to leave a place ❷ to drive away a thought or feeling from your mind

banisters PLURAL NOUN a handrail with upright supports beside a staircase

banjo NOUN a musical instrument like a small guitar with a round body

bank NOUN ❶ a business that looks after people's money ❷ a reserve supply ❸ a sloping piece of ground at either side of a river ❹ a long raised mass of earth, sand or snow ❺ a long thick mass of cloud or fog ❻ a row of lights or switches

bank VERB ❶ to put money in a bank ❷ to pile up to form a bank ❸ to tilt sideways while changing direction

banker NOUN a person who runs a bank

bank holiday NOUN (British) a public holiday, when banks are officially closed

43

banknote NOUN a piece of paper money issued by a bank

bankrupt ADJECTIVE not able to pay your debts

banner NOUN ① a strip of cloth with a design or slogan on it, carried on a pole or two poles in a procession or demonstration ② a flag

banns PLURAL NOUN an announcement in a church that the two people named are going to marry each other

banquet NOUN a large formal dinner for invited guests which includes several courses

bantam NOUN a kind of small hen

banter NOUN playful teasing or joking

Bantu NOUN ① a member of a group of central and southern African peoples ② the group of languages spoken by these peoples

baptism NOUN the ceremony in which a person is formally baptized

Baptist NOUN a member of a group of Christians who believe that a person should not be baptized until he or she is old enough to understand what baptism means

baptize (also **baptise**) VERB to receive someone into the Christian Church in a ceremony in which they are sprinkled with or dipped in water and usually given a name or names

bar NOUN ① a long straight piece of metal ② a block of something solid ③ a band of colour or light ④ a counter or room where refreshments, especially alcoholic

drinks, are served ⑤ one of the small equal sections into which music is divided

bar VERB ① to fasten something with a bar or bars ② to bar someone's way or path is to stop them getting past ③ to forbid or ban someone from doing something

barb NOUN the backward-pointing spike of a spear, arrow or fish hook, which makes it difficult to pull out

barbarian NOUN an uncivilized or brutal person

barbaric, barbarous ADJECTIVE savage and cruel

barbecue NOUN ① a metal frame for grilling food over an open fire outdoors ② a party where food is cooked in this way

barbecue VERB to cook food on a barbecue

barbed ADJECTIVE ① having a barb or barbs ② a barbed comment or remark is deliberately hurtful

barbed wire NOUN wire with small spikes in it, used to make fences

barber NOUN a men's hairdresser

bar chart NOUN a diagram that shows amounts as bars of equal width but varying height

bar code NOUN a set of black lines that are printed on goods, library books, etc. and can be read by a computer to give information about the goods, books, etc.

bard NOUN (literary) a poet or minstrel

bare ADJECTIVE ① without clothing or covering ② empty ③ plain and simple, without details ④ only

44

just enough

bare VERB to uncover or reveal something

bareback ADJECTIVE & ADVERB riding on a horse without a saddle

barefaced ADJECTIVE a barefaced lie is one that is told boldly without any shame or guilt

barely ADVERB only just; with difficulty

bargain NOUN ❶ an agreement about doing something in return for something else ❷ something that you buy cheaply

bargain VERB to argue over the price to be paid or what you will do in return for something

barge NOUN a long flat-bottomed boat used on canals

barge VERB to barge into someone is to bump clumsily into them or push them out of the way

baritone NOUN a male singer with a voice between a tenor and a bass

barium (say **bair**-ee-um) NOUN a soft silvery-white metal

bark NOUN ❶ the short harsh sound made by a dog or fox ❷ the outer covering of a tree's branches or trunk

bark VERB ❶ to make the sound of a bark ❷ to speak loudly and harshly

barley NOUN a cereal plant from which malt is made

barley sugar NOUN a sweet made from boiled sugar

bar mitzvah NOUN a religious ceremony for Jewish boys aged 13, when they take on the responsibilities of an adult under Jewish law

barn NOUN a farm building for storing hay or grain

barnacle NOUN a shellfish that attaches itself to rocks and the bottoms of ships

barn dance NOUN a kind of country dance; an informal gathering for dancing

barnyard NOUN a farmyard next to a barn

barometer (say ba-**rom**-it-er) NOUN an instrument that measures air pressure, used in forecasting the weather

baron NOUN ❶ a member of the lowest rank of noblemen ❷ a powerful owner of an industry or business

baroness NOUN a female baron or a baron's wife

baronet NOUN a nobleman with a knighthood inherited from his father

baroque (say ba-**rok**) NOUN an elaborately decorated style of architecture used in the 17th and 18th centuries

barracks NOUN a large building or group of buildings for soldiers to live in

barrage (say ba-**rahzh**) NOUN ❶ a dam built across a river ❷ heavy gunfire ❸ a large number of questions or comments that come quickly

barrel NOUN ❶ a large rounded container with flat ends ❷ the metal tube of a gun, through which the shot is fired

barrel organ NOUN a musical instrument which you play by

barren ADJECTIVE ❶ barren land is not able to produce crops or has no vegetation ❷ a barren woman is not able to have children ❸ a barren plant or tree is one that cannot bear fruit

barricade NOUN a barrier, especially one put up hastily across a street or door

barricade VERB to block a street or door with a barricade

barrier NOUN ❶ a fence or wall that prevents people from getting past ❷ something that stops you doing something

barrier reef NOUN a coral reef close to the shore but separated from it by a channel of deep water

barrister NOUN a lawyer in England or Wales who represents people in the higher law courts

barrow NOUN ❶ (British) a wheelbarrow ❷ (British) a small cart that is pushed or pulled by hand ❸ a mound of earth over a prehistoric grave

barter VERB to exchange goods for other goods, without using money

barter NOUN the system of bartering

basalt (say bas-awlt) NOUN a kind of dark volcanic rock

base NOUN ❶ the lowest part of something; the part on which a thing stands ❷ a starting point or foundation; a basis ❸ a headquarters ❹ each of the four corners that must be reached by a runner in baseball ❺ a substance that can combine with an acid to form a salt ❻ (in mathematics) the

number in terms of which other numbers can be expressed in a number system. 10 is the base of the decimal system and 2 is the base of the binary system.

base VERB ❶ to base one thing on another thing is to use the second thing as the starting point for the first ❷ to be based somewhere is to live there or work from there

base ADJECTIVE ❶ showing no honour or moral principles ❷ a base metal is one that has no great value

baseball NOUN ❶ a game in which runs are scored by hitting a ball and running round a series of four bases, played mainly in North America ❷ the ball used in this game

basement NOUN a room or part of a building below ground level

bash VERB to hit something or someone hard

bash NOUN ❶ a hard hit ❷ (informal) a try

bashful ADJECTIVE shy and self-conscious

basic ADJECTIVE forming an essential part or starting point

basically ADVERB at the simplest or most fundamental level

basil NOUN a Mediterranean herb used in cooking

basilica (say ba-zil-ik-a) NOUN a large oblong church with two rows of columns and an apse at one end

basilisk (say baz-il-isk) NOUN a mythical reptile that was said to be able to kill people just by looking at them

basin NOUN ❶ a deep bowl for mixing food in ❷ a washbasin ❸ a sheltered area of water for mooring boats ❹ the area from which water drains into a river

basis NOUN bases ❶ something to start from or add to; the main principle or ingredient ❷ the way in which something is done or organized

bask VERB to sit or lie comfortably warming yourself in the sun

basket NOUN a container for holding or carrying things, made of strips of flexible material or wire woven together

basketball NOUN ❶ a game in which goals are scored by putting a ball through high nets ❷ the ball used in this game

bass (say bayss) ADJECTIVE deep-sounding; the bass part of a piece of music is the lowest part

bass (say bayss) NOUN ❶ a male singer with a very deep voice ❷ a bass instrument or part

bass (say bas) NOUN a fish of the perch family

basset NOUN a short-legged dog with drooping ears

bassoon NOUN a bass woodwind instrument

bastard NOUN ❶ (old use) an illegitimate child ❷ (offensive) an unpleasant or difficult person or thing

baste VERB ❶ to moisten meat with fat while it is cooking ❷ to sew fabric together loosely with long stitches

bastion NOUN ❶ a part of a fortified building that sticks out from the rest ❷ something that protects a belief or way of life

bat NOUN ❶ a shaped piece of wood used to hit the ball in sports like cricket, baseball and table tennis ❷ a flying mammal that looks like a mouse with wings

bat VERB to have a turn at using a bat in cricket or baseball

batch NOUN a set of things or people dealt with together

bated ADJECTIVE ➤ **with bated breath** waiting anxiously

bath NOUN ❶ washing your whole body while sitting in water ❷ a large container for water in which to wash your whole body; the water in a bath ❸ a liquid in which something is placed

bath VERB (British) to give someone a bath

bathe VERB ❶ (British) to go swimming in the sea or a river ❷ to wash something gently ❸ to be bathed in light is to have light shining all over you

bathe NOUN (British) a swim

bathroom NOUN a room containing a bath or shower, a washbasin and often a toilet

baths PLURAL NOUN ❶ (British) a public swimming pool ❷ a place where people went in the past to wash or have a bath

bat mitzvah NOUN a religious ceremony for Jewish girls aged 13, when they take on the responsibilities of an adult under Jewish law

baton NOUN a short stick, e.g. one used to conduct an orchestra or in

a
b
c
d
e
f
g
h
i
j
k
l
m
n
o
p
q
r
s
t
u
v
w
x
y
z

a relay race

batsman *NOUN* a player who uses a bat in cricket

battalion *NOUN* an army unit containing two or more companies

batten *NOUN* a strip of wood or metal that holds something in place

batten *VERB* to fasten something down firmly

batter *VERB* to hit something hard and often

batter *NOUN* ❶ a beaten mixture of flour, eggs and milk, used for making pancakes or coating food to be fried ❷ a player who is batting in baseball

battered *ADJECTIVE* no longer looking new; damaged or out of shape

battering ram *NOUN* a heavy pole that is used to break down walls or gates

battery *NOUN* ❶ a device for storing and supplying electricity ❷ a set of pieces of equipment that are used together, especially a group of large guns ❸ a series of cages in which poultry or animals are kept close together

battle *NOUN* ❶ a fight between two armies ❷ a struggle

battle *VERB* to fight or struggle

battlefield *NOUN* a piece of ground on which a battle is or was fought

battlements *PLURAL NOUN* the top of a castle wall, often with gaps from which the defenders could fire at the enemy

battleship *NOUN* a heavily armed warship

batty *ADJECTIVE* (informal) (British) crazy or eccentric

bauble *NOUN* ❶ a bright and showy ornament that has little value ❷ a decorative ball hung on a Christmas tree

bauxite *NOUN* the clay-like substance from which aluminium is obtained

bawl *VERB* ❶ to shout loudly ❷ to cry noisily

bay *NOUN* ❶ an area of the sea and coast where the shore curves inwards ❷ an area that is marked out to be used for parking vehicles, storing things, etc.

bay *ADJECTIVE* a bay horse is reddish-brown in colour

bay *VERB* to howl or cry, like a hunting dog chasing its prey

bayonet *NOUN* a blade that can be fixed to the end of a rifle and used for stabbing

bay window *NOUN* a window that sticks out from the main wall of a house

bazaar *NOUN* ❶ a sale held to raise money for charity ❷ a market place in a Middle Eastern country

bazooka *NOUN* a tube-shaped portable weapon for firing anti-tank rockets

BC *ABBREVIATION* before Christ (used with dates counting back from the birth of Jesus Christ)

be *VERB* am, are, is; was, were; being, been ❶ to exist; to occupy a position ❷ to happen; to take place

be This verb is also used ❶ to describe a person or thing or give more information about them (*He is my teacher.*), ❷ to form parts of other verbs (*It is raining.*)

beach NOUN the part of the seashore nearest to the water

beached ADJECTIVE a beached whale is one that is stranded on a beach

beacon NOUN a light or fire used as a signal or warning

bead NOUN ❶ a small piece of glass, wood or plastic with a hole through it for threading with others on a string or wire, e.g. to make a necklace ❷ a drop of liquid

beady ADJECTIVE beady eyes are small and bright

beagle NOUN a small hound with long ears, used for hunting hares

beak NOUN the hard horny part of a bird's mouth

beaker NOUN (*British*) ❶ a tall drinking mug, often without a handle ❷ a glass container used for pouring liquids in a laboratory

beam NOUN ❶ a long thick bar of wood or metal ❷ a ray or stream of light or other radiation ❸ a happy smile

beam VERB ❶ to smile happily ❷ to send out radio or TV signals ❸ to send out light and warmth

bean NOUN ❶ a kind of plant with seeds growing in pods ❷ its seed or pod eaten as food ❸ the seed of a coffee plant

bear NOUN a large heavy animal with thick fur and large teeth and claws

bear VERB bears, bearing, bore, born or borne ❶ to carry or support the weight of something

❷ to have or show a mark, signature, etc. ❸ to accept something and be able to deal with it; to put up with something ❹ to produce fruit or give birth to a child

bearable ADJECTIVE that you can accept and deal with; able to be put up with

beard NOUN hair on a man's chin

bearer NOUN someone who carries or brings something important

bearing NOUN ❶ the way that you stand, walk or behave ❷ to have a bearing on something is to be relevant to it or to have an effect on it

beast NOUN ❶ any large four-footed animal ❷ (*informal*) a cruel or vicious person

beastly ADJECTIVE (*informal*) cruel or unkind

beat VERB beats, beating, beat, beaten ❶ to hit someone repeatedly, especially with a stick ❷ to defeat someone or do better than them ❸ to shape or flatten something by hitting it repeatedly ❹ to stir a cooking mixture quickly so that it becomes thicker ❺ a heart beats when it makes regular movements ❻ a bird or insect beats its wings when it flaps them repeatedly

beat NOUN ❶ a regular rhythm or stroke ❷ emphasis in rhythm; a strong rhythm in pop music ❸ a policeman's regular route

beautiful ADJECTIVE attractive to look at; giving pleasure to your senses or your mind

beautifully ADVERB in a beautiful or

pleasing way

beautify *VERB* to make someone or something beautiful

beauty *NOUN* ❶ a quality that gives pleasure to your senses or your mind ❷ a beautiful person or thing ❸ an excellent example of something

beaver *NOUN* an animal with soft brown fur and strong teeth; it builds its home in a deep pool which it makes by damming a stream

beaver *VERB* to beaver away at something is to work hard at it

because *CONJUNCTION* for the reason that

beck *NOUN* ➤ at someone's beck and call always ready and waiting to do what he or she asks

beckon *VERB* to make a sign to someone asking them to come towards you

become *VERB* becomes, becoming, became, become ❶ to begin to be something; to come or grow to be something ❷ to make a person look attractive

bed *NOUN* ❶ a piece of furniture that you sleep or rest on, especially one with a mattress and coverings ❷ an area of ground in a garden where plants are grown ❸ the bottom of the sea or of a river ❹ a layer that other things lie or rest on ❺ a layer of rock or soil

bedclothes *PLURAL NOUN* sheets, blankets and duvets for covering a bed

bedding *NOUN* mattresses, pillows and bedclothes

bedlam *NOUN* a scene full of noise and confusion

Bedouin (say **bed**-oo-in) *NOUN* a member of an Arab people living in tents in the desert regions of Arabia and North Africa

bedpan *NOUN* a container used as a toilet by a person who is bedridden

bedraggled (say bid-**rag**-eld) *ADJECTIVE* looking untidy or messy, especially after getting very wet

bedridden *ADJECTIVE* too weak or ill to get out of bed

bedrock *NOUN* ❶ solid rock beneath soil ❷ the fundamental facts or principles on which an idea or belief is based

bedroom *NOUN* a room for sleeping in

bedside *NOUN* a space beside a bed

bedsitter, bedsit *NOUN* a room used for both living and sleeping in

bedspread *NOUN* a covering spread over a bed during the day

bedstead *NOUN* the framework of a bed

bedtime *NOUN* the time for going to bed

bee *NOUN* a stinging insect with four wings that makes honey

beech *NOUN* a tree with smooth bark and glossy leaves

beef *NOUN* meat from an ox, bull or cow

beefeater *NOUN* one of the guards at the Tower of London, who wear a uniform based on Tudor dress

beefy *ADJECTIVE* having a solid muscular body

beehive *NOUN* a box or other

50

container for bees to live in

beeline NOUN ➤ **make a beeline for something** to go straight or quickly towards something

beep VERB ❶ to give out a short high-pitched sound ❷ to sound a car horn as a signal

beep NOUN a short high-pitched sound

beer NOUN an alcoholic drink made from malt and hops

beeswax NOUN a yellow substance produced by bees, used for polishing wood and making candles

beet NOUN a plant with a thick root used as a vegetable or for making sugar

beetle NOUN an insect with hard shiny wing covers

beetroot NOUN (chiefly British) the dark red root of beet used as a vegetable

befall VERB befalls, befalling, befell, befallen (formal) to happen to someone

before ADVERB at an earlier time

before PREPOSITION & CONJUNCTION ❶ earlier than ❷ in front of

beforehand ADVERB earlier or before something else happens

befriend VERB to make friends with someone

beg VERB ❶ to ask other people for money or food to live on ❷ to ask someone for something something seriously or desperately

beget VERB begets, begetting, begot, begotten (old use) ❶ to be the father of someone ❷ to produce or cause something

beggar NOUN ❶ a person who lives by begging in the street ❷ (informal) a person

begin VERB begins, beginning, began, begun ❶ to do the earliest or first part of something; to start doing something ❷ to start to happen or exist ❸ to have something as its first part

beginner NOUN a person who is just beginning to learn a subject or skill

beginning NOUN the first part of something or the time when it starts

begonia (say big-oh-nee-a) NOUN a garden plant with brightly coloured flowers

begot past tense of beget

begrudge VERB ❶ to resent the fact that someone has something ❷ to resent having to do something

beguile (say big-yl) VERB ❶ to amuse or fascinate someone ❷ to deceive someone

behalf NOUN ➤ **on behalf of** for the benefit of someone else or as their representative ➤ **on my behalf** for me

behave VERB ❶ to act in a particular way ❷ to show good manners

behaviour NOUN the way that someone behaves or acts

behead VERB to cut the head off a person or thing; to execute a person in this way

behest NOUN (formal) ➤ **at a person's behest** done because they have asked or commanded you to do it

behind ADVERB ❶ at or to the back; at a place people have left ❷ not making good progress; late

behind PREPOSITION ❶ at or to the back of; on the further side of ❷ having made less progress than ❸ causing or being the reason for something ❹ supporting or encouraging a person or thing

behind NOUN (informal) a person's bottom

behold VERB (old use) to see something in front of you

beige (say bayzh) NOUN & ADJECTIVE a very light brown colour

being NOUN ❶ the state of existing ❷ a living creature

belated ADJECTIVE coming very late or too late

belch VERB ❶ to send out wind from your stomach through your mouth noisily ❷ to send out fire or smoke from an opening

belch NOUN an act of belching

belfry NOUN a tower or part of a tower in which bells hang

belie VERB to give a false idea of something

belief NOUN ❶ the feeling that something exists or is true ❷ something that a person believes

believable ADJECTIVE able to be believed

believe VERB to think that something is true or that someone is telling the truth

belittle VERB to talk about something as if it were unimportant or of little value

bell NOUN ❶ a cup-shaped metal instrument that makes a ringing sound when struck by the clapper hanging inside it ❷ any device that makes a ringing or buzzing sound to attract attention ❸ a bell-shaped object

belligerent (say bil-ij-er-ent) ADJECTIVE aggressive; keen to start a fight

bellow VERB ❶ to shout loudly and deeply ❷ to make a loud deep sound, like a bull does

bellow NOUN ❶ a deep shout ❷ the loud deep sound made by a bull or other large animal

bellows PLURAL NOUN a device for pumping air into a fire, organ pipes, etc.

belly NOUN your stomach or abdomen

belong VERB ❶ to belong to someone is to be owned by them ❷ to belong to a club or group is to be a member of it ❸ to belong somewhere is to have a special place where it goes

belongings PLURAL NOUN your belongings are the things that you own

beloved ADJECTIVE dearly loved

below ADVERB at or to a lower position; underneath

below PREPOSITION lower than; under

belt NOUN ❶ a strip of cloth or leather etc. that you wear round your waist ❷ a continuous moving band used in engines and machinery ❸ a long narrow area

belt VERB ❶ (informal) to hit someone very hard ❷ (informal) to run or travel very fast

bemused ADJECTIVE puzzled or confused

bench NOUN ❶ a long seat ❷ a long table for working at in a workshop or laboratory ❸ the seat where judges or magistrates sit; the judges or magistrates hearing a case

bend VERB bends, bending, bent ❶ to make something curved and no longer straight ❷ to be or become curved ❸ to move the top of your body downwards; to stoop

bend NOUN a place where something bends; a curve or turn

beneath PREPOSITION ❶ under ❷ not good enough for someone

beneath ADVERB underneath

benediction NOUN a blessing

benefactor NOUN a person who gives money or other help

beneficial ADJECTIVE having a good or helpful effect

benefit NOUN ❶ an advantage or good effect that something brings ❷ money that the government pays to help people who are poor, sick or out of work

benefit VERB ❶ to receive an advantage from something ❷ to give an advantage to someone or something

benevolence NOUN kindness or being helpful

benevolent ADJECTIVE ❶ kind and helpful ❷ formed for charitable purposes

benign (say bin-**yn**) ADJECTIVE ❶ kind and gentle; not hurting anyone ❷ a benign tumour is not dangerous or likely to cause death

bent ADJECTIVE curved or crooked

bent NOUN a liking or talent for something

bequeath VERB to leave something to a person in a will

bequest NOUN something left to a person in a will

bereaved ADJECTIVE suffering from the recent death of a close relative

beret (say **bair**-ay) NOUN a round flat cap with no peak

berry NOUN any small round juicy fruit without a stone

berserk (say ber-**zerk**) ADJECTIVE
➤ go berserk to become extremely angry or violent, often in an uncontrolled way

berth NOUN ❶ a sleeping place on a ship or train ❷ a place where a ship can moor

berth VERB to moor in a berth

beryl NOUN a pale-green precious stone

beseech VERB to ask or beg someone earnestly to do something; to implore someone

beset VERB besets, besetting, beset to be beset by problems or difficulties is to be badly affected by them

beside PREPOSITION by the side of; near

besides PREPOSITION & ADVERB in addition to; also

besiege VERB ❶ to surround a place in order to capture it ❷ to crowd round a person or group

besotted ADJECTIVE so much in love with a person or thing that you cannot think or behave normally

best ADJECTIVE of the most excellent kind; most able to do something

best ADVERB ❶ in the best way; most ❷ most usefully; most wisely

best NOUN ❶ the best person or thing; the one that is better than all the others ❷ to do your best is to do as well as you can

bestial (say best-ee-al) ADJECTIVE to do with or like a beast; cruel and disgusting

best man NOUN a man who helps and supports the bridegroom at a wedding

bestow VERB to give something to someone, especially to show how much they are respected

bestseller NOUN a book that has sold in large numbers

bet NOUN ❶ an agreement that you will receive money if you are correct in choosing the winner of a race or game or in saying something will happen and will lose money if you are not correct ❷ the amount of money you risk losing in a bet

bet VERB bets, betting, bet or betted ❶ to make a bet ❷ (informal) to think that something is likely to happen or be true

beta (say beet-a) NOUN the second letter of the Greek alphabet, equivalent to Roman B, b

betide VERB ➤ woe betide there will be trouble for

betray VERB ❶ to be disloyal to a person or country; to do harm to someone who trusts you ❷ to reveal something without meaning to

betrayal NOUN betraying someone or something

betrothed ADJECTIVE (formal) engaged to be married

better ADJECTIVE ❶ more excellent; more satisfactory ❷ no longer ill

better ADVERB ❶ in a better way; more ❷ if you had better do something, you should do it or ought to do it

better VERB to improve on something

between PREPOSITION & ADVERB ❶ in the space or time that separates two points or limits ❷ connecting two or more people, places or things ❸ shared by ❹ separating; comparing

bevel VERB to give a sloping edge to something

beverage NOUN any kind of drink

bevy NOUN a large group

beware VERB to be careful

bewilder VERB to puzzle or confuse someone completely

bewitch VERB ❶ to put a magic spell on someone ❷ to delight or fascinate someone very much

beyond PREPOSITION & ADVERB ❶ further than; further on ❷ outside the range of; too difficult for

Bhagavadgita NOUN a sacred book in Hinduism

bhangra NOUN a style of music that combines traditional Punjabi music with rock music

bias NOUN ❶ a strong feeling in favour of one person or side and against another; a prejudice ❷ a tendency to swerve

biased _ADJECTIVE_ showing that you prefer one person or side over another

bib _NOUN_ ❶ a cloth or covering put under a baby's chin during meals ❷ the part of an apron above the waist

Bible _NOUN_ the sacred book of the Jews (the Old Testament) and of the Christians (the Old and New Testament)

biblical _ADJECTIVE_ to do with or mentioned in the Bible

bibliography (say bib-lee-**og**-ra-fee) _NOUN_ a list of books about a subject or by a particular author

bicarbonate _NOUN_ a kind of carbonate

bicentenary (say by-sen-**teen**-er-ee) _NOUN_ a 200th anniversary

biceps (say **by**-seps) _NOUN_ the large muscle at the front of the arm above the elbow

bicker _VERB_ to quarrel over unimportant things; to squabble

bicycle _NOUN_ a two-wheeled vehicle that you ride by pushing down on pedals with your feet

bid _NOUN_ ❶ the offer of an amount you are willing to pay for something, especially at an auction ❷ an attempt

bid _VERB_ bids, bidding, bid to make a bid

bid _VERB_ bids, bidding, bid (or _old use_) bade, bid or bidden ❶ to say something as a greeting or farewell ❷ to command someone to do something

bidding _NOUN_ if you do someone's bidding, you do what they tell

you to do

bide _VERB_ bides, biding, bided ➤ **bide your time** to wait for the right time to do something

bidet (say bee-**day**) _NOUN_ a low washbasin to sit on for washing the lower part of the body

biennial (say by-**en**-ee-al) _ADJECTIVE_ ❶ a biennial plant lives for two years, flowering and dying in the second year ❷ happening once every two years

biennial _NOUN_ a plant that lives for two years, flowering and dying in the second year

bier (say beer) _NOUN_ a movable stand on which a coffin or a dead body is placed before it is buried

bifocal (say by-**foh**-kal) _ADJECTIVE_ bifocal lenses for glasses are made in two sections, with the upper part for looking at distant objects and the lower part for reading

bifocals _PLURAL NOUN_ bifocal glasses

big _ADJECTIVE_ ❶ more than the normal size; large ❷ important ❸ more grown-up; elder

bigot _NOUN_ a person who holds strong and unreasonable opinions and is not willing to listen to other people's opinions

bigoted _ADJECTIVE_ holding strong and unreasonable opinions and not willing to listen to other people's opinions

bike _NOUN_ (_informal_) a bicycle or motorcycle

bikini _NOUN_ a woman's two-piece swimsuit

bilateral _ADJECTIVE_ ❶ between two people or groups ❷ affecting both

a
b
c
d
e
f
g
h
i
j
k
l
m
n
o
p
q
r
s
t
u
v
w
x
y
z

bilberry NOUN a small dark-blue edible berry

bile NOUN a bitter liquid produced by the liver, helping to digest fats

bilge NOUN ❶ **(the bilges)** the bottom of a ship or the water that collects there ❷ (informal) nonsense; worthless ideas

bilingual (say by-**ling**-wal) ADJECTIVE ❶ able to speak two languages well ❷ written in two languages

bill NOUN ❶ a piece of paper that shows how much money you owe for goods or services ❷ a list of events and performers in a show or concert ❸ a poster or notice ❹ the draft of a proposed law to be discussed by parliament ❺ (North American) a banknote ❻ a bird's beak

billboard NOUN a large board near a road where advertisements are displayed

billet NOUN a temporary lodging for soldiers, especially in a private house

billet VERB to house soldiers in a billet

billiards NOUN a game in which three balls are struck with long sticks (called cues) on a cloth-covered table

billion NOUN & ADJECTIVE ❶ a thousand million (1,000,000,000) ❷ (old use) a million million (1,000,000,000,000)

billow VERB ❶ to fill with air and swell outwards ❷ to move in large clouds through the air

billow NOUN a large rolling mass of cloud, smoke or steam

billy goat NOUN a male goat. Compare with nanny goat.

bin NOUN (British) a large or deep container, especially one for rubbish or litter

binary (say **by**-ner-ee) ADJECTIVE involving sets of two; consisting of two parts

binary digit NOUN either of the two digits (0 and 1) used in the binary system

binary number NOUN a number expressed in the binary system

binary system, binary notation NOUN a system of expressing numbers by using the digits 0 and 1 only, used in computing

bind VERB binds, binding, bound ❶ to tie things together or tie someone up ❷ to fasten a strip of material round something ❸ to fasten the pages of a book into a cover ❹ to make people feel that they have a close connection with something ❺ to make someone agree to do something

bind NOUN (informal) something that you find boring or annoying; a nuisance

binder NOUN a cover for holding magazines or loose papers together

binding ADJECTIVE a binding agreement or promise is one that must be carried out or obeyed

binding NOUN the covers and glue that hold the pages of a book together

binge NOUN (informal) a time spent

eating or drinking too much

bingo NOUN a game using cards on which numbered squares are crossed out as the numbers are called out at random

binoculars PLURAL NOUN a device with lenses for both eyes, making distant objects seem nearer

biochemistry NOUN the study of the chemical composition and processes of living things

biodegradable ADJECTIVE able to be broken down by bacteria in the environment

biodiversity NOUN the existence of a large number of different kinds of animals and plants in an area

biography (say by-*og*-ra-fee) NOUN the story of a person's life

biological ADJECTIVE to do with biology

biology NOUN the scientific study of the life and structure of living things

bionic (say by-*on*-ik) ADJECTIVE a bionic body part is operated by electronic devices

biopsy (say *by*-op-see) NOUN an examination of tissue from a living body

biosphere NOUN all the parts of the Earth which contain living things

biplane NOUN an aeroplane with two sets of wings, one above the other

birch NOUN ❶ a deciduous tree with slender branches ❷ a bundle of birch twigs used in the past for flogging people

bird NOUN an animal with feathers, two wings and two legs

birdie NOUN ❶ (*informal*) a bird ❷ a score in golf of one stroke under par for a hole

bird of prey NOUN a bird that feeds on animal flesh, such as an eagle or hawk

bird's-eye view NOUN a view of something from above

Biro NOUN (*British*) (*trademark*) a kind of ballpoint pen

birth NOUN ❶ birth is when a baby or young animal comes out from its mother's body at the beginning of its life ❷ a person's family origin ❸ the beginning of something

birth control NOUN ways of avoiding conceiving a baby

birthday NOUN the anniversary of the day you were born

birthmark NOUN a coloured mark that has been on a person's skin since they were born

birthplace NOUN the house or town where someone was born

birth rate NOUN the number of children born in one year for every 1,000 people

birthright NOUN a right or privilege to which a person is entitled through being born into a particular family or country

biscuit NOUN a small flat kind of cake that has been baked until it is crisp

bisect (say by-*sekt*) VERB to divide something into two equal parts

bishop NOUN ❶ a high-ranking member of the Christian clergy in charge of all the churches in a city or district ❷ a chess piece shaped like a bishop's mitre

bismuth NOUN ❶ a greyish-white metal ❷ a compound of this used in medicine

bison (say **by**-son) NOUN bison a wild ox found in North America and Europe, with a large shaggy head

bistro NOUN a small restaurant

bit NOUN ❶ a small piece or amount of something ❷ the metal part of a horse's bridle that is put into its mouth ❸ the part of a tool that cuts or grips things when twisted ❹ (in computing) the smallest unit of information in a computer

bit VERB past tense of **bite**

bitch NOUN ❶ a female dog, fox or wolf ❷ (offensive) a woman who behaves in a spiteful or nasty way

bitchy ADJECTIVE talking about other people in a spiteful way

bite VERB bites, biting, bit, bitten ❶ to cut or take something with your teeth ❷ to pierce skin with a sting or teeth ❸ fish bite when they accept an angler's bait

bite NOUN ❶ a mouthful cut off by biting ❷ a wound or mark made by biting ❸ a snack

biting ADJECTIVE a biting wind is cold and unpleasant

bitter ADJECTIVE ❶ tasting sharp, not sweet ❷ feeling hurt or resentful ❸ causing hurt or sorrow ❹ very cold

bitterly ADVERB ❶ in an angry and disappointed way ❷ extremely, unpleasantly

bittern NOUN a marsh bird, the male of which makes a booming cry

bitumen (say **bit**-yoo-min) NOUN a black sticky substance used for covering roads or roofs

bivalve NOUN a shellfish, such as an oyster or mussel, that has a shell with two hinged parts

bivouac (say **biv**-oo-ak) NOUN a temporary camp without tents

bivouac VERB to camp in a bivouac

bizarre (say biz-**ar**) ADJECTIVE very odd in appearance or effect

blab VERB to let out a secret

black ADJECTIVE ❶ of the very darkest colour, like coal or soot ❷ having dark skin; of African or Australian Aboriginal ancestry ❸ black coffee or tea has no milk added to it ❹ very dirty ❺ dismal; not hopeful ❻ hostile or angry

black NOUN a black colour

black VERB to make a thing black

blackberry NOUN a sweet black berry

blackbird NOUN a European songbird, the male of which is black

blackboard NOUN a dark board for writing on with chalk

black box NOUN the flight recorder of an aircraft, which records technical information about its flight

blacken VERB ❶ to make something black or to become black ❷ to blacken someone's name or reputation is to damage it

black eye NOUN an eye with a bruise round it

blackguard (say **blag**-erd) NOUN (old use) a man who behaves in a wicked or dishonourable way

blackhead NOUN a small black spot in the skin

black hole NOUN a region in outer space with such a strong gravitational field that no matter or radiation can escape from it

black ice NOUN thin transparent ice on roads

blacklist NOUN a list of people who are disapproved of

black magic NOUN magic used for evil purposes

blackmail VERB to demand money from someone by threatening to reveal something that they want to keep secret

blackmail NOUN the crime of blackmailing someone

black market NOUN illegal trading in goods

blackout NOUN ❶ a period of darkness when no light must be shown ❷ a temporary loss of consciousness

black sheep NOUN a member of a family or other group who is seen as a disgrace to it

blacksmith NOUN a person who makes and repairs iron things, especially one who makes and fits horseshoes

black spot NOUN a dangerous place where accidents often happen

bladder NOUN the bag-like part of the body in which urine collects

blade NOUN ❶ the flat cutting edge of a knife, sword or axe ❷ the flat wide part of an oar, spade or propeller ❸ a long flat narrow leaf of grass ❹ a broad flat bone

blame VERB ❶ to say that somebody or something has caused what is wrong ❷ to find fault with someone

blame NOUN responsibility for what is wrong

blameless ADJECTIVE deserving no blame; innocent

blanch VERB to turn pale

blancmange (say bla-**monj**) NOUN (British) a jelly-like pudding made with milk

bland ADJECTIVE ❶ having a mild flavour rather than a strong one ❷ not having any interesting features or qualities

blank ADJECTIVE ❶ empty, with nothing written, printed or recorded on it ❷ showing no interest or expression ❸ empty of thoughts

blank NOUN ❶ an empty space ❷ a blank cartridge

blank cartridge NOUN a cartridge for a gun that makes a noise but does not fire a bullet

blank cheque NOUN a cheque with the amount not yet filled in

blanket NOUN ❶ a warm cloth covering for a bed ❷ a thick soft layer covering something completely

blanket VERB to cover something completely with a thick soft layer

blanket ADJECTIVE covering all cases or instances

blank verse NOUN verse written without rhyme, usually in lines of ten syllables

blare VERB to make a loud harsh sound

59

blasé (say blah-zay) ADJECTIVE not interested in or impressed by something because you are used to it

blaspheme (say blas-**feem**) VERB to talk or write in a rude or disrespectful way about God or religion

blasphemy (say **blas**-fim-ee) NOUN rude or disrespectful talk about God or religion

blast NOUN ❶ a strong rush of wind or air ❷ a sharp or loud noise ❸ an explosion, especially one caused by a bomb

blast VERB ❶ to make a hole in something with an explosion; to blow something up ❷ to hit or kick something with a lot of force ❸ to make a loud noise

blast furnace NOUN a furnace for smelting ore, which works by having hot air driven into it

blast-off NOUN the launch of a rocket or spacecraft

blatant (say **blay**-tant) ADJECTIVE very obvious

blaze NOUN a very bright flame, fire or light

blaze VERB ❶ to burn or shine brightly ❷ to show great feeling

blazer NOUN a kind of jacket, often with a badge or in the colours of a school or team

bleach NOUN a chemical substance used to make clothes white or to clean things and kill germs

bleach VERB to make something white or pale by using a chemical or by leaving it in the sun

bleak ADJECTIVE ❶ bare and cold

❷ dreary or miserable

bleary ADJECTIVE bleary eyes are tired and do not see clearly

bleat NOUN the cry of a lamb, goat or calf

bleat VERB to cry with a bleat

bleed VERB bleeds, bleeding, bled to lose blood

bleep NOUN a short high sound made by a piece of electronic equipment

bleep VERB to make a bleep

bleeper NOUN (British) a small electronic device that bleeps when the wearer is contacted

blemish NOUN ❶ a mark or flaw that spoils a thing's appearance ❷ something that spoils a person's character or reputation

blench VERB to back away in fear; to flinch

blend VERB ❶ to mix things together smoothly or easily ❷ things blend when they combine well with each other

blend NOUN a mixture

blender NOUN an electric machine used to mix food or turn it into liquid

bless VERB ❶ to ask God to protect a person or thing ❷ to make something holy so that it can be used in a religious ceremony ❸ to be blessed with something is to be lucky enough to have it

blessing NOUN ❶ a prayer that blesses a person or thing ❷ something that you are grateful for

blight NOUN ❶ a disease that withers plants ❷ something that spoils or damages something

blight VERB ❶ to affect a plant with blight ❷ to spoil or damage something

blind ADJECTIVE ❶ without the ability to see ❷ without any thought or understanding ❸ a blind bend or corner is one where you cannot see clearly ahead

blind VERB ❶ to make someone blind ❷ to dazzle someone with a bright light

blind NOUN ❶ a screen for a window ❷ something used to hide your real intentions

blind date NOUN a date between people who have not met before

blindfold NOUN a strip of cloth tied round someone's eyes so that they cannot see

blindfold VERB to cover someone's eyes with a blindfold

blindfold ADVERB with a blindfold covering your eyes

blindly ADVERB ❶ without being able to see what you are doing ❷ without thinking about what you are doing

blind spot NOUN a subject that you do not understand or know much about

bling NOUN (informal) showy and expensive jewellery and clothes

blink VERB ❶ to shut and open your eyes rapidly ❷ a light blinks when it shines unsteadily

blink NOUN when you shut and open your eyes rapidly

blinkers PLURAL NOUN leather pieces fixed on a bridle to prevent a horse from seeing sideways

bliss NOUN extreme happiness

blissful ADJECTIVE feeling or causing extreme happiness

blister NOUN a swelling like a bubble, especially on skin

blister VERB ❶ to form blisters ❷ when a surface blisters it swells and cracks

blithe ADJECTIVE casual and carefree

blitz NOUN ❶ a sudden violent attack, especially from aircraft ❷ the German bombing of London in 1940

blizzard NOUN a severe snowstorm

bloated ADJECTIVE swollen by fat, gas or liquid

bloater NOUN a salted smoked herring

blob NOUN a small round lump or drop of something

bloc NOUN a group of parties or countries who have formed an alliance

block NOUN ❶ a solid piece of something ❷ a large building divided into flats or offices ❸ a group of buildings ❹ an obstacle or obstruction

block VERB to get in the way of something; to obstruct something

blockade NOUN the blocking of the entrance to a city or port in order to prevent people and goods from going in or out

blockade VERB to set up a blockade of a place

blockage NOUN something that blocks a pipe or passageway

block letters PLURAL NOUN plain capital letters

blog NOUN a personal website on which someone writes regularly

blog VERB to write on a blog

blogger NOUN someone who keeps a blog or who writes fiction and posts it on the Internet

bloke NOUN (British) (informal) a man

blond, blonde ADJECTIVE fair-haired; fair

blond NOUN a fair-haired girl or woman

blood NOUN ❶ the red liquid that flows through veins and arteries ❷ family background or ancestry

blood bank NOUN a place where supplies of blood and plasma for transfusions are stored

bloodbath NOUN a massacre

blood group NOUN any of the classes or types of human blood

bloodhound NOUN a large dog that was used to track people by their scent

bloodshed NOUN the killing or wounding of people

bloodshot ADJECTIVE bloodshot eyes are streaked with red

blood sport NOUN a sport that involves wounding or killing animals

bloodstream NOUN the blood circulating in the body

bloodthirsty ADJECTIVE enjoying killing and violence

blood vessel NOUN a tube carrying blood in the body; an artery, vein or capillary

bloody ADJECTIVE ❶ stained with blood ❷ with much bloodshed

bloody-minded ADJECTIVE (British) deliberately awkward and not helpful

bloom NOUN ❶ a flower ❷ the fine powder on fresh ripe grapes etc.

bloom VERB to produce flowers

blossom NOUN a flower or a mass of flowers, especially on a fruit tree

blossom VERB ❶ to produce flowers ❷ to develop into something

blot NOUN ❶ a spot of ink ❷ a flaw or fault; something ugly

blot VERB ❶ to make a blot or blots on something ❷ to remove liquid from a surface by pressing paper or cloth on it

blotch NOUN an untidy patch of colour

blotter NOUN a pad of blotting paper; a holder for blotting paper

blotting paper NOUN absorbent paper for soaking up ink from writing

blouse NOUN a loose piece of clothing like a shirt, worn by women

blow VERB blows, blowing, blew, blown ❶ to send air out of your mouth or nose ❷ to move in or with a current of air ❸ to form something or make a sound by blowing ❹ a fuse or light bulb blows when it melts or breaks because the electric current is too strong

blow NOUN ❶ a hard knock or hit ❷ a shock or disappointment ❸ the action of blowing

blowlamp, blowtorch NOUN a portable device for aiming a very hot flame at a surface, used to remove old paint

blowpipe NOUN a tube for sending out a dart or pellet by blowing

blubber NOUN the fat on a whale

bludgeon (say **bluj**-on) NOUN a short stick with a thickened end, used as a weapon

bludgeon VERB to hit someone several times with a heavy stick or other object

blue NOUN the colour of a cloudless sky

blue ADJECTIVE ❶ of the colour blue ❷ unhappy or depressed

bluebell NOUN a plant with blue bell-shaped flowers

bluebottle NOUN a large bluish fly

blueprint NOUN a detailed plan for making or doing something

blues NOUN a style of music made up of slow sad songs or tunes

bluff VERB to try to deceive someone, especially by pretending to be someone else or to be able to do something

bluff NOUN ❶ bluffing; a threat that you make but do not intend to carry out ❷ a cliff with a broad steep front

bluff ADJECTIVE frank and direct, in a good-natured way

bluish ADJECTIVE having a blue tinge

blunder NOUN a stupid mistake

blunder VERB ❶ to make a blunder ❷ to move clumsily and uncertainly

blunderbuss NOUN an old type of gun that fired many balls in one shot

blunt ADJECTIVE ❶ not sharp ❷ saying what you mean without trying to be polite or tactful

blunt VERB to make a point or edge blunt

blur VERB to make something less clear or distinct

blur NOUN something that you cannot see or remember clearly

blurb NOUN a short description of a book that is printed on the back and meant to make you want to buy it

blurred ADJECTIVE not clear in outline; out of focus

blurt VERB to say something suddenly or tactlessly

blush VERB to become red in the face because you are ashamed or embarrassed

blush NOUN reddening in the face

bluster VERB to talk loudly and aggressively, making empty threats

blustery ADJECTIVE blustery weather is when the wind is blowing strongly in gusts

boa (say **boh**-a) (or **boa constrictor**) NOUN a large South American snake that squeezes its prey so that it suffocates it

boar NOUN ❶ a wild pig ❷ a male pig

board NOUN ❶ a long flat piece of wood, used in building ❷ a flat piece of stiff material ❸ a group of people who run a company or organization ❹ daily meals provided in return for payment or work

board VERB ❶ to get on a boat, ship, train or aircraft ❷ to receive meals and accommodation for payment

boarder NOUN ❶ a pupil who lives

at a boarding school during the term ❷ a lodger who receives meals

boarding school NOUN a school where pupils live during the term

boast VERB ❶ to speak with too much pride about yourself and try to impress people ❷ to have something to be proud of

boast NOUN a boastful statement

boastful ADJECTIVE boasting a lot

boat NOUN a vehicle built to travel on water

boater NOUN a hard flat straw hat

boatswain (say boh-sun) NOUN a ship's officer in charge of rigging, boats and anchors

bob VERB to move quickly up and down

bobbin NOUN a small spool holding thread or wire in a machine

bobble NOUN a small ball of wool, used to decorate a hat or jumper

bobsleigh, bobsled NOUN (British) a sledge with two sets of runners

bode VERB to bode well (or ill) is to be a sign that something good (or bad) will happen

bodice NOUN the upper part of a dress

bodily ADJECTIVE to do with your body

bodily ADVERB by taking hold of someone's body

body NOUN ❶ the whole physical structure of a person or animal; the main part of this apart from the head and limbs ❷ a corpse ❸ the main part of something ❹ an organized group of people ❺ a quantity of something

regarded as a unit ❻ an object or piece of matter

bodyguard NOUN a guard whose job is to protect an important person

Boer (say boh-er) NOUN ❶ an Afrikaner ❷ (historical) an early Dutch inhabitant of South Africa

boffin NOUN (British) (informal) a person involved in scientific or technical research

bog NOUN an area of wet spongy ground

bogeyman NOUN an imaginary man used in stories to frighten children

boggle VERB to be amazed or puzzled

boggy ADJECTIVE boggy ground is wet and spongy

bogus ADJECTIVE not real or genuine

boil VERB ❶ to become hot enough to bubble and give off steam ❷ to heat a liquid so that it boils ❸ to cook something in boiling water ❹ to be very hot

boil NOUN ❶ the point at which a liquid starts to boil ❷ an inflamed swelling under the skin

boiler NOUN a container for heating water or making steam

boiling point NOUN the temperature at which a liquid boils

boisterous ADJECTIVE noisy and lively

bold ADJECTIVE ❶ brave and confident; not afraid to say what you feel or to take risks ❷ a bold colour or design is strong and vivid ❸ printed in thick black type

bollard NOUN ❶ a short post for keeping vehicles off a road ❷ a short thick post on a quayside to which a ship's rope may be tied

bolster NOUN a long pillow for placing across a bed under other pillows

bolster VERB to add extra strength or support to something

bolt NOUN ❶ a sliding bar for fastening a door or window ❷ a thick metal pin for fastening things together ❸ a sliding bar that opens and closes the breech of a rifle ❹ a shaft of lightning ❺ an arrow shot from a crossbow ❻ the action of bolting

bolt VERB ❶ to fasten a door or window with a bolt or bolts ❷ to fasten things together with bolts ❸ to run away or escape ❹ to swallow food quickly

bomb NOUN an explosive device

bomb VERB to attack a place with bombs

bombard VERB ❶ to attack a place with gunfire or many missiles ❷ to direct a large number of questions or comments at somebody

bombardment NOUN a heavy attack with guns or missiles

bomber NOUN ❶ someone who plants or sets off a bomb ❷ an aeroplane from which bombs are dropped

bombshell NOUN a great shock

bona fide (say **boh**-na **fy**-dee) ADJECTIVE genuine; without fraud

bond NOUN ❶ a close friendship or connection between two or more people ❷ bonds are ropes or chains used to tie someone up ❸ a document stating an agreement

bond VERB to become closely linked or connected

bondage NOUN slavery or captivity

bone NOUN ❶ one of the hard whitish parts that make up the skeleton of a person's or animal's body ❷ the substance from which these parts are made

bone VERB to remove the bones from meat or fish

bone dry ADJECTIVE completely dry

bonfire NOUN an outdoor fire to burn rubbish or celebrate something

bonnet NOUN ❶ the hinged cover over a car engine ❷ a hat with strings that tie under the chin ❸ a flat cap, often with a bobble, worn by Scottish men

bonny ADJECTIVE (Scottish) good-looking or pretty

bonus (say **boh**-nus) NOUN ❶ an extra payment in addition to a person's normal wages ❷ an extra benefit

bon voyage (say bawn vwah-**yah** zh) EXCLAMATION said to wish someone a good journey

bony ADJECTIVE ❶ so thin that you can see the shape of the bones ❷ full of bones ❸ looking or feeling like bone

boo EXCLAMATION ❶ shouted out to show that you do not like something ❷ said to take someone by surprise and startle them

boo VERB to shout 'boo' in disapproval

booby prize NOUN a prize given as a joke to someone who comes last in a contest

booby trap NOUN something designed to hit or injure someone unexpectedly

book NOUN a set of sheets of paper, usually with printing or writing on them, fastened together inside a cover

book VERB ❶ to reserve a place or ticket in advance ❷ to enter a person in a police record ❸ to make a note of a player who has committed a foul in a football match

bookcase NOUN a piece of furniture with shelves for books

bookkeeping NOUN recording details of the money that is spent and received by a business

booklet NOUN a small thin book with paper covers

bookmaker NOUN a person whose business is taking bets, especially bets made on horse races

bookmark NOUN ❶ something to mark a place in a book ❷ a record of the address of a computer file or Internet page so that you can find it again quickly

bookworm NOUN a person who loves reading

boom VERB ❶ to make a deep hollow sound ❷ to speak in a loud deep voice ❸ to be growing and successful

boom NOUN ❶ a deep hollow sound ❷ a period of increased growth or prosperity ❸ a long pole at the bottom of a sail to keep it stretched ❹ a long pole carrying a microphone or film camera ❺ a chain or floating barrier that

can be placed across a river or a harbour entrance

boomerang NOUN a curved piece of wood that can be thrown so that it returns to the thrower, originally used by Australian Aborigines

boon NOUN something that makes life easier

boon companion NOUN a close friend

boost VERB to increase the strength, value or reputation of a person or thing

boost NOUN ❶ an increase or improvement ❷ something that encourages or helps someone

booster NOUN ❶ a rocket that gives a spacecraft extra power when it leaves the earth ❷ a second dose of a vaccine which renews the effect of an earlier one

boot NOUN ❶ a shoe that covers the foot and ankle or leg ❷ the compartment for luggage in a car

boot VERB ❶ to kick something hard ❷ to boot up a computer is to switch it on and get it ready to use

bootee NOUN a baby's knitted boot

booth NOUN an enclosed compartment, e.g. for a public telephone or for voting at elections

booty NOUN valuable goods taken away by soldiers after a battle

booze VERB (informal) to drink a lot of alcohol

booze NOUN (informal) alcoholic drink

border NOUN ❶ the line dividing two countries or other areas ❷ a band or line around the edge of

something, often for decoration
❸ a long flower bed

border VERB to form a border around or along something

borderline NOUN a boundary

borderline ADJECTIVE only just belonging to a particular group or category

bore VERB ❶ to make someone feel uninterested by being dull ❷ to drill a hole through something ❸ past tense of **bear** VERB

bore NOUN ❶ a dull and uninteresting person or thing ❷ the width of the inside of a pipe or gun barrel ❸ a tidal wave with a steep front that moves up some estuaries

boredom NOUN a feeling of being bored

boring ADJECTIVE dull and uninteresting

born ADJECTIVE ❶ to be born is to have come into existence by birth. (See the note on **borne**.) ❷ having a certain natural quality or ability

borne past participle of **bear** VERB

borough (say burra) NOUN a town or district that has its own council

borrow VERB ❶ to get something to use for a time, with the intention of giving it back afterwards ❷ to obtain money as a loan ❸ to take something and use it as your own

bosom NOUN a woman's breasts

boss NOUN ❶ (informal) a person who is in charge of a business or group of workers ❷ a round raised knob or stud

boss VERB (informal) to order someone about

bossy ADJECTIVE fond of ordering people about

botany NOUN the study of plants

botch VERB to spoil something by poor or clumsy work

both DETERMINER & PRONOUN the two of them, not only one

both ADVERB ➤ **both ... and** not only ... but also

bother VERB ❶ to cause somebody trouble or worry ❷ to take the time or trouble to do something

bother NOUN trouble or worry

bottle NOUN ❶ a narrow-necked container for liquids ❷ (informal) courage

bottle VERB to put or store something in bottles

bottle bank NOUN (British) a large container in which used glass bottles are collected for recycling

bottleneck NOUN a narrow place where something, especially traffic, cannot flow freely

bottom NOUN ❶ the lowest part of something; the base ❷ the part furthest away ❸ your buttocks

bottom ADJECTIVE lowest

bottomless ADJECTIVE extremely deep

boudoir (say boo-dwar) NOUN a woman's bedroom or other private room

bough NOUN a large branch coming from the trunk of a tree

boulder NOUN a very large rock

boulevard (say bool-ev-ard) NOUN a wide street, often with trees on each side

bounce VERB ❶ to spring back when thrown against something

67

A
B
C
D
E
F
G
H
I
J
K
L
M
N
O
P
Q
R
S
T
U
V
W
X
Y
Z

❷ to make a ball or other object bounce **❸** to jump up and down repeatedly; to move in a lively manner **❹** a cheque bounces when it is sent back by the bank because there is not enough money in the account

bounce NOUN **❶** the action of bouncing **❷** a lively confident manner

bouncer NOUN **❶** a person who stands at the door of a club and stops unwanted people coming in or makes troublemakers leave **❷** a ball in cricket that bounces high

bouncy ADJECTIVE **❶** lively and full of energy **❷** that bounces well or can make things bounce

bound VERB **❶** to move or run with large leaps **❷** to be the boundary of something; to limit something **❸** past tense of bind

bound NOUN a large leap

bound ADJECTIVE **❶** obstructed or hindered by something **❷** going towards a place

boundary NOUN **❶** a line that marks a limit **❷** a hit to the boundary of a cricket field

boundless ADJECTIVE without limits

bounds PLURAL NOUN limits

bountiful ADJECTIVE **❶** plentiful; producing a lot **❷** giving generously

bounty NOUN **❶** a reward paid for capturing or killing someone **❷** generosity in giving things

bouquet (say boh-**kay**) NOUN a bunch of flowers

bout NOUN **❶** a boxing or wrestling contest **❷** a period of exercise or work or illness

boutique (say boo-**teek**) NOUN a small shop selling fashionable clothes

bovine (say **boh**-vyn) ADJECTIVE **❶** to do with or like cattle **❷** dull and stupid

bow (rhymes with go) NOUN **❶** a knot made with two loops and two loose ends **❷** a strip of wood curved by a tight string joining its ends, used for shooting arrows **❸** a wooden rod with horsehair stretched between its ends, used for playing a violin or similar string instrument

bow (rhymes with cow) VERB **❶** to bend your body forwards to show respect or as a greeting **❷** to bend a part of your body downwards

bow (rhymes with cow) NOUN **❶** a movement of bowing your body **❷** the front end of a ship

bowels PLURAL NOUN your intestines

bower NOUN a pleasant shady place under trees

bowl NOUN **❶** a round open container for food or liquid **❷** the rounded part of a spoon **❸** a heavy ball used in the game of bowls or in bowling

bowl VERB **❶** to send a ball to be played by a batsman in cricket **❷** to get a batsman out by hitting the wicket with the ball **❸** to send a ball rolling along the ground

bow-legged ADJECTIVE having legs that curve outwards at the knees

bowler NOUN **❶** a person who bowls **❷** (also **bowler hat**) (chiefly British) a man's stiff felt hat with a rounded top

bowling NOUN ❶ the game of knocking down skittles with a heavy ball ❷ the game of bowls

bowls NOUN a game played on a smooth piece of grass, in which you roll heavy wooden balls towards a smaller target ball

bow tie NOUN a tie in the form of a bow, worn by men as part of formal dress

bow window NOUN a curved window

box NOUN ❶ a container made of wood, cardboard, etc., usually with a top or lid ❷ a rectangular space that you fill in on a form or computer screen ❸ a compartment for seating several people in a theatre ❹ an enclosed area for the jury or witnesses in a law court ❺ a small evergreen shrub

box VERB ❶ to fight with your fists as a sport ❷ to put something into a box

boxer NOUN ❶ a person who boxes ❷ a dog that looks like a bulldog

Boxing Day NOUN (British) the first weekday after Christmas Day

box office NOUN an office for booking seats at a theatre or cinema

boy NOUN ❶ a male child ❷ a young man

boycott VERB to refuse to use or buy something because you do not approve of it

boyfriend NOUN a person's regular male friend or lover

boyhood NOUN the time when a man was boy

boyish ADJECTIVE like a boy or suitable for a boy

bra NOUN a piece of underwear worn by women to support their breasts

brace NOUN ❶ a device for holding things in place ❷ a wire device fitted in your mouth to straighten your teeth ❸ a pair of something

brace VERB to support something or make it steady

bracelet NOUN a small band or chain you wear round your wrist

braces PLURAL NOUN straps to hold trousers up, which pass over your shoulders

bracing ADJECTIVE making you feel refreshed and healthy

bracken NOUN a type of large fern that grows in open country; a mass of these ferns

bracket NOUN ❶ a mark used in pairs to enclose words or figures. There are round brackets ( ) and square brackets [ ]. ❷ a support attached to a wall to hold a shelf or light fitting ❸ a group or range between certain limits

bracket VERB ❶ to enclose words or figures in brackets ❷ to group things together because they are similar

brag VERB to boast

braggart NOUN a person who brags

Brahmin NOUN a member of the highest Hindu class, originally priests

braid NOUN ❶ a plait of hair ❷ a strip of cloth with a woven decorative pattern, used as trimming

braid VERB ❶ to plait hair ❷ to trim something with braid

Braille (rhymes with *mail*) NOUN a system of representing letters by raised dots which blind people can read by touch

brain NOUN ❶ the organ inside the top of the head that controls the body ❷ your mind or intelligence

brainwash VERB to force a person to give up one set of ideas or beliefs and accept new ones

brainwave NOUN a sudden bright idea

brainy ADJECTIVE (*informal*) clever; intelligent

braise VERB to cook food slowly in a little liquid in a closed container

brake NOUN a device for slowing down or stopping a moving vehicle

brake VERB to use a brake

bramble NOUN a blackberry bush or a prickly bush like it

bran NOUN ground-up husks of grain which have been sifted out from flour

branch NOUN ❶ a woody arm-like part of a tree or shrub ❷ a local shop, bank or office that belongs to a large organization ❸ a part of a railway, road or river that leads off from the main part ❹ a part of an academic subject

branch VERB to form a branch or divide into branches

brand NOUN ❶ a particular make of goods ❷ a mark made on cattle or sheep by branding ❸ a piece of burning wood

brand VERB ❶ to mark cattle or sheep with a piece of hot iron to identify them ❷ to identify or class someone as something bad ❸ to sell goods under a particular trademark

brandish VERB to wave something about

brand name NOUN a name given to a product or range of products

brand new ADJECTIVE completely new

brandy NOUN a strong alcoholic drink, usually made from wine

brash ADJECTIVE too confident in a rude or aggressive way

brass NOUN ❶ a metal that is an alloy of copper and zinc ❷ wind instruments made of brass, such as trumpets and trombones

brass band NOUN a musical band made up of brass instruments

brassiere (say bras-ee-air) NOUN a bra

brat NOUN (*informal*) a badly behaved child

bravado (say brav-ah-doh) NOUN a display of boldness to impress people

brave ADJECTIVE having or showing courage

brave VERB to face and endure something dangerous or unpleasant

brave NOUN a Native American warrior

bravery NOUN brave actions; courage

bravo (say brah-voh) EXCLAMATION well done!

brawl NOUN a noisy quarrel or fight

brawl VERB to take part in a brawl

brawn NOUN physical strength

brawny ADJECTIVE strong and muscular

bray VERB a donkey brays when it makes a loud harsh cry

bray NOUN the loud harsh cry of a donkey

brazen ADJECTIVE ❶ bold and shameless ❷ made of brass

brazen VERB ➤ **brazen it out** to behave, after doing something wrong, as if you have nothing to be ashamed of

brazier (say bray-zee-er) NOUN a metal basket in which coals can be burned to keep people warm outdoors

breach NOUN ❶ the breaking of an agreement or rule ❷ a gap or broken place in a wall or barrier

breach VERB to break through something; to make a gap

bread NOUN a food made by baking flour and water, usually with yeast

breadth NOUN ❶ the distance across something, from one side to another ❷ a wide range

breadwinner NOUN the member of a family who earns money to support the others

break VERB breaks, breaking, broke, broken ❶ to divide something into pieces by hitting or dropping it ❷ to fall into pieces because of being hit ❸ to damage something so that it stops working properly ❹ to fail to keep a promise, rule or law ❺ to stop something for a time; to end something ❻ weather breaks when it changes suddenly after being hot ❼ a boy's voice breaks

when it becomes suddenly deeper at puberty ❽ waves break when they fall in foam on a shore ❾ to go suddenly or with force ❿ to appear suddenly

break NOUN ❶ a broken place; a gap ❷ an escape; a sudden dash ❸ a short rest from work ❹ a number of points scored continuously in snooker ❺ the winning of a tennis game against the other player's serve ❻ (informal) a piece of luck; a fair chance

breakable ADJECTIVE easy to break

breakage NOUN something that is broken

breakdown NOUN ❶ a sudden failure to work properly, especially by a car ❷ a failure or collapse of something ❸ a period of mental illness caused by anxiety or depression ❹ an analysis of accounts or statistics

breaker NOUN a large wave breaking on the shore

breakfast NOUN the first meal of the day

breakneck ADJECTIVE breakneck speed is dangerously fast

breakthrough NOUN an important development or discovery

breakwater NOUN a wall built out into the sea to protect a coast from heavy waves

bream NOUN a kind of fish with an arched back

breast NOUN ❶ one of the two fleshy parts on the upper front of a woman's body that produce milk to feed a baby ❷ a person's or animal's chest

breastbone NOUN the flat bone down the centre of your chest, joined to your ribs

breastplate NOUN a piece of armour covering the chest

breaststroke NOUN a way of swimming on your front in which you push your arms forward and bring them round and back

breath (say breth) NOUN ❶ air that is drawn into your lungs and sent out again ❷ a gentle blowing

breathalyser NOUN a device for measuring the amount of alcohol in a person's breath

breathe (say breeth) VERB ❶ to take air into your body and send it out again ❷ to say or speak about something

breather (say bree-ther) NOUN (informal) a pause for rest

breathless ADJECTIVE out of breath

breathtaking ADJECTIVE very impressive or beautiful

breech NOUN the back part of a gun barrel, where the bullets are put in

breeches (say brich-iz) PLURAL NOUN trousers reaching to just below your knees

breed VERB breeds, breeding, bred ❶ to produce children or offspring ❷ to keep animals in order to produce young ones from them ❸ to create or produce something ❹ to be bred in a particular way is to be brought up or trained that way

breed NOUN a variety of animal that has been specially developed

breeze NOUN a gentle wind

brethren PLURAL NOUN (old use) brothers

breve (say breev) NOUN a note in music, lasting eight times as long as a crotchet

brevity NOUN being brief or short

brew VERB ❶ to make tea or coffee by mixing it with hot water ❷ to make beer by boiling and fermentation ❸ something bad is brewing when it is growing or developing

brew NOUN a brewed drink

brewer NOUN a person who brews beer for sale

brewery NOUN a place where beer is brewed

briar NOUN a thorny bush, especially the wild rose

bribe NOUN money or a gift offered to someone to influence them to do something

bribe VERB to persuade someone to do something by offering them a bribe

brick NOUN ❶ a small hard block of baked clay used to build walls ❷ a rectangular block of something

brick VERB ➤ brick something up to block an entrance or window with bricks

bricklayer NOUN a worker who builds with bricks

bridal ADJECTIVE to do with a bride or a wedding

bride NOUN a woman on her wedding day

bridegroom NOUN a man on his wedding day

bridesmaid NOUN a woman or girl who accompanies a bride at her

72

wedding

bridge NOUN ❶ a structure built over and across a river, railway or road to allow people or vehicles to cross it ❷ a high platform above a ship's deck, for the officer in charge ❸ the bony upper part of your nose ❹ a card game rather like whist

bridge VERB to make or form a bridge over something

bridle NOUN the part of a horse's harness that fits over its head

bridle VERB ❶ to put a bridle on a horse ❷ to show you are angry or offended by something

bridleway, bridle path NOUN (British) a road suitable for horses but not for vehicles

brief ADJECTIVE lasting for a short time or using only a few words

brief NOUN instructions and information given to someone before they start a piece of work

brief VERB to give someone the instructions and information they need before they start a piece of work

briefcase NOUN a flat case for carrying documents

briefly ADVERB ❶ for a short time ❷ using only a few words

briefs PLURAL NOUN short knickers or underpants

brier NOUN a different spelling of briar

brigade NOUN ❶ a large unit of an army ❷ a group of people organized for a special purpose

brigadier NOUN an army officer who commands a brigade, higher

in rank than a colonel

brigand NOUN a member of a band of robbers

bright ADJECTIVE ❶ giving out a strong light; filled with light or sunlight ❷ a bright colour is strong and vivid ❸ clever ❹ cheerful

brighten VERB to become brighter or more cheerful; to make something brighter

brilliance NOUN ❶ bright light ❷ great intelligence or cleverness

brilliant ADJECTIVE ❶ very clever or talented ❷ excellent; very enjoyable ❸ shining very brightly

brim NOUN ❶ the edge round the top of a cup, bowl or other container ❷ the bottom part of a hat that sticks out

brim VERB to be full of something

brimful ADJECTIVE full to the brim

brimstone NOUN (old use) sulphur

brine NOUN salt water

bring VERB brings, bringing, brought ❶ to carry or take a person or thing with you to a place ❷ to make something come or happen ❸ to move something somewhere

brink NOUN ❶ the edge of a steep place or of a stretch of water ❷ the point beyond which something will happen

brisk ADJECTIVE ❶ quick and lively ❷ wanting to get things done quickly and efficiently

bristle NOUN ❶ a short stiff hair ❷ one of the stiff pieces of hair, wire or plastic in a brush

73

bristle VERB ❶ an animal bristles when it raises its bristles in anger or fear ❷ someone bristles when they show indignation

Britain NOUN the island made up of England, Scotland and Wales, with the small adjacent islands; Great Britain

British Isles PLURAL NOUN the island group which includes Great Britain, Ireland and all the smaller nearby islands

brittle ADJECTIVE hard but easy to break or snap

broach VERB ❶ to start a discussion of something ❷ to make a hole in something and draw out liquid

broad ADJECTIVE ❶ large across; wide ❷ in general terms; not detailed ❸ strong and unmistakable

broadband NOUN (in computing) a system for connecting computers to the Internet at very high speed

broad bean NOUN a bean with large flat seeds

broadcast NOUN a programme sent out on television or the radio

broadcast VERB to send out a programme on television or the radio

broaden VERB to become broader; to make something broader

broadly ADVERB ❶ generally; on the whole ❷ widely

broad-minded ADJECTIVE tolerant; not easily shocked

broadside NOUN ❶ a round of firing by all the guns on one side of a ship ❷ a strong verbal attack

brocade NOUN a rich fabric woven with raised patterns

broccoli NOUN a kind of cauliflower with greenish flower heads

brochure (say **broh**-shoor) NOUN a booklet or pamphlet containing information

brogue (rhymes with rogue) NOUN ❶ a strong kind of shoe ❷ a strong regional accent

broil VERB ❶ to cook food using a direct heat, such as a grill ❷ to be broiling is to be very hot

broke ADJECTIVE (informal) having spent all your money

broken-hearted ADJECTIVE feeling great sadness or grief

broken home NOUN a family in which the parents are divorced or separated

broker NOUN a person who buys and sells things, especially shares, for other people

brolly NOUN (British) (informal) an umbrella

bromide NOUN a substance used in medicine to calm the nerves

bronchial (say **bronk**-ee-al) ADJECTIVE to do with the tubes that lead from your windpipe to your lungs

bronchitis (say bronk-**y**-tiss) NOUN a disease that causes inflammation of the bronchial tubes, which makes you cough a lot

bronze NOUN ❶ a metal that is an alloy of copper and tin ❷ something made of bronze ❸ a bronze medal, awarded as third prize ❹ a yellowish-brown colour

Bronze Age NOUN the period in human history when tools and

74

weapons were made of bronze

brooch (rhymes with *coach*) NOUN an ornament with a hinged pin for fastening it on to clothes

brood NOUN young birds that were hatched together

brood VERB ❶ to keep thinking and worrying about something ❷ to sit on eggs to hatch them

broody ADJECTIVE ❶ a broody hen is ready to sit on her eggs ❷ quietly worried and unhappy about something ❸ a woman who is broody is eager to have children

brook NOUN a small stream

brook VERB to allow or tolerate something

broom NOUN ❶ a brush with a long handle, for sweeping floors ❷ a shrub with yellow, white or pink flowers

broomstick NOUN the handle of a broom, which in stories witches use to ride on

broth NOUN a kind of thin soup

brother NOUN ❶ a son of the same parents as another person ❷ a member of a Christian religious order of men

brotherhood NOUN ❶ friendliness and companionship between men ❷ a society or association of men

brother-in-law NOUN the brother of a married person's husband or wife; the husband of a person's sister

brow NOUN ❶ an eyebrow ❷ your forehead ❸ the top of a hill

brown NOUN a colour between orange and black, like the colour of dark wood

brown ADJECTIVE ❶ of the colour brown ❷ having a brown skin; suntanned

brown VERB ❶ to make something brown, especially by cooking it ❷ to become brown

Brownie NOUN a member of a junior branch of the Guides

brownie NOUN a flat chocolate cake, served in squares

browse VERB ❶ to read or look at something casually ❷ to look for information on the Internet ❸ animals browse when they feed on grass or leaves

browser NOUN (*in computing*) a piece of computer software that allows you to search and look at websites on the Internet

bruise NOUN a dark mark made on the skin by hitting it

bruise VERB ❶ to make a bruise or bruises appear on a person's skin ❷ to develop a bruise

brunch NOUN (*informal*) a late-morning meal combining breakfast and lunch

brunette NOUN a woman with dark-brown hair

brunt NOUN the chief impact of something

brush NOUN ❶ an object used for cleaning or painting things or for smoothing the hair, usually with bristles set in a solid base ❷ using a brush ❸ a fox's bushy tail ❹ an unpleasant experience or encounter ❺ undergrowth, bushes and shrubs that often grow under trees

brush VERB ❶ to use a brush on something ❷ to touch something lightly while passing it

brusque (say bruusk) ADJECTIVE abrupt and offhand in manner

Brussels sprouts PLURAL NOUN the edible buds of a kind of cabbage

brutal ADJECTIVE cruel and violent

brute NOUN ❶ a cruel or violent man ❷ an animal

brute ADJECTIVE brute force or strength is purely physical, without using any skill

BSc ABBREVIATION Bachelor of Science

BSE ABBREVIATION bovine spongiform encephalopathy; a fatal disease of cattle that affects the nervous system and makes the cow stagger about. BSE is sometimes known as 'mad cow disease'

bubble NOUN ❶ a thin transparent ball of liquid filled with air or gas ❷ a small ball of air in something, such as a fizzy drink

bubble VERB ❶ to send up bubbles or rise to the surface in bubbles ❷ to show great liveliness

bubblegum NOUN chewing gum that can be blown into large bubbles

bubbly ADJECTIVE ❶ full of bubbles ❷ cheerful and lively

buccaneer NOUN a pirate

buck NOUN ❶ a male deer, rabbit or hare ❷ (North American & Australian/NZ) a dollar

buck VERB a horse bucks when it jumps with its back arched

bucket NOUN a container with a handle, for carrying liquids, sand, etc.

buckle NOUN a clip at the end of a belt or strap for fastening it

buckle VERB ❶ to fasten something with a buckle ❷ to bend or give way under a strain

bud NOUN a flower or leaf before it opens

Buddhism (say buud-izm) NOUN a religion that started in Asia and follows the teachings of Siddharta Gautama who lived in India in the 5th century BC and became known as 'the Buddha'

budding ADJECTIVE beginning to develop

buddy NOUN (informal) a friend

budge VERB if you cannot budge something, you cannot move it at all

budgerigar NOUN an Australian bird often kept as a pet in a cage

budget NOUN ❶ a plan for spending money wisely ❷ an amount of money set aside for a purpose

budget VERB to plan how much you are going to spend

budgie NOUN (informal) a budgerigar

buff NOUN (informal) a person who is very interested in a subject and knows a lot about it

buff ADJECTIVE of a dull yellow colour

buff VERB to polish something with soft material

buffalo NOUN buffalo or buffaloes a large ox. Different kinds are found in Asia, Africa and North America (where they are also called bison)

buffer NOUN ❶ something that reduces an impact or protects something ❷ (*British*) a device on a railway engine or wagon or at the end of a track, for reducing the shock if there is a collision ❸ (*in computing*) a memory in which text or data can be stored temporarily

buffet (say **buu**-fay) NOUN ❶ a room or counter selling light meals or snacks ❷ a meal where guests serve themselves

buffet (say **buf**-it) VERB to hit or knock something repeatedly

buffoon NOUN a person who acts like a fool

bug NOUN ❶ a tiny insect ❷ an error in a computer program that prevents it working properly ❸ (*informal*) a germ or virus ❹ a secret hidden microphone

bug VERB ❶ to fit a room with a secret hidden microphone ❷ (*informal*) to pester or annoy someone

bugbear NOUN something you fear or dislike

buggy NOUN ❶ a kind of chair on wheels for pushing young children around ❷ a small open-topped vehicle used on beaches or golf courses ❸ a light, horse-drawn carriage

bugle NOUN a brass instrument like a small trumpet, used for sounding military signals

build VERB builds, building, built ❶ to make something by putting parts together ❷ to develop or increase something gradually

build NOUN the shape of someone's body

builder NOUN someone who puts up buildings

building NOUN ❶ a structure with walls and a roof, such as a house or office block ❷ the process of constructing houses and other structures

building society NOUN (*British*) an organization that accepts deposits of money and lends to people who want to buy houses

built-in ADJECTIVE made into a permanent part of something

built-up ADJECTIVE a built-up area is one with a lot of buildings

bulb NOUN ❶ a glass globe that produces electric light ❷ a thick rounded part of a plant from which a stem grows up and roots grow down ❸ a rounded part of something

bulbous ADJECTIVE round and fat in an ugly way

bulge NOUN a rounded swelling; an outward curve

bulge VERB to swell or stick out in a curve

bulimia (say bew-**lim**-ia) NOUN an illness that makes someone alternately overeat and fast, often making themselves vomit after eating

bulk NOUN ❶ the size of something, especially when it is large ❷ the greater part or the majority

bulk VERB ➤ bulk something out to increase the size or thickness of something

bulky ADJECTIVE taking up a lot

of space

bull NOUN ❶ a fully-grown male of the cattle family ❷ a male seal, whale or elephant

bulldog NOUN a dog of a powerful breed with a short thick neck

bulldoze VERB to clear an area with a bulldozer

bulldozer NOUN a powerful tractor with a wide metal blade or scoop in front, used for shifting soil or clearing ground

bullet NOUN a small piece of shaped metal shot from a rifle or revolver

bulletin NOUN ❶ a short announcement of news on radio or television ❷ a regular newsletter or report

bulletin board NOUN (in computing) a site on a computer system where people can read or write messages

bullet point NOUN an important item in a list, printed with a black dot in front of it

bulletproof ADJECTIVE able to keep out bullets

bullfight NOUN in Spain, a public entertainment in which bulls are fought and usually killed, in an arena

bullfinch NOUN a bird with a strong beak and a pink breast

bullion NOUN bars of gold or silver

bullock NOUN a young castrated bull

bull's-eye NOUN ❶ the centre of a target ❷ a hard round peppermint sweet

bully VERB to use strength or power

to hurt or frighten another person

bully NOUN someone who bullies people

bulrush NOUN a tall plant which grows in marshes, with a thick velvety head

bum NOUN (British) (informal) a person's bottom

bumble VERB to move or behave or speak clumsily

bumblebee NOUN a large bee with a loud hum

bump VERB ❶ to knock against something ❷ to move along with jolts

bump NOUN ❶ knocking against something or the sound of this ❷ a swelling or lump

bumper NOUN a bar along the front or back of a motor vehicle to protect it in collisions

bumper ADJECTIVE unusually large or plentiful

bumpkin NOUN a country person with awkward manners

bumpy ADJECTIVE having a lot of bumps

bun NOUN ❶ a small round sweet cake ❷ hair twisted into a round bunch at the back of the head

bunch NOUN a number of things joined or fastened together

bundle NOUN a number of things tied or wrapped together

bundle VERB ❶ to wrap or tie things into a bundle ❷ to push someone hurriedly or carelessly

bungalow NOUN a house without any upstairs rooms

bungee jumping NOUN the sport of jumping from a height with a special elastic rope (called a **bungee**) tied to your legs to stop you from hitting the ground

bungle VERB to make a mess of doing something

bunion NOUN a swelling at the side of the joint where your big toe joins your foot

bunk NOUN ❶ a narrow bed built like a shelf ❷ (also **bunk bed**) one of a pair of single beds mounted one above the other

bunk VERB ➤ **bunk off** (*British*) (*informal*) to sneak away from where you are supposed to be, especially school

bunker NOUN ❶ a sandy hollow built as an obstacle on a golf course ❷ an underground shelter for use in wartime ❸ an outdoor container for storing coal

bunny NOUN (*informal*) a rabbit

Bunsen burner NOUN a small gas burner used in laboratories

bunting NOUN ❶ a kind of small bird ❷ strips of small flags hung up to decorate streets and buildings

buoy (say boi) NOUN a floating object anchored to mark a channel or underwater rocks

buoy VERB ❶ to keep something afloat ❷ to encourage someone or keep their spirits up

buoyant (say boy-ant) ADJECTIVE ❶ able to float ❷ light-hearted; cheerful

bur NOUN a different spelling of **burr** (seed case)

burble VERB ❶ to make a gentle murmuring sound ❷ to speak in a confused way

burden NOUN ❶ a heavy load that you have to carry ❷ something troublesome that you have to put up with

burden VERB ❶ to load someone heavily ❷ to cause someone worry or trouble

bureau (say bewr-oh) NOUN bureaux ❶ a writing desk with drawers ❷ an office or department

bureaucracy (say bewr-ok-ra-see) NOUN the use of too many rules and forms by officials, especially in government departments

bureaucrat (say bewr-ok-rat) NOUN a person who works in a government department

burger NOUN a hamburger

burglar NOUN a person who breaks into a building in order to steal things

burglary NOUN the crime of breaking into a building and stealing things

burgle VERB (*British*) to break into a house and steal things

burgundy NOUN a rich red or white wine

burial NOUN burying somebody

burlesque (say ber-lesk) NOUN a comical imitation that makes fun of something

burly ADJECTIVE having a strong heavy body

burn VERB burns, burning, burned or burnt ❶ to be on fire; to blaze or glow with fire ❷ to damage or destroy something by fire or heat ❸ to hurt yourself with fire or heat ❹ to spoil food by cooking it for too long ❺ to feel very hot

a
b
c
d
e
f
g
h
i
j
k
l
m
n
o
p
q
r
s
t
u
v
w
x
y
z

burn NOUN ❶ a mark or injury made by burning ❷ the firing of a spacecraft's rockets ❸ (*Scottish*) a small stream

burner NOUN the part of a lamp or cooker that gives out the flame

burning ADJECTIVE ❶ a burning desire or ambition is one that is very intense ❷ a burning issue or question is one that is very topical and important

burnish VERB to polish a surface by rubbing

burp VERB to make a noise through your mouth by letting air come up from your stomach

burp NOUN the act or sound of burping

burr NOUN ❶ a plant's seed case or flower that clings to hair or clothes ❷ a whirring sound ❸ a strong pronunciation of the letter 'r', as in some regional accents

burrow NOUN a hole or tunnel dug by a rabbit or fox as a place to live

burrow VERB ❶ to dig a burrow ❷ to push your way through or into something; to search deeply

bursar NOUN (*British*) a person who manages the finances and other business of a school or college

bursary NOUN (*British*) a grant given to a student

burst VERB bursts, bursting, burst ❶ to come apart or tear open suddenly ❷ to break or force something apart ❸ to burst into a room is to go in suddenly in a rush ❹ to start doing something suddenly ❺ to be very full

burst NOUN ❶ a split caused by something bursting ❷ something short and forceful

bury VERB ❶ to put a dead body in the ground ❷ to put something underground ❸ to cover something up or hide it

bus NOUN buses a large vehicle for passengers to travel in

busby NOUN a tall fur cap worn by some regiments on ceremonial occasions

bush NOUN ❶ a woody plant smaller than a tree; a shrub ❷ wild uncultivated land, especially in Africa and Australia

bushel NOUN a measure for grain and fruit equal to 8 gallons (36.4 litres)

bushman NOUN a person who lives or travels in the Australian or African bush

bushy ADJECTIVE thick and hairy

busily ADVERB in a busy way

business (say biz-niss) NOUN ❶ buying and selling things; trade ❷ a shop or firm ❸ a person's concern or responsibilities ❹ an affair or subject

businesslike ADJECTIVE dealing with things in a direct and practical way

businessman NOUN a man or woman who works in business

businesswoman NOUN a woman who works in business

busker NOUN a person who plays music in the street for money

bust NOUN ❶ a sculpture of a person's head, shoulders and chest ❷ a woman's breasts or chest

bust VERB (*informal*) to break something

bust ADJECTIVE (*informal*) ❶ broken or damaged ❷ bankrupt

bustle VERB to hurry in a busy or excited way

bustle NOUN ❶ hurried or excited activity ❷ padding used to puff out the top of a long skirt at the back

busy ADJECTIVE ❶ having a lot to do; working on something ❷ full of activity ❸ a busy telephone line or number is one that is engaged

busy VERB ➤ busy yourself to do things to occupy yourself; to keep busy

busybody NOUN a person who meddles or interferes

but CONJUNCTION however; nevertheless

but PREPOSITION except

but ADVERB only; no more than

butcher NOUN ❶ a person who cuts up meat and sells it ❷ a person who kills people in a cruel way

butcher VERB to kill people in a cruel way

butler NOUN a male servant in charge of other servants in a large private house

butt NOUN ❶ the thicker end of a weapon or tool ❷ the stub of a cigar or cigarette ❸ a large cask or barrel ❹ someone who is a target for ridicule or teasing

butt VERB an animal butts something when it pushes or hits it with its head and horns

butter NOUN a soft fatty food made by churning cream

butter VERB to spread something with butter

buttercup NOUN a wild plant with bright yellow cup-shaped flowers

butter-fingers NOUN a clumsy person who often drops things

butterfly NOUN ❶ an insect with large white or brightly coloured wings ❷ a swimming stroke in which both arms are lifted forwards at the same time

buttermilk NOUN the liquid that is left after butter has been made

butterscotch NOUN a kind of hard toffee

buttock NOUN either of the two fleshy rounded parts of your bottom

button NOUN ❶ a knob or disc sewn on clothes as a fastening or ornament ❷ a small knob that you press to work an electric device

button VERB to fasten a piece of clothing with a button or buttons

buttonhole NOUN ❶ a slit through which you push a button to fasten clothes ❷ a flower worn on a lapel

buttonhole VERB to come up to someone so that you can talk to them

buttress NOUN a support built against a wall

buy VERB buys, buying, bought to get something by paying for it

buy NOUN something that is bought

buzz NOUN a vibrating humming sound

buzz VERB ❶ to make a buzz ❷ to be full of excitement or activity ❸ to threaten an aircraft by deliberately flying close to it

buzzard NOUN a kind of hawk

buzzer NOUN a device that makes a buzzing sound as a signal

by PREPOSITION This word is used to show ❶ closeness to something (*Sit by me.*), ❷ direction or route (*We got here by a short cut.*), ❸ the time before which something happens (*Try to get there by 6 o'clock.*), ❹ manner or method (*cooking by gas*), ❺ distance or amount (*You missed it by inches.*)

by ADVERB past

bye NOUN ❶ a run scored in cricket when the ball goes past the batsman without being touched ❷ an opportunity to go to the next round of a tournament without having won the current round, because you have no opponent

bye-bye EXCLAMATION (*informal*) goodbye

by-election NOUN (*British*) an election to replace a Member of Parliament who has died or resigned

bygone ADJECTIVE belonging to the past

by-law NOUN a law that applies only to a particular town or district

bypass NOUN ❶ a road taking traffic round the edge of a town or city rather than going through the centre ❷ an operation on the heart to make an alternative passage for the blood so that it does not flow through a part that is damaged or blocked

bypass VERB to avoid something by means of a bypass

by-product NOUN something useful produced while something else is being made

byroad NOUN a minor road

bystander NOUN a person standing near but taking no part when something happens

byte NOUN (*in computing*) a unit of information in a computer

byway NOUN a minor road or path

byword NOUN a person or thing spoken of as a famous example

Cc

cab NOUN ❶ a taxi ❷ a compartment for the driver of a lorry, train, truck or crane

cabaret (*say* **kab**-er-ay) NOUN an entertainment provided for the customers in a restaurant or nightclub

cabbage NOUN a vegetable with layers of closely packed green or purple leaves

caber NOUN a tree trunk used in the Scottish Highland sport of 'tossing the caber'

cabin NOUN ❶ a wooden hut or shelter ❷ a room for sleeping on a ship ❸ the part of an aircraft where the passengers sit ❹ a driver's cab

Cabinet NOUN the group of chief ministers, chosen by the Prime Minister, who meet to decide government policy

cabinet NOUN a cupboard with drawers or shelves for storing things

cable NOUN ❶ a thick rope of fibre or wire; a thick chain ❷ a covered group of wires laid underground for transmitting electrical signals ❸ cable television ❹ (old use) a telegram sent overseas

cable car NOUN a small cabin suspended on a moving cable, used for carrying people up and down a mountainside

cable television NOUN a broadcasting service with signals transmitted by cable to the sets of people who have paid to receive it

cacao (say ka-**kay**-oh) NOUN a tropical tree with a seed from which cocoa and chocolate are made

cache (say kash) NOUN a hidden store of things, especially valuable things

cackle NOUN ❶ a loud unpleasant laugh ❷ noisy chatter ❸ the loud clucking noise a hen makes

cackle VERB ❶ to laugh in a loud and unpleasant way ❷ hens cackle when they make loud clucking noises

cacophony (say kak-**off**-on-ee) NOUN a harsh mixture of loud unpleasant sounds

cactus NOUN cacti a fleshy plant, usually with prickles, from a hot dry climate

cad NOUN a dishonourable man

caddie NOUN a person who carries a golfer's clubs during a game

caddy NOUN a small box for holding tea

cadence (say **kay**-denss) NOUN ❶ rhythm; the rise and fall of the voice in speaking ❷ the final notes of a musical phrase

cadenza (say ka-**den**-za) NOUN an elaborate passage for a solo instrument or singer, to show the performer's skill

cadet NOUN a young person being trained for the armed forces or the police

cadge VERB (British) to get something from someone without paying for it

cadmium NOUN a metal that looks like tin

Caesarean, Caesarean section (say siz-**air**-ee-an) NOUN a surgical operation for taking a baby out of the mother's womb

caesura (say siz-**yoor**-a) NOUN a short pause in a line of verse

cafe (say **kaf**-ay) NOUN a small restaurant that sells light meals and drinks

cafeteria (say kaf-it-**eer**-ee-a) NOUN a self-service cafe

caffeine (say **kaf**-een) NOUN the substance found in tea and coffee that makes you feel more awake and full of energy

caftan NOUN a long loose coat or dress with wide sleeves

cage NOUN a container or structure made of bars or wires, in which birds or animals are kept

cagoule (say kag-**ool**) NOUN (British) a lightweight waterproof jacket

cairn NOUN a pile of loose stones set up as a landmark or monument

cajole VERB to persuade someone to do something by saying nice

cake NOUN ❶ a sweet food made by baking a mixture of flour, fat, eggs, sugar, etc. ❷ something shaped into a lump or block

caked ADJECTIVE covered with something that has dried hard

calamine NOUN a pink powder used to make a soothing lotion for the skin

calamity NOUN an event that causes a lot of damage or harm

calcium NOUN a chemical substance found in teeth, bones and lime

calculate VERB ❶ to work something out by using mathematics ❷ if something is calculated to have an effect, it is intended or designed to have that effect

calculating ADJECTIVE planning things carefully so that you get what you want

calculation NOUN something you work out by using mathematics

calculator NOUN a small electronic device for making calculations

calculus NOUN mathematics for working out problems about rates of change

calendar NOUN a chart or set of pages showing the dates of the month or year

calf NOUN calves ❶ a young cow or bull ❷ a young whale, seal or elephant ❸ the fleshy back part of your leg below your knee

calibre (say kal-ib-er) NOUN ❶ the diameter of the inside of a tube or gun barrel or of a bullet or shell ❷ ability or quality

calico NOUN a kind of cotton cloth

caliper NOUN a support for a weak or injured leg

calipers PLURAL NOUN compasses for measuring the width of tubes or of round objects

caliph (say kal-if or kay-lif) NOUN the former title of the ruler in certain Muslim countries

call VERB ❶ to name or describe a person or thing ❷ to be called something is to have that as your name ❸ to shout or speak loudly, e.g. to attract someone's attention ❹ to telephone someone ❺ to tell or ask someone to come to you ❻ to make a short visit

call NOUN ❶ a shout or cry to attract someone's attention ❷ a short visit ❸ telephoning someone ❹ a request for someone to come

call box NOUN a telephone box

caller NOUN a person who telephones or visits someone

calligram NOUN a poem in which the form of the writing relates to the content of the poem, e.g. a poem about growth shown with the letters getting larger

calligraphy (say kal-ig-raf-ee) NOUN the art of beautiful handwriting

calling NOUN ❶ a person's profession or trade ❷ a strong feeling that you should follow a particular occupation; a vocation

callous (say kal-us) ADJECTIVE hard-hearted; not caring about other people's feelings

callow ADJECTIVE immature and inexperienced

callus NOUN a small patch of skin that has become thick and hard through being continually pressed or rubbed

calm ADJECTIVE ❶ not excited, worried or angry ❷ quiet and still; not windy

calm VERB to become or make someone calm

calorie NOUN a unit for measuring an amount of heat or the energy produced by food

calumny (say kal-um-nee) NOUN an untrue statement that damages a person's reputation

calve VERB to give birth to a calf

calypso NOUN a West Indian song about current happenings, made up as the singer goes along

calyx (say kay-liks) NOUN a ring of leaves (sepals) forming the outer case of a bud

camaraderie (say kam-er-ah-der-ee) NOUN trust and comradeship between friends

camber NOUN a slight curved shape from the middle of a road down to the sides

camel NOUN a large animal with a long neck and either one or two humps on its back, used in desert countries for riding and for carrying goods

camellia NOUN a kind of evergreen flowering shrub

cameo (say kam-ee-oh) NOUN ❶ a small raised piece of stone carved with a raised design in its upper layer ❷ a short part in a play or film, usually one played by a well-known actor

camera NOUN a device for taking photographs, films or television pictures

camomile NOUN a plant with sweet-smelling daisy-like flowers

camouflage (say kam-off-lahzh) NOUN a way of hiding things by making them look like part of their surroundings

camouflage VERB to hide something by camouflage

camp NOUN a place where people live in tents or huts for a short time

camp VERB ❶ to put up a tent or tents ❷ to have a holiday in a tent

campaign NOUN ❶ a planned series of actions, especially to get people to support you or become interested in something ❷ a series of battles in one area or with one purpose

campaign VERB to take part in a campaign

camphor NOUN a strong-smelling white substance used in medicine and mothballs and in making plastics

campsite NOUN a place for camping

campus NOUN the grounds and buildings of a university or college

can AUXILIARY VERB past tense could ❶ to be able to ❷ to be allowed to

can NOUN ❶ a sealed tin in which food or drink is preserved ❷ a metal or plastic container for liquids

can VERB cans, canning, canned to preserve food in a sealed can

canal NOUN ❶ an artificial water channel cut through land so that boats can sail along it or for irrigating land ❷ a tube through which food or air passes in a plant or animal body

canary NOUN a small yellow bird that sings

cancan NOUN a lively dance in which the legs are kicked very high

cancel VERB ❶ to decide that something planned will not be done or will not take place ❷ to stop an order or instruction for something ❸ to mark a stamp or ticket etc. so that it cannot be used again

cancellation NOUN something that has been cancelled

cancer NOUN ❶ a serious disease in which harmful growths form in the body ❷ a harmful tumour

candelabrum (say kan-dil-**ab**-rum) NOUN a candlestick with several branches for holding candles

candid ADJECTIVE frank and honest

candidate NOUN ❶ a person who wants to be elected or chosen for a particular job or position ❷ a person taking an examination

candle NOUN a stick of wax with a wick running through it, giving light when it is burning

candlestick NOUN a holder for a candle or candles

candour (say kan-der) NOUN being candid; frankness and honesty

candy NOUN (North American) sweets or a sweet

candyfloss NOUN (British) a fluffy mass of very thin strands of spun sugar wrapped round a stick

cane NOUN ❶ the hollow stem

of a reed or tall grass ❷ a long thin stick

cane VERB to beat someone with a long thin stick as a punishment

canine (say **kayn**-yn) ADJECTIVE to do with dogs

canine NOUN ❶ a dog ❷ a pointed tooth at the front of the mouth

canister NOUN a round metal container

cannabis NOUN hemp smoked as a drug

cannibal NOUN ❶ a person who eats human flesh ❷ an animal that eats animals of its own kind

cannon NOUN ❶ a large heavy gun that fires heavy balls made of metal or stone ❷ (chiefly British) the hitting of two balls in billiards by the third ball

cannon VERB (chiefly British) to cannon into something is to collide with it clumsily or heavily

cannon ball NOUN a large solid ball fired from a cannon

cannot can not

canny ADJECTIVE clever and cautious; shrewd

canoe NOUN a narrow lightweight boat, moved forwards with paddles

canoe VERB to travel in a canoe

canon NOUN ❶ a general principle; a rule ❷ a clergyman of a cathedral

canonize (also **canonise**) VERB to declare officially that someone is a saint

canopy NOUN ❶ a hanging cover forming a shelter above a throne or bed ❷ a natural covering, e.g. of leaves and branches ❸ the part of

a parachute that spreads in the air

cant VERB to slope or tilt

cant NOUN insincere talk about moral behaviour

can't (*mainly spoken*) cannot

cantaloupe NOUN a small round orange-coloured melon

cantankerous ADJECTIVE bad-tempered and always complaining

cantata (say kant-**ah**-ta) NOUN a musical composition for singers, usually with a chorus and orchestra

canteen NOUN ❶ a restaurant for workers in a factory or office ❷ a case or box containing a set of cutlery ❸ a small water flask carried by a soldier or camper

canter NOUN a gentle gallop by a horse

canter VERB to go or ride at a gentle gallop

cantilever NOUN a beam or girder fixed at only one end and used to support a bridge

canton NOUN each of the districts into which a country, especially Switzerland, is divided

canvas NOUN ❶ a kind of strong coarse cloth ❷ a piece of canvas for painting on; a painting

canvass VERB to visit people to ask them for their support, especially in an election

canyon NOUN a deep valley, usually with a river running through it

cap NOUN ❶ a soft hat without a brim but often with a peak ❷ a special headdress, e.g. that worn by a nurse ❸ a cap awarded to members of a sports team ❹ a

cover or top ❺ something that makes a bang when fired in a toy pistol

cap VERB ❶ to put a cap or cover on something ❷ to award a sports cap to someone chosen to be in a team ❸ to cap a story or joke is to tell one that is better

capable ADJECTIVE able to do something

capacity NOUN ❶ the amount that something can hold ❷ ability to do something ❸ the position that someone occupies

cape NOUN ❶ a short cloak ❷ a large piece of high land that sticks out into the sea

caper VERB to jump about playfully

caper NOUN ❶ jumping about playfully ❷ (*informal*) an adventure or prank ❸ the pickled bud of a prickly shrub, used in cooking

capillary (say ka-**pil**-er-ee) NOUN any of the very fine blood vessels that connect veins and arteries

capillary ADJECTIVE to do with or occurring in a very narrow tube; to do with a capillary

capital NOUN ❶ a capital city ❷ a capital letter ❸ money or property that can be used to produce more wealth ❹ the top part of a pillar

capital ADJECTIVE (*old use*) very good or excellent

capital city NOUN the most important city in a country, usually where the government is based

capitalism (say **kap**-it-al-izm) NOUN an economic system in which a country's trade and industry are controlled by private owners

capitalist (say **kap**-it-al-ist) NOUN ❶ a rich person who has a lot of their wealth invested ❷ a person who is in favour of capitalism

capitalize (also **capitalise**) (say **kap**-it-al-yz) VERB ❶ to write or print a word with a capital letter ❷ to capitalize on something is to use it to your own advantage

capital letter NOUN a large letter of the kind used at the start of a name or sentence

capital punishment NOUN punishing criminals by putting them to death

capitulate VERB to admit that you are defeated and surrender

cappuccino NOUN milky coffee made frothy by putting steam through it under pressure

capricious (say ka-**prish**-us) ADJECTIVE deciding or changing your mind in an impulsive way

capsize VERB a boat or ship capsizes when it overturns in the water

capstan NOUN a thick post that can be turned to wind up a rope or cable

capsule NOUN ❶ a hollow pill containing medicine ❷ a plant's seed case that splits open when ripe ❸ a compartment of a spacecraft that can be separated from the main part

captain NOUN ❶ a person in command of a ship or aircraft ❷ the leader of a sports team ❸ an army officer ranking next below a naval officer

ranking next below a commodore
captain VERB to be the captain of a sports team

captaincy NOUN the position of captain of a team

caption NOUN ❶ the words printed next to a picture to describe it ❷ a short title or heading in a newspaper or magazine

captivate VERB to charm or delight someone

captive NOUN someone who has been taken prisoner

captive ADJECTIVE taken prisoner; unable to escape

captivity NOUN ❶ the state of being held prisoner ❷ the state of being kept in a zoo or wildlife park rather than living in the wild

captor NOUN someone who has captured a person or animal

capture VERB ❶ to catch or imprison a person or animal ❷ to take control of a place using force ❸ to make someone interested in something ❹ to succeed in representing or describing something ❺ (in computing) to put data in a form that can be stored in a computer

capture NOUN the act of capturing someone or something

car NOUN ❶ a road vehicle with four wheels that can carry a small number of people ❷ a railway carriage

carafe (say ka-**raf**) NOUN a glass bottle holding wine or water for pouring out at the table

caramel NOUN ❶ a kind of soft toffee made from sugar and butter

❷ burnt sugar used for colouring and flavouring food

carat NOUN ❶ a measure of weight for precious stones ❷ a measure of the purity of gold

caravan NOUN ❶ a vehicle towed by a car and used for living in, especially by people on holiday ❷ a group of people travelling together across desert country

caraway NOUN a plant with spicy seeds that are used for flavouring food

carbohydrate NOUN a compound of carbon, oxygen and hydrogen (e.g. sugar or starch), found in food and a source of energy

carbolic NOUN a kind of disinfectant

carbon NOUN ❶ an element that is present in all living things and that occurs in its pure form as diamond and graphite ❷ carbon dioxide

carbonate NOUN a compound that gives off carbon dioxide when mixed with acid

carbonated ADJECTIVE a carbonated drink has carbon dioxide added to make it fizzy

carbon copy NOUN an exact copy of something

carbon dating NOUN the use of a kind of radioactive carbon that decays at a steady rate, to find out how old something

carbon dioxide NOUN a gas formed when things burn or breathed out by humans and animals

carboniferous ADJECTIVE producing coal

carbon monoxide NOUN a poisonous gas found especially in the exhaust fumes of motor vehicles

carbuncle NOUN ❶ a large boil or abscess in the skin ❷ a bright-red gem

carburettor NOUN a device for mixing fuel and air in an engine

carcass NOUN ❶ the dead body of an animal ❷ the bony part of a bird's body after the meat has been eaten

carcinogen NOUN any substance that can cause cancer

card NOUN ❶ thick stiff paper or thin cardboard ❷ a small piece of stiff paper for writing or printing on, especially to send messages or greetings or to record information ❸ a small, oblong piece of plastic issued to a customer by a bank or shop for drawing out money and making payments ❹ a playing card

cardboard NOUN a kind of thin board made of layers of paper or wood fibre

cardiac (say **kard**-ee-ak) ADJECTIVE to do with the heart

cardigan NOUN a knitted jumper fastened with buttons down the front

cardinal NOUN a senior priest in the Roman Catholic Church

cardinal ADJECTIVE chief or most important

cardinal number NOUN a number for counting things, e.g. one, two, three, etc. Compare with **ordinal** number.

cardiology NOUN the study of the

heart and its diseases

care NOUN ❶ serious attention and thought ❷ caution to avoid damage or loss ❸ protection or supervision ❹ worry or anxiety

care VERB ❶ to feel interested or concerned about someone or something ❷ to feel affection

career NOUN the series of jobs that someone has as they make progress in their occupation

career VERB to rush along wildly

carefree ADJECTIVE without worries or responsibilities

careful ADJECTIVE ❶ thinking about what you are doing so that you do not make a mistake, have an accident, etc. ❷ giving serious thought and attention to something

careless ADJECTIVE not taking enough care to avoid mistakes or harm

caress NOUN a gentle loving touch

caress VERB to touch someone lovingly

caret NOUN a mark (^) showing where something is to be inserted in writing or printing

caretaker NOUN a person employed to look after a school, block of flats, etc.

cargo NOUN goods carried in a ship or aircraft

Caribbean ADJECTIVE to do with or from the Caribbean Sea, a part of the Atlantic Ocean east of Central America

caribou (say ka-rib-oo) NOUN a North American reindeer

caricature NOUN an amusing or

exaggerated picture or description of someone

caries (say kair-eez) NOUN decay in teeth or bones

carnage NOUN the killing of large numbers of people

carnation NOUN a garden flower with a sweet smell

carnival NOUN a festival, often with a procession of people in fancy dress

carnivore (say kar-niv-or) NOUN an animal that feeds on the flesh of other animals. Compare with **herbivore**.

carnivorous (say kar-niv-er-us) ADJECTIVE a carnivorous animal feeds on the flesh of other animals. Compare with **herbivorous**.

carol NOUN a Christmas hymn

carousel (say ka-roo-sel) NOUN ❶ a roundabout at a fair ❷ a conveyor belt that goes round in a circle for passengers to collect their baggage at an airport

carp NOUN an edible freshwater fish

carp VERB to keep complaining or finding fault

car park NOUN (British) an area where cars may be parked

carpenter NOUN a person who makes things out of wood

carpet NOUN ❶ a thick soft covering for a floor ❷ a thick layer of something on the ground

carport NOUN a shelter with a roof and open sides for a car

carriage NOUN ❶ one of the separate parts of a train, where passengers sit ❷ a passenger vehicle pulled by horses

❸ carrying goods from one place to another or the cost of this ❹ a moving part carrying or holding something in a machine

carriageway NOUN (British) the part of a road on which vehicles travel

carrier NOUN a person or thing that carries something

carrier bag NOUN (British) a plastic or paper bag with handles

carrier pigeon NOUN a pigeon used to carry messages

carrion NOUN the decaying flesh of a dead animal

carrot NOUN a plant with a thick orange-coloured root used as a vegetable

carry VERB ❶ to take something from one place to another ❷ to support the weight of something ❸ to take an amount into the next column when adding figures ❹ to be heard a long way away ❺ if a motion is carried, it is approved by most people at the meeting

cart NOUN an open vehicle for carrying loads

cart VERB ❶ (informal) to carry something heavy or tiring ❷ to carry something in a cart

carthorse NOUN a large strong horse used for pulling heavy loads

cartilage NOUN tough white flexible tissue attached to a bone

cartography NOUN the art of drawing maps

carton NOUN a light cardboard or plastic container

cartoon NOUN ❶ an amusing drawing, especially one in a newspaper or magazine ❷ a series of drawings that tell a story ❸ an animated film

cartridge NOUN ❶ a case containing the explosive for a bullet or shell ❷ a container holding film for a camera, ink for a printer or pen, etc.

cartwheel NOUN ❶ a circular movement in which you do a sideways handstand by balancing on each hand in turn with arms and legs spread like spokes of a wheel ❷ the wheel of a cart

carve VERB ❶ to cut wood or stone in order to make something or to put a pattern or writing on it ❷ to cut cooked meat into slices

carving NOUN an object or design that has been carved

cascade NOUN a small waterfall

cascade VERB to pour down in large amounts

case NOUN ❶ an instance of something existing or occurring ❷ something that the police are investigating or that is being decided in a law trial ❸ a set of facts or arguments to support something ❹ the form of a word that shows how it is related to other words. *Fred's* is the possessive case of *Fred*; *him* is the objective case of *he*. ❺ a container ❻ a suitcase

casement NOUN a window that opens on hinges at its side

cash NOUN ❶ money in coin or notes ❷ immediate payment for goods

cash VERB to cash a cheque is to exchange it for cash

cash dispenser NOUN (*British*) a machine, usually outside a bank or building society, from which people can draw out cash by using a cash card

cashew NOUN a kind of small nut

cashier NOUN a person who takes in and pays out money in a bank or takes payments in a shop

cashmere NOUN very fine soft wool

cashpoint NOUN a cash dispenser

cash register NOUN a machine that records and stores the money received in a shop

casing NOUN a protective case or covering

casino NOUN a public building or room for gambling

cask NOUN a large barrel

casket NOUN a small box for jewellery or other valuable objects

cassava NOUN a tropical plant with starchy roots that are an important source of food in tropical countries

casserole NOUN ❶ a covered dish in which food is cooked and served ❷ a kind of stew cooked in a casserole

cassette NOUN a small sealed case containing recording tape, film, etc.

cassock NOUN a long piece of clothing worn by clergy and members of a church choir

cast VERB casts, casting, cast ❶ to throw something with force ❷ to shed something or throw it off ❸ to make a light or shadow fall on something ❹ to direct your eyes or thoughts to something ❺ to make a vote in an election ❻ to make something out of metal or plaster in a mould ❼ to choose the performers for a play or film

cast NOUN ❶ a shape made by pouring liquid metal or plaster into a mould ❷ all the performers in a play or film

castanets PLURAL NOUN two pieces of wood or ivory held in one hand and clapped together to make a clicking sound, especially in Spanish dancing

castaway NOUN a shipwrecked person

caste NOUN (in India) each of the social classes into which Hindus are born

caster sugar NOUN (*British*) finely ground white sugar

casting vote NOUN the vote that decides which group wins when the votes on each side are equal

cast iron NOUN a hard alloy of iron made by casting it in a mould

castle NOUN ❶ a large fortified building that was built in the past to defend people against attack ❷ a piece in chess, also called a rook

castor NOUN a small wheel on the leg of a table, chair, etc.

castor oil NOUN oil from the seeds of a tropical plant, used as a laxative

castrate VERB to remove the testicles of a male animal. Compare with **spay**.

casual ADJECTIVE ❶ happening by chance and not planned ❷ not carefully done or thought out ❸ relaxed and not bothered by something ❹ suitable for informal occasions ❺ not permanent

casually ADVERB in a casual way

casualty NOUN ❶ a person who is killed or injured in war or in an accident ❷ a casualty department in a hospital

casualty department NOUN (British) the department of a hospital that deals with emergency patients

cat NOUN ❶ a small furry domestic animal ❷ a wild animal of the same family as a domestic cat, e.g. a lion, tiger or leopard

cataclysm (say **kat**-a-klizm) NOUN a violent upheaval or disaster, such as a flood or war

catacombs (say **kat**-a-koomz) PLURAL NOUN underground passages with compartments for tombs

catalogue NOUN ❶ a list of things (e.g. of books in a library), usually arranged in order ❷ a book containing a list of things that can be bought

catalogue VERB to list a collection of things in a catalogue

catalyst (say **kat**-a-list) NOUN ❶ something that starts or speeds up a chemical reaction ❷ something that brings about a change

catamaran NOUN a boat with twin parallel hulls

catapult NOUN ❶ a forked stick with elastic fastened to each prong, used for shooting small stones ❷ an ancient military weapon for hurling stones

catapult VERB to hurl something or rush violently

cataract NOUN ❶ a large waterfall or rush of water ❷ a cloudy area that forms in the eye and causes blurred vision

catarrh (say ka-**tar**) NOUN inflammation in your nose that makes it drip a watery fluid

catastrophe (say ka-**tass**-trof-ee) NOUN a sudden great disaster

catastrophic (say kat-a-**strof**-ik) ADJECTIVE absolutely disastrous

catch VERB catches, catching, caught ❶ to take hold of something moving ❷ to capture a person or animal ❸ to reach someone who has been ahead of you ❹ to be in time to get on a bus or train ❺ to become infected with an illness ❻ to hear what someone says ❼ to discover someone doing something wrong ❽ to get something snagged or entangled ❾ to hit or strike something

catch NOUN ❶ catching something, e.g. a ball ❷ something caught or worth catching ❸ a hidden difficulty ❹ a device for fastening a door or window

catching ADJECTIVE a disease is catching when it is infectious

catchment area NOUN ❶ the area from which a hospital takes patients or a school takes pupils ❷ the whole area from which water drains into a river or reservoir

catchphrase NOUN a well-known phrase, especially one that a famous person has used

catchy ADJECTIVE a catchy tune is pleasant and easy to remember

catechism (say kat-ik-izm) NOUN a set of questions and answers that give the basic beliefs of a religion

categorical (say kat-ig-o-rik-al) ADJECTIVE completely clear and definite

category NOUN a set of people or things classified as being similar to each other

cater VERB ❶ to provide food for a lot of people at a social occasion ❷ to provide what is needed

caterpillar NOUN the creeping worm-like creature that turns into a butterfly or moth

cathedral NOUN the most important church of a district, usually with a bishop in charge of it

cathode NOUN the electrode by which electric current leaves a device. Compare with **anode**.

cathode ray tube NOUN a tube used in televisions and computers, in which a beam of electrons from a cathode produces an image on a fluorescent screen

Catholic ADJECTIVE belonging to the Roman Catholic Church

Catholic NOUN a Roman Catholic

catholic ADJECTIVE including a wide range of things

catkin NOUN a spike of small soft flowers on trees such as hazel and willow

catnap NOUN a short sleep during the day

Catseye NOUN (trademark) one of a line of reflecting studs that mark the centre or edge of a road

cattle PLURAL NOUN cows and bulls kept by farmers for their milk and beef

catty ADJECTIVE saying unkind and spiteful things about someone

catwalk NOUN a long narrow platform that models walk along at a fashion show

caucus NOUN a small group within a political party, influencing decisions and policy

cauldron NOUN a large deep pot for boiling things in

cauliflower NOUN a cabbage with a large head of white flowers

cause NOUN ❶ a person or thing that makes something happen or produces an effect ❷ a good reason ❸ a purpose for which people work; an organization or charity

cause VERB to be the cause of something or to make it happen

causeway NOUN a raised road across low or marshy ground

caustic ADJECTIVE ❶ able to burn or wear things away by chemical action ❷ very critical or sarcastic

caution NOUN ❶ care you take to avoid difficulty or danger ❷ a warning

caution VERB to give someone a warning

cautionary ADJECTIVE giving a warning

cautious ADJECTIVE taking care to avoid difficulty or danger

cavalcade NOUN a procession of vehicles or people on horseback

Cavalier NOUN a supporter of King

Charles I in the English Civil War (1642-9)

cavalry NOUN soldiers who fight on horseback or in an armoured vehicles. Compare with **infantry**.

cave NOUN a large hollow place in the side of a hill or cliff or underground

cave VERB ➤ **cave in** ❶ to collapse or fall inwards ❷ to give way in an argument

caveman NOUN a person living in a cave in prehistoric times

cavern NOUN a large cave

cavernous ADJECTIVE a cavernous room or space is huge and often empty or dark

caviare (say kav-ee-ar) NOUN the pickled roe of sturgeon or other large fish

cavity NOUN a hollow or hole

cavort (say ka-vort) VERB to jump or run about excitedly

caw NOUN the harsh cry of a crow or other large bird

cc ABBREVIATION ❶ cubic centimetre(s) ❷ used to show that a copy of an email is being sent to another person

CD ABBREVIATION compact disc

CD-ROM ABBREVIATION compact disc read-only memory; a compact disc on which large amounts of data can be stored and then displayed on a computer screen

cease VERB to stop happening or stop doing something

ceasefire NOUN an agreement between the two sides in a conflict for fighting to stop for a time

ceaseless ADJECTIVE not stopping; going on continuously

cedar NOUN an evergreen tree with hard fragrant wood

cedilla (say sid-il-a) NOUN a mark under c in certain languages to show that it is pronounced as s, e.g. in façade

ceilidh (say kay-lee) NOUN an informal gathering for music, singing and dancing, originating from Scotland and Ireland

ceiling NOUN ❶ the flat surface at the top of a room ❷ the highest limit that something can reach

celandine NOUN a small wild plant with yellow flowers

celebrate VERB ❶ to do something special or enjoyable to show that a day or event is important ❷ to perform a religious ceremony

celebrated ADJECTIVE famous

celebration NOUN ❶ celebrating something ❷ a party or other event that celebrates something

celebrity NOUN ❶ a celebrity is a famous person ❷ celebrity is fame or being famous

celery NOUN a vegetable with crisp white or green stems

celestial (say sil-est-ee-al) ADJECTIVE ❶ to do with the sky ❷ to do with heaven; divine

celibate (say sel-ib-at) ADJECTIVE remaining unmarried or not having sex, especially for religious reasons

cell NOUN ❶ a small room where a prisoner is locked up ❷ a small room in a monastery or convent ❸ a microscopic unit of living matter. All plants and

a b c d e f g h i j k l m n o p q r s t u v w x y z

animals are made up of cells. ④ a compartment of a honeycomb ⑤ a device for producing electric current chemically ⑥ a small group or unit in an organization

cellar NOUN an underground room

cello (say **chel**-oh) NOUN a musical instrument like a large violin, played upright between the knees of a player

Cellophane NOUN (*trademark*) a thin transparent wrapping material

cellular ADJECTIVE ① to do with or containing cells ② with an open mesh ③ a cellular telephone uses a network of radio stations to allow messages to be sent over a wide area

celluloid NOUN a kind of plastic, used in the past for making cinema films

cellulose NOUN tissue that forms the main part of all plants and trees

Celsius (say **sel**-see-us) ADJECTIVE measuring temperature on a scale using 100 degrees, where water freezes at 0° and boils at 100°

Celtic (say **kel**-tik) ADJECTIVE to do with the languages or inhabitants of ancient Britain and France before the Romans came or of their descendants, e.g. Irish, Welsh, Gaelic

cement NOUN ① a mixture of lime and clay used in building, to join bricks together ② a strong glue

cement VERB ① to build something with cement ② to strengthen or join something firmly

cemetery (say **sem**-et-ree) NOUN a place where dead people are buried

cenotaph (say **sen**-o-taf) NOUN a monument, especially a war memorial, to people who are buried in other places

censor NOUN a person who examines films, books, letters, etc. and removes or bans anything that is thought to be offensive or unacceptable

censor VERB to ban or remove parts of a film, book, letter, etc. that are thought to be offensive or unacceptable

censure (say **sen**-sher) NOUN strong criticism or disapproval of something

censure VERB to criticize someone severely and openly

census NOUN an official count or survey of the population of a country or area

cent NOUN a coin worth one-hundredth of a dollar

centaur (say **sen**-tor) NOUN (in Greek myths) a creature with the upper body, head and arms of a man and the lower body of a horse

centenarian (say sent-in-**air**-ee-an) NOUN a person who is 100 years old or more

centenary (say sen-**teen**-er-ee) NOUN (*British*) a 100th anniversary of an important event

centigrade ADJECTIVE Celsius

centilitre NOUN one-hundredth of a litre

centimetre NOUN one-hundredth of a metre

centipede NOUN a small crawling

creature with a long body and many legs

central ADJECTIVE ❶ to do with or at the centre ❷ most important or main

central heating NOUN a system of heating a building from one source by circulating hot water or hot air or steam in pipes or by linked radiators

centre NOUN ❶ the middle point or part ❷ an important place ❸ a building or place for a special purpose

centre VERB to place something at the centre

centre forward NOUN the player in the middle of the forward line in football or hockey

centre of gravity NOUN the point in an object around which its mass is perfectly balanced

centrifugal ADJECTIVE moving away from the centre; using centrifugal force

centrifugal force NOUN a force that makes a thing that is travelling round a central point fly outwards off its circular path

centurion (say sent-**yoor**-ee-on) NOUN an officer in the ancient Roman army, originally commanding a hundred men

century NOUN ❶ a period of one hundred years ❷ a hundred runs scored by a batsman in an innings at cricket

cephalopod (say **sef**-al-o-pod) NOUN a mollusc (such as an octopus or squid) that has a head with a ring of tentacles round the mouth

ceramic ADJECTIVE to do with or made of pottery

ceramics PLURAL NOUN pottery-making

cereal NOUN ❶ a grass producing seeds which are used as food, e.g. wheat, barley or rice ❷ a breakfast food made from these seeds

cerebral (say **se**-rib-ral) ADJECTIVE to do with the brain

cerebral palsy NOUN a condition caused by brain damage before birth that makes a person suffer from spasms of the muscles and jerky movements

ceremonial ADJECTIVE to do with or used in a ceremony; formal

ceremonious ADJECTIVE full of ceremony; elaborately performed

ceremony NOUN ❶ a formal religious or public occasion celebrating an important event ❷ the formal actions carried out on an important occasion, e.g. at a wedding or a funeral

certain ADJECTIVE ❶ something is certain when it is definitely true or going to happen ❷ you are certain about something when you know it is definitely true

certainly ADVERB ❶ for certain ❷ yes

certainty NOUN ❶ something that is sure to happen ❷ being sure

certificate NOUN an official document giving information about a person or event

certify VERB to declare formally that something is true

cervix NOUN the entrance to the womb

a b c d e f g h i j k l m n o p q r s t u v w x y z

cessation NOUN the stopping or ending of something

cesspit, cesspool NOUN a covered pit where liquid waste or sewage is stored temporarily

CFC ABBREVIATION chlorofluorocarbon; a gas containing chlorine and fluorine that is thought to be harmful to the ozone layer in the Earth's atmosphere

chafe VERB ❶ to make something sore or become sore by rubbing ❷ to become irritated or impatient

chaff NOUN husks of corn, separated from the seed

chaff VERB to tease someone

chaffinch NOUN a kind of finch

chagrin (say **shag**-rin) NOUN a feeling of being annoyed or disappointed

chain NOUN ❶ a row of metal rings fastened together ❷ a connected series of things ❸ a number of shops, hotels or other businesses owned by the same company

chain VERB to fasten something with a chain or chains

chain reaction NOUN a series of happenings in which each causes the next

chain store NOUN one of a number of similar shops owned by the same firm

chair NOUN ❶ a movable seat, with a back, for one person ❷ the person who is in charge of a meeting

chair VERB to chair a meeting is to be in charge of it and run it

chairman, chairwoman NOUN

the person who is in charge of a meeting

chairperson NOUN a chairman or chairwoman

chalet (say **shal**-ay) NOUN ❶ a Swiss hut or cottage ❷ a hut in a holiday camp etc.

chalice NOUN a large goblet for holding wine, especially one from which the Communion wine is drunk in Christian services

chalk NOUN ❶ a soft white or coloured stick used for writing on blackboards or for drawing ❷ soft white limestone

chalky ADJECTIVE containing chalk or like chalk

challenge NOUN ❶ a task or activity that is new and exciting but also difficult ❷ a call to someone to take part in a contest or to show their ability or strength

challenge VERB ❶ to make a challenge to someone ❷ to be a challenge to someone ❸ to question whether something is true or correct

chamber NOUN ❶ (old use) a room ❷ a hall used for meetings of a parliament or council; the members of the group using it ❸ a compartment in machinery etc.

chamberlain NOUN an official who manages the household of a sovereign or great noble

chambermaid NOUN a woman employed to clean bedrooms at a hotel etc.

chamber music NOUN classical music for a small group of players

chamber pot NOUN a bowl kept in

a bedroom and used as a toilet

chameleon (say kam-**ee**-lee-on) NOUN a small lizard that can change its colour to match that of its surroundings

chamois NOUN ❶ (say **sham**-wa) a small wild antelope living in the mountains ❷ (say **sham**-ee) a piece of soft yellow leather used for washing and polishing things

champ VERB to munch or bite something noisily

champagne (say sham-**payn**) NOUN a bubbly white wine from the region of Champagne in France

champion NOUN ❶ a person or thing that has defeated all the others in a sport or competition ❷ someone who supports a cause by fighting or speaking for it

champion VERB to support a cause by fighting or speaking for it

championship NOUN a competition to find the best player or team in a particular sport or game

chance NOUN ❶ an opportunity or possibility ❷ the way things happen without being planned

chance VERB ❶ to happen by chance ❷ to risk something

chancel NOUN the part of a church nearest to the altar

chancellor NOUN ❶ an important government or legal official ❷ the chief minister of the government in some European countries

Chancellor of the Exchequer NOUN the government minister in charge of a country's finances and taxes

chancy ADJECTIVE risky or uncertain

chandelier (say shand-il-**eer**) NOUN a large hanging light with branches for several light bulbs or candles

change VERB ❶ to make something different or become different ❷ to exchange one thing for another ❸ to put on different clothes ❹ to go from one train or bus to another ❺ to give smaller units of money or money in another currency, for an amount of money

change NOUN ❶ changing; a difference in doing something ❷ coins or notes of small values ❸ money given back to the payer when the price is less than the amount handed over ❹ a fresh set of clothes ❺ something different from what is usual

changeable ADJECTIVE likely to change; changing frequently

changeling NOUN a child who is believed to have been substituted secretly for another, especially by fairies

channel NOUN ❶ a stretch of water connecting two seas ❷ a broadcasting wavelength ❸ a way for water to flow along ❹ the part of a river or sea that is deep enough for ships

channel VERB ❶ to use something for a particular purpose ❷ to make something move along a particular channel, path or route

chant NOUN ❶ a tune to which words with no regular rhythm are fitted, especially one used in church music ❷ a rhythmic call or shout

chant VERB ❶ to sing a chant ❷ to call out words in a rhythm

chaos (say **kay**-oss) NOUN great disorder

chaotic (say kay-ot-ik) ADJECTIVE in a state of complete confusion and disorder

chap NOUN (British) (informal) a man

chapatti NOUN a flat cake of unleavened bread, used in Indian cookery

chapel NOUN ❶ a small building or room used for Christian worship ❷ a section of a large church, with its own altar

chaperone (say **shap**-er-ohn) NOUN an older woman in charge of a young one on social occasions

chaplain NOUN a member of the clergy who regularly works in a college, hospital, prison, regiment, etc.

chapped ADJECTIVE with skin split or cracked from cold etc.

chapter NOUN ❶ a section or division of a book ❷ the clergy of a cathedral or members of a monastery

char VERB to make something black by burning

char NOUN (British) (old use) a charwoman

character NOUN ❶ a person in a story, film or play ❷ all the qualities that make a person or thing what he, she or it is ❸ a letter of the alphabet or other written symbol

characteristic NOUN a quality that forms part of a person's or thing's character

characteristic ADJECTIVE typical of a person or thing

characterize (also **characterise**) VERB ❶ to be a characteristic of something ❷ to describe a person's character in a certain way

charade (say sha-**rahd**) NOUN ❶ a scene in the game of charades, in which people try to guess a word from other people's acting ❷ a pretence

charcoal NOUN a black substance made by burning wood slowly. Charcoal can be used for drawing with.

charge NOUN ❶ the price asked for something ❷ an accusation that someone has committed a crime ❸ a rushing attack ❹ the amount of electricity in something ❺ the amount of explosive needed to fire a gun ❻ a person or thing in someone's care

charge VERB ❶ to ask a particular price for something ❷ to accuse someone of committing a crime ❸ to rush forward in an attack ❹ to give an electric charge to something ❺ to give someone a responsibility or task

charger NOUN ❶ a piece of equipment for charging a battery with electricity ❷ (old use) a cavalry horse

chariot NOUN a horse-drawn vehicle with two wheels, used in ancient times for fighting and racing

charisma (say ka-**riz**-ma) NOUN the special quality that makes a person attractive or influential

charismatic (say ka-riz-**mat**-ik)

ADJECTIVE having charisma

charitable *ADJECTIVE* ❶ giving money and help to people who need it; to do with a charity ❷ kind in your attitude to other people

charity *NOUN* ❶ an organization set up to help people who are poor, ill or disabled or have suffered a disaster ❷ giving money or help to people who need it ❸ kindness and sympathy towards others; being unwilling to think badly of people

charlatan (say *shar*-la-tan) *NOUN* a person who falsely claims to be an expert

charm *NOUN* ❶ the power to please or delight people; attractiveness ❷ a magic spell ❸ a small object that is believed to bring good luck ❹ an ornament worn on a bracelet

charm *VERB* ❶ to give pleasure or delight to people ❷ to put a spell on someone; bewitch

charming *ADJECTIVE* pleasant and attractive

chart *NOUN* ❶ a map for people sailing ships or flying aircraft ❷ an outline map showing special information ❸ a diagram, list or table giving information in an orderly way

chart *VERB* to make a chart or map of something

charter *NOUN* ❶ an official document stating the rights or aims of an organization or group of people ❷ hiring an aircraft, ship or vehicle

charter *VERB* to hire an aircraft, ship or vehicle

chartered accountant *NOUN* an accountant who is qualified according to the rules of a professional association that has a royal charter

charwoman *NOUN* (*British*) (*old use*) a woman employed as a cleaner

chase *VERB* to go quickly after a person or thing in order to capture or catch them up or drive them away

chase *NOUN* chasing someone or something

chasm (say kazm) *NOUN* a deep opening in the ground

chassis (say *shas*-ee) *NOUN* the framework under a car etc., on which other parts are mounted

chaste *ADJECTIVE* not expressing sexual feelings

chasten (say *chay*-sen) *VERB* to make someone realize that they have behaved badly or done something wrong

chastise *VERB* to punish or scold someone severely

chastity (say *chas*-ti-ti) *NOUN* the state of not having sex with anyone

chat *NOUN* a friendly informal conversation

chat *VERB* ❶ to have a friendly informal conversation ❷ to exchange messages with other people on the Internet

chateau (say *shat*-oh) *NOUN* a castle or large country house in France

chat room *NOUN* an area on the Internet where people can have a

a
b
c
d
e
f
g
h
i
j
k
l
m
n
o
p
q
r
s
t
u
v
w
x
y
z

conversation by sending messages to each other

chatter VERB ❶ to talk quickly about unimportant things; to keep on talking ❷ your teeth chatter when they make a rattling sound because you are cold or frightened

chatter NOUN chattering talk or sound

chatterbox NOUN a talkative person

chatty ADJECTIVE ❶ liking to talk a lot in a friendly way ❷ in an informal style

chauffeur (say shoh-fer) NOUN a person employed to drive a car

chauvinism (say shoh-vin-izm) NOUN ❶ prejudiced belief that your own country is superior to any other ❷ the belief of some men that men are superior to women

cheap ADJECTIVE ❶ low in price; not expensive ❷ of poor quality; of low value

cheat VERB ❶ to try to do well in an exam or game by breaking the rules ❷ to trick or deceive someone so they lose something

cheat NOUN a person who cheats

check VERB ❶ to make sure that something is correct or in good condition ❷ to make something stop or go slower

check NOUN ❶ checking something ❷ stopping or slowing; a pause ❸ (North American) a bill in a restaurant ❹ the situation in chess when a king may be captured ❺ a pattern of squares

checked ADJECTIVE marked with a pattern of squares

checkmate NOUN the winning situation in chess, where one player's king is threatened and cannot be moved out of danger

checkout NOUN a place where goods are paid for in a self-service shop

check-up NOUN a routine medical or dental examination

cheek NOUN ❶ the side of your face below your eye ❷ rude or disrespectful talk or behaviour

cheeky ADJECTIVE rude or disrespectful

cheer NOUN ❶ a shout of praise or pleasure or encouragement ❷ good cheer is being cheerful and enjoying yourself

cheer VERB ❶ to give a cheer ❷ to comfort or encourage someone

cheerful ADJECTIVE ❶ looking or sounding happy ❷ pleasantly bright or colourful

cheerio EXCLAMATION (informal) goodbye

cheers EXCLAMATION (informal) ❶ a word that people say to each other as they lift up their glasses to drink ❷ goodbye ❸ thank you

cheery ADJECTIVE bright and cheerful

cheese NOUN a solid food made from milk

cheesecake NOUN a dessert made of a mixture of sweetened curds on a layer of biscuit

cheetah NOUN a large spotted animal of the cat family that can run extremely fast

chef (say shef) NOUN the cook in a hotel or restaurant

chemical ADJECTIVE to do with or produced by chemistry

chemical NOUN a substance obtained by or used in chemistry

chemist NOUN ❶ a person who makes or sells medicines ❷ a shop selling medicines, cosmetics, etc. ❸ an expert in chemistry

chemistry NOUN ❶ the way that substances combine and react with one another ❷ the study of substances and their reactions etc.

chemotherapy NOUN the treatment of disease, especially cancer, by the use of chemical substances

cheque NOUN a printed form on which you write instructions to a bank to pay out money from your account

chequered ADJECTIVE marked with a pattern of squares

cherish VERB ❶ to look after a person or thing lovingly ❷ to keep something in your mind for a long time

cherry NOUN a small soft round fruit with a stone

cherub NOUN an angel, often pictured as a chubby child with wings

chess NOUN a game for two players with sixteen pieces each (called **chessmen**) on a board of 64 squares (a **chessboard**)

chest NOUN ❶ the front part of the body between the neck and the waist ❷ a large strong box for storing things in

chestnut NOUN ❶ a tree that produces hard brown nuts ❷ the

nut of this tree ❸ an old joke or story

chest of drawers NOUN a piece of furniture with drawers for storing clothes etc.

chew VERB to grind food between your teeth

chewing gum NOUN a sticky flavoured type of sweet for chewing

chewy ADJECTIVE chewy food is tough and needs a lot of chewing

chic (say sheek) ADJECTIVE stylish and elegant

chick NOUN a very young bird

chicken NOUN ❶ a young hen ❷ a hen's flesh used as food

chicken ADJECTIVE (informal) afraid to do something; cowardly

chicken VERB ➤ **chicken out** (informal) to refuse to take part in something because you are afraid

chickenpox NOUN a disease that produces red spots on the skin

chickpea NOUN the yellow seed of a plant of the pea family, eaten as a vegetable

chicory NOUN a plant whose leaves are used in salads

chide VERB to tell someone off

chief NOUN ❶ a leader or ruler of a people, especially of a Native American tribe ❷ a person with the highest rank or authority

chief ADJECTIVE ❶ most important; main ❷ having the highest rank or authority

chiefly ADVERB mainly or mostly

chieftain NOUN the chief of a tribe or clan

a
b
c
d
e
f
g
h
i
j
k
l
m
n
o
p
q
r
s
t
u
v
w
x
y
z

chiffon (say **shif**-on) NOUN a very thin, almost transparent, fabric

chilblain NOUN a sore swollen place, usually on a hand or foot, caused by cold weather

child NOUN children ① a young person; a boy or girl ② someone's son or daughter

childhood NOUN the time when a person is a child

childish ADJECTIVE ① like a child; unsuitable for a grown person ② silly and immature

childless ADJECTIVE having no children

childminder NOUN (British) a person who is paid to look after children while their parents are out at work

chill NOUN ① unpleasant coldness ② an illness that makes you shiver

chill VERB ① to make a person or thing cold ② (informal) to relax completely

chilli NOUN the hot-tasting pod of a red pepper

chilli con carne NOUN a stew of chilli-flavoured minced beef and beans

chilly ADJECTIVE ① rather cold ② unfriendly

chime NOUN a series of ringing sounds made by a set of bells or clock

chime VERB to make a chime

chimney NOUN a tall pipe or structure that carries smoke away from a fire

chimney pot NOUN a pipe fitted to the top of a chimney

chimney sweep NOUN a person

who cleans soot from inside chimneys

chimpanzee NOUN an intelligent African ape, smaller than a gorilla

chin NOUN the lower part of the face below the mouth

china NOUN thin delicate pottery

chink NOUN ① a narrow opening that lets light through ② a chinking sound

chink VERB to make a sound like glasses or coins being struck together

chintz NOUN a shiny cotton cloth used for making curtains etc.

chip NOUN ① a thin piece cut or broken off something hard ② a fried oblong strip of potato ③ a place where a small piece has been knocked off something ④ a small counter used in gambling games ⑤ a microchip

chip VERB ① to knock a small piece off something by accident ② to cut a potato into chips

chipboard NOUN board made from chips of wood pressed and stuck together

chipolata NOUN (British) a small spicy sausage

chiropody (say ki-**rop**-od-ee) NOUN (chiefly British) medical treatment of the feet, e.g. corns

chirp VERB to make short sharp sounds like a small bird

chirpy ADJECTIVE lively and cheerful

chisel NOUN a tool with a sharp end for shaping wood or stone

chisel VERB to shape or cut wood or stone with a chisel

chivalry (say **shiv**-al-ree) NOUN

❶ the code of good behaviour and brave fighting that medieval knights used to follow ❷ behaviour that is considerate and helpful, especially by men towards women

chive NOUN a small herb with leaves that taste like onions

chlorine (say **klor**-een) NOUN a greenish-yellow gas used to disinfect water etc.

chloroform (say **klo**-ro-form) NOUN a liquid that gives off a vapour that makes people unconscious

chlorophyll (say **klo**-ro-fil) NOUN the substance that makes plants green

choc ice NOUN (British) a bar of ice cream covered with chocolate

chock NOUN a block or wedge used to prevent an aircraft from moving

chock-full ADJECTIVE crammed full of good things

chocolate NOUN ❶ a solid brown food or powder made from roasted cacao seeds ❷ a drink made with this powder ❸ a sweet made of or covered with chocolate

choice NOUN ❶ the opportunity to choose between things ❷ the range of things from which someone can choose ❸ a person or thing that someone has chosen

choice ADJECTIVE of the best quality

choir NOUN a group of people trained to sing together, especially in a church

choke VERB ❶ to be unable to breathe properly because something is blocking your

windpipe ❷ to stop someone breathing properly by blocking their windpipe ❸ to block up or clog something

choke NOUN a device controlling the flow of air into the engine of a motor vehicle

cholera (say **kol**-er-a) NOUN an infectious disease that is often fatal

cholesterol (say kol-**est**-er-ol) NOUN a fatty substance that can clog the arteries

choose VERB chooses, choosing, chose, chosen to decide which you want from among a number of people or things

choosy ADVERB (informal) careful or fussy about what you choose

chop VERB ❶ to cut something into pieces with a knife ❷ to cut or hit something with a heavy blow

chop NOUN ❶ a chopping blow ❷ a small thick slice of meat, usually on a rib

chopper NOUN ❶ a chopping tool; a small axe ❷ (informal) a helicopter

choppy ADJECTIVE the sea is choppy when it is not smooth but full of small waves

chopsticks PLURAL NOUN a pair of thin sticks used for lifting Chinese and Japanese food to your mouth

chop suey NOUN a Chinese dish of meat fried with bean sprouts and vegetables served with rice

choral ADJECTIVE to do with or sung by a choir or chorus

chord (say kord) NOUN ❶ a number of musical notes sounded together

② a straight line joining two points on a curve

chore (say chor) NOUN a regular or dull task

choreography (say ko-ree-og-ra-fee) NOUN the art of writing the steps for ballets or stage dances

chorister (say ko-rist-er) NOUN a member of a choir

chortle VERB to chuckle loudly

chortle NOUN a loud chuckle

chorus NOUN **①** the words repeated after each verse of a song or poem **②** a piece of music sung by a group of people **③** a group singing together

chorus VERB to all say something at the same time

chow mein NOUN a Chinese dish of fried noodles with shredded meat or shrimps etc. and vegetables

christen VERB **①** to baptize a child and give them a name **②** to give a name or nickname to a person or thing

christening NOUN the church ceremony at which a child is baptized

Christian NOUN a person who believes in Jesus Christ and his teachings

Christian ADJECTIVE to do with Christians or their beliefs

Christian name NOUN a name given to a person at his or her christening; a person's first name

Christmas NOUN the day (25 December) when Christians commemorate the birth of Jesus Christ; the days round it

chromatic scale NOUN a musical

scale going up or down in semitones

chrome (say krohm) NOUN chromium

chromium (say kroh-mee-um) NOUN a shiny silvery metal

chromosome (say kroh-mos-ohm) NOUN a tiny thread-like part of an animal cell or plant cell, carrying genes

chronic ADJECTIVE lasting for a long time

chronicle NOUN a record of events in the order that they happened

chronological ADJECTIVE arranged in the order that things happened

chronology (say kron-ol-oj-ee) NOUN the arrangement of events in the order in which they happened, e.g. in history or geology

chrysalis NOUN the hard cover a caterpillar makes round itself before it changes into a butterfly or moth

chrysanthemum NOUN a garden flower that blooms in autumn

chubby ADJECTIVE plump and healthy

chuck VERB (informal) to throw something roughly or carelessly

chuck NOUN **①** the part of a drill that holds the bit **②** the gripping part of a lathe

chuckle NOUN a quiet laugh

chuckle VERB to laugh quietly

chug VERB to move making the sound of an engine running slowly

chum NOUN (informal) a friend

chunk NOUN a thick piece of something

chunky ADJECTIVE thick and big

chupatty (say chup-**at**-ee) NOUN a different spelling of **chapatti**

church NOUN ❶ a building where Christians go to worship ❷ a religious service in a church ❸ a particular Christian religion, e.g. the Church of England

churchyard NOUN the ground round a church, often used as a graveyard

churlish ADJECTIVE rude and bad-tempered

churn NOUN ❶ a large can in which milk is carried from a farm ❷ a machine in which milk is beaten to make butter

churn VERB ❶ to stir something or move it around vigorously ❷ your stomach churns when you feel very nervous or excited ❸ to make butter in a churn

chute (say shoot) NOUN a steep channel for people or things to slide down

chutney NOUN a strong-tasting mixture of fruit, peppers, etc., eaten with meat or cheese

cider NOUN an alcoholic drink made from apples

cigar NOUN a roll of compressed tobacco leaves for smoking

cigarette NOUN a small roll of shredded tobacco in thin paper for smoking

cinder NOUN a small piece of partly burnt coal or wood

cinema NOUN (chiefly British) ❶ a place where films are shown ❷ the business or art of making films

cinnamon (say **sin**-a-mon) NOUN a

yellowish-brown spice

cinquain (say sin-kayn) NOUN a poem of five lines with a total of 22 syllables arranged in the pattern 2, 4, 6, 8, 2

cipher (say **sy**-fer) NOUN a secret system of writing used for sending messages; a code

circle NOUN ❶ a perfectly round flat shape or thing ❷ the balcony of a cinema or theatre ❸ a number of people with similar interests

circle VERB to move round something in a circle

circuit (say **ser**-kit) NOUN ❶ a circular line or journey ❷ a track for motor racing ❸ the path of an electric current

circular ADJECTIVE ❶ shaped like a circle; round ❷ moving round in a circle

circular NOUN a letter or advertisement sent to a number of people

circulate VERB ❶ to go round something continuously ❷ to spread or be passed from one person to another ❸ to send something round to a number of people

circulation NOUN ❶ the movement of blood around the body ❷ the number of copies of each issue of a newspaper or magazine that are sold or distributed

circumcise VERB to cut off the fold of skin at the tip of the penis

circumference NOUN the line or distance round something, especially round a circle

circumflex accent NOUN a mark

(ˆ) over a vowel

circumnavigate *VERB* to sail completely round something

circumstance *NOUN* a fact or condition connected with an event or person or action

circumstantial (say ser-kum-**stan**-shal) *ADJECTIVE* circumstantial evidence consists of facts that strongly suggest something but do not actually prove it

circumvent *VERB* to find a way of avoiding something

circus *NOUN* a travelling show usually performed in a tent, with clowns, acrobats and sometimes trained animals

cirrus (say si-rus) *NOUN* cloud made up of light wispy streaks

cistern *NOUN* a tank for storing water

citadel *NOUN* a fortress protecting a city

cite (say sight) *VERB* to quote or name something as an example

citizen *NOUN* a person belonging to a particular city or country

citizenship *NOUN* the rights or duties of a citizen

citrus fruit *NOUN* a lemon, orange, grapefruit or other sharp-tasting fruit

city *NOUN* a large important town, often having a cathedral

civic *ADJECTIVE* to do with a city or its citizens

civics *NOUN* the study of the rights and duties of citizens

civil *ADJECTIVE* ❶ polite and courteous ❷ to do with citizens

❸ to do with civilians; not military

civil engineering *NOUN* the work of designing or maintaining roads, bridges, dams, etc.

civilian *NOUN* a person who is not serving in the armed forces

civility *NOUN* polite and courteous behaviour

civilization (also **civilisation**) *NOUN* ❶ a society or culture at a particular time in history ❷ a developed or organized way of life

civilize (also **civilise**) *VERB* ❶ to bring culture and education to a primitive community ❷ to improve a person's behaviour and manners

civil partnership *NOUN* (in some countries) a legal union of a couple of the same sex, with rights similar to those of marriage

civil rights *PLURAL NOUN* the rights of citizens, especially to have freedom, equality and the right to vote

civil service *NOUN* all the officials who work for the government to run its affairs

civil war *NOUN* war between groups of people of the same country

clad *ADJECTIVE* to be clad in something is to be wearing it or covered by it

claim *VERB* ❶ to state something without being able to prove it ❷ to ask for something to which you believe you have a right

claim *NOUN* ❶ a statement that something is true, without any proof ❷ a statement that you have a right to something ❸ a piece of ground claimed by someone for mining etc.

clairvoyant NOUN a person who is said to be able to predict future events or know about things that are happening out of sight

clam NOUN a large shellfish

clamber VERB to climb with difficulty, using your hands and feet

clammy ADJECTIVE damp and slimy

clamour NOUN ❶ a loud confused noise ❷ a loud protest or demand

clamour VERB to make a loud protest or demand

clamp NOUN a device for holding things tightly

clamp VERB ❶ to fix something with a clamp ❷ to hold something firmly in position

clan NOUN a group of families sharing the same ancestor, especially in Scotland

clandestine (say klan-**dest**-in) ADJECTIVE done secretly; kept secret

clang NOUN a loud ringing sound

clang VERB to make a loud ringing sound

clank NOUN a sound like heavy pieces of metal banging together

clank VERB to make a sound like heavy pieces of metal banging together

clap VERB ❶ to strike the palms of the hands together loudly, especially as applause ❷ to slap someone in a friendly way ❸ to put someone somewhere quickly or with force

clap NOUN ❶ a sudden sharp noise ❷ a round of clapping ❸ a friendly slap

clapper NOUN the hanging piece inside a bell that strikes against the bell to make it sound

claret NOUN a kind of red wine

clarify VERB to make something clear or easier to understand

clarinet NOUN a woodwind instrument

clarity NOUN the quality of being clear or easy to understand

clash VERB ❶ to make a loud sound like that of cymbals banging together ❷ two events clash when they happen inconveniently at the same time ❸ people clash when they have a fight or argument ❹ colours clash when they do not go well together

clash NOUN ❶ a loud sound like that of cymbals banging together ❷ a fight or argument

clasp NOUN ❶ a device for fastening things, with interlocking parts ❷ a tight grasp

clasp VERB ❶ to grasp or hold someone or something tightly ❷ to fasten something with a clasp

class NOUN ❶ a group of children or students who are taught together ❷ a group of similar people, animals or things ❸ people of the same social or economic level ❹ a level of quality

class VERB to put something in a particular class or group; to classify something

classic ADJECTIVE ❶ generally agreed to be excellent or important

a
b
c
d
e
f
g
h
i
j
k
l
m
n
o
p
q
r
s
t
u
v
w
x
y
z

❷ very typical or common

classic NOUN a book, film or song that is well known and generally agreed to be excellent or important

classical ADJECTIVE **❶** to do with ancient Greek or Roman literature or art **❷** serious or conventional in style and of lasting value

classics NOUN the study of ancient Greek and Latin languages and literature

classified ADJECTIVE **❶** put into classes or groups **❷** classified information is officially secret and available only to certain people

classify VERB to arrange things in classes or groups

classmate NOUN someone in the same class at school

classroom NOUN a room where a class of children or students is taught

clatter VERB to make a sound like hard objects rattling together

clatter NOUN a clattering noise

clause NOUN **❶** a single part of a treaty, law or contract **❷** (in grammar) a part of a sentence, with its own verb

claustrophobia NOUN an extreme fear of being inside an enclosed space

claw NOUN **❶** a sharp nail on a bird's or animal's foot **❷** a claw-like part or device used for grasping things

claw VERB to grasp, pull or scratch something with a claw or hand

clay NOUN a kind of stiff sticky earth that becomes hard when baked, used for making bricks and pottery

clean ADJECTIVE **❶** without any dirt or marks or stains **❷** fresh; not yet used **❸** done or played in a fair way according to the rules **❹** not rude or indecent **❺** a clean catch is one made skilfully with no fumbling

clean VERB to make something clean

clean ADVERB (informal) completely

cleaner NOUN **❶** a person who cleans things, especially rooms etc. **❷** something used for cleaning things

cleanliness (say klen-li-nis) NOUN being clean or keeping things clean

cleanly (say kleen-lee) ADVERB easily or smoothly in one movement; neatly

cleanse (say klenz) VERB **❶** to clean something **❷** to make something pure

clear ADJECTIVE **❶** transparent; not muddy or cloudy **❷** easy to see or hear **❸** easy to understand; without doubt **❹** free from obstacles or unwanted things **❺** a clear conscience is one that doesn't make you feel guilty **❻** complete

clear ADVERB **❶** in a way that is easy to see or hear; distinctly **❷** completely **❸** at a distance from something; not too close to something

clear VERB **❶** to make something clear or become clear **❷** to show that someone is innocent or reliable **❸** to jump over something without touching it **❹** to get approval or authorization for something

clearance NOUN **❶** official permission to do something

❷ getting rid of unwanted goods
❸ the space between one thing
and another thing that is passing
under or beside it

clearing NOUN an open space in
a forest

clearly ADVERB ❶ in a way that is
easy to see, hear or understand
❷ without doubt; obviously

cleave VERB cleaves, cleaving; *past
tense* cleaved, clove or cleft; *past
participle* cleft or cloven ❶ to
divide something by chopping it;
to split something ❷ to make a
way through something

cleave VERB cleaves, cleaving,
cleaved (*old use*) to cling to
something

cleaver NOUN a butcher's chopping
tool

clef NOUN a symbol on a stave in
music, showing the pitch of the
notes

cleft *past tense* of **cleave** VERB

cleft NOUN a split in something

clench VERB to close your teeth or
fingers tightly

clergy NOUN the people who
have been ordained as priests or
ministers of the Christian Church

clerical ADJECTIVE ❶ to do with the
routine work in an office, such as
filing and writing letters ❷ to do
with the clergy

clerk (say klark) NOUN a person
employed to keep records or
accounts, deal with papers in an
office, etc.

clever ADJECTIVE ❶ quick at
learning and understanding things
❷ showing intelligence and

imagination

cliché (say klee-shay) NOUN a
phrase or idea that is used so often
that it has little meaning

click NOUN a short sharp sound

click VERB ❶ to make a short sharp
sound ❷ to press a button on a
computer mouse

client NOUN a person who gets
help or advice from a professional
person such as a lawyer,
accountant, architect, etc.; a
customer

cliff NOUN a steep rock face,
especially on a coast

cliffhanger NOUN a tense and
exciting ending to an episode of
a story

climate NOUN the normal weather
conditions of an area

climax NOUN the most interesting
or important point of a story, series
of events, etc.

climb VERB ❶ to go up towards
the top of something ❷ to move
somewhere with difficulty or
effort ❸ to go higher ❹ to grow
upwards

climb NOUN an act of climbing

climber NOUN someone who climbs
mountains as a sport

clinch VERB ❶ to settle something
definitely ❷ boxers clinch when
they clasp each other during a
fight

cling VERB clings, clinging, clung to
hold on tightly

cling film NOUN (*British*) a thin
clinging transparent film, used as a
covering for food

clinic NOUN a place where people

clinical *ADJECTIVE* ❶ to do with the medical treatment of patients ❷ cool and unemotional

clink *NOUN* a thin sharp sound like glasses being struck together

clink *VERB* to make a thin sharp sound like glasses being struck together

clip *NOUN* ❶ a fastener for keeping things together, usually worked by a spring ❷ a short piece of film shown on its own ❸ (*informal*) a hit on the head

clip *VERB* ❶ to fasten something with a clip ❷ to cut something with shears or scissors ❸ (*informal*) to hit someone or something

clipper *NOUN* an old type of fast sailing ship

clippers *PLURAL NOUN* an instrument for cutting hair

clique (say kleek) *NOUN* a small group of people who stick together and keep others out

clitoris *NOUN* the small sensitive piece of flesh near the opening of a woman's vagina

cloak *NOUN* a sleeveless piece of outdoor clothing that hangs loosely from the shoulders

cloak *VERB* to cover or conceal something

cloakroom *NOUN* ❶ a place where people can leave coats and bags while visiting a building ❷ a toilet

cloche (say klosh) *NOUN* a glass or plastic cover to protect outdoor plants

clock *NOUN* ❶ a device that shows what the time is ❷ a measuring device with a dial or digital display

clock *VERB* (*informal*) to notice or recognize someone

clockwise *ADVERB & ADJECTIVE* moving round a circle in the same direction as a clock's hands

clockwork *NOUN* a mechanism with a spring that has to be wound up

clod *NOUN* a lump of earth or clay

clog *NOUN* a shoe with a wooden sole

clog *VERB* to block something up

cloister *NOUN* a covered path along the side of a church or monastery etc., round a courtyard

clone *NOUN* an animal or plant made from the cells of another animal or plant and therefore exactly like it

clone *VERB* to produce a clone of an animal or plant

close (say klohss) *ADJECTIVE* ❶ near ❷ detailed or careful ❸ that you know well and have a strong friendship with; related to you directly ❹ a close fit is tight, with little space to spare ❺ a close contest or fight is one in which competitors are nearly equal ❻ warm and stuffy, without fresh air

close (say klohss) *ADVERB* at a close distance

close (say klohss) *NOUN* (*British*) ❶ a street that is closed at one end ❷ an enclosed area, especially round a cathedral

close (say klohz) *VERB* ❶ to shut something ❷ to be no longer open ❸ to end a meeting or activity

close (say klohz) NOUN the close of an activity is when it ends

closed ADJECTIVE not open; shut

closely ADVERB ❶ carefully, with attention ❷ in a way that is very similar or shows a strong connection ❸ so that people or things are close together

closet NOUN (North American) a cupboard or storeroom

closet VERB to shut yourself away in a private room

close-up NOUN a photograph or piece of film taken at close range

closure NOUN the closing of something permanently

clot NOUN ❶ a small mass of blood, cream, etc. that has become solid ❷ (informal) a stupid person

clot VERB to form clots

cloth NOUN ❶ woven material or felt ❷ a piece of this material ❸ a tablecloth

clothe VERB to put clothes on someone

clothes PLURAL NOUN things worn to cover the body

clothing NOUN clothes

clotted cream NOUN (chiefly British) cream thickened by being scalded

cloud NOUN ❶ a mass of condensed water vapour floating in the sky ❷ a mass of smoke, dust, etc., in the air

cloud VERB ❶ to become difficult to see through ❷ if a person's face clouds, their expression becomes more serious, worried or angry

cloudburst NOUN a sudden heavy rainstorm

cloudy ADJECTIVE ❶ full of clouds ❷ a cloudy liquid is not clear or transparent

clout VERB (informal) to hit someone roughly

clove NOUN ❶ the dried bud of a tropical tree, used as a spice ❷ one of the separate sections in a bulb of garlic

clove VERB past tense of cleave

cloven past participle of cleave

clover NOUN a small plant usually with three leaves on each stalk

clown NOUN ❶ a performer who does amusing tricks and actions, especially in a circus ❷ a person who does silly things

clown VERB to fool about and do silly things

cloying ADJECTIVE sickeningly sweet

club NOUN ❶ a heavy stick used as a weapon ❷ a stick with a shaped head used to hit the ball in golf ❸ a group of people who meet because they are interested in the same thing; the building where they meet ❹ a playing card with black clover leaves on it

club VERB to hit someone with a heavy stick

cluck VERB to make a hen's throaty cry

clue NOUN something that helps you to solve a puzzle or a mystery

clump NOUN a cluster or mass of things

clump VERB ❶ to walk with a heavy tread ❷ to form a cluster or mass

clumsy ADJECTIVE ❶ careless and likely to knock things over or drop things ❷ not skilful or tactful

cluster *NOUN* a group of people or things that stand or grow close together

cluster *VERB* to form a cluster

clutch *VERB* to grasp something tightly

clutch *NOUN* ❶ a tight grasp ❷ a device for connecting and disconnecting the engine of a motor vehicle from its gears ❸ a set of eggs laid at the same time

clutter *NOUN* a lot of things lying about untidily

clutter *VERB* to fill a place with clutter

Co. *ABBREVIATION* Company

c/o *ABBREVIATION* care of

coach *NOUN* ❶ a comfortable bus used for long journeys ❷ a carriage of a railway train ❸ a large horse-drawn carriage with four wheels ❹ an instructor who gives training in sports ❺ a teacher giving private tuition in a subject

coach *VERB* to instruct or train somebody, especially in sports

coal *NOUN* a hard black mineral substance used for burning to supply heat; a piece of this

coalition *NOUN* a temporary alliance, especially of two or more political parties in order to form a government

coarse *ADJECTIVE* ❶ not smooth or delicate; rough ❷ made up of large particles; not fine ❸ rude or vulgar

coast *NOUN* the seashore or the land close to it

coast *VERB* to ride downhill without using power

coastal *ADJECTIVE* by the coast or near the coast

coastguard *NOUN* a person whose job is to keep watch on the coast, detect or prevent smuggling, etc.

coastline *NOUN* the shape or outline of a coast

coat *NOUN* ❶ a piece of clothing with sleeves, worn over other clothes ❷ the hair or fur on an animal's body ❸ a layer of something that covers a surface

coat *VERB* to cover a thing with a layer of something

coating *NOUN* a thin layer that covers something

coat of arms *NOUN* a design on a shield, used as an emblem by a family, city, etc.

coax *VERB* to persuade someone gently or patiently to do something

cob *NOUN* ❶ the central part of an ear of maize, on which the corn grows ❷ (*British*) a round loaf of bread ❸ a sturdy horse for riding ❹ a male swan (The female is a **pen**.)

cobalt *NOUN* a hard silvery-white metal

cobble *NOUN* cobbles are a surface of cobblestones on a street

cobble *VERB* to cobble something together is to make it quickly and without much care

cobbler *NOUN* someone who mends shoes

cobblestone *NOUN* a small smooth rounded stone sometimes used in large numbers to pave roads in towns

cobra (say koh-bra) NOUN a poisonous snake that can rear up

cobweb NOUN the thin sticky net made by a spider to trap insects

cocaine NOUN a drug made from the leaves of a tropical plant called coca ①

cock NOUN ① a male chicken ② a male bird ③ a lever in a gun

cock VERB ① to make a gun ready to fire by raising the cock ② to turn part of your body upwards or in a particular direction

cockatoo NOUN a crested parrot

cockerel NOUN a young male chicken

cocker spaniel NOUN a kind of small spaniel with long hanging ears

cockle NOUN an edible shellfish

cockney NOUN ① a person born in the East End of London ② the dialect or accent of cockneys

cockpit NOUN the compartment where the pilot of an aircraft sits

cockroach NOUN a dark brown beetle-like insect, often found in dirty houses

cocktail NOUN ① a mixed alcoholic drink ② a dish consisting of small pieces of shellfish or mixed fruit

cocky ADJECTIVE (informal) too self-confident and cheeky

cocoa NOUN ① a hot drink made from a powder of crushed cacao seeds ② this powder

coconut NOUN ① a large round nut that grows on a kind of palm tree ② its white lining, used in sweets and cookery

cocoon NOUN ① the covering round a chrysalis ② a protective wrapping

cocoon VERB to protect something by wrapping it up

cod NOUN a large edible sea fish

coddle VERB to treat someone in a way that protects them too much

code NOUN ① a system of words, letters or numbers used instead of the real letters or words to make a message or information secret ② a set of signals or signs used in sending messages ③ a set of numbers used for an area in making telephone calls ④ a set of laws or rules

code VERB to put a message into code

co-education NOUN educating boys and girls together

coefficient NOUN a number by which another number is multiplied; a factor

coexist VERB to exist together or at the same time

coffee NOUN ① a hot drink made from the roasted ground seeds (**coffee beans**) of a tropical plant ② these seeds

coffer NOUN a large strong box for holding money and valuables

coffin NOUN a long box in which a body is buried or cremated

cog NOUN one of a number of tooth-like parts round the edge of a wheel, fitting into and pushing those on another wheel

cogent (say koh-jent) ADJECTIVE a cogent argument is strong and convincing

cognac (say **kon**-yak) NOUN brandy, especially from Cognac in France

cogwheel NOUN a wheel with cogs

coherent (say koh-**heer**-ent) ADJECTIVE clear, reasonable and making sense

cohesion NOUN the ability to combine or fit together well to form a whole

coil NOUN something wound into a spiral or series of loops

coil VERB to wind something into a coil

coin NOUN a piece of metal, usually round, used as money

coin VERB ❶ to manufacture coins ❷ to invent a word or phrase

coinage NOUN ❶ coins; a system of money ❷ a new word or phrase that someone has invented

coincide VERB ❶ to happen at the same time as something else ❷ to be the same

coincidence NOUN the happening of similar events at the same time by chance

coke NOUN the solid fuel left when gas and tar have been extracted from coal

colander NOUN a bowl-shaped container with holes in it, used for straining water from vegetables etc. after cooking

cold ADJECTIVE ❶ having or at a low temperature; not warm ❷ not friendly or loving; showing no kindness or understanding

cold NOUN ❶ lack of warmth; low temperature; cold weather ❷ an infectious illness that makes your nose run, your throat sore, etc.

cold-blooded ADJECTIVE ❶ having a body temperature that changes according to the surroundings ❷ showing no feelings or pity for other people

coldly ADVERB in an unfriendly or distant way

cold war NOUN a situation where nations are enemies without actually fighting

colic NOUN pain in a baby's stomach

collaborate VERB to work together on a job

collage (say kol-**ah** zh) NOUN a picture made by fixing small objects to a surface

collapse VERB ❶ to fall down or fall in suddenly, often after breaking apart ❷ to fall down because of being very weak or ill ❸ to fold up

collapse NOUN ❶ collapsing ❷ a failure or breakdown

collar NOUN ❶ the part of a piece of clothing that goes round your neck ❷ a band that goes round the neck of a dog, cat, horse, etc.

collar VERB (informal) to seize or catch someone

collarbone NOUN the bone joining the breastbone and shoulder blade

collate VERB to collect and arrange pieces of information in an organized way

colleague NOUN a person you work with

collect (say kol-**ekt**) VERB ❶ to bring people or things together from various places ❷ to get and keep together examples of things as a hobby ❸ to come together ❹ to ask for money or contributions etc. from people ❺ to go to fetch someone or something

collection NOUN ❶ a number of things someone has collected ❷ collecting something ❸ money collected for a charity or some other purpose

collective ADJECTIVE to do with a group taken as a whole

collective noun NOUN a noun that is singular in form but refers to many individuals taken as a unit, e.g. *army*, *herd*, *choir*

collector NOUN someone who collects things as a hobby or as part of their job

college NOUN a place where people can continue learning something after they have left school

collide VERB to crash into something

collie NOUN a dog with a long pointed face

colliery NOUN (*British*) a coal mine and its buildings

collision NOUN an accident in which two moving vehicles or people crash into each other

colloquial (say col-**oh**-kwee-al) ADJECTIVE suitable for conversation but not for formal speech or writing

cologne (say kol-**ohn**) NOUN eau de Cologne or a similar liquid

colon NOUN ❶ a punctuation mark (:), often used to introduce lists or an explanation ❷ the largest part of the intestine

colonel (say **ker**-nel) NOUN an army officer in charge of a regiment

colonial ADJECTIVE to do with a colony

colonialism NOUN the policy of acquiring and keeping colonies

colonist NOUN a person who goes to live in a colony abroad

colonize (also **colonise**) VERB to establish a colony in a country

colony NOUN ❶ an area of land that the people of another country settle in and control ❷ the people of a colony ❸ a group of people or animals of the same kind living close together

coloration NOUN colouring

colossal ADJECTIVE extremely large; enormous

colossus NOUN ❶ a huge statue ❷ a person of immense importance

colour NOUN ❶ the effect produced by waves of light of a particular wavelength ❷ the use of various colours, not only black and white ❸ the colour of someone's skin ❹ a substance used to colour things ❺ the special flag of a ship or regiment

colour VERB ❶ to put colour on something, using paint, crayons, etc. ❷ to blush ❸ to influence what someone says or believes

colour-blind ADJECTIVE unable to see the difference between certain colours

coloured ADJECTIVE having colour

colourful ADJECTIVE ❶ with bright colours ❷ lively; with vivid details

colouring NOUN ❶ a substance that you add to something, especially food, to give it a special

colour ❷ a person's colouring is the colour of their skin and hair

colourless ADJECTIVE without colour

colt NOUN a young male horse

column NOUN ❶ a pillar ❷ something long or tall and narrow ❸ a vertical section of a page ❹ a regular article or feature in a newspaper or magazine

coma (say **koh**-ma) NOUN a state of deep unconsciousness, especially in someone who is ill or injured

comb NOUN ❶ a strip of wood, plastic or metal with a row of teeth, used to tidy hair or hold it in place ❷ something used like this, e.g. to separate strands of wool ❸ the red crest on a fowl's head ❹ a honeycomb

comb VERB ❶ to tidy your hair with a comb ❷ to search a place thoroughly

combat NOUN fighting, especially in a war

combat VERB to combat something bad or unpleasant is to fight it and try to get rid of it

combatant (say **kom**-ba-tant) NOUN someone who takes part in a fight

combination NOUN ❶ a number of people or things that have been joined or mixed together ❷ joining or mixing things ❸ a series of numbers or letters used to open a combination lock

combine (say komb-**yn**) VERB to join or mix things together; to come together to form something

combine harvester NOUN (British) a machine that both reaps and

threshes grain

combustible ADJECTIVE able to be set on fire and burn

combustion NOUN the process of burning, a chemical process in which substances combine with oxygen in air and produce heat

come VERB comes, coming, came, come ❶ to move or travel to the place where you are ❷ to arrive at or reach a place or condition or result ❸ to happen ❹ to occur or be present ❺ to result

comedian NOUN someone who entertains people by making them laugh

comedy NOUN ❶ a play or film etc. that makes people laugh ❷ humour

comet NOUN an object moving across the sky with a bright tail of light

comfort NOUN ❶ a feeling of being physically relaxed and satisfied ❷ soothing somebody who is worried or unhappy ❸ a person or thing that gives comfort

comfort VERB to make a person feel less worried or unhappy

comfortable ADJECTIVE ❶ at ease; free from worry or pain ❷ pleasant to use or wear; making you feel relaxed

comfy ADJECTIVE (informal) comfortable

comic NOUN ❶ a children's magazine full of comic strips ❷ a comedian

comic ADJECTIVE making people laugh; funny

comical ADJECTIVE making people

laugh; funny

comic strip NOUN a series of drawings telling a story, especially a funny one

comma NOUN a punctuation mark (,) used to mark a pause in a sentence or to separate items in a list

command NOUN ❶ a statement telling someone to do something; an order ❷ to be in command is to have authority or control over someone ❸ a command of a subject or language is a good knowledge of it and an ability to use it well

command VERB ❶ to give a command to someone; to order someone to do something ❷ to have authority over a group of people ❸ to deserve and get something

commandant (say kom-an-dant) NOUN a military officer in charge of a fortress etc.

commander NOUN a person in command of a group of people

commandment NOUN a sacred command, especially one of the Ten Commandments given to Moses

commando NOUN a soldier trained for making dangerous raids

commemorate VERB to be a celebration or reminder of some past event or person

commence VERB (formal) to begin

commend VERB ❶ to praise someone ❷ (formal) to entrust a person or thing to someone

commendable ADJECTIVE deserving praise

comment NOUN an opinion given about something or to explain something

comment VERB to make a comment

commentary VERB ❶ a description of an event by someone who is watching it, especially for radio or television ❷ a set of explanatory comments on a text

commentator NOUN a person who gives a radio or television commentary

commerce NOUN the business of buying and selling goods and services; trade

commercial ADJECTIVE ❶ to do with commerce ❷ paid for by advertising ❸ making a profit

commercial NOUN a broadcast advertisement

commiserate VERB to sympathize with someone

commission NOUN ❶ a task formally given to someone ❷ an appointment to be an officer in the armed forces ❸ a group of people given authority to do or investigate something ❹ extra money that a person gets for selling goods

commission VERB to give someone a task or assignment

commissionaire NOUN (British) an attendant in uniform at the entrance to a theatre, large shop, offices, etc.

commissioner NOUN ❶ an official appointed by commission ❷ a member of a commission

commit VERB ❶ to commit a

crime is to do something against the law ❷ to commit yourself to something is to promise to do it or to devote all your energy to doing it ❸ to promise that you will make your time etc. available for a particular purpose ❹ to place a person in someone's care or custody

commitment NOUN ❶ the work, belief and loyalty that a person gives to something because they think it is important ❷ something that regularly takes up some of your time

committee NOUN a group of people appointed to deal with something

commodity NOUN a product or material that can be bought and sold

common ADJECTIVE ❶ ordinary or usual; occurring frequently ❷ affecting all or most people ❸ shared ❹ vulgar; showing a lack of education

common NOUN a piece of land that everyone can use

commoner NOUN a member of the ordinary people, not of the nobility

commonly ADVERB usually or frequently

commonplace ADJECTIVE not exciting or unusual; ordinary

common room NOUN (*chiefly British*) a room for students or teachers at a school or college to use when they are not involved in lessons

common sense NOUN normal good sense in thinking or behaviour

commonwealth NOUN ❶ a group

of countries cooperating together ❷ a country made up of an association of states

commotion NOUN great noise or excitement; an uproar

communal (say kom-yoo-nal) ADJECTIVE shared by several people

commune (say **kom**-yoon) NOUN ❶ a group of people living together and sharing everything ❷ a district of local government in France and some other countries

commune (say kom-**mewn**) VERB to share your thoughts and feelings with someone or with nature without speaking

communicate VERB ❶ to pass news or information to other people ❷ rooms communicate when there is a door leading from one to the other

communication NOUN ❶ communicating with other people ❷ a written or spoken message

communicative ADJECTIVE willing to talk

communion NOUN religious fellowship

communiqué (say ko-mew-nik-ay) NOUN an official message giving a report

communism NOUN a political system in which property is shared by everyone and the state controls the country's industry and resources. Compare with capitalism.

communist NOUN a person who believes in communism

community NOUN ❶ the people

living in one area ❷ a group with similar interests or origins

commute VERB ❶ to travel a fairly long way by train, bus or car to and from your daily work ❷ to alter a punishment to something less severe

commuter NOUN a person who commutes to and from work

compact ADJECTIVE ❶ neat and small ❷ closely or neatly packed together

compact NOUN ❶ a small flat container for face powder ❷ an agreement or contract

compact VERB to press something firmly together

compact disc NOUN a small plastic disc on which music or information is stored as digital signals and is read by a laser beam

companion NOUN ❶ a person who you spend time with or travel with ❷ a guidebook or reference book

companionship NOUN being with someone and enjoying their friendship

company NOUN ❶ a business firm ❷ a group of people who perform together ❸ having people with you; being with someone ❹ visitors ❺ a section of a battalion

comparable (say kom-per-a-bul) ADJECTIVE able to be compared, similar

comparative ADJECTIVE compared with something else

comparative NOUN the form of an adjective or adverb that expresses 'more'

compare VERB ❶ to put or consider things together so that you can see in what ways they are similar or different ❷ to form the comparative and superlative of an adjective or adverb

comparison NOUN comparing things

compartment NOUN ❶ one of the spaces into which something is divided; a separate room or enclosed space ❷ a division of a railway carriage

compass NOUN an instrument that shows direction, with a magnetized needle pointing to the north

compassion NOUN pity or mercy you show to someone who is suffering

compatible ADJECTIVE ❶ able to live or exist together without trouble ❷ able to be used together

compatriot (say kom-**pat**-ri-ot) NOUN a person from the same country as another

compel VERB to force someone to do something

compelling ADJECTIVE forcing you to pay attention or believe something

compendium NOUN ❶ an encyclopedia or handbook in one volume ❷ a set of different board games in one box

compensate VERB ❶ to give a person money etc. to make up for a loss or injury ❷ to have a balancing effect

compensation NOUN ❶ money paid to someone to make up for a loss or injury ❷ a thing

a
b
c
d
e
f
g
h
i
j
k
l
m
n
o
p
q
r
s
t
u
v
w
x
y
z

that reduces the bad effect of something

compère (say kom-pair) NOUN (British) a person who introduces the performers in a show or broadcast

compete VERB ❶ to take part in a competition ❷ to try to be better or more successful than someone else

competent ADJECTIVE having the skill or knowledge to do something in a satisfactory way

competition NOUN ❶ a game or race or other contest in which people try to win ❷ trying to be better or more successful than someone else ❸ the people who compete with you

competitive ADJECTIVE ❶ a competitive person enjoys competing with other people ❷ involving competition between people or firms

competitor NOUN someone who competes; a rival

compile VERB to put together a book, list, etc. by collecting together information from various places

complacent ADJECTIVE smugly satisfied with the way things are and feeling that no change or action is necessary

complain VERB to say that you are annoyed or unhappy about something

complaint NOUN ❶ a statement complaining about something ❷ a minor illness

complement NOUN ❶ the

quantity needed to fill or complete something ❷ the word or words used after verbs such as be and become to complete the sense. In *She was brave* and *He became king of England*, the complements are *brave* and *king of England*

complement VERB one thing complements another when they go well together or when one makes the other complete

complementary ADJECTIVE going together well or going together to make a whole

complementary angle NOUN either of two angles that add up to 90°

complementary medicine NOUN (British) medical methods that are not considered part of ordinary medicine, but may be used alongside it, e.g. acupuncture and homoeopathy

complete ADJECTIVE ❶ having all its parts, with nothing missing ❷ finished, with everything done ❸ thorough; in every way

complete VERB ❶ to finish something or make it complete ❷ to complete a form is to write on it all the information you are asked for

completely ADVERB in every way; totally

completion NOUN making a thing complete; finishing something

complex ADJECTIVE ❶ made up of many different parts ❷ difficult or complicated

complex NOUN ❶ a set of buildings made up of related parts ❷ a group of feelings or ideas that influence a person's behaviour or make them worry about something

complexion NOUN ❶ the natural colour and appearance of the skin of the face ❷ the way things seem

complicate VERB to make something more difficult to understand or deal with

complicated ADJECTIVE ❶ made up of many different parts ❷ difficult to understand or deal with

complication NOUN ❶ something that complicates things or adds difficulties ❷ a new illness that you get when you are already ill

compliment NOUN something you say or do to show that you approve of a person or thing

compliment VERB to pay someone a compliment; to congratulate someone

complimentary ADJECTIVE ❶ expressing a compliment ❷ given free of charge

comply VERB to obey an order, rule or request

component NOUN each of the parts of which a thing is made up

compose VERB ❶ to write music ❷ to write a letter, speech or poem ❸ to be composed of several people or things is to contain or include them ❹ to compose yourself is to become calm after being excited or angry

composed ADJECTIVE calm and in control of your feelings

composer NOUN a person who composes music

composite (say kom-poz-it) ADJECTIVE made up of a number of

parts or different styles

composition NOUN ❶ composing music or poetry ❷ something composed, especially a piece of music ❸ an essay or story written as a school exercise ❹ the composition of a substance is the way that it is made up

compost NOUN ❶ decayed leaves and grass etc. used as a fertilizer ❷ a soil-like mixture for growing seedlings, cuttings, etc.

composure NOUN calmness of manner

compound ADJECTIVE made of two or more parts or ingredients

compound NOUN ❶ a compound substance ❷ (in grammar) a word or expression made from other words joined together, e.g. 'football' and 'newspaper' ❸ a fenced area containing buildings

compound VERB to make something worse

comprehend VERB to understand something

comprehensible ADJECTIVE able to be understood

comprehension NOUN ❶ understanding something ❷ an exercise that tests how well you understand something written or spoken in another language

comprehensive ADJECTIVE including all or many kinds of people or things

comprehensive NOUN (British) a comprehensive school

comprehensive school NOUN (British) a secondary school for all or most of the children in an area

compress (say kom-**press**) VERB
① to press or squeeze something together or into a smaller space
② to alter the form of computer data to reduce the amount of space needed to store it

compress (say kom-**press**) NOUN
a soft pad or cloth pressed on the body to stop bleeding or cool inflammation etc.

comprise VERB to include or consist of

compromise (say kom-prom-yz) NOUN settling a dispute by each side accepting less than it wanted or asked for

compromise VERB to accept less than you wanted or asked for in order to settle a dispute

compulsion NOUN a strong and uncontrollable desire to do something

compulsive ADJECTIVE having or resulting from a strong and uncontrollable desire

compulsory ADJECTIVE something is compulsory when you have to do it and cannot choose

compute VERB to calculate something

computer NOUN an electronic machine for making calculations, storing and analysing information put into it or controlling machinery automatically

computerize (also **computerise**) VERB to use computers to do a job or to store information

computing NOUN the use of computers

comrade NOUN a companion who shares in your activities

con VERB (informal) to swindle someone

concave ADJECTIVE curved like the inside of a ball or circle. (The opposite is **convex**.)

conceal VERB to hide something or keep it secret

concede VERB ① to admit that something is true ② to admit that you have been defeated ③ to give up a possession or right

conceit NOUN too much pride in your abilities and achievements

conceited ADJECTIVE too proud of yourself and your abilities

conceivable ADJECTIVE able to be imagined or believed

conceive VERB ① to become pregnant; to form a baby in the womb ② to form an idea or plan in your mind

concentrate VERB ① to give your full attention or effort to something ② to bring something together in one place

concentrated ADJECTIVE a concentrated liquid has been made stronger by removing water

concentration NOUN
① concentrating on something
② the amount dissolved in each part of a liquid

concentration camp NOUN a prison camp where political prisoners are kept together, especially one set up by the Nazis during World War II

concentric ADJECTIVE having the same centre

concept NOUN an idea

conception NOUN ❶ conceiving a baby ❷ forming an idea in your mind

concern VERB ❶ to be important to or affect someone ❷ to worry someone ❸ to be about something; to have something as its subject

concern NOUN ❶ something that is important to you or that affects you; a responsibility ❷ a worry or a feeling of worry ❸ a business

concerned ADJECTIVE ❶ worried or anxious ❷ involved in or affected by something

concerning PREPOSITION on the subject of; about

concert NOUN a performance of music

concerted ADJECTIVE done in cooperation with others

concertina NOUN a portable musical instrument with bellows, played by squeezing

concerto (say kon-**chert**-oh) NOUN a piece of music for a solo instrument and an orchestra

concession NOUN ❶ something that you agree to let someone have or do in order to end an argument or to be helpful ❷ a reduction in price for a certain category of person

concise ADJECTIVE brief; giving a lot of information in a few words

conclave NOUN a private meeting

conclude VERB ❶ to decide about something; to form an opinion by reasoning ❷ to end or to bring something to an end

conclusion NOUN ❶ an ending

❷ an opinion formed by reasoning

conclusive ADJECTIVE putting an end to all doubt

concoct VERB ❶ to make something by putting ingredients together ❷ to invent something or make it up

concord NOUN friendly agreement or harmony

concourse NOUN an open area through which people pass, e.g. at an airport

concrete NOUN cement mixed with sand and gravel, used in building

concrete ADJECTIVE ❶ based on facts, not ideas or guesses ❷ definite and clear, not general

concrete poem NOUN a poem printed in a special way, so that the words form a pattern on the page that has something to do with the meaning of the poem

concur VERB to agree

concussion NOUN a temporary injury to the brain caused by a hard knock

condemn VERB ❶ to say that you strongly disapprove of something ❷ to convict or sentence a criminal ❸ to be condemned to something unpleasant is to have to suffer it ❹ to declare that a building is not fit to be used

condensation NOUN ❶ water from humid air collecting as tiny drops on a cold surface ❷ the process of changing from gas or vapour to liquid

condense VERB ❶ to make a liquid denser or more compact ❷ to put something into fewer words or less

125

space ❸ to change from gas or vapour to liquid

condescend VERB ❶ to behave towards someone in a way which shows that you think you are superior to them ❷ to allow yourself to do something that you think is unworthy of you or beneath you

condescending ADJECTIVE behaving towards someone in a way which shows that you think you are superior to them

condiment NOUN a seasoning (e.g. salt or pepper) for food

condition NOUN ❶ the state or fitness of a person or thing ❷ the situation or surroundings that affect people ❸ something required as part of an agreement

condition VERB ❶ to bring something into a healthy or proper condition ❷ to train someone to behave in a particular way or become used to a particular situation

conditional ADJECTIVE containing a condition; depending on something else

conditioner NOUN a substance you put on your hair to keep it in good condition

condolence NOUN an expression of sympathy, especially for someone who is bereaved

condom NOUN a rubber sheath worn on the penis during sexual intercourse as a contraceptive and as a protection against sexual disease or infection

condone VERB to accept or ignore wrongdoing

condor NOUN a kind of large vulture

conducive ADJECTIVE helping to cause or produce something

conduct (say kon-**dukt**) VERB ❶ to manage something or carry it out ❷ to lead or guide someone to a place ❸ to be the conductor of an orchestra or choir ❹ to allow heat, light, sound or electricity to pass along or through something ❺ to behave in a particular way

conduct (say **kon**-dukt) NOUN a person's behaviour

conduction NOUN the conducting of heat or electricity etc

conductor NOUN ❶ a person who directs the performance of an orchestra or choir by movements of the arms ❷ something that conducts heat or electricity etc. ❸ a person who collects the fares on a bus etc.

conduit (say **kon**-dit) NOUN ❶ a pipe or channel for liquid ❷ a tube protecting electric wire

cone NOUN ❶ an object that is circular at one end and narrows to a point at the other end ❷ an ice cream cornet ❸ the dry cone-shaped fruit of a pine, fir or cedar tree

confection NOUN something made of various things, especially sweet ones, put together

confectioner NOUN someone who makes or sells sweets

confederacy NOUN a union of states; a confederation

confederate ADJECTIVE allied; joined by an agreement or treaty

confederate NOUN ❶ a member of a confederacy ❷ an ally or accomplice

confederation NOUN ❶ the process of joining in an alliance ❷ a group of people, organizations or states joined together by an agreement or treaty

confer VERB ❶ to have a discussion before deciding ❷ to grant a right or privilege to someone

conference NOUN a meeting at which formal discussions take place

confess VERB to state openly that you have done something wrong or have a weakness; to admit something

confession NOUN ❶ admitting that you have done wrong ❷ (in the Roman Catholic Church) an act of telling a priest that you have sinned

confessional NOUN a small room where a priest hears confessions

confessor NOUN a priest who hears confessions

confetti NOUN tiny pieces of coloured paper thrown by wedding guests at the bride and bridegroom

confidant NOUN (**confidante** is used of a woman) a person you confide in

confide VERB to tell someone a secret

confidence NOUN ❶ a feeling of being sure that you are right or can do something ❷ firm trust in someone or something ❸ something told as a secret

confidence trick NOUN swindling a person after persuading him or her to trust you

confident ADJECTIVE showing or feeling confidence

confidential ADJECTIVE meant to be kept secret

configuration NOUN the way in which the parts of something or a group of things are arranged.

confine VERB ❶ to keep something within limits; to restrict something ❷ to keep someone in a place and not let them leave

confined ADJECTIVE a confined space is narrow or enclosed

confinement NOUN ❶ being forced to stay somewhere ❷ (old use) the time of giving birth to a baby

confines (say **kon**-fynz) PLURAL NOUN the limits or boundaries of an area

confirm VERB ❶ to show definitely that something is true or correct ❷ to make an arrangement definite ❸ to make a person a full member of the Christian Church

confirmation NOUN ❶ a statement showing that something is true, correct or definite ❷ a ceremony in which a person is made a full member of the Christian Church

confiscate VERB to take something away from someone as a punishment

conflict (say **kon**-flikt) NOUN a fight, struggle or disagreement

conflict (say kon-**flikt**) VERB two things conflict when they contradict or disagree with one another

confluence NOUN the place where two rivers meet

conform VERB to keep to accepted rules, customs or ideas

confound VERB to astonish or confuse someone

confront VERB ❶ to confront someone is to challenge them face to face for a fight or argument ❷ to confront a problem or difficulty is to deal with it rather than ignoring it ❸ if a problem or difficulty confronts you, you have to deal with it

confrontation NOUN meeting someone face to face for a fight or argument

confuse VERB ❶ to make a person puzzled or muddled ❷ to mistake one person or thing for another

confusing ADJECTIVE difficult to understand; not clear

confusion NOUN ❶ not being able to think clearly or not knowing what to do ❷ mistaking one thing for another

congeal (say kon-jeel) VERB to become jelly-like instead of liquid, especially in cooling

congenial ADJECTIVE pleasant through being similar to yourself or suiting your tastes

congenital (say kon-jen-it-al) ADJECTIVE existing in a person from birth

congested ADJECTIVE ❶ a congested place is crowded or blocked up with traffic or people ❷ your breathing and a part of your body are congested when they become blocked with mucus

congestion NOUN ❶ when a place is crowded and full of traffic or people ❷ when your nose is blocked with mucus and you cannot breathe properly

conglomerate NOUN a large business group formed by merging several different companies

congratulate VERB to tell a person that you are pleased about what they have achieved or something good that has happened to them

congratulations PLURAL NOUN what you say to congratulate someone

congregate VERB to come together in a crowd or group

congregation NOUN a group of people who have come together to take part in religious worship

Congress NOUN the parliament of the USA

congress NOUN a large meeting or conference

congruent ADJECTIVE (in mathematics) having exactly the same shape and size

conical ADJECTIVE cone-shaped

conifer (say kon-if-er) NOUN an evergreen tree with cones

conjecture NOUN guesswork or a guess

conjecture VERB to guess about something

conjoined twins PLURAL NOUN twins who are born with their bodies joined together

conjugate VERB to give all the different forms of a verb

128

conjunction NOUN a word that joins words, phrases or sentences, e.g. *and*, *but* and *because*

conjure VERB to perform tricks that look like magic

conker NOUN (British) the hard shiny brown nut of the horse chestnut tree

connect VERB ❶ to join things together; to link one thing with another ❷ to think of things or people as being associated with each other

connection NOUN ❶ a link or relationship between things ❷ a place where two wires, pipes, etc are joined together ❸ a train, bus, etc. that leaves a station soon after another arrives, so that passengers can change from one to the other

connective NOUN a word that joins words, clauses or sentences. Some connectives (e.g. *but*, *and* and *because*) are conjunctions, while some (e.g. *however* and *in addition*) are adverbials.

conning tower NOUN the part on top of a submarine, containing the periscope

connive (say kon-**yv**) VERB ➤ **connive at something** to ignore something wrong or quietly approve of it ➤ **connivance** NOUN

connoisseur (say kon-a-**ser**) NOUN a person with great experience and appreciation of something

conquer VERB ❶ to defeat and take control of a country and its people ❷ to succeed in controlling a difficult feeling

conquest NOUN ❶ a victory over someone ❷ conquered territory

conscience (say **kon**-shens) NOUN knowing what is right and wrong, especially in your own actions

conscientious (say kon-shee-en-shus) ADJECTIVE careful and honest about doing your work properly

conscientious objector NOUN a person who refuses to serve in the armed forces because he or she believes it is morally wrong

conscious (say **kon**-shus) ADJECTIVE ❶ awake and knowing what is happening ❷ aware of something ❸ done deliberately

conscript (say kon-**skript**) VERB to make a person join the armed forces

conscript (say kon-**skript**) NOUN a person who has been conscripted

consecrate VERB to officially say that a thing, especially a building, is holy

consecutive ADJECTIVE following one after another

consensus NOUN general agreement; the opinion of most people

consent NOUN agreement to what someone wishes; permission

consent VERB to say that you are willing to do or allow what someone wishes

consequence NOUN ❶ something that happens as the result of an event or action ❷ the importance that something has

consequently ADVERB as a result

conservation NOUN ❶ the preservation of the natural environment ❷ not allowing something valuable from being spoilt or wasted

conservationist NOUN a person who believes in preserving the natural environment

Conservative NOUN a person who supports the Conservative Party, a British political party that favours private enterprise and freedom from state control

conservative ADJECTIVE ❶ liking traditional ways and disliking changes ❷ lower than what is probably the real amount

conservatory NOUN a room with a glass roof and large windows, built against an outside wall of a house with a connecting door from the house

conserve VERB to prevent something valuable from being changed, spoilt or wasted

consider VERB ❶ to think carefully about or give attention to something, especially in order to make a decision ❷ to have something as an opinion; to think something

considerable ADJECTIVE fairly great or large

considerate ADJECTIVE always thinking of other people's needs, wishes or feelings

consideration NOUN ❶ careful thought or attention ❷ considerate behaviour ❸ a fact that must be kept in mind

considering PREPOSITION taking something into consideration

consign VERB to put something somewhere in order to get rid of it

consignment NOUN a batch of goods etc. sent to someone

consist VERB to be made up or formed of

consistency NOUN ❶ how thick or smooth a liquid is ❷ being consistent

consistent ADJECTIVE ❶ keeping to a regular pattern, style or standard; not changing ❷ agreeing with something else; not contradictory

consolation NOUN ❶ consolation is giving comfort or sympathy to someone ❷ a consolation is something that comforts someone who is unhappy or disappointed

console (say kon-sohl) VERB to comfort someone who is unhappy or disappointed

console (say kon-sohl) NOUN a panel or unit containing the controls for electrical or other equipment

consolidate VERB ❶ to make something secure and strong ❷ to combine two or more organizations, funds, etc. into one

consonant NOUN a letter that is not a vowel

consort (say kon-sort) NOUN a husband or wife, especially of a monarch

consort (say kon-sort) VERB to consort with someone is to be often in their company

consortium NOUN a group of companies working together

conspicuous ADJECTIVE easy to see or notice; standing out very clearly

conspiracy NOUN a secret plan

130

made by a group of people to do something illegal

conspirator NOUN a person who takes part in a conspiracy

conspire VERB to take part in a conspiracy

constable NOUN a police officer of the lowest rank

constant ADJECTIVE ❶ not changing; happening all the time ❷ faithful or loyal

constant NOUN ❶ a thing that does not vary ❷ (in science and mathematics) a number or value that does not change

constantly ADVERB all the time; again and again

constellation NOUN a group of stars

constipated ADJECTIVE unable to empty the bowels easily or regularly

constituency NOUN a district represented by a Member of Parliament elected by the people who live there

constituent NOUN ❶ one of the parts that form a whole thing ❷ someone who lives in a particular constituency

constitute VERB ❶ to make up or form something ❷ to be considered to be something

constitution NOUN ❶ the group of laws or principles that state how a country is to be organized and governed ❷ the condition of your body in terms of its general physical health

constrain VERB to force someone to act in a certain way

constraint NOUN ❶ something that limits you; a restriction ❷ forcing someone to act in a certain way

constrict VERB to become tighter and narrower or to make something do this

construct VERB to make something by placing parts together; to build something from parts

construction NOUN ❶ constructing something ❷ something constructed; a building ❸ two or more words put together to form a phrase or clause or sentence

constructive ADJECTIVE helpful and positive

consul NOUN ❶ a government official appointed to live in a foreign city to help people from his or her own country who visit there ❷ either of the two chief magistrates in ancient Rome

consulate NOUN the building where a consul works

consult VERB ❶ to go to a person or book etc. for information or advice ❷ to discuss something with someone before taking a decision

consultant NOUN ❶ a person who is qualified to give expert advice ❷ a senior hospital doctor who is an expert in one type of medicine

consultation NOUN ❶ a discussion between people before a decision is taken ❷ meeting someone to get information or advice or looking for it in a book

consume VERB ❶ to eat or drink something ❷ to use something up ❸ to destroy something

a
b
c
d
e
f
g
h
i
j
k
l
m
n
o
p
q
r
s
t
u
v
w
x
y
z

consumer NOUN a person who buys or uses goods or services

consummate (say kon-**sum**-at) ADJECTIVE perfect; highly skilled

consummate (say **kon**-sum-ayt) VERB to make something complete or perfect

consumption NOUN ❶ the using up of something, especially food or fuel ❷ (old use) tuberculosis of the lungs

contact NOUN ❶ communication with someone, by speaking or writing to them regularly ❷ if two things are in contact with one another, they are touching ❸ a person to communicate with when you need information or help

contact VERB to get in touch with a person

contact lens NOUN a tiny plastic lens worn against the eyeball, instead of glasses

contagion NOUN a contagious disease

contagious ADJECTIVE a contagious disease is one that spreads by contact with an infected person

contain VERB ❶ to have something inside ❷ to consist of ❸ to restrain or hold back a strong feeling

container NOUN ❶ a box or bottle etc. designed to contain something ❷ a large box-like object of standard design in which goods are transported

contaminate VERB to make a thing dirty or impure or diseased; to pollute something

contemplate VERB ❶ to look at

something thoughtfully ❷ to consider or think about doing something

contemplation NOUN thinking deeply about something

contemporary ADJECTIVE ❶ living or happening in the same period ❷ belonging to the present time; modern

contemporary NOUN a person who is about the same age as another or is living at the same time

contempt NOUN a feeling of despising a person or thing

contemptible ADJECTIVE deserving contempt

contemptuous ADJECTIVE feeling or showing contempt

contend VERB ❶ to contend with a problem or difficulty is to have to deal with it ❷ to compete in a contest ❸ to declare or claim that something is true

contender NOUN a person who may win a competition

content (say kon-**tent**) ADJECTIVE happy or satisfied

content (say kon-**tent**) NOUN a happy or satisfied feeling

content (say **kon**-tent) NOUN ❶ the amount of a substance in something ❷ the subject and ideas dealt with in a book, television programme, speech, etc.

content (say kon-**tent**) VERB to make a person happy or satisfied

contented ADJECTIVE happy with what you have; satisfied

contention NOUN ❶ a point of view or opinion that someone puts forward ❷ strong disagreement or arguing

contentment NOUN a feeling of being happy or satisfied

contents (say **kon**-tents) PLURAL NOUN ❶ the contents of a box or other container are what is inside it ❷ the contents of a book, magazine, etc. are the things you read in it

contest (say **kon**-test) NOUN ❶ a competition; a struggle in which rivals try to obtain something or to be the best

contest (say kon-**test**) VERB ❶ to try to win a competition, election, etc. ❷ to dispute something or argue that it is wrong or not legal

contestant NOUN a person taking part in a contest; a competitor

context NOUN ❶ the words that come before and after a particular word or phrase and help to fix its meaning ❷ the background to an event that helps to explain it

continent NOUN one of the main masses of land in the world

contingency NOUN something that may happen but cannot be known for certain

continual ADJECTIVE happening all the time, usually with breaks in between

continuance NOUN (formal) continuing something

continue VERB ❶ to do something without stopping ❷ to begin again after stopping

continuous ADJECTIVE going on and on; without a break

contort VERB to twist or force something out of the usual shape

contour NOUN ❶ a line on a map joining the points that are the same height above sea level ❷ an outline

contraband NOUN smuggled goods

contraception NOUN the use of contraceptives to prevent pregnancy; birth control

contraceptive NOUN a substance or device that prevents pregnancy

contract (say **kon**-trakt) NOUN ❶ a formal agreement to do something ❷ a document stating the terms of an agreement

contract (say kon-**trakt**) VERB ❶ to become smaller or shorter ❷ to get an illness ❸ to make a contract

contraction NOUN ❶ getting smaller or shorter ❷ a shortened form of a word or words. Can't is a contraction of cannot.

contractor NOUN a person or company that has a contract to do work for someone else, especially in the building industry

contradict VERB ❶ to say that something said is not true or that someone is wrong ❷ to say the opposite of something

contradiction NOUN a statement that is opposite to or different from another one

contradictory ADJECTIVE being opposite to or not matching something else

contraflow NOUN (British) a special arrangement of traffic when a motorway is being repaired, with traffic going in both directions using the carriageway on the other side

contralto NOUN a female singer with a low voice

contraption NOUN a strange-looking or complicated device or machine

contrary ADJECTIVE ① (say kon-tra-ree) completely different or opposed to something ② (say kon-**trair**-ee) awkward and obstinate

contrary (say **kon**-tra-ree) NOUN the opposite

contrast (say **kon**-trahst) NOUN ① a difference clearly seen when things are compared ② something showing a clear difference compared with something else

contrast (say kon-**trahst**) VERB ① to compare two things in order to show that they are clearly different ② to be clearly different when compared

contravene VERB to do something that breaks a rule or law

contribute VERB ① to give money or help jointly with others ② to write something for a newspaper or magazine etc. ③ to help to cause something

contribution NOUN money or help that someone gives jointly with others

contrite ADJECTIVE very sorry for having done wrong

contrive VERB ① to find a way of doing something although it is difficult ② to plan or make something cleverly

control VERB ① to have the power to make other people or things do what you want ② to operate a machine ③ to hold something, especially anger, in check

control NOUN controlling a person or thing; authority

controls PLURAL NOUN the switches, buttons, etc. used to control a machine

controversial ADJECTIVE likely to cause people to have strong opinions and disagree about it

controversy (say **kon**-tro-ver-see or kon-**trov**-er-see) NOUN a long argument or disagreement

contusion NOUN a bruise

conundrum NOUN a riddle or difficult question

conurbation NOUN a large urban area where towns have spread into each other

convalesce VERB to be recovering from an illness

convection NOUN the passing on of heat within liquid, air or gas by circulation of the warmed parts

convector NOUN a heater that circulates warm air by convection

convene VERB to bring people together or come together for a meeting

convenience NOUN ① the quality of being easy to use or of making it easy for you to do something ② something that is convenient ③ a public toilet

convenience food NOUN food sold in a form that is already partly prepared and so is easy to use

convenient ADJECTIVE easy to use or deal with or reach

convent NOUN a place where nuns live and work

convention NOUN ① an accepted

134

way of doing things ❷ a large meeting or conference

conventional ADJECTIVE ❶ done or doing things in the normal or accepted way; traditional ❷ conventional weapons are those that are not nuclear

converge VERB to come to or towards the same point from different directions

conversation NOUN an informal talk between two or more people

conversational ADJECTIVE informal; as used in conversation

converse (say kon-verss) VERB to have a conversation

converse (say kon-verss) NOUN the opposite of something

conversion NOUN ❶ changing something from one form, system or use to another ❷ changing your religion

convert (say kon-vert) VERB ❶ to change something from one form, system or use to another ❷ to change to a different religion ❸ to kick a goal after scoring a try at rugby football

convert (say kon-vert) NOUN a person who has changed his or her religion

convertible ADJECTIVE able to be converted

convertible NOUN a car with a roof that can be folded down or taken off

convex ADJECTIVE curved like the outside of a ball or circle. (The opposite is **concave**.)

convey VERB ❶ to communicate a message, idea or feeling ❷ to

transport people or goods

conveyance NOUN ❶ transporting people or goods ❷ (formal) a vehicle for transporting people

conveyancing NOUN transferring the legal ownership of land or property from one person to another

conveyor belt NOUN a continuous moving belt for moving objects from one place to another

convict (say kon-vikt) VERB to convict someone of a crime is to decide at their trial that they are guilty of it

convict (say kon-vikt) NOUN a convicted person who is in prison

conviction NOUN ❶ being convicted of a crime ❷ being firmly convinced of something ❸ a firm opinion or belief

convince VERB to make someone feel certain that something is true; to persuade someone to do something

convivial ADJECTIVE sociable and lively

convoluted ADJECTIVE ❶ complicated and difficult to follow ❷ having lots of twists and curves

convoy NOUN a group of ships or vehicles travelling together

convulse VERB to be convulsed is to have violent movements of the body that you cannot control

convulsion NOUN a violent movement of the body that you cannot control

coo VERB to make a soft murmuring sound like a dove

cook VERB to make food ready to eat by heating it

cook NOUN a person who cooks

cooker NOUN (British) a piece of equipment for cooking food

cookery NOUN (chiefly British) the skill of cooking food

cookie NOUN (North American) a sweet biscuit

cool ADJECTIVE ❶ fairly cold; not hot or warm ❷ calm and not easily excited ❸ not friendly or enthusiastic ❹ (informal) very good or fashionable

cool VERB to become cool or make something cool

coolly ADVERB ❶ in a calm way ❷ in a slightly unfriendly way

coop NOUN a cage for poultry

cooped up ADJECTIVE having to stay in a place which is small and uncomfortable

cooperate VERB ❶ to work helpfully with other people ❷ to be helpful by doing what someone asks

cooperation NOUN ❶ working helpfully with other people ❷ being helpful by doing what someone asks

coordinate VERB to organize people or things to work properly together

coordinate NOUN either of the pair of numbers or letters used to fix the position of a point on a graph or map

coordination NOUN ❶ organizing people or things to work properly together ❷ the ability to control the movements of your body well

coot NOUN a waterbird with a horny white patch on its forehead

cop VERB ➤ **cop it** to get into trouble or be punished

cop NOUN (informal) a police officer

cope VERB to manage or deal with something successfully

copier NOUN a machine for copying pages

co-pilot NOUN a second pilot who helps the main pilot in an aircraft

coping NOUN the top row of stones or bricks in a wall, usually slanted so that rainwater will run off

copious ADJECTIVE plentiful; in large amounts

copper NOUN ❶ a reddish-brown metal used to make wire, coins, etc. ❷ a reddish-brown colour ❸ (British) coppers are brown coins of low value made of copper or bronze ❹ (British) (informal) a policeman

coppice NOUN a small group of trees

copse NOUN a small group of trees

copulate VERB to have sexual intercourse

copy NOUN ❶ a thing made to look like another ❷ something written or typed out again from its original form ❸ a single book, newspaper, CD, etc. that is one of many produced at the same time

copy VERB ❶ to make a copy of something ❷ to do the same as someone else; to imitate someone ❸ to copy a computer file or program or piece of text is to make another one that is exactly the

same, usually one that you store
somewhere else

copyright NOUN the legal right to
print a book, reproduce a picture,
record a piece of music, etc.

coral NOUN ❶ a hard red, pink or
white substance formed by the
skeletons of tiny sea creatures
massed together ❷ a pink colour

cord NOUN ❶ strong thick string
made of twisted threads or strands
❷ a piece of flex ❸ a cord-like
structure in the body

cordial NOUN a fruit-flavoured
drink

cordial ADJECTIVE warm and friendly

cordon NOUN a line of police,
soldiers or vehicles placed round
an area to guard or enclose it

cordon VERB ➤ **cordon something
off** to stop people entering an area
by surrounding it with a ring of
police, soldiers or vehicles

cordon bleu (say kor-dawn **bler**)
ADJECTIVE of the highest class in
cookery

cords PLURAL NOUN trousers made
of corduroy

corduroy NOUN a thick cotton cloth
with velvety ridges

core NOUN ❶ the hard central
part of an apple or pear etc.,
containing the seeds ❷ the part
in the middle of something ❸ the
most important or basic part of
something

corgi NOUN a small dog with short
legs and upright ears

cork NOUN ❶ the lightweight bark
of a kind of oak tree ❷ a stopper
for a bottle, made of cork or other
material

cork VERB to close a bottle or other
container with a cork

corkscrew NOUN ❶ a device for
removing corks from bottles
❷ a spiral

corm NOUN a part of a plant rather
like a bulb

cormorant NOUN a large black
seabird

corn NOUN ❶ the seed of wheat
and similar plants ❷ a plant, such
as wheat, grown for its grain
❸ a small hard painful lump on
the foot

cornea NOUN the transparent
covering over the pupil of the eye

corner NOUN ❶ the angle or area
where two lines or sides or walls
meet or where two streets join ❷ a
free hit or kick from the corner
of a hockey or football field ❸ a
remote or distant region

corner VERB ❶ to drive someone
into a corner or other position
from which it is difficult to escape
❷ to go round a corner or a bend
in the road ❸ to corner the market
is to get possession of all or most
of something that people want

cornerstone NOUN ❶ a stone built
into the corner at the base of a
building ❷ a vitally important part
that everything else depends on

cornet NOUN ❶ a cone-shaped
wafer for holding ice cream ❷ a
musical instrument rather like a
trumpet but shorter and wider

cornflakes PLURAL NOUN toasted
maize flakes eaten as a breakfast
cereal

cornflour NOUN (British) flour made from maize or rice, used in sauces and milk puddings

cornflower NOUN a plant with blue flowers that grows wild in fields of corn

cornice NOUN a band of ornamental moulding on walls just below a ceiling or at the top of a building

cornucopia NOUN ① a plentiful supply of good things ② a horn-shaped container overflowing with fruit and flowers

corny ADJECTIVE (informal) a corny joke or remark is one that is silly or repeated so often that it no longer has much effect

corona (say kor-**oh**-na) NOUN a circle of light round something

coronary NOUN short for **coronary thrombosis**, blockage of an artery carrying blood to the heart

coronation NOUN the ceremony of crowning a king or queen

coroner NOUN an official who holds an inquiry into the cause of a death thought to be from unnatural causes

coronet NOUN a small crown

corporal NOUN a soldier ranking next below a sergeant

corporal punishment NOUN punishment by hitting or beating someone

corporate ADJECTIVE shared by members of a group, especially in business

corporation NOUN ① a large business company ② a group of people elected to govern a town

corps (say kor) NOUN corps (say

korz) ① a special army unit ② a large group of soldiers ③ a set of people doing the same job

corpse NOUN a dead body

corpuscle NOUN one of the red or white cells in blood

corral (say kor-**ahl**) NOUN (North American) an enclosure for horses or cattle on a farm or ranch

correct ADJECTIVE ① true or accurate; without any mistakes ② correct behaviour is behaving properly or in a way that people approve of

correct VERB ① to make a thing correct by altering or adjusting it ② to mark the mistakes in something ③ to tell someone what mistake they have just made

correction NOUN ① a change made in something in order to correct it ② correcting something

correctly ADVERB in the right way, without any mistakes

correspond VERB ① to agree or match ② to be similar or equivalent ③ people correspond when they write letters to each other

correspondence NOUN ① letters or writing letters ② similarity or agreement between things

correspondent NOUN ① a person who writes letters to someone else ② a person employed to gather news and send reports to a newspaper or broadcasting station

corridor NOUN a passage in a building

corroborate VERB to help to confirm a statement etc.

corrode VERB to destroy metal gradually by chemical action

corrosive ADJECTIVE able to corrode something

corrugated ADJECTIVE shaped into alternate ridges and grooves

corrupt ADJECTIVE ❶ dishonest; willing to accept bribes ❷ wicked or immoral ❸ (in computing) corrupt data is unreliable because of errors or faults

corrupt VERB ❶ to cause someone to become dishonest or wicked ❷ (in computing) a bug or other fault corrupts data when it makes it unreliable or impossible to read

corruption NOUN dishonest behaviour by people in authority

corset NOUN a close-fitting piece of underwear worn to shape or support the body

cortège (say kort-**ay** zh) NOUN a funeral procession

cosh NOUN (British) a thick heavy stick used as a weapon

cosine NOUN in a right-angled triangle, the ratio of the length of a side adjacent to one of the acute angles to the length of the hypotenuse. Compare with sine.

cosmetic NOUN a substance put on the face to make it look more attractive, e.g. lipstick or face powder

cosmetic surgery NOUN surgery carried out to make people look more attractive

cosmic ADJECTIVE ❶ to do with the universe ❷ to do with outer space

cosmonaut NOUN a Russian astronaut

cosmopolitan ADJECTIVE from many countries; containing people from many countries

cosmos (say **koz**-moss) NOUN the universe

Cossack NOUN a member of a people of south Russia, famous as horsemen

cost NOUN ❶ the amount of money needed to buy, do or make something ❷ the effort or loss needed to achieve something

cost VERB costs, costing, cost ❶ to have a certain amount as the price or charge ❷ to cause the loss of something ❸ past tense is costed to estimate the cost of something

costly ADJECTIVE expensive

cost of living NOUN the average amount each person in a country spends on food, clothing and housing

costume NOUN ❶ a set or style of clothes, especially for a particular purpose or of a particular place or period ❷ the clothes worn by an actor

cosy ADJECTIVE warm and comfortable

cosy NOUN a cover placed over a teapot or boiled egg to keep it hot

cot NOUN (British) a baby's bed with high sides

cottage NOUN a small simple house, especially in the country

cottage cheese NOUN soft white cheese made from curds of skimmed milk

cottage pie NOUN (British) a dish of minced meat covered with mashed potato and baked

a b c d e f g h i j k l m n o p q r s t u v w x y z

cotton NOUN ❶ a soft white substance covering the seeds of a tropical plant; the plant itself ❷ thread made from this substance ❸ cloth made from cotton thread

cotton wool NOUN soft fluffy wadding originally made from cotton

couch NOUN ❶ a long soft seat like a sofa but with only one end raised ❷ a sofa or settee

couch VERB to express something in words of a certain kind

cougar (say koo-ger) NOUN (North American) a puma

cough (say kof) VERB to send out air from the lungs with a sudden sharp sound

cough NOUN ❶ the act or sound of coughing ❷ an illness that makes you cough

could past tense of can VERB

council NOUN a group of people chosen or elected to organize or discuss something, especially those elected to organize the affairs of a town or county

councillor NOUN a member of a town or county council

counsel NOUN ❶ (formal) advice given by someone ❷ a barrister or group of barristers representing someone in a lawsuit

counsel VERB to give advice to someone

counsellor NOUN a person whose job is to give advice

count VERB ❶ to find the total of something by using numbers ❷ to say a sequence of numbers

in their proper order ❸ to include something in a total ❹ to be important ❺ to regard or consider something in a particular way

count NOUN ❶ a number reached by counting ❷ each of the points being considered, e.g. in accusing someone of crimes ❸ a foreign nobleman

countdown NOUN counting numbers backwards to zero before an event, especially the launching of a space rocket

countenance NOUN a person's face or the expression on a person's face

countenance VERB to give approval to or allow something

counter NOUN ❶ a flat surface over which customers are served in a shop, bank or office ❷ a small round playing piece used in certain board games ❸ a device for counting things

counter VERB ❶ to reply to someone by trying to prove that what they said is not true ❷ to try to reduce or prevent the bad effects of something

counter ADVERB contrary to something

counteract VERB to act against something and reduce or prevent its effects

counter-attack VERB to attack in response to an enemy's attack

counterbalance NOUN a weight or influence that balances another

counterfeit (say kownt-er-feet) ADJECTIVE fake; not genuine

counterfeit NOUN a forgery or imitation

counterfeit *VERB* to forge or make an imitation of something

counterpart *NOUN* a person or thing that corresponds to another

counterpoint *NOUN* a method of combining melodies in harmony

countersign *VERB* to add another signature to a document to give it authority

counterweight *NOUN* a counterbalancing weight or influence

countess *NOUN* the wife or widow of a count or earl; a female count

countless *ADJECTIVE* too many to count

country *NOUN* ❶ the land occupied by a nation ❷ all the people of a country ❸ the countryside

country dance *NOUN* a folk dance

countryman *NOUN* ❶ a man who lives in the countryside ❷ a man who comes from the same country as you do

countryside *NOUN* an area with fields, woods, villages, etc. away from towns

countrywoman *NOUN* ❶ a woman who lives in the countryside ❷ a woman who comes from the same country as you do

county *NOUN* each of the main areas that a country is divided into for local government

coup (say koo) *NOUN* ❶ the sudden overthrow of a government; a coup d'état ❷ a sudden action taken to win power; a clever victory

coup de grâce (say koo der **grahs**) *NOUN* a stroke or blow that puts an end to something

coup d'état (say koo day-**tah**) *NOUN* the sudden overthrow of a government

couple *NOUN* two people or things considered together; a pair

couple *VERB* to fasten or link two things together

couplet *NOUN* a pair of lines in rhyming verse

coupon *NOUN* a piece of paper that gives you the right to receive or do something

courage *NOUN* the ability to face danger or difficulty or pain even when you are afraid; bravery

courageous *ADJECTIVE* ready to face danger or difficulty or pain even when you are afraid

courgette (say koor-zh **et**) *NOUN* (*British*) a kind of small vegetable marrow

courier (say **koor**-ee-er) *NOUN* ❶ a messenger who takes goods or documents ❷ a person employed to guide and help a group of tourists

course *NOUN* ❶ the direction followed by something ❷ a series of events or actions; a way of proceeding ❸ a series of lessons or exercises in learning something ❹ part of a meal ❺ a racecourse or golf course

course *VERB* to move or flow freely

court *NOUN* ❶ the royal household ❷ a law court; the judges and lawyers in a law court ❸ an enclosed area for games such as tennis or netball ❹ a courtyard

court *VERB* ❶ to try to get someone's support ❷ (*old use*) to try to win someone's love

a
b
c
d
e
f
g
h
i
j
k
l
m
n
o
p
q
r
s
t
u
v
w
x
y
z

courteous (say ker-tee-us)
ADJECTIVE polite and helpful

courtesy (say ker-tiss-ee) NOUN
polite behaviour towards other
people

courtier NOUN (old use) one of
a king's or queen's companions
at court

courtly ADJECTIVE dignified and
polite

court martial NOUN ❶ a court
for trying members of the armed
services who have broken military
law ❷ a trial in this court

court-martial VERB to try a person
by a court martial

courtship NOUN ❶ (old use) a
period of courting someone in
the hope of marrying them ❷ the
mating ritual of some birds and
animals

courtyard NOUN a space
surrounded by walls or buildings

cousin NOUN a child of your uncle
or aunt

cove NOUN a small bay

coven (say kuv-en) NOUN a group
of witches

covenant (say kuv-en-ant) NOUN a
formal agreement or contract

cover VERB ❶ to place one thing
over or round another; to conceal
something ❷ to deal with or
include a particular subject ❸ to
travel a certain distance ❹ to aim
a gun at or near somebody ❺ to
protect something by insurance
or a guarantee ❻ to be enough
money to pay for something

cover NOUN ❶ a thing used for
covering something else; a lid,

wrapper, envelope, etc. ❷ the
binding of a book ❸ a place where
you can hide or take shelter

coverage NOUN the amount of time
or space given to reporting an
event in a newspaper or broadcast

coverlet NOUN a bedspread

covert (say kuv-ert) NOUN an area
of thick bushes in which birds and
animals hide

covert (say koh-vert) ADJECTIVE
done secretly

cover-up NOUN an attempt
to conceal information about
something, especially a crime or
mistake

covet (say kuv-it) VERB to wish to
have something that belongs to
someone else

cow NOUN ❶ the fully-grown
female of cattle ❷ the fully-grown
female of certain large animals,
e.g. the elephant, whale or seal

cow VERB to frighten someone into
doing what you want them to

coward NOUN a person who has
no courage and shows fear in a
shameful way

cowboy NOUN a man in charge
of grazing cattle on a ranch in
the USA

cower VERB to crouch or shrink
back in fear

cowl NOUN ❶ a monk's hood ❷ a
hood-shaped covering, e.g. on a
chimney

cowshed NOUN a shed for cattle

cowslip NOUN a wild plant with
small yellow flowers in spring

cox NOUN a person who steers a
rowing boat

coxswain (say kok-swayn or kok-sun) NOUN ❶ a cox ❷ a sailor with special duties

coy ADJECTIVE pretending to be shy or modest

coyote (say koi-oh-ti) NOUN ❶ a North American mammal, similar to but smaller than a wolf

crab NOUN a shellfish with ten legs, the first pair being a set of pincers

crack NOUN ❶ a line on the surface of something where it has broken but not come completely apart ❷ a narrow gap ❸ a sudden sharp noise ❹ a hard knock or blow ❺ (informal) a joke; a wisecrack ❻ a drug made from cocaine

crack ADJECTIVE (informal) first-class

crack VERB ❶ to make a crack in something ❷ to split without breaking ❸ to make a sudden sharp noise ❹ to break down ❺ to solve a problem

cracker NOUN ❶ a paper tube that bangs when pulled apart ❷ a thin biscuit

crackle VERB to make small cracking sounds

cradle NOUN ❶ a small cot for a baby ❷ a supporting framework

cradle VERB to hold someone or something gently and protectively

craft NOUN ❶ a job that needs skill, especially with the hands ❷ skill in doing your work ❸ cunning or trickery ❹ a ship or boat; an aircraft or spacecraft

craftsman, craftswoman NOUN a person who is good at a craft

crafty ADJECTIVE cunning or deceitful

crag NOUN a steep piece of rough rock

craggy ADJECTIVE ❶ steep and rocky ❷ a craggy face is strong and has deep lines in it

cram VERB ❶ to push many things into something so that it is very full ❷ to learn as many facts as you can in a short time just before an examination

cramp NOUN pain caused by a muscle tightening suddenly

cramp VERB to hinder someone's freedom or growth

cramped ADJECTIVE in a space that is too small or tight

cranberry NOUN a small sour red berry used for making jelly and sauce

crane NOUN ❶ a machine for lifting and moving heavy objects ❷ a large wading bird with long legs and a long slender neck

crane VERB to crane your neck is to stretch it to try to see something

crane fly NOUN a flying insect with very long legs

cranium NOUN the skull

crank NOUN ❶ an L-shaped part used for changing the direction of movement in machinery ❷ a person with strange or fanatical ideas

crank VERB to turn or move something using a crank

cranny NOUN a narrow hole or space; a crevice

crash NOUN ❶ the loud noise of something breaking or colliding ❷ an accident in which a vehicle hits something violently and is badly damaged ③ a sudden drop or failure

crash VERB ① a vehicle crashes when it hits something violently and is badly damage ② to move or fall with a crash ③ a computer system crashes when it stops working suddenly

crash ADJECTIVE done rapidly and intensively

crash helmet NOUN a padded helmet worn by cyclists and motorcyclists to protect the head

crash landing NOUN an emergency landing of an aircraft, which usually damages it

crass ADJECTIVE very stupid or insensitive

crate NOUN ① a packing case made of strips of wood ② an open container with compartments for carrying bottles

crater NOUN ① the mouth of a volcano ② a wide hole in the ground caused by an explosion or by something hitting it

cravat NOUN a short wide scarf worn by men round the neck and tucked into an open-necked shirt

crave VERB ① to want something very strongly ② (formal) to beg for something

craving NOUN a strong desire; a longing

crawl VERB ① to move with the body close to the ground or other surface or on hands and knees ② traffic crawls when it moves slowly ③ a place is crawling with unpleasant things or people when there are a lot of them there

crawl NOUN ① a crawling movement ② a very slow pace ③ an overarm swimming stroke

crayon NOUN a stick or pencil of coloured wax etc. for drawing

craze NOUN a brief enthusiasm for something

crazy ADJECTIVE ① insane ② very foolish

crazy paving NOUN (British) paving made of pieces of stone of different shapes and sizes fitted together

creak NOUN a harsh squeak like that of a stiff door hinge

creak VERB to make a creak

creaky ADJECTIVE making creaks

cream NOUN ① the fatty part of milk ② a yellowish-white colour ③ a food containing or looking like cream ④ a soft substance ⑤ the best people or things

cream VERB to make something creamy; to beat a mixture until it is soft like cream

crease NOUN ① a line made in something by folding, pressing or crushing it ② a line on a cricket pitch marking a batsman's or bowler's position

crease VERB to make a crease or creases in something

create VERB ① to make or produce something, especially something that no one has made before ② to bring something into existence; to make something happen

creation NOUN ① the act of creating something ② something that has been created

creative ADJECTIVE showing

imagination and thought as well as skill

creator NOUN a person who creates something

creature NOUN a living being, especially an animal

crèche (say kresh) NOUN a place where babies and young children are looked after while their parents are at work

credentials PLURAL NOUN ❶ documents showing a person's identity, qualifications, etc. ❷ a person's past achievements that make them suitable for something

credible ADJECTIVE able to be believed; convincing

credit NOUN ❶ a source of pride or honour ❷ praise or acknowledgement given for some achievement or good quality ❸ an arrangement allowing a person to buy something and not pay for it until later on ❹ an amount of money in an account at a bank etc. or entered in a financial account as paid in. Compare with **debit**. ❺ belief or trust

credit VERB ❶ to believe something ❷ to believe or say that a person has done or achieved something ❸ to enter something as a credit in a financial account. Compare with **debit**.

creditable ADJECTIVE deserving praise

credit card NOUN a plastic card that you can use to buy something and pay for it later on

creditor NOUN a person to whom money is owed

credulous ADJECTIVE too ready to believe things; gullible

creed NOUN a set or formal statement of religious beliefs

creek NOUN ❶ (British) a narrow inlet ❷ (North American & Australian) a small stream

creep VERB creeps, creeping, crept ❶ to move quietly and slowly ❷ to move along close to the ground ❸ to appear or increase gradually ❹ your flesh creeps when it prickles with fear

creep NOUN (informal) an unpleasant person, especially one who is always trying to get other people's approval

creeper NOUN a plant that grows along the ground or up a wall

creepy ADJECTIVE (informal) slightly frightening and sinister

cremate VERB to burn a dead body to ashes

crematorium NOUN a place where dead people are cremated

creosote NOUN an oily brown liquid painted on wood to prevent it from rotting

crêpe (say krayp) NOUN a thin pancake

crêpe paper NOUN paper with a wrinkled surface

crescendo (say krish-**end**-oh) NOUN a gradual increase in loudness

crescent NOUN ❶ a narrow curved shape coming to a point at each end ❷ a curved street forming an arc

cress NOUN a plant with hot-tasting leaves, used in salads and sandwiches

a
b
c
d
e
f
g
h
i
j
k
l
m
n
o
p
q
r
s
t
u
v
w
x
y
z

crest NOUN ❶ a tuft of hair, skin or feathers on an animal's or bird's head ❷ the top of a hill or wave ❸ a design used as the symbol of a family or organization

crestfallen ADJECTIVE disappointed or dejected

crevasse (say kri-**vass**) NOUN a deep open crack, especially in a glacier

crevice NOUN a narrow opening, especially in a rock or wall

crew NOUN ❶ the people working in a ship or aircraft ❷ a group working together

crew VERB past tense of **crow** VERB

crib NOUN ❶ a baby's cot ❷ a framework holding fodder for animals ❸ a model representing the Nativity of Jesus Christ ❹ a piece of paper with answers to questions on it, used dishonestly by a student in an examination ❺ cribbage

crib VERB to copy someone else's work

cribbage NOUN a card game

crick NOUN painful stiffness in the neck or back

cricket NOUN ❶ a game played outdoors between teams with a ball, bats and two wickets ❷ a brown insect like a grasshopper

crime NOUN ❶ breaking the law ❷ an act that breaks the law

criminal NOUN a person who has committed a crime or crimes

criminal ADJECTIVE to do with crime or criminals

criminology NOUN the study of crime

crimp VERB to press something into small ridges

crimson ADJECTIVE deep red

cringe VERB ❶ to shrink back in fear; to cower ❷ to feel embarrassed

crinkle VERB to make something have creases or wrinkles in it

crinoline NOUN a long skirt worn over a framework that makes it stand out

cripple NOUN a person who is permanently lame

cripple VERB ❶ to make a person lame ❷ to weaken or damage something seriously

crisis NOUN crises an important and dangerous or difficult situation

crisp ADJECTIVE ❶ very dry so that it breaks with a snap ❷ fresh and stiff ❸ cold and dry ❹ brisk and sharp

crisp NOUN a very thin fried slice of potato, usually sold in packets

criss-cross ADJECTIVE & ADVERB with crossing lines

criss-cross VERB to form a pattern of crossing lines

criterion (say kry-**teer**-ee-on) NOUN criteria a standard or principle by which something is judged or decided

critic NOUN ❶ a person who gives opinions on books, plays, films, music, etc. ❷ a person who criticizes

critical ADJECTIVE ❶ pointing out faults or weaknesses in a person or thing ❷ to do with or at a crisis; very serious ❸ to do with critics or criticism

critically ADVERB ❶ extremely and

seriously ❷ in a critical way

criticism NOUN ❶ pointing out faults and weaknesses ❷ the work of a critic

criticize (also **criticise**) VERB to say that a person or thing has faults or weaknesses

croak NOUN a deep hoarse sound like that of a frog

croak VERB to make a croak

crochet (say kroh-shay) NOUN a kind of needlework done by using a hooked needle to loop a thread into patterns

crock NOUN ❶ a piece of crockery ❷ (British) (informal) an old person or an old car in a bad condition

crockery NOUN dishes, plates, cups, etc.

crocodile NOUN ❶ a large tropical reptile with a thick skin, long tail and huge jaws ❷ a long line of schoolchildren walking in pairs

crocus NOUN a small plant with yellow, purple or white flowers

croft NOUN (British) a small rented farm in Scotland

croissant (say krwah-sahn) NOUN a flaky crescent-shaped bread roll

crone NOUN a very old woman

crony NOUN a close friend or companion

crook NOUN ❶ (informal) a thief or other criminal ❷ a shepherd's stick with a curved end ❸ a bend at the elbow

crook VERB to crook a finger is to bend or curl it

crook ADJECTIVE (Australian/NZ) (informal) bad or unwell

crooked ADJECTIVE ❶ bent or twisted; not straight ❷ dishonest or criminal

croon VERB to sing softly and gently

crop NOUN ❶ a plant grown in large quantities for food ❷ a very short haircut ❸ a whip with a loop instead of a lash ❹ a pouch in a bird's throat, where it stores food

crop VERB ❶ to cut something or bite the top off it ❷ to produce a crop

cropper NOUN ➤ come a cropper (informal) ❶ to have a bad fall ❷ to fail badly

croquet (say kroh-kay) NOUN a game played on a lawn with wooden balls and mallets

cross NOUN ❶ a mark or shape made like + or x ❷ an upright post with another piece of wood across it, used in ancient times for crucifixion; **the Cross** the cross on which Christ was crucified, used as a symbol of Christianity ❸ a mixture of two different things

cross VERB ❶ to go across something ❷ to cross your arms, legs or fingers is to put one over the other ❸ to draw a line or lines across something ❹ to make the sign or shape of a cross ❺ to cross animals or plants of different kinds is to produce a new animal or plant from them

cross ADJECTIVE ❶ annoyed or bad-tempered ❷ going from one side to another

crossbar NOUN a horizontal bar between two uprights

crossbow NOUN a powerful bow with a mechanism for pulling and

a b c d e f g h i j k l m n o p q r s t u v w x y z

releasing the string

cross-breed *VERB* to breed by mating an animal with one of a different kind

crosse *NOUN* a hooked stick with a net across it, used in lacrosse

cross-examine *VERB* to question a witness called by the other side in a law court, to check the evidence they have already given

cross-eyed *ADJECTIVE* with eyes that look or seem to look towards the nose

crossfire *NOUN* lines of gunfire that cross each other

cross-hatch *VERB* to shade part of a drawing with two sets of parallel lines crossing each other

crossing *NOUN* a place where people can cross a road or railway

cross-legged *ADJECTIVE & ADVERB* with ankles crossed and knees spread apart

cross-question *VERB* to question someone carefully in order to test answers they have already given

cross-reference *NOUN* a note telling readers to look at another part of a book etc. for more information

crossroads *NOUN* a place where two or more roads cross one another

cross-section *NOUN* ❶ a drawing of something as if it has been cut through ❷ a typical sample from a larger group

crossword *NOUN* a puzzle in which words have to be guessed from clues and then written into the blank squares in a diagram

crotch *NOUN* the part between the legs where they join the body; a similar angle in a forked part

crotchet *NOUN* a note in music, which usually represents one beat (written ♩)

crotchety *ADJECTIVE* bad-tempered or irritable

crouch *VERB* to lower your body, with your arms and legs bent

croup (say kroop) *NOUN* a disease causing a hard cough and difficulty in breathing

crow *NOUN* ❶ a large black bird ❷ a shrill cry like that of a cock

crow *VERB* crows, crowing, crowed or crew ❶ to make a shrill cry as a cock does ❷ to boast or be triumphant

crowbar *NOUN* an iron bar used as a lever

crowd *NOUN* a large number of people in one place

crowd *VERB* ❶ to come together in large numbers; to form a crowd ❷ to make a place uncomfortably full of people

crowded *ADJECTIVE* full of people

crown *NOUN* ❶ an ornamental headdress worn by a king or queen ❷ (often **Crown**) the king or queen ❸ the highest part ❹ a former coin worth 5 shillings (25p)

crown *VERB* ❶ to place a crown on someone as a symbol of royal power or victory ❷ to form or cover or decorate the top of something ❸ to reward something; to make a successful end to something ❹ (*informal*) to hit someone on the head

crow's nest NOUN a lookout platform high up on a ship's mast

crucial (say kroo-shal) ADJECTIVE extremely important because it will affect other things

crucible NOUN a melting pot for metals

crucifix NOUN a model of a cross with a figure of Christ on it

crucify VERB to put a person to death by nailing or tying their hands and feet to a cross

crude ADJECTIVE ❶ in a natural state; not yet processed or refined ❷ not well finished; rough and simple ❸ rude or coarse

cruel ADJECTIVE deliberately causing pain or suffering to others

cruelty NOUN cruel behaviour

cruet NOUN a set of small containers for salt, pepper, oil, etc. for use at the table

cruise NOUN a voyage on a ship, taken as a holiday

cruise VERB ❶ to sail or travel at a gentle or steady speed ❷ to have a cruise

cruiser NOUN ❶ a fast warship ❷ a large motor boat

crumb NOUN a tiny piece of bread, cake or biscuit

crumble VERB ❶ to break something into small pieces ❷ to fall or break into small pieces

crumble NOUN (British) a dessert made with fruit cooked with a crumbly topping

crumbly ADJECTIVE that easily breaks into small pieces

crumpet NOUN a soft flat cake made with yeast, eaten toasted

with butter

crumple VERB to crush something or become crushed, into creases or folds

crunch VERB to crush something noisily, for example between your teeth or under your feet

crunch NOUN a crunching sound

crunchy ADJECTIVE crunchy food is firm and crisp and makes a noise when you bite it

Crusade NOUN a military expedition made by Christians in the Middle Ages to recover the Holy Land from the Muslims who had conquered it

crusade NOUN a campaign against something you believe is wrong or to achieve something you believe is right

crush VERB ❶ to press or squeeze something so that it gets broken or harmed ❷ to break something into very small pieces or powder ❸ to defeat someone completely

crush NOUN ❶ a crowd of people pressed together ❷ a drink made with crushed fruit

crust NOUN ❶ the hard outer layer of something, especially bread ❷ the rocky outer layer of the earth

crustacean (say krust-ay-shon) NOUN an animal with a shell that lives in water, e.g. a crab, lobster or shrimp

crusty ADJECTIVE ❶ having a crisp crust ❷ bad-tempered or irritable

crutch NOUN a support like a long walking stick for helping a lame person to walk

a b c d e f g h i j k l m n o p q r s t u v w x y z

cry NOUN ❶ a loud wordless sound expressing pain, grief, joy, etc. ❷ a shout ❸ the special sound made by a bird or animal ❹ crying

cry VERB ❶ to shed tears; to weep ❷ to call out loudly

crypt NOUN a room under a church, used as a chapel or burial place

cryptic ADJECTIVE having a hidden meaning that is not easy to understand

crystal NOUN ❶ a transparent colourless mineral rather like glass ❷ very clear high-quality glass ❸ a small solid piece of a substance with a symmetrical shape

crystalline ADJECTIVE made of crystals or having the structure of crystals

crystallize (also **crystallise**) VERB ❶ to form into crystals ❷ to become definite in form

Cub, Cub Scout NOUN a member of the junior branch of the Scout Association

cub NOUN a young lion, tiger, fox, bear, etc.

cubbyhole NOUN a small compartment or snug place

cube NOUN ❶ an object that has six equal square sides, like a box or dice ❷ the number you get by multiplying a number by itself twice

cube VERB ❶ to multiply a number by itself twice ❷ to cut something into small cubes

cube root NOUN the number that gives a particular number if it is multiplied by itself twice

cubic ADJECTIVE shaped like a cube

cubicle NOUN a small room made by separating off part of a larger room

cuboid (say kew-boid) NOUN an object with six rectangular sides

cuckoo NOUN a bird that makes a sound like 'cuck-oo' and lays its eggs in other birds' nests

cucumber NOUN a long green-skinned vegetable eaten raw or pickled

cud NOUN half-digested food that a cow brings back from its first stomach to chew again

cuddle VERB to put your arms closely round a person in a loving way

cuddle NOUN to give someone a cuddle is to put your arms closely round them in a loving way

cuddly ADJECTIVE soft and pleasant to cuddle

cudgel NOUN a short thick stick used as a weapon

cudgel VERB to beat someone with a cudgel

cue NOUN ❶ something said or done that acts as a signal for an actor to say something or come on stage ❷ a long stick for striking the ball in billiards or snooker

cuff NOUN ❶ the end of a sleeve that fits round the wrist ❷ a light hit or slap with the hand

cuff VERB to hit someone lightly with your hand

cufflink NOUN each of a pair of fasteners for shirt cuffs, used instead of buttons

cuisine (say kwiz-een) NOUN a style

or method of cooking

cul-de-sac NOUN a street or passage closed at one end; a dead end

culinary ADJECTIVE to do with cooking

cull VERB ❶ to collect information or ideas from different places ❷ to pick out and kill a number of animals from a group to reduce the population

cull NOUN the act of culling a group of animals

culminate VERB to reach its highest point or final result

culprit NOUN the person who has done something wrong

cult NOUN ❶ a small religious group with special beliefs and practices ❷ a film, TV programme, rock group, etc. that is very popular with a particular group of people

cultivate VERB ❶ to use land to grow crops ❷ to try to make something grow or develop

cultivated ADJECTIVE having good manners and education

cultural ADJECTIVE ❶ to do with the customs and traditions of a people ❷ to do with literature, art, music, etc.

culture NOUN ❶ appreciation and understanding of literature, art, music, etc. ❷ the customs and traditions of a people ❸ (in science) a quantity of bacteria or cells grown for study

cultured ADJECTIVE educated to appreciate literature, art, music, etc.

cumbersome ADJECTIVE difficult or awkward to carry or use

cumin NOUN a plant with spicy seeds that are used for flavouring foods

cummerbund NOUN a broad sash worn round the waist

cumulative ADJECTIVE increasing by continuous additions

cumulus NOUN a type of cloud consisting of rounded heaps on a horizontal base

cunning ADJECTIVE ❶ clever at deceiving people ❷ cleverly designed or planned

cunning NOUN ❶ skill in deceiving people; craftiness ❷ skill or ingenuity

cup NOUN ❶ a small bowl-shaped container for drinking from ❷ anything shaped like a cup ❸ a trophy shaped like a cup with a stem, given as a prize

cup VERB to form your hands into the curved shape of a cup

cupboard NOUN a piece of furniture or compartment with a door, for storing things

cupola (say kew-pol-a) NOUN a small dome on a roof

cur NOUN a scruffy or bad-tempered dog

curable ADJECTIVE a curable illness is one that can be cured

curate NOUN a member of the clergy who helps a vicar

curator (say kewr-ay-ter) NOUN a person in charge of a museum or other collection

curb VERB to keep something in check; to restrain something

curb NOUN a limit or restraint on something

curd NOUN (or **curds**) PLURAL NOUN a thick substance formed when milk turns sour

curdle VERB to form into curds or lumps

cure VERB ❶ to get rid of someone's illness ❷ to stop something bad ❸ to treat meat or fish in order to preserve it

cure NOUN ❶ something that cures a person or thing; a remedy ❷ a return to good health; being cured

curfew NOUN a time or signal after which people must remain indoors until the next day

curio NOUN a rare or unusual object

curiosity NOUN ❶ curiosity is being curious ❷ a curiosity is something unusual and interesting

curious ADJECTIVE ❶ wanting to find out about things; inquisitive ❷ strange or unusual

curl NOUN a curve or coil, e.g. of hair

curl VERB ❶ to form into curls ❷ to move in a curve or spiral

curler NOUN a device for curling the hair

curlew NOUN a wading bird with a long curved bill

curling NOUN a game played on ice with large flat stones

curly ADJECTIVE full of curls

currant NOUN ❶ a small black dried grape used in cookery ❷ a small round red, black or white berry

currency NOUN ❶ the money in use in a country ❷ the general use of something

current ADJECTIVE happening or being used now

current NOUN ❶ water or air etc. moving in one direction ❷ the flow of electricity along a wire etc. or through something

current affairs PLURAL NOUN political events in the news at the moment

currently ADVERB at present; at the moment

curriculum NOUN curricula the subjects forming a course of study in a school or university

curry NOUN food cooked with spices that make it taste hot

curry VERB ➤ **curry favour** to try to win someone's approval or support by flattering them

curse NOUN ❶ a call or prayer for a person or thing to be harmed; the evil produced by this ❷ something very unpleasant ❸ an angry or offensive word or expression

curse VERB ❶ to say offensive words; to swear ❷ to use a curse against a person or thing

cursor NOUN a movable indicator, usually a flashing light or arrow, on a computer screen, showing where new data will go

cursory ADJECTIVE hasty and not thorough

curt ADJECTIVE brief and hasty or rude

curtail VERB ❶ to cut something short ❷ to reduce something

curtain NOUN ❶ a piece of material hung at a window or door ❷ the large cloth screen hung at the front of a stage

curtsy NOUN a movement of respect made by women and girls, putting one foot behind the other and bending the knees

curtsy VERB to make a curtsy

curvature NOUN a curving or bending, especially of the earth's horizon

curve NOUN a line or shape that bends gradually and smoothly

curve VERB to bend gradually and smoothly; to form a curve

curved ADJECTIVE forming a curve

cushion NOUN ❶ a bag, usually of cloth, filled with soft material so that it is comfortable to sit on or lean against ❷ anything soft or springy that protects or supports something

cushion VERB to protect someone from the effects of a knock or shock etc.

cushy ADJECTIVE (informal) pleasant and easy

custard NOUN ❶ a sweet yellow sauce made with milk ❷ a pudding made with beaten eggs and milk

custodian NOUN a person who is responsible for looking after something; a keeper

custody NOUN ❶ the legal right or duty to take care of a person or thing ❷ to be in custody is to be in prison awaiting trial

custom NOUN ❶ the usual way of behaving or doing something ❷ regular business from customers

customary ADJECTIVE according to custom; usual

customer NOUN a person who buys goods and services from a shop or business

customs PLURAL NOUN ❶ the place at a port or airport where officials examine your luggage to check that you are not carrying anything illegal ❷ taxes charged on goods brought into a country

cut VERB cuts, cutting, cut ❶ to divide or separate something by using a knife, axe, scissors, etc. ❷ to wound someone with a sharp object or weapon ❸ to make a thing shorter or smaller; to remove part of something ❹ to divide a pack of playing cards ❺ to hit a ball with a chopping movement ❻ to go through or across something ❼ to switch off electrical power or an engine ❽ in a film, to move from one shot or scene to another ❾ to make a sound recording

cut NOUN ❶ cutting; the result of cutting ❷ a small wound ❸ (informal) a share of profits

cute ADJECTIVE (informal) pretty or attractive

cuticle (say kew-tik-ul) NOUN the skin round a nail

cutlass NOUN a short sword with a broad curved blade

cutlery NOUN knives, forks and spoons used for eating

cutlet NOUN a thick slice of meat for cooking

cut-out NOUN a shape cut out of paper, cardboard, etc.

cut-price ADJECTIVE for sale at a reduced price

cutter NOUN ❶ a person or thing that cuts ❷ a small fast sailing ship

cutting NOUN ❶ something cut out of a newspaper or magazine ❷ a piece cut from a plant to form a new plant ❸ a steep-sided passage cut through high ground for a road or railway

cuttlefish NOUN a sea creature with ten arms, which sends out a black liquid when attacked

cyanide NOUN a very poisonous chemical

cycle NOUN ❶ a bicycle or motorcycle ❷ a series of events that are regularly repeated in the same order

cycle VERB to ride a bicycle or tricycle

cyclical, cyclic ADJECTIVE repeated regularly in the same order

cyclist NOUN a person who rides a bicycle

cyclone NOUN a violent tropical storm in which strong winds rotate round a calm central area

cygnet (say **sig**-nit) NOUN a young swan

cylinder NOUN an object with straight sides and circular ends

cylindrical ADJECTIVE shaped like a cylinder

cymbal NOUN a percussion instrument consisting of a metal plate that is hit to make a ringing sound

cynic (say **sin**-ik) NOUN a person who believes that people's reasons for doing things are usually selfish or bad

cynical ADJECTIVE believing that people's reasons for doing things are usually selfish or bad

cypress NOUN an evergreen tree with dark leaves

cyst (say sist) NOUN an abnormal swelling in the body containing fluid or soft matter

czar (say zar) NOUN a different spelling of tsar

Dd

dab NOUN ❶ a quick gentle touch, usually with something wet ❷ a small amount of something put on a surface

dab VERB to touch something quickly and gently

dabble VERB ❶ to splash something about in water ❷ to do something as a hobby or not very seriously

dachshund (say **daks**-huund) NOUN a small dog with a long body and very short legs

dad, daddy NOUN (informal) father

daddy-long-legs NOUN a crane fly

daffodil NOUN a yellow flower that grows from a bulb

daft ADJECTIVE (British) (informal) silly or stupid

dagger NOUN a pointed knife with two sharp edges, used as a weapon

dahlia (say **day**-lee-a) NOUN a garden plant with brightly-coloured flowers

daily ADVERB & ADJECTIVE every day

dainty ADJECTIVE small, delicate and pretty

dairy NOUN a place where milk, butter, etc. are produced or sold

dairy ADJECTIVE to do with the production of milk; made from milk

dais (say day-iss) NOUN a low platform, especially at the end of a room

daisy NOUN a small flower with white petals and a yellow centre

dale NOUN a valley

dally VERB to dawdle or waste time

dam NOUN a barrier built across a river to hold water back

dam VERB to hold water back with a dam

damage NOUN harm or injury done to something

damage VERB to harm or spoil something

damages PLURAL NOUN money paid as compensation for an injury or loss

Dame NOUN the title of a woman who has been given the equivalent of a knighthood

dame NOUN a comic middle-aged woman in a pantomime, usually played by a man

damn VERB ❶ to condemn someone to eternal punishment in hell ❷ to swear at someone or curse them

damn EXCLAMATION (informal) said to show you are angry or annoyed

damnation NOUN being condemned to hell

damned ADJECTIVE hateful or annoying

damp ADJECTIVE slightly wet; not quite dry

damp NOUN moisture in the air or on a surface or all through something

damp VERB ❶ to make something slightly wet ❷ to reduce the strength of something

dampen VERB ❶ to make something damp ❷ to reduce the strength of something

damper NOUN ❶ a felt pad that presses against a piano string to stop it vibrating ❷ a metal plate that can be moved to increase or decrease the amount of air flowing into a fire or furnace

damsel NOUN (old use) a young woman

damson NOUN a small dark purple plum

dance VERB to move about in time to music

dance NOUN ❶ a set of movements used in dancing ❷ a piece of music for dancing to ❸ a party or gathering where people dance

dancer NOUN a person who dances

dandelion NOUN a yellow wild flower with jagged leaves

dandruff NOUN tiny white flakes of dead skin in a person's hair

D and T ABBREVIATION design and technology

dandy NOUN a man who likes to look very smart

danger NOUN ❶ the possibility of suffering harm or death or that something bad might happen ❷ a bad effect that happens as a result of doing something

dangerous ADJECTIVE likely to kill or harm you

dangle VERB ❶ to swing or hang down loosely ❷ to hold or carry something so that it swings loosely

a
b
c
d
e
f
g
h
i
j
k
l
m
n
o
p
q
r
s
t
u
v
w
x
y
z

dank ADJECTIVE damp and chilly

dapper ADJECTIVE dressed neatly and smartly

dappled ADJECTIVE marked with patches of a different colour or with patches of shade

dare VERB dares, daring, dared ❶ to be brave or bold enough to do something ❷ to challenge a person to do something risky

dare NOUN a challenge to do something risky

daredevil NOUN a person who enjoys doing dangerous things

daring ADJECTIVE bold or courageous

daring NOUN adventurous courage

dark ADJECTIVE ❶ with little or no light ❷ not light in colour ❸ having dark hair ❹ sinister or unpleasant

dark NOUN ❶ absence of light ❷ the time when it becomes dark

darken VERB ❶ to become dark or darker ❷ to make something dark or darker

darkness NOUN being dark, without any light

darkroom NOUN a room kept dark for developing and printing photographs

darling NOUN someone who is loved very much

darn VERB to mend a hole by weaving threads across it

darn NOUN a place that has been darned

dart NOUN ❶ an object with a sharp point, thrown at a target ❷ a sudden swift movement ❸ a tapering tuck stitched in something to make it fit

dart VERB ❶ to run suddenly and quickly ❷ you dart a look or glance at someone when you look at them suddenly and briefly

darts NOUN a game in which darts are thrown at a circular board (**dartboard**)

dash VERB ❶ to run quickly; to rush ❷ to throw a thing violently against something hard ❸ to destroy a hope or expectation

dash NOUN ❶ a short quick run; a rush ❷ a small amount of something ❸ a short line (–) used in writing or printing

dashboard NOUN a panel with dials and controls in front of the driver of a vehicle

dashing ADJECTIVE attractive in an exciting and stylish way

dastardly ADJECTIVE (old use) wicked and cruel

data (say **day**-ta) NOUN pieces of information

database NOUN a store of information held in a computer

date NOUN ❶ the time when something happens or happened, stated as the day, month and year (or any of these) ❷ an appointment to meet someone, especially at the start of a romantic relationship ❸ a small sweet brown fruit that grows on a kind of palm tree

date VERB ❶ to give a date to something ❷ to have existed from a particular time ❸ to seem old-fashioned

daub VERB to paint or smear something clumsily

daughter NOUN a girl or woman who is someone's child

daughter-in-law NOUN a son's wife

daunt VERB to make someone feel worried and not confident about doing something

daunting ADJECTIVE a daunting task makes you feel worried because it seems so difficult

dauphin (say daw-fin) NOUN the title of the eldest son of each of the kings of France between 1349 and 1830

dawdle VERB to walk or do things slowly and lazily

dawn NOUN ① the time when the sun rises ② the beginning of something

dawn VERB ① to begin to grow light in the morning ② to begin to be realized

day NOUN ① the 24 hours between midnight and the next midnight ② the light part of this time; the daytime ③ a period of time

daybreak NOUN the first light of day; dawn

daydream NOUN pleasant thoughts of something you would like to happen

daydream VERB to have daydreams

daylight NOUN ① the light of day; sunlight ② dawn

daytime NOUN the time of daylight

day-to-day ADJECTIVE ordinary; happening every day

daze NOUN ➤ in a daze unable to think or see clearly

dazed ADJECTIVE unable to think or see clearly

dazzle VERB ① a light dazzles you when it is so bright that you cannot see clearly because of it ② to amaze or impress a person by a splendid display

deacon NOUN ① a member of the clergy ranking below a priest in Catholic, Anglican and Orthodox Christian Churches ② a church officer who is not a member of the clergy in some Christian Churches

dead ADJECTIVE ① no longer alive ② not at all lively ③ no longer working or in use ④ exact or complete

deaden VERB to make a pain, feeling or sound weaker

dead end NOUN ① a road or passage with one end closed ② a situation where there is no chance of making progress

dead heat NOUN a race in which two or more winners finish exactly together

deadline NOUN a time by which you have to finish something

deadlock NOUN a situation in which two sides cannot reach an agreement

deadly ADJECTIVE & ADVERB ① likely to kill ② complete or completely

deaf ADJECTIVE ① unable to hear ② refusing to listen

deafen VERB to make someone unable to hear by making a very loud noise

deafening ADJECTIVE extremely loud

deal VERB deals, dealing, dealt ① to hand something out ② to give out cards for a card game ③ to do business; to buy and sell goods

❹ to deal someone or something a blow is to hit or harm them

deal NOUN ❶ an agreement or bargain ❷ someone's turn to deal at cards

dean NOUN ❶ an important member of the clergy in a cathedral ❷ the head of a university, college or department

dear ADJECTIVE ❶ loved very much ❷ a polite greeting in letters ❸ expensive

dearly ADVERB very much; a lot

death NOUN dying; the end of life

deathly ADJECTIVE & ADVERB like death

debatable ADJECTIVE not certain; that people might argue about

debate NOUN a formal discussion about a subject

debate VERB ❶ to discuss or argue about something ❷ to think about something before deciding what to do

debit NOUN an entry in an account showing how much money is owed. Compare with **credit**.

debit VERB to enter an amount as a debit in an account; to remove money from an account

debonair (say deb-on-air) ADJECTIVE fashionable and and confident

debris (say deb-ree) NOUN scattered broken pieces that are left after something has been destroyed

debt (say det) NOUN something, especially money, that you owe someone

debtor (say det-or) NOUN a person who owes money to someone

debut (say day-bew) NOUN

someone's first public appearance as a performer

decade (say dek-ayd) NOUN a period of ten years

decadent (say dek-a-dent) ADJECTIVE falling to a lower standard of morality or behaviour, especially in order to enjoy pleasure

decaffeinated ADJECTIVE decaffeinated coffee or tea has had caffeine removed from it

decant (say dik-ant) VERB to pour wine or other liquid gently from one container into another

decanter (say dik-ant-er) NOUN a decorative glass bottle into which wine etc. is poured for serving

decapitate VERB to cut someone's head off; to behead someone

decathlon NOUN an athletic contest in which each competitor takes part in ten events

decay VERB ❶ to go bad or rot ❷ to become less good or less strong

decay NOUN going bad or rotting

decease (say dis-eess) NOUN (formal) a person's death

deceased ADJECTIVE (formal) dead

deceit (say dis-eet) NOUN making a person believe something that is not true

deceitful ADJECTIVE dishonest; trying to make someone believe something that is not true

deceive VERB to make a person believe something that is not true

December NOUN the twelfth month of the year

decency NOUN respectable and honest behaviour

decent ADJECTIVE ❶ respectable and honest ❷ of a good enough standard or quality ❸ (*informal*) kind or generous

deception NOUN ❶ deceiving someone ❷ something that deceives people

deceptive ADJECTIVE not what it seems to be; giving a false impression

decibel (say dess-ib-el) NOUN a unit for measuring the loudness of sound

decide VERB ❶ to make up your mind; to make a choice ❷ to settle a contest or argument

decided ADJECTIVE ❶ noticeable or definite ❷ having clear and definite opinions

deciduous (say dis-id-yoo-us) ADJECTIVE a deciduous tree is one that loses its leaves in autumn

decimal ADJECTIVE decimal numbers or fractions are expressed in tens or tenths

decimal NOUN a decimal fraction

decimal currency NOUN a currency in which each unit is ten or one hundred times the value of the one next below it

decimal fraction NOUN a fraction with tenths shown as numbers after a dot (¼ is 0.25; 1½ is 1.5)

decimalize (also **decimalise**) VERB ❶ to express a number as a decimal ❷ to change something, especially coinage, to a decimal system

decimal point NOUN the dot in a decimal fraction

decimate (say dess-im-ayt) VERB to kill or destroy a large part of something

decipher (say dis-y-fer) VERB ❶ to work out the meaning of a coded message ❷ to work out the meaning of something that is hard to read

decision NOUN ❶ a decision is what someone has decided ❷ decision is deciding or making a judgment about something

decisive (say dis-y-siv) ADJECTIVE ❶ that settles or ends something ❷ able to make decisions quickly and firmly

deck NOUN ❶ a floor or level on a ship or bus ❷ a pack of playing cards ❸ a part of a music system for playing discs or tapes

deck VERB to decorate a place with something

deckchair NOUN a folding chair with a canvas or plastic seat

declaim VERB to speak or say something loudly and dramatically

declare VERB ❶ to say something clearly or firmly ❷ to tell customs officials that you have goods on which you ought to pay duty ❸ to end a cricket innings before all the batsmen are out

decline VERB ❶ to refuse something politely ❷ to become weaker or smaller ❸ to state the forms of a noun, pronoun or adjective that correspond to particular cases, numbers and genders

decline NOUN a gradual decrease or loss of strength

decode VERB to work out the meaning of something written in code

decompose VERB to decay or rot

decompression NOUN reducing air pressure

decor (say **day-kor**) NOUN the style of furnishings and decorations used in a room

decorate VERB ❶ to make something look more beautiful or colourful ❷ to put fresh paint or paper on walls ❸ to give somebody a medal or other award

decoration NOUN ❶ something used to decorate a room, table, etc. on special occasions ❷ the process of decorating a room or building ❸ a medal or other award given as an honour

decorative ADJECTIVE attractive to look at

decorator NOUN a person whose job is to paint and decorate rooms and buildings

decorum (say dik-**or**-um) NOUN polite and dignified behaviour

decoy (say **dee**-koi) NOUN something used to tempt a person or animal into a trap or into danger

decoy (say dik-**oi**) VERB to tempt a person or animal into a trap or danger

decrease VERB ❶ to become smaller or fewer ❷ to make something smaller or fewer in number

decrease NOUN decreasing; the amount by which something decreases

decree NOUN an official order or decision

decree VERB to give an official order that something must happen

decrepit (say dik-**rep**-it) ADJECTIVE old and weak

dedicate VERB ❶ to devote all your time or energy to something ❷ to name a person as a mark of respect or friendship, e.g. at the beginning of a book

dedication NOUN ❶ hard work and effort ❷ a message at the beginning of a book, naming a person as a mark of respect or friendship

deduce VERB to work something out from facts that you already know are true

deduct VERB to subtract an amount from a total

deduction NOUN ❶ something you work out from facts that you already know are true ❷ an amount taken away from a total

deed NOUN ❶ something that someone has done; an act ❷ a legal document that shows who owns something

deem VERB (formal) to consider something in a certain way

deep ADJECTIVE ❶ going a long way down or back in ❷ measured from top to bottom or front to back ❸ a deep feeling is intense or strong ❹ a deep colour is dark and intense ❺ low-pitched, not shrill

deepen VERB to become deeper or more intense

deep-freeze NOUN a freezer

deeply ADVERB very or very much

deer NOUN deer a fast-running graceful animal, the male of which usually has antlers

deface VERB to spoil the surface of something, e.g. by scribbling on it

default VERB to fail to do what you have agreed to do, especially to pay back a loan

default NOUN ❶ failure to do something, especially to pay back a loan ❷ (*in computing*) what a computer does unless you give it another command

defeat VERB ❶ to win a victory over someone ❷ to baffle someone or be too difficult for them

defeat NOUN ❶ being defeated; a lost game or battle ❷ defeating someone

defecate (say **def**-ik-ayt) VERB to get rid of faeces from your body

defect (say **dee**-fect) NOUN a fault or flaw in something

defect (say dif-**ekt**) VERB to desert your own country or cause and join the other side

defective ADJECTIVE having defects; incomplete

defence NOUN ❶ protecting someone or something from an attack or from criticism ❷ all the soldiers, weapons, etc. that a country uses to protect itself from attack ❸ something that defends or protects you ❹ the case put forward by or on behalf of a defendant in a trial; the lawyers who put forward this case ❺ the players in a defending position in a game

defenceless ADJECTIVE having no defences; not able to defend yourself

defend VERB ❶ to protect someone,

especially against an attack or accusation ❷ to argue in support of something ❸ to try to prove that an accused person is not guilty ❹ to try to stop the other team from scoring

defendant NOUN a person accused of something in a law court

defensible ADJECTIVE able to be defended

defensive ADJECTIVE ❶ used or done to defend something; protective ❷ anxious about being criticized

defer VERB ❶ to put something off to a later time; to postpone something ❷ to give way to a person's wishes or authority

deference (say **def**-er-ens) NOUN polite respect

defiance NOUN open disobedience

defiant ADJECTIVE openly showing that you refuse to obey someone

deficiency NOUN ❶ a lack or shortage ❷ a defect or failing

deficit (say **def**-iss-it) NOUN ❶ the amount by which a total is smaller than what is required ❷ the amount by which spending is greater than income

defile VERB to make a thing dirty or impure

define VERB ❶ to explain what a word or phrase means ❷ to show clearly what something is ❸ to show a thing's outline

definite ADJECTIVE ❶ clearly stated; exact ❷ certain or settled

definite article NOUN the word 'the'. The word 'a' is called the indefinite article.

definitely ADVERB without doubt;

certainly

definition NOUN ❶ a statement of what a word or phrase means or of what a thing is ❷ being distinct; clearness of outline (e.g. in a photograph)

definitive (say dif-**in**-it-iv) ADJECTIVE ❶ finally settling something; conclusive ❷ not able to be bettered

deflate VERB ❶ to let out air from a tyre or balloon etc. ❷ to make someone feel less proud or less confident ❸ to reduce or reverse inflation

deflect VERB to make something turn aside

deforest VERB to clear away the trees from an area

deforestation NOUN the cutting down of a lot of trees in an area

deform VERB to spoil a thing's shape or appearance

deformed ADJECTIVE not properly shaped because it has grown wrongly

defraud VERB to get money from someone by fraud

defrost VERB ❶ to thaw out frozen food ❷ to remove the ice and frost from a refrigerator or windscreen

deft ADJECTIVE skilful and quick

defunct ADJECTIVE no longer in use or existing

defuse VERB ❶ to remove the fuse from a bomb so that it cannot explode ❷ to make a situation less dangerous or tense

defy VERB ❶ to refuse to obey someone or something; to openly resist something ❷ to challenge

a person to do something you believe cannot be done ❸ to prevent something being done

degenerate VERB to become worse or lower in standard

degenerate ADJECTIVE having become immoral or bad

degrade VERB ❶ to humiliate or dishonour someone ❷ to reduce a chemical substance to a simpler molecular form

degree NOUN ❶ a unit for measuring temperature ❷ a unit for measuring angles ❸ extent or amount ❹ an award to someone at a university or college who has successfully finished a course

dehydrated ADJECTIVE ❶ someone who is dehydrated has lost a lot of water from their body ❷ a dehydrated substance has had all its moisture removed

deign (say dayn) VERB to do something that you think is below your dignity

deity (say **dee**-it-ee or **day**-it-ee) NOUN a god or goddess

déjà vu (say day-zha **vew**) NOUN a feeling that you have already experienced what is happening now

dejected ADJECTIVE sad or disappointed

delay VERB ❶ to make someone or something late ❷ to postpone something until later ❸ to wait or hesitate before doing something

delay NOUN ❶ delaying or waiting ❷ the amount of time by which something is delayed

delectable ADJECTIVE delightful or

delicious

delegate (say del-ig-at) NOUN a person who represents others and acts on their instructions

delegate (say del-ig-ayt) VERB ❶ to choose someone to carry out a task or duty that you are responsible for ❷ to appoint someone as a delegate

delegation (say del-ig-ay-shon) NOUN ❶ a group of delegates ❷ delegating

delete (say dil-eet) VERB to cross out or remove something written or printed or stored on a computer

deliberate (say dil-ib-er-at) ADJECTIVE ❶ done on purpose; intentional ❷ slow and careful

deliberate (say dil-ib-er-ayt) VERB to think over or discuss something carefully before reaching a decision

deliberately ADVERB on purpose

delicacy NOUN ❶ a delicious food ❷ being delicate

delicate ADJECTIVE ❶ fine and graceful ❷ fragile and easily damaged ❸ pleasant and not strong or intense ❹ becoming ill easily ❺ using or needing great care

delicatessen NOUN a shop that sells cooked meats, cheeses, salads, etc.

delicious ADJECTIVE tasting or smelling very pleasant

delight VERB ❶ to please someone greatly ❷ to take great pleasure in something

delight NOUN great pleasure

delighted ADJECTIVE extremely pleased

delightful ADJECTIVE giving great pleasure; very pleasant

delinquent (say dil-ing-kwent) NOUN a young person who breaks the law

delirious (say di-li-ri-us) ADJECTIVE ❶ in a state of mental confusion and agitation during a feverish illness ❷ extremely excited or enthusiastic

delirium (say dil-irri-um) NOUN ❶ a state of mental confusion and agitation during a feverish illness ❷ wild excitement

deliver VERB ❶ to take letters or goods to the person or place they are addressed to ❷ to give a speech or lecture ❸ to help with the birth of a baby ❹ to aim or strike a blow or an attack ❺ to rescue someone or set them free

delivery NOUN ❶ delivering letters or goods ❷ the way a person gives a speech or lecture ❸ giving birth to a baby ❹ a ball bowled in cricket

dell NOUN a small valley with trees

delphinium NOUN a garden plant with tall spikes of flowers, usually blue

delta NOUN a triangular area at the mouth of a river where it spreads into branches

delude VERB to deceive someone into believing something that is not true

deluge NOUN ❶ a large flood ❷ a heavy fall of rain ❸ something coming in great numbers

deluge VERB to be deluged with something is to be overwhelmed by a great number of them

delusion NOUN a false belief

de luxe ADJECTIVE of very high quality

delve VERB ❶ to delve into a subject is to study it closely ❷ to search for something inside a bag or container

demand VERB ❶ to ask for something firmly or forcefully ❷ to need something

demand NOUN ❶ a firm or forceful request ❷ a desire to have or buy something

demanding ADJECTIVE ❶ needing skill or effort ❷ needing a lot of attention

demean VERB to lower a person's dignity

demeanour (say dim-**een**-er) NOUN a person's behaviour or manner

demented ADJECTIVE driven mad; crazy

demerara (say dem-er-**air**-a) NOUN light-brown cane sugar

demigod NOUN a partly divine being

demise (say dim-**yz**) NOUN (formal) ❶ a person's death ❷ the end or failure of something

demisemiquaver NOUN (chiefly British) a note in music, equal in length to one-eighth of a crotchet

demist VERB (British) to remove misty condensation from a windscreen etc.

demo NOUN (informal) a demonstration

democracy NOUN ❶ government of a country by representatives elected by all the people ❷ a country governed in this way

Democrat NOUN a member of the Democratic Party in the USA

democrat NOUN a person who believes in or supports democracy

democratic ADJECTIVE ❶ based on the system of democracy ❷ taking account of the views of all people involved

demolish VERB ❶ to pull or knock down a building ❷ to destroy something completely

demon NOUN ❶ a devil or evil spirit ❷ a fierce or forceful person

demonstrate VERB ❶ to show that something is true; to prove something ❷ to show someone how to do something or how something works ❸ to take part in a demonstration

demonstration NOUN ❶ demonstrating; showing how to do or work something ❷ a march or meeting held to show everyone what you think about something

demonstrative (say dim-**on**-strat-iv) ADJECTIVE ❶ showing feelings or affections openly ❷ (in grammar) pointing out the person or thing referred to. *This, that, these* and *those* are demonstrative adjectives and pronouns.

demoralize (also **demoralise**) VERB to make someone lose confidence or the courage to continue doing something

demote VERB to move someone to a lower position or rank than they had before

demure ADJECTIVE shy and modest

den NOUN ❶ a wild animal's lair
❷ a place where something illegal
happens ❸ a secret place where
children go to play

denial NOUN a statement that
something is not true

denim NOUN a kind of strong,
usually blue, cotton cloth used to
make jeans etc.

denomination NOUN ❶ a person's
name or title ❷ a branch of a
Church or religion ❸ a unit of
money

denominator NOUN the number
below the line in a fraction,
showing how many parts the
whole is divided into, e.g. 4 in ¼.
Compare with numerator.

denote VERB to mean or indicate
something

dénouement (say day-**noo**-mahn)
NOUN the final outcome of a plot or
story, which is revealed at the end

denounce VERB to speak strongly
against someone or something; to
accuse someone of something

dense ADJECTIVE ❶ thick and not
easy to see through ❷ packed
closely together ❸ (informal)
stupid

densely ADVERB thickly; closely
together

density NOUN ❶ how thick or
tightly packed something is ❷ (in
science) the proportion of mass
to volume

dent NOUN a hollow left in a surface
where something has pressed
or hit it

dent VERB to make a dent in
something

dental ADJECTIVE to do with your
teeth or with dentistry

dentist NOUN a person who is
trained to treat people's teeth
and gums

dentures PLURAL NOUN a set of
false teeth

denunciation NOUN denouncing
someone or something

deny VERB ❶ to say that something
is not true ❷ to refuse to give or
allow something

deodorant (say dee-**oh**-der-ant)
NOUN a substance that removes
unpleasant smells

depart VERB to go away or leave

department NOUN one section of a
large organization or shop

department store NOUN a large
shop that sells many different
kinds of goods

departure NOUN leaving or going
away from a place

depend VERB ❶ to rely on someone
or something ❷ to be controlled
or decided by something else

dependable ADJECTIVE that you can
depend on; reliable

dependant NOUN a person who
depends on another, especially
financially

dependence NOUN being
dependent on someone or
something

dependency NOUN a country that
is controlled by another

dependent ADJECTIVE ❶ relying
on someone else financially

② controlled by or needing something

depict VERB **①** to show something in a painting or a drawing etc. **②** to describe something in words

deplete (say dip-**leet**) VERB to reduce the supply of something by using up large amounts

deplorable ADJECTIVE extremely bad or shocking

deplore VERB to strongly dislike something because you think it is wrong

deploy VERB **①** to place troops or weapons in good positions so that they are ready to be used effectively **②** to use something effectively

deport VERB to send an unwanted foreign person out of a country

depose VERB to remove a person from power

deposit NOUN **①** an amount of money paid into a bank or other account **②** a sum of money paid as a first instalment **③** a layer of solid matter in or on the earth

deposit VERB **①** to put something down **②** to pay money as a deposit

deposition NOUN a written piece of evidence, given under oath

depot (say **dep**-oh) NOUN **①** a place where things are stored **②** a place where buses or trains are kept or repaired

depraved ADJECTIVE behaving wickedly; of bad character

deprecate (say **dep**-rik-ayt) VERB to say that you disapprove of something

depreciate (say dip-**ree**-shee-ayt)

VERB to become lower in value over a period of time

depress VERB **①** to make someone feel very sad and gloomy **②** to lower the value of something **③** to press something down

depressed ADJECTIVE feeling very sad and without hope

depression NOUN **①** a feeling of great sadness or hopelessness, often with physical symptoms **②** a long period when trade is very slack because no one can afford to buy things, with widespread unemployment **③** a shallow hollow in the ground or on a surface **④** an area of low air pressure which may bring rain

deprive VERB to take or keep something away from someone

deprived ADJECTIVE not having enough of the things that are essential for a comfortable life, e.g. food, money, etc.

depth NOUN **①** being deep; how deep something is **②** how strong or intense something is **③** the deepest or lowest part

deputize (also **deputise**) VERB to act as someone's deputy

deputy NOUN a person appointed to help someone else in their job and to take their place when they are away

derail VERB to cause a train to come off the tracks

deranged ADJECTIVE insane; wild and out of control

derby (say **dar**-bi) NOUN a sports match between two teams from the same city or area

derelict (say **de**rri-likt) ADJECTIVE abandoned and left to fall into ruin

deride VERB to laugh at someone or something with contempt or scorn

derision NOUN scorn or ridicule

derisory ADJECTIVE ❶ so small that it is ridiculous ❷ scornful

derivation NOUN the origin of a word from another language or from another word

derivative ADJECTIVE derived from something; not original

derive VERB ❶ to obtain something from a source ❷ to originate from a language or from another word

derogatory (say di-**rog**-at-er-ee) ADJECTIVE scornful or critical

derrick NOUN ❶ a kind of crane for lifting things ❷ a tall framework holding the machinery used in drilling an oil well

descant NOUN a tune sung or played above the main tune

descend VERB ❶ to go or come down ❷ to surprise someone with a sudden visit

descendant NOUN a person who is descended from someone

descent NOUN ❶ the process of going down; a climb down ❷ a way down; a downward path or slope ❸ a person's family origin

describe VERB ❶ to say what someone or something is like ❷ to move or draw something in a particular pattern or shape

description NOUN ❶ describing someone or something ❷ an account or picture in words

descriptive ADJECTIVE giving a description; full of details

desecrate (say **dess**-ik-rayt) VERB to treat a sacred thing without respect

desert (say **dez**-ert) NOUN a large area of dry land, often covered with sand

desert (say diz-**ert**) VERB ❶ to leave a person or place without intending to return ❷ to run away from the army

deserted ADJECTIVE empty or abandoned

desert island NOUN an uninhabited island

deserts (say diz-**erts**) PLURAL NOUN what a person deserves

deserve VERB to have a right to something; to be worthy of something

desiccated ADJECTIVE dried, in order to preserve it

design NOUN ❶ the way something is made or arranged ❷ a drawing that shows how something is to be made ❸ lines and shapes that form a decoration; a pattern ❹ a plan or scheme in the mind

design VERB ❶ to draw a design for something ❷ to plan or intend something for a special purpose

designate VERB ❶ to mark or describe a thing as something particular ❷ to appoint someone to a position

designate ADJECTIVE appointed to a job but not yet doing it

designer NOUN someone who designs things, especially clothes

desirable ADJECTIVE worth having or doing

a b c d e f g h i j k l m n o p q r s t u v w x y z

desire NOUN a feeling of wanting something very much

desire VERB to want something very much

desist (say diz-**ist**) VERB (formal) to stop doing something

desk NOUN ❶ a piece of furniture with a flat top and often drawers, used when writing or doing work ❷ a counter at which a cashier or receptionist sits

desktop NOUN ❶ a screen on a computer that shows the icons of the programs that you can use ❷ a computer that is designed to be used on a desk

desolate ADJECTIVE ❶ lonely and sad ❷ uninhabited or barren

despair NOUN a feeling of hopelessness

despair VERB to lose all hope

despatch VERB a different spelling of **dispatch**

desperado (say dess-per-**ah**-doh) NOUN a reckless criminal

desperate ADJECTIVE ❶ extremely serious or hopeless ❷ needing or wanting something very much ❸ reckless and ready to do anything

desperately ADVERB ❶ in a desperate way ❷ very much; extremely

despicable ADJECTIVE very unpleasant or evil; deserving to be despised

despise VERB to hate someone or something or have no respect for them

despite PREPOSITION in spite of

despondent ADJECTIVE sad or gloomy

despot (say **dess**-pot) NOUN a tyrant

dessert (say diz-**ert**) NOUN fruit or a sweet food served as the last course of a meal

dessertspoon NOUN a medium-sized spoon used for eating puddings etc.

destination NOUN the place to which a person or thing is travelling or being sent

destined ADJECTIVE intended by fate; meant to happen

destiny NOUN what will happen or has happened to someone or something, in a way that seems to be beyond human control; fate

destitute ADJECTIVE left without anything; living in extreme poverty

destroy VERB to damage something so badly that it can no longer be used or no longer exists

destroyer NOUN a fast warship

destruction NOUN destroying something or being destroyed

destructive ADJECTIVE causing a lot of harm or damage

desultory (say **dess**-ul-ter-ee) ADJECTIVE half-hearted, without enthusiasm or a definite plan

detach VERB to unfasten or separate something

detached ADJECTIVE ❶ separated; not connected ❷ a detached house is one that is not joined to another ❸ able to stand back from a situation and not get emotionally involved in it

detachment NOUN ❶ the ability

to stand back from a situation and not get emotionally involved in it ❷ a small group of soldiers sent away from a larger group for a special duty

detail NOUN ❶ a very small part of a design, plan or decoration ❷ a small piece of information

detailed ADJECTIVE giving many details

detain VERB ❶ to keep someone waiting ❷ to keep someone at a place

detect VERB to discover or notice something

detective NOUN a person, especially a police officer, who investigates crimes

detector NOUN a device that detects something

detention NOUN ❶ detaining or being detained ❷ being made to stay late in school as a punishment

deter VERB to discourage or prevent a person from doing something

detergent NOUN a substance used for cleaning or washing things

deteriorate (say dit-**eer**-ee-er-ayt) VERB to become worse

determination NOUN the firm intention to achieve what you have decided to achieve

determine VERB ❶ to decide something ❷ to cause or influence something ❸ to find out or calculate something

determined ADJECTIVE full of determination; with your mind firmly made up

determiner NOUN (in grammar) a word (such as a, the, many) that

introduces a noun and gives you some information about it

deterrent NOUN something that may deter people, e.g. a nuclear weapon that deters countries from making war on the one that has it

detest VERB to strongly dislike a person or thing

detonate (say **det**-on-ayt) VERB to explode or make a bomb or mine explode

detour (say dee-**toor**) NOUN a roundabout route you use instead of the normal one

detract VERB to make something seem less good or valuable

detriment (say **det**-rim-ent) NOUN something is to the detriment of a thing if it is harmful or damaging to it

detrimental (say det-rim-**en**-tal) ADJECTIVE harmful or damaging

deuce NOUN a score in tennis where both sides have 40 points and must gain two consecutive points to win

devastate VERB ❶ to ruin or cause great destruction to something ❷ to overwhelm someone with shock or grief

develop VERB ❶ to create or improve something gradually ❷ to become bigger or better; to grow ❸ to come gradually into existence ❹ to begin to have or use something ❺ to use an area of land for building houses, shops, factories, etc. ❻ to treat photographic film with chemicals so that pictures appear

developing country NOUN a poor country that is building up its

169

industry and trying to improve its living conditions

development NOUN ❶ developing or being developed ❷ a recent event that changes a situation ❸ an area of land with new buildings on it

deviate (say dee-vee-ayt) VERB to turn aside from a course or from what is usual or true

device NOUN a tool or piece of equipment used for a particular purpose

devil NOUN ❶ an evil spirit ❷ a wicked, cruel or annoying person

devilish ADJECTIVE extremely cruel or cunning

devious (say dee-vee-us) ADJECTIVE ❶ cunning and dishonest; underhand ❷ a devious route is roundabout and not direct

devise VERB to invent a way of doing something

devoid ADJECTIVE lacking or without something

devolution NOUN handing over power from central government to local or regional government

devolve VERB a task or power devolves on a deputy or successor when it is passed on to them

devote VERB to devote yourself or your time to something is to spend all your time doing it

devoted ADJECTIVE very loving or loyal

devotee (say dev-o-tee) NOUN a person who likes something very much; an enthusiast

devotion NOUN great love or loyalty

devotions PLURAL NOUN prayers

devour VERB ❶ to eat or swallow something hungrily or greedily ❷ to read or look at something eagerly

devout ADJECTIVE deeply religious

dew NOUN tiny drops of water that form during the night on the ground and other surfaces in the open air

dexterity (say deks-terri-tee) NOUN skill in handling things

dhal NOUN an Indian dish of cooked lentils

dhoti NOUN a loincloth worn by male Hindus

diabetes (say dy-a-bee-teez) NOUN a disease in which there is too much sugar in a person's blood

diabolical ADJECTIVE ❶ like a devil; very wicked ❷ very bad or annoying

diadem (say dy-a-dem) NOUN a crown or headband worn by a royal person

diagnose VERB to find out and say what disease a person has or what is wrong

diagnosis NOUN diagnoses saying what is wrong with someone who is ill after examining them

diagonal (say dy-ag-on-al) NOUN a straight line joining opposite corners

diagonal ADJECTIVE slanting; crossing from corner to corner

diagram NOUN a kind of drawing or picture that shows the parts of something or how it works

dial NOUN ❶ a circular object with numbers or letters round it, used

170

for measuring something ❷ a round control on a radio, cooker, etc. that you turn to change something

dial VERB to press the numbers on a telephone dial or keypad in order to call a telephone number

dialect NOUN the words and pronunciations used by people in one district but not in the rest of a country

dialogue NOUN ❶ the words spoken by characters in a play, film or story ❷ a conversation

dialysis (say dy-**al**-iss-iss) NOUN a way of removing harmful substances from a person's blood by letting it flow through a machine

diameter (say dy-**am**-it-er) NOUN ❶ a line drawn straight across a circle or sphere and passing through its centre ❷ the length of this line

diamond NOUN ❶ a very hard precious stone, a form of carbon, that looks like clear glass ❷ a shape with four equal sides and four angles that are not right angles ❸ a playing card with red diamond shapes on it

diamond wedding NOUN a couple's 60th wedding anniversary

diaphanous (say dy-**af**-an-us) ADJECTIVE diaphanous fabric is thin, light and almost transparent

diaphragm (say **dy**-a-fram) NOUN ❶ the muscular layer inside your body that separates your chest from your abdomen and is used in breathing ❷ a dome-shaped contraceptive device that fits over

the neck of the womb

diarrhoea (say dy-a-**ree**-a) NOUN too frequent and too watery emptying of the bowels

diary NOUN a book in which someone writes down what happens each day

dice NOUN a small cube marked with dots (1 to 6) on its sides, used in games

dice VERB ❶ to cut meat, vegetables, etc. into small cubes ❷ to play gambling games using dice

dictate VERB ❶ to speak or read something aloud for someone else to write down ❷ to give orders in a bossy way

dictates (say **dik**-tayts) PLURAL NOUN rules or principles that must be obeyed

dictation NOUN ❶ a test in which students write down what is being read to them, especially in a language lesson ❷ speaking or reading something aloud for someone else to write down

dictator NOUN a ruler who has complete power over the people of a country

diction NOUN ❶ a person's way of speaking words ❷ a writer's choice of words

dictionary NOUN a book that contains words in alphabetical order so that you can find out how to spell them and what they mean; a similar product for use on a computer

diddle VERB (informal) to cheat or swindle someone

a
b
c
d
e
f
g
h
i
j
k
l
m
n
o
p
q
r
s
t
u
v
w
x
y
z

didgeridoo NOUN an Australian Aboriginal musical instrument which consists of a long thin pipe that you blow into to make a low humming sound

die VERB ❶ to stop living or existing ❷ to stop working or burning

die NOUN ❶ singular of dice ❷ dies a device that stamps a design on coins etc. or that cuts or moulds metal

diehard NOUN a person who obstinately refuses to give up old ideas or policies

diesel (say dee-zel) NOUN ❶ an engine that works by burning oil in compressed air ❷ fuel for this kind of engine

diet NOUN ❶ special meals that someone eats in order to be healthy or to lose weight ❷ the sort of foods usually eaten by a person or animal ❸ the parliament of certain countries, such as Japan

diet VERB to keep to a diet

dietitian (say dy-it-ish-an) NOUN an expert in diet and nutrition

differ VERB ❶ to be different ❷ to disagree in opinion

difference NOUN ❶ being different; the way in which things differ ❷ the remainder left after one number is subtracted from another ❸ a disagreement

different ADJECTIVE ❶ unlike; not the same ❷ separate or distinct

differential ADJECTIVE ❶ a difference in wages between one group of workers and another ❷ a differential gear

differential gear NOUN a system

of gears that makes a vehicle's driving wheels revolve at different speeds when going round corners

differentiate VERB ❶ to be a difference between things; to make one thing different from another ❷ to recognize differences between things

differently ADVERB in a different way

difficult ADJECTIVE ❶ needing a lot of effort or skill; not easy to do or understand ❷ not easy to please or satisfy

difficulty NOUN ❶ being difficult ❷ something that causes a problem

diffident (say dif-id-ent) ADJECTIVE shy and not self-confident; hesitating to put yourself or your ideas forward

diffract VERB to break up a beam of light

diffuse (say dif-yooz) VERB ❶ to spread something widely or thinly ❷ if a gas or liquid diffuses in a substance, it becomes slowly mixed with that substance

diffuse (say dif-yooss) ADJECTIVE ❶ spread widely; not concentrated ❷ using many words; not concise

dig VERB digs, digging, dug ❶ to break up soil and move it; to make a hole or tunnel by moving soil ❷ to poke or jab something sharply ❸ to seek or discover something by investigating

dig NOUN ❶ a place where archaeologists dig to look for ancient remains ❷ a sharp poke ❸ an unpleasant remark

digest (say dy-jest) VERB ❶ to

soften and break down food in the stomach so that the body can absorb it ❷ to take information into your mind and think it over

digest (say **dy**-jest) NOUN a summary of news or information

digestion NOUN the process of digesting food

digestive ADJECTIVE to do with digestion

digestive biscuit NOUN a wholemeal biscuit

digger NOUN ❶ a machine for digging ❷ (*informal*) (*Australian/NZ*) a friendly form of address for a man

digit (say **dij**-it) NOUN ❶ any of the numbers from 0 to 9 ❷ a finger or toe

digital ADJECTIVE ❶ to do with or using digits ❷ a digital watch or clock shows the time with a row of figures ❸ a digital image or sound is represented as a series of binary digits ❹ a digital camera or recorder records digital sound and images

dignified ADJECTIVE having or showing dignity

dignitary NOUN an important official

dignity NOUN a calm and serious manner

digress VERB to stray from the main subject

dike NOUN a different spelling of dyke

dilapidated ADJECTIVE falling to pieces; in disrepair

dilate VERB to become or to make something wider or larger

dilemma (say dil-**em**-a) NOUN a situation where someone has to choose between two or more possible actions, either of which would bring difficulties

diligence NOUN careful and thorough work or effort

diligent (say **dil**-ij-ent) ADJECTIVE careful and hard-working

dilute VERB to make a liquid weaker by adding water or other liquid

dilute ADJECTIVE diluted

dim ADJECTIVE ❶ not bright or clear; only faintly lit ❷ not distinct or vivid ❸ (*informal*) stupid

dim VERB to become or make something dim

dime NOUN (*North American*) a ten-cent coin

dimension NOUN ❶ a measurement such as length, width, area or volume ❷ the size or extent of something

diminish VERB ❶ to become smaller or less important ❷ to make something smaller or less important

diminutive (say dim-**in**-yoo-tiv) ADJECTIVE very small

dimly ADVERB ❶ not brightly or clearly ❷ not distinctly or vividly

dimple NOUN a small hollow or dent, especially in the skin of a person's cheek or chin

din NOUN a loud annoying noise

dine VERB (*formal*) to have dinner

diner NOUN ❶ a person who is dining ❷ (*North American*) a small, inexpensive restaurant

dinghy (say **ding**-ee) NOUN a kind of small boat

dingo NOUN an Australian wild dog

dingy (say **din**-jee) ADJECTIVE dark and dirty-looking

dinner NOUN ❶ the main meal of the day, eaten either in the middle of the day or in the evening ❷ a formal evening meal in honour of something

dinosaur (say **dy**-noss-or) NOUN a prehistoric reptile, often of enormous size

dint NOUN ➤ **by dint of** by means of; using

diocese (say **dy**-oss-iss) NOUN a district under the care of a bishop in the Christian Church

dioxide NOUN an oxide with two atoms of oxygen to one of another element

dip VERB ❶ to put something into a liquid and then take it out again ❷ to go or slope downwards ❸ to move or point something downwards

dip NOUN ❶ dipping ❷ a downward slope ❸ a quick swim ❹ a creamy mixture into which you can dip pieces of food

diphtheria (say dif-**theer**-ee-a) NOUN a serious disease that causes inflammation in the throat

diphthong (say **dif**-thong) NOUN a compound vowel sound made up of two sounds, e.g. *oi* in *point*, (made up of 'aw' + 'ee') or *ou* in *loud* ('ah' + 'oo')

diploma NOUN a certificate awarded by a college etc. for skill in a particular subject

diplomacy NOUN ❶ the work of making agreements with other countries ❷ skill in dealing with other people without upsetting or offending them; tact

diplomat NOUN ❶ a person who represents their country officially abroad ❷ a tactful person

diplomatic ADJECTIVE ❶ to do with diplomats or diplomacy ❷ tactful; careful not to offend people

dipper NOUN ❶ a kind of bird that dives for its food ❷ a ladle

dire ADJECTIVE dreadful or serious

direct ADJECTIVE ❶ as straight as possible; not changing direction ❷ with no one or nothing in between ❸ going straight to the point; frank ❹ exact or complete

direct VERB ❶ to tell or show someone the way ❷ to guide or aim something in a certain direction ❸ to control or manage someone or something ❹ to order someone to do something

direct current NOUN electric current flowing only in one direction

direction NOUN ❶ the line along which something moves or faces ❷ managing or controlling someone or something

directions PLURAL NOUN information on how to use or do something or how to get somewhere

directive NOUN an official command

directly ADVERB ❶ by a direct route or in a direct line ❷ immediately; without delay

direct object NOUN (*in grammar*) the word that receives the action of the verb. In *she hit him*, 'him' is the direct object.

director NOUN ❶ a person who is in charge of something, especially one of a group of people managing a company ❷ a person who decides how a film, programme or play should be made or performed

directory NOUN ❶ a book containing a list of people with their telephone numbers, addresses, etc. ❷ (*in computing*) a file containing a group of other files

direct speech NOUN someone's words written down exactly in the way they were said

dirge NOUN a slow sad song

dirt NOUN ❶ anything that is not clean, such as mud or dust ❷ loose earth or soil

dirty ADJECTIVE ❶ covered with dirt; not clean ❷ unfair or dishonourable ❸ indecent or obscene

disability NOUN a physical or mental condition that restricts someone's movements or senses

disable VERB to stop something from working properly

disabled ADJECTIVE unable to use part of your body properly because of illness or injury

disadvantage NOUN something that hinders you or is unhelpful

disagree VERB ❶ to have or express a different opinion from someone ❷ to have a bad effect

disagreeable ADJECTIVE unpleasant

disagreement NOUN a situation in which people have different opinions about something and

often also argue

disappear VERB ❶ to stop being visible; to vanish ❷ to stop happening or existing

disappoint VERB to make you sad by failing to do or be what you hoped for or expected

disappointment NOUN ❶ a feeling of being disappointed ❷ a person or thing that disappoints you

disapproval NOUN a feeling that someone is behaving badly

disapprove VERB to think that something is wrong or bad, especially the way someone is behaving

disarm VERB ❶ to reduce the size of armed forces ❷ to take away someone's weapons ❸ to overcome a person's anger or doubt

disarmament NOUN reduction of a country's armed forces or weapons

disarray NOUN disorder or confusion

disassemble VERB to take something to pieces

disaster NOUN ❶ an event or accident that causes a lot of harm or damage; a very bad misfortune ❷ a complete failure

disastrous ADJECTIVE causing great harm or failing completely

disband VERB a group or organization disbands when it breaks up

disbelief NOUN a feeling of not being able to believe something

disc NOUN ❶ any round flat object ❷ a CD or DVD ❸ a layer of cartilage between vertebrae in

a b c d e f g h i j k l m n o p q r s t u v w x y z

A
B
C
D
E
F
G
H
I
J
K
L
M
N
O
P
Q
R
S
T
U
V
W
X
Y
Z

your spine

discard VERB to get rid of something because it is useless or unwanted

discern (say dis-**sern**) VERB to see or recognize something that is not obvious

discerning ADJECTIVE showing good judgement about the quality of something

discharge VERB ❶ to allow a person to leave a place ❷ to send something out ❸ to discharge a debt or promise is to pay it off or do what has been agreed

discharge NOUN ❶ an act of discharging someone or something ❷ something that is discharged

disciple NOUN ❶ a follower or pupil of a leader or of a religion or philosophy ❷ any of the original followers of Jesus Christ

discipline NOUN ❶ training people to obey rules and behave well and punishing them if they do not ❷ self-control; the ability to work or behave in a controlled way ❸ a subject for study

discipline VERB ❶ to train yourself to work or behave in a controlled way ❷ to punish someone

disc jockey NOUN a person who introduces and plays records on the radio or at a club

disclaim VERB to say that you are not responsible for something or have no knowledge of something

disclose VERB you disclose a fact or information when you reveal it or make it known

disco NOUN an event where pop

music is played for people to dance to

discolour VERB to spoil or change the colour of something

discomfort NOUN ❶ slight pain ❷ being uneasy or embarrassed

disconcert (say dis-kon-**sert**) VERB to make a person feel uneasy or worried

disconnect VERB to break a connection; to detach something

disconnected ADJECTIVE not joined together in a logical way or order

discontent NOUN a feeling of being unhappy and not satisfied

discontinue VERB to stop doing or producing something

discord NOUN ❶ disagreement; quarrelling ❷ musical notes sounded together and producing a harsh or unpleasant sound

discount NOUN an amount by which a price is reduced

discount VERB to ignore or disregard something

discourage VERB ❶ to take away someone's enthusiasm or confidence ❷ to try to persuade someone not to do something

discourse NOUN a formal speech or piece of writing about something

discourse VERB to speak or write at length about something

discourteous ADJECTIVE not courteous or polite; rude

discover VERB ❶ to find or find out something, especially by searching ❷ to be the first person to find something

discovery NOUN ❶ discovering something or being discovered

❷ something that is discovered

discredit VERB ❶ to cause an idea or theory to be doubted ❷ to damage someone's reputation

discredit NOUN damage to someone's reputation

discreet ADJECTIVE ❶ being careful in what you say and not giving away secrets ❷ not likely to attract attention

discrepancy (say dis-**krep**-an-see) NOUN lack of agreement between things which should be the same

discretion (say dis-**kresh**-on) NOUN ❶ being discreet; keeping secrets ❷ freedom to decide things and take action according to your own judgement

discriminate VERB ❶ to notice and understand the differences between things; to prefer one thing to another ❷ to treat people differently or unfairly because of their race, gender or religion

discrimination NOUN ❶ different or unfair treatment of people because of their race, gender or religion ❷ the ability to notice and understand the differences between things

discus NOUN a thick heavy disc thrown in athletic contests

discuss VERB to talk with other people about a subject or to write about it in detail

discussion NOUN ❶ a conversation about a subject ❷ a piece of writing in which the writer examines a subject from different points of view

disdain NOUN scorn or contempt

disdain VERB ❶ to regard or treat someone or something with disdain ❷ to not do something because of disdain

disease NOUN an unhealthy condition; an illness

disembark VERB to get off a ship or aircraft

disembodied ADJECTIVE a disembodied voice comes from an invisible or unknown source

disembowel VERB to take out the bowels or inside parts of something

disentangle VERB to free something from tangles or confusion

disfigure VERB to spoil a person's or thing's appearance

disgrace NOUN ❶ shame; loss of approval or respect ❷ something that is shameful or unacceptable

disgrace VERB to bring disgrace upon someone

disgraceful ADJECTIVE shameful or unacceptable

disgruntled ADJECTIVE discontented or in a bad mood

disguise VERB ❶ to make a person or thing look different so that people will not recognize them ❷ to conceal your feelings

disguise NOUN something you wear or use to change your appearance so that nobody recognizes you

disgust NOUN a feeling that something is very unpleasant or disgraceful

disgust VERB to make someone feel disgust

dish NOUN ❶ a plate or bowl for

food ❷ food prepared for eating ❸ a bowl-shaped aerial for receiving broadcasting signals transmitted by satellite

dish VERB (informal) ➤ **dish something out** to give out portions of something to people

dishcloth NOUN a cloth you use for washing dishes

dishearten VERB to cause a person to lose hope or confidence

dishevelled (say dish-ev-eld) ADJECTIVE untidy in appearance

dishonest ADJECTIVE not honest or truthful

dishonour NOUN loss of honour or respect; disgrace

dishwasher NOUN a machine for washing dishes etc. automatically

disinfect VERB to destroy the germs in something

disinfectant NOUN a substance used for disinfecting things

disinherit VERB to deprive a person of the right to inherit something

disintegrate VERB to break up into small parts or pieces

disinterested ADJECTIVE not influenced by the hope of gaining something yourself; impartial

disjointed ADJECTIVE disjointed talk or writing is not well joined together and so is difficult to understand

disk NOUN a flat circular object on which computer data can be stored

dislike VERB to not like someone or something

dislike NOUN a feeling of not liking someone or something

dislocate VERB a bone is dislocated when it moves or is forced from its proper position in one of your joints

dislodge VERB to move or force something from its place

disloyal ADJECTIVE not loyal

dismal ADJECTIVE ❶ gloomy or dreary ❷ of poor quality

dismantle VERB to take something to pieces

dismay NOUN a feeling of strong disappointment and surprise

dismember VERB to tear or cut the limbs from a body

dismiss VERB ❶ to send someone away ❷ to tell someone that you will no longer employ them ❸ to put something out of your thoughts because it is not worth thinking about

dismissive ADJECTIVE saying or showing that you think something is not worth taking seriously

dismount VERB to get off a horse or bicycle

disobedient ADJECTIVE not obedient

disobey VERB to refuse to do what you are told to do

disorder NOUN ❶ untidiness or lack of order ❷ an illness ❸ violent behaviour by a large number of people

disorganized (also **disorganised**) ADJECTIVE muddled and badly organized

disown VERB to refuse to acknowledge that a person has any connection with you

disparity NOUN difference or

inequality

dispatch VERB ① to send someone or something off to a destination ② to kill a person or animal

dispatch NOUN ① dispatching ② a report or message sent ③ to do something with dispatch is to do it promptly and efficiently

dispatch box NOUN a container for carrying official documents

dispatch rider NOUN (British) a messenger who travels by motorcycle

dispel VERB ① to drive or clear something away ② to get rid of a fear or doubt

dispensary NOUN a place where medicines are dispensed

dispense VERB ① to distribute something to a number of people ② a machine dispenses money or goods when it gives them out to customers ③ to prepare medicine according to prescriptions

dispenser NOUN a device that supplies a quantity of something

disperse VERB ① to separate and go off in different directions; to scatter ② to force a crowd to break up

displace VERB ① to take a person's or thing's place ② to force someone or something to move from their usual place

display VERB ① to show or arrange something so that it can be clearly seen ② to show a quality or emotion

display NOUN ① the displaying of something ② a collection of things displayed in a shop window, museum, etc. ③ an electronic device for visually presenting data

displease VERB to annoy or offend someone

disposable ADJECTIVE made to be thrown away after it has been used

disposal NOUN getting rid of something

dispose VERB ① to dispose of something is to get rid of it ② to be disposed to do something is to be ready or willing to do it

disposition NOUN a person's nature or qualities

disprove VERB to show that something is not true

dispute VERB ① to argue about something ② to question the truth of something

dispute NOUN a disagreement or argument

disqualify VERB to bar someone from a competition because they have broken the rules or are not properly qualified to take part

disquiet NOUN anxiety or worry

disregard VERB to take no notice of something; to ignore something

disregard NOUN the act of ignoring something

disrepair NOUN bad condition caused by not doing repairs

disreputable ADJECTIVE not respectable in character

disrepute NOUN bad reputation

disrespect NOUN lack of respect; rudeness

disrupt VERB to stop something running smoothly; to throw something into confusion

179

disruptive ADJECTIVE causing so much disorder that a lesson, meeting, etc. cannot continue

dissatisfied ADJECTIVE not satisfied or pleased

dissect (say dis-**sekt**) VERB to cut something up so that you can examine it

dissent NOUN a difference of opinion; disagreement

dissent VERB to express a difference of opinion about something

dissertation NOUN a long essay on an academic subject, written as part of a university degree

dissident NOUN a person who disagrees, especially someone who opposes their government

dissipate VERB ① to disappear or scatter ② to waste or squander something

dissolution NOUN ① putting an end to a marriage or partnership ② formally ending a parliament or assembly

dissolve VERB ① to mix something with a liquid so that it becomes part of the liquid ② to break up and become mixed with a liquid ③ to put an end to a marriage or partnership ④ to formally end a parliament or assembly

dissuade VERB to persuade someone not to do something

distance NOUN ① the amount of space between two places or things ② being far away in space or time

distant ADJECTIVE ① far away ② not closely related ③ not friendly or sociable

distaste NOUN a feeling of dislike for something

distasteful ADJECTIVE unpleasant or offensive

distemper NOUN ① a disease of dogs and certain other animals ② a kind of paint

distil VERB to purify a liquid by boiling it and condensing the vapour

distillery NOUN a place where whisky or other alcoholic spirit is made

distinct ADJECTIVE ① easily heard or seen; noticeable ② clearly separate or different

distinction NOUN ① a difference between things ② excellence or honour ③ an award for excellence; a high mark in an examination

distinctive ADJECTIVE clearly different from others and therefore easy to recognize

distinctly ADVERB ① clearly or noticeably ② particularly; definitely

distinguish VERB ① to make or notice differences between things ② to see or hear something clearly ③ if you distinguish yourself you do something that brings you honour or respect

distinguished ADJECTIVE ① excellent and famous ② dignified in appearance

distort VERB ① to pull or twist something out of its normal shape ② to give a false account or impression of something

distract VERB to take a person's attention away from what they

are doing

distracted ADJECTIVE greatly upset by worry or distress; distraught

distraction NOUN ① something that distracts a person's attention ② an amusement or entertainment ③ great worry or distress

distraught (say dis-**trawt**) ADJECTIVE greatly upset by worry or distress

distress NOUN great sorrow, pain or trouble

distress VERB to make someone feel very upset or worried

distribute VERB ① to give or share something out to a number of people ② to spread or scatter something around

distribution NOUN ① the way that something is shared out or spread over an area ② giving or delivering something to a number of people or places

district NOUN part of a town or country

distrust NOUN lack of trust; suspicion

distrust VERB to have no trust in someone or something

disturb VERB ① to spoil someone's peace or rest ② to make someone feel upset or worried ③ to move a thing from its position

disturbance NOUN ① something that makes you stop what you are doing ② fighting or noisy behaviour in a public place

disuse NOUN the state of being no longer used

disused ADJECTIVE no longer used

ditch NOUN a trench dug to hold

water or carry it away or to serve as a boundary

ditch VERB ① (*informal*) to abandon or get rid of something ② to bring an aircraft down in a forced landing on the sea

dither VERB to hesitate nervously

ditto NOUN used in a list with the meaning 'the same again'

ditty NOUN a short simple song

divan NOUN a bed or couch without a raised back or sides

dive VERB dives, diving, dived ① to jump into water with your arms and head first ② to swim under water using breathing equipment ③ to move down quickly

dive NOUN ① diving into water ② a quick downwards movement

diver NOUN ① someone who dives ② a person who works under water in a special suit with an air supply ③ a bird that dives for its food

diverge VERB to go aside or in different directions

diverse (say dy-**verss**) ADJECTIVE varied; of several different kinds

diversion NOUN ① diverting something from its course ② something intended to take people's attention away from something ③ an alternative route for traffic when a road is closed ④ something amusing or entertaining

diversity NOUN the wide variety of something

divert VERB ① to make something change its direction or path ② to entertain or amuse someone

divide VERB ❶ to separate something into smaller parts; to split something up ❷ to share something out ❸ to find how many times one number is contained in another ❹ to cause people to disagree

dividend NOUN ❶ a share of a business's profit ❷ a number that is to be divided by another. Compare with **divisor**.

dividers PLURAL NOUN a pair of compasses for measuring distances

divine ADJECTIVE ❶ belonging to or coming from God ❷ like a god ❸ (*informal*) excellent; extremely beautiful

divine VERB to discover something by guessing or instinct

divinity NOUN ❶ being divine ❷ a god or goddess ❸ the study of religion

division NOUN ❶ the process of dividing numbers or things ❷ a dividing line or partition ❸ one of the parts into which something is divided ❹ a difference of opinion within a group of people

divisor NOUN a number by which another is to be divided. Compare with **dividend**.

divorce NOUN the legal ending of a marriage

divorce VERB a husband and wife divorce when they end their marriage by law

divulge VERB to reveal information

Diwali (say di-**wah**-lee) NOUN a Hindu religious festival at which lamps are lit, held in October or November

DIY ABBREVIATION do-it-yourself; the activity of doing your own house repairs and improvements instead of paying someone to do them

dizzy ADJECTIVE having or causing the feeling that everything is spinning round; giddy

DJ ABBREVIATION disc jockey

DNA ABBREVIATION deoxyribonucleic acid; a substance in chromosomes that stores genetic information

do VERB does, doing, did, done

do This word has many different uses, most of which mean performing or dealing with something (*Do your best. I can't do this. She is doing well at school.*) or being suitable or enough (*This will do*). The verb is also used with other verbs: ❶ in questions (*Do you want this?*), ❷ in statements with 'not' (*He does not want it.*), ❸ for emphasis (*I do like nuts.*), ❹ to avoid repeating a verb that has just been used (*We work as hard as they do.*)

do NOUN (*informal*) a party or other social event

docile (say doh-syl) ADJECTIVE quiet, obedient and easy to control

dock NOUN ❶ a part of a harbour where ships are loaded, unloaded or repaired ❷ the place in a law court where the prisoner on trial sits or stands ❸ a weed with broad leaves

dock VERB ❶ a ship docks when it comes into a dock ❷ when two spacecraft dock, they join together in space ❸ to cut short an animal's tail ❹ to reduce or take away part of someone's wages or the number of points they have

docker NOUN a worker in a port who loads and unloads ships

docket NOUN a document or label listing the contents of a package

dockyard NOUN an open area with docks and equipment for building or repairing ships

doctor NOUN ① a person who is trained to treat sick or injured people ② a person who holds an advanced degree (a **doctorate**) at a university

doctrine NOUN a belief held by a religious, political or other group

document NOUN ① a written or printed paper giving information or evidence about something ② (in computing) a computer file that contains text or images and that has a name

documentary ADJECTIVE ① consisting of documents ② showing real events or situations

documentary NOUN a film or television programme giving information about real events

doddery, doddering ADJECTIVE shaking and walking unsteadily because of old age

dodge VERB ① to move quickly to avoid someone or something ② to avoid doing something

dodge NOUN (informal) a trick; a clever way of doing something

dodgem NOUN (British) a small electrically driven car at a funfair, in which each driver tries to bump some cars and dodge others

dodgy ADJECTIVE (British) (informal) ① awkward or tricky ② not working properly ③ dishonest or unreliable

dodo NOUN a large heavy bird that used to live on an island in the Indian Ocean but has been extinct for over 200 years

doe NOUN a female deer, rabbit or hare

doer NOUN a person who does things

doff VERB to take off your hat, especially to show respect for someone

dog NOUN a four-legged animal that barks, often kept as a pet

dog VERB to follow someone closely or persistently

dog-eared ADJECTIVE a dog-eared book has the corners of its pages bent from constant use

dogfish NOUN a kind of small shark

dogged (say dog-id) ADJECTIVE determined and persistent; not giving up easily

doggerel NOUN bad or comic verse

dogsbody NOUN (British) (informal) a person who is given boring or unimportant jobs to do

doh NOUN a name for the keynote of a scale in music or the note C

doily NOUN a small ornamental table-mat, made of paper or lace

doldrums PLURAL NOUN the ocean regions near the equator where there is little or no wind

dole VERB NOUN (informal) money paid by the state to unemployed people

183

doleful ADJECTIVE sad or sorrowful

doll NOUN a toy model of a person, especially a baby or child

dollar NOUN a unit of money in the USA and some other countries

dollop NOUN (*informal*) a lump of something soft

dolly NOUN (*informal*) a doll

dolphin NOUN a sea animal like a small whale with a beak-like snout

domain (say dom-**ayn**) NOUN ① a kingdom ② an area of knowledge or interest ③ a group of Internet addresses that end with the same letters, such as .com

dome NOUN a roof shaped like the top half of a ball

domestic ADJECTIVE ① to do with your home or household ② to do with your own country; not foreign or international ③ domestic animals are kept by people and are not wild

domesticated ADJECTIVE domesticated animals are trained to live with and are kept by humans

dominant ADJECTIVE more important or powerful than others

dominate VERB ① to control someone or something by being stronger or more powerful ② to be the highest or most noticeable thing in a place

domineer VERB to behave in a forceful or arrogant way towards others

dominion NOUN ① authority to rule others; control ② an area over which someone rules

domino NOUN a small flat oblong piece of wood or plastic with dots (1 to 6) or a blank space at each end, used in the game of dominoes

don VERB (*formal*) to put on a piece of clothing

donate VERB to present money or a gift to a charity or organization

donkey NOUN an animal that looks like a small horse with long ears

donor NOUN someone who gives something

don't (*mainly spoken*) do not

doodle VERB to scribble or draw something absent-mindedly

doodle NOUN a drawing made by doodling

doom NOUN a grim fate that you cannot avoid, especially death or destruction

doom VERB to make it certain that someone will suffer a grim fate

doomed ADJECTIVE ① certain to suffer a grim fate ② bound to fail or be destroyed

doomsday NOUN the day of the Last Judgement; the end of the world

door NOUN a movable barrier on hinges (or one that slides or revolves), used to open or close an entrance; the entrance itself

doorstep NOUN the step or piece of ground just outside a door

door-to-door ADJECTIVE done at each house in turn

doorway NOUN the opening into which a door fits

dope NOUN (*informal*) ① a drug, especially one taken or given illegally ② a stupid person

dope VERB (*informal*) to give a drug to a person or animal

dormant ADJECTIVE ❶ sleeping ❷ living or existing but not active; not extinct

dormitory NOUN a room for several people to sleep in, especially in a school or institution

dormouse NOUN an animal like a large mouse that hibernates in winter

dorsal ADJECTIVE to do with or on the back

dosage NOUN ❶ the giving of medicine in doses ❷ the size of a dose

dose NOUN the amount of a medicine that you are meant to take at one time

dose VERB to give a dose of medicine to a person or animal

dossier (say doss-ee-er or doss-ee-ay) NOUN a set of documents containing information about a person or event

dot NOUN a small round mark or spot

dot VERB ❶ to mark something with dots ❷ an area is dotted with things when they are scattered all over it

dotage (say doh-tij) NOUN someone is in their dotage when they are old, weak and not able to think clearly

dote VERB ➤ dote on someone to be very fond of someone

double ADJECTIVE ❶ twice as much; twice as many ❷ having two things or parts that form a pair ❸ suitable for two people

double NOUN ❶ a double quantity or thing ❷ a person or thing that looks exactly like another

double VERB ❶ to become twice as much or as many ❷ to make something twice as much or as many ❸ to bend or fold something in two

double bass NOUN a musical instrument with strings, like a very large cello

double-cross VERB to deceive or cheat someone who thinks you are working with them

double-decker NOUN a bus with two floors, one above the other

doublet NOUN a man's close-fitting jacket worn in the 15th-17th centuries

doubly ADVERB twice as much; more than usual

doubt NOUN a feeling of not being sure about something

doubt VERB to feel unsure about something; to think that something is unlikely

doubtful ADJECTIVE ❶ feeling doubt; unsure ❷ not certain to happen

doubtless ADVERB certainly; without any doubt

dough NOUN ❶ a thick mixture of flour and water used for making bread or pastry ❷ (informal) money

doughnut NOUN a round or ring-shaped bun that has been fried and covered in sugar

doughty (say dow-tee) ADJECTIVE brave and determined

dour (say doo-er) ADJECTIVE stern

and gloomy-looking

douse VERB ❶ to pour water or other liquid over something ❷ to put out a light or fire

dove NOUN a kind of pigeon, often used as a symbol of peace

dovetail NOUN a wedge-shaped joint used to join two pieces of wood

dovetail VERB ❶ to join pieces of wood with a dovetail ❷ to fit neatly together

dowager NOUN a woman who holds a title or property after her husband has died

dowdy ADJECTIVE shabby and unfashionable; not stylish

dowel NOUN a headless wooden or metal pin for holding together two pieces of wood or stone

down ADVERB ❶ to or in a lower place or position or level ❷ in writing ❸ to a source or place

down PREPOSITION downwards through or along or into

down ADJECTIVE ❶ unhappy or depressed ❷ not connected or working properly

down VERB to finish a drink

down NOUN ❶ very fine soft feathers or hair ❷ a grass-covered hill

downcast ADJECTIVE ❶ looking downwards ❷ sad or dejected

downfall NOUN a person's fall from power or prosperity; the thing that causes this

downgrade VERB to reduce a person or thing to a lower grade or rank

downhill ADVERB & ADJECTIVE down

a slope

download VERB to transfer data or programs to your computer from the Internet or a large computer system

download NOUN a computer program or file that you have downloaded

downpour NOUN a heavy fall of rain

downright ADVERB & ADJECTIVE complete or completely

Down's syndrome NOUN a medical condition caused by a chromosome defect that causes intellectual impairment and physical abnormalities such as short stature and a broad flattened skull

downstairs ADVERB & ADJECTIVE to or on a lower floor

downstream ADJECTIVE & ADVERB in the direction in which a stream or river flows

down-to-earth ADJECTIVE sensible and practical

downward ADJECTIVE & ADVERB going towards what is lower

dowry NOUN property or money brought by a bride to her husband when she marries him

doze VERB to sleep lightly

doze NOUN a short light sleep

dozen NOUN a set of twelve

drab ADJECTIVE ❶ not colourful ❷ dull or uninteresting

draft NOUN ❶ a rough plan of a piece of writing, not the final version ❷ a written order for a bank to pay out money

draft VERB ❶ to make a rough plan of something you are going to write ❷ to select someone for a special duty

drag VERB ❶ to pull something heavy along ❷ to search a river or lake with nets and hooks ❸ to continue slowly in a boring manner

drag NOUN ❶ (*informal*) something that is tedious or a nuisance ❷ women's clothes worn by men

dragon NOUN ❶ a mythological monster, usually with wings and able to breathe out fire ❷ a fierce person, especially a woman

dragonfly NOUN an insect with a long thin body and two pairs of transparent wings

dragoon NOUN a member of certain cavalry regiments

dragoon VERB to force someone into doing something

drain NOUN ❶ a pipe or ditch for taking away water or other liquid ❷ something that takes away your strength or resources

drain VERB ❶ to make an area dry by taking the water away ❷ to flow or trickle away ❸ to pour off liquid in which something has been cooked ❹ to take away your strength gradually; to exhaust someone

drainage NOUN a system of drains for taking water away

drainpipe NOUN a pipe used for carrying water or sewage from a building

drake NOUN a male duck

drama NOUN ❶ a play ❷ writing or performing plays ❸ a series of exciting or emotional events

dramatic ADJECTIVE ❶ to do with

drama ❷ exciting and impressive ❸ sudden and very noticeable

dramatis personae (say dram-a-tis per-**sohn**-eye) PLURAL NOUN the characters in a play

dramatist NOUN a person who writes plays

dramatize (also **dramatise**) VERB ❶ to make a story into a play ❷ to make something seem more exciting than it really is

drape VERB to arrange cloth or clothing loosely over something

drastic ADJECTIVE having a strong or violent effect

draught (say drahft) NOUN ❶ a current of cold air indoors ❷ a swallow of liquid

draughts NOUN (*British*) a game played with 24 round pieces on a chessboard

draughtsman NOUN ❶ a person who makes drawings or is good at drawing ❷ (*British*) a piece used in the game of draughts

draw VERB draws, drawing, drew, drawn ❶ to produce a picture or outline by making marks on a surface ❷ to pull something along ❸ to take something out ❹ to attract people or their attention ❺ to end a game or contest with the same score on both sides ❻ to move or come gradually ❼ to draw curtains is to open or close them ❽ to get a prize or ticket in a raffle or lottery

draw NOUN ❶ a game or match that ends with the same score on both sides ❷ a raffle or similar competition in which the winner is chosen by picking tickets

a b c d e f g h i j k l m n o p q r s t u v w x y z

or numbers at random ❸ an attraction ❹ the drawing out of a gun

drawback NOUN a disadvantage

drawbridge NOUN a bridge over a moat, hinged at one end so that it can be raised or lowered

drawer NOUN ❶ a sliding box-like compartment in a piece of furniture ❷ a person who draws something

drawing NOUN ❶ a picture drawn with a pencil, pen or crayon ❷ making pictures in this way

drawing pin NOUN (*British*) a short pin with a flat top that you use for fastening paper to a surface

drawing room NOUN (*old use*) a sitting room

drawl VERB to speak very slowly or lazily

drawl NOUN a drawling way of speaking

dray NOUN a strong low flat cart for carrying heavy loads

dread NOUN great fear or worry

dread VERB to fear something very much

dreadful ADJECTIVE (*informal*) very bad or unpleasant

dreadfully ADVERB (*chiefly British*) extremely; or very badly

dreadlocks PLURAL NOUN hair worn in many ringlets or plaits, especially by Rastafarians

dream NOUN ❶ a series of pictures or events in your mind while you are asleep ❷ something you imagine; an ambition or ideal

dream VERB dreams, dreaming, dreamt or dreamed ❶ to have

a dream or dreams ❷ to have an ambition ❸ to think something might happen

dreary ADJECTIVE ❶ dull or boring ❷ gloomy or depressing

dredge VERB to drag something up, especially by scooping at the bottom of a river or the sea

dregs PLURAL NOUN the last drops of a liquid at the bottom of a glass, barrel, etc., together with any sediment

drench VERB to make someone or something wet all through; to soak someone or something

dress NOUN ❶ a woman's or girl's piece of clothing which has a skirt and also covers the top part of the body ❷ clothes or costume

dress VERB ❶ to put clothes on someone or yourself ❷ to clean a wound and put a dressing on it ❸ to put a dressing on a salad

dressage (say *dress*-ahzh) NOUN the training of a horse to perform various manoeuvres in order to show its obedience

dresser NOUN ❶ a sideboard with shelves at the top for displaying plates etc. ❷ a person who dresses in a particular way

dressing NOUN ❶ a bandage, plaster or ointment etc. for a wound ❷ a sauce of oil, vinegar, etc. for a salad

dressing gown NOUN (*British*) a loose light indoor coat you wear when you are not fully dressed

dressmaker NOUN a person who makes women's clothes

dress rehearsal NOUN the final

rehearsal of a play at which the cast wear their costumes

dribble VERB ❶ to let saliva trickle out of your mouth ❷ liquid dribbles when it flows in drops ❸ to move the ball forward in football or hockey with slight touches of your feet or stick

drier NOUN a device for drying hair or laundry

drift VERB ❶ to be carried gently along by water or air ❷ to move along slowly and casually ❸ to live casually with no definite plan or purpose

drift NOUN ❶ a drifting movement ❷ a mass of snow or sand piled up by the wind ❸ the general meaning of what someone says

driftwood NOUN wood floating on the sea or washed ashore by it

drill NOUN ❶ a tool for making holes; a machine for boring holes or wells ❷ repeated exercises, e.g. in military training ❸ (informal) a set way of doing something

drill VERB ❶ to make a hole or well with a drill ❷ to teach someone to do something by making them do repeated exercises

drily ADVERB you speak drily when you say something funny in a clever and sarcastic way

drink VERB drinks, drinking, drank, drunk ❶ to swallow liquid ❷ to drink a lot of alcoholic drinks

drink NOUN ❶ a liquid for drinking; an amount of liquid swallowed ❷ an alcoholic drink

drip VERB ❶ to fall in drops ❷ to let liquid fall in drops

drip NOUN ❶ liquid falling in drops; the sound it makes ❷ a piece of medical equipment for dripping liquid or a drug into the veins of a sick person

drive VERB drives, driving, drove, driven ❶ to operate a motor vehicle or a train; to go or take someone to a place in a car ❷ to make something or someone move ❸ to force or compel someone to do something ❹ to force someone into a state ❺ to force something into place by hitting it ❻ to move or fall rapidly

drive NOUN ❶ a journey in a vehicle ❷ a hard stroke in cricket or golf ❸ a track for vehicles through the grounds of a house ❹ energy or enthusiasm ❺ an organized effort ❻ the part of a computer that reads and stores information on disks

drive-in ADJECTIVE that you can use without getting out of your car

drivel NOUN silly talk; nonsense

drizzle NOUN very fine rain

drizzle VERB to rain gently

droll ADJECTIVE amusing in an odd way

dromedary NOUN a camel with one hump, bred for riding on

drone VERB ❶ to make a deep humming sound ❷ to talk for a long time in a boring way

drone NOUN ❶ a droning sound ❷ a male bee

drool VERB to dribble continuously

droop VERB to bend or hang down weakly

drop NOUN ❶ a tiny amount of

189

liquid ❷ a fall or decrease ❸ a distance down from a high point to a lower point

drop VERB ❶ to let something fall ❷ to fall downwards ❸ to become lower or less ❹ to abandon or stop dealing with something ❺ to leave a passenger, parcel, etc. at a destination

droplet NOUN a small drop

droppings PLURAL NOUN the dung of animals or birds

drought (say drowt) NOUN a long period of dry weather

drove NOUN a moving herd or flock

drown VERB ❶ to die or kill someone by suffocation under water ❷ to make so much noise that another sound cannot be heard ❸ to cover something completely in liquid

drowsy ADJECTIVE sleepy

drudge NOUN a person who does hard or boring work

drug NOUN ❶ a substance used in medicine ❷ a substance that affects your senses or your mind, e.g. a narcotic or stimulant, especially one causing addiction

drug VERB to give a drug to someone, especially to make them unconscious

Druid (say droo-id) NOUN a priest of an ancient Celtic religion in Britain and France

drum NOUN ❶ a musical instrument made of a cylinder with a skin or parchment stretched over one or both ends ❷ a cylindrical object or container

drum VERB ❶ to play a drum or drums ❷ to tap repeatedly on something ❸ you drum a lesson or fact into someone when you make them remember it by constant repetition

drummer NOUN a person who plays the drums

drumstick NOUN ❶ a stick for beating a drum ❷ the lower part of a cooked bird's leg

drunk ADJECTIVE not able to control your behaviour because of drinking too much alcohol

drunk NOUN a person who is drunk

drunkard NOUN a person who is often drunk

drunken ADJECTIVE ❶ drunk ❷ caused by drinking alcohol

dry ADJECTIVE ❶ without water or moisture ❷ thirsty ❸ boring or dull ❹ funny in a clever and not obvious way

dry VERB ❶ to make something dry ❷ to become dry

dryad NOUN a wood nymph

dry-cleaning NOUN a method of cleaning clothes using a liquid that evaporates quickly

dry dock NOUN a dock that can be emptied of water so that ships can float in and then be repaired

DT ABBREVIATION design technology

dual ADJECTIVE having two parts or aspects; double

dual carriageway NOUN (British) a road with a dividing strip between lanes of traffic in opposite directions

dub VERB ❶ to change or add new sound to the soundtrack of a

film or to a recording ❷ to give
a person or thing a nickname or
title ❸ to make a man a knight
by touching him on the shoulder
with a sword

dubious (say **dew**-bee-us) ADJECTIVE
❶ doubtful or suspicious about
something ❷ not to be relied on;
probably not honest

duchess NOUN a duke's wife or
widow

duchy NOUN the territory of a duke

duck NOUN ❶ a swimming bird with
a flat beak; the female of this bird
❷ a batsman's score of nought
at cricket

duck VERB ❶ to bend down quickly
to avoid being hit or seen ❷ to
push someone's head under water
for a short time ❸ to avoid doing
something

duckling NOUN a young duck

duct NOUN a tube or channel
through which liquid, gas, air or
cables can pass

ductile ADJECTIVE ductile metal is
able to be drawn out into fine
strands

dud NOUN (*informal*) something that
is useless or a fake or fails to work

dudgeon (say **duj**-on) NOUN ➤ **in
high dudgeon** very resentful or
indignant

due ADJECTIVE ❶ expected;
scheduled to do something or to
arrive ❷ owing; needing to be paid
❸ that ought to be given; rightful

due ADVERB exactly or directly

due NOUN ❶ something you deserve
or have a right to; proper respect
❷ a fee

duel NOUN a fight between two
people, especially with pistols or
swords

duet NOUN a piece of music for two
players or singers

duffel coat NOUN a thick overcoat
with a hood, fastened with toggles

dugout NOUN ❶ an underground
shelter ❷ a shelter at the side of
a sports field for a team's coaches
and substitutes ❸ a canoe made
by hollowing out a tree trunk

duke NOUN a member of the highest
rank of noblemen

dulcet (say **dul**-sit) ADJECTIVE sweet-
sounding

dulcimer NOUN a musical
instrument with strings that are
struck by two small hammers

dull ADJECTIVE ❶ not bright or clear
❷ not interesting or exciting;
boring ❸ not sharp ❹ stupid; slow
to understand

duly ADVERB in the due or proper
way; as expected

dumb ADJECTIVE ❶ without the
ability to speak ❷ silent; unable
or unwilling to speak ❸ (*informal*)
stupid or foolish

dumbfounded ADJECTIVE unable to
say anything because you are so
astonished

dummy NOUN ❶ a model of a
person used to display clothes ❷ a
rubber teat given to a baby to suck
❸ an imitation of something

dump NOUN ❶ a place where
rubbish is left or stored
❷ (*informal*) a dull or unattractive
place

dump VERB ❶ to get rid of something you do not want ❷ to put something down carelessly

dumpling NOUN a ball of dough cooked in a stew or baked with fruit inside

dumps PLURAL NOUN (informal) ➤ **in the dumps** feeling depressed or unhappy

dumpy ADJECTIVE short and fat

dunce NOUN a person who is slow at learning

dune NOUN a mound of loose sand shaped by the wind

dung NOUN solid waste matter excreted by an animal

dungarees PLURAL NOUN trousers with a piece in front covering your chest, held up by straps over your shoulders

dungeon (say **dun**-jon) NOUN an underground cell for prisoners

dunk VERB to dip something into liquid

duo (say **dew**-oh) NOUN a pair of people, especially playing music

duodenum (say dew-o-**deen**-um) NOUN the part of the small intestine that is just below the stomach

dupe VERB to deceive or trick someone

duplicate (say **dyoop**-lik-at) NOUN ❶ something that is exactly the same as something else ❷ an exact copy

duplicate (say **dyoop**-lik-ayt) VERB ❶ to make an exact copy of something ❷ to do something that has already been done

durable ADJECTIVE strong and likely to last

duration NOUN the length of time something lasts

duress (say dewr-**ess**) NOUN the use of force or threats to make someone do something against their will

during PREPOSITION throughout or within a period of time

dusk NOUN the darker stage of twilight

dusky ADJECTIVE dark or shadowy

dust NOUN tiny particles of earth or other solid material

dust VERB ❶ to wipe away dust ❷ to sprinkle something with powder

dustbin NOUN (British) a bin for household rubbish

duster NOUN a cloth for dusting things

dustman NOUN (British) a person employed to empty dustbins and take away household rubbish

dustpan NOUN a pan into which dust is brushed from a floor

dusty ADJECTIVE covered with or full of dust

dutiful ADJECTIVE doing your duty; obedient

duty NOUN ❶ what you ought to do or must do ❷ a task that must be done, often as part of your job ❸ a tax charged on imports and on certain other things

duty-free ADJECTIVE duty-free goods are goods on which duty is not charged

duvet (say **doo**-vay) NOUN (British) a thick soft quilt used instead of other bedclothes

DVD ABBREVIATION digital video disc; a disc used for storing large amounts of audio or video information, especially films

dwarf NOUN dwarfs or dwarves ❶ a very small person or thing ❷ a creature in stories like a small human being, sometimes with magical powers

dwarf VERB to make something seem small by contrast

dwell VERB dwells, dwelling, dwelt (formal) to dwell in a place is to live there

dwelling NOUN a house or other place to live in

dwindle VERB to get smaller or less gradually

dye NOUN a substance used to change the colour of something

dye VERB to change the colour of something with dye

dyke NOUN ❶ a long wall or embankment to hold back water and prevent flooding ❷ a ditch for draining water from land

dynamic ADJECTIVE ❶ a dynamic person is energetic and forceful ❷ a dynamic force produces motion

dynamics NOUN ❶ the scientific study of force and motion ❷ (in music) the different levels of loudness and softness in a piece of music

dynamite NOUN ❶ a powerful explosive ❷ something likely to make people very excited or angry

dynamo NOUN (chiefly British) a machine that makes electricity

dynasty (say **din**-a-stee) NOUN a line of rulers or powerful people all from the same family

dysentery (say **dis**-en-tree) NOUN a disease causing severe diarrhoea

dyslexia (say dis-**leks**-ee-a) NOUN special difficulty in being able to read and spell, caused by a brain condition

dystrophy (say **dis**-trof-ee) NOUN a disease that weakens the muscles

Ee

E. ABBREVIATION east; eastern

each DETERMINER & PRONOUN every one of two or more people or things

eager ADJECTIVE wanting very much to do or have something; very keen

eagle NOUN a large bird of prey with very strong sight

ear NOUN ❶ the organ of the body that is used for hearing ❷ the ability to recognize and repeat sounds ❸ the spike of seeds at the top of a stalk of corn

earache NOUN pain inside the ear

eardrum NOUN a membrane in the ear that vibrates when sounds reach it

earl NOUN a British nobleman

early ADJECTIVE & ADVERB ❶ before the usual or expected time ❷ near the beginning of something ❸ near the beginning of the day

earmark VERB to put something aside for a particular purpose

earn VERB ❶ to get money as an income for doing work ❷ to win or receive something because you deserve it

earnest ADJECTIVE very serious and sincere

earnings PLURAL NOUN money earned

earphones PLURAL NOUN a listening device that fits over or in your ears

earring NOUN an ornament worn on your ear

earshot NOUN the distance within which a sound can be heard

earth NOUN ❶ the planet that we live on ❷ the ground; soil ❸ the hole or burrow where a fox or badger lives ❹ connection to the ground to complete an electrical circuit

earth VERB to connect an electrical circuit to the ground

earthenware NOUN pottery made of coarse baked clay

earthly ADJECTIVE to do with life on earth rather than with life after death

earthquake NOUN a violent movement of part of the earth's surface

earthworm NOUN a worm that lives in the soil

earthy ADJECTIVE ❶ like earth or soil ❷ crude and vulgar

earwig NOUN a crawling insect with pincers at the end of its body

ease NOUN ❶ a lack of difficulty or trouble ❷ to be at ease with someone is to feel comfortable and relaxed with them

ease VERB ❶ to make something less painful or troublesome ❷ to move something gently into position ❸ to become less severe

easel NOUN a stand for supporting a painting or a blackboard

easily ADVERB ❶ without difficulty; with ease ❷ by far ❸ very likely

east NOUN ❶ the direction where the sun rises ❷ the eastern part of a country, city or other area

east ADJECTIVE & ADVERB towards or in the east; coming from the east

Easter NOUN the Sunday (in March or April) when Christians commemorate the resurrection of Christ; the days around it

eastward ADJECTIVE & ADVERB towards the east

easy ADJECTIVE able to be done or used or understood without trouble

easy ADVERB ➤ **take it easy** to relax or calm down

easy chair NOUN a comfortable armchair

eat VERB eats, eating, ate, eaten ❶ to chew and swallow something as food ❷ to have a meal ❸ to use something up; to destroy something gradually

eatable ADJECTIVE fit to be eaten

eau de Cologne (say oh der kol-**ohn**) NOUN a light perfume first made at Cologne, in Germany

eaves PLURAL NOUN the overhanging edges of a roof

eavesdrop VERB to listen secretly to a private conversation

ebb NOUN the movement of the tide when it is going out, away from the land

ebb VERB ❶ the tide ebbs when it flows away from the land ❷ your strength or courage ebbs when it weakens or fades

ebony NOUN a hard black wood

e-book NOUN a book in electronic form that you can read on a screen

eccentric (say ik-**sen**-trik) ADJECTIVE behaving strangely

ecclesiastical (say ik-lee-zee-**ast**-ik-al) ADJECTIVE to do with the Christian Church or the clergy

echo NOUN a sound that is heard again as it is reflected off something

echo VERB ❶ to make an echo ❷ to repeat a sound or what someone has said

eclair (say ay-**klair**) NOUN a finger-shaped cake of pastry with a creamy filling

eclipse NOUN the blocking of the sun's or moon's light when the moon or the earth is in the way

eclipse VERB ❶ to block the light and cause an eclipse ❷ to seem better or more important than others

ecology (say ee-**kol**-o-jee) NOUN the study of living things in relation to each other and to where they live

economic (say ee-kon-**om**-ik) ADJECTIVE ❶ to do with the economy or economics ❷ making enough money; profitable

economical ADJECTIVE using money and resources in a careful way that avoids waste

economics NOUN the study of how money is used and how goods and services are provided and used

economize (also **economise**)

VERB to be economical; to use or spend less

economy NOUN ❶ the system of trade and industry that a country uses to produce wealth ❷ careful use of money or resources ❸ a way of saving money

ecosystem (say ee-koh-sis-tum) NOUN all the plants and animals in a particular area considered in terms of their relationship with their environment

ecstasy (say **ek**-sta-see) NOUN ❶ a feeling of great delight ❷ an illegal drug that makes people feel very energetic and can cause hallucinations

ecstatic (say ik-**stat**-ik) ADJECTIVE extremely happy

eczema (say **eks**-im-a) NOUN a skin disease that causes rough itching patches

eddy NOUN a swirling patch of water, air or smoke

eddy VERB to swirl

edge NOUN ❶ the part along the side or end of something ❷ the sharp part of a knife or axe or other cutting instrument

edge VERB ❶ to move gradually and carefully ❷ to put something around the edge of something ❸ to be the edge or border of something

edgeways ADVERB ➤ not get a word in edgeways to not be able to say something because someone else is talking a lot

edgy ADJECTIVE tense and irritable

edible ADJECTIVE suitable for eating, not poisonous

edict (say **ee**-dikt) *NOUN* an official command

edifice (say **ed**-if-iss) *NOUN* a large building

edit *VERB* ❶ to make written material ready for publishing ❷ to make changes to text on a computer screen ❸ to be the editor of a newspaper or other publication ❹ to choose and put the parts of a film or tape recording into order

edition *NOUN* ❶ the form in which something is published ❷ all the copies of a book etc. published at the same time ❸ an individual television or radio programme in a series

editor *NOUN* ❶ the person in charge of a newspaper or a section of it ❷ a person who edits something

editorial *ADJECTIVE* to do with editing or editors

editorial *NOUN* a newspaper article giving the editor's comments on something

educate *VERB* to provide people with education

educated *ADJECTIVE* showing a high standard of knowledge and culture, as a result of a good education

education *NOUN* the process of training people's minds and abilities so that they acquire knowledge and develop skills

educational *ADJECTIVE* to do with education; teaching you something

eel *NOUN* a long fish that looks like a snake

eerie *ADJECTIVE* strange in a frightening or mysterious way

effect *NOUN* ❶ a change that is produced by an action or cause; a result ❷ an impression that is produced by something

effect *VERB* to make something happen

effective *ADJECTIVE* ❶ producing the effect that is wanted ❷ impressive and striking

effeminate *ADJECTIVE* an effeminate man looks or behaves like a woman

effervesce (say ef-er-**vess**) *VERB* liquid effervesces when it fizzes or gives off bubbles of gas

efficient *ADJECTIVE* able to work well without making mistakes or wasting time

effigy *NOUN* a model or sculptured figure

effort *NOUN* ❶ the use of physical or mental energy; the energy used ❷ something difficult or tiring ❸ an attempt

effortless *ADJECTIVE* done with little or no effort

effusive *ADJECTIVE* showing a great deal of affection or enthusiasm

e.g. *ABBREVIATION* for example

egg *NOUN* ❶ an oval or round object produced by the female of birds, fishes, reptiles and insects, which may develop into a new individual if fertilized ❷ a hen's or duck's egg used as food ❸ an ovum

egg *VERB* ➤ **egg someone on** to encourage someone to do something with taunts or dares

eggplant *NOUN* (North American)

an aubergine

ego (say **eeg**-oh) NOUN the opinion that you have of yourself and your own importance

egotist (say **eg**-oh-tist) NOUN a conceited person who is always talking about himself or herself

Eid (say eed) NOUN a Muslim festival marking the end of the fast of Ramadan

eiderdown NOUN a quilt stuffed with soft material

eight NOUN & ADJECTIVE the number 8

eighteen NOUN & ADJECTIVE the number 18

eighty NOUN & ADJECTIVE the number 80

eisteddfod (say eye-**ste** th-vod) NOUN an annual Welsh gathering of poets and musicians for competitions

either DETERMINER & PRONOUN ❶ one or the other of two ❷ both of two

either ADVERB also; similarly

either CONJUNCTION (used with or) the first of two possibilities

ejaculate VERB ❶ to produce semen from the penis ❷ (formal) to suddenly say something

eject VERB ❶ to force someone to leave ❷ to send something out forcefully ❸ a pilot ejects when they are deliberately thrown out of an aircraft in a special seat in an emergency ❹ to remove a disk or tape from a machine, usually by pressing a button

eke (say eek) VERB ➤ **eke something out** to manage to make something last as long as possible by only using small amounts of it

elaborate (say il-**ab**-er-at) ADJECTIVE having many parts or details; complicated

elaborate (say il-**ab**-er-ayt) VERB to explain or work something out in detail

elapse VERB an amount of time elapses when it passes

elastic NOUN cord or material woven with strands of rubber so that it can stretch

elastic ADJECTIVE able to be stretched or squeezed and then go back to its original length or shape

elated ADJECTIVE feeling very pleased and excited

elbow NOUN the joint in the middle of your arm, where it bends

elbow VERB to push or prod someone with your elbow

elder ADJECTIVE older

elder NOUN ❶ an older person ❷ an official in some Christian Churches ❸ a tree with white flowers and black berries

elderberry NOUN a small black berry, the fruit of the elder tree

elderly ADJECTIVE rather old

eldest ADJECTIVE oldest

elect VERB ❶ to choose someone by voting ❷ to choose or decide to do something

elect ADJECTIVE chosen by a vote but not yet in office

election NOUN a time when people choose someone to do a political or official job by voting

elector NOUN a person who has the right to vote in an election

electorate NOUN all the people who have a right to vote in an

electric **ADJECTIVE** ① to do with or worked by electricity ② very tense or exciting

electrical **ADJECTIVE** to do with or worked by electricity

electric chair **NOUN** an electrified chair used for capital punishment in the USA

electrician **NOUN** a person whose job is to fit and repair electrical equipment

electricity **NOUN** a form of energy carried by certain particles of matter (electrons and protons), used for lighting and heating and for making machines work

electrify **VERB** ① to supply something with electric power to make it work ② to give an electric charge to something ③ to make someone feel very excited

electrocute **VERB** to kill someone with electricity that goes through the body

electrode **NOUN** a solid conductor through which electricity enters or leaves a battery or other piece of electrical equipment

electromagnet **NOUN** a magnet worked by electricity

electron **NOUN** a particle of matter with a negative electric charge

electronic **ADJECTIVE** ① worked by microchips, etc. that control an electric current ② done using a computer or the Internet

electronics **NOUN** the use or study of electronic devices

elegant **ADJECTIVE** graceful and stylish

elegy (say el-ij-ee) **NOUN** a sad or sorrowful poem

element **NOUN** ① each of about 100 substances that cannot be split up into simpler substances, composed of atoms that have the same number of protons ② each of the parts that make up a whole thing ③ a basic or elementary principle ④ a wire or coil that gives out heat in an electric fire or cooker ⑤ the environment or circumstances that suit you best

elementary **ADJECTIVE** dealing with the simplest stages of something; easy

elephant **NOUN** a very large animal with a trunk, large ears and tusks

elevate **VERB** ① to lift or raise something to a higher position ② to give someone a higher position or rank

elevation **NOUN** ① moving to a higher position or rank ② the height of a place above sea level ③ a drawing of a building seen from the side

elevator **NOUN** ① something that raises things ② (North American) a lift

eleven **NOUN & ADJECTIVE** the number 11

elf **NOUN** elves in fairy stories, a small being with pointed ears and magic powers

elicit (say ill-**iss**-It) **VERB** to manage to get information or a reaction from someone

eligible (say el-ij-ib-ul) **ADJECTIVE** qualified or suitable for something

eliminate **VERB** ① to get rid of

someone or something ② to defeat someone and stop them going further in a competition

elite (say ay-**leet**) NOUN a group of people given privileges which are not given to others

elixir (say il-**iks**-er) NOUN a liquid that is believed to have magic powers, such as restoring youth to someone who is old

Elizabethan (say il-iz-a-**beeth**-an) ADJECTIVE from the time of Queen Elizabeth I (1558-1603)

elk NOUN a large kind of deer

ellipse (say il-**ips**) NOUN an oval shape

ellipsis NOUN omitting a word or words from a sentence, usually so that the sentence can still be understood

elm NOUN a tall tree with rough leaves

elocution (say el-o-**kew**-shon) NOUN the art of speaking clearly and correctly

elongated ADJECTIVE made longer; lengthened

elope VERB two people elope if they run away secretly to get married

eloquent ADJECTIVE speaking well and expressing ideas clearly and effectively

else ADVERB ① besides; other ② otherwise; if not

elsewhere ADVERB somewhere else

elude (say il-**ood**) VERB ① to avoid being caught by someone ② to be too difficult for you to remember or understand

elusive ADJECTIVE difficult to find,

catch or remember

emaciated (say im-**ay**-see-ay-tid) ADJECTIVE very thin from illness or starvation

email NOUN ① a system of sending messages and data from one computer to another by means of a network ② a message sent in this way

email VERB to send an email to someone

emancipate (say im-**an**-sip-ayt) VERB to set someone free from slavery or other restrictions

embalm VERB to preserve a corpse from decay by using spices or chemicals

embankment NOUN a long bank of earth or stone to hold back water or support a road or railway

embargo NOUN embargoes an official ban, especially on trade with a country

embark VERB to go on board a ship or aircraft

embarrass VERB to make someone feel shy, awkward or ashamed

embarrassing ADJECTIVE making you feel shy, awkward or ashamed

embarrassment NOUN the feeling you have when you are embarrassed

embassy NOUN ① an ambassador and his or her staff ② the building where they work

embed VERB to fix something firmly in something solid

embellish VERB to decorate something or add extra details to it

embers PLURAL NOUN small pieces of glowing coal or wood in a

A　dying fire

B　**emblazon** VERB ❶ to decorate
something with a coat of arms
C　❷ to decorate something with
bright or eye-catching designs
D　or words

E　**emblem** NOUN a symbol that
represents something

F　**embody** VERB ❶ to express
principles or ideas in a visible form
G　❷ to include or contain something

H　**emboss** VERB to decorate a flat
surface with a raised design

I　**embrace** VERB ❶ to hold someone
closely in your arms ❷ to accept
J　or adopt a cause or belief ❸ to
include a number of things
K　**embrace** NOUN a hug

L　**embroider** VERB ❶ to decorate
cloth by sewing designs or pictures
M　into it ❷ to add made-up details to
a story to make it more interesting
N
embroidery NOUN designs or
pictures sewn into cloth; the art of
O　decorating cloth in this way

P　**embroil** VERB to involve someone
in an argument or quarrel
Q
embryo (say **em**-bree-oh) NOUN
R　❶ a baby or young animal as it
starts to grow in the womb; a
S　young bird growing in an egg
❷ anything in its earliest stages of
T　development

U　**emerald** NOUN ❶ a bright-green
precious stone ❷ a bright green
V　colour

W　**emerge** VERB ❶ to come out or
appear ❷ to become known
X
emergency NOUN a sudden serious
Y　happening that needs to be dealt
with very quickly
Z

emery paper NOUN paper with a
gritty coating like sandpaper

emetic (say im-**et**-ik) NOUN a
medicine used to make a person
vomit

emigrate VERB to leave your own
country and go and live in another

eminent ADJECTIVE famous and
respected

emir (say em-**eer**) NOUN a Muslim
ruler

emission NOUN ❶ emitting
something ❷ something that
is emitted, especially fumes or
radiation

emit VERB to send out light, heat,
fumes or sound

emotion NOUN a strong feeling
in the mind, such as love, anger
or hate

emotional ADJECTIVE ❶ causing
strong feelings ❷ expressing
your feelings openly ❸ to do with
people's feelings

emotive ADJECTIVE causing emotion
or strong feelings

empathy NOUN the ability to
understand and share in someone
else's feelings

emperor NOUN a man who rules
an empire

emphasis (say **em**-fa-sis) NOUN
emphases ❶ special importance
given to something ❷ stress put
on a word or part of a word

emphasize (also **emphasise**) VERB
to put emphasis on something

emphatic (say im-**fat**-ik) ADJECTIVE
using or showing emphasis

empire NOUN ❶ a group of

200

countries controlled by one person or government ❷ a large business organization controlled by one person or group

empirical ADJECTIVE based on observation or experiment, not on theory

employ VERB ❶ to pay a person to work for you ❷ to make use of something

employee NOUN someone who is employed in a job

employer NOUN a person or organization that has people working for them

employment NOUN having a paid job

empower VERB to give someone the power or authority to do something

empress NOUN ❶ a woman who rules an empire ❷ an emperor's wife

empty ADJECTIVE ❶ with nothing in it ❷ with nobody in it ❸ with no meaning or no effect

empty VERB ❶ to remove the contents from something ❷ to become empty

emu NOUN a large Australian bird rather like an ostrich

emulate VERB to try to do as well as someone or something, especially by imitating them

emulsion NOUN ❶ a creamy or slightly oily liquid ❷ a kind of water-based paint ❸ the coating on photographic film which is sensitive to light

enable VERB to give someone the means or ability to do something

enact VERB ❶ to make a law by a formal process ❷ to perform a play or act out a scene

enamel NOUN ❶ a shiny substance for coating metal ❷ paint that dries hard and shiny ❸ the hard shiny surface of teeth

enamel VERB to coat or decorate a surface with enamel

encampment NOUN a camp, especially a military one

encase VERB to surround or cover something completely

enchant VERB ❶ to put someone under a magic spell ❷ to fill someone with intense delight

enchanted ADJECTIVE placed under a magic spell

enchantment NOUN ❶ being under a magic spell ❷ a feeling of intense delight

encircle VERB to surround someone or something

enclose VERB ❶ to put a wall or fence round an area; to shut something in on all sides ❷ to put something into an envelope or packet with something else

enclosure NOUN ❶ a piece of ground with a wall or fence round it ❷ something enclosed with a letter or packet

encompass VERB ❶ to contain or include a number of things ❷ to surround something

encore (say **on**-kor) NOUN an extra item performed at a concert after previous items have been applauded

encounter VERB ❶ to meet someone unexpectedly ❷ to

experience something

encounter NOUN ❶ an unexpected meeting ❷ a battle

encourage VERB ❶ to give someone confidence or hope ❷ to urge or try to persuade someone to do something ❸ to help something to develop or happen more easily

encroach VERB to take or use too much of something

encrusted ADJECTIVE covered with a layer or crust

encrypt VERB to put information into a special code in order to stop people reading it if they are not allowed to

encyclopedia NOUN a book or set of books containing information about many subjects

encyclopedic ADJECTIVE giving information about many different subjects

end NOUN ❶ the last part of something or the point where it stops ❷ the half of a sports pitch or court defended or occupied by one team or player ❸ destruction or death ❹ a person's goal or purpose

end VERB ❶ to come to an end ❷ to bring something to an end

endanger VERB to cause danger to someone or something

endangered species NOUN a species in danger of extinction

endear VERB if you endear yourself to someone, you make them fond of you

endearment NOUN a word or phrase that expresses love or affection

endeavour (say in-**dev**-er) VERB to try hard to do something

endeavour NOUN an attempt

ending NOUN the last or final part of something

endless ADJECTIVE ❶ never stopping; having no end ❷ an endless belt or loop has the ends joined to make a continuous strip for use in machinery

endorse VERB ❶ to give your approval or support to something ❷ to sign your name on the back of a cheque or document ❸ to make an official entry on a licence about an offence committed by its holder

endow VERB ❶ to provide money to establish something ❷ to be endowed with an ability or quality is to possess it

endurance NOUN the ability to put up with difficulty or pain for a long period

endure VERB ❶ to suffer or put up with difficulty or pain ❷ to continue to exist; to last

enemy NOUN ❶ a person who hates someone else and wants to harm them ❷ a nation or army that is at war with another

energetic ADJECTIVE full of or needing energy

energy NOUN ❶ strength to do things, liveliness ❷ the ability of matter or radiation to do work. Energy is measured in joules ❸ power obtained from fuel and other resources and used for light and heat or to operate machinery

enforce VERB to make people obey

a law or rule

engage VERB ❶ to attract and keep a person's interest or attention ❷ to give someone a job ❸ to begin a battle against someone

engaged ADJECTIVE ❶ someone who is engaged has promised to marry another person ❷ in use; occupied

engagement NOUN ❶ a promise to marry someone ❷ an arrangement to meet someone or do something ❸ a battle

engaging ADJECTIVE attractive or charming

engine NOUN ❶ a machine that provides power ❷ a vehicle that pulls a railway train; a locomotive

engineer NOUN an expert in engineering

engineer VERB ❶ to arrange for something to happen ❷ to plan and construct something

engineering NOUN the design and building or control of machinery or of structures such as roads and bridges

engrave VERB to cut words or a design onto a hard surface such as metal or stone

engraving NOUN a picture or design that has been cut into metal or stone

engrossed ADJECTIVE so interested in something that you give it all your attention

engulf VERB to flow over something and cover it completely

enhance VERB to improve something or make it more attractive or valuable

enigma (say in-**ig**-ma) NOUN

something very difficult to understand; a puzzle

enigmatic (say en-ig-**mat**-ik) ADJECTIVE mysterious and puzzling

enjoy VERB ❶ to get pleasure from something ❷ to enjoy yourself is to have a good time

enjoyable ADJECTIVE giving pleasure

enjoyment NOUN a feeling of pleasure; something that you enjoy doing

enlarge VERB to make something bigger

enlighten VERB to give someone more knowledge or information about something

enlist VERB ❶ to join the armed forces ❷ to enlist someone's help or support is to ask for and get it

enliven VERB to make something more lively or interesting

en masse (say ahn **mass**) ADVERB all together; in large numbers

enormity NOUN ❶ great wickedness ❷ great size; hugeness

enormous ADJECTIVE very large; huge

enough DETERMINER, NOUN & ADVERB as much or as many as necessary

enquire VERB (chiefly British) ❶ to ask for information ❷ to enquire into something is to find out about it

enquiry NOUN (chiefly British) ❶ a question ❷ an investigation

enrage VERB to make someone very angry

enrich VERB ❶ to improve the quality of something ❷ to make someone or something richer

enrol VERB to arrange for yourself or someone else to join a course or school

en route (say ahn **root**) ADVERB on the way

ensconce VERB to be ensconced in a place is to be settled there comfortably

ensemble (say on-**sombl**) NOUN ❶ a group of musicians or actors who perform together ❷ a matching outfit of clothes ❸ a group of things that go together

enshrine VERB to preserve an idea or memory with love or respect

ensign NOUN a military or naval flag

enslave VERB to make a slave of someone; to force someone into slavery

ensue VERB to happen afterwards or as a result

ensure VERB to make sure that something happens or is done

entail VERB to involve something or make it necessary

entangle VERB two or more things are entangled when they are tangled together

enter VERB ❶ to come or go into a place ❷ to join an organization ❸ to key something into a computer ❹ to put something into a list or book ❺ to put your name down to take part in a competition or examination

enterprise NOUN ❶ being bold and adventurous ❷ a difficult or important task or project ❸ business activity

enterprising ADJECTIVE willing to take on new or adventurous projects

entertain VERB ❶ to amuse and interest someone ❷ to have people as guests and give them food and drink ❸ to consider something

entertainer NOUN someone whose job is to amuse and please an audience, such as a singer or comedian

entertainment NOUN ❶ entertaining people; being entertained ❷ something performed in front of an audience to amuse or interest them

enthral (say in-**thrawl**) VERB to hold someone's complete attention; to fascinate someone

enthusiasm NOUN a strong liking, interest or excitement

enthusiastic ADJECTIVE full of enthusiasm

entice VERB to persuade someone to do something or go somewhere by offering them something pleasant

entire ADJECTIVE whole or complete

entirely ADVERB completely; in every way

entirety (say in-**ty**-rit-ee) NOUN the whole of something

entitle VERB to give someone the right to have or do something

entitled ADJECTIVE having as a title

entity NOUN something that exists as a distinct and separate thing

entomb (say in-**toom**) VERB to place a body in a tomb

entomology (say en-tom-ol-o-jee) NOUN the study of insects

entourage (say on-toor-**ah** zh) NOUN the people who accompany an important person

entrails PLURAL NOUN the intestines of a person or animal

entrance (say **en**-trans) NOUN ❶ the way into a place ❷ coming or going into a place

entrance (say in-**trahns**) VERB to entrance someone with delight and wonder

entrant NOUN someone who takes part in an examination or competition

entreat VERB to beg or plead with someone to do something

entreaty NOUN a serious and emotional request

entrench VERB ❶ to fix or establish something firmly so that it is difficult to change ❷ to settle in a well-defended position

entrepreneur (say on-tru-pren-er) NOUN a person who starts a new business or sets up business deals, especially risky ones, in order to make a profit

entrust VERB to make someone responsible for doing something or looking after someone

entry NOUN ❶ coming or going into a place; the right to enter a place ❷ something entered in a list, diary or reference book ❸ something entered in a competition

entwine VERB to twist or wind something round something else

enumerate VERB to list things one by one

envelop (say en-**vel**-op) VERB to cover or wrap round something completely

envelope (say **en**-vel-ohp) NOUN a wrapper or covering, especially a folded cover for a letter

enviable ADJECTIVE likely to be envied

envious ADJECTIVE feeling envy; wanting something that someone else has

environment NOUN ❶ your surroundings, especially as they affect your life ❷ the natural world of the land, sea and air

environmental ADJECTIVE to do with the environment

environmentalist NOUN a person who wishes to protect or improve the environment

environmentally-friendly ADJECTIVE not harmful to the environment

environs (say in-**vy**-ronz) PLURAL NOUN the surrounding districts

envisage (say in-**viz**-ij) VERB to picture something in the mind; to imagine something

envoy NOUN an official representative, especially one sent by one government to another

envy NOUN ❶ a feeling of discontent you have when someone possesses things that you would like to have for yourself ❷ something causing this feeling

envy VERB to feel envy towards someone

enzyme NOUN a kind of substance that assists chemical processes such as digestion

epaulette (say **ep**-al-et) NOUN an

ornamental flap on the shoulder of a coat

ephemeral (say if-**em**-er-al) *ADJECTIVE* lasting only a very short time

epic *NOUN* ❶ a long poem or story about heroic deeds or history ❷ a spectacular film

epicentre *NOUN* the point where an earthquake reaches the earth's surface

epidemic *NOUN* an outbreak of a disease that spreads quickly among the people of an area

epidermis *NOUN* the outer layer of the skin

epigram *NOUN* a short witty saying

epilepsy *NOUN* a disease of the nervous system which causes convulsions

epilogue (say **ep**-il-og) *NOUN* a short section at the end of a book or play

episode *NOUN* ❶ one event in a series of happenings ❷ one programme in a television or radio serial

epistle *NOUN* a letter, especially one forming part of the New Testament

epitaph *NOUN* words written on a tomb or describing a person who has died

epithet *NOUN* a word or phrase used to describe someone and often forming part of their name, e.g. 'the Great' in *Alfred the Great*

epitome (say ip-**it**-om-ee) *NOUN* a person or thing that is a perfect example of something

epoch (say **ee**-pok) *NOUN* a period of time in the past during which

important events happened

eponym (say **ep**-o-nim) *NOUN* a word that is derived from the name of a person

equal *ADJECTIVE* ❶ the same in amount, size or value ❷ having the necessary strength, courage or ability to do something

equal *NOUN* a person or thing that is equal to another

equal *VERB* ❶ to be the same in amount, size or value ❷ to be as good as someone or something

equality *NOUN* being equal

equalize (also **equalise**) *VERB* ❶ to make things equal ❷ to score a goal that makes the score equal

equalizer (also **equaliser**) *NOUN* a goal or point that makes the score equal

equally *ADVERB* in the same way or to the same extent

equation *NOUN* (*in mathematics*) a statement that two amounts etc. are equal, e.g. $3 + 4 = 2 + 5$

equator *NOUN* an imaginary line round the Earth at an equal distance from the North and South Poles

equatorial (say ek-wa-**tor**-ee-al) *ADJECTIVE* to do with or near the equator

equestrian (say ik-**wes**-tree-an) *ADJECTIVE* to do with horse riding

equidistant (say ee-kwi-**dis**-tant) *ADJECTIVE* at an equal distance

equilateral (say ee-kwi-**lat**-er-al) *ADJECTIVE* an equilateral triangle has all its sides equal

equilibrium (say ee-kwi-**lib**-ree-um) *NOUN* ❶ a balance between different forces or influences ❷ a calm and balanced state of mind

equine (say ek-wyn) ADJECTIVE to do with or like a horse

equinox (say ek-win-oks) NOUN the time of year when day and night are equal in length (about 20 March in spring and about 22 September in autumn)

equip VERB to supply someone or something with what is needed

equipment NOUN the things needed for a particular purpose

equity (say ek-wit-ee) NOUN fairness

equivalent ADJECTIVE equal in importance, meaning or value

equivalent NOUN a thing that is equivalent to something else

equivocal (say ik-wiv-ok-al) ADJECTIVE able to be interpreted in two ways and deliberately vague; ambiguous

era (say eer-a) NOUN a period of history

eradicate VERB to get rid of something completely; to remove all traces of something

erase VERB ❶ to rub something out ❷ to wipe out a recording on magnetic tape

erect ADJECTIVE standing straight up

erect VERB to set up or build something

erection NOUN ❶ the process of erecting something ❷ a building or structure that has been erected ❸ the swelling and hardening of a man's penis when he becomes sexually excited

ermine NOUN ❶ a kind of weasel with brown fur that turns white in winter ❷ this valuable white fur

erode VERB to wear away the surface of something over time

erosion NOUN the wearing away of the earth's surface by the action of water and wind

erotic ADJECTIVE arousing sexual feelings

err (say er) VERB to make a mistake or be incorrect

errand NOUN a short journey to take a message or fetch something

errant (say e-rant) ADJECTIVE ❶ misbehaving ❷ wandering; travelling in search of adventure

erratic (say ir-at-ik) ADJECTIVE not regular or reliable

erroneous (say ir-oh-nee-us) ADJECTIVE incorrect; based on wrong information

error NOUN a mistake

erudite (say e-rew-dyt) ADJECTIVE having great knowledge or learning

erupt VERB ❶ a volcano erupts when it shoots out lava ❷ to start suddenly and powerfully; to break out

eruption NOUN ❶ when a volcano erupts ❷ a sudden bursting out

escalate VERB to become greater, more serious or more intense

escalator NOUN a staircase with an endless line of steps moving up or down

escapade (say es-ka-payd) NOUN a reckless adventure

escape VERB ❶ to get yourself free; to get out or away ❷ to avoid something unpleasant ❸ to be forgotten or not noticed

escape NOUN ❶ escaping from somewhere or something ❷ a way to escape

escapism NOUN escaping from the difficulties of life by thinking about or doing more pleasant things

escarpment NOUN a steep slope at the edge of some high level ground

escort (say ess-kort) NOUN a person or group accompanying a person or thing, especially to protect or guard them

escort (say iss-kort) VERB to act as an escort to someone or something

Eskimo NOUN a member of a people living near the Arctic coast of North America, Greenland and Siberia

especial ADJECTIVE special or particular

especially ADVERB specially; more than anything else

espionage (say ess-pee-on-ahzh) NOUN spying on other countries or organizations

espresso NOUN strong black coffee made by forcing steam through ground coffee beans

Esq. ABBREVIATION (short for **Esquire**) a title written after a man's surname where no title is used before his name

essay (say ess-ay) NOUN a short piece of writing on one subject

essay (say ess-ay) VERB (formal) to attempt to do something

essence NOUN ❶ the most important quality or element of

something ❷ a concentrated liquid

essential ADJECTIVE completely necessary; that you cannot do without

essential NOUN something that you cannot do without

essentially ADVERB basically; when you consider the basic or most important part of something

establish VERB ❶ to set up a business, government or relationship on a firm basis ❷ to show that something is true; to prove something

establishment NOUN ❶ establishing something ❷ a business firm or other institution

estate NOUN ❶ an area of land with a set of houses or factories on it ❷ a large area of land owned by one person ❸ all that a person owns when he or she dies

estate agent NOUN (British) a person whose business is selling or letting houses and land

estate car NOUN (British) a car with a door or doors at the back and rear seats that can be removed or folded away

esteem VERB to respect and admire someone very much

esteem NOUN respect and admiration

ester NOUN a kind of chemical compound

estimate (say ess-tim-at) NOUN a rough calculation or guess about an amount or value

estimate (say ess-tim-ayt) VERB to make an estimate

estranged ADJECTIVE no longer

friendly or in contact with someone who was once close to you

estuary (say **ess**-tew-er-ee) NOUN the mouth of a river where it reaches the sea and the tide flows in and out

etc. ABBREVIATION (short for **et cetera**) and other similar things; and so on

etch VERB ❶ to engrave a picture with acid on a metal plate, especially for printing ❷ if something is etched on your mind or memory, it has made a deep impression and you will never forget it

etching NOUN a picture printed from an etched metal plate

eternal ADJECTIVE lasting for ever; not ending or changing

eternity NOUN ❶ time that goes on for ever ❷ (informal) a very long time

ether (say **ee**-ther) NOUN ❶ a colourless liquid that evaporates easily into fumes that are used as an anaesthetic ❷ the upper air

ethereal (say ith-**eer**-ee-al) ADJECTIVE light and delicate

ethical (say **eth**-ik-al) ADJECTIVE ❶ to do with ethics ❷ morally right; honourable

ethics (say **eth**-iks) PLURAL NOUN standards of right behaviour; moral principles

ethnic ADJECTIVE belonging to a particular national or racial group within a larger set of people

ethnic cleansing NOUN the mass killing of people from other ethnic or religious groups within a certain area

etiquette (say **et**-ik-et) NOUN the rules of correct behaviour

etymology (say et-im-**ol**-oj-ee) NOUN ❶ a description of the origin and history of a particular word ❷ the study of the origins of words

EU ABBREVIATION European Union

eucalyptus (say yoo-kal-**ip**-tus) NOUN ❶ a kind of evergreen tree ❷ a strong-smelling oil obtained from its leaves

Eucharist (say **yoo**-ker-ist) NOUN the Christian sacrament in which bread and wine are consecrated and swallowed, commemorating the Last Supper of Christ and his disciples

eulogy (say **yoo**-loj-ee) NOUN a speech or piece of writing in praise of a person or thing

eunuch (say **yoo**-nuk) NOUN a man who has been castrated

euphemism (say **yoo**-fim-izm) NOUN a mild word or phrase used instead of an offensive or frank one; 'to pass away' is a euphemism for 'to die'

euphonium (say yoof-**oh**-nee-um) NOUN a large brass wind instrument

euphoria (say yoo-**for**-ee-a) NOUN a feeling of general happiness

eureka (say yoor-**eek**-a) EXCLAMATION a cry of triumph at a great discovery

euro NOUN the single currency introduced in the EU in 1999. Its symbol is €.

European ADJECTIVE to do with

Europe or its people

euthanasia (say yooth-an-**ay**-zee-a) NOUN causing someone to die gently and without pain when they are suffering from a painful incurable disease

evacuate VERB ❶ to move people away from a dangerous place

evacuee NOUN a person who has been evacuated

evade VERB ❶ to avoid being caught or meeting someone ❷ to avoid dealing with something

evaluate VERB to estimate the value or quality of something; to assess something

evangelist NOUN a person who preaches the Christian faith enthusiastically

evaporate VERB ❶ to change from liquid into steam or vapour ❷ to disappear completely

evaporation NOUN the process of changing from liquid into steam or vapour

evasion NOUN ❶ evading someone or something ❷ an evasive answer or excuse

evasive ADJECTIVE trying to avoid answering something; not frank or straightforward

eve NOUN ❶ the day or evening before an important day or event ❷ (old use) evening

even ADJECTIVE ❶ level and smooth ❷ not changing or varying; regular ❸ calm and not easily upset ❹ equal or equally balanced ❺ able to be divided exactly by two Compare with **odd**.

even VERB ❶ to make something even ❷ things even up or even out when they become even

even ADVERB used to emphasize a word or statement

even NOUN (old use) evening

even-handed ADJECTIVE fair and impartial

evening NOUN the time at the end of the day between the late afternoon and bedtime

evenly ADVERB in a smooth, regular or equal way

event NOUN ❶ something that happens, especially something important ❷ a race or competition that forms part of a sports contest

eventful ADJECTIVE full of happenings

eventual ADJECTIVE happening in the end

eventuality (say iv-en-tew-**al**-it-ee) NOUN something that may happen

eventually ADVERB finally; in the end

ever ADVERB ❶ at any time ❷ always; at all times ❸ (informal) used for emphasis

evergreen ADJECTIVE an evergreen tree or shrub has green leaves all through the year

evergreen NOUN an evergreen tree or shrub

everlasting ADJECTIVE lasting for ever or for a very long time

every DETERMINER ❶ each without any exceptions ❷ used for saying how often something happens

everybody PRONOUN every person; everyone

everyday *ADJECTIVE* ordinary or usual

everyone *PRONOUN* every person; all people

everything *PRONOUN* ❶ all things; all ❷ the only or most important thing

everywhere *ADVERB* in every place

evict *VERB* to make people move out from where they are living

evidence *NOUN* ❶ anything that gives people reason to believe something ❷ statements made or objects produced in a law court to prove something

evident *ADJECTIVE* obvious; clearly seen or understood

evil *ADJECTIVE* morally bad; wicked

evil *NOUN* ❶ wickedness ❷ something bad or harmful

evoke *VERB* to bring a memory or feeling into your mind

evolution (say ee-vol-**oo**-shon) *NOUN* ❶ gradual change into something different ❷ the development of animals and plants from earlier or simpler forms of life

evolve *VERB* ❶ to develop gradually or naturally ❷ animals and plants evolve when they develop from earlier or simpler forms of life

ewe (say yoo) *NOUN* a female sheep

ewer (say yoo-er) *NOUN* a large water jug

ex- *PREFIX* former

exacerbate (say eks-**ass**-er-bayt) *VERB* to make a pain or disease or other problem worse

exact *ADJECTIVE* ❶ completely correct ❷ clearly stated; giving all the details

exact *VERB* ❶ to demand and get something from someone ❷ to exact revenge on someone is to take revenge on them

exacting *ADJECTIVE* needing a lot of effort and care

exactly *ADVERB* ❶ in an exact manner; precisely ❷ used for agreeing with someone

exaggerate *VERB* to make something seem bigger, better or worse than it really is

exaggeration *NOUN* making something seem bigger, better or worse than it really is

exalt (say ig-**zawlt**) *VERB* ❶ to raise someone in rank or status ❷ to praise someone or something highly

exam *NOUN* (*informal*) an examination

examination *NOUN* ❶ a test of a person's knowledge or skill ❷ examining something; an inspection

examine *VERB* ❶ to look at something closely or in detail ❷ to test a person's knowledge or skill

examinee *NOUN* a person being tested in an examination

example *NOUN* ❶ anything that shows what others of the same kind are like or how they work ❷ a person or thing good enough to be worth imitating

exasperate *VERB* to annoy someone very much

excavate *VERB* ❶ to dig in the ground in order to find things from the past ❷ to uncover something

a
b
c
d
e
f
g
h
i
j
k
l
m
n
o
p
q
r
s
t
u
v
w
x
y
z

by digging

exceed VERB ❶ to be more than a particular number or amount ❷ to go beyond the limit of what is normal or allowed

exceedingly ADVERB very; extremely

excel VERB to be better than others at doing something

excellence NOUN the quality of being extremely good

Excellency NOUN the title of high officials such as ambassadors and governors

excellent ADJECTIVE extremely good

except PREPOSITION not including; apart from

except VERB to not include someone or something; to leave someone or something out

excepting PREPOSITION except for; apart from

exception NOUN a person or thing that is left out or does not follow the general rule

exceptional ADJECTIVE ❶ very unusual ❷ outstandingly good

excerpt (say **ek**-serpt) NOUN a passage taken from a book, speech or film

excess NOUN too much of something

excessive ADJECTIVE too much or too great

exchange VERB to give something and receive something else for it

exchange NOUN ❶ exchanging things ❷ a place where things (especially stocks and shares) are bought and sold ❸ a place where

telephone lines are connected to each other when a call is made

exchequer NOUN a national treasury into which public funds (such as taxes) are paid

excise (say **eks**-yz) NOUN a tax charged on certain goods and licences

excitable ADJECTIVE easily excited

excite VERB ❶ to make someone eager and enthusiastic about something ❷ to cause a feeling or reaction

excited ADJECTIVE feeling eager and enthusiastic about something

excitement NOUN a strong feeling of eagerness or pleasure

exciting ADJECTIVE causing strong feelings or pleasure and interest

exclaim VERB to shout or cry out in eagerness or surprise

exclamation NOUN ❶ exclaiming ❷ a word or words cried out expressing joy, pain or surprise

exclamation mark NOUN the punctuation mark (!) placed after an exclamation

exclude VERB ❶ to keep someone or something out of a place ❷ to leave something out

exclusive ADJECTIVE ❶ allowing only a few people to be involved ❷ not shared with others

excommunicate VERB to cut a person off from membership of a Church

excrement (say **eks**-krim-ent) NOUN waste matter excreted from the bowels

excrete VERB to get rid of waste

matter from the body

excursion NOUN a short journey made for pleasure

excusable ADJECTIVE able to be excused

excuse (say iks-**kewz**) VERB ❶ to forgive someone ❷ to allow someone not to do something ❸ to allow someone to leave a room, table or meeting

excuse (say iks-**kewss**) NOUN a reason given to explain why something wrong has been done

execute VERB ❶ to put someone to death as a punishment ❷ to perform or produce something

executioner NOUN a person whose job is to execute people

executive (say ig-**zek**-yoo-tiv) NOUN a senior person with authority in a business or government organization

executive ADJECTIVE having the authority to carry out plans or laws

exemplary (say ig-**zem**-pler-ee) ADJECTIVE very good; being a good example to others

exemplify VERB to be a typical example of something

exempt ADJECTIVE not having to do something that others have to do

exempt VERB to make someone or something exempt

exercise NOUN ❶ using your body to make it strong and healthy ❷ a piece of work done for practice

exercise VERB ❶ to do exercises ❷ to give exercise to an animal ❸ to use something

exert VERB to use power, strength or influence

exertion NOUN physical effort or exercise

exeunt (say **eks**-ee-unt) VERB a stage direction meaning 'they leave the stage'

exhale VERB to breathe out

exhaust VERB ❶ to make someone very tired ❷ to use something up completely

exhaust NOUN ❶ the waste gases or steam from an engine ❷ the pipe through which they are sent out

exhaustion NOUN being very tired

exhaustive ADJECTIVE thorough; including everything possible

exhibit VERB to show or display something in public

exhibit NOUN something on display in a gallery or museum

exhibition NOUN a collection of things put on display for people to look at, for example at a museum or gallery

exhilarate (say ig-**zil**-er-ayt) VERB to make someone very happy and excited

exhort (say ig-**zort**) VERB to try hard to persuade someone to do something

exile VERB to banish someone from a country

exile NOUN ❶ to be in exile is to be forced to live away from your own country ❷ someone who has been banished from their own country

exist VERB ❶ to be present as part of what is real ❷ to stay alive

existence NOUN ❶ existing or being ❷ a way of living

existing ADJECTIVE that is already

a
b
c
d
e
f
g
h
i
j
k
l
m
n
o
p
q
r
s
t
u
v
w
x
y
z

there or being used

exit NOUN ❶ the way out of a building ❷ going off the stage

exit VERB an actor or performer exits when they leave the stage

exodus NOUN the departure of many people

exonerate VERB to say or prove that a person is not to blame for something

exorbitant ADJECTIVE much too great; excessive

exorcize (also **exorcise**) VERB to drive out an evil spirit

exotic ADJECTIVE ❶ very unusual and colourful ❷ from a foreign country, especially a distant or tropical one

expand VERB ❶ to become larger or fuller ❷ to make something larger or fuller

expanse NOUN a wide area of open land, sea or sky

expansion NOUN becoming larger or making something larger

expatriate (say eks-**pat**-ree-at) NOUN a person living away from his or her own country

expect VERB ❶ to think or believe that something will happen or that someone will come ❷ to think that something ought to happen

expectant ADJECTIVE ❶ expecting something to happen; hopeful ❷ an expectant mother is a woman who is pregnant

expectation NOUN ❶ expecting something; being hopeful ❷ something you expect to happen or get

expecting ADJECTIVE (informal)

a woman who is expecting is pregnant

expedient (say iks-**pee**-dee-ent) ADJECTIVE ❶ suitable or convenient ❷ useful and practical though perhaps unfair

expedient NOUN a convenient means of achieving something

expedition NOUN ❶ a journey or voyage made in order to do something ❷ (formal) speed or promptness

expel VERB ❶ to send or force something out ❷ to make a person leave a school or country

expend VERB to use or spend time, money or energy doing something

expendable ADJECTIVE no longer useful or necessary and so not worth keeping or saving

expenditure NOUN the spending of money or the amount spent

expense NOUN the cost of doing something

expensive ADJECTIVE costing a lot

experience NOUN ❶ what you learn from doing or seeing things ❷ something that has happened to you

experience VERB to have something happen to you

experienced ADJECTIVE having a lot of skill or knowledge from much experience

experiment NOUN a test made in order to find out what happens or to prove something

experiment VERB ❶ to carry out an experiment ❷ to try out new things

experimental ADJECTIVE to do

with experiments or trying out new ideas

expert NOUN a person with great knowledge or skill in something

expert ADJECTIVE having great knowledge or skill

expertise (say eks-per-**teez**) NOUN expert ability or knowledge

expire VERB ❶ to come to an end or stop being usable ❷ to die

explain VERB ❶ to make something clear to someone else; to show its meaning ❷ to give or be a reason for something

explanation NOUN a statement or fact that explains something or gives a reason for it

explanatory (say iks-**plan**-at-er-ee) ADJECTIVE giving an explanation

explicit (say iks-**pliss**-it) ADJECTIVE stated or stating something openly and exactly. Compare with **implicit**.

explode VERB ❶ to burst or suddenly release energy with a loud noise ❷ to cause a bomb to go off ❸ to burst into anger or laughter suddenly ❹ to increase suddenly or quickly

exploit (say **eks**-ploit) NOUN a brave or exciting deed

exploit (say iks-**ploit**) VERB ❶ to exploit someone is to treat them unfairly for your own advantage ❷ to exploit resources is to use or develop them

exploration NOUN exploring a place

exploratory (say iks-**plor**ra-ter-ee) ADJECTIVE for the purpose of exploring

explore VERB ❶ to travel through a place in order to learn about it ❷ to examine a subject or idea carefully

explorer NOUN someone who explores a remote place to find out what is there

explosion NOUN ❶ the exploding of a bomb; the noise made by exploding ❷ a sudden great increase

explosive ADJECTIVE able to explode

explosive NOUN a substance that is used for causing explosions

exponent NOUN ❶ someone who is very good at an activity ❷ a person who puts forward an idea or theory ❸ (in mathematics) the raised number etc. written to the right of another (e.g. 3 in 2^3) showing how many times the first one is to be multiplied by itself

export VERB to send goods abroad to be sold

export NOUN ❶ exporting goods ❷ something that is exported

expose VERB ❶ to reveal or uncover something ❷ to put someone in a situation where they could be harmed ❸ to allow light to reach a photographic film so as to take a picture

exposure NOUN ❶ the harmful effects of being exposed to cold weather without enough protection ❷ exposing film to the light so as to take a picture or a piece of film exposed in this way

express ADJECTIVE ❶ going or sent quickly ❷ clearly stated

express NOUN a fast train stopping at only a few stations

express VERB to put ideas or feelings into words; to make your feelings known

expression NOUN ① the look on a person's face that shows his or her feelings ② a word or phrase ③ a way of speaking or of playing music that shows your feelings ④ expressing something

expressive ADJECTIVE showing your thoughts and feelings

expressly ADVERB ① clearly and plainly ② specially

expulsion NOUN expelling someone or something or being expelled

exquisite (say eks-kwiz-it) ADJECTIVE very beautiful or delicate

extend VERB ① to spread or stretch out ② to make something become longer or larger ③ to offer or give something

extension NOUN ① a section added on to a building ② an extra period that is allowed for something to be done ③ one of a set of telephones in an office or house

extensive ADJECTIVE ① covering a large area ② large in scope; wide-ranging

extent NOUN ① the area or length over which something extends ② the amount, level or scope of something

extenuating ADJECTIVE making a crime seem less great by providing a partial excuse

exterior ADJECTIVE outer

exterior NOUN ① the outside of something ② a person's outward appearance

exterminate VERB to kill all the

members of a group of people or animals

external ADJECTIVE on or from the outside of something

extinct ADJECTIVE ① not existing any more ② an extinct volcano is no longer burning or active

extinction NOUN becoming extinct

extinguish VERB ① to put out a fire or light ② to put an end to something

extinguisher NOUN a portable device for sending out water, chemicals or gases to put out a fire

extortionate ADJECTIVE an extortionate price or fee is much too high

extra ADJECTIVE additional; more than is usual

extra ADVERB more than usually

extra NOUN ① an extra person or thing ② a person acting as part of a crowd in a film or play

extract (say iks-trakt) VERB ① to take something out; to remove something ② to obtain information from someone, usually with difficulty

extract (say eks-trakt) NOUN ① a passage taken from a book, film, piece of music, etc. ② a substance separated or obtained from another

extraction NOUN ① extracting something ② a person's family history

extraordinary ADJECTIVE very unusual or strange

extrasensory ADJECTIVE outside the range of the known human senses

extraterrestrial ADJECTIVE from

beyond the earth's atmosphere;
from outer space

extraterrestrial NOUN a being
from outer space

extravagant ADJECTIVE ❶ spending
or using too much of something
❷ too much; more than is
reasonable

extravaganza NOUN a very
spectacular show

extreme ADJECTIVE ❶ very great or
intense ❷ furthest away ❸ going
to great lengths in actions or
opinions; not moderate

extreme NOUN ❶ something
extreme ❷ either end of
something

extremely ADVERB very

extremist NOUN a person who
holds extreme (not moderate)
opinions in political or other
matters

extremity (say iks-**trem**-it-ee)
NOUN ❶ an extreme point; the
very end of something ❷ your
extremities are your hands and
feet ❸ an extreme need, feeling
or danger

extricate (say eks-trik-ayt) VERB to
free someone or something from a
difficult position or situation

extrovert NOUN a person who is
generally lively and confident and
likes company. (The opposite is
introvert.)

exuberant (say ig-**zew**-ber-ant)
ADJECTIVE very lively and cheerful

exude VERB ❶ to give off moisture
or a smell ❷ to display a feeling or
quality openly

exult VERB to show great pleasure

and excitement about something

eye NOUN ❶ the organ of the body
that is used for seeing ❷ the
power of seeing ❸ the small hole
in a needle ❹ the centre of a storm

eye VERB to look at something with
interest

eyeball NOUN the ball-shaped part
of the eye inside the eyelids

eyebrow NOUN the fringe of hair
growing on your face above
each eye

eye-catching ADJECTIVE striking or
attractive

eyelash NOUN one of the short hairs
that grow on an eyelid

eyelid NOUN either of the two
folds of skin that can close over
the eyeball

eyepiece NOUN the lens of a
telescope or microscope that you
put to your eye

eyesight NOUN the ability to see

eyesore NOUN something that is
ugly to look at

eyewitness NOUN a person who
actually saw an accident or crime

eyrie (say **ee**-ree) NOUN the nest of
an eagle or other bird of prey

Ff

fable NOUN a short story that
teaches a lesson about how people
should behave, often with animals
as characters

fabric NOUN ❶ cloth ❷ the
basic framework of something,
especially the walls, floors and roof
of a building

fabricate VERB ❶ to construct or manufacture something ❷ to invent a story or excuse

fabulous ADJECTIVE ❶ wonderful; really good ❷ incredibly great ❸ told of in fables and myths

facade (say fas-**ahd**) NOUN ❶ the front of a building ❷ an outward appearance, especially a deceptive one

face NOUN ❶ the front part of the head ❷ the expression on a person's face ❸ the front or upper side of something ❹ a flat surface

face VERB ❶ to look or have the front towards something ❷ to have to deal with something difficult or dangerous ❸ to cover a surface with a layer of different material

facelift NOUN surgery to remove wrinkles by tightening the skin of the face, done to make someone look younger

facet (say **fas**-it) NOUN ❶ one of the many sides of a cut stone or jewel ❷ one aspect of a situation or problem

facetious (say fas-**ee**-shus) ADJECTIVE trying to be funny at an unsuitable time

facial (say **fay**-shal) ADJECTIVE to do with the face

facilitate (say fas-**il**-it-ayt) VERB to make something easier to do

facility (say fas-**il**-it-ee) NOUN ❶ a building or service that provides you with the means to do things ❷ ease or skill in doing something

facsimile (say fak-**sim**-il-ee) NOUN an exact reproduction of a document

fact NOUN something that is known to have happened or to be true

faction NOUN a small united group within a larger one, especially in politics

factor NOUN ❶ something that helps to bring about a result ❷ a number by which a larger number can be divided exactly

factory NOUN a large building where machines are used to make things in large quantities

factual ADJECTIVE based on facts; containing facts

faculty NOUN ❶ any of the powers of the body or mind (e.g. sight, speech, understanding) ❷ a department teaching a particular subject in a university or college

fad NOUN a fashion or interest that only lasts a short time

fade VERB ❶ to lose colour, freshness or strength ❷ to disappear gradually ❸ to make a sound etc. become gradually weaker (*fade it out*) or stronger (*fade it in* or *up*)

faeces (say **fee**-seez) PLURAL NOUN solid waste matter passed out of the body

faggot NOUN ❶ a meat ball made with chopped liver and baked ❷ a bundle of sticks bound together, used for firewood

Fahrenheit ADJECTIVE measuring temperature on a scale where water freezes at 32° and boils at 212°

fail VERB ❶ to try to do something but not be able to do it ❷ to become weak or useless; to stop working ❸ to not do something when you should ❹ to not get enough marks to pass an examination ❺ to judge that someone has not passed an examination

fail NOUN a mark which does not pass an examination

failing NOUN a weakness or a fault

failure NOUN ❶ a lack of success; not being able to do something ❷ not doing something that you were expected to do ❸ a person or thing that has failed

faint ADJECTIVE ❶ pale or dim; not clear or distinct ❷ slight ❸ feeling weak and dizzy; nearly unconscious

faint VERB to become unconscious for a short time

faintly ADVERB ❶ not in a clear or strong way ❷ slightly

fair ADJECTIVE ❶ just or reasonable; treating everyone equally ❷ fair hair or skin is light in colour and a fair person has hair that is light in colour ❸ fair weather is fine and without clouds ❹ of a reasonable size, amount or number ❺ quite good ❻ (old use) beautiful

fair ADVERB fairly, according to the rules

fair NOUN ❶ an outdoor entertainment with rides, amusements and stalls ❷ an exhibition or market

fairground NOUN an open outdoor space where a fair is held

fairly ADVERB ❶ justly; according to the rules ❷ quite or rather

fairy NOUN an imaginary very small creature with magic powers

fairy tale NOUN a story about fairies or magic

faith NOUN ❶ strong belief or trust ❷ a religion

faithful ADJECTIVE ❶ loyal and trustworthy ❷ true to the facts; accurate ❸ sexually loyal to one partner

fake NOUN something that looks genuine but is not; a forgery

fake ADJECTIVE not real or genuine

fake VERB ❶ to make something that looks genuine, in order to deceive people ❷ to pretend to have something

fakir (say *fay-keer*) NOUN a Muslim or Hindu religious beggar regarded as a holy man

falcon NOUN a kind of hawk often used in the sport of hunting other birds or game

fall VERB falls, falling, fell, fallen ❶ to come or go down without being pushed or thrown ❷ to decrease or become lower ❸ to be captured or overthrown ❹ to die in battle ❺ to happen ❻ to become

fall NOUN ❶ the action of falling ❷ (North American) autumn, when leaves fall

Fallopian tube NOUN one of the two tubes in a woman's body along which the eggs travel from the ovaries to the uterus

fallout NOUN particles of radioactive material carried in the air after a nuclear explosion

fallow ADJECTIVE fallow land is ploughed but left without crops in

219

order to make it fertile again

fallow deer NOUN a kind of light-brown deer

falls PLURAL NOUN a waterfall

false ADJECTIVE ❶ untrue or incorrect ❷ not genuine; artificial ❸ treacherous or deceitful

falsehood NOUN ❶ a lie ❷ telling lies

falsetto NOUN a man's voice forced into speaking or singing higher than is natural

falsify VERB to alter a document or evidence dishonestly

falter VERB ❶ to hesitate when you move or speak ❷ to become weaker; to begin to give way

fame NOUN being famous

famed ADJECTIVE very well known

familiar ADJECTIVE ❶ well-known; often seen or experienced ❷ knowing something well ❸ very friendly

familiarize (also **familiarise**) VERB to make yourself familiar with something

family NOUN ❶ parents and their children, sometimes including grandchildren and other relations ❷ a group of related plants or animals ❸ a group of things that are alike in some way

family planning NOUN the use of contraceptives to control pregnancies; birth control

family tree NOUN a diagram showing how people in a family are related

famine NOUN a very bad shortage of food in an area

famished ADJECTIVE very hungry

famous ADJECTIVE known to very many people

famously ADVERB (informal) very well

fan NOUN ❶ a device or machine for making air move about in order to cool people or things ❷ an enthusiastic admirer or supporter

fan VERB to send a current of air on something

fanatic NOUN a person who is very enthusiastic or too enthusiastic about something

fanatical ADJECTIVE very enthusiastic or too enthusiastic about something

fanciful ADJECTIVE ❶ imagined; not based on reality or reason ❷ imagining things

fancy NOUN ❶ a liking or desire for something ❷ something that you imagine

fancy ADJECTIVE decorated or elaborate; not plain

fancy VERB ❶ to have a liking or desire for something ❷ to imagine something ❸ to believe or suppose something

fancy dress NOUN unusual costume worn for a party, often to make you look like a famous person

fanfare NOUN a short piece of loud music played on trumpets, especially as part of a ceremony

fang NOUN a long sharp tooth

fanlight NOUN a window above a door

fantasize (also **fantasise**) VERB to imagine something pleasant or strange that you would like to happen

fantastic ADJECTIVE ❶ (*informal*) excellent ❷ strange or unusual; showing a lot of imagination

fantasy NOUN ❶ something pleasant that you imagine but is not likely to happen; imagining things ❷ a very imaginative story that is not based on real life

far ADVERB ❶ at or to a great distance ❷ much; by a great amount

far ADJECTIVE ❶ distant or remote ❷ the far side or end of something is the side or end facing you or furthest away

farce NOUN ❶ a comedy in which the humour is exaggerated ❷ a situation or series of events that is ridiculous or a pretence

fare NOUN ❶ the price charged for a passenger to travel ❷ food and drink

fare VERB to get on or make progress

farewell EXCLAMATION & NOUN goodbye

far-fetched ADJECTIVE unlikely to be true, difficult to believe

farm NOUN ❶ an area of land and its buildings used for growing crops or keeping animals for food or other use ❷ a farmhouse

farm VERB ❶ to grow crops or keep animals for food etc. ❷ to use land for growing crops

farmer NOUN a person who owns or manages a farm

farmyard NOUN the yard or area round farm buildings

farrier (say **fa-ree-er**) NOUN a smith

who shoes horses

farther ADVERB & ADJECTIVE at or to a greater distance; more distant

farthest ADVERB & ADJECTIVE at or to the greatest distance; most distant

farthing NOUN a former British coin worth one-quarter of a penny

fascinate VERB to be very attractive or interesting to someone

fascination NOUN great interest in something

Fascist (say **fash-ist**) NOUN a person who supports a type of government in which a country is ruled by a powerful dictator and people are not allowed to hold opposing political views

fashion NOUN ❶ the style of clothes or other things that most people like at a particular time ❷ a way of doing something

fashion VERB to make something in a particular shape or style

fashionable ADJECTIVE following the fashion of the time; popular

fast ADJECTIVE ❶ moving or done quickly ❷ allowing fast movement ❸ showing a time later than the correct time ❹ firmly fixed or attached ❺ a fast colour or dye is not likely to fade or run

fast ADVERB ❶ quickly ❷ firmly

fast VERB to go without food, especially for religious or medical reasons

fast NOUN a period of fasting

fasten VERB ❶ to fix one thing firmly to another ❷ to close or lock something firmly

fastener, fastening NOUN a device used to fasten something

fast food NOUN restaurant food that is quickly prepared and served

fastidious ADJECTIVE ① fussy and hard to please ② very careful about small details of dress or cleanliness

fat NOUN ① the white greasy part of meat ② oil or grease used in cooking

fat ADJECTIVE ① having a very thick round body ② thick

fatal ADJECTIVE ① causing or ending in death ② likely to have bad results

fatality (say fa-**tal**-it-ee) NOUN a death caused by an accident, war or other disaster

fate NOUN ① a person's fate is what will happen or has happened to them ② a power that is thought to make things happen

fated ADJECTIVE destined by fate; doomed

fateful ADJECTIVE bringing events that are important and often disastrous

father NOUN ① a male parent ② the title of certain priests

father VERB to become a father

father-in-law NOUN the father of a married person's husband or wife

fathom NOUN a unit used to measure the depth of water, equal to 1.83 metres or 6 feet

fathom VERB to understand something difficult; to work something out

fatigue NOUN ① extreme tiredness ② weakness in metals, caused by stress

fatten VERB to feed a person or animal to make them fatter

fatty ADJECTIVE fatty meat or food contains a lot of fat

fatwa NOUN a ruling on a religious matter given by an Islamic authority

faucet NOUN (North American) a tap

fault NOUN ① anything that makes a person or thing imperfect; a flaw or mistake ② the responsibility for something wrong ③ a break in a layer of rock, caused by movement of the earth's crust ④ an incorrect serve in tennis

fault VERB to find faults in something

faultless ADJECTIVE without a fault; perfect

faulty ADJECTIVE having a fault or faults; not working or made properly

faun NOUN an ancient Roman god with a man's body and goat's legs, horns and tail

fauna NOUN the animals of a certain area or period of time. Compare with **flora**.

favour NOUN ① something kind or helpful that you do for someone ② approval or liking

favour VERB ① to approve of or prefer something ② to help or support one person or group more than others

favourable ADJECTIVE ① helpful or advantageous ② showing or earning approval

favourite ADJECTIVE liked more than others

favourite NOUN ❶ a person or thing that you like most ❷ a competitor that is generally expected to win

favouritism NOUN unfairly being kinder to one person than to others

fawn NOUN ❶ a young deer ❷ a light-brown colour

fawn VERB to get someone to like you by flattering or praising them too much

fax NOUN ❶ a machine that sends an exact copy of a document electronically ❷ a copy produced by this

fax VERB to send a copy of a document using a fax machine

faze VERB (*informal*) to make someone feel confused or shocked, so that they do not know what to do

fear NOUN a feeling that you are in danger or that something unpleasant may happen

fear VERB ❶ to feel fear; to be afraid of someone or something ❷ to be anxious or sad about something

fearful ADJECTIVE ❶ afraid or worried ❷ causing fear or horror ❸ (*informal*) very great or bad

fearless ADJECTIVE without fear

fearsome ADJECTIVE frightening or dreadful

feasible ADJECTIVE ❶ able to be done; possible ❷ likely or probable

feast NOUN ❶ a large splendid meal for a lot of people ❷ a religious festival

feast VERB to eat a feast or a large amount

feat NOUN a deed or achievement that shows a lot of skill, strength or courage

feather NOUN one of the very light coverings that grow from a bird's skin

featherweight NOUN a boxer weighing between 54 and 57 kg

feathery ADJECTIVE light and soft; like a feather

feature NOUN ❶ any part of the face (e.g. mouth, nose, eyes) ❷ an important or noticeable part of something; a characteristic ❸ a special newspaper article or programme that deals with a particular subject ❹ the main film in a cinema programme

feature VERB ❶ to include something as an important part ❷ to play an important part in something

February NOUN the second month of the year

fed *past tense of* **feed**

federal ADJECTIVE to do with a system in which several states are ruled by a central government but have the power to make some of their own laws

federation NOUN a group of states that have joined together under a central government

fee NOUN a charge for something

feeble ADJECTIVE weak; without strength or force

feed VERB feeds, feeding, fed ❶ to give food to a person or animal ❷ to take and eat food ❸ to put something into a machine

feed NOUN food for animals or babies

feedback NOUN ❶ the response you get from people to something you have done ❷ the harsh noise produced when some of the sound from an amplifier goes back into it

feel VERB feels, feeling, felt ❶ to touch something to find out what it is like ❷ to think or have something as an opinion ❸ to experience an emotion ❹ to be affected by something ❺ to give a certain sensation

feel NOUN what something is like when you touch it

feeler NOUN ❶ either of the two long thin parts that stick out from an insect's or crustacean's body, used for feeling ❷ a cautious question or suggestion to test people's reactions

feeling NOUN ❶ the ability to feel things; the sense of touch ❷ what a person feels in the mind; emotion ❸ what you think about something

feign (say fayn) VERB to pretend to have a feeling or to be ill

feint (say faynt) NOUN a pretended attack or punch meant to deceive an opponent

feint VERB to pretend to attack or hit someone

feline (say feel-yn) ADJECTIVE to do with cats; cat-like

fell past tense of **fall**

fell VERB ❶ to cut down a tree ❷ to knock someone down with a hard blow

fell NOUN a piece of wild hilly country, especially in the north of England

fellow NOUN ❶ a friend or companion; one who belongs to the same group ❷ a man or boy ❸ a member of a learned society

fellow ADJECTIVE of the same group or kind

fellowship NOUN ❶ friendship between people ❷ a group of friends; a society

felon (say fel-on) NOUN a criminal

felony (say fel-on-ee) NOUN a serious crime

felt past tense of **feel**

felt NOUN a thick fabric made of wool fibres pressed together

female ADJECTIVE of the sex that can bear offspring or produce eggs or fruit

female NOUN a female person, animal or plant

feminine ADJECTIVE ❶ to do with or like women; thought to be suitable for a woman ❷ belonging to the class of words (in some languages) which includes the words referring to women

feminist NOUN a person who believes that women should have the same rights and opportunities as men

femur (say fee-mer) NOUN the thigh bone

fen NOUN an area of low-lying marshy or flooded ground

fence NOUN ❶ a barrier made of wood or wire etc. round an area ❷ a structure for a horse to jump over ❸ a person who buys stolen goods and sells them again

fence VERB ❶ to put a fence round or along something ❷ to fight with long narrow swords (called foils) as a sport

fend VERB ➤ **fend for yourself** to take care of yourself ➤ **fend someone** or **something off** to defend yourself from a person or thing that is attacking you

fender NOUN ❶ something placed round a fireplace to stop coals from falling into the room ❷ something hung over the side of a boat to protect it from knocks

fennel NOUN a herb with yellow flowers whose seeds and root are used for flavouring

ferment (say fer-ment) VERB to bubble and change chemically by the action of a substance such as yeast

ferment (say fer-ment) NOUN a state of great excitement or agitation

fern NOUN a plant with feathery leaves and no flowers

ferocious ADJECTIVE fierce or savage

ferocity NOUN violence or fierceness

ferret NOUN a small weasel-like animal used for catching rabbits and rats

ferret VERB ❶ to hunt with a ferret ❷ to search or rummage about for something

ferric, ferrous ADJECTIVE containing iron

ferry NOUN a boat or ship used for carrying people or things across a short stretch of water

ferry VERB to carry people or things across water or for a short distance

fertile ADJECTIVE ❶ fertile soil is rich and produces good crops ❷ people or animals that are fertile can produce babies or young animals ❸ a fertile brain or imagination is able to produce ideas

fertility NOUN being fertile

fertilize (also **fertilise**) VERB ❶ to add substances to the soil to make it more fertile ❷ to put pollen into a plant or sperm into an egg or female animal so that it develops seed or young

fertilizer (also **fertiliser**) NOUN chemicals or manure added to the soil to make it more fertile

fervent ADJECTIVE showing warm or strong feelings about something

fester VERB ❶ a wound festers if it becomes septic and fills with pus ❷ to cause resentment for a long time

festival NOUN ❶ a time of celebration, especially for religious reasons ❷ an organized series of concerts, films, performances, etc., especially one held every year

festive ADJECTIVE ❶ to do with a festival ❷ suitable for a festival; joyful

festivity NOUN ❶ festivities are the parties and other events that are held to celebrate something ❷ festivity is being happy and celebrating something

festoon VERB to hang decorations, such as chains of flowers or paper, across something

fetch VERB ❶ to go for something

and bring it back ❷ to be sold for a particular price

fete (say fayt) NOUN an outdoor event with stalls, games and things for sale, often held to raise money

fete VERB to honour a person with celebrations

fetlock NOUN the part of a horse's leg above and behind the hoof

fetter NOUN a chain or shackle put round a prisoner's ankle

fetter VERB to put fetters on a prisoner

fettle NOUN ➤ in fine fettle in good health

feud (say fewd) NOUN a long-lasting quarrel, especially between two families

feud VERB to keep up a quarrel for a long time

feudal (say few-dal) ADJECTIVE to do with the system used in the Middle Ages in which people could farm land in exchange for work done for the owner

fever NOUN ❶ an abnormally high body temperature, usually with an illness ❷ excitement or agitation

feverish ADJECTIVE ❶ having a fever or high temperature ❷ showing great excitement or agitation

few DETERMINER not many

few PRONOUN a small number of people or things

fez NOUN a high flat-topped red hat with a tassel, worn by men in some Muslim countries

fiancé (say fee-ahn-say) NOUN a woman's fiancé is the man who she is engaged to be married to

fiancée (say fee-ahn-say) NOUN a

man's fiancée is the woman who he is engaged to be married to

fiasco (say fee-as-koh) NOUN a complete and embarrassing failure

fib NOUN a lie about something unimportant

fib VERB to tell a lie about something unimportant

fibre NOUN ❶ a very thin thread ❷ a substance made of thin threads ❸ parts of certain foods that your body cannot digest but that move the rest of the food quickly through your body

fibreglass NOUN ❶ fabric made from glass fibres ❷ plastic containing glass fibres

fickle ADJECTIVE constantly changing your mind; not staying loyal to one person or group

fiction NOUN ❶ writings about events that have not really happened; stories and novels ❷ something made up or untrue

fictional ADJECTIVE existing only in a story, not in real life

fictitious ADJECTIVE made up by someone and not true or real

fiddle NOUN ❶ (informal) a violin ❷ (informal) a swindle

fiddle VERB ❶ (informal) to play the violin ❷ to keep touching or playing with something, using your fingers ❸ (informal) to alter accounts or records dishonestly

fiddly ADJECTIVE (British) small and awkward to use or do

fidelity NOUN ❶ faithfulness or loyalty ❷ accuracy; the exactness with which sound is reproduced

fidget VERB to make small restless

movements because you are bored or nervous

fidget NOUN a person who fidgets

field NOUN ① a piece of land with grass or crops growing on it ② an area of interest or study ③ those who are taking part in a race or outdoor game ④ (*in computing*) one area of a database, where one particular type of information is stored

field VERB ① to stop or catch the ball in cricket or other ball games ② to be on the side not batting in cricket ③ to put a team into a match

field events PLURAL NOUN athletic sports other than track races, such as jumping and throwing events

Field Marshal NOUN an army officer of the highest rank

fieldwork NOUN practical work or research done in various places outside, not in a school, college or laboratory

fiend (say feend) NOUN ① an evil spirit or devil ② a very wicked or cruel person ③ a person who is enthusiastic about doing or having something

fiendish ADJECTIVE ① very wicked or cruel ② extremely difficult or complicated

fierce ADJECTIVE ① angry and violent and likely to attack you ② strong or intense

fiery ADJECTIVE ① full of flames or heat ② easily made angry ③ full of emotion and passion

fifteen NOUN & ADJECTIVE the number 15

fifth ADJECTIVE & NOUN next after the fourth

fifty NOUN & ADJECTIVE the number 50

fifty-fifty ADJECTIVE & ADVERB ① shared equally between two people or groups ② evenly balanced

fig NOUN a soft fruit full of small seeds

fight NOUN ① a struggle against someone using hands or weapons ② an attempt to achieve or overcome something

fight VERB fights, fighting, fought ① to have a fight ② to try to achieve or overcome something

fighter NOUN ① someone who fights ② a fast military plane that attacks other aircraft

figment NOUN ➤ a figment of your imagination something that you only imagine and is not real

figurative ADJECTIVE figurative language uses words or phrases for special effect and not in their literal meanings

figure NOUN ① the symbol of a number ② an amount or value ③ a diagram or illustration ④ a shape ⑤ the shape of a person's, especially a woman's, body ⑥ a person ⑦ a representation of a person or animal in painting, sculpture, etc.

figure VERB ① to appear or take part in something ② (*informal, chiefly North American*) to think that something is probably true

figurehead NOUN ① a carved figure decorating the prow of a sailing ship ② a person who is

227

head of a country or organization but has no real power

figure of speech NOUN a word or phrase used for special effect and not intended literally, e.g. 'flood' in *a flood of emails*

filament NOUN a thread or thin wire, especially one in a light bulb

filch VERB to steal something slyly

file NOUN ❶ a folder or box for keeping papers in order ❷ a collection of data stored under one name in a computer ❸ a line of people one behind the other ❹ a metal tool with a rough surface that is rubbed on things to shape them or make them smooth

file VERB ❶ to put something into a file ❷ to walk in a line one behind the other ❸ to shape or smooth something with a file

filigree NOUN delicate lace-like decoration made from twisted metal wire

filings PLURAL NOUN tiny pieces of metal rubbed off by a metal file

fill VERB ❶ to make something full or to become full ❷ to block up a hole or cavity ❸ to appoint a person to a vacant post

fill NOUN enough to make you full

fillet NOUN a piece of fish or meat without bones

fillet VERB remove the bones from fish or meat

filling NOUN something used to fill a hole or gap, e.g. in a tooth ❷ something put in pastry to make a pie or between layers of bread to make a sandwich

filly NOUN a young female horse

film NOUN ❶ a story or event recorded by a camera as a series of moving pictures and shown in cinemas, on television, etc. ❷ a rolled strip or sheet of thin plastic coated with material that is sensitive to light, used, especially in the past, for taking photographs or cinema images ❸ a very thin layer of something

film VERB to record moving pictures using a camera; to make a film of a story

filmy ADJECTIVE thin and almost transparent

filter NOUN a device for holding back dirt or other unwanted material from a liquid or gas that passes through it

filter VERB ❶ to pass something through a filter ❷ to move gradually

filth NOUN disgusting dirt

filthy ADJECTIVE ❶ extremely dirty ❷ obscene or offensive

fin NOUN ❶ a thin flat part sticking out from a fish's body, that helps it to swim ❷ a flat part that sticks out from an aircraft or rocket and helps it to balance

final ADJECTIVE ❶ coming at the end; last ❷ that cannot be argued with or changed

final NOUN the last in a series of contests, that decides the overall winner

finale (say fin-**ah**-lee) NOUN the final section of a piece of music or entertainment

finalist NOUN a person or team taking part in a final

finalize (also **finalise**) VERB to put

something into its final form

finally ADVERB ❶ after a long time; at last ❷ as the last thing

finance NOUN ❶ the use or management of money ❷ the money used to pay for something

finance VERB to provide the money for something

financial ADJECTIVE to do with finance

finch NOUN a small bird with a short stubby bill

find VERB finds, finding, found ❶ to get or see something by looking for it or by chance ❷ to learn something by experience ❸ something is found in a particular place when it lives, grows or exists there ❹ to decide and give a verdict

find NOUN something interesting or valuable that has been found

findings PLURAL NOUN the conclusions reached from an investigation

fine ADJECTIVE ❶ of high quality; excellent ❷ dry and clear; sunny ❸ very thin or delicate ❹ consisting of small particles ❺ in good health; well

fine ADVERB ❶ finely ❷ (informal) very well

fine NOUN money which has to be paid as a punishment

fine VERB to make someone pay a fine

fine arts PLURAL NOUN painting, sculpture and music

finely ADVERB ❶ into very small grains or pieces ❷ carefully and delicately

finery NOUN fine clothes or decorations

finesse (say fin-**ess**) NOUN skill and elegance in doing something

finger NOUN ❶ one of the long thin parts sticking out from the hand ❷ something shaped like a finger

finger VERB to touch or feel something with your fingers

fingernail NOUN the hard covering at the end of a finger

fingerprint NOUN a mark made by the tiny ridges on your fingertip, used as a way of identifying someone

fingertip NOUN the tip of a finger

finish VERB ❶ to complete something or reach the end of it ❷ to come to an end

finish NOUN ❶ the last stage of something; the end ❷ the surface or coating on woodwork etc.

finite verb NOUN a verb that agrees with its subject in person and number; 'was', 'went' and 'says' are finite verbs; 'going' and 'to say' are not

fiord (say fee-**ord**) NOUN a different spelling of fjord

fir NOUN an evergreen tree with needle-like leaves, that produces cones

fire NOUN ❶ the flames, heat and light produced when something burns ❷ coal and wood etc. burning in a grate or furnace to give heat ❸ a device using electricity or gas to heat a room ❹ the shooting of guns

fire VERB ❶ to set fire to something ❷ to bake pottery or bricks in a kiln ❸ to shoot a gun; to send out a bullet or missile ❹ to tell someone that you will no longer employ them ❺ to produce a strong feeling in someone

firearm NOUN a gun that you can carry; a rifle, pistol or revolver

fire brigade NOUN (*British*) a team of people organized to fight fires

fire drill NOUN a rehearsal of the procedure that needs to be followed in case of a fire

fire engine NOUN a large vehicle that carries firefighters and equipment to put out large fires

fire escape NOUN a special staircase by which people may escape from a burning building

fire extinguisher NOUN a metal cylinder from which water or foam can be sprayed to put out a fire

firefighter NOUN a member of a fire brigade

firefly NOUN a kind of beetle that gives off a glowing light

fireman NOUN firemen a man who is a member of a fire brigade

fireplace NOUN an opening in the wall of a room for holding a fire

fireproof ADJECTIVE able to stand fire or great heat without burning

fireside NOUN the part of the room near a fireplace

firewood NOUN wood for use as fuel

firework NOUN a device containing chemicals that burn or explode attractively and noisily

firing squad NOUN a group of soldiers given the duty of shooting a condemned person

firm NOUN a business organization

firm ADJECTIVE ❶ not giving way when pressed; hard or solid ❷ steady; not shaking or moving ❸ definite and not likely to change

firm ADVERB firmly

firm VERB to make something firm or definite

firmament NOUN (*poetical use*) the sky with its clouds and stars

firmly ADVERB ❶ in a strong or definite way ❷ in a fixed or steady way

first ADJECTIVE coming before all others in time or order or importance

first ADVERB before everything else

first NOUN a person or thing that is first

first aid NOUN treatment given to an injured person before a doctor comes

first-class ADJECTIVE ❶ using the best class of a service ❷ excellent

first-hand ADJECTIVE & ADVERB obtained directly, rather than from other people or from books

firstly ADVERB as the first thing

firth NOUN an estuary or inlet of the sea on the coast of Scotland

fish NOUN fish or fishes an animal with gills and fins that always lives and breathes in water

fish VERB ❶ to try to catch fish ❷ to search for something; to try to get something

fisherman NOUN a person who catches fish either as a job or as a sport

fishery NOUN ❶ the part of the sea

230

where fishing is carried on ❷ the business of fishing

fishmonger NOUN a shopkeeper who sells fish

fishy ADJECTIVE ❶ smelling or tasting of fish ❷ (*informal*) causing doubt or suspicion

fission NOUN ❶ splitting something ❷ splitting the nucleus of an atom so as to release energy

fissure (say **fish**-er) NOUN a narrow opening made where something splits

fist NOUN a tightly closed hand with the fingers bent into the palm

fit ADJECTIVE ❶ suitable or good enough ❷ healthy, in good physical condition ❸ ready or likely

fit VERB fits, fitting, fitted ❶ to be the right size and shape for something ❷ to be suitable for something ❸ to put something into place ❹ to alter something to make it the right size and shape ❺ to make someone suitable for something

fit NOUN ❶ the way something fits ❷ a sudden illness, especially one that makes you move violently or become unconscious ❸ a sudden outburst

fitful ADJECTIVE happening in short periods, not steadily

fitness NOUN ❶ being healthy and in good physical condition ❷ being suitable for something

fitting ADJECTIVE proper or appropriate

fitting NOUN having a piece of clothing fitted

fittings PLURAL NOUN pieces of furniture or equipment in a room or building

five NOUN & ADJECTIVE the number 5

fiver NOUN (*informal*) a five-pound note; £5

fix VERB ❶ to fasten or place something firmly ❷ to make something permanent and unable to change ❸ to decide or arrange something ❹ to repair something that is broken

fix NOUN ❶ (*informal*) an awkward situation ❷ finding the position of something, by using a compass, radar, etc.

fixation NOUN a strong interest or a concentration on one idea; an obsession

fixed ADJECTIVE not changing

fixture NOUN ❶ something fixed in its place, such as a cupboard or washbasin ❷ a sports event planned for a particular day

fizz VERB to make a hissing or spluttering sound; to produce a lot of small bubbles

fizzle VERB to make a slight fizzing sound

fizzy ADJECTIVE a fizzy drink has a lot of small bubbles

fjord (say fee-**ord**) NOUN an inlet of the sea between high cliffs, as in Norway

flabbergasted ADJECTIVE greatly astonished

flabby ADJECTIVE fat and soft, not firm

flag NOUN ❶ a piece of cloth with a coloured pattern or shape on it, used as the symbol of a country or organization or as a signal ❷ a small piece of paper or plastic that looks like a flag ❸ a flagstone

flag VERB to become weak or droop because of tiredness

flagon NOUN a large bottle or container for drink, especially wine

flagpole, flagstaff NOUN a pole used for flying a flag

flagrant (say **flay**-grant) ADJECTIVE very bad and noticeable

flagship NOUN ❶ a main ship in a navy's fleet, which has the fleet's admiral on board ❷ a company's best or most important product or store

flagstone NOUN a flat slab of stone used for paving

flail NOUN an old-fashioned tool for threshing grain

flail VERB to flail your arms or legs to wave them about wildly

flair NOUN a natural ability or talent

flak NOUN ❶ shells fired by anti-aircraft guns ❷ strong criticism

flake NOUN ❶ a very light thin piece of something ❷ a small flat piece of falling snow

flake VERB to come off in flakes

flamboyant ADJECTIVE very showy in appearance or manner

flame NOUN a tongue-shaped portion of fire or burning gas

flame VERB ❶ to produce flames ❷ to become bright red

flamenco (say fla-**menk**-oh) NOUN a lively Spanish style of guitar playing and dance

flaming ADJECTIVE ❶ burning brightly ❷ bright red or orange

flamingo NOUN a wading bird with long legs, a long neck and pinkish feathers

flammable ADJECTIVE able to be set on fire

flan NOUN a pastry or sponge shell with no cover over the filling

flank NOUN the side of something, especially an animal's body or an army

flank VERB to be positioned at the side of something

flannel NOUN ❶ a soft cloth for washing your face ❷ a soft woollen material

flap VERB ❶ to move loosely back and forth in the wind or air ❷ to make something move back and forth in the air ❸ (informal) to panic or fuss about something

flap NOUN ❶ a part that is fixed at one edge onto something else, often to cover an opening ❷ the action or sound of flapping ❸ (informal) a panic or fuss

flapjack NOUN a cake made from oats and golden syrup

flare VERB ❶ to blaze with a sudden bright flame ❷ to become angry suddenly ❸ to become gradually wider

flare NOUN ❶ a sudden bright flame or light, especially one fired into the sky as a signal ❷ a gradual widening, especially in skirts or trousers

flash NOUN ❶ a sudden bright flame or light ❷ a device for making a sudden bright light for taking photographs ❸ a sudden display of anger, wit, etc. ❹ a short item of news

232

flash VERB ❶ to make a flash of light ❷ to appear or move suddenly and quickly

flashback NOUN going back in a film or story to something that happened earlier

flashy ADJECTIVE showy and expensive

flask NOUN ❶ a bottle with a narrow neck ❷ a vacuum flask

flat ADJECTIVE ❶ with no curves or bumps; smooth and level ❷ spread out; lying at full length ❸ a flat tyre has no air inside ❹ flat feet do not have the normal arch underneath ❺ firm and absolute ❻ dull; showing no interest or emotion ❼ a drink that is flat is no longer fizzy ❽ (*British*) a flat battery is unable to produce any more electric current ❾ (*in music*) one semitone lower than the natural note

flat ADVERB ❶ so as to be flat ❷ (*informal*) exactly and no more ❸ (*in music*) below the correct pitch

flat NOUN ❶ (*chiefly British*) a set of rooms for living in, usually on one floor of a building ❷ (*in music*) a note one semitone lower than the natural note; the sign (♭) that indicates this ❸ a punctured tyre

flatly ADVERB ❶ in a definite way, leaving no room for doubt ❷ in a way that shows no interest or emotion

flatten VERB ❶ to make something flat ❷ to become flat

flatter VERB ❶ to praise someone more than they deserve ❷ to make a person or thing seem better

or more attractive than they really are

flattery NOUN flattering someone

flaunt VERB to display something proudly in a way that annoys people; to show something off

flavour NOUN the taste of something

flavour VERB to give something a flavour; to season food

flaw NOUN something that makes a person or thing imperfect

flawless ADJECTIVE without a flaw; perfect

flax NOUN a plant that produces fibres from which linen is made and seeds from which linseed oil is obtained

flaxen ADJECTIVE pale yellow like flax fibres

flay VERB ❶ to strip the skin from an animal ❷ to whip or beat someone

flea NOUN a small jumping insect that sucks blood

flea market NOUN a street market that sells cheap or second-hand goods

fleck NOUN ❶ a very small patch of colour ❷ a very small piece of something

flecked ADJECTIVE with small spots of colour

fledged ADJECTIVE young birds are fledged when they have grown feathers and are able to fly

fledgeling NOUN a young bird that is just fledged

flee VERB flees, fleeing, fled to run or hurry away from something

a b c d e f g h i j k l m n o p q r s t u v w x y z

fleece NOUN ❶ the woolly hair of a sheep or similar animal ❷ a warm piece of clothing made from a soft fabric

fleece VERB ❶ to shear the fleece from a sheep ❷ to swindle a person out of some money

fleecy ADJECTIVE made of soft material like fleece; soft and light

fleet NOUN a number of ships, aircraft or vehicles owned by one country or company

fleet ADJECTIVE able to run or move swiftly

fleeting ADJECTIVE passing quickly; brief

Flemish ADJECTIVE to do with Flanders in Belgium or its people or language

flesh NOUN ❶ the soft substance of the bodies of people and animals, consisting of muscle and fat ❷ the body as opposed to the mind or soul ❸ the pulpy part of fruits and vegetables

flex VERB to bend or stretch a limb or muscle

flex NOUN (British) flexible insulated wire for carrying electric current

flexible ADJECTIVE ❶ easy to bend or stretch without breaking ❷ able to be changed or adapted

flick NOUN a quick light hit or movement

flick VERB ❶ to hit or move something with a flick ❷ to flick through a book or magazine etc. is to turn its pages quickly, without reading carefully

flicker VERB ❶ to burn or shine unsteadily ❷ to move quickly to and fro

flicker NOUN a flickering light or movement

flick knife NOUN (British) a knife with a blade that springs out when a button is pressed

flier NOUN a different spelling of flyer

flight NOUN ❶ flying ❷ a journey in an aircraft ❸ a series of stairs ❹ a group of flying birds or aircraft ❺ the feathers or fins on a dart or arrow ❻ fleeing; an escape

flight recorder NOUN an electronic device in an aircraft that records technical information about its flight. It may be used after an accident to help find the cause.

flighty ADJECTIVE silly and frivolous

flimsy ADJECTIVE ❶ made of something thin or weak; fragile ❷ not convincing

flinch VERB to make a sudden movement backwards because you are afraid or in pain

fling VERB flings, flinging, flung to throw something violently or carelessly

fling NOUN ❶ a short time of enjoyment ❷ a brief romantic affair ❸ a vigorous dance

flint NOUN ❶ a very hard kind of stone ❷ a piece of flint or hard metal used to produce sparks

flip VERB ❶ to turn something over with a quick movement ❷ (informal) to become crazy or very angry

flip NOUN a flipping movement

flippant ADJECTIVE not being serious when you should be

flipper NOUN ❶ a limb that water

animals use for swimming ❷ a kind of flat rubber shoe, shaped like a duck's foot, that you wear on your feet to help you to swim

flirt VERB ❶ to behave as though you are attracted to someone, in a playful rather than a serious way ❷ to take an interest in an idea without being too serious about it

flirt NOUN a person who flirts

flit VERB to fly or move lightly and quickly

flitter VERB to flit about

float VERB ❶ to stay or move on the surface of a liquid or in air ❷ to make something move on the surface of a liquid ❸ to launch a business by getting financial support from the sale of shares

float NOUN ❶ a device designed to float ❷ a vehicle with a platform used for delivering milk or for carrying a display in a parade or carnival ❸ a small amount of money kept for paying small bills or giving change

floating voter NOUN (British) a person who has not yet decided who to vote for in an election

flock NOUN ❶ a number of birds flying or resting together ❷ a number of sheep or goats kept together ❸ a tuft of wool or cotton

flock VERB to gather or move in a crowd or in large numbers

floe NOUN a sheet of floating ice

flog VERB ❶ to beat a person or animal hard with a whip or stick as a punishment ❷ (British) (informal) to sell something

flood NOUN ❶ a large amount of

water spreading over a place that is usually dry ❷ a large number of things ❸ the movement of the tide when it is coming in towards the land

flood VERB ❶ to cover an area with a flood ❷ a river floods when its waters flow over the banks ❸ to come in large quantities

floodlight NOUN a lamp that makes a broad bright beam to light up a stadium or a public building

floor NOUN ❶ the part of a room that people walk on ❷ a storey of a building; all the rooms at the same level

floor VERB ❶ to knock a person down ❷ to baffle someone

floorboard NOUN one of the boards forming the floor of a room

flop VERB ❶ to fall or sit down clumsily ❷ to hang or sway heavily and loosely ❸ (informal) to be a failure

flop NOUN ❶ a flopping movement or sound ❷ (informal) a failure or disappointment

floppy ADJECTIVE hanging loosely; not firm or rigid

flora NOUN the plants of a particular area or period. Compare with **fauna**.

floral ADJECTIVE decorated with a pattern of flowers or made of flowers

florid (say **flo-rid**) ADJECTIVE ❶ red and flushed ❷ elaborate and ornate

florist NOUN a person who sells flowers

floss NOUN ❶ silky thread or fibres

235

② a soft medicated thread pulled between the teeth to clean them

flotation NOUN floating something

flotilla (say flot-**il**-a) NOUN a fleet of boats or small ships

flotsam NOUN wreckage or cargo found floating after a shipwreck

flounce VERB to go in an impatient or annoyed manner

flounce NOUN **①** a flouncing movement **②** a wide frill on a skirt or dress

flounder VERB **①** to move clumsily and with difficulty **②** to make mistakes or become confused when trying to do something

flounder NOUN a small flat edible sea fish

flour NOUN a fine powder of wheat or other grain, used in cooking

flourish VERB **①** to grow or develop strongly **②** to be successful; to prosper **③** to wave something about dramatically

flourish NOUN a showy or dramatic sweeping movement, curve or passage of music

flout VERB to disobey a rule or instruction openly and scornfully

flow VERB **①** to move along smoothly or continuously **②** to gush out **③** to hang loosely **④** the tide flows when it comes in towards the land

flow NOUN **①** a flowing movement or mass **②** a steady continuous stream of something **③** the movement of the tide when it is coming in towards the land

flow chart NOUN a diagram that shows how the different stages of

a process or parts of a system are connected

flower NOUN **①** the part of a plant from which seed and fruit develops **②** a blossom and its stem used for decoration, usually in groups

flower VERB to produce flowers

flowerpot NOUN a pot in which a plant may be grown

flowery ADJECTIVE **①** full of flowers **②** flowery language is elaborate and fully of fancy phrases

flu NOUN influenza

fluctuate VERB to keep changing, especially by rising and falling

flue NOUN a pipe or tube that takes smoke and fumes away from a stove or boiler

fluent (say **floo**-ent) ADJECTIVE **①** skilful at speaking clearly and without hesitating **②** able to speak a foreign language easily and well

fluff NOUN the small soft pieces that come off wool and cloth

fluff VERB (informal) to make a mistake

fluffy ADJECTIVE having a mass of soft fur or fibres

fluid NOUN a substance that is able to flow freely as liquids and gases do

fluid ADJECTIVE **①** able to flow freely and smoothly **②** not fixed and able to be changed

fluke NOUN a success that you achieve by unexpected good luck

fluorescent (say floo-er-**ess**-ent) ADJECTIVE **①** creating light from radiation **②** very bright and shining in the dark

fluoridation NOUN adding fluoride

to drinking water in order to help prevent tooth decay

fluoride NOUN a chemical substance that is thought to prevent tooth decay

flurry NOUN ❶ a sudden whirling gust of wind, rain or snow ❷ a short period of activity or excitement

flush VERB ❶ to become red in the face; to blush ❷ to clean or remove something with a fast flow of water

flush NOUN ❶ a slight blush ❷ a fast flow of water ❸ a hand of playing cards of the same suit

flush ADJECTIVE ❶ level with the surrounding surface ❷ (*informal*) having plenty of money

fluster NOUN ➤ **in a fluster** nervous and confused

flute NOUN a musical instrument consisting of a long pipe with holes that are stopped by fingers or keys, which you play by blowing across a hole at one end

flutter VERB ❶ to flap wings quickly ❷ to move or flap quickly and lightly

flutter NOUN a fluttering movement

flux NOUN continual change or flow

fly VERB flies, flying, flew, flown ❶ to move through the air by means of wings or in an aircraft ❷ to move quickly or suddenly, especially through the air ❸ to wave in the air ❹ to make something fly ❺ a period of time flies when it passes quickly

fly NOUN ❶ a small flying insect with two wings ❷ a real or artificial fly used as bait in fishing ❸ the front opening of a pair of trousers

flyer NOUN ❶ a person or vehicle that flies ❷ a small poster advertising an event

flying saucer NOUN a mysterious saucer-shaped object that some people say they have seen in the sky and believe to be an alien spacecraft

flyleaf NOUN a blank page at the beginning or end of a book

flyover NOUN a bridge that carries one road over another

foal NOUN a young horse

foal VERB to give birth to a foal

foam NOUN ❶ a white mass of tiny bubbles on a liquid; froth ❷ a spongy kind of rubber or plastic

foam VERB to form a white mass of tiny bubbles; to froth

fob NOUN ❶ a chain for a pocket watch ❷ a tab on a key ring

fob VERB ➤ **fob someone off** to get rid of someone by an excuse or a trick

focal ADJECTIVE to do with or at a focus

focal point NOUN ❶ the point on a lens at which rays seem to meet ❷ something that is a centre of interest or attention

focus NOUN focuses or foci ❶ the distance from an eye or lens at which an object appears clearest ❷ the point at which rays seem to meet ❸ something that is a centre of interest or attention

focus VERB ❶ to adjust the focus of your eye or a lens so that objects

237

appear clearly ❷ to concentrate on something

fodder NOUN food for horses and farm animals

foe NOUN (old use) an enemy

foetus (say fee-tus) NOUN a developing embryo, especially an unborn human baby

fog NOUN thick mist

foggy ADJECTIVE full of fog

foghorn NOUN a loud horn for warning ships in fog

foible (say foy-bel) NOUN a slight peculiarity in someone's character or tastes

foil NOUN ❶ a very thin sheet of metal ❷ a person or thing that makes another look better in contrast ❸ a long narrow sword used in the sport of fencing

foil VERB to prevent something from being successful

foist VERB to force a person to accept something that they do not want

fold VERB ❶ to bend or wrap one part of something over another part ❷ to bend or move in this way ❸ you fold your arms when you put one of your arms over the other one and hold them against your chest

fold NOUN ❶ a line where something is folded ❷ an enclosure for sheep

folder NOUN ❶ a folding cover for loose papers ❷ a place where a set of files are grouped together in a computer

foliage NOUN the leaves of a tree or plant

folk PLURAL NOUN people

folk dance NOUN a dance in the traditional style of a country

folklore NOUN old beliefs and legends

folk music NOUN the traditional music of a country

folk song NOUN a song in the traditional style of a country

follow VERB ❶ to go or come after someone or something ❷ to do a thing after something else ❸ to act according to someone's instructions, advice or example ❹ to go along a road or path ❺ to take an interest in the progress of events or a sport or team ❻ to understand someone or something ❼ to result from something ❽ to receive the messages that a particular person sends on social networking websites such as Twitter

follower NOUN a person who follows or supports someone or something

following PREPOSITION after, as a result of

folly NOUN foolishness; a foolish action

fond ADJECTIVE ❶ loving or liking a person or thing ❷ pleasant and affectionate

fondle VERB to touch or stroke someone or something lovingly

font NOUN ❶ a basin (often of carved stone) in a Christian church, to hold water for baptism ❷ a set of characters used in printing and computer documents

food NOUN any substance that a

plant or animal can take into its body to help it to grow and be healthy

food chain NOUN a series of plants and animals each of which serves as food for the one above it in the series

foodstuff NOUN something that can be used as food

food technology NOUN the study of foods, what they are made of and how they are prepared

fool NOUN ❶ a stupid person; someone who acts unwisely ❷ a jester or clown ❸ (*British*) a creamy pudding with crushed fruit in it

fool VERB to trick or deceive someone

foolhardy ADJECTIVE bold but foolish; reckless

foolish ADJECTIVE without good sense or judgement; unwise

foolproof ADJECTIVE easy to use or do without anything going wrong

foot NOUN feet ❶ the lower part of your leg below the ankle ❷ any similar part, e.g. one used by certain animals to move or attach themselves to things ❸ the lowest part or end of something ❹ a measure of length, 12 inches (30.48 centimetres) ❺ a unit of rhythm in a line of poetry, e.g. each of the four divisions in *Jack / and Jill / went up / the hill*

footage NOUN an amount of film showing something

foot-and-mouth disease NOUN a serious contagious disease that affects cattle, sheep and other animals

football NOUN ❶ a game played by two teams of eleven players who try to kick a ball into their opponents' goal ❷ the round ball used in this game

footballer NOUN a person who plays football

foothill NOUN a low hill near the bottom of a mountain or range of mountains

foothold NOUN ❶ a place to put your foot when climbing ❷ a small but firm position from which further progress can be made

footing NOUN ❶ having your feet firmly placed on something ❷ the status or nature of a relationship

footlights PLURAL NOUN a row of lights along the front of the floor of a stage

footman NOUN a male servant who opens doors, serves at table, etc.

footnote NOUN a note printed at the bottom of the page

footpath NOUN a path for people to walk along, especially one in the countryside

footprint NOUN a mark made by a foot or shoe

footsore ADJECTIVE having feet that are painful or sore from walking

footstep NOUN ❶ a step taken in walking or running ❷ the sound of a step being taken

footstool NOUN a stool for resting your feet on when you are sitting

footwear NOUN shoes, boots and other coverings for the feet

for PREPOSITION This word is used to

show **①** purpose or direction (*This letter is for you; We set out for home.*) **②** distance or time (*They walked for three miles; We've been waiting for hours.*) **③** price or exchange (*We bought it for £5; New lamps for old.*) **④** cause or reason (*She was fined for speeding.*) **⑤** defence or support (*He fought for his country; Are you for us or against us?*) **⑥** what something refers to or relates to (*She has a good ear for music; What's the Russian for 'goodbye'?*) **⑦** similarity or correspondence (*We took him for a fool.*)

for CONJUNCTION because

forage VERB to go searching for something, especially food or fuel

foray NOUN a sudden attack or raid

forbear VERB **①** to avoid or refrain from doing something something **②** to be patient or tolerant

forbid VERB forbids, forbidding, forbade, forbidden **①** to order someone not to do something **②** to refuse to allow something

forbidding ADJECTIVE looking stern or unfriendly

force NOUN **①** strength or power **②** (*in science*) an influence, which can be measured, that causes something to move **③** an organized group of police, soldiers or workers

force VERB **①** to get someone to do something by using force or power **②** to break something open by force

forceful ADJECTIVE strong and vigorous

forceps NOUN pincers or tongs used by dentists or surgeons

forcible ADJECTIVE done by force; forceful

ford NOUN a shallow place where you can walk across a river

ford VERB to cross a river at a ford

fore ADJECTIVE & ADVERB at or towards the front

fore NOUN the front part

forearm NOUN the arm from the elbow to the wrist or fingertips

forearm VERB to be forearmed is to be prepared in advance against possible danger

forebears PLURAL NOUN your forebears are your ancestors

foreboding NOUN a feeling that trouble is coming

forecast NOUN a statement that tells in advance what is likely to happen

forecast VERB to say in advance what is likely to happen

forecastle (say **foh**-ksul) NOUN the forward part of certain ships

forecourt NOUN an open area in front of a large building or petrol station

forefathers PLURAL NOUN your forefathers are your ancestors (both male and female)

forefinger NOUN the finger next to your thumb

forefoot NOUN an animal's front foot

forefront NOUN the leading position; the position at the front

foregoing ADJECTIVE preceding; previously mentioned

foregone conclusion NOUN a

result that is certain to happen

foreground NOUN the part of a scene, picture or view that is nearest to you

forehand NOUN a stroke made in tennis etc. with the palm of the hand turned forwards

forehead (say forrid or for-hed) NOUN the part of your face above your eyes

foreign ADJECTIVE ① belonging to or in another country ② not belonging naturally to a place or to someone's nature

foreigner NOUN a person from another country

foreleg NOUN an animal's front leg

foreman NOUN ① a worker in charge of a group of other workers ② a member of a jury who is in charge of the jury's discussions and who speaks on its behalf

foremost ADJECTIVE & ADVERB first in position or rank; most important

forensic (say fer-en-sik) ADJECTIVE ① to do with or used in law courts ② using scientific tests to find out about a crime

forensic medicine NOUN medical knowledge needed in legal matters or in solving crimes

forerunner NOUN a person or thing that comes before another; a sign of what is to come

foresee VERB foresees, foreseeing, foresaw, foreseen to realize that something is likely to happen

foreseeable ADJECTIVE a foreseeable event is one that you should realize is likely to happen

foreshorten VERB to draw or

paint an object with some lines shortened to give an effect of distance or depth

foresight NOUN the ability to realize what is likely to happen in the future and be prepared for it

foreskin NOUN the fold of skin covering the end of a penis

forest NOUN trees and undergrowth covering a large area

forestall VERB to prevent something from happening or someone from doing something by taking action first

forestry NOUN planting forests and looking after them

foretell VERB to know or say what will happen in the future; to predict something

forethought NOUN careful thought and planning for the future

forever ADVERB ① for all time or for a long time ② continually or constantly

forewarn VERB to warn someone beforehand

forewoman NOUN ① a female worker in charge of other workers ② a female member of a jury who is in charge of the jury's discussions and who speaks on its behalf

foreword NOUN a short introduction at the beginning of a book

forfeit (say for-fit) VERB to pay or give up something as a penalty

forfeit NOUN something forfeited

forge NOUN a place where metal is heated and shaped; a blacksmith's workshop

forge VERB ❶ to shape metal by heating and hammering it ❷ to copy a banknote, document or painting in order to deceive people

forgery NOUN ❶ the crime of copying something in order to deceive people ❷ a copy of something made to deceive people

forget VERB forgets, forgetting, forgot, forgotten ❶ to fail to remember something ❷ to stop thinking or worrying about something

forgetful ADJECTIVE frequently forgetting things

forget-me-not NOUN a plant with small blue flowers

forgive VERB to stop feeling angry towards someone for something they have done

forgiveness NOUN forgiving someone

forgo VERB forgoes, forgoing, forwent, forgone to decide to give something up; to go without something

fork NOUN ❶ a small device with prongs for lifting food to your mouth ❷ a large device with prongs used for digging or lifting things ❸ a place where a road or river separates into two or more parts

fork VERB ❶ to lift or dig something with a fork ❷ a road or river forks when it separates into two or more branches ❸ to follow one fork of a road or river

forklift truck NOUN a truck with two metal bars at the front for lifting and moving heavy loads

forlorn ADJECTIVE left alone and unhappy

form NOUN ❶ the shape, appearance or condition of something ❷ a kind or type of something ❸ a class in school ❹ a piece of paper with spaces to be filled in

form VERB ❶ to shape or construct something; to create something ❷ to come into existence or develop

formal ADJECTIVE ❶ strictly following the accepted rules or customs; not casual ❷ rather serious and stiff in your manner ❸ official or ceremonial

formality NOUN ❶ formal behaviour ❷ something done to obey a rule or custom

formally ADVERB in a formal way

format NOUN ❶ the shape and size of something ❷ the way something is arranged or organized ❸ (in computing) the way data is organized for processing or storage by a computer

format VERB (in computing) to organize data in a particular format

formation NOUN ❶ the act of forming something ❷ something that has been formed ❸ a special arrangement or pattern

formative ADJECTIVE having an important and lasting influence on how a person develops

former ADJECTIVE of an earlier time Compare with **latter**.

formerly ADVERB at an earlier time; previously

formidable (say **for**-mid-a-bul) ADJECTIVE ❶ difficult to deal with or do ❷ impressive and frightening

formula NOUN formulae or formulas ❶ a set of chemical symbols showing what a substance consists of ❷ a rule or statement expressed in symbols or numbers ❸ a list of the ingredients you need to make something ❹ a fixed wording for a speech or ceremony ❺ one of the groups into which racing cars are placed according to the size of their engines

formulate VERB to express an idea or plan clearly and exactly

forsake VERB forsakes, forsaking, forsook, forsaken ❶ to give something up; to leave a place ❷ to abandon someone

fort NOUN a building that has been strongly built against attack

forth ADVERB ❶ out; into view ❷ onwards or forwards

forthcoming ADJECTIVE ❶ due to happen soon ❷ made available when needed ❸ willing to talk or give information

forthright ADJECTIVE frank and outspoken

fortification NOUN ❶ fortifying something ❷ a wall or building constructed to make a place strong against attack

fortify VERB ❶ to make a place strong against attack, especially by building fortifications ❷ to make someone feel stronger

fortissimo ADVERB (in music) to be played very loudly

fortitude NOUN courage in bearing pain or trouble

fortnight NOUN a period of two weeks

fortress NOUN a castle or town that has been strongly built against attack

fortunate ADJECTIVE having or caused by good luck; lucky

fortunately ADVERB by good luck

fortune NOUN ❶ luck, especially good luck ❷ a large amount of money

forty NOUN & ADJECTIVE the number 40

forum NOUN ❶ the public square in an ancient Roman city ❷ a place or meeting where people can exchange and discuss ideas

forward ADJECTIVE ❶ going forwards ❷ placed in the front ❸ too eager or bold

forward ADVERB forwards or ahead

forward NOUN a player in the front line of a team in football, hockey, etc.

forward VERB to send on a letter, parcel or email to a new address

forwards ADVERB ❶ to or towards the front ❷ in the direction you are facing

fossil NOUN the remains or traces of a prehistoric animal or plant that has been buried in the ground for a very long time and become hardened in rock

fossil fuel NOUN a natural fuel such as coal or gas formed in the geological past

fossilized (also **fossilised**) ADJECTIVE formed into a fossil

foster VERB ❶ to take care of and

a
b
c
d
e
f
g
h
i
j
k
l
m
n
o
p
q
r
s
t
u
v
w
x
y
z

bring up a child who is not your own ❷ to help something to grow or develop

foul ADJECTIVE ❶ disgusting; tasting or smelling unpleasant ❷ foul weather is wet and stormy ❸ unfair; breaking the rules of a game

foul NOUN an action that breaks the rules of a game

foul VERB ❶ to commit a foul against a player in a game ❷ to make something foul or unpleasant

foul play NOUN a violent crime, especially murder

found past tense of **find**

found VERB ❶ to start or set up an organization or institution, especially by providing money ❷ to be founded on something is to be based on it

foundation NOUN ❶ a building's foundations are the solid base under the ground on which it is built ❷ the basis for something ❸ the founding of an organization or institution ❹ a fund of money set aside for a charitable purpose

founder NOUN a person who founds something

founder VERB ❶ to fill with water and sink ❷ to fail completely

foundry NOUN a factory or workshop where metal or glass is made

fount NOUN (poetical use) a fountain

fountain NOUN an ornamental structure in which a jet of water shoots up into the air

fountain pen NOUN a pen that can be filled with a supply of ink

four NOUN & ADJECTIVE the number 4

fourteen NOUN & ADJECTIVE the number 14

fourth ADJECTIVE next after the third

fourth NOUN ❶ the fourth person or thing ❷ one of four equal parts; a quarter

fowl NOUN a bird, especially one kept on a farm for its eggs or meat

fox NOUN a wild animal that looks like a dog with a long furry tail

fox VERB to deceive or puzzle someone

foxglove NOUN a tall plant with flowers like the fingers of gloves

foyer (say foy-ay) NOUN the entrance hall of a theatre, cinema or hotel

fraction NOUN ❶ a number that is not a whole number, e.g. ½ or 0.5 ❷ a tiny part or amount of something

fractious (say frak-shus) ADJECTIVE irritable or bad-tempered

fracture NOUN the breaking of something, especially of a bone

fracture VERB to break something, especially a bone

fragile ADJECTIVE easy to break or damage

fragment NOUN ❶ a small piece broken off ❷ a small part of something

fragrance NOUN a pleasant smell or perfume

fragrant ADJECTIVE having a pleasant smell

frail ADJECTIVE not strong or healthy; physically weak

frailty NOUN weakness in someone's

body or character

frame NOUN ❶ a holder that fits round the outside of a picture or mirror ❷ a rigid structure that supports something ❸ a human or animal body ❹ each of the single photographs that a cinema film or video is made from

frame VERB ❶ to put a frame on or round something ❷ to express something in a particular way ❸ to make an innocent person seem guilty by arranging false evidence

framework NOUN ❶ a frame supporting something ❷ a basic plan or system

franc NOUN a unit of money in Switzerland and formerly in France, Belgium and some other countries (until replaced by the euro)

franchise NOUN ❶ the right to vote in elections ❷ a licence to sell a firm's goods or services in a certain area

frank ADJECTIVE honest and saying exactly what you think

frank VERB to mark a letter or parcel automatically in a machine to show that postage has been paid

frankincense NOUN a sweet-smelling gum burnt as incense

frantic ADJECTIVE ❶ wildly anxious or frightened ❷ done in a hurried and urgent way

fraternal (say fra-**tern**-al) ADJECTIVE to do with brothers; brotherly

fraternity NOUN ❶ a brotherly feeling ❷ a group of people who have the same interests or occupation

fraud NOUN ❶ the crime of getting money by tricking people ❷ a dishonest trick ❸ a person who is not what they pretend to be

fraudulent (say **fraw**-dew-lent) ADJECTIVE involving fraud; deceitful or dishonest

fraught ADJECTIVE ❶ filled with problems or difficulties ❷ tense or upset

fray VERB ❶ material frays or becomes frayed when some of the threads become loose and start to come apart ❷ a person's temper or nerves fray when they become strained or upset

fray NOUN a fight or conflict

freak NOUN ❶ a very strange or abnormal person, animal or thing ❷ a person with a very strong interest in something

freckle NOUN a small brown spot on the skin

free ADJECTIVE ❶ able to do what you want to do or go where you want to go ❷ not costing anything ❸ not fixed or not having or being affected by something ❹ available; not being used or occupied ❺ not already having things to do ❻ generous

free VERB to set someone or something free

freedom NOUN ❶ the right to do or say what you like ❷ being free; not being a prisoner

freehand ADJECTIVE & ADVERB a freehand drawing is done without a ruler or compasses or without tracing it

freely ADVERB ❶ without being controlled or limited ❷ without anything stopping the movement or flow of something

free-range ADJECTIVE ① free-range hens are not kept in small cages but are allowed to move about freely ② free-range eggs are ones laid by these hens

free verse NOUN poetry that does not rhyme or have a regular rhythm

freeway NOUN (North American) a dual-carriageway main road

freewheel VERB to ride a bicycle without pedalling

freeze VERB freezes, freezing, froze, frozen ① to turn into ice or to become covered with ice ② to feel very cold ③ to keep food to store it at a low temperature to preserve it ④ to suddenly stand completely still ⑤ to keep wages or prices at a fixed level

freeze NOUN ① a period of freezing weather ② the freezing of wages or prices

freezer NOUN a refrigerator in which food can be frozen quickly and stored

freezing ADJECTIVE very cold

freezing point NOUN the temperature at which a liquid freezes

freight (say frayt) NOUN goods carried by road or in a ship or aircraft

freighter (say fray-ter) NOUN a ship or aircraft used for carrying goods

French window NOUN a long window that serves as a door on an outside wall

frenzy NOUN wild and uncontrolled

excitement or anger

frequency NOUN ① being frequent; happening often ② how often something happens ③ the number of vibrations made each second by a wave of sound, radio or light

frequent (say freek-went) ADJECTIVE happening often

frequent (say frik-went) VERB to visit a place or be seen there, often

frequently ADVERB often

fresco NOUN a picture painted on a wall or ceiling before the plaster is dry

fresh ADJECTIVE ① newly made or produced or arrived; not stale ② not tinned or preserved ③ fresh air is cool and refreshing ④ fresh water is not salty ⑤ full of energy and not tired

freshen VERB ① to make something fresh ② to become fresh

freshwater ADJECTIVE living in rivers or lakes, not the sea

fret VERB to worry or be upset about something

fret NOUN a bar or ridge on the fingerboard of a guitar etc.

friar NOUN a man who is a member of a Roman Catholic religious order and has vowed to live a life of poverty

friary NOUN a building where friars live

friction NOUN ① the rubbing of one thing against another ② (in science) the resistance that one surface or object meets when it moves over another ③ bad feeling between people; quarrelling

Friday NOUN the day of the week

following Thursday

fridge NOUN (British) a refrigerator

friend NOUN ❶ a person you like and who likes you ❷ a person you send messages to on a social networking site ❸ a helpful or kind person

friendly ADJECTIVE ❶ behaving like a friend; kind and pleasant ❷ helpful and easy to use; not harmful

friendly NOUN (British) a sports match that is not part of a formal competition

friendship NOUN friendly feelings between people; being friends

frieze (say freez) NOUN a strip of designs or pictures round the top of a wall or building

frigate NOUN a small warship

fright NOUN ❶ sudden great fear ❷ (informal) a person or thing that looks ridiculous

frighten VERB to make someone afraid

frightful ADJECTIVE (British) awful; very great or bad

frigid ADJECTIVE ❶ extremely cold ❷ unfriendly; not affectionate

frill NOUN ❶ a decorative gathered or pleated trimming on a dress, shirt, curtain, etc. ❷ something extra that is pleasant but unnecessary

fringe NOUN ❶ a decorative edging with many threads hanging down loosely ❷ a straight line of hair hanging down over your forehead ❸ the edge of something

fringe VERB ➤ be fringed with something to have something as a border or around the edge

frisk VERB ❶ to jump or run about playfully ❷ to search someone by running your hands over his or her clothes

frisky ADJECTIVE playful or lively

fritter NOUN a slice of meat, potato or fruit coated in batter and fried

fritter VERB if you fritter away your time or money, you waste it on trivial things

frivolous ADJECTIVE without a serious purpose; light-hearted when you should be serious

frizzy ADJECTIVE frizzy hair is in tight stiff curls

fro ADVERB ➤ to and fro backwards and forwards

frock NOUN (British) a girl's or woman's dress

frog NOUN a small jumping animal that can live both in water and on land

frogman NOUN a swimmer equipped with a rubber suit, flippers and breathing apparatus for swimming and working underwater

frolic NOUN a lively cheerful game or entertainment

frolic VERB to play about in a lively cheerful way

from PREPOSITION This word is used to show ❶ a starting point in space or time or order (We flew from London to Paris. We work from 9 to 5 o'clock. Count from one to ten.) ❷ distance (We are a mile from home.) ❸ source or origin (Get water from the tap.) ❹ separation or release (Take the gun from him. She was freed from *prison.*) ❺ difference (*How do you tell one twin from the other?*) ❻ cause (*We were all suffering from exhaustion.*)

frond NOUN ❶ a leaf-like part of a fern, palm tree, etc.

front NOUN ❶ the part or side that comes first or is the most important or furthest forward ❷ a road or promenade along the seashore ❸ the place where fighting is happening in a war ❹ in weather systems, the forward edge of an approaching mass of air

front ADJECTIVE of the front; in front

frontage NOUN the front of a building; the land beside this

frontier NOUN the boundary between two countries or regions

frontispiece NOUN an illustration opposite the title page of a book

frost NOUN ❶ powdery ice that forms on things in freezing weather ❷ weather with a temperature below freezing point

frost VERB ➤ **frost up** or **over** to become covered with frost

frostbite NOUN harm done to the body by very cold weather

frosted glass NOUN glass made cloudy so that you cannot see clearly through it

frosting NOUN sugar icing for cakes

frosty ADJECTIVE ❶ so cold that there is frost ❷ unfriendly and unwelcoming

froth NOUN a white mass of tiny bubbles on a liquid

froth VERB to form a froth

frown VERB to wrinkle your forehead because you are angry

or worried

frown NOUN a frowning movement or look

frozen ADJECTIVE ❶ frozen food is stored at a low temperature in order to preserve it ❷ very cold ❸ with a layer of ice on the surface

frugal (say froo-gal) ADJECTIVE ❶ spending very little money ❷ small and meagre; costing very little money

fruit NOUN ❶ the seed container that grows on a tree or plant and is often used as food ❷ the result of doing something

fruit VERB a tree or plant fruits when it produces fruit

fruitful ADJECTIVE producing good results

fruition (say froo-ish-on) NOUN the achievement of what was hoped or worked for

fruitless ADJECTIVE producing no results

fruit machine NOUN (*British*) a gambling machine worked by putting a coin in a slot

frustrate VERB ❶ to make someone annoyed and upset because they are prevented from doing something ❷ to prevent something from being successful

frustrating ADJECTIVE making you annoyed or upset because you cannot do what you want

frustration NOUN a feeling of annoyance when you have been prevented from doing something

fry VERB to cook food in very hot fat

fry PLURAL NOUN very young fishes

frying pan NOUN a shallow pan for frying things

fuchsia (say few-sha) NOUN an ornamental plant with flowers that hang down

fudge NOUN a soft sugary sweet

fudge VERB to avoid giving clear and accurate information or a clear answer

fuel NOUN something that is burnt to produce heat or power

fuel VERB ❶ to supply something with fuel ❷ to strengthen a feeling or belief

fugitive (say few-jit-iv) NOUN a person who is running away from something, especially from the police

fugue (say fewg) NOUN a piece of music in which tunes are repeated in a complicated pattern

fulcrum NOUN the point on which something balances or turns

fulfil VERB ❶ to do what is required; to carry something out ❷ to make something come true ❸ to give you a feeling of satisfaction

fulfilment NOUN the feeling of satisfaction you have when you have achieved something

full ADJECTIVE ❶ containing as much or as many as possible ❷ having many people or things ❸ complete ❹ the greatest possible ❺ fitting loosely; with many folds

full ADVERB completely and directly

full-blown ADJECTIVE fully developed

full moon NOUN the moon when you can see the whole of it as a bright disc

full stop NOUN (*British*) the dot (.) used as a punctuation mark at the end of a sentence or an abbreviation or after an initial

full-time ADJECTIVE & ADVERB for all the normal working hours of the day

fully ADVERB completely

fully-fledged ADJECTIVE fully trained or developed

fumble VERB to handle or feel for something something clumsily

fume VERB ❶ to give off fumes ❷ to be very angry

fumes PLURAL NOUN strong-smelling smoke or gas

fun NOUN amusement or enjoyment

function NOUN ❶ what someone or something is there to do ❷ an important event or party ❸ a basic operation in a computer or calculator ❹ (*in mathematics*) a variable quantity whose value depends on the value of other variable quantities

function VERB to perform a function; to work properly

functional ADJECTIVE ❶ working properly ❷ practical and useful without being decorative or luxurious

fund NOUN ❶ an amount of money collected or kept for a special purpose ❷ a stock or supply

fund VERB to supply someone or something with money

fundamental ADJECTIVE basic; involving the central and most important part of something

funeral NOUN the ceremony when a dead person is buried or cremated

funereal (say few-*neer*-ee-al) ADJECTIVE gloomy or depressing

funfair NOUN (British) a fair consisting of amusements and sideshows

fungus NOUN fungi (say *fung*-eye) a plant without leaves or flowers that grows on other plants or on decayed material, such as mushrooms and toadstools

funk VERB (British) (old-fashioned use) to be afraid of doing something and avoid it

funk NOUN a style of popular music with a strong rhythm, based on jazz and blues

funnel NOUN ❶ a metal chimney on a ship or steam engine ❷ a tube that is wide at the top and narrow at the bottom to help you pour things into a narrow opening

funny ADJECTIVE ❶ that makes you laugh or smile ❷ strange or odd

funny bone NOUN part of your elbow which produces a tingling feeling if you knock it

fur NOUN ❶ the soft hair that covers some animals ❷ animal skin with the fur on it, used for clothing ❸ fabric that looks like animal fur

furious ADJECTIVE ❶ very angry ❷ violent or intense

furl VERB to roll up a sail, flag or umbrella

furlong NOUN one-eighth of a mile, 220 yards (201 metres)

furnace NOUN a type of large oven that produces great heat for making glass or melting metals

furnish VERB ❶ to put furniture in a room or building ❷ to provide someone with something

furnishings PLURAL NOUN furniture, curtains and fittings for a room or house

furniture NOUN tables, chairs and other movable things that you need in a house, school or office

furrow NOUN ❶ a long cut in the ground made by a plough ❷ a deep wrinkle in the skin

furrow VERB to make furrows in something

furry ADJECTIVE like fur; covered with fur

further ADVERB & ADJECTIVE ❶ at or to a greater distance; more distant ❷ more; additional

further VERB to help something to progress

further education NOUN (British) education for people above school age

furthermore ADVERB also; moreover

furthest ADVERB & ADJECTIVE at or to the greatest distance; most distant

furtive ADJECTIVE stealthy; trying not to be seen

fury NOUN wild anger; rage

fuse NOUN ❶ a safety device containing a short piece of wire that melts if too much electricity is passed through it ❷ a length of material that burns easily, used for setting off an explosive

fuse VERB ❶ an electrical device fuses when it stops working because a fuse has melted ❷ to fuse things is to blend them together, especially through melting

fuselage (say **few**-zel-ahzh) NOUN the main body of an aircraft

fusion NOUN ❶ the action of blending or uniting things ❷ the uniting of atomic nuclei, usually releasing energy

fuss NOUN ❶ unnecessary excitement or worry about something ❷ angry complaints about something

fuss VERB to be too anxious about something that is not important

fussy ADJECTIVE ❶ worrying too much about something that is not important ❷ choosing very carefully; hard to please ❸ full of unnecessary details or decorations

futile (say **few**-tyl) ADJECTIVE useless or pointless; having no chance of success

futon (say **foo**-ton) NOUN a seat with a mattress that rolls out to form a bed

future NOUN ❶ the time that will come ❷ what is going to happen to someone or something in the time to come ❸ (in grammar) the use of verbs and phrases such as 'will', 'shall', 'be going to', or 'be about to' to talk about something happening in the future

future ADJECTIVE belonging or referring to the future

futuristic ADJECTIVE very modern, as if belonging to the future rather than the present

fuzz NOUN something soft and fluffy like soft hair

fuzzy ADJECTIVE ❶ a fuzzy picture

or image is blurred and not clear ❷ covered with short soft hair or fur

Gg

gabble VERB to talk so quickly that it is difficult to hear the words

gable NOUN the pointed triangular part at the top of an outside wall, between two sloping roofs

gadget NOUN any small useful tool or device

Gaelic (say **gay**-lik) NOUN the Celtic languages of Scotland and Ireland

gag NOUN ❶ something put into a person's mouth or tied over it to prevent them speaking ❷ a joke

gag VERB ❶ to put a gag on a person ❷ to prevent someone from making comments ❸ to retch

gaggle NOUN ❶ a flock of geese ❷ a group of noisy people

gaiety NOUN being cheerful and having fun

gaily ADVERB in a cheerful way

gain VERB ❶ to get something that you did not have before ❷ a clock or watch gains when it shows a time later than the correct time ❸ (literary) to reach or arrive at a place

gain NOUN something that you gain; a profit or improvement

gait NOUN a way of walking or running

gaiter NOUN a leather or cloth covering for the lower part of the leg

gala (say **gah**-la) NOUN ❶ a festival

or celebration ❷ a set of sports contests, especially in swimming

galaxy NOUN a very large group of stars

gale NOUN a very strong wind

gall (say gawl) NOUN being bold or cheeky enough to do something

gall VERB to annoy or upset someone, especially because something is unfair

gallant (say **gal**-lant) ADJECTIVE ❶ brave or heroic ❷ courteous towards women

gall bladder NOUN an organ attached to the liver, in which bile is stored

galleon NOUN a large Spanish sailing ship used in the 16th and 17th centuries

gallery NOUN ❶ a room or building for showing works of art ❷ the highest balcony in a cinema or theatre ❸ a long room or passage ❹ a platform jutting out from the wall in a church or hall

galley NOUN ❶ an ancient type of ship driven by oars ❷ the kitchen in a ship or aircraft

galling (say **gawl**-ing) ADJECTIVE annoying and upsetting because of being unfair

gallon NOUN a unit used to measure liquids, 8 pints or 4.546 litres

gallop NOUN ❶ the fastest pace that a horse can go ❷ a fast ride on a horse

gallop VERB to go or ride at a gallop

gallows NOUN a framework with a noose for hanging criminals

galore ADVERB in great numbers; in a large amount

galoshes PLURAL NOUN a pair of waterproof shoes worn over ordinary shoes

galvanize (also **galvanise**) VERB ❶ to shock or stimulate someone into sudden activity ❷ to coat iron with zinc to protect it from rust

gambit NOUN ❶ a kind of opening move in chess ❷ an action or remark intended to gain an advantage

gamble VERB ❶ to bet on the result of a game, race or other event ❷ to take risks in the hope of gaining something

gamble NOUN ❶ a bet or chance ❷ something you do that is a risk

gambol VERB to jump or skip about in play

game NOUN ❶ something that you can play, usually with rules ❷ a section of a long game such as tennis or whist ❸ a scheme or plan; a trick ❹ wild animals or birds hunted for sport or food

game ADJECTIVE willing to do or try something

gamekeeper NOUN a person employed to protect game birds and animals, especially from poachers

games PLURAL NOUN ❶ a meeting for sporting contests ❷ athletics or sports as a subject taught at school

gaming NOUN ❶ gambling ❷ playing computer games

gamma NOUN the third letter of the Greek alphabet, equivalent to Roman G, g

gamma rays PLURAL NOUN very short X-rays emitted by radioactive substances

gammon NOUN (British) a kind of ham

gamut (say **gam**-ut) NOUN the whole range or scope of anything

gander NOUN a male goose

gang NOUN ① a group of people who do things together ② a group of young people who cause trouble and fight other groups ③ a group of criminals

gang VERB ▸ **gang up on someone** to form a group to fight or oppose someone

gangling ADJECTIVE tall, thin and awkward-looking

gangplank NOUN a plank placed so that people can walk on or off a boat

gangrene (say **gang**-green) NOUN decay of body tissue in a living person

gangster NOUN a member of a gang of violent criminals

gangway NOUN ① a gap left for people to pass between rows of seats, e.g. in a theatre or aircraft ② a movable bridge placed so that people can walk onto or off a ship

gannet NOUN a large seabird which catches fish by flying above the sea and then diving in

gaol (say jayl) NOUN (British) a different spelling of **jail**

gap NOUN ① a break or opening in something continuous such as a hedge or fence ② an interval or break ③ a wide difference in ideas

gape VERB ① to stare in amazement with your mouth open ② to be wide open

garage (say **ga**-rahzh or **ga**-rij) NOUN ① a building for keeping a motor vehicle or vehicles ② a place where petrol is sold and vehicles are repaired and serviced

garb NOUN special clothing

garbage NOUN (esp. North American) rubbish, especially household rubbish

garbled ADJECTIVE a garbled message or story is mixed up so that it is difficult to understand

garden NOUN a piece of ground where flowers, fruit or vegetables are grown

gargantuan (say gar-**gan**-tew-an) ADJECTIVE gigantic

gargle VERB to hold a liquid at the back of the mouth and push air through it to wash the inside of the throat

gargoyle NOUN an ugly or comical face or figure carved on a building, especially on a waterspout

garish (say **gair**-ish) ADJECTIVE too bright or highly coloured; gaudy

garland NOUN a wreath of flowers worn or hung as a decoration

garland VERB to decorate something with a garland

garlic NOUN a plant with a bulb divided into smaller bulbs (called cloves), which have a strong smell and taste and are used for flavouring food

garment NOUN a piece of clothing

garnet NOUN a dark red stone used as a gem

garnish VERB to decorate something, especially food

a b c d e f g h i j k l m n o p q r s t u v w x y z

garnish NOUN something used to decorate food or give it extra flavour

garret NOUN a dingy attic room

garrison NOUN ❶ troops who stay in a town or fort to defend it ❷ the building they live in

garter NOUN a band of elastic to hold up a sock or stocking

gas NOUN ❶ a substance, such as oxygen, that can move freely and is not liquid or solid at ordinary temperatures ❷ a gas that can be burned, used for lighting, heating or cooking ❸ (*North American*) (*informal*) short for gasoline

gas VERB ❶ to kill or injure someone with gas ❷ (*informal*) to chatter idly

gas chamber NOUN a room that can be filled with poisonous gas to kill people or animals

gaseous (say **gas**-ee-us) ADJECTIVE in the form of a gas

gash NOUN a long deep cut or wound

gash VERB to make a gash in something

gasket NOUN a flat ring or strip of soft material for sealing a joint between metal surfaces in machinery

gasoline NOUN (*North American*) petrol

gasometer (say gas-**om**-it-er) NOUN a large round tank in which gas is stored

gasp VERB ❶ to breathe in suddenly when you are shocked or surprised ❷ to struggle to breathe with your mouth open when you are tired or

ill ❸ to speak in a breathless way

gasp NOUN a sudden deep breath, especially one caused by shock or surprise

gassy ADJECTIVE fizzy

gastric ADJECTIVE to do with the stomach

gastronomy (say gas-**tron**-om-ee) NOUN the art or practice of good eating

gastropod NOUN an animal (e.g. a snail or slug) that moves by means of a fleshy 'foot' on its stomach

gate NOUN ❶ a movable barrier, usually on hinges, used as a door in a wall or fence ❷ a barrier for controlling the flow of water in a dam or lock ❸ a place where you wait before you board an aircraft ❹ the number of people attending a football match or other sports event

gateau (say **gat**-oh) NOUN a large rich cream cake

gatecrash VERB to go to a private party without being invited

gateway NOUN ❶ an opening containing a gate ❷ a way to reach something

gather VERB ❶ to come together ❷ to bring people or things together ❸ to collect something; to obtain something gradually ❹ to collect crops as harvest; to pick plants or fruit ❺ to understand or learn something ❻ to pull cloth into folds by running a thread through it

gathering NOUN an assembly or meeting of people; a party

gaudy ADJECTIVE very showy and

bright

gauge (say gayj) NOUN ❶ a measuring instrument ❷ a standard measurement ❸ the distance between the rails on a railway track

gauge VERB ❶ to measure something ❷ to estimate or form a judgement about something

gaunt ADJECTIVE lean and haggard

gauntlet NOUN a glove with a wide cuff covering the wrist

gauze NOUN ❶ thin transparent woven material ❷ fine wire mesh

gay ADJECTIVE ❶ homosexual ❷ cheerful ❸ brightly coloured

gaze VERB to look at something steadily for a long time

gaze NOUN a long steady look

gazelle NOUN a small antelope, usually fawn and white, from Africa or Asia

gazette NOUN ❶ a newspaper ❷ an official journal of an organization

gazetteer (say gaz-it-eer) NOUN a dictionary or list of place names

GCSE ABBREVIATION (British) General Certificate of Secondary Education

gear NOUN ❶ a set of toothed wheels in a motor vehicle that turn power from the engine into movement of the wheels ❷ equipment or apparatus ❸ (informal) clothing

gear VERB to gear one thing to another is to make it match or be suitable for the other thing

gearbox NOUN a set of gears in a casing

Geiger counter (say gy-ger) NOUN an instrument that detects and measures radioactivity

gel NOUN a jelly-like substance, especially one used to give a style to hair

gelatin, gelatine NOUN a clear jelly-like substance made by boiling animal tissue and used to make jellies and other foods and in photographic film

geld VERB to castrate a male animal

gelding NOUN a castrated horse or other male animal

gelignite (say jel-ig-nyt) NOUN a kind of explosive

gem NOUN ❶ a precious stone ❷ an excellent person or thing

gender NOUN ❶ the group in which a noun is classed in the grammar of some languages, e.g. masculine, feminine or neuter ❷ a person's sex

gene (say jeen) NOUN the part of a living cell that controls which characteristics (such as the colour of hair or eyes) are inherited from parents

genealogy (say jeen-ee-al-o-jee) NOUN ❶ a list or diagram showing how people are descended from an ancestor ❷ the study of family history and ancestors

genera (say jen-e-ra) PLURAL NOUN plural of **genus**

general ADJECTIVE ❶ to do with or involving most people or things ❷ not detailed; broad ❸ chief or head

general NOUN a senior army officer

general election NOUN an election of Members of Parliament for the whole country

255

generalize (also **generalise**) VERB to make a statement that is true in most cases

generally ADVERB ❶ by or to most people ❷ usually ❸ in a general sense; without regard to details

general practitioner NOUN a doctor who treats all kinds of diseases and is the first doctor that people see when they are ill

generate VERB to produce or create something

generation NOUN ❶ generating something ❷ a single stage in a family ❸ all the people born at about the same time

generator NOUN a machine for converting mechanical energy into electricity

generic (say jin-**e-rik**) ADJECTIVE belonging to a whole class, group or genus

generosity NOUN the quality of being generous

generous ADJECTIVE ❶ willing to give things or share them ❷ given freely; larger than usual

genesis NOUN the beginning or origin of something

genetic (say jin-**et-ik**) ADJECTIVE ❶ to do with genes ❷ to do with characteristics inherited from parents or ancestors

genetics NOUN the study of genes and genetic behaviour

genial (say **jee**-nee-al) ADJECTIVE friendly and cheerful

genie (say **jee**-nee) NOUN in Arabian tales, a spirit with strange powers, especially one who can grant wishes

genital (say **jen**-it-al) ADJECTIVE to do with the reproductive organs of a person or animal

genitals (say **jen**-it-alz) PLURAL NOUN external reproductive organs

genius NOUN ❶ an unusually clever person; a person with very great creativity or natural ability ❷ unusual cleverness; very great creativity or natural ability

genocide (say **jen**-o-syd) NOUN the deliberate killing of large numbers of people from a particular nation or ethnic group

genome (say **jee**-ohm) NOUN (in science) the complete set of genes in one cell of a living thing

genre (say **zhahnr**) NOUN a particular kind or style of art or literature, e.g. epic, romance or western

gent NOUN (informal) a gentleman; a man

genteel (say jen-**teel**) ADJECTIVE trying to seem polite and refined

gentile NOUN a person who is not Jewish

gentle ADJECTIVE ❶ mild or kind; not rough ❷ not harsh or severe

gentleman NOUN ❶ a well-mannered or honourable man ❷ a man of good social position ❸ (in polite use) a man

gently ADVERB in a gentle way

gentry PLURAL NOUN (old use) upper-class people

genuine ADJECTIVE ❶ real; not faked or pretending ❷ sincere and honest

genus (say **jee**-nus) NOUN genera (say **jen**-e-ra) a group of similar animals or plants

geo- PREFIX earth

geographical ADJECTIVE to do with geography or where something is

geography (say jee-**og**-ra-fee) NOUN the study of the earth's surface and of its climate, peoples and products

geology (say jee-**ol**-o-jee) NOUN the study of the structure of the earth's crust and its layers

geometric, geometrical ADJECTIVE consisting of regular shapes and lines

geometry (say jee-**om**-it-ree) NOUN the study of lines, angles, surfaces and solids in mathematics

Georgian ADJECTIVE belonging to the time of the British kings George I–IV (1714–1830) or George V–VI (1910–52)

geranium NOUN a garden plant with red, pink or white flowers

gerbil (say **jer**-bil) NOUN a small brown rodent with long hind legs, often kept as a pet

geriatric (say jee-ree-**at**-rik) ADJECTIVE to do with the care of old people and their health

germ NOUN ❶ a micro-organism, especially one that can cause disease ❷ a tiny living structure from which a plant or animal may develop ❸ part of the seed of a cereal plant ❹ a first stage from which something might develop

Germanic NOUN ❶ a group of languages spoken in northern Europe and Scandinavia ❷ an unrecorded language believed to be the ancestor of this group

German measles NOUN rubella

German shepherd dog NOUN a large strong dog, often used by the police

germicide NOUN a substance that kills germs

germinate VERB when a seed germinates, it begins to develop and roots and shoots grow from it

gerund (say **je**-rund) NOUN (in grammar) a form of a verb (in English ending in -ing) that functions as a noun, e.g. telling in do you mind my telling her?

gestation (say jes-**tay**-shun) NOUN the process of carrying a foetus in the womb between conception and birth; the time this takes

gesticulate (say jes-**tik**-yoo-layt) VERB to make movements with your hands and arms in order to express something

gesture (say **jes**-cher) NOUN ❶ a movement that expresses what a person feels ❷ an action that shows goodwill

gesture VERB to tell a person something by making a gesture

get VERB gets, getting, got ❶ to obtain or receive something ❷ to become ❸ to reach a place ❹ to put or move something into position ❺ to make or prepare something ❻ to persuade or order someone to do something ❼ to catch or suffer from an illness ❽ (informal) to understand something

getaway NOUN an escape after committing a crime

geyser (say **gee**-zer or **gy**-zer) NOUN

❶ a natural spring that shoots up columns of hot water ❷ a kind of water heater

ghastly ADJECTIVE ❶ very unpleasant or bad ❷ looking pale and ill

gherkin (say **ger**-kin) NOUN a small cucumber used for pickling

ghetto (say **get**-oh) NOUN an area of a city, often a slum area, where a group of people live who are treated unfairly in comparison with others

ghost NOUN the spirit of a dead person that a living person believes they can see or hear

ghostly ADJECTIVE looking or sounding like a ghost

ghoulish (say **gool**-ish) ADJECTIVE enjoying watching ot thinking about things to do with death, murder and suffering

giant NOUN ❶ (in myths or fairy tales) a creature like a huge man ❷ a man, animal or plant that is much larger than the usual size

giant ADJECTIVE much larger than the usual size

gibberish (say **jib**-er-ish) NOUN meaningless speech; nonsense

gibbet (say **jib**-it) NOUN ❶ a gallows ❷ an upright post with an arm from which a criminal's body was hung after execution, as a warning to others

gibbon NOUN a small ape from south-east Asia. Gibbons have very long arms to help them swing through the trees where they live

giblets (say **jib**-lits) PLURAL NOUN the parts of the inside of a bird, such as

the heart, liver, etc., that are taken out before it is cooked

giddy ADJECTIVE ❶ feeling that everything is spinning round and that you might fall ❷ causing this feeling

gift NOUN ❶ a present ❷ a natural talent

gifted ADJECTIVE having a special talent or ability

gig NOUN (informal) a live performance by a musician, comedian, etc.

gigabyte (say **gi**-ga-byt) NOUN (in computing) a unit of information equal to one thousand million bytes or (more precisely) 2^{30} bytes

gigantic (say jy-**gan**-tik) ADJECTIVE extremely large; huge

giggle VERB to laugh in a silly way

giggle NOUN ❶ a silly laugh ❷ (informal) something amusing; a bit of fun

gild VERB gilds, gilding, gilded to cover something with a thin layer of gold or gold paint

gills PLURAL NOUN the part of the body through which fish and certain other water animals breathe

gilt NOUN a thin covering of gold or gold paint

gilt ADJECTIVE gilded; gold-coloured

gimmick NOUN something unusual or silly done or used just to attract people's attention

gin NOUN ❶ a clear alcoholic drink flavoured with juniper berries ❷ a machine for separating the fibres of the cotton plant from its seeds

ginger NOUN ❶ the hot-tasting

root of a tropical plant or a flavouring made from this root, used especially in drinks and Eastern cooking ❷ a reddish-yellow colour

ginger ADJECTIVE reddish-yellow

ginger VERB to make something more lively or exciting

gingerbread NOUN a ginger-flavoured cake or biscuit

gingerly ADVERB in a cautious or careful way

gipsy NOUN a different spelling of **gypsy**

giraffe NOUN an African animal with long legs and a very long neck, the world's tallest mammal

girder NOUN a metal beam supporting part of a building or a bridge

girdle NOUN ❶ a belt or cord worn round the waist ❷ a woman's elastic corset covering from the waist to the thigh

girl NOUN ❶ a female child ❷ a young woman

girlfriend NOUN a person's regular female friend or lover

girlhood NOUN the time when a woman was a girl

girlish ADJECTIVE like a girl or suitable for a girl

giro (say **jy**-roh) NOUN a system of sending money directly from one bank account or post office account to another

girth NOUN ❶ the measurement round something, especially a person's waist ❷ a band passing under a horse's body to hold the saddle in place

gist (say jist) NOUN the essential points or general sense of what someone says

give VERB gives, giving, gave, given ❶ to let someone have something ❷ to make or do something ❸ to present or perform something ❹ be flexible or springy; to bend or collapse when pressed

given ADJECTIVE named or stated in advance

glacé (say **glas**-ay) ADJECTIVE iced with sugar; crystallized

glacial (say **glay**-shal) ADJECTIVE ❶ made of ice or formed by glaciers ❷ icy or very cold

glaciation (say glay-see-**ay**-shun) NOUN the process or state of being covered with glaciers or ice sheets

glacier (say **glas**-ee-er) NOUN a mass of ice that moves very slowly down a mountain valley

glad ADJECTIVE ❶ pleased or happy; expressing joy ❷ giving pleasure or happiness ❸ to be glad of something is to be grateful for it or pleased with it

gladden VERB to make a person glad

glade NOUN an open space in a forest

gladiator (say **glad**-ee-ay-ter) NOUN a man trained to fight for public entertainment in ancient Rome

gladly ADVERB with pleasure or willingly

glamorous ADJECTIVE excitingly attractive

glamour NOUN exciting attractiveness or romantic charm

glance VERB ❶ to look at something briefly ❷ to strike something at an angle and slide off it

glance NOUN a quick look

gland NOUN an organ of the body that separates substances from the blood so that they can be used or passed out of the body

glare VERB ❶ to stare angrily or fiercely at someone ❷ to shine with a bright or dazzling light

glare NOUN ❶ an angry stare ❷ a strong light

glaring ADJECTIVE very obvious

glass NOUN ❶ a hard brittle substance that is usually transparent ❷ a container made of glass for drinking from ❸ (*old use*) a mirror

glasses PLURAL NOUN a pair of lenses in a frame, worn over the eyes to help improve eyesight

glaze VERB ❶ to fit a window or building with glass ❷ to give a shiny surface to pottery or food ❸ your eyes glaze when they lose expression or interest

glaze NOUN a shiny surface or coating, especially on pottery or food

glazier (say **glay-zee-er**) NOUN a person whose job is to fit glass in windows

gleam NOUN ❶ a beam of soft light, especially one that comes and goes ❷ a small amount of hope, humour, etc.

gleam VERB ❶ to shine brightly, especially after cleaning or polishing

glean VERB ❶ to gather information bit by bit ❷ to pick up grain left by harvesters

glee NOUN great delight

glen NOUN a narrow valley, especially in Scotland

glib ADJECTIVE speaking or writing fluently but not sincerely or thoughtfully

glide VERB ❶ to move along smoothly ❷ to fly without using an engine ❸ birds glide when they fly without beating their wings

glider NOUN an aircraft without an engine that flies by floating on warm air currents called thermals

glimmer NOUN ❶ a faint light that flickers ❷ a small sign or trace of something

glimmer VERB to shine with a faint, flickering light

glimpse NOUN a brief view of something

glimpse VERB to see something briefly

glint NOUN a very brief flash of light

glint VERB to shine with small flashes of light

glisten (say **glis-en**) VERB to shine like something wet or oily

glitter VERB to shine with tiny flashes of light; to sparkle

glitter NOUN tiny sparkling pieces used for decoration

gloat VERB to be pleased in an unkind way that you have succeeded or that someone else has failed or had problems

global ADJECTIVE ❶ to do with the whole world; worldwide ❷ to do with the whole of a system

globalization (also **globalisation**) NOUN the fact

that different economies and cultures around the world are becoming connected and similar to each other because of improved communication and the influence of very large companies

global warming NOUN the increase in the temperature of the earth's atmosphere, caused by the greenhouse effect

globe NOUN ❶ something shaped like a ball, especially one with a map of the whole world on it ❷ the world ❸ a hollow round glass object

gloom NOUN ❶ darkness ❷ sadness or despair

gloomy ADJECTIVE ❶ almost dark; not well lit ❷ depressed or depressing

glorify VERB ❶ to give great praise or great honour to someone ❷ to make a thing seem more splendid or attractive than it really is

glorious ADJECTIVE splendid or magnificent

glory NOUN ❶ fame and honour you get for achieving something ❷ praise and worship of God ❸ beauty or magnificence

glory VERB to rejoice over an achievement and take great pride in it

gloss NOUN the shine on a smooth surface

gloss VERB ➤ **gloss over something** to mention a fault or mistake only briefly to make it seem less serious than it really is

glossary NOUN a list of difficult words with their meanings explained

gloss paint NOUN a paint with a glossy finish

glossy ADJECTIVE smooth and shiny

glove NOUN a covering for the hand, usually with separate divisions for each finger and thumb

glow NOUN ❶ brightness and warmth without flames ❷ a warm or cheerful feeling

glow VERB to shine with a soft, warm light

glower (rhymes with *flower*) VERB to stare with an angry look; to scowl

glowing ADJECTIVE very enthusiastic or favourable

glow-worm NOUN a kind of beetle whose tail gives out a green light

glucose NOUN a form of sugar found in fruit juice and honey

glue NOUN a sticky substance used for joining things together

glue VERB ❶ to stick something with glue ❷ to be glued to something is to pay close attention to it for a long period

glum ADJECTIVE miserable or depressed

glut NOUN more of something than is needed

gluten (say gloo-ten) NOUN a sticky protein substance in flour

glutinous (say gloo-tin-us) ADJECTIVE glue-like or sticky

glutton NOUN a person who eats too much

gluttony NOUN eating too much

glycerine (say glis-er-een) NOUN a thick sweet colourless liquid used in ointments and medicines and in

a b c d e f g h i j k l m n o p q r s t u v w x y z

explosives

gm *ABBREVIATION* gram

GMT *ABBREVIATION* Greenwich Mean Time

gnarled (say narld) *ADJECTIVE* twisted and knobbly, like an old tree

gnash (say nash) *VERB* to grind your teeth together, especially because you are angry

gnat (say nat) *NOUN* a tiny fly that bites

gnaw (say naw) *VERB* to keep on biting something hard so that it wears away

gnome (say nohm) *NOUN* a kind of dwarf in fairy tales, usually living underground

gnu (say noo) *NOUN* a large ox-like antelope

go *VERB* goes, going, went, gone This word has many uses, including ❶ to move or travel from one place to another ❷ to leave ❸ to disappear or be used up ❹ to lead from one place to another ❺ to become ❻ to make a sound ❼ to work properly ❽ to belong in some place or position ❾ to be sold

go *NOUN* ❶ a turn or try ❷ (*informal*) energy or liveliness

goad *NOUN* a stick with a pointed end for prodding cattle to move onwards

goad *VERB* to stir someone into action by being annoying

go-ahead *NOUN* permission to do something

goal *NOUN* ❶ the area between two posts where a ball must go to score a point in football, hockey, etc. ❷ a

successful shot at goal, scoring a point ❸ something that you are trying to reach or achieve

goalkeeper *NOUN* the player in football or hockey who stands in the goal and tries to keep the ball out

goat *NOUN* a mammal with horns and a beard, closely related to the sheep. Domestic goats are kept for their milk.

gobble *VERB* to eat something quickly and greedily

gobbledegook *NOUN* (*informal*) pompous and technical language that is difficult to understand, especially in official documents

go-between *NOUN* a person who acts as a messenger or negotiator between others

goblet *NOUN* a drinking glass with a long stem and a base

goblin *NOUN* a mischievous ugly elf in stories

God *NOUN* the creator of the universe in many religions

god *NOUN* a male being that is worshipped

godchild *NOUN* a child that a godparent promises to see brought up as a Christian

goddess *NOUN* a female being that is worshipped

godly *ADJECTIVE* sincerely religious

godparent *NOUN* a person at a child's christening who promises to see that it is brought up as a Christian

godsend *NOUN* a piece of unexpected good luck

goggle VERB to stare with wide-open eyes

goggles PLURAL NOUN large glasses that you wear to protect your eyes from wind, water, dust, etc.

going present participle of go ➤ be **going to do something** to be ready or likely to do it

going NOUN ➤ **good going** quick progress

go-kart NOUN a kind of small lightweight racing car

gold NOUN ❶ a precious yellow metal ❷ a deep yellow colour ❸ a **gold medal**, awarded as first prize

gold ADJECTIVE ❶ made of gold ❷ deep yellow in colour

golden ADJECTIVE ❶ made of gold ❷ coloured like gold ❸ precious or excellent

golden wedding NOUN a couple's fiftieth wedding anniversary

goldfinch NOUN a bird with yellow feathers in its wings

goldfish NOUN a small red or orange fish, often kept as a pet

gold leaf NOUN gold that has been beaten into a very thin sheet

goldsmith NOUN a person who makes things in gold

golf NOUN an outdoor game played by hitting a small white ball with a club into a series of holes on a specially prepared ground (a **golf course**) and taking as few strokes as possible

golfer NOUN a person who plays golf

gondola (say gond-ol-a) NOUN a boat with high pointed ends used on the canals in Venice

gondolier NOUN the person who moves a gondola along with a pole

gone past participle of **go**

gone ADJECTIVE not present any longer; completely used or finished

gong NOUN a large metal disc that makes an echoing sound when it is hit

good ADJECTIVE better, best ❶ having the right qualities; of the kind that people like ❷ kind ❸ well-behaved ❹ skilled or talented ❺ healthy; giving benefit ❻ thorough ❼ large; considerable

good NOUN ❶ something good ❷ benefit or advantage

goodbye EXCLAMATION a word used when you leave someone or at the end of a phone call

Good Friday NOUN the Friday before Easter, when Christians commemorate the Crucifixion of Christ

good-looking ADJECTIVE attractive or handsome

goodness NOUN ❶ being good ❷ the good part of something

goods PLURAL NOUN ❶ things that are bought and sold ❷ things that are carried on trains or lorries

goodwill NOUN a kindly or helpful feeling towards another person

goody NOUN (informal) ❶ something good or attractive, especially to eat ❷ a good person, especially one of the heroes in a story

gooey ADJECTIVE sticky or slimy

goose NOUN geese a long-necked water bird with webbed feet, larger than a duck

a b c d e f g h i j k l m n o p q r s t u v w x y z

gooseberry NOUN ❶ a small green fruit that grows on a prickly bush ❷ (*informal*) an unwanted extra person when two people want to be alone together

goose pimples, **goosebumps** PLURAL NOUN skin that has turned rough with small bumps on it because a person is cold or afraid

gore VERB to wound a person or animal by piercing them with a horn or tusk

gore NOUN thickened blood from a cut or wound

gorge NOUN a narrow valley with steep sides

gorge VERB to eat something greedily; to stuff yourself with food

gorgeous ADJECTIVE very attractive or beautiful

gorilla NOUN a large powerful African ape, the largest of all the apes

gorse NOUN a prickly bush with small yellow flowers

gory ADJECTIVE ❶ involving a lot of violence and bloodshed ❷ covered with blood

gosh EXCLAMATION an exclamation of surprise

gosling NOUN a young goose

gospel NOUN ❶ the teachings of Jesus Christ ❷ something you can safely believe to be true

gospel music NOUN a style of black American religious singing

gossamer NOUN ❶ fine cobwebs made by small spiders ❷ any fine delicate material

gossip VERB to talk a lot about other people

gossip NOUN ❶ talk, especially rumours, about other people ❷ a person who enjoys gossiping

got past tense of **get**

Gothic NOUN the style of building common in the 12th-16th centuries, with pointed arches and much decorative carving

gouge (say gowj) VERB to scoop or force something out by pressing

goulash (say goo-lash) NOUN a Hungarian meat stew seasoned with paprika

gourd (say goord) NOUN the rounded hard-skinned fruit of a climbing plant

gourmet (say goor-may) NOUN a person who knows about and enjoys good food and drink

gout NOUN a disease that causes painful swelling in the legs and feet

govern VERB to be in charge of the public affairs of a country or region

governess NOUN a woman employed to teach children in a private household

government NOUN ❶ the group of people who are in charge of the public affairs of a country ❷ the process of governing

governor NOUN ❶ a person who governs a state or a colony etc. ❷ a member of the group of people who manage a school or other institution ❸ the person in charge of a prison

gown NOUN ❶ a woman's long dress ❷ a loose robe worn by lawyers, members of a university, etc.

GP *ABBREVIATION* general practitioner (a doctor who treats all kinds of diseases and who is the first doctor that people see when they are ill)

grab *VERB* to take hold of something firmly or suddenly

grace *NOUN* ① beauty, especially of movement ② dignity or good manners ③ extra time that is allowed for something ④ a short prayer of thanks before or after a meal ⑤ the title of a duke, duchess or archbishop

grace *VERB* to bring honour or dignity to something

graceful *ADJECTIVE* beautiful and elegant in movement or shape

gracious *ADJECTIVE* generous and pleasant

grade *NOUN* ① a mark showing the quality of a student's work ② a step in a scale of quality or value or rank

grade *VERB* to sort or divide things into grades

gradient (say gray-dee-ent) *NOUN* a slope or the steepness of a slope

gradual *ADJECTIVE* happening slowly but steadily

gradually *ADVERB* slowly but steadily; bit by bit

graduate (say grad-yoo-ayt) *VERB* ① to get a university or college degree ② to divide something into graded sections; to mark something with units of measurement

graduate (say grad-yoo-at) *NOUN* a person who has a university or college degree

graduation *NOUN* graduating from a university or college; a ceremony at which degrees are given out

graffiti *NOUN* words or drawings scribbled or sprayed on a wall

graft *NOUN* ① a shoot from one plant or tree fixed into another to form a new growth ② a piece of living tissue transplanted by a surgeon to replace what is diseased or damaged ③ (*British*) (*informal*) hard work

graft *VERB* to insert or transplant something as a graft

grain *NOUN* ① a small hard seed or similar particle ② cereal plants when they are growing or after being harvested ③ a very small amount ④ the pattern of lines made by the fibres in a piece of wood or paper

grainy *ADJECTIVE* ① a grainy photograph or film is not clear because the image looks like it is made up of small spots ② with grains in it

gram *NOUN* a unit of mass or weight in the metric system

grammar *NOUN* ① the rules for putting words together to form sentences ② a book about these rules

grammar school *NOUN* a secondary school for children with high academic ability

grammatical *ADJECTIVE* following the rules of grammar

gramophone *NOUN* (*old use*) a record player

granary *NOUN* a storehouse for grain

a b c d e f g h i j k l m n o p q r s t u v w x y z

grand ADJECTIVE ❶ large and impressive ❷ most important or highest-ranking ❸ (informal) very good or pleasant

grandad NOUN (informal) grandfather

grandchild NOUN the child of a person's son or daughter

grandeur (say grand-yer) NOUN impressive beauty; splendour

grandfather NOUN the father of a person's father or mother

grandfather clock NOUN a clock in a tall wooden case

grandma NOUN (informal) grandmother

grandmother NOUN the mother of a person's father or mother

grandpa NOUN (informal) grandfather

grandparent NOUN a grandfather or grandmother

grand piano NOUN a large piano with the strings fixed horizontally

grandstand NOUN a building with a roof and rows of seats for spectators at a racecourse or sports ground

grand total NOUN the sum of other totals

grange NOUN a large country house

granite NOUN a very hard kind of rock used for building

granny NOUN (informal) grandmother

grant VERB ❶ to give or allow someone what they have asked for ❷ to admit something or agree that it is true

grant NOUN a sum of money awarded for a special purpose

Granth (say grunt) NOUN the sacred scriptures of the Sikhs

granulated sugar NOUN white sugar in the form of small grains

granule NOUN a small grain; a small hard piece of something

grape NOUN a small green or purple berry that grows in bunches on a vine. Grapes are used to make wine

grapefruit NOUN a large round yellow citrus fruit

grapevine NOUN ❶ a vine on which grapes grow ❷ a way by which news spreads unofficially, with people passing it on from one to another

graph NOUN a diagram showing how two quantities or variables are related

grapheme NOUN a letter or combination of letters which can be used to represent a sound, for example f and ph to represent the same sound at the beginning of the words face and phase

graphic ADJECTIVE ❶ to do with drawing or painting ❷ very detailed and lively

graphics PLURAL NOUN diagrams, lettering and drawings, especially pictures that are produced by a computer

graphite NOUN a soft black form of carbon used for the lead in pencils, as a lubricant and in nuclear reactors

grapple VERB ❶ to struggle or wrestle with someone ❷ to seize or hold something firmly ❸ to try to deal with a problem

grasp VERB ❶ to seize something and hold it firmly ❷ to understand something

grasp NOUN ❶ a person's understanding of something ❷ a firm hold

grasping ADJECTIVE greedy for money or possessions

grass NOUN ❶ a plant with green blades and stalks that are eaten by animals ❷ ground covered with grass; lawn

grasshopper NOUN a jumping insect that makes a shrill noise

grassland NOUN a wide area covered in grass with few trees

grass roots PLURAL NOUN the ordinary people in a political party or other group

grate NOUN ❶ a metal framework that keeps fuel in a fireplace ❷ a fireplace

grate VERB ❶ to shred something into small pieces by rubbing it on a rough surface ❷ to make a harsh sound by rubbing on something

grateful ADJECTIVE feeling or showing that you want to thank someone for what they have done for you

grater NOUN a device with a jagged surface for grating food

gratify VERB ❶ to give pleasure to someone ❷ to satisfy a feeling or desire

grating NOUN a framework of metal bars placed across an opening

gratis (say grah-tiss) ADVERB & ADJECTIVE free of charge

gratitude NOUN a feeling of being

grateful

grave NOUN the place where a dead person is buried

grave ADJECTIVE serious or solemn

grave accent (rhymes with starve) NOUN a backward-sloping mark over a vowel, as in vis-à-vis

gravel NOUN small stones mixed with coarse sand, used to make paths

gravelly ADJECTIVE ❶ a gravelly voice is deep and rough-sounding ❷ containing many small stones

gravely ADVERB seriously or solemnly

gravestone NOUN a stone monument put over a grave

graveyard NOUN a burial ground

gravitate VERB to move or be attracted towards something

gravitation NOUN the force of gravity

gravity NOUN ❶ the force that pulls all objects in the universe towards each other ❷ the force that pulls everything towards the earth ❸ the seriousness or importance of something

gravy NOUN a hot brown sauce made from meat juices

graze VERB ❶ animals graze when they feed on growing grass ❷ to scrape your skin slightly ❸ to touch something lightly in passing

graze NOUN a raw place where skin has been scraped

grease NOUN ❶ any thick oily substance ❷ melted fat

grease VERB to put grease on something

greasy ADJECTIVE oily like grease

great ADJECTIVE ❶ very large; much above average ❷ very important or talented ❸ (*informal*) very good or enjoyable ❹ older or younger by one generation

Great Britain NOUN the island made up of England, Scotland and Wales, with the small islands close to it

greatly ADVERB very much

grebe (say greeb) NOUN a kind of diving bird

greed NOUN being greedy

greedy ADJECTIVE wanting more food, money or other things than you need

green NOUN ❶ the colour of grass, leaves, etc. ❷ an area of grassy land

green ADJECTIVE ❶ of the colour green ❷ concerned with the natural environment ❸ inexperienced and likely to make mistakes

green belt NOUN an area kept as open land round a city

greenery NOUN green leaves or plants

greenfly NOUN a small green insect that feeds on and damages plants

greengrocer NOUN (*British*) a person who keeps a shop that sells fruit and vegetables

greenhouse NOUN a glass building where plants are protected from cold

greenhouse effect NOUN the warming up of the earth's surface when heat from the sun is trapped in the earth's atmosphere by gases such as carbon dioxide and methane

greenhouse gas NOUN any of the gases, especially carbon dioxide and methane, that are found in the earth's atmosphere and contribute to the greenhouse effect

greens PLURAL NOUN green vegetables, such as cabbage and spinach

Greenwich Mean Time (say gren-ich) NOUN the time on the line of longitude which passes through Greenwich in London, used as a basis for calculating time throughout the world

greet VERB ❶ to say hello to someone or to welcome them when they arrive ❷ to respond to something in a certain way ❸ to be the first thing that you notice

greeting NOUN words or actions used to greet someone

greetings PLURAL NOUN good wishes

gregarious (say grig-**air**-ee-us) ADJECTIVE ❶ fond of company ❷ living in flocks or communities

grenade (say grin-**ayd**) NOUN a small bomb thrown by hand

grey NOUN the colour between black and white, like ashes or dark clouds

grey ADJECTIVE of the colour grey

greyhound NOUN a slender dog with smooth hair and long legs, used in racing

grid NOUN ❶ a framework or pattern of bars or lines crossing each other ❷ a network of cables or wires for carrying electricity over a large area

grid reference NOUN a set of numbers that allows you to

describe the exact position of something on a map

grief NOUN deep sorrow, especially because a close relative or friend has died

grievance NOUN something that people are unhappy or angry about

grieve VERB ❶ to feel deep sorrow, especially because a close relative or friend has died ❷ to make a person feel very sad

grievous (say gree-vus) ADJECTIVE very serious

griffin NOUN a creature in fables, with an eagle's head and wings on a lion's body

grill NOUN ❶ (British) a heated element on a cooker, for sending heat downwards ❷ food cooked under this ❸ a grille

grill VERB ❶ (British) to cook food under a grill ❷ to question someone closely and severely

grille NOUN a metal grating covering a window or similar opening

grim ADJECTIVE ❶ stern or severe ❷ unpleasant or unattractive

grimace (say grim-ayss or grim-as) NOUN a twisted expression on the face made in pain or disgust

grimace VERB to make a grimace

grime NOUN dirt in a layer on a surface or on the skin

grimy ADJECTIVE very dirty

grin NOUN a broad smile showing your teeth

grin VERB to smile broadly showing your teeth

grind VERB grinds, grinding, ground ❶ to crush something into tiny pieces or powder ❷ to

sharpen or smooth something by rubbing it on a rough surface ❸ to grind your teeth is to rub the upper and lower teeth harshly together, often as sign of anger or impatience

grindstone NOUN a thick round rough revolving stone for sharpening or grinding things

grip VERB ❶ to hold something firmly ❷ to hold a person's attention

grip NOUN ❶ a firm hold ❷ a handle, especially on a sports racket or bat ❸ a travelling bag ❹ control or power

gripe VERB (informal) to grumble or complain

gripe NOUN (informal) a complaint

gripping ADJECTIVE very interesting and exciting in a way that holds your attention

grisly ADJECTIVE causing horror or disgust; gruesome

grist NOUN corn for grinding

gristle NOUN tough rubbery tissue in meat

grit NOUN ❶ tiny pieces of stone or sand ❷ courage and determination to do something difficult

grit VERB to spread a road or path with grit

grizzle VERB (British) (informal) a baby or young child grizzles when it cries or whimpers

grizzled ADJECTIVE streaked with grey hairs

grizzly ADJECTIVE grey-haired

grizzly bear NOUN a large fierce bear of North America

groan VERB ❶ to make a long

deep sound in pain, distress or disapproval ❷ to creak loudly under a heavy load

groan NOUN the sound of groaning

grocer NOUN a person who keeps a shop that sells food and household goods

groceries PLURAL NOUN goods sold by a grocer

grocery NOUN a grocer's shop

groggy ADJECTIVE dizzy and unsteady, especially after illness or injury

groin NOUN the hollow between your thigh and the trunk of the body

groom NOUN ❶ a person whose job is to look after horses ❷ a bridegroom

groom VERB ❶ to clean and brush a horse or other animal ❷ to make something, especially hair or a beard, neat and trim ❸ to prepare or train a person for a certain job or position

groove NOUN a long narrow furrow or channel cut in the surface of something

grope VERB to feel about for something you cannot see

gross (say grohss) ADJECTIVE ❶ fat and ugly ❷ very obvious or shocking ❸ having bad manners; crude or vulgar ❹ (informal) disgusting ❺ total; without anything being deducted Compare with **net**.

gross NOUN twelve dozen (144) of something

grotesque (say groh-**tesk**) ADJECTIVE very strange and ugly

grotto NOUN ❶ an attractive cave ❷ an artificial cave, especially one that is brightly decorated

ground NOUN ❶ the solid surface of the earth ❷ a sports field ❸ land of a certain kind ❹ the amount of a subject that is dealt with

ground VERB ❶ to prevent a plane from flying ❷ to stop a child from going out, as a punishment ❸ an idea or story is grounded on something when it is based on it

ground past tense of **grind**

ground control NOUN the people and machinery that control and monitor an aircraft or spacecraft from the ground

groundless ADJECTIVE having no good reason or cause

grounds PLURAL NOUN ❶ the gardens of a large house ❷ small solid pieces that sink to the bottom of a drink ❸ good reasons

groundsheet NOUN (British) a piece of waterproof material for spreading on the ground inside a tent

groundsman NOUN (chiefly British) a person whose job is to look after a sports ground

groundwork NOUN work that lays the basis for something

group NOUN ❶ a number of people, animals or things that come together or belong together in some way ❷ a band of musicians

group VERB to put people or things together in a group or groups; to gather into a group

grouse NOUN a bird with feathered feet, hunted as game

grouse VERB (*informal*) to grumble or complain

grove NOUN a small wood or group of trees

grovel VERB ❶ to crawl on the ground, especially in a show of fear or humility ❷ to act in an excessively humble way, for example by apologizing a lot

grow VERB grows, growing, grew, grown ❶ to become bigger or greater ❷ a plant or seed grows when it develops in the ground ❸ to put a plant in the ground or a pot and look after it ❹ to become

growl VERB to make a deep angry sound in the throat

growl NOUN the sound of growling

grown-up NOUN an adult person

growth NOUN ❶ growing or developing ❷ something that has grown ❸ a lump that has grown on or inside a person's body; a tumour

grub NOUN ❶ a tiny worm-like creature that will become an insect; a larva ❷ (*informal*) food

grub VERB ❶ to turn things over or move them about while looking for something ❷ to dig something up by the roots

grubby ADJECTIVE rather dirty

grudge NOUN unfriendly feelings towards someone because you are angry about what has happened in the past

grudge VERB to be unhappy that someone has something or that you have to do something

grudging ADJECTIVE given or done although you do not want to

gruelling ADJECTIVE difficult and exhausting

gruesome ADJECTIVE horrible or shocking

gruff ADJECTIVE having a rough unfriendly voice or manner

grumble VERB to complain in a bad-tempered way

grumble NOUN a bad-tempered complaint

grumpy ADJECTIVE bad-tempered

grunt VERB to make a gruff snorting sound like a pig

grunt NOUN the sound of grunting

guarantee NOUN a formal promise to do something or to repair something you have sold if it breaks or goes wrong

guarantee VERB ❶ to give a guarantee; to make a formal promise ❷ to make it certain that something will happen

guard VERB ❶ to protect a place or thing from danger; to keep something safe ❷ to watch over a prisoner and prevent them from escaping

guard NOUN ❶ guarding or protecting people or things ❷ someone who guards a person or place ❸ a group of soldiers or police officers etc. acting as a guard ❹ a railway official in charge of a train ❺ a protecting device or screen

guardian NOUN ❶ someone who guards or protects something ❷ a person who is legally in charge of a child whose parents cannot look after him or her

guerrilla (say ger-il-a) NOUN a member of a small unofficial army who fights by making surprise attacks

guess NOUN an opinion or answer that you give without making careful calculations or without being certain

guess VERB to make a guess

guesswork NOUN something you do or think by guessing

guest NOUN ❶ a person who is invited to your house for a meal or a visit or to a special event ❷ a person staying at a hotel ❸ a person who takes part in another's show as a visiting performer

guest house NOUN a kind of small hotel

guffaw VERB to laugh noisily

guffaw NOUN a noisy laugh

guidance NOUN help and advice

Guide NOUN a member of the Guide Association, an organization for girls

guide NOUN ❶ a person who shows others the way or points out interesting sights ❷ a book giving information about a place or subject

guide VERB to show someone the way or how to do something

guidebook NOUN a book of information about a place, for travellers or visitors

guided missile NOUN an explosive rocket that is guided to its target by remote control or by equipment inside it

guide dog NOUN a dog trained to lead a blind person

guidelines PLURAL NOUN statements that give general advice about how

something should be done

guild (say gild) NOUN a society of people with similar skills or interests

guile (rhymes with mile) NOUN craftiness and deceit

guillotine (say gil-ot-een) NOUN ❶ a machine with a heavy blade for beheading criminals, used in the past in France ❷ a machine with a long sharp blade for cutting paper

guillotine VERB to cut off someone's head with a guillotine

guilt NOUN ❶ an unpleasant feeling you have when you have done wrong or are to blame for something bad that has happened ❷ the fact that you have committed a crime or done wrong

guilty ADJECTIVE ❶ having done wrong ❷ feeling or showing guilt

guinea (say gin-ee) NOUN ❶ a former British gold coin worth 21 shillings (£1.05) ❷ this amount of money

guinea pig NOUN ❶ a small furry animal without a tail, kept as a pet ❷ a person who is used to try out something new

guise (say guys) NOUN an outward disguise or pretence

guitar NOUN a musical instrument played by plucking its strings

gulf NOUN ❶ a large area of the sea that is partly surrounded by land ❷ a wide gap; a great difference

gull NOUN a seagull

gullet NOUN the tube from the throat to the stomach

gullible ADJECTIVE easily deceived or

persuaded to believe something

gully NOUN a narrow channel that carries water

gulp VERB ❶ to swallow something hastily or greedily ❷ to make a loud swallowing noise, especially because of fear

gulp NOUN ❶ the act of gulping food or drink ❷ a large mouthful of liquid

gum NOUN ❶ the firm flesh in which your teeth are rooted ❷ a sticky substance produced by some trees and shrubs, used as glue ❸ a sweet made with gum or gelatin ❹ chewing gum ❺ a gum tree

gum VERB to cover or stick something with gum

gumption NOUN (*informal*) common sense

gum tree NOUN a eucalyptus

gun NOUN ❶ a weapon that fires shells or bullets from a metal tube ❷ a starting pistol ❸ a device that forces a substance out of a tube

gun VERB ➤ **gun someone down** to shoot and kill someone with a gun

gunboat NOUN a small warship

gunfire NOUN the rapid firing of guns

gunman NOUN a criminal with a gun

gunner NOUN a person in the armed forces who operates a large gun

gunpowder NOUN an explosive made from a powdered mixture of potassium nitrate, charcoal and sulphur

gunshot NOUN the sound of a gun being fired

gurdwara NOUN a Sikh temple

gurgle VERB to make a low bubbling sound

gurgle NOUN a low bubbling sound

guru NOUN ❶ a spiritual teacher in Hinduism and Sikhism ❷ an influential teacher; an expert on a subject whose ideas people follow

gush VERB ❶ to flow out suddenly or quickly ❷ to talk too enthusiastically or emotionally

gust NOUN a short sudden rush of wind

gust VERB to blow in gusts

gusto NOUN great enjoyment and enthusiasm

gusty ADJECTIVE with the wind blowing in gusts

gut NOUN the lower part of the digestive system; the intestine

gut VERB ❶ to remove the guts from a dead fish or other animal ❷ to remove or destroy the inside of something

guts PLURAL NOUN ❶ the digestive system; the insides of a person or thing ❷ (*informal*) courage and determination

gutted ADJECTIVE (*British*) (*informal*) extremely disappointed or upset

gutter NOUN a long narrow channel at the side of a road or along the edge of a roof, for carrying away rainwater

gutter VERB a candle gutters when it burns unsteadily so that melted wax runs down

guttural (say gut-er-al) ADJECTIVE a guttural voice is throaty and harsh-sounding

guy NOUN ❶ a figure representing Guy Fawkes, burnt on 5 November in memory of the Gunpowder Plot which planned to blow up Parliament on that day in 1605 ❷ (*informal*) a man ❸ (also **guy-rope**) a rope used to hold something in place, especially a tent

guzzle VERB to eat or drink greedily

gym (say jim) NOUN (*informal*) ❶ a gymnasium ❷ gymnastics

gymkhana (say jim-**kah**-na) NOUN a series of horse-riding contests and other sports events

gymnasium NOUN a large room or building with equipment for doing physical exercise

gymnast NOUN a person trained in gymnastics

gymnastics PLURAL NOUN exercises performed to develop the muscles or to show the performer's agility

gynaecology (say guy-ni-**kol**-o-ji) NOUN the branch of medicine concerned with the female reproductive system

gypsy NOUN a member of a community of people, also called travellers, who live in caravans or similar vehicles and travel from place to place

gyrate (say jy-**rayt**) VERB to move round in circles or spirals

gyroscope (say **jy**-ro-skohp) NOUN a device used in navigation, that keeps steady because of a heavy wheel spinning inside it

Hh

habit NOUN ❶ something that you do regularly or often; a settled way of behaving ❷ something that is hard to give up ❸ a piece of clothing like a long dress worn by a monk or nun

habitat NOUN where an animal or plant lives or grows naturally

habitual ADJECTIVE done regularly; usual or typical of someone

hack VERB ❶ to chop or cut something roughly ❷ (*informal*) to break into a computer system

hacker NOUN a person who breaks into a computer system, especially that of a company or government

hackles PLURAL NOUN ➤ **make someone's hackles rise** to make someone angry or indignant

hacksaw NOUN a saw for cutting metal

haddock NOUN a sea fish like cod but smaller, used as food

haemoglobin (say heem-a-**gloh**-bin) NOUN the red substance that carries oxygen in the blood

haemophilia (say heem-o-**fil**-ee-a) NOUN a disease that causes people to bleed dangerously from even a slight cut

haemorrhage (say **hem**-er-ij) NOUN severe bleeding, especially inside a person's body

hag NOUN an ugly old woman

haggard ADJECTIVE looking ill or very tired

haggis NOUN a Scottish food made from sheep's offal

haggle *VERB* to argue about a price or agreement

haiku (say **hy**-koo) *NOUN* A Japanese form of poem, written in three lines of five, seven and five syllables

hail *NOUN* ❶ frozen drops of rain ❷ a hail of bullets or arrows is a large number of them coming quickly

hail *VERB* ❶ it is hailing when rain is falling in frozen drops ❷ to call out or wave to someone to get their attention

hail *EXCLAMATION* (old use) an exclamation of greeting

hailstone *NOUN* a frozen drop of rain

hair *NOUN* ❶ a soft covering that grows on the heads and bodies of people and animals ❷ one of the threads that make up this covering

haircut *NOUN* ❶ cutting a person's hair when it gets too long ❷ the style in which someone's hair is cut

hairdresser *NOUN* a person whose job is to cut and arrange people's hair

hairpin *NOUN* a U-shaped pin for keeping hair in place

hairpin bend *NOUN* a sharp bend in a road

hair-raising *ADJECTIVE* terrifying but also exciting

hairstyle *NOUN* a way or style of arranging your hair

hairy *ADJECTIVE* ❶ with a lot of hair ❷ (informal) dangerous and frightening

hajj *NOUN* the pilgrimage to Mecca which all Muslims are expected to make at least once

hake *NOUN* a sea fish used as food

halal *ADJECTIVE* halal meat is prepared according to Muslim law

halcyon (say **hal**-see-on) *ADJECTIVE* halcyon days are happy and peaceful days that you long for from the past

hale *ADJECTIVE* ➤ hale and hearty strong and healthy

half *NOUN* halves one of the two equal parts or amounts into which something is or can be divided

half *ADVERB* partly; not completely

half-baked *ADJECTIVE* (informal) not properly planned or thought out

half-brother *NOUN* a brother to whom you are related by one parent but not by both parents

half-hearted *ADJECTIVE* not very keen or enthusiastic

half-life *NOUN* the time taken for the radioactivity of a substance to fall to half its original value

half mast *NOUN* a point about halfway up a flagpole, to which a flag is lowered as a mark of respect for a person who has died

halfpenny (say **hayp**-nee) *NOUN* a former British coin worth half a penny

half-sister *NOUN* a sister to whom you are related by one parent but not by both parents

half-term *NOUN* (in British schools) a short holiday in the middle of a school term

half-time *NOUN* the point or interval halfway through a game

halfway *ADJECTIVE & ADVERB* at a

A

point half the distance or amount between two places or times

halibut NOUN a large flat fish used as food

hall NOUN ❶ a space or passage just inside the front entrance of a house ❷ a large room or building used for meetings, concerts or social events ❸ a large country house

hallelujah EXCLAMATION & NOUN alleluia

hallmark NOUN ❶ an official mark made on gold, silver and platinum to show its quality ❷ a typical quality or feature by which you can recognize a person or thing

hallo EXCLAMATION a different spelling of hello

hallowed ADJECTIVE honoured as being holy

Hallowe'en NOUN 31 October, traditionally a time when ghosts and witches are believed to appear

hallucination NOUN something you think you can see or hear that is not really there, usually because of illness or drugs

halo NOUN a circle of light round something, especially round the head of a saint or other holy person in paintings

halt VERB to stop or to make something stop

halt NOUN ❶ a stop or standstill ❷ a small stopping place on a railway

halter NOUN a rope or strap put round a horse's head so that it can be led or fastened to something

halting ADJECTIVE slow and

uncertain

halve VERB ❶ to reduce something to half its size or amount ❷ to divide something into halves

ham NOUN ❶ meat from a pig's leg ❷ (informal) an actor who acts in a very exaggerated way ❸ (informal) someone who operates a radio to send and receive messages as a hobby

hamburger NOUN a flat round cake of minced beef served fried, often in a bread roll

hamlet NOUN a small village

hammer NOUN a tool with a heavy metal head used for hitting nails into things

hammer VERB ❶ to hit something with a hammer ❷ to knock loudly ❸ (informal) to criticize or defeat someone

hammock NOUN a bed made of a strong net or piece of cloth hung up above the ground or floor

hamper NOUN a large box-shaped basket with a lid

hamper VERB to hinder someone or prevent them from moving or working freely

hamster NOUN a small furry animal with cheek pouches for carrying grain

hamstring NOUN any of the five tendons at the back of a person's knee

hand NOUN ❶ the end part of the arm below the wrist ❷ a pointer on a clock or dial ❸ a worker; a member of a ship's crew ❹ the cards held by one player in a card game ❺ side or direction ❻ help

276

or assistance

hand VERB to give or pass something to someone

handbag NOUN a bag for holding a purse and other personal items

handbook NOUN a small book that gives useful facts about something

handcuff NOUN one of a pair of metal rings linked by a chain, for fastening wrists together

handcuff VERB to put handcuffs on someone

handful NOUN ❶ as much as you can hold in one hand ❷ a few people or things ❸ (*informal*) a difficult or awkward person or task

handicap NOUN ❶ a disadvantage ❷ (*offensive*) a physical or mental disability

handicraft NOUN artistic work done with your hands, e.g. woodwork or needlework

handiwork NOUN ❶ something made by hand ❷ something done

handkerchief NOUN a small square of cloth for wiping your nose or face

handle NOUN the part of a thing by which you can hold, carry or control it

handle VERB ❶ to touch or feel something with your hands ❷ to deal with or manage something

handlebar NOUN (or **handlebars**) PLURAL NOUN the bar, with a handle at each end, that steers a bicycle or motorcycle

handout NOUN ❶ money given to a needy person ❷ a sheet of information given out in a lesson,

lecture, etc.

handrail NOUN a narrow rail for people to hold as a support

handset NOUN ❶ the part of a telephone that you hold up to speak into and listen to ❷ a hand-held control device for a piece of electronic equipment

handshake NOUN shaking hands with someone as a greeting or to show you agree to something

handsome ADJECTIVE ❶ attractive or good-looking ❷ large and generous

hands-on ADJECTIVE involving actual experience of using equipment or doing something

handstand NOUN balancing on your hands with your feet in the air

handwriting NOUN writing done by hand; a person's style of writing

handwritten ADJECTIVE written by hand, not typed or printed

handy ADJECTIVE ❶ convenient or useful; within easy reach ❷ good at using the hands

handyman NOUN a person who does household repairs or odd jobs

hang VERB hangs, hanging, hung ❶ to fix the top part of something to a hook or nail etc. so that the lower part is free; to be supported in this way ❷ to stick wallpaper to a wall ❸ to decorate something with drapery or hanging ornaments etc. ❹ to lean or lie over something ❺ to remain in the air or as something unpleasant ❻ with *past tense & past participle* hanged to execute someone by hanging them from a rope that tightens round the neck

hang NOUN ➤ **get the hang of** (*informal*) to learn how to do or use something

hangar NOUN a large shed where aircraft are kept

hanger NOUN a curved piece of wood, plastic or wire with a hook at the top, for hanging clothes from a rail

hang-glider NOUN a framework like a large kite from which a person can hang and glide through the air

hangman NOUN a man whose job it is to hang people condemned to death

hangover NOUN a headache and sick feeling after drinking too much alcohol

hanker VERB to hanker after something is to feel a longing for it

hanky NOUN (*informal*) a handkerchief

Hanukkah (say **hah**-noo-ka) NOUN the eight-day Jewish festival of lights beginning in December

haphazard ADJECTIVE done or chosen at random, with no particular order or plan

hapless ADJECTIVE having no luck

happen VERB ❶ to take place; to occur ❷ to do something by chance

happening NOUN something that happens; an event

happily ADVERB ❶ in a happy way ❷ it is lucky that

happy ADJECTIVE ❶ pleased or contented ❷ willing to do something ❸ fortunate

harangue (say ha-**rang**) VERB to speak to someone at length in a loud aggressive way, often to criticize someone

harangue NOUN a long aggressive speech criticizing someone

harass (say ha-ras) VERB to trouble or annoy someone continually

harassed ADJECTIVE tired and anxious because you have too much to do

harbour NOUN a place where ships can shelter or unload

harbour VERB ❶ to keep something in your mind for a long time ❷ to give shelter to someone, especially a criminal

hard ADJECTIVE ❶ firm or solid; not soft ❷ strong and violent ❸ difficult to do or understand ❹ severe or harsh ❺ causing suffering ❻ using or needing great effort ❼ hard drugs are strong and addictive ❽ hard water contains minerals that prevent soap from making much lather

hard ADVERB ❶ so as to be hard ❷ with great effort or force ❸ with difficulty

hardback NOUN a book bound in stiff covers

hardboard NOUN stiff board made of compressed wood pulp

hard disk NOUN a disk fixed inside a computer, able to store large amounts of data

harden VERB ❶ to make something hard or to become hard ❷ to become more serious and unfriendly

hard-hearted ADJECTIVE unkind or unsympathetic

hardly ADVERB only just; only with difficulty

hardship NOUN difficult conditions that cause discomfort or suffering

hard shoulder NOUN (British) a strip at the edge of a motorway where vehicles can stop in an emergency

hardware NOUN ❶ tools and other pieces of equipment that you use in the house and garden ❷ the machinery of a computer as opposed to the software. Compare with software.

hard-wearing ADJECTIVE able to stand a lot of wear

hardwood NOUN hard heavy wood from deciduous trees, e.g. oak and teak

hardy ADJECTIVE able to endure cold or difficult conditions

hare NOUN a fast-running animal like a large rabbit

hare VERB (British) to hare about or hare off is to rush away at great speed

harem (say har-eem) NOUN the part of a Muslim palace or house where the women live; the women living there

hark VERB (old use) to listen

harm VERB to damage or injure someone or something

harm NOUN damage or injury

harmful ADJECTIVE causing harm or likely to cause harm

harmless ADJECTIVE not able or likely to cause harm

harmonic ADJECTIVE to do with harmony in music

harmonica NOUN a mouth organ

harmonious ADJECTIVE
❶ combining together in a pleasant, attractive or effective way ❷ sounding pleasant ❸ peaceful and friendly

harmonize (also **harmonise**) VERB ❶ to combine together in a pleasant, attractive or effective way ❷ musicians or singers harmonize when they play or sing together with notes that combine in a pleasant way with the main tune

harmony NOUN ❶ a pleasant combination of musical notes played or sung at the same time ❷ being friendly to each other and not quarrelling

harness NOUN the straps put round a horse's head and neck for controlling it

harness VERB ❶ to put a harness on a horse ❷ to control and use something

harp NOUN a musical instrument made of strings stretched across a frame and plucked with the fingers

harp VERB to harp on about something is to keep on talking about it in a tiresome way

harpoon NOUN NOUN a spear attached to a rope, used for catching whales or large fish

harpoon VERB to spear a whale or fish with a harpoon

harpsichord NOUN an instrument like a piano but with strings that are plucked (not struck) when keys are pressed

harrow NOUN a heavy device pulled over the ground to break up the soil

harrowing ADJECTIVE very upsetting or distressing

harsh ADJECTIVE ❶ rough and unpleasant ❷ severe or cruel

hart NOUN a male deer. Compare with hind.

harvest NOUN ❶ the time when farmers gather in the corn, fruit or vegetables that they have grown ❷ the crop that is gathered in

harvest VERB to gather in a crop

hash NOUN ❶ a mixture of small pieces of meat and vegetables, usually fried ❷ (chiefly British) the symbol #

hashtag NOUN a word or phrase with the symbol # in front of it, used on websites such as Twitter to identify the subject of a message

hassle (informal) NOUN something that is difficult or troublesome

hassle VERB to annoy or pester someone

haste NOUN doing something in a short time or too quickly

hasten VERB ❶ to be quick to do or say something ❷ to make something happen or be done earlier or more quickly

hasty ADJECTIVE hurried; done too quickly

hat NOUN a covering for the head, worn out of doors

hatch NOUN an opening in a floor, wall or door, usually with a covering

hatch VERB ❶ to break out of an egg ❷ to keep an egg warm until a baby bird comes out ❸ to plan something ❹ to shade part of a drawing with close parallel lines

hatchback NOUN a car with a sloping back hinged at the top

hatchet NOUN a small axe

hate VERB to dislike someone or something very strongly

hate NOUN ❶ extreme dislike ❷ something you dislike very much

hateful ADJECTIVE extremely unkind or unpleasant; horrible

hatred NOUN extreme dislike

hatter NOUN a person who makes hats

hat-trick NOUN getting three goals, wickets or victories one after the other

haughty ADJECTIVE proud of yourself and looking down on other people

haul VERB to pull or drag something with great effort

haul NOUN ❶ an amount taken or obtained by an effort ❷ a distance to be covered

haulage NOUN (British) ❶ transporting goods by road ❷ a charge for this

haunches PLURAL NOUN the buttocks and top part of the thighs

haunt VERB ❶ a ghost haunts a place or person when it appears often ❷ to visit a place often ❸ to stay for a long time in your mind

haunt NOUN a place that you often visit

haunted ADJECTIVE a haunted place is one that people think is visited by ghosts

haunting ADJECTIVE so beautiful and sad that it stays in your mind

have VERB has, having, had This

word has many uses, including ❶ to possess or own something ❷ to contain something ❸ to experience something ❹ to be obliged or forced to do something ❺ to allow something to happen ❻ to receive or accept something ❼ to get something done; to organize something ❽ (*informal*) to be had is to be cheated or deceived

have AUXILIARY VERB used to form the past tense of verbs, e.g. *He has gone*

haven NOUN a safe place for people or animals

haven't (*mainly spoken*) have not

haversack NOUN a strong bag carried on your back or over your shoulder

havoc NOUN great destruction or disorder

hawk NOUN a bird of prey with very strong eyesight

hawk VERB to carry goods about and try to sell them

hawthorn NOUN a thorny tree with small red berries (called *haws*)

hay NOUN dried grass for feeding to animals

hay fever NOUN an allergy to pollen that causes irritation of the nose, throat and eyes

haystack NOUN a large neat pile of hay packed for storing

haywire ADJECTIVE (*informal*) out of control

hazard NOUN ❶ a danger or risk ❷ an obstacle on a golf course

hazard VERB to put something at risk

hazardous ADJECTIVE dangerous or risky

haze NOUN thin mist

hazel NOUN ❶ a bush with small nuts ❷ a light brown colour

hazy ADJECTIVE ❶ misty ❷ vague or uncertain

he PRONOUN ❶ the male person or animal being talked about ❷ a person (male or female)

head NOUN ❶ the part of the body containing the brains, eyes and mouth ❷ your brains or mind; intelligence ❸ a talent or ability ❹ heads is the side of a coin on which someone's head is shown ❺ a person ❻ the top or front of something ❼ the person in charge of an organization or group of people ❽ a headteacher

head VERB ❶ to be at the top or front of something ❷ to be in charge of or lead something ❸ to hit a ball with your head ❹ to start to go in a particular direction

headache NOUN ❶ a pain in the head ❷ (*informal*) a worrying problem

headdress NOUN a covering or decoration for the head

header NOUN a shot or pass made with the head in football

heading NOUN a word or words put at the top of a piece of printing or writing

headland NOUN a large piece of high land that sticks out into the sea

headlight NOUN a powerful light at the front of a car, engine, etc.

headline NOUN a heading in a

newspaper, printed in large type

headlong ADVERB & ADJECTIVE
① falling head first ② in a hasty or thoughtless way

headmaster NOUN (chiefly British) a male headteacher

headmistress NOUN (chiefly British) a female headteacher

head-on ADVERB & ADJECTIVE with the front parts hitting each other

headphones PLURAL NOUN a pair of earphones on a band that fits over the head

headquarters NOUN & PLURAL NOUN the place from which an organization is controlled

headstone NOUN a stone set up on a grave, with the name of the person buried there

headstrong ADJECTIVE determined to do what you want

headteacher NOUN the person in charge of a school

headway NOUN ▸ make headway to make good progress

heal VERB ① a wound or injury heals when it gets better ② to make a wound or injury better ③ (old use) to cure someone who is ill

health NOUN ① the condition of a person's body or mind ② being healthy and not ill

health food NOUN food that contains only natural substances and is thought to be good for your health

healthy ADJECTIVE ① being well; free from illness ② producing good health

heap NOUN a pile, especially an

untidy one

heap VERB ① to put things in a pile ② to put large amounts on something ③ to give a lot of something, such as praise or criticism, to someone

hear VERB hears, hearing, heard ① to take in sounds through the ears ② to receive news or information ③ to listen to and try a case in a law court ④ to hear from someone is to get a phone call, letter or email from them

hearing NOUN ① the ability to hear ② a chance to give your opinion or to defend yourself ③ a trial in a law court

hearing aid NOUN a device to help a partially deaf person to hear

hearsay NOUN something you have heard from another person or as a rumour, which may or may not be true

hearse NOUN a vehicle for taking the coffin to a funeral

heart NOUN ① the organ in your chest that pumps the blood around your body ② a person's feelings or emotions; sympathy ③ enthusiasm or courage ④ the middle or most important part of something ⑤ a curved shape representing a heart ⑥ a playing card with red heart shapes on it

heart attack NOUN a sudden failure of the heart to work properly, which results in great pain or sometimes death

heartbroken ADJECTIVE very unhappy

hearten VERB to make a person feel encouraged

heart failure NOUN gradual failure of the heart to work properly, especially as a cause of death

heartfelt ADJECTIVE felt deeply and sincerely

hearth NOUN the floor of a fireplace or the area in front of it

heartless ADJECTIVE cruel or without pity

hearty ADJECTIVE ❶ strong and healthy ❷ enthusiastic and sincere ❸ a hearty meal is large and filling

heat NOUN ❶ hotness or (in scientific use) the form of energy that causes things to be hot ❷ hot weather ❸ strong feeling, especially anger ❹ a race or contest to decide who will take part in the final

heat VERB ❶ to make something hot ❷ to become hot

heater NOUN a device for heating a room or vehicle

heath NOUN an area of flat open land with low shrubs

heathen NOUN a person who does not believe in any of the world's chief religions

heather NOUN an evergreen plant with small purple, pink or white flowers

heatwave NOUN a long period of hot weather

heave VERB ❶ to lift or move something heavy ❷ (informal) to throw something ❸ to rise and fall ❹ if your stomach heaves, you feel like vomiting

heave NOUN an act of heaving; a strong pull or shove

heaven NOUN ❶ the place where, in some religions, good people are thought to go when they die and where God and angels are thought to live ❷ a very pleasant place or state

heavenly ADJECTIVE ❶ to do with heaven ❷ a heavenly body is a star or planet in the sky ❸ (informal) very pleasing

heavily ADVERB ❶ to a great degree; in large amounts ❷ with a lot of force or effort ❸ in a slow and sad way

heavy ADJECTIVE ❶ weighing a lot; difficult to lift or carry ❷ used to ask or say how much something weighs ❸ great in amount or force ❹ needing much effort ❺ full of sadness or worry

heavy industry NOUN industry producing metal, large machines, etc.

heavyweight NOUN ❶ a heavy person ❷ a boxer of the heaviest weight

Hebrew NOUN the language of the Jews in ancient Palestine and modern Israel

heckle VERB to interrupt a speaker with awkward questions

hectare (say **hek**-tar) NOUN a unit of area equal to 10,000 square metres or nearly 2.5 acres

hectic ADJECTIVE full of frantic activity

hedge NOUN a row of bushes forming a barrier or boundary

hedge VERB ❶ to surround a field or other area with a hedge ❷ to avoid giving a definite answer

hedgehog NOUN a small animal

covered with long prickles

hedgerow NOUN a hedge of bushes bordering a field

heed VERB to pay attention to someone or something

heed NOUN ➤ take or pay heed to give your attention to something

heel NOUN ❶ the back part of the foot ❷ the part of a sock or shoe round or under your heel

heel VERB ❶ to repair the heel of a shoe ❷ a ship heels when it leans over to one side

hefty ADJECTIVE large and strong

Hegira (say hej-ir-a) NOUN the flight of Muhammad from Mecca in AD 622. The Muslim era is reckoned from this date.

heifer (say hef-er) NOUN a young cow

height NOUN ❶ how high something is; the distance from the base to the top or from head to foot ❷ a high place ❸ the highest or most intense part

heighten VERB ❶ to become or make something more intense ❷ to make something higher

heinous (say hay-nus or hee-nus) ADJECTIVE very bad or wicked

heir (say air) NOUN a person who inherits money or a title

heiress (say air-ess) NOUN a female heir, especially to great wealth

heirloom (say air-loom) NOUN a valued possession that has been handed down in a family for several generations

helicopter NOUN a kind of aircraft with a large horizontal propeller or rotor

helium (say hee-lee-um) NOUN a light colourless gas that does not burn and is sometimes used to fill balloons

helix (say hee-liks) NOUN a spiral

hell NOUN ❶ a place where, in some religions, wicked people are thought to be punished after they die ❷ a very unpleasant place or situation ❸ (informal) an exclamation of anger

hellish ADJECTIVE (informal) very difficult or unpleasant

hello EXCLAMATION a word used to greet someone or to attract their attention

helm NOUN the handle or wheel used to steer a ship

helmet NOUN a strong hat or covering worn to protect the head

help VERB ❶ to do something useful for someone ❷ to make something better or easier ❸ if you cannot help doing something, you cannot avoid doing it ❹ to serve food or drink to someone

help NOUN ❶ helping someone ❷ a person or thing that helps

helpful ADJECTIVE giving help; useful

helping NOUN a portion of food at a meal

helpless ADJECTIVE not able to do things or look after yourself

helpline NOUN a telephone service giving advice on problems

helter-skelter ADVERB in great haste

helter-skelter NOUN a tall spiral slide at a fair

hem NOUN the edge of a piece of cloth that is folded over and sewn down

hem VERB to put a hem on something

hemisphere NOUN ❶ half a sphere ❷ half the earth, divided into north and south

hemp NOUN ❶ a plant that produces coarse fibres from which cloth and ropes are made ❷ the drug cannabis, made from this plant

hen NOUN ❶ a female bird ❷ a female fowl

hence ADVERB ❶ as a result; therefore ❷ from now on ❸ (*old use*) from here

henceforth ADVERB from now on

henchman NOUN a trusty supporter

henna NOUN a reddish-brown dye, especially used for colouring hair

hepatitis NOUN a disease causing inflammation of the liver

heptagon NOUN a flat shape with seven sides and seven angles

heptathlon NOUN an athletic contest in which each competitor takes part in seven events

her PRONOUN the form of **she** used as the object of a verb or after a preposition

her DETERMINER belonging to her

herald NOUN ❶ an official in former times who made announcements and carried messages for a king or queen ❷ a person or thing that is a sign of something to come

herald VERB to show that something is coming

heraldry NOUN the study of coats of arms

herb NOUN a plant used for flavouring or for making medicine

herbaceous (say her-**bay**-shus) ADJECTIVE containing many flowering plants

herbal ADJECTIVE made of or using herbs

herbivore (say **her**-biv-or) NOUN an animal that feeds on plants and not on the flesh of other animals. Compare with **carnivore**.

herbivorous (say her-**biv**-er-us) ADJECTIVE a herbivorous animal feeds on plants and not on the flesh of other animals. Compare with **carnivorous**.

Herculean (say her-kew-**lee**-an) ADJECTIVE needing great strength or effort

herd NOUN ❶ a group of cattle or other animals that feed together ❷ a mass of people; a mob

herd VERB ❶ to gather or move in a large group ❷ to move people or animals together in a large group ❸ to look after a herd of animals

here ADVERB in or to this place

hereafter ADVERB from now on; in future

hereby ADVERB as a result of this act or statement.

hereditary ADJECTIVE passed down to a child from a parent

heredity (say hir-**ed**-it-ee) NOUN the process of inheriting physical or mental characteristics from parents or ancestors

heresy (say **herri**-see) NOUN an opinion or belief that disagrees with those that are generally accepted, especially in Christianity

heretic (say **herri**-tik) NOUN a

285

person who supports a heresy

heritage NOUN things that have been passed from one generation to another; a country's history and traditions

hermetically ADVERB so as to be airtight

hermit NOUN a person who lives alone and keeps away from people, often for religious reasons

hernia NOUN a condition in which an internal part of the body pushes through a weak point in another part

hero NOUN heroes ❶ a man or boy who is admired for doing something very brave or great ❷ the chief male character in a story, play or film

heroic ADJECTIVE showing great courage or determination

heroin NOUN a very strong drug, made from morphine

heroine NOUN ❶ a woman or girl who is admired for doing something very brave or great ❷ the chief female character in a story, play or film

heroism NOUN great courage

heron NOUN a wading bird with long legs and a long neck

herring NOUN a sea fish used as food

hers POSSESSIVE PRONOUN belonging to her

herself PRONOUN she or her and nobody else. The word is used to refer back to the subject of a sentence (e.g. She cut herself.) or for emphasis (e.g. She herself has said it.)

hertz NOUN a unit of frequency of electromagnetic waves, equal to one cycle per second

hesitant ADJECTIVE slow to speak or do something because you are not sure if you should or not

hesitate VERB to pause before doing or saying something, because you are uncertain or worried

hesitation NOUN a pause before doing or saying something, because you are uncertain or worried

hessian NOUN (chiefly British) a type of strong coarse cloth, used for making sacks

heterosexual ADJECTIVE attracted to people of the opposite sex; not homosexual

hew VERB hews, hewing, hewn to chop or cut wood or stone with an axe or other tool

hexagon NOUN a flat shape with six sides and six angles

hey EXCLAMATION an exclamation used to attract attention or to express surprise or interest

heyday NOUN the time of a person's or thing's greatest success or popularity

hi EXCLAMATION an exclamation used as a friendly greeting

hiatus (say hy-ay-tus) NOUN a gap in something that is otherwise continuous

hibernate VERB an animal hibernates when it spends the winter in a state like deep sleep

hiccup NOUN ❶ a high gulping sound made when your breath is briefly interrupted ❷ a brief hitch or setback

hiccup VERB to make a sound of hiccups

hide VERB hides, hiding, hid, hidden ❶ to get into a place where you cannot be seen ❷ to keep a person or thing from being seen ❸ to keep a thing secret

hide NOUN ❶ an animal's skin ❷ (British) a camouflaged shelter used to observe wildlife at close quarters

hide-and-seek NOUN a game in which one person looks for others who are hiding

hideous ADJECTIVE very ugly or unpleasant

hideout NOUN a place where someone hides

hiding NOUN ❶ being hidden ❷ a thrashing or beating

hierarchy (say hyr-ark-ee) NOUN an organization that ranks people one above another according to the power or authority that they hold

hieroglyphics (say hyr-o-glif-iks) PLURAL NOUN pictures or symbols used in ancient Egypt to represent words

hi-fi NOUN (informal) equipment for playing CDs or other recorded music

higgledy-piggledy ADVERB & ADJECTIVE completely mixed up; not in any order

high ADJECTIVE ❶ reaching a long way upwards ❷ far above the ground or above sea level ❸ measuring from top to bottom ❹ above average level in

importance, quality or amount ❺ a high note is one at the top end of a musical scale ❻ meat is high when it is beginning to go bad ❼ (informal) affected by a drug

high ADVERB ❶ far above the ground or a long way up ❷ at or to a high level

highbrow ADJECTIVE having serious or intellectual tastes

Higher NOUN the advanced level of the Scottish Certificate of Education

higher education NOUN education at a university or college

high explosive NOUN a powerful explosive

high fidelity NOUN reproducing recorded sound with very little distortion

high jump NOUN an athletic contest in which competitors try to jump over a high bar

highlands PLURAL NOUN mountainous country

highlight NOUN ❶ the most interesting part of something ❷ a light area in a painting or photograph ❸ highlights are light-coloured streaks in a person's hair

highlight VERB ❶ to draw special attention to something ❷ to mark part of a text with a different colour so that people give it more attention

highlighter NOUN a felt-tip pen that you use to spread bright colour over lines of text to draw attention to them

highly ADVERB ❶ extremely; to a high degree ❷ very well or

a b c d e f g **h** i j k l m n o p q r s t u v w x y z

favourably

highly-strung ADJECTIVE nervous and easily upset

Highness NOUN the title of a prince or princess

high-pitched ADJECTIVE high in sound

high-rise ADJECTIVE a high-rise building is tall with many storeys

high school NOUN a secondary school

high spirits PLURAL NOUN cheerful and lively behaviour

high street NOUN (*British*) a town's main street

high-tech ADJECTIVE using the most advanced technology, especially electronic devices and computers

highway NOUN a main road or route for vehicles

highwayman NOUN a man who robbed travellers on highways in former times

hijack VERB to seize control of an aircraft or vehicle by force during a journey

hike NOUN a long walk in the countryside

hike VERB to go on a hike

hilarious ADJECTIVE very funny

hilarity NOUN great amusement and laughter

hill NOUN a piece of land that is higher than the ground around it

hillock NOUN a small hill or mound

hilly ADJECTIVE having a lot of hills

hilt NOUN the handle of a sword, dagger or knife

him PRONOUN the form of **he** used as the object of a verb or after a preposition

himself PRONOUN he or him and nobody else. The word is used to refer back to the subject of a sentence (e.g. *He has hurt himself*) or for emphasis (e.g. *He himself has told us*)

hind ADJECTIVE at the back

hind NOUN a female deer. Compare with **hart**.

hinder VERB to get in your way or make things difficult for you

Hindi NOUN one of the languages of India

hindquarters PLURAL NOUN an animal's hind legs and rear parts

hindrance NOUN a person or thing that gets in your way or makes it difficult for you to do something

Hindu NOUN a person who believes in Hinduism, which is one of the religions of India

hinge NOUN a joining device on which a lid or door etc. turns when it opens

hinge VERB ❶ to be hinged is to be fixed with a hinge ❷ to hinge on something is to depend on it

hint NOUN ❶ a slight indication or suggestion ❷ a useful idea or piece of advice

hint VERB to suggest something without actually saying it

hip NOUN ❶ your hips are the bony parts at the side of your body between your waist and your thighs ❷ the fruit of the wild rose

hip hop NOUN a type of popular dance music with spoken words and a steady beat, played on electronic instruments

hippie NOUN (informal) a young person who joins with others to live in an unconventional way, often based on ideas of peace and love. Hippies first appeared in the 1960s.

hippo NOUN (informal) a hippopotamus

hippopotamus NOUN hippopotamuses a very large African animal that lives near water

hire VERB ❶ to pay to have use of something for a time ❷ to lend something in return for payment ❸ to pay someone to do a job for you

hire NOUN ➤ **for hire** available for people to hire

hire purchase NOUN (British) buying something by paying for it in instalments

his DETERMINER & POSSESSIVE PRONOUN belonging to him

hiss VERB ❶ to make a sound like a continuous s ❷ to say something in a quiet angry voice

hiss NOUN the sound of hissing

histogram NOUN a chart showing amounts as rectangles of varying sizes

historian NOUN a person who writes or studies history

historic ADJECTIVE famous or important in history; likely to be remembered

historical ADJECTIVE ❶ to do with history ❷ that actually existed or took place in the past

history NOUN ❶ what happened in the past ❷ the study of

past events ❸ a description of important events

hit VERB hits, hitting, hit ❶ to come forcefully against a person or thing. or to give them a blow ❷ to have a bad effect on a place or group of people ❸ something hits you when you suddenly realize or feel it ❹ to reach something

hit NOUN ❶ hitting; a knock or stroke ❷ a shot that hits the target ❸ a success ❹ a successful song or show ❺ a result of a search on a computer, especially on the Internet

hit-and-run ADJECTIVE a hit-and-run driver is one who injures someone in an accident and drives off without stopping

hitch VERB ❶ to raise or pull something with a slight jerk ❷ to fasten something with a loop or hook ❸ to hitch-hike

hitch NOUN ❶ a slight difficulty causing delay ❷ a knot

hitch-hike VERB to travel by getting lifts from passing vehicles

hi-tech ADJECTIVE a different spelling of **high-tech**

hither ADVERB (old use) to or towards this place

hitherto ADVERB until this time

HIV ABBREVIATION human immunodeficiency virus; a virus that causes Aids

hive NOUN ❶ a beehive ❷ the bees living in a beehive

hoard NOUN a carefully saved store of money, treasure, food, etc.

hoard VERB to collect and store away large quantities of something

hoarding NOUN (British) a tall fence covered with advertisements

hoar frost NOUN the white frost that forms on the ground in the morning after a cold night

hoarse ADJECTIVE having a rough or croaking voice

hoax NOUN a trick played on someone in which they are told about something that is not true

hob NOUN a flat surface on the top of a cooker, for cooking or heating food

hobble VERB to walk with difficulty because your feet or legs hurt

hobby NOUN something you enjoy doing in your spare time

hobby horse NOUN ❶ a stick with a horse's head, used as a toy ❷ a subject that a person likes to talk about whenever they get the chance

hobgoblin NOUN a mischievous or evil spirit

hobnob VERB to spend a lot of time with someone famous or important

hock NOUN the middle joint of an animal's hind leg

hockey NOUN a game played by two teams with curved sticks and a hard ball

hoe NOUN a gardening tool with a long handle and a metal blade, used for scraping up weeds and making soil loose

hoe VERB to scrape or dig the ground with a hoe

hog NOUN ❶ a male pig ❷ (informal) a greedy person

hog VERB (informal) to take more than your fair share of something

Hogmanay NOUN New Year's Eve in Scotland

hoist VERB hoists, hoisting, hoisted to lift something up, especially by using ropes or pulleys

hold VERB holds, holding, held ❶ to have something in your hands ❷ to keep something in a certain position ❸ to contain or have room for a certain amount ❹ to support something ❺ to stay the same; to continue ❻ to have or possess something ❼ to believe or consider something ❽ to arrange something or cause it to take place ❾ to keep someone somewhere or stop them getting away

hold NOUN ❶ holding something; a grasp ❷ a place where you can put your hand or foot when climbing ❸ the part of a ship where cargo is stored, below the deck

holdall NOUN (British) a large portable bag or case

holder NOUN a person or thing that holds something

hold-up NOUN ❶ a brief delay ❷ a robbery with threats or force

hole NOUN ❶ a hollow place; a gap or opening made in something ❷ an animal's burrow ❸ one of the small holes into which you have to hit the ball in golf ❹ (informal) an unpleasant place

hole VERB ❶ to make a hole or holes in something, especially a boat or ship ❷ to hit a golf ball into one of the holes

Holi NOUN a Hindu festival held in the spring

holiday NOUN (*chiefly British*)
❶ a day or time when people do not go to work or to school ❷ a time when you go away to enjoy yourself

holiness NOUN being holy or sacred

hollow ADJECTIVE ❶ with an empty space inside; not solid ❷ loud and echoing ❸ not sincere

hollow NOUN a hollow or sunken place

hollow VERB to make a thing hollow

holly NOUN an evergreen bush with shiny prickly leaves and red berries

hollyhock NOUN a plant with large flowers on a very tall stem

holocaust NOUN large-scale destruction, especially by fire or in a war

hologram NOUN a type of photograph made by laser beams that produces a three-dimensional image

holster NOUN a leather case in which a pistol or revolver is carried

holy ADJECTIVE ❶ to do with God or a particular religion ❷ a holy person is religious and leads a pure life

homage NOUN an act or expression of respect or honour

home NOUN ❶ the place where you live ❷ the place where you were born or where you feel you belong ❸ a place where those who need help are looked after ❹ the place to be reached in a race or in certain games

home ADJECTIVE ❶ to do with your own home or country ❷ played on a team's own ground

home ADVERB ❶ to or at home ❷ to the point aimed at

home VERB ➤ **home in on something** to aim at something and move straight towards it

home economics NOUN the study of cookery and how to run a home

homeland NOUN a person's native country

homeless ADJECTIVE having no home

homely ADJECTIVE simple and ordinary

home-made ADJECTIVE made at home, not bought from a shop

homeopath NOUN a person who practises homeopathy

homeopathy NOUN the treatment of disease by tiny doses of drugs that in a healthy person would produce symptoms of the disease

home page NOUN an introductory page on a website

homesick ADJECTIVE sad or upset because you are away from home

homestead NOUN a farmhouse, usually with the land and buildings round it

homeward ADJECTIVE & ADVERB going towards home

homework NOUN school work that you have to do at home

homicide NOUN the crime of killing another person

homily NOUN a lecture about behaviour

homing ADJECTIVE ❶ trained or having the natural ability, to find its way home from a long distance away ❷ programmed to find and hit its target

homograph NOUN a word that is spelt like another but has a different meaning or origin, e.g. *bat* (a flying animal) and *bat* (for hitting a ball)

homonym (say hom-o-nim) NOUN a homograph or homophone

homophone NOUN a word with the same sound as another but a different spelling and meaning, e.g. *son*, *sun*

Homo sapiens NOUN human beings regarded as a species of animal

homosexual ADJECTIVE attracted to people of the same sex; not heterosexual

honest ADJECTIVE not stealing or cheating or telling lies; truthful

honestly ADVERB ❶ in an honest way ❷ speaking truthfully

honesty NOUN being honest and truthful

honey NOUN a sweet sticky food made by bees

honeycomb NOUN a wax structure of small six-sided sections made by bees to hold their honey and eggs

honeycombed ADJECTIVE with many holes or tunnels

honeymoon NOUN a holiday spent together by a newly-married couple

honeysuckle NOUN a climbing plant with fragrant yellow or pink flowers

honk NOUN a loud sound like that made by a goose or an old-fashioned car horn

honk VERB to make a honking sound

honorary ADJECTIVE ❶ given or received as an honour ❷ unpaid

honour NOUN ❶ great respect or reputation ❷ a person or thing that brings honour ❸ something a person is proud to do ❹ honesty and loyalty ❺ an award given as a mark of respect

honour VERB ❶ to feel or show honour for a person ❷ to keep to the terms of an agreement or promise

honourable ADJECTIVE able to be trusted and always trying to do the right thing; deserving honour and respect

hood NOUN ❶ a covering of soft material for the head and neck ❷ a folding hood or cover

hoodie NOUN ❶ a jacket or sweatshirt with a hood that goes over the head ❷ a person who wears a hoodie

hoodwink VERB to deceive someone

hoof NOUN hoofs or hooves the hard horny part of the feet of horses and some other animals

hook NOUN a bent or curved piece of metal or plastic for hanging things on or for catching hold of something

hook VERB ❶ to fasten something with or on a hook ❷ to catch a fish with a hook ❸ to hit a ball in a curving path

hookah NOUN an oriental tobacco pipe with a long tube passing through a jar of water

hooked ADJECTIVE hook-shaped

hooligan NOUN a rough and violent young person

hoop NOUN a large ring made of

metal, wood or plastic

hoopla NOUN a game in which people try to throw hoops round an object, which they then win as a prize

hooray EXCLAMATION a different spelling of **hurray**

hoot NOUN ❶ the sound made by an owl or a vehicle's horn or a steam whistle ❷ a cry of scorn or disapproval ❸ a loud laugh ❹ something funny

hoot VERB ❶ to make the sound of a hoot ❷ to laugh loudly

Hoover NOUN (trademark) (British) a vacuum cleaner

hoover VERB to clean a carpet with a vacuum cleaner

hop VERB ❶ to jump on one foot ❷ an animal hops when it springs from all its feet at once ❸ (informal) to move quickly

hop NOUN ❶ a hopping movement ❷ a climbing plant used to give beer its flavour

hope NOUN ❶ the feeling of wanting something to happen and thinking that it will happen ❷ a person or thing that gives hope

hope VERB to feel hope; to want and expect something

hopeful ADJECTIVE ❶ feeling hope ❷ likely to be good or successful

hopefully ADVERB ❶ in a hopeful way ❷ it is to be hoped; I hope that

hopeless ADJECTIVE ❶ without hope ❷ very bad at something

hopper NOUN a large funnel-shaped container for grain or sand

hopscotch NOUN a game of hopping into squares drawn on the ground

horde NOUN a large group or crowd

horizon NOUN the line where the earth and the sky seem to meet

horizontal ADJECTIVE level or flat; going across from side to side, not up and down. (The opposite is **vertical**.)

hormone NOUN a substance produced by glands in the body and carried by the blood to stimulate other organs in the body

horn NOUN ❶ a hard substance that grows into a point on the head of a bull, cow, ram, etc. ❷ a brass musical instrument played by blowing ❸ a device for making a warning sound

hornet NOUN a large kind of wasp

horny ADJECTIVE hard like horn

horoscope NOUN an astrologer's forecast of what is going to happen to someone in the future

horrendous ADJECTIVE extremely unpleasant

horrible ADJECTIVE ❶ shocking or horrifying ❷ very unpleasant or nasty

horrid ADJECTIVE nasty or unkind; horrible

horrific ADJECTIVE shocking or horrifying

horrify VERB to make someone feel shocked or disgusted

horror NOUN ❶ great fear or disgust ❷ a person or thing causing horror ❸ (informal) a badly behaved child

hors-d'oeuvre (say or-**dervr**)

a
b
c
d
e
f
g
h
i
j
k
l
m
n
o
p
q
r
s
t
u
v
w
x
y
z

NOUN food served as an appetizer at the start of a meal

horse *NOUN* ❶ a large four-legged animal used for riding on and for pulling carts etc. ❷ a padded wooden block for vaulting over in gymnastics

horseback *NOUN* ➤ **on horseback** riding on a horse

horse chestnut *NOUN* a large tree that produces dark-brown nuts (conkers)

horseman *NOUN* a man who rides a horse, especially a skilled rider

horsemanship *NOUN* skill in riding horses

horseplay *NOUN* rough play

horsepower *NOUN* a unit for measuring the power of an engine, equal to 746 watts

horseshoe *NOUN* a U-shaped piece of metal nailed to a horse's hoof

horsewoman *NOUN* a woman who rides a horse, especially a skilled rider

horticulture *NOUN* the art of planning and looking after gardens

hose *NOUN* ❶ a flexible tube for taking water to something ❷ (*old use*) men's breeches

hose *VERB* to water or spray something with a hose

hosiery *NOUN* socks, stockings and tights sold in shops

hospice (say hosp-iss) *NOUN* a nursing home for people who are very ill or dying

hospitable *ADJECTIVE* welcoming and friendly to guests and visitors

hospital *NOUN* a place where ill or injured people are given medical treatment

hospitality *NOUN* welcoming guests and visitors and giving them food and entertainment

host *NOUN* ❶ a person who has guests and looks after them ❷ the presenter of a television or radio programme ❸ a large number of people or things ❹ in the Christian Church, the bread consecrated at Communion

host *VERB* to organize a party, event, etc. and look after the people who come

hostage *NOUN* a person who is held prisoner until the people who are holding them get what they want

hostel *NOUN* a building where travellers, students or other groups can stay or live

hostess *NOUN* a woman who has guests and looks after them

hostile *ADJECTIVE* ❶ unfriendly and angry ❷ opposed to something ❸ to do with an enemy

hostility *NOUN* unfriendliness and strong dislike

hot *ADJECTIVE* ❶ having great heat or a high temperature ❷ giving a burning sensation in the mouth; spicy ❸ passionate or excitable

hot *VERB* ➤ **hot up** (*British*) (*informal*) to become hotter or more exciting

hot cross bun *NOUN* a spicy bun marked with a cross, eaten at Easter

hot dog *NOUN* a hot sausage in a long bread roll

hotel *NOUN* a building where people

pay to stay for the night when they are travelling or on holiday

hotfoot *ADVERB* in eager haste

hothead *NOUN* an impetuous person

hothouse *NOUN* a heated greenhouse

hotplate *NOUN* a heated surface for cooking food or keeping it hot

hotpot *NOUN* (*British*) a kind of stew

hot-water bottle *NOUN* a container that is filled with hot water and used to warm a bed

hound *NOUN* a dog used in hunting or racing

hound *VERB* to keep on chasing and bothering someone

hour *NOUN* ❶ one of the twenty four parts into which a day is divided; sixty minutes ❷ a particular time

hourglass *NOUN* a glass container with a very narrow part in the middle through which sand runs from the top half to the bottom half, taking one hour

hourly *ADVERB & ADJECTIVE* every hour

house (say howss) *NOUN* ❶ a building made for people to live in, usually designed for one family ❷ a building or establishment for a special purpose ❸ a building for a government assembly; the assembly itself ❹ one of the divisions in some schools for sports competitions and other events ❺ a family or dynasty

house (say howz) *VERB* to provide a place for someone to live or a place where something can be kept

houseboat *NOUN* a barge-like boat

for living in

household *NOUN* all the people who live together in the same house

householder *NOUN* a person who owns or rents a house

housekeeper *NOUN* a person employed to look after a household

housekeeping *NOUN* ❶ looking after a household ❷ the money for food and the other things that you need at home

house-proud *ADJECTIVE* very careful to keep a house clean and tidy

house-trained *ADJECTIVE* an animal that is house-trained is trained to be clean in the house

house-warming *NOUN* a party to celebrate moving into a new home

housewife *NOUN* a woman who does the housekeeping for her family and does not have a paid job

housework *NOUN* the regular work that has to be done in a house, such as cleaning and cooking

housing *NOUN* ❶ buildings in which people live ❷ a stiff cover or guard for a piece of machinery

housing estate *NOUN* (*British*) a set of houses planned and built together in one area

hove *past tense* of **heave** (when used of ships).

hovel *NOUN* a small shabby house

hover *VERB* ❶ to stay in one place in the air ❷ to wait about near someone or something

hovercraft *NOUN* a vehicle that

travels just above the surface of land or water, supported by a strong current of air sent downwards from its engines

how ADVERB ❶ in what way; by what means ❷ to what extent or amount etc. ❸ in what condition ❹ used for emphasis

however ADVERB ❶ in whatever way; to whatever extent ❷ all the same; nevertheless

however CONJUNCTION in any way

howl NOUN a long loud sad-sounding cry or sound, such as that made by a dog or wolf

howl VERB ❶ to make a howl ❷ to weep loudly

howler NOUN (informal) a silly and embarrassing mistake

HQ ABBREVIATION headquarters

hub NOUN ❶ the central part of a wheel ❷ the central point of interest or activity

hubbub NOUN a loud confused noise of voices

huddle VERB ❶ people huddle when they crowd together, often for warmth ❷ to curl up your body closely

huddle NOUN a small group of people crowded together

hue NOUN a colour or tint

huff VERB to breathe out noisily

hug VERB ❶ to clasp someone tightly in your arms ❷ to keep close to something

hug NOUN clasping someone tightly in your arms

huge ADJECTIVE extremely large; enormous

hugely ADVERB extremely; very much

hulk NOUN ❶ the body or wreck of an old ship ❷ a large clumsy person or thing

hulking ADJECTIVE large and heavy in appearance

hull NOUN the main framework of a ship

hullabaloo NOUN an uproar or commotion

hullo EXCLAMATION a different spelling of hello

hum VERB ❶ to sing a tune with your lips closed ❷ to make a low continuous sound like that of a bee

hum NOUN a humming sound

human ADJECTIVE to do with human beings

human NOUN a human being

human being NOUN a person; a man, woman or child

humane (say hew-mayn) ADJECTIVE showing kindness and a wish to cause as little suffering or pain as possible

humanist NOUN a person who believes that people can live using reason and understanding of others, rather than using religious belief

humanitarian ADJECTIVE concerned with people's welfare and the reduction of suffering

humanity NOUN ❶ human beings as a whole; people ❷ being human ❸ compassion and understanding

humble ADJECTIVE ❶ modest; not proud or showy ❷ not special or important

humble VERB to make someone feel humble or humiliated

humbug NOUN ❶ insincere or dishonest talk or behaviour ❷ a hard peppermint sweet

humdrum ADJECTIVE dull and boring; commonplace

humid (say hew-mid) ADJECTIVE humid air is warm and damp

humiliate VERB to make a person feel ashamed or foolish in front of other people

humility NOUN being humble

hummingbird NOUN a small tropical bird that makes a humming sound by beating its wings rapidly

humorous ADJECTIVE amusing or funny

humour NOUN ❶ being amusing; what makes people laugh ❷ the ability to enjoy things that are funny ❸ a person's mood

humour VERB to keep a person happy by doing what they want or agreeing with them

hump NOUN ❶ a rounded lump or mound ❷ an abnormal outward curve at the top of a person's back

hump VERB to carry something heavy with difficulty

humpback bridge NOUN (British) a small bridge that steeply curves upwards in the middle

humus (say hew-mus) NOUN rich earth made by decayed plants

hunch NOUN a feeling that you can guess what is going to happen

hunch VERB to hunch your shoulders is to raise them so that your back is rounded

hunchback NOUN (old use) someone with a hump on their back

hundred NOUN & ADJECTIVE the number 100

hundredweight NOUN a unit of weight equal to 112 pounds (about 50.8 kilograms)

hunger NOUN ❶ the feeling that you have when you need to eat ❷ a strong desire for something

hunger VERB to hunger for something is to want it very much

hunger strike NOUN refusing to eat, as a way of making a protest

hungry ADJECTIVE ❶ wanting or needing to eat ❷ wanting something very much

hunk NOUN ❶ a large piece of something ❷ (informal) a muscular, good-looking man

hunt VERB ❶ to chase and kill animals for food or as a sport ❷ to search for something

hunt NOUN ❶ hunting or searching ❷ a group of hunters

hunter, huntsman NOUN someone who hunts for sport

hurdle NOUN ❶ an upright frame that runners jump over in hurdling ❷ a difficulty or problem that you need to overcome

hurdling NOUN racing in which the runners jump over hurdles

hurl VERB to throw something with great force

hurray, hurrah EXCLAMATION a shout of joy or approval; a cheer

hurricane NOUN a storm with violent wind

hurriedly ADVERB in a hurry

hurry VERB ❶ to move or do

a
b
c
d
e
f
g
h
i
j
k
l
m
n
o
p
q
r
s
t
u
v
w
x
y
z

something quickly **2** to try to make someone be quick

hurry NOUN hurrying; a need to hurry

hurt VERB hurts, hurting, hurt **1** to cause pain or injury to someone **2** to feel painful **3** to upset or offend someone

hurt NOUN physical or mental pain or injury

hurtful ADJECTIVE upsetting and unkind

hurtle VERB to move rapidly, sometimes in an uncontrolled way

husband NOUN the man someone is married to

hush VERB to become silent or quiet or to make someone do this

hush NOUN silence or quiet

husk NOUN the dry outer covering of some seeds and fruits

husky ADJECTIVE a husky voice is low-pitched and slightly hoarse

husky NOUN a large powerful dog used in the Arctic for pulling sledges

hustle VERB **1** to push or shove someone roughly **2** to hurry

hut NOUN a small roughly-made house or shelter

hutch NOUN a box or cage for a rabbit or other pet animal

hyacinth NOUN a sweet-smelling flower that grows from a bulb

hybrid NOUN **1** a plant or animal produced by combining two different species or varieties **2** something that combines parts or characteristics of two different things

hydra NOUN a microscopic

freshwater animal with a tubular body

hydrangea (say hy-**drayn**-ja) NOUN a shrub with pink, blue or white flowers growing in large clusters

hydrant NOUN an outdoor water tap with a nozzle that a fire hose can be attached to

hydraulic ADJECTIVE worked by the force of water or other fluid

hydrochloric acid NOUN a strong colourless acid containing hydrogen and chlorine

hydroelectric ADJECTIVE using water power to produce electricity

hydrofoil NOUN a boat designed to skim over the surface of water

hydrogen NOUN a lightweight gas that combines with oxygen to form water

hyena NOUN a wild animal that looks like a wolf and makes a shrieking howl

hygiene (say hy-jeen) NOUN keeping things clean in order to remain healthy and prevent disease

hygienic ADJECTIVE clean and healthy and free of germs

hymn NOUN a Christian religious song, usually one praising God

hype NOUN (*informal*) extravagant publicity or advertising

hyperactive ADJECTIVE unable to relax and always moving about or doing things

hyperbola (say hy-**per**-bol-a) NOUN (*in mathematics*) a kind of curve

hyperbole (say hy-**per**-bol-ee) NOUN a dramatic exaggeration that is not meant to be taken literally, e.g. 'I've got a stack of work a mile high.'

hyperlink NOUN a place in a computer document that is linked to another computer document

hypermarket NOUN (*British*) a very large supermarket, usually outside a town

hypertext NOUN a computer document that contains links that allow the user to move from one document to another

hyphen NOUN a short dash (-) used to join words or parts of words together (e.g. in *hitch-hiker*)

hypnosis (say hip-**noh**-sis) NOUN a condition like a deep sleep in which a person can be made to follow the commands of someone else

hypnotic ADJECTIVE ❶ having a regular, repeated sound or movement which makes you feel sleepy ❷ to do with hypnosis

hypnotize (also **hypnotise**) VERB to put someone in a state of hypnosis

hypochondriac (say hy-po-**kon**-dree-ak) NOUN a person who constantly imagines that they are ill even though there is nothing wrong with them

hypocrite (say **hip**-o-krit) NOUN someone who pretends to be a better person than they really are

hypodermic ADJECTIVE a hypodermic needle or syringe is one used to inject something under the skin

hypotenuse (say hy-**pot**-i-newz) NOUN the side opposite the right angle in a right-angled triangle

hypothermia NOUN the condition of having a body temperature well below normal

hypothesis (say hy-**poth**-i-sis) NOUN hypotheses a suggestion or guess that tries to explain something but has not yet been proved to be true or correct

hypothetical (say hy-po-**thet**-ikal) ADJECTIVE based on a theory or possibility, not on proven facts

hysteria NOUN wild uncontrollable excitement or emotion

hysterical ADJECTIVE ❶ in a state of hysteria ❷ (*informal*) extremely funny

hysterics (say hiss-**te**-riks) PLURAL NOUN a fit of hysteria

Ii

I PRONOUN a word used by a person to refer to himself or herself

ice NOUN ❶ solid frozen water ❷ an ice cream

ice VERB ❶ to become covered with ice ❷ to put icing on a cake

ice age NOUN a period in the past when most of the earth's surface was covered with ice

iceberg NOUN a large mass of ice floating in the sea with most of it under water

ice cap NOUN a permanent covering of ice and snow at the North or South Pole

ice cream NOUN a sweet creamy frozen food

ice hockey NOUN a form of hockey played on ice

299

ice lolly NOUN (*British*) frozen juice on a small stick

ice rink NOUN a place made for skating

icicle NOUN a pointed hanging piece of ice formed when dripping water freezes

icing NOUN a sugary liquid mixture for decorating cakes

icon (say **eye**-kon) NOUN ① a small symbol or picture on a computer screen, representing a program, window, etc. that you can select ② a sacred painting or mosaic of a holy person

ICT ABBREVIATION information and communication technology

icy ADJECTIVE ① covered with ice ② very cold ③ very unfriendly

Id NOUN a different spelling of Eid

idea NOUN ① a plan or thought that you form in your mind ② an opinion or belief ③ what you know about something

ideal ADJECTIVE perfect; completely suitable

ideal NOUN ① a person or thing that seems to be a perfect example of something ② a high standard or principle that people try to follow

idealist NOUN a person who has high ideals and wishes to achieve them

ideally ADVERB if things were perfect

identical ADJECTIVE exactly the same

identification NOUN ① any document, such as a passport or driving licence, that proves who you are ② identifying someone or something

identify VERB ① to recognize a person or thing as being who or what they are ② to treat something as being identical to something else ③ to think of yourself as sharing someone else's feelings or experiences

identity NOUN who or what a person or thing is

ideology (say eye-dee-**ol**-o-jee) NOUN a set of beliefs and aims, especially in politics

idiocy NOUN stupid behaviour

idiom NOUN a phrase that means something different from the meanings of the words in it, e.g. *in hot water* (= in trouble) or *hell for leather* (= at great speed)

idiosyncrasy (say id-ee-o-**sink**-ra-see) NOUN one person's own way of behaving or doing something

idiot NOUN a stupid or foolish person

idiotic ADJECTIVE stupid or foolish

idle ADJECTIVE ① doing no work; lazy ② not being used ③ useless; with no real purpose

idle VERB ① to be idle or lazy ② an engine idles when it is working slowly

idol NOUN ① a statue or image that is worshipped as a god ② a famous person who is widely admired

idolize (also **idolise**) VERB to admire or love someone very much

idyll (say **id**-il) NOUN ① a beautiful or peaceful scene or situation ② a poem describing a peaceful or romantic scene

idyllic (say id-**il**-ik) ADJECTIVE

beautiful and peaceful

i.e. ABBREVIATION that is

if CONJUNCTION ❶ on condition that; supposing that ❷ even though ❸ whether

igloo NOUN an Inuit round house built of blocks of hard snow

igneous ADJECTIVE igneous rock is formed when hot liquid rock from a volcano cools and becomes hard

ignite VERB ❶ to set fire to something ❷ to catch fire

ignition NOUN ❶ igniting ❷ the part of a motor engine that starts the fuel burning

ignoble ADJECTIVE not noble; shameful

ignoramus NOUN an ignorant person

ignorance NOUN a lack of information or knowledge

ignorant ADJECTIVE ❶ not knowing about something ❷ knowing very little

ignore VERB to take no notice of a person or thing

iguana (say ig-wah-na) NOUN a large tree-climbing tropical lizard

ilk NOUN ➤ of that ilk (informal) of that kind

ill ADJECTIVE ❶ unwell; in bad health ❷ bad or harmful

ill ADVERB badly

illegal ADJECTIVE not legal; against the law

illegible ADJECTIVE illegible writing is not clear enough to read

illegitimate ADJECTIVE (old use) an illegitimate child is born of parents who are not married to each other

ill-fated ADJECTIVE bound to fail or have bad luck

illicit ADJECTIVE done in a way that is against the law; not allowed

illiterate ADJECTIVE unable to read or write

illness NOUN ❶ being ill ❷ a particular form of bad health; a disease

illogical ADJECTIVE not logical; not reasoning correctly

ills PLURAL NOUN problems and difficulties

illuminate VERB ❶ to light something up ❷ to decorate streets or buildings with lights ❸ to decorate a manuscript with coloured designs ❹ to help to explain something or make it clearer

illusion NOUN ❶ something that seems to be real or actually happening but is not, especially something that deceives the eye ❷ a false idea or belief

illusionist NOUN an entertainer who performs tricks that deceive the eye

illustrate VERB ❶ to show or explain something by pictures or examples ❷ to illustrate a book is to put illustrations in it

illustration NOUN ❶ a picture in a book etc. ❷ an example that helps to explain something ❸ illustrating something

illustrator NOUN a person who produces the illustrations in a book

illustrious ADJECTIVE famous and respected

ill will NOUN unkind feelings

towards a person

image NOUN ❶ a picture or statue of a person or thing ❷ what you see in a mirror or through a lens ❸ a person or thing that looks very much like another ❹ a word or phrase that describes something in an imaginative way ❺ a person's or company's public reputation

imagery NOUN a writer's or speaker's use of words to produce pictures in the mind of the reader or hearer

imaginable ADJECTIVE able to be imagined

imaginary ADJECTIVE existing only in your mind; not real

imagination NOUN the ability to imagine things, especially in a creative or inventive way

imaginative ADJECTIVE having or showing imagination

imagine VERB ❶ to form pictures or ideas in your mind ❷ to suppose or think something

imam NOUN a Muslim religious leader

imbecile (say **imb-i-seel**) NOUN a very stupid person

imitate VERB to copy or mimic something

imitation NOUN ❶ a copy of something else ❷ copying something

immaculate ADJECTIVE ❶ perfectly clean; spotless ❷ without any faults or mistakes

immaterial ADJECTIVE not important; not mattering at all

immature ADJECTIVE ❶ not fully grown or developed ❷ behaving in

a silly or childish way

immediate ADJECTIVE ❶ happening or done without any delay ❷ nearest; with nothing or no one between

immediately ADVERB at once; without any delay

immemorial ADJECTIVE ➤ **from time immemorial** further back in time than anyone can remember

immense ADJECTIVE extremely large or great; huge

immensely ADVERB extremely; very much

immerse VERB ❶ to put something completely into a liquid ❷ to be immersed in something is to be concentrating fully on it

immersion heater NOUN a device that heats up water by means of an electric element immersed in the water in a tank

immigrant NOUN a person who has come into a country to live there

immigration NOUN the process by which people come into a country to live there

imminent ADJECTIVE likely to happen at any moment

immobile ADJECTIVE not moving or not able to move

immoral ADJECTIVE morally wrong; wicked

immortal ADJECTIVE ❶ living for ever; not mortal ❷ famous for all time

immortalize (also **immortalise**) VERB to make someone famous for all time

immovable ADJECTIVE unable to

A
B
C
D
E
F
G
H
I
J
K
L
M
N
O
P
Q
R
S
T
U
V
W
X
Y
Z

be moved

immune ADJECTIVE ❶ not able to catch a disease ❷ not affected by something ❸ protected from something and able to avoid it

immune system NOUN the body's means of resisting infection

immunize (also **immunise**) VERB to make a person immune from a disease etc., e.g. by vaccination

imp NOUN ❶ a small devil ❷ a mischievous child

impact NOUN ❶ the force of one thing hitting another ❷ an influence or effect

impair VERB to damage or weaken something

impala (say im-**pah**-la) NOUN a small African antelope

impale VERB to pierce or fix something on a sharp pointed object

impart VERB ❶ to impart news or information is to tell it to someone ❷ to give something a certain taste, smell or quality

impartial ADJECTIVE not favouring one side more than the other; treating everyone equally

impassive ADJECTIVE not showing any emotion

impasto (say im-**past**-oh) NOUN (in art) the technique of applying paint so thickly that it stands out from the surface of the picture

impatient ADJECTIVE ❶ not able to wait for something without getting annoyed ❷ eager to do something and not wanting to wait

impeach VERB to bring an important person to trial for a

serious crime against their country

impeccable ADJECTIVE without any mistakes or faults; perfect

impede VERB to hinder someone or get in their way

impediment NOUN ❶ a hindrance ❷ a fault or defect

impel VERB to urge or drive someone to do something

impending ADJECTIVE about to happen; imminent

impenetrable ADJECTIVE ❶ impossible to get through or see through ❷ impossible to understand

imperative ADJECTIVE ❶ (in grammar) expressing a command or instruction ❷ essential

imperative NOUN (in grammar) the form of a verb used in making commands (e.g. 'come' in Come here!)

imperceptible ADJECTIVE too small or gradual to be noticed

imperfect ADJECTIVE ❶ with faults or problems; not perfect ❷ the imperfect tense of a verb shows a continuous action in the past, e.g. She was singing.

imperial ADJECTIVE ❶ to do with an empire or its rulers ❷ imperial weights and measures are the non-metric ones formerly in use in Britain and still used for some purposes

imperious ADJECTIVE haughty and bossy

impermeable ADJECTIVE not allowing liquid or gas to pass through it

impersonal ADJECTIVE ❶ not

a
b
c
d
e
f
g
h
i
j
k
l
m
n
o
p
q
r
s
t
u
v
w
x
y
z

showing friendly human feelings ❷ not referring to any particular person

impersonate VERB to pretend to be another person

impertinent ADJECTIVE rude to someone and not showing them proper respect

impervious ADJECTIVE ❶ not affected by something and not noticing it ❷ not allowing water, heat, etc. to pass through

impetuous ADJECTIVE acting hastily without thinking

impetus NOUN ❶ the force that makes an object start moving and that keeps it moving ❷ the influence that causes something to develop more quickly

impinge VERB to have an effect or influence on something

impish ADJECTIVE mischievous

implant VERB to fix something into a person's body by means of an operation

implant NOUN an organ or piece of tissue implanted into a person's body

implement NOUN a tool or device you use for something

implement VERB to put a plan or idea into action

implicate VERB to involve a person in a crime etc. or to show that a person is involved

implication NOUN ❶ something that someone suggests without actually saying it ❷ a possible effect or result of something

implicit (say im-**pliss**-it) ADJECTIVE ❶ suggested but not stated

openly. Compare with **explicit**. ❷ absolute or unquestioning

implode VERB to burst or explode inwards

implore VERB to beg someone to do something

imply VERB to suggest something without actually saying it

impolite ADJECTIVE not polite; having bad manners

import VERB to bring in goods from another country

import NOUN ❶ importing goods ❷ something that is imported ❸ (formal) meaning or importance

importance NOUN being important

important ADJECTIVE ❶ having a great effect or value ❷ having great authority or influence

impose VERB ❶ to make someone have to put up with or accept something ❷ to make people have to pay something

imposing ADJECTIVE grand and impressive

imposition NOUN ❶ an unfair burden or inconvenience ❷ imposing something

impossible ADJECTIVE ❶ not possible ❷ (informal) very annoying; unbearable

impostor NOUN a person who dishonestly pretends to be someone else

impotent ADJECTIVE ❶ powerless; unable to take action ❷ a man is impotent when he is unable to have an erection

impoverished ADJECTIVE ❶ poor ❷ poor in quality

impractical ADJECTIVE not practical or sensible

impregnable ADJECTIVE strong enough to be safe against attack

impregnated ADJECTIVE something is impregnated with a substance when the substance has spread all the way through it

impresario NOUN a person who organizes concerts, shows, etc.

impress VERB ❶ to make a person admire something or think it is very good ❷ to impress something on someone is to make them realize its importance ❸ to press a mark into something

impression NOUN ❶ an effect produced on the mind ❷ a vague idea that you have about something ❸ an imitation of a person or a sound ❹ a reprint of a book

impressionable ADJECTIVE easily influenced or affected

Impressionism NOUN a style of painting that gives the general effect of a scene but without details

impressionist NOUN an entertainer who does impressions of famous people

impressive ADJECTIVE making a strong impression; seeming to be very good

imprint NOUN a mark pressed into or on something

imprison VERB to put someone in prison; to shut someone up in a place

improbable ADJECTIVE unlikely

impromptu ADJECTIVE done without any rehearsal or preparation

improper ADJECTIVE ❶ unsuitable or wrong ❷ rude or indecent

improper fraction NOUN a fraction that is greater than 1, with the numerator greater than the denominator, e.g. ¾

improve VERB to make something better or to become better

improvement NOUN making something better or becoming better

improvise VERB ❶ to perform something by making it up as you go along, rather than following a score or script ❷ to make something quickly with whatever is available

impudent ADJECTIVE cheeky or disrespectful

impulse NOUN ❶ a sudden desire or urge to do something ❷ (in science) a force acting on something for a very short time

impulsive ADJECTIVE done or acting on impulse, not after careful thought

impure ADJECTIVE not pure

impurity NOUN a small amount of something in a substance that makes it not pure

in PREPOSITION This word is used to show position or condition, e.g. ❶ at or inside something (I was in the kitchen; He fell in a puddle.) ❷ within the limits of something (I will see you in an hour.) ❸ arranged as; consisting of (a serial in four parts) ❹ a member of (He is in the army.) ❺ by means of (We paid in cash.)

in ADVERB ❶ so as to be in something or inside (*Get in.*) ❷ inwards (*The top caved in.*) ❸ at home; indoors (*Is anybody in?*) ❹ having arrived (*The train will be in soon.*)

inability NOUN being unable to do something

inaccessible ADJECTIVE not able to be reached

inaccurate ADJECTIVE not accurate

inactive ADJECTIVE not active or working

inadequate ADJECTIVE ❶ not enough; not good enough ❷ not able to cope or deal with something

inadvertently ADVERB by accident; without intending to

inane ADJECTIVE silly; without sense

inanimate ADJECTIVE ❶ not living ❷ showing no sign of life

inappropriate ADJECTIVE not appropriate or suitable

inarticulate ADJECTIVE ❶ not able to speak or express yourself clearly ❷ not expressed in words

inaudible ADJECTIVE not loud enough to be heard

inaugurate VERB ❶ to start or introduce something new and important ❷ to formally establish a person in office

inborn ADJECTIVE present in a person or animal from birth

inbox NOUN the place on a computer where new email messages are shown

inbred ADJECTIVE ❶ inborn ❷ produced by inbreeding

inbreeding NOUN breeding from closely related individuals over many generations

in camera ADVERB in a judge's private room, not in public

incandescent ADJECTIVE ❶ giving out a bright light when heated; shining ❷ very angry

incantation NOUN a set of words spoken as a spell or charm

incapable ADJECTIVE not able to do something

incapacitate VERB to make a person too ill or weak to be able to do things normally

incapacity NOUN inability; lack of sufficient strength or power

incarcerate VERB to shut in or imprison a person

incarnate ADJECTIVE having a body or human form

incarnation NOUN ❶ a period of life in a particular form ❷ a perfect example of a certain quality

incendiary ADJECTIVE an incendiary bomb or device is one that is designed to start a fire

incense (say in-sens) NOUN a substance making a spicy smell when it is burnt

incense (say in-sens) VERB to make a person very angry

incentive NOUN something that encourages a person to do something or to work harder

inception NOUN the beginning of something

incessant ADJECTIVE continuing for a long time without a pause

incest NOUN sexual intercourse between two people who are so closely related that they cannot marry each other

inch NOUN a measure of length, one-twelfth of a foot (about 2½ centimetres)

inch VERB to move slowly and gradually

incidence NOUN the extent or frequency of something

incident NOUN an event, especially an unusual or unpleasant one

incidental ADJECTIVE happening as a minor part of something else

incidentally ADVERB by the way

incinerate VERB to destroy something by burning it

incinerator NOUN a device for burning rubbish

incise VERB to cut or engrave something into a surface

incision NOUN a cut, especially one made in a surgical operation

incisive ADJECTIVE clear and sharp

incisor (say in-**sy**-zer) NOUN each of the sharp-edged front teeth in the upper and lower jaws

incite VERB to urge a person to do something; to stir people up

inclement ADJECTIVE (formal) cold, wet or stormy

inclination NOUN ❶ a feeling that makes you want to do something ❷ a tendency to do something ❸ a slope or the angle of a slope

incline (say in-**klyn**) VERB ❶ to lean or slope ❷ to bend the head or body forward, as in a nod or bow ❸ to influence someone to act or think in a certain way

incline (say in-**klyn**) NOUN a slope

include VERB to make or consider something as part of a group of things

inclusive ADJECTIVE including everything; including all the things mentioned

incognito (say in-kog-**neet**-oh or in-**kog**-nit-oh) ADJECTIVE & ADVERB with your name or identity concealed

incoherent ADJECTIVE not speaking or reasoning in a way that can be understood

income NOUN money received regularly from doing work or from investments

income tax NOUN tax charged on income

incoming ADJECTIVE ❶ arriving or being received ❷ about to take over from someone else

incomparable (say in-**komp**-er-abul) ADJECTIVE so good or great that it does not have an equal

incompatible ADJECTIVE not able to exist or be used together

incompetent ADJECTIVE not able or skilled enough to do something properly

incomplete ADJECTIVE not complete

incomprehensible ADJECTIVE not able to be understood

inconceivable ADJECTIVE not able to be imagined; most unlikely

inconclusive ADJECTIVE not leading to a definite decision or result

incongruous ADJECTIVE out of place or unsuitable

a
b
c
d
e
f
g
h
i
j
k
l
m
n
o
p
q
r
s
t
u
v
w
x
y
z

inconsiderable ADJECTIVE small or unimportant

inconsiderate ADJECTIVE not considerate towards other people

inconsistent ADJECTIVE not consistent

inconspicuous ADJECTIVE not attracting attention or clearly visible

incontinent ADJECTIVE not able to control the bladder or bowels

inconvenience NOUN difficulty or problems caused by something

inconvenience VERB to cause slight difficulty for someone

inconvenient ADJECTIVE not convenient; awkward

incorporate VERB to include something as a part of something larger

incorrect ADJECTIVE not correct; wrong

incorrigible ADJECTIVE not able to be reformed or changed

increase VERB ❶ to become larger or more ❷ to make something larger or more

increase NOUN increasing; the amount by which a thing increases

increasingly ADVERB more and more

incredible ADJECTIVE ❶ very difficult to believe ❷ (informal) extremely good or big

incredibly ADVERB ❶ extremely ❷ in a way that is very difficult to believe

incredulous ADJECTIVE finding it difficult to believe someone; doubtful that something is true

incriminate VERB to make it seem as if a person is guilty of a crime or doing something wrong

incubate VERB ❶ to hatch eggs by keeping them warm ❷ to cause bacteria or a disease to develop

incubation period NOUN the time it takes for symptoms of a disease to be seen in an infected person

incubator NOUN ❶ a device in which a baby born prematurely can be kept warm and supplied with oxygen ❷ a device for incubating eggs

incumbent ADJECTIVE if it is incumbent on you to do something, it is your duty to do it

incumbent NOUN a person who holds a particular office or position

incur VERB to bring something upon yourself

incurable ADJECTIVE not able to be cured

incursion NOUN a raid or brief invasion

indebted ADJECTIVE owing money or gratitude to someone

indecent ADJECTIVE something that is indecent is rude or shocking because it involves sex or the body

indecision NOUN being unable to make up your mind; hesitation

indecisive ADJECTIVE not able to make decisions easily

indeed ADVERB ❶ used to strengthen a meaning ❷ really and truly; in fact

indefinable ADJECTIVE not able to be defined or described clearly

indefinite ADJECTIVE not definite or fixed

indefinite article NOUN the word 'a' or 'an'. The word 'the' is called the definite article.

indefinitely ADVERB for an indefinite or unlimited time

indelible ADJECTIVE impossible to rub out or remove

indelicate ADJECTIVE ❶ slightly indecent ❷ tactless

indent VERB to start a line of writing or printing further in from the margin than other lines

indentation NOUN a dent or notch made in something

independence NOUN ❶ the freedom to live your life without being dependent on someone else ❷ the freedom of a country from foreign rule and the ability to govern itself

independent ADJECTIVE ❶ not dependent on any other person or thing for help, money or support ❷ an independent country is one that governs itself ❸ not connected or involved with something

indescribable ADJECTIVE unable to be described

indestructible ADJECTIVE unable to be destroyed

indeterminate ADJECTIVE not fixed or decided exactly; left vague

index NOUN ❶ indexes an alphabetical list of things, especially at the end of a book ❷ a number showing how prices or wages have changed from a previous level ❸ (in mathematics) indices the raised number etc. written to the right of another (e.g. 3 in 2^3) showing how many times the first one is to be multiplied by itself

index VERB to make an index to a book etc.; to put something into an index

index finger NOUN the finger next to your thumb; the forefinger

Indian ADJECTIVE ❶ to do with India or its people ❷ to do with Native Americans

Indian summer NOUN a period of warm weather in autumn

indicate VERB ❶ to point something out or make it known ❷ to be a sign of something ❸ when drivers indicate, they signal which direction they are turning by using their indicators

indication NOUN a sign of something

indicative ADJECTIVE being a sign of something

indicative NOUN the form of a verb used in making a statement (e.g. 'he said' or 'He is coming.'), not in a command, question or wish

indicator NOUN ❶ a thing that indicates or points to something ❷ a flashing light used to signal that a motor vehicle is turning ❸ (in science) a chemical compound (such as litmus) that changes colour in the presence of a particular substance or condition

indict (say ind-yt) VERB to charge a person with having committed a serious crime

indifferent ADJECTIVE ❶ not caring about something; not interested in something at all ❷ not very good

indigenous (say in-dij-in-us) ADJECTIVE growing or originating in a particular country; native

indigestible ADJECTIVE difficult or impossible to digest

indigestion NOUN pain or discomfort caused by difficulty in digesting food

indignant ADJECTIVE angry at something you think is wrong or unfair

indignation NOUN anger about something you think is wrong or unfair

indignity NOUN treatment that makes a person feel undignified or humiliated; an insult

indigo NOUN a deep-blue colour

indirect ADJECTIVE not direct or straight

indirect speech NOUN a speaker's words given in a changed form reported by someone else, as in *He said that he would come.* (reporting the words 'I will come.')

indiscreet ADJECTIVE ① not discreet; revealing secrets or too much information ② not cautious; rash

indiscriminate ADJECTIVE showing no discrimination; not making a careful choice

indispensable ADJECTIVE that you cannot do without; essential

indisposed ADJECTIVE slightly unwell so that you are unable to do something

indisputable ADJECTIVE definitely true; that cannot be shown to be wrong

indistinct ADJECTIVE not distinct or clear

indistinguishable ADJECTIVE not able to be told apart

individual ADJECTIVE ① of or for one person ② single or separate

individual NOUN one person, animal or plant

individuality NOUN the things that make one person or thing different from another; distinctive identity

individually ADVERB separately; one by one

indivisible ADJECTIVE not able to be divided or separated

indomitable ADJECTIVE not able to be overcome or conquered

indoor ADJECTIVE used, placed or done inside a building

indoors ADVERB inside a building

induce VERB ① to persuade someone to do something ② to produce or cause something ③ if a pregnant woman is induced, the birth is brought on artificially with the use of drugs

inducement NOUN something that is offered to someone to persuade them to do something

indulge VERB to allow a person to have or do whatever they want

indulgent ADJECTIVE allowing someone to have or do whatever they want; kind and lenient

industrial ADJECTIVE to do with industry; working or used in industry

industrial action NOUN (chiefly British) ways for workers to protest, such as striking or working to rule

industrialist NOUN a person who owns or manages an industrial business

industrialized (also **industrialised**) ADJECTIVE an industrialized country or district has many industries

Industrial Revolution NOUN the expansion of British industry by the use of machines in the late 18th and early 19th century

industrious ADJECTIVE working hard

industry NOUN ❶ making or producing goods, especially in factories ❷ a particular branch of this or any business activity ❸ hard work and effort

inedible ADJECTIVE not suitable for eating

ineffective ADJECTIVE not producing the effect or result that you want

ineffectual ADJECTIVE not achieving anything

inefficient ADJECTIVE not working well and wasting time or energy

inelegant ADJECTIVE not elegant

ineligible ADJECTIVE not eligible

inept ADJECTIVE lacking any skill

inequality NOUN not being equal

inert ADJECTIVE not moving or reacting

inert gas NOUN a gas that almost never combines with other substances

inertia (say in-**er**-sha) NOUN ❶ being unwilling to move or take action ❷ (in science) the tendency for a moving thing to keep moving in a straight line

inescapable ADJECTIVE unavoidable

inevitable ADJECTIVE something is inevitable when it cannot be avoided and is sure to happen

inexcusable ADJECTIVE not able to be excused or justified

inexhaustible ADJECTIVE so great that it cannot be used up completely

inexorable (say in-**eks**-er-a-bul) ADJECTIVE not able to be stopped; relentless

inexpensive ADJECTIVE not expensive; cheap

inexperience NOUN lack of experience

inexplicable ADJECTIVE impossible to explain

infallible ADJECTIVE ❶ never wrong ❷ never failing

infamous (say in-**fam**-us) ADJECTIVE famous for being bad or wicked

infancy NOUN ❶ the time when you are a baby or young child ❷ an early stage of development

infant NOUN a baby or young child

infantile ADJECTIVE ❶ very childish and silly ❷ to do with babies or young children

infantry NOUN soldiers who fight on foot. Compare with **cavalry**.

infatuated ADJECTIVE filled with an unreasonably strong feeling of love that does not last long

infect VERB to pass on a disease or bacteria to a person, animal or plant

infection NOUN ❶ infecting someone or something ❷ an infectious disease or condition

a
b
c
d
e
f
g
h
i
j
k
l
m
n
o
p
q
r
s
t
u
v
w
x
y
z

infectious ADJECTIVE ❶ an infectious disease is able to be spread by air, water, etc. Compare with **contagious**. ❷ quickly spreading to others

infer VERB to form an opinion or work something out from what someone says or does, even though they do not actually say it

inferior ADJECTIVE less good or less important; low or lower in position, quality, etc.

inferior NOUN a person who is lower in position or rank than someone else

infernal ADJECTIVE ❶ (informal) awful; very annoying ❷ to do with or like hell

inferno NOUN a raging fire

infertile ADJECTIVE not fertile

infest VERB insects or other pests infest a place when they are numerous and troublesome there

infidel (say in-fid-el) NOUN (old use) a person who does not believe in a religion

infidelity NOUN being unfaithful to your husband, wife or partner

infiltrate VERB to get into a place or organization gradually and without being noticed

infinite ADJECTIVE ❶ endless; without a limit ❷ too great to be measured

infinitely ADVERB very much; with no limit

infinitive NOUN (in grammar) the form of a verb that does not change to indicate a particular tense, number or person, in English used with or without to, e.g. go in

'Let him go.' or 'Allow him to go.'

infinity NOUN an infinite number, distance or time

infirm ADJECTIVE weak, especially from old age or illness

infirmary NOUN ❶ a hospital ❷ a place where sick people are cared for in a school, monastery, etc.

inflame VERB ❶ to produce strong feelings or anger in people ❷ a part of the body is inflamed when it becomes painfully red and swollen

inflammable ADJECTIVE able to be set on fire

inflammation NOUN painful redness or swelling in a part of the body

inflammatory ADJECTIVE likely to make people angry

inflatable ADJECTIVE able to be inflated

inflate VERB ❶ to fill something with air or gas so that it expands ❷ to increase something too much

inflation NOUN a general rise in prices and fall in the purchasing power of money

inflect VERB ❶ (in grammar) to change the ending or form of a word to show its tense or its grammatical relation to other words, e.g. sing changes to sang or sung, child changes to children ❷ to alter the voice in speaking

inflection NOUN ❶ (in grammar) an ending or form of a word used to inflect, e.g. -ed in killed and -es in bunches ❷ the rise and fall in your voice when you are speaking

inflexible ADJECTIVE not able to be bent, changed or persuaded

inflict VERB to make someone suffer something

influence NOUN ❶ the power to affect other people or things ❷ a person or thing with this power

influence VERB to have an influence on a person or thing

influential ADJECTIVE having great influence

influenza NOUN an infectious disease that causes fever, catarrh and pain

influx NOUN a flowing in, especially of people or things coming in

inform VERB to tell someone something or give them information about it

informal ADJECTIVE not formal; casual and relaxed

informant NOUN a person who gives information

information NOUN facts or knowledge about something

information technology NOUN the study or use of ways of storing, arranging and giving out information, especially computers and telecommunications

informative ADJECTIVE giving a lot of useful information

informed ADJECTIVE knowing about something

informer NOUN a person who gives information against someone, especially to the police

infra-red ADJECTIVE below or beyond red in the spectrum

infrastructure NOUN the basic services and systems that a country needs in order for its society and economy to work properly, such as buildings, roads, transport and power supplies

infrequent ADJECTIVE not happening often

infringe VERB ❶ to break a rule, law or agreement ❷ to reduce or limit a person's rights

infuriate VERB to make a person very angry

infuse VERB ❶ to fill someone or something with a feeling or quality ❷ to soak or steep tea, herbs, etc. in a liquid to extract the flavour

ingenious ADJECTIVE ❶ cleverly made or done ❷ clever at inventing things

ingenuity NOUN cleverness in inventing things or solving problems

ingenuous ADJECTIVE without cunning; innocent

ingot NOUN a lump of gold or silver that is cast in a brick shape

ingrained ADJECTIVE ❶ ingrained feelings or habits are deeply fixed in people's minds ❷ ingrained dirt marks a surface deeply

ingratiate VERB ➤ ingratiate yourself to get yourself into favour with someone, especially by flattering them or always agreeing with them

ingratitude NOUN lack of gratitude

ingredient NOUN one of the parts of a mixture; one of the things used in a recipe

inhabit VERB to live in a place

inhabitant NOUN a person or

animal that lives in a place

inhale *VERB* to breathe in

inhaler *NOUN* a device used for relieving asthma by inhaling medicine into your mouth

inherent (say in-**heer**-ent) *ADJECTIVE* existing in something as one of its natural or permanent qualities

inherit *VERB* ❶ to receive money, property or a title when its previous owner dies ❷ to get certain qualities or characteristics from your parents or predecessors

inheritance *NOUN* inheriting something; the money, property, etc. that you inherit

inhibition *NOUN* a feeling of embarrassment or worry that prevents you from doing something or expressing your emotions

inhospitable *ADJECTIVE* ❶ unfriendly to visitors ❷ an inhospitable place is difficult to live in because it gives no shelter from the weather

inhuman *ADJECTIVE* cruel; without pity or kindness

inhumane *ADJECTIVE* not humane

inimitable *ADJECTIVE* impossible to imitate

initial *NOUN* the first letter of a word or name

initial *VERB* to mark or sign something with the initials of your names

initial *ADJECTIVE* at the beginning

initially *ADVERB* at the beginning; at first

initiate *VERB* ❶ to start something

❷ to admit a person as a member of a society or group, often with special ceremonies

initiative (say in-**ish**-a-tiv) *NOUN* ❶ the power or right to get something started ❷ the ability to make decisions and take action on your own without being told what to do

inject *VERB* ❶ to put a medicine or drug into the body by means of a hollow needle ❷ to put liquid into something by means of a syringe etc. ❸ to add a new quality

injunction *NOUN* a command given with authority, e.g. by a law court

injure *VERB* to harm or hurt someone

injury *NOUN* harm or damage done to someone

injustice *NOUN* lack of justice; unjust treatment

ink *NOUN* a black or coloured liquid used in writing and printing

inkling *NOUN* a slight idea or suspicion

inky *ADJECTIVE* ❶ stained with ink ❷ black like ink

inland *ADJECTIVE & ADVERB* in or towards the middle part of a country, away from the coast

in-laws *PLURAL NOUN* (*informal*) relatives by marriage, especially the parents of your husband or wife

inlay *VERB* inlays, inlaying, inlaid to set pieces of wood or metal into a surface to form a design

inlay *NOUN* a design formed by inlaying

inlet *NOUN* a strip of water reaching

into the land from a sea or lake

inmate NOUN one of the people kept in a prison or mental hospital

inmost ADJECTIVE most inward

inn NOUN a hotel or public house, especially in the country

innards PLURAL NOUN (*informal*) the internal organs of a person or animal; the inner parts of a machine

innate ADJECTIVE an innate ability or quality is one that you were born with

inner ADJECTIVE inside; nearer to the centre

innermost ADJECTIVE ❶ nearest to the centre; furthest inside ❷ most secret or private

innings NOUN the time when a cricket team or player is batting

innocence NOUN ❶ not being guilty of doing something wrong ❷ lack of experience of the world, especially of bad things

innocent ADJECTIVE ❶ not guilty of doing something wrong ❷ lacking experience of the world, especially of bad things ❸ harmless

innocuous ADJECTIVE harmless

innovation NOUN ❶ introducing new things or new methods ❷ a completely new process or way of doing things that has just been introduced

innovative ADJECTIVE an innovative design or way of doing something is new and clever

innuendo NOUN indirect reference to something insulting or rude

innumerable ADJECTIVE too many

to be counted

inoculate VERB to inject or treat someone with a vaccine or serum as a protection against a disease

inoffensive ADJECTIVE not likely to upset or offend anyone

inorganic ADJECTIVE not of living organisms; of mineral origin

in-patient NOUN a patient who stays at a hospital for treatment

input NOUN what you put into something, especially data put into a computer

input VERB inputs, inputting, input or inputted to put data into a computer

inquest NOUN an official inquiry to find out how a person died

inquire VERB ❶ to investigate something carefully ❷ to ask for information

inquiry NOUN ❶ an official investigation ❷ a question

inquisition NOUN a detailed questioning or investigation

inquisitive ADJECTIVE always asking questions or trying to find out things

inroads PLURAL NOUN ➤ **make inroads on** or **into something** to take away or use up large quantities of something

insane ADJECTIVE not sane; mad

insanitary ADJECTIVE unclean and likely to be harmful to health

insatiable (say in-**say**-sha-bul) ADJECTIVE impossible to satisfy

inscribe VERB to write or carve words or symbols on something

inscription NOUN words written

or carved on a monument, coin, stone, etc. or written in the front of a book

inscrutable ADJECTIVE mysterious; impossible to interpret

insect NOUN a small animal with six legs, no backbone and a body divided into three parts (head, thorax, abdomen)

insecticide NOUN a substance for killing insects

insectivorous ADJECTIVE feeding on insects and other small invertebrate creatures

insecure ADJECTIVE ① not secure or safe ② lacking confidence about yourself

insensitive ADJECTIVE not sensitive or thinking about other people's feelings

inseparable ADJECTIVE ① liking to be constantly together ② not able to be separated

insert VERB to put a thing into something else or between two things

inshore ADVERB & ADJECTIVE near or nearer to the shore

inside NOUN the inner side, surface or part

inside ADJECTIVE on or coming from the inside; in or nearest to the middle

inside ADVERB & PREPOSITION on or to the inside of something; in

insidious ADJECTIVE causing harm gradually, without being noticed

insight NOUN ① the ability to see the truth about things ② an understanding of something

insignia SINGULAR NOUN & PLURAL NOUN a badge or symbol that shows that you belong to something or hold a particular office

insignificant ADJECTIVE not important or influential

insincere ADJECTIVE not sincere

insinuate VERB ① to hint something unpleasant ② to introduce a thing or yourself gradually or craftily into a place

insinuation NOUN an unpleasant hint or suggestion that someone makes

insipid ADJECTIVE ① lacking flavour ② not lively or interesting

insist VERB to be very firm in saying or asking for something

insistent ADJECTIVE ① insisting on doing or having something ② continuing for a long time in a way that you cannot ignore

insolent ADJECTIVE very rude and disrespectful

insoluble ADJECTIVE ① impossible to solve ② impossible to dissolve

insolvent ADJECTIVE unable to pay your debts

insomnia NOUN being unable to sleep

inspect VERB to examine something carefully to check that everything is as it should be

inspector NOUN ① a person whose job is to inspect or supervise things ② a police officer ranking next above a sergeant

inspiration NOUN ① a sudden brilliant idea ② a person or thing that fills you with ideas or enthusiasm

inspire VERB to fill a person with ideas, enthusiasm or creative feeling

instability NOUN lack of stability

install VERB ❶ to put something in position and ready to use ❷ to put a person into an important position with a ceremony

instalment NOUN ❶ each of a series of payments made for something over a period of time ❷ each part of a television serial or of a series of publications

instance NOUN an example

instant ADJECTIVE ❶ happening immediately ❷ instant food or drink is designed to be prepared quickly and easily

instant NOUN a moment

instantaneous ADJECTIVE happening immediately

instantly ADVERB without delay; immediately

instead ADVERB in place of something else

instep NOUN the top of the foot between the toes and the ankle

instigate VERB to make something start to happen; to stir something up

instil VERB to put ideas into a person's mind gradually

instinct NOUN a natural tendency or ability

instinctive ADJECTIVE following instinct, not thought

institute NOUN a society or organization; the building used by this

institute VERB to establish or introduce something

institution NOUN ❶ an institute; a public organization, e.g. a hospital or university ❷ an established habit or custom ❸ instituting something

instruct VERB ❶ to teach a person a subject or skill ❷ to tell a person what they must do

instruction NOUN ❶ teaching a subject or skill ❷ an order or piece of information

instructive ADJECTIVE giving useful information or knowledge

instructor NOUN a person who teaches a practical skill or sport

instrument NOUN ❶ a device for producing musical sounds ❷ a tool used for delicate or scientific work ❸ a measuring device

instrumental ADJECTIVE ❶ performed on musical instruments, without singing ❷ to be instrumental in doing something is to play an important part in it

instrumentalist NOUN a person who plays a musical instrument

insubordinate ADJECTIVE disobedient or rebellious

insufferable ADJECTIVE annoying and difficult to bear

insufficient ADJECTIVE not enough

insular ADJECTIVE ❶ to do with or like an island ❷ narrow-minded

insulate VERB to cover or protect something to prevent heat, cold or electricity from passing in or out

insulin NOUN a substance that controls the amount of sugar in the blood. The lack of insulin causes diabetes.

insult (say in-**sult**) VERB to speak to or treat someone in a rude way that offends them

insult (say **in**-sult) NOUN an insulting remark or action

insurance NOUN an agreement to compensate someone for a loss, damage or injury etc., in return for a payment (called a **premium**) made in advance

insure VERB to protect something with insurance

insurmountable ADJECTIVE unable to be overcome

insurrection NOUN a rebellion

intact ADJECTIVE not damaged; complete

intake NOUN ❶ taking something in ❷ the number of people or things taken in

intangible ADJECTIVE difficult to describe or measure; not able to be touched

integer NOUN a whole number (e.g. 0, 3, 19), not a fraction

integral (say in-**tig**-ral) ADJECTIVE that is an essential part of a whole thing

integrate VERB ❶ to make parts into a whole; to combine things ❷ to bring people together harmoniously into a single community

integrity (say in-**teg**-rit-ee) NOUN being honest and behaving well

intellect NOUN the ability to think and work things out with your mind

intellectual ADJECTIVE ❶ to do with or using the intellect ❷ having a good intellect ❸ a liking for

knowledge

intellectual NOUN an intellectual person

intelligence NOUN ❶ being intelligent ❷ information, especially of military value; the people who collect and study this information

intelligent ADJECTIVE able to learn and understand things; having great mental ability

intelligible ADJECTIVE able to be understood

intend VERB ❶ to have something in mind as what you want to do ❷ to plan that something should have a particular meaning or purpose

intense ADJECTIVE ❶ very strong or great ❷ feeling things very strongly and seriously

intensify VERB to make something more intense or to become more intense

intensity NOUN the intensity of something is how strong or great it is

intensive ADJECTIVE concentrated; using a lot of effort over a short time

intensive care NOUN medical treatment of a patient who is dangerously ill, with constant supervision

intent NOUN what someone intends; an intention

intent ADJECTIVE showing great attention and interest

intention NOUN what someone intends; a purpose or plan

intentional ADJECTIVE deliberate,

not accidental

inter *VERB* to bury a corpse

interact *VERB* ❶ to talk to or mix with other people ❷ to have an effect upon one another

interactive *ADJECTIVE* (*in computing*) allowing information to be sent immediately in either direction between a computer system and its user

intercede *VERB* to speak or act on behalf of another person or as a peacemaker

intercept *VERB* to stop or catch a person or thing that is going from one place to another

interchange *VERB* ❶ to put each of two things into the other's place ❷ to exchange things

interchange *NOUN* ❶ interchanging ❷ a road junction where vehicles can move from one motorway etc. to another

interchangeable *ADJECTIVE* things are interchangeable when they can be changed or swapped around

intercom *NOUN* a system of communication between rooms or compartments, operating rather like a telephone

intercourse *NOUN* ❶ communication or dealings between people ❷ sexual intercourse

interdependent *ADJECTIVE* dependent upon each other

interest *NOUN* ❶ a feeling of wanting to know about or be involved with something ❷ a thing that interests someone ❸ an advantage or benefit ❹ money

paid regularly in return for money lent or deposited

interest *VERB* to attract a person's interest

interesting *ADJECTIVE* catching and holding your attention

interface *NOUN* a connection between two parts of a computer system

interfere *VERB* ❶ to take part in something that has nothing to do with you ❷ to get in the way of something

interference *NOUN* ❶ interfering in something ❷ a crackling or distorting of a radio or television signal

interim *NOUN* an interval of time between two events

interim *ADJECTIVE* in use for the time being until something more permanent is arranged

interior *NOUN* the inside of something; the central or inland part of a country

interior *ADJECTIVE* inner

interject *VERB* to break in with a remark while someone is speaking

interjection *NOUN* a word or words exclaimed expressing joy or pain or surprise, such as *oh!* or *wow!* or *good heavens!*

interlock *VERB* things interlock when they fit into each other

interloper *NOUN* an intruder

interlude *NOUN* ❶ an interval ❷ something happening in an interval or between other events

intermediary *NOUN* someone who tries to settle a dispute by negotiating with both sides; a mediator

intermediate ADJECTIVE coming between two things in time, place or order

interminable ADJECTIVE seeming to go on for ever; long and boring

intermission NOUN an interval between parts of a film or show

intermittent ADJECTIVE happening at intervals; not continuous

intern VERB to imprison someone in a special camp or area, usually in wartime

internal ADJECTIVE inside; within something

internal-combustion engine NOUN an engine that produces power by burning fuel inside the engine itself

international ADJECTIVE to do with or belonging to more than one country; agreed between nations

international NOUN ❶ a sports contest between teams representing different countries ❷ a sports player who plays for his or her country

Internet NOUN a computer network that allows users all over the world to communicate and exchange information

internment NOUN being interned in wartime

interplanetary ADJECTIVE between planets

interpret VERB ❶ to explain what something means ❷ to translate what someone says into another language as they are speaking ❸ to perform music, a part in a play, etc. in a way that shows your

feelings about its meaning

interregnum NOUN an interval between the reign of one ruler and that of his or her successor

interrogate VERB to question someone closely or aggressively

interrogative ADJECTIVE questioning; expressing a question

interrupt VERB ❶ to stop someone while they are in the middle of speaking or concentrating by saying something to them ❷ to stop something continuing for a short time

interruption NOUN interrupting someone or something

intersect VERB ❶ lines or roads intersect when they cross each other ❷ to divide a thing by passing or lying across it

intersection NOUN a place where lines or roads cross each other

intersperse VERB to be interspersed with things is to have them mixed in here and there

interval NOUN ❶ a time between two events or parts of a play or show ❷ (in music) the musical difference between the pitches of two notes

intervene VERB ❶ to come between two events ❷ to interrupt a discussion or fight to try and stop it or change its result

interview NOUN a meeting with someone to ask him or her questions or to obtain information

interview VERB to have an interview with someone

intestine NOUN the long tube along which food passes while being absorbed by the body, between the stomach and the anus

intimacy *NOUN* having a very close friendship or relationship with someone

intimate (say **in**-tim-at) *ADJECTIVE* ❶ very friendly with someone ❷ private and personal ❸ detailed

intimate (say **in**-tim-ayt) *VERB* to hint at something

intimidate *VERB* to frighten a person into doing something by using threats

into *PREPOSITION* ❶ used to express movement to the inside of something (*Go into the room.*) ❷ used to express a change of condition or state (*It broke into pieces. She went into politics.*) ❸ used to show division (*4 into 20 = 20 divided by 4*)

intolerable *ADJECTIVE* too much to bear

intolerant *ADJECTIVE* not tolerant or willing to put up with people

intonation *NOUN* the tone or pitch of the voice in speaking

intone *VERB* to recite something in a chanting voice

intoxicate *VERB* ❶ to make someone very drunk ❷ to make someone wildly excited

intransitive *ADJECTIVE* an intransitive verb is one that is used without a direct object after it, e.g. *hear* in *We can hear.* (but not in *We can hear you.*) Compare with **transitive**.

intravenous (say in-tra-**veen**-us) *ADJECTIVE* an intravenous injection is made directly into a vein

intrepid *ADJECTIVE* fearless and brave

intricate *ADJECTIVE* very complicated, with a lot of fine details

intrigue (say in-**treeg**) *VERB* to interest someone very much and make them curious

intrigue (say in-**treeg**) *NOUN* ❶ plotting; an underhand plot ❷ (*old use*) a secret love affair

intrinsic *ADJECTIVE* being part of the essential nature or character of something

introduce *VERB* ❶ to bring an idea or practice into use ❷ to make a person known to other people ❸ to announce a broadcast, etc.

introduction *NOUN* ❶ introducing someone or something ❷ an explanation put at the beginning of a book, speech, etc.

introspective *ADJECTIVE* examining your own thoughts and feelings

introvert *NOUN* a shy person who does not like to talk about their own thoughts and feelings with other people. (The opposite is extrovert.)

intrude *VERB* to come in or join in without being wanted

intruder *NOUN* someone who forces their way into a place where they are not supposed to be

intuition *NOUN* the power to know or understand things without having to think hard or without being taught

Inuit (say in-yoo-it) *NOUN* ❶ a member of a people living in northern Canada and Greenland; an Eskimo ② the language of the Inuit

inundate VERB to send someone so many things that they cannot deal with them all

invade VERB ① to attack and enter a country ② to crowd into a place

invalid (say **in**-va-leed) NOUN a person who is ill or who is weakened by illness

invalid (say in-**val**-id) ADJECTIVE not valid; not able to be used legally

invaluable ADJECTIVE having a value that is too great to be measured; extremely valuable

invariable ADJECTIVE not variable; never changing

invariably ADVERB without exception; always

invasion NOUN ① attacking and entering a country ② crowding into a place

invective NOUN abusive words

invent VERB ① to be the first person to make or think of a particular thing ② to make up a false story

invention NOUN ① a thing that has been made or designed by someone for the first time ② inventing something

inventive ADJECTIVE having clever new ideas

inventor NOUN a person who has invented something

inventory (say **in**-ven-ter-ee) NOUN a detailed list of goods or furniture

inverse ADJECTIVE opposite or reverse

invert VERB to turn something

upside down

invertebrate NOUN an animal without a backbone

inverted commas PLURAL NOUN punctuation marks (" " or ' ') which are put round quotations and spoken words

invest VERB ① to use money to make a profit, e.g. by lending it in return for interest to be paid or by buying stocks and shares or property ② to give someone an honour, medal or special title in a formal ceremony

investigate VERB to find out as much as you can about something

investigation NOUN a careful search for information about something

investiture NOUN the ceremony of investing someone with an honour etc.

investment NOUN ① an amount of money invested ② something in which money is invested

inveterate ADJECTIVE always doing something and not likely to stop

invigilate VERB (British) to supervise the people taking an examination

invigorate VERB to make someone feel healthy and full of energy

invincible ADJECTIVE not able to be defeated

invisible ADJECTIVE not visible; not able to be seen

invitation NOUN a request for a person to do or come to something

invite VERB ① to ask a person to come or do something ② to be likely to cause something unpleasant to happen

inviting *ADJECTIVE* attractive or tempting

invoice *NOUN* a list of goods sent or work done, with the prices charged

invoke *VERB* ❶ to mention a law or someone's authority to support what you are doing ❷ to call upon a god in prayer asking for help etc.

involuntary *ADJECTIVE* not deliberate; done without thinking

involve *VERB* ❶ to have or include something as a necessary part ❷ to make or let someone share or take part in something

involved *ADJECTIVE* ❶ taking part in something; closely connected with something ❷ long and complicated

invulnerable *ADJECTIVE* not able to be harmed

inward *ADJECTIVE* ❶ on the inside ❷ going or facing inwards

inward *ADVERB* inwards

inwardly *ADVERB* in your thoughts; privately

inwards *ADVERB* towards the inside

iodine *NOUN* a chemical substance used as an antiseptic

ion *NOUN* an electrically charged particle

ionosphere (say eye-**on**-os-feer) *NOUN* a region of the upper atmosphere, containing ions

iota *NOUN* a tiny amount of something

IOU *NOUN* a signed note acknowledging that you owe someone some money

IQ *ABBREVIATION* intelligence

quotient; a number showing how a person's intelligence compares with that of an average person

irascible (say ir-**as**-ib-ul) *ADJECTIVE* easily becoming angry; irritable

irate (say eye-**rayt**) *ADJECTIVE* angry

iridescent *ADJECTIVE* showing rainbow-like colours

iris *NOUN* ❶ the coloured part of your eyeball ❷ a plant with long pointed leaves and large flowers

irk *VERB* to annoy someone

irksome *ADJECTIVE* annoying or tiresome

iron *NOUN* ❶ a hard grey metal ❷ a device with a flat base that is heated for smoothing clothes or cloth ❸ a tool made of iron

iron *VERB* to smooth clothes or cloth with an iron

Iron Age *NOUN* the time when tools and weapons were made of iron

ironic (say eye-**ron**-ik) *ADJECTIVE* ❶ an ironic situation is strange because the opposite happens to what you might expect ❷ you are being ironic when you say the opposite of what you mean

ironmonger *NOUN* (*British*) a shopkeeper who sells tools and other metal objects

irons *PLURAL NOUN* shackles or fetters

irony (say **eye**-ron-ee) *NOUN* ❶ saying the opposite of what you mean in order to emphasize it or as a joke, e.g. saying 'What a lovely day.' when it is pouring with rain ❷ a situation that is the opposite of what you might have expected

irrational *ADJECTIVE* not rational; illogical

irrefutable (say ir-**ef**-yoo-ta-bul) ADJECTIVE unable to be proven wrong

irregular ADJECTIVE ❶ not regular; uneven ❷ not following the normal rules or usual custom

irrelevant (say ir-**el**-iv-ant) ADJECTIVE not relevant; not having anything to do with what is being discussed

irreplaceable ADJECTIVE unable to be replaced

irrepressible ADJECTIVE unable to be repressed; always lively and cheerful

irresistible ADJECTIVE too strong or attractive or tempting to resist

irresolute ADJECTIVE feeling uncertain; hesitant

irrespective ADJECTIVE not taking something into account

irresponsible ADJECTIVE not thinking enough about the effects of your actions

irretrievable ADJECTIVE not able to be retrieved

irreverent ADJECTIVE not reverent or respectful

irrigate VERB to supply land with water so that crops can grow

irritable ADJECTIVE easily annoyed; bad-tempered

irritate VERB ❶ to annoy someone ❷ to make a part of your body itch or feel sore

irritation NOUN ❶ being annoyed ❷ something that annoys you

Islam NOUN the religion of Muslims

island NOUN ❶ a piece of land surrounded by water ❷ something

that resembles an island because it is isolated or detached

islander NOUN someone who lives on an island

isle (rhymes with *mile*) NOUN (*poetic & in names*) an island

isobar (say **eye**-so-bar) NOUN a line on a map connecting places that have the same atmospheric pressure

isolate VERB to place or keep a person or thing apart from other people or things

isolation NOUN being separate or alone

isosceles (say eye-**soss**-il-eez) ADJECTIVE an isosceles triangle has two sides of equal length

isotope NOUN (*in science*) a form of an element that differs from other forms in the structure of its nucleus but has the same chemical properties as the other forms

ISP ABBREVIATION Internet service provider, a company providing individual users with a connection to the Internet

issue VERB ❶ to supply something or give it out to people ❷ to send something out ❸ to put something out for sale; to publish something ❹ to come or go out; to flow out

issue NOUN ❶ a subject for discussion or concern ❷ a particular edition of a newspaper or magazine ❸ issuing something ❹ (*formal*) the birth of children

isthmus (say **iss**-mus) NOUN a narrow strip of land connecting two larger pieces of land

IT ABBREVIATION information

technology

it *PRONOUN* ❶ the thing being talked about ❷ used in statements about the weather, the time or a distance ❸ used to refer to a phrase ❹ used as an indefinite object

italic (say it-**al**-ik) *ADJECTIVE* printed with sloping letters (called **italics**) *like this*

itch *VERB* ❶ to have or feel a tickling sensation in the skin that makes you want to scratch it ❷ to long to do something

itch *NOUN* ❶ an itching feeling ❷ a longing

itchy *ADJECTIVE* making you want to scratch your skin

item *NOUN* ❶ one thing in a list or group of things ❷ one piece of news, article, etc. in a newspaper or bulletin

itinerary (say eye-**tin**-er-er-ee) *NOUN* a list of places to be visited on a journey; a route

its *DETERMINER* belonging to it

it's (mainly spoken) ❶ it is ❷ it has

itself *PRONOUN* it and nothing else. The word is used to refer back to the subject of a sentence (e.g. *The cat has hurt itself.*) or for emphasis (e.g. *The house itself is quite small.*).

ivory *NOUN* ❶ the hard creamy-white substance that forms elephants' tusks ❷ a creamy-white colour

ivy *NOUN* a climbing evergreen plant with shiny leaves

Jj

jab *VERB* ❶ to poke someone roughly with your finger or something pointed ❷ to push a thing roughly into something else

jab *NOUN* ❶ a rough push or hit with something pointed or a fist ❷ (informal) an injection

jabber *VERB* to speak quickly and not clearly; to chatter

jack *NOUN* ❶ a device for lifting something heavy off the ground, especially a car ❷ a playing card with a picture of a young man ❸ a small white ball that players aim at in the game of bowls

jack *VERB* to lift something with a jack

jackal *NOUN* a wild animal rather like a dog

jackass *NOUN* ❶ a male donkey ❷ (informal) a stupid person

jackdaw *NOUN* a kind of small crow

jacket *NOUN* ❶ a short coat, usually reaching to your hips ❷ a cover to keep the heat in a water tank or boiler ❸ a paper wrapper for a book ❹ the skin of a potato that is baked without being peeled

jack-in-the-box *NOUN* a toy figure that springs out of a box when the lid is lifted

jackknife *VERB* an articulated lorry jackknifes if it folds against itself in an accidental skidding movement

jackpot *NOUN* an amount of prize money that increases until someone wins it

Jacobean *ADJECTIVE* from the reign

a b c d e f g h i j k l m n o p q r s t u v w x y z

of James I of England (1603-25)

Jacobite NOUN a supporter of the exiled Stuarts after the abdication of James II of England (1688)

Jacuzzi (say ja-**koo**-zi) NOUN (trademark) a large bath in which underwater jets of water massage your body

jade NOUN a hard green stone that is carved to make ornaments and jewellery

jaded ADJECTIVE tired and bored after doing the same thing for too long

jagged (say jag-id) ADJECTIVE a jagged line or outline has an uneven edge with sharp points

jaguar NOUN a large fierce South American animal of the cat family rather like a leopard

jail NOUN a prison

jail VERB to put someone in prison

jailer NOUN a person in charge of a jail

Jain (say Jane) NOUN a follower of Jainism

Jainism (say **jayn**-izm) NOUN an ancient philosophy originating in India and closely linked to Hinduism

jam NOUN ❶ a sweet food made of fruit boiled with sugar until it is thick ❷ a lot of people, cars or logs etc. crowded together so that movement is difficult

jam VERB ❶ to become or make something fixed and difficult to move ❷ to squeeze something into a space where there is not much room ❸ to push something with a lot of force ❹ to block a broadcast

by causing interference with the transmission

jamb (say jam) NOUN a side post of a doorway or window frame

jamboree NOUN a large party or celebration

jangle VERB ❶ to make a loud harsh ringing sound ❷ your nerves are jangling when you feel anxious

janitor NOUN a caretaker

January NOUN the first month of the year

jar NOUN a container made of glass or pottery

jar VERB ❶ to cause an unpleasant jolt or shock ❷ to make a harsh sound, especially in an annoying way

jargon NOUN words or expressions used by a profession or group that are difficult for other people to understand

jasmine NOUN a shrub with yellow or white flowers

jaundice NOUN a disease in which the skin becomes yellow

jaunt NOUN a short trip for fun

jaunty ADJECTIVE lively and cheerful

javelin NOUN a lightweight spear used for throwing in athletics competitions

jaw NOUN ❶ either of the two bones that form the framework of the mouth ❷ the lower part of the face; the mouth and teeth of a person or animal ❸ the part of a tool that grips something

jay NOUN a noisy brightly-coloured bird

jazz NOUN a kind of music with

strong rhythm, often improvised

jealous ADJECTIVE ❶ angry or upset because someone you love seems to be showing interest in someone else ❷ unhappy or resentful because you feel that someone is more successful or luckier than you or has something that you would like to have ❸ careful in keeping something

jealousy NOUN a jealous feeling

jeans PLURAL NOUN trousers made of denim or another strong cotton fabric

Jeep NOUN (*trademark*) a small sturdy motor vehicle with four-wheel drive, especially one used in the army

jeer VERB ❶ to laugh rudely at someone and shout insults at them

jeer VERB a rude or scornful remark

jelly NOUN ❶ a soft transparent food with a fruit flavour ❷ any soft slippery substance

jellyfish NOUN a sea animal with a body like jelly and stinging tentacles

jeopardize (also **jeopardise**) (say **jep**-er-dyz) VERB to put something at risk

jeopardy (say jep-er-dee) NOUN danger of harm or failure

jerk VERB ❶ to make a sudden sharp movement ❷ to pull something suddenly

jerk NOUN ❶ a sudden sharp movement ❷ (*informal*) a stupid person

jerkin NOUN a sleeveless jacket

jerky ADJECTIVE moving with sudden sharp movements

jersey NOUN ❶ a pullover with sleeves ❷ a plain machine-knitted material used for making clothes

jest NOUN a joke

jest VERB to make jokes

jester NOUN a professional entertainer at a royal court in the Middle Ages

jet NOUN ❶ a stream of water, gas, flame, etc. shot out from a narrow opening ❷ a spout or nozzle from which a jet comes ❸ an aircraft driven by engines that send out a high-speed jet of hot gases at the back ❹ a hard black mineral substance ❺ a deep glossy black colour

jet VERB ❶ to come out or send something out in a strong stream ❷ (*informal*) to travel in a jet aircraft

jet lag NOUN extreme tiredness that a person feels after a long flight between different time zones

jetsam NOUN goods thrown overboard from a ship in difficulty and washed ashore

jettison VERB ❶ to throw something overboard ❷ to release or drop something from an aircraft or spacecraft in flight ❸ to get rid of something that you no longer want

jetty NOUN a small landing stage for boats

Jew NOUN ❶ a member of a people descended from the ancient tribes of Israel ❷ someone who believes in Judaism

jewel NOUN ❶ a precious stone ❷ an ornament containing precious stones

jeweller NOUN a person who sells or makes jewellery

jewellery NOUN jewels and similar ornaments for wearing

jib NOUN ❶ a triangular sail stretching forward from a ship's front mast ❷ the arm of a crane

jib VERB to be unwilling to do or accept something

jibe NOUN a remark that is meant to hurt someone's feelings or make them look silly

jibe VERB to make hurtful remarks; to mock someone

jiffy NOUN (informal) a brief moment

jig NOUN ❶ a lively jumping dance ❷ a device that holds something in place while you work on it with tools

jig VERB to move up and down quickly and jerkily

jiggle VERB to move around with short quick movements

jigsaw NOUN ❶ a puzzle made of differently shaped pieces that you have to fit together to make a picture ❷ a saw that can cut curved shapes

jihad NOUN (among Muslims) a war or struggle against unbelievers or a spiritual struggle

jilt VERB to abandon a boyfriend or girlfriend, especially after promising to marry them

jingle VERB ❶ metal objects jingle when they make a tinkling sound like small bells ❷ to shake metal objects together so that they make a tinkling sound like small bells

jingle NOUN ❶ a jingling sound ❷ a catchy verse or tune, especially one used in advertising

jingoism NOUN an extremely strong and unreasonable belief that your country is superior to others

jinx NOUN a person or thing that is thought to bring bad luck

jitters PLURAL NOUN (informal) a feeling of extreme nervousness

job NOUN ❶ work that someone does regularly to earn a living ❷ a piece of work that needs to be done ❸ (informal) a difficult task ❹ (informal) a thing; a state of affairs

jobcentre NOUN a government office with information about available jobs

jockey NOUN a person who rides horses in races

jocular ADJECTIVE joking or humorous

jodhpurs (say jod-perz) PLURAL NOUN trousers for horse riding, fitting closely from the knee to the ankle

joey NOUN (Australian) a young animal, especially a kangaroo, still young enough to be carried in its mother's pouch

jog VERB ❶ to run or trot slowly, especially for exercise ❷ to give something a slight knock or push

jog NOUN a slow run or trot

joggle VERB to shake slightly or move jerkily

join VERB ❶ two things join when they come together ❷ to put things together; to fasten or connect things ❸ to take part with others in doing something or going somewhere ❹ to become a member of a group or organization

join NOUN a place where things join

joiner NOUN a person whose job is to make doors, window frames, etc. and furniture out of wood

joint NOUN ❶ a place where two things are joined ❷ the place where two bones fit together ❸ a large piece of meat cut ready for cooking ❹ (*informal*) a cannabis cigarette

joint ADJECTIVE shared or done by two or more people, groups or countries

joist NOUN any of the long beams supporting a floor or ceiling

joke NOUN ❶ something said or done to make people laugh ❷ a ridiculous person or thing

joke VERB ❶ to make jokes ❷ to tease someone or not be serious

joker NOUN ❶ someone who likes making jokes ❷ an extra playing card with a picture of a jester on it

jolly ADJECTIVE cheerful and good-humoured

jolly ADVERB (British) (*informal*) very

jolly VERB (British) (*informal*) ➤ **jolly someone along** to keep someone in a cheerful mood

jolt VERB ❶ to shake or dislodge something with a sudden sharp movement ❷ to move along jerkily, e.g. on a rough road ❸ to give someone a shock

jolt NOUN ❶ a jolting movement ❷ a shock

jostle VERB to push someone roughly, especially in a crowd

jot VERB to jot something down is to

write it down quickly

jot NOUN a tiny amount

joule (say jool) NOUN (*in science*) a unit of work or energy

journal NOUN ❶ a newspaper or magazine ❷ a diary

journalist NOUN a person who writes for a newspaper or magazine or who prepares news broadcasts on television or radio

journey NOUN ❶ going from one place to another ❷ the distance or time taken to travel somewhere

journey VERB to make a journey

joust (say jowst) VERB to fight on horseback with lances, as knights did in medieval times

jovial ADJECTIVE cheerful and good-humoured

jowl NOUN ❶ the jaw or cheek ❷ loose skin on the neck

joy NOUN ❶ a feeling of great pleasure or happiness ❷ a thing that causes joy ❸ satisfaction or success

joyful ADJECTIVE very happy

joyous ADJECTIVE full of joy; causing joy

joyride NOUN a drive in a stolen car for amusement

joystick NOUN ❶ the control lever of an aircraft ❷ a device for moving a cursor or image on a computer screen, especially in computer games

jubilant ADJECTIVE very happy because you have won or succeeded

jubilee (say joo-bil-ee) NOUN a special anniversary of an important event

Judaism (say **joo**-day-izm) *NOUN* the religion of the Jewish people

judder *VERB* (*British*) to shake noisily or violently

judge *NOUN* ① a person appointed to hear cases in a law court and decide what should be done ② a person who decides the winner of a contest or competition ③ someone who is good at forming opinions or making decisions about things

judge *VERB* ① to act as a judge ② to form and give an opinion ③ to estimate something

judgement *NOUN* ① judging ② the decision made by a law court ③ someone's opinion ④ the ability to make decisions wisely ⑤ something considered as a punishment from God

judicial *ADJECTIVE* to do with law courts, judges or legal judgements

judiciary (say joo-**dish**-er-ee) *NOUN* all the judges in a country

judicious (say joo-**dish**-us) *ADJECTIVE* having or showing good sense or good judgement

judo *NOUN* a Japanese method of self-defence without using weapons

jug *NOUN* a container for holding and pouring liquids, with a handle and a lip

juggernaut *NOUN* (*British*) a huge lorry

juggle *VERB* ① to toss and catch a number of objects skilfully for entertainment, keeping one or more in the air at any time ② to try to deal with several jobs or activities at the same time

jugular *ADJECTIVE* to do with your throat or neck

juice *NOUN* ① the liquid from fruit, vegetables or other food ② a liquid produced by the body

juicy *ADJECTIVE* full of juice

jukebox *NOUN* a machine that automatically plays a record you have selected when you put a coin in

July *NOUN* the seventh month of the year

jumble *VERB* to mix things up in a confused and untidy way

jumble *NOUN* a confused mixture of things; a muddle

jumble sale *NOUN* (*British*) a sale of second-hand goods to raise money

jumbo *NOUN* ① something very large ② a jumbo jet

jumbo jet *NOUN* a very large jet aircraft

jump *VERB* ① to move up suddenly from the ground into the air ② to go over something by jumping ③ to move suddenly in surprise ④ to get into or out of a vehicle quickly ⑤ to pass over something; to miss out part of a book etc. ⑥ to pass quickly to a higher level

jump *NOUN* ① a jumping movement ② an obstacle to jump over ③ a sudden rise or change

jumper *NOUN* a pullover with sleeves

jumpy *ADJECTIVE* nervous and edgy

junction *NOUN* a place where roads or railway lines meet

June *NOUN* the sixth month of the year

jungle NOUN a thick tangled forest, especially in the tropics

junior ADJECTIVE ❶ younger ❷ for young children ❸ lower in rank or importance

junior NOUN a junior person

juniper NOUN an evergreen shrub

junk NOUN ❶ old worthless things that should be thrown away ❷ a Chinese sailing boat

junk food NOUN food that is not nourishing

junkie NOUN (*informal*) a drug addict

junk mail NOUN unwanted advertising material sent by post or mail

jurisdiction NOUN authority; official power, especially to interpret and apply the law

juror NOUN a member of a jury

jury NOUN ❶ a group of people (usually twelve) appointed to give a verdict about a case in a law court ❷ a group of people chosen to judge a competition

just ADJECTIVE ❶ fair and right; giving proper consideration to everyone's claims ❷ deserved; right in amount etc.

just ADVERB ❶ exactly ❷ only; simply ❸ barely; by only a small amount ❹ at this moment or only a little while ago

justice NOUN ❶ being just; fair treatment ❷ the system by which courts deal with people who break the law ❸ a judge or magistrate

justifiable ADJECTIVE that you can accept because there is good reason for it

justify VERB ❶ to show that something is fair, just or reasonable ❷ to arrange lines of printed text so that one or both edges are straight

jut VERB to stick out

jute NOUN fibre from tropical plants, used for making sacks etc.

juvenile ADJECTIVE ❶ to do with or for young people ❷ childish

juvenile NOUN a young person, not old enough to be legally considered an adult

Kk

kale NOUN a kind of cabbage with curly leaves

kaleidoscope (say kal-y-dos-kohp) NOUN ❶ a tube that you look through to see brightly coloured patterns which change as you turn the end of the tube ❷ something full of colour and variety

kangaroo NOUN an Australian animal that jumps along on its strong hind legs. (See **marsupial**.)

kaolin NOUN fine white clay used in making porcelain and in medicine

karaoke NOUN a form of entertainment in which people sing well-known songs against a pre-recorded backing

karate (say ka-**rah**-tee) NOUN a Japanese method of self-defence in which the hands and feet are used as weapons

karoo NOUN (*S. African*) a dry plateau in southern Africa

kayak NOUN a small canoe with a covering that fits round the canoeist's waist

KB, Kb *ABBREVIATION* kilobytes

kebab *NOUN* small pieces of meat or vegetables cooked on a skewer

keel *NOUN* the long piece of wood or metal along the bottom of a boat

keel *VERB* ➤ keel over to fall down or overturn

keen *ADJECTIVE* ❶ enthusiastic or eager ❷ to be keen on a person or thing is to like or be interested in them ❸ very sharp ❹ piercingly cold

keen *VERB* to wail in grief for a dead person

keep *VERB* keeps, keeping, kept ❶ to have something and look after it or not get rid of it ❷ to stay or cause something to stay in the same condition etc. ❸ to do something continually or repeatedly ❹ food or drink keeps when it lasts without going bad ❺ to keep a promise or your word is to respect and not break it ❻ to keep a diary is to make regular entries in it

keep *NOUN* ❶ the food, clothes, etc. that a person needs to live ❷ a strong tower in a castle

keeper *NOUN* ❶ a person who looks after an animal, building, etc. ❷ a goalkeeper or wicketkeeper

keeping *NOUN* something is in your keeping when you are looking after it

keepsake *NOUN* a gift to be kept in memory of the person who gave it

keg *NOUN* a small barrel

kelp *NOUN* a large type of seaweed

kelvin *NOUN* the SI unit of thermodynamic temperature

kennel *NOUN* a shelter for a dog

kennels *NOUN* a place where dogs are bred or where they can be looked after while their owners are away

kenning *NOUN* a type of expression or riddle from Anglo-Saxon times, in which something is described without using its name, e.g. *bar-steed* meaning 'ship'

kerb *NOUN* the edge of a pavement

kernel *NOUN* the part inside the shell of a nut

kerosene (say ke-ro-seen) *NOUN* paraffin

kestrel *NOUN* a small falcon

ketchup *NOUN* a thick sauce made from tomatoes and vinegar

kettle *NOUN* a container with a spout and handle, for boiling water

kettledrum *NOUN* a drum consisting of a large metal bowl with skin or plastic over the top

key *NOUN* ❶ a piece of metal shaped so that it will open a lock ❷ a device for winding up a clock or clockwork toy ❸ a small lever or button to be pressed by a finger, e.g. on a piano, typewriter or computer ❹ a system of notes in music ❺ a fact or clue that explains or solves something ❻ a list of symbols used in a map or table

key *VERB* ➤ key something in to type information into a computer using a keyboard

keyboard *NOUN* the set of keys on a piano, computer, etc.

keyhole *NOUN* the hole through

which a key is put into a lock

keyhole surgery NOUN surgery carried out through a very small cut in the patient's body, using special instruments

keynote NOUN ❶ the note on which a key in music is based ❷ the main idea or theme in something that is said, written or done

keypad NOUN a small keyboard or set of buttons used to operate a telephone, television, etc.

keystone NOUN the central wedge-shaped stone in an arch, locking the others together

keyword NOUN a word that you type into a computer search engine so that it will search for that word on the Internet

kg ABBREVIATION kilogram

khaki NOUN a dull yellowish-brown colour, used for military uniforms

Khalsa NOUN members of the Sikh religion who vow to wear five signs of their faith known as the five Ks

kibbutz NOUN a farming commune in Israel

kick VERB ❶ to hit or move a person or thing with your foot ❷ to move your legs about vigorously ❸ a gun kicks if it moves back sharply when it is fired

kick NOUN ❶ a kicking movement ❷ the sudden backwards movement a gun makes when it is fired ❸ (informal) a feeling of great excitement or pleasure ❹ (informal) an interest or activity

kick-off NOUN the start of a football match

kid NOUN ❶ (informal) a child ❷ a young goat ❸ fine leather made from goatskin

kid VERB (informal) to tease or fool someone in fun

kidnap VERB to take someone away by force, especially in order to obtain a ransom

kidney NOUN either of the two organs in the body that remove waste products from the blood and turn them into urine

kidney bean NOUN a dark red bean with a curved shape like a kidney

kill VERB ❶ to make a person or animal die ❷ to destroy or put an end to something ❸ (informal) to cause a person pain or mental suffering

kill NOUN ❶ killing an animal ❷ an animal that has been hunted and killed

killer NOUN a person, animal or thing that kills

killing NOUN an act causing death; a murder

kiln NOUN an oven for hardening pottery or bricks, or for drying hops

kilo NOUN a kilogram

kilobyte NOUN (in computing) a unit of memory or data equal to 1,024 bytes

kilogram NOUN a unit of mass or weight equal to 1,000 grams (about 2.2 pounds)

kilometre (say **kil**-o-meet-er or kil-**om**-it-er) NOUN a unit of length equal to 1,000 metres (about ⅔ of a mile)

kilowatt NOUN a unit of electrical power equal to 1,000 watts

kilt NOUN a kind of pleated skirt worn by men as part of traditional Scottish dress

kimono NOUN a long loose Japanese robe with wide sleeves

kin NOUN a person's relatives

kind NOUN a class of similar things or animals; a sort or type

kind ADJECTIVE friendly and helpful; considerate

kindergarten NOUN a school or class for very young children

kindle VERB ❶ to start a flame; to set light to something ❷ to begin burning

kindling NOUN small pieces of wood used for lighting fires

kindly ADVERB ❶ in a kind manner ❷ please

kindly ADJECTIVE kind or friendly

kindred NOUN a person's family and relatives

kindred ADJECTIVE related or similar

kinetic ADJECTIVE to do with or produced by movement

king NOUN ❶ a man who is the ruler of a country through inheriting the position ❷ a person or thing regarded as supreme ❸ the most important piece in chess ❹ a playing card with a picture of a king

kingdom NOUN ❶ a country ruled by a king or queen ❷ a division of the natural world

kingfisher NOUN a small bird with blue feathers that dives to catch fish

king-size, king-sized ADJECTIVE extra large

kink NOUN ❶ a short twist in a rope, wire or length of hair ❷ a peculiarity

kiosk NOUN ❶ a telephone booth ❷ a small hut or stall where newspapers, sweets, etc. are sold

kip NOUN (British informal) a sleep

kipper NOUN a smoked herring

kirk NOUN (Scottish) a church

kiss NOUN touching someone with your lips as a sign of affection or greeting

kiss VERB to give someone a kiss

kiss of life NOUN blowing air from your mouth into someone else's to help them start breathing again, especially after an accident

kit NOUN ❶ equipment or clothes that you need to do a sport, a job or some other activity ❷ a set of parts sold ready to be fitted together

kitchen NOUN a room in which meals are prepared and cooked

kitchenette NOUN a small kitchen

kite NOUN ❶ a light framework covered with cloth or paper that you fly in the wind on the end of a long piece of string ❷ a large hawk

kith and kin PLURAL NOUN friends and relatives

kitten NOUN a very young cat

kitty NOUN ❶ a fund of money for use by several people ❷ an amount of money that you can win in a card game

kiwi (say kee-wee) NOUN ❶ a New Zealand bird that cannot fly ❷ (informal) (Kiwi) someone who comes from or lives in New Zealand

kiwi fruit NOUN a fruit with thin

hairy skin, green flesh and black seeds

kloof NOUN (*S. African*) a narrow valley or mountain pass, usually wooded

km ABBREVIATION kilometre

knack NOUN a special skill or talent

knapsack NOUN a bag carried on the back by soldiers, hikers, etc.

knave NOUN ❶ (*old use*) a dishonest man; a rogue ❷ a jack in a pack of playing cards

knead VERB to press and stretch something soft (especially dough) with your hands

knee NOUN the joint in the middle of your leg

kneecap NOUN the small bone covering the front of your knee joint

kneel VERB kneels, kneeling, knelt to be or get yourself in a position where you are resting on your knees

knell NOUN the sound of a bell rung solemnly after a death or at a funeral

knickers PLURAL NOUN underpants worn by women and girls

knick-knack NOUN a small ornament

knife NOUN knives a cutting instrument or weapon consisting of a sharp blade set in a handle

knife VERB to stab someone with a knife

knight NOUN ❶ a man who has been given the rank that allows him to put 'Sir' before his name ❷ a warrior of high social rank in the Middle Ages, usually mounted and in armour ❸ a piece in chess, with a horse's head

knight VERB to make someone a knight

knit VERB knits, knitting, knitted or knit ❶ to make something by looping together wool or other yarn, using long needles or a machine ❷ broken bones knit together when they join back together and heal

knitting NOUN ❶ the activity of making things by knitting ❷ something that is being knitted

knob NOUN ❶ the round handle of a door or drawer ❷ a round lump on something ❸ a round button or switch on a dial or machine ❹ a small round piece of something

knobbly ADJECTIVE having many small hard lumps or bumps

knock VERB ❶ to make a noise by hitting a thing hard ❷ to hit something hard or bump into it, especially by accident ❸ to produce something by hitting ❹ (*informal*) to criticize someone or something

knock NOUN the act or sound of knocking

knocker NOUN a hinged metal device for knocking on a door

knockout NOUN ❶ knocking someone out ❷ a contest in which the loser in each round has to drop out ❸ (*informal*) an extremely attractive or outstanding person or thing

knoll NOUN a small round hill; a mound

knot NOUN ❶ a fastening made by tying or looping two ends of string, rope or cloth together ❷ a lump where hair or threads have become tangled together ❸ a round spot on a piece of wood where a branch once joined it ❹ a small group of people standing close together ❺ a unit for measuring the speed of ships and aircraft, equal to 2,025 yards (1,852 metres or 1 nautical mile) per hour

knot VERB ❶ to tie or fasten something with a knot ❷ to become tangled up

knotty ADJECTIVE ❶ full of knots ❷ difficult or puzzling

know VERB knows, knowing, knew, known ❶ to have something in your mind that you have learned or discovered ❷ to recognize or be familiar with a person or place ❸ to understand or realize something

know-all NOUN (British) a person who behaves as if they know everything

know-how NOUN practical knowledge or skill for a particular job

knowing ADJECTIVE showing that you know or are aware of something

knowingly ADVERB ❶ in a knowing way ❷ deliberately

knowledge NOUN ❶ information and skills you have through experience and education ❷ knowing about a particular thing ❸ all that is known

knowledgeable ADJECTIVE knowing a lot about something; well-informed

knuckle NOUN a joint in your finger

knuckle VERB ➤ **knuckle down** to begin to work hard ➤ **knuckle under** to accept someone else's authority

koala (say koh-**ah**-la) NOUN a furry Australian animal that looks like a small bear

koppie (say **kop**-i) NOUN (S. African) a small hill

Koran, Qur'an (say kor-**ahn**) NOUN the sacred book of Islam

kosher (say koh-**sher**) ADJECTIVE keeping to Jewish laws about the preparation of food

kraal (say krahl) NOUN (S. African) ❶ a traditional African village of huts ❷ an enclosure for sheep and cattle

krill NOUN a mass of tiny shrimp-like creatures, the chief food of certain whales

krypton NOUN an inert gas that is present in the earth's atmosphere and is used in fluorescent lamps

kung fu NOUN a Chinese method of self-defence, similar to karate

kW ABBREVIATION kilowatt

Ll

L ABBREVIATION learner, a person learning to drive a car

lab NOUN (informal) a laboratory

label NOUN a small piece of paper, cloth or metal fixed on or beside something to show what it is or what it costs or its owner, destination, etc.

336

label VERB ❶ to put a label on something ❷ to describe something in a particular way

laboratory NOUN a room or building equipped for scientific experiments

laborious ADJECTIVE ❶ needing or using a lot of hard work ❷ explaining something at great length and with obvious effort

Labour NOUN the Labour Party, a British political party formed to represent the interests of working people and believing in social equality and socialism

labour NOUN ❶ hard work ❷ a task ❸ workers ❹ the contractions of the womb when a baby is being born

labour VERB ❶ to work hard at something ❷ to explain or discuss something at great length and with obvious effort

labourer NOUN a person who does hard manual work, especially outdoors

Labrador NOUN a large black or light-brown dog

laburnum NOUN a tree with hanging yellow flowers

labyrinth NOUN a complicated arrangement of passages or paths; a maze

lace NOUN ❶ net-like material with decorative patterns of holes in it ❷ a piece of thin cord or leather for fastening a shoe, etc.

lace VERB ❶ to fasten something with a lace ❷ to thread a cord through something ❸ to add spirits to a drink

lack NOUN being without something or not having enough of it

lack VERB to be without something

lackey NOUN a servant; a person who behaves or is treated like a servant

lacking ADJECTIVE not having any or enough of something

laconic ADJECTIVE using few words; terse

lacquer NOUN a hard glossy varnish

lacrosse NOUN a game using a stick with a net on it (called a *crosse*) to catch and throw a ball

lacy ADJECTIVE made of lace or like lace

lad NOUN a boy or young man

ladder NOUN ❶ two upright pieces of wood or metal and crosspieces (rungs), used for climbing up or down ❷ (*British*) a vertical ladder-like flaw in a pair of tights or stockings where a stitch has become undone

ladder VERB (*British*) to get a ladder in a pair of tights or stockings

laden ADJECTIVE carrying something heavy or a lot of something

ladle NOUN a large deep spoon with a long handle, used for lifting and pouring liquids

ladle VERB to lift and pour a liquid with a ladle

lady NOUN ❶ a polite word for a woman ❷ a well-mannered woman ❸ a woman of good social position

ladybird NOUN (*British*) a small flying beetle, usually red with black spots

lady-in-waiting NOUN a woman of

ladylike *ADJECTIVE* behaving in a well mannered and refined way that was traditionally thought to be suitable for a woman

ladyship *NOUN* a title used in speaking to or about a woman of the rank of 'Lady'

lag *VERB* ❶ to go too slowly and fail to keep up with others ❷ (*British*) to wrap a pipe or boiler in insulating material (*lagging*) to prevent loss of heat

lag *NOUN* a delay

lager (say *lah-ger*) *NOUN* a light beer

lagoon *NOUN* a salt-water lake separated from the sea by sandbanks or reefs

laid *past tense of* lay

laid-back *ADJECTIVE* (*informal*) relaxed and easy-going

lain *past participle of* lie

lair *NOUN* a sheltered place where a wild animal lives

lake *NOUN* a large area of water entirely surrounded by land

lakh (say *lak*) *NOUN* (*Indian*) a hundred thousand (rupees etc.)

lama *NOUN* a Buddhist priest or monk in Tibet and Mongolia

lamb *NOUN* ❶ a young sheep ❷ meat from a lamb

lame *ADJECTIVE* ❶ not able to walk normally because of an injury to the leg or foot ❷ weak and not very convincing

lament *VERB* to express grief or disappointment about something

good social position who attends a queen or princess

lament *NOUN* a statement, song or poem expressing grief or regret

laminated *ADJECTIVE* made of thin layers or sheets joined one upon the other

lamp *NOUN* a device for producing light from electricity, gas or oil

lamp post *NOUN* a tall post in a street or path, with a lamp at the top

lampshade *NOUN* a cover for the bulb of an electric lamp, to soften the light

lance *NOUN* a long spear

lance *VERB* to cut open a boil on someone's skin with a surgical knife

lance corporal *NOUN* a soldier ranking between a private and a corporal

land *NOUN* ❶ the part of the earth's surface not covered by sea ❷ the ground or soil; an area of country ❸ the area occupied by a nation; a country

land *VERB* ❶ to arrive on land from a ship or aircraft ❷ to reach the ground after jumping or falling ❸ to come down through the air and settle on something ❹ to bring a fish out of the water ❺ to succeed in getting something ❻ to give someone something unpleasant to do

landed *ADJECTIVE* ❶ owning land ❷ consisting of land

landing *NOUN* ❶ the level area at the top of a flight of stairs ❷ bringing an aircraft to the ground ❸ a place where people can get on and off a boat

landlady NOUN ① a woman who lets rooms to lodgers ② a woman who runs a pub

landline NOUN a telephone connection that uses wires carried on poles or under the ground

landlocked ADJECTIVE almost or entirely surrounded by land

landlord NOUN ① a person who lets a house, room or land to a tenant ② a person who runs a pub

landmark NOUN ① an object that is easily seen in a landscape ② an important event in the history or development of something

landmine NOUN an explosive mine laid on or just under the surface of the ground

landowner NOUN a person who owns a large amount of land

landscape NOUN ① a view of a particular area of countryside or town ② a picture of a scene in the countryside

landslide NOUN ① a landslip ② an overwhelming victory in an election

landslip NOUN (*chiefly British*) a huge mass of soil and rocks sliding down a slope

lane NOUN ① a narrow road, especially in the country ② a strip of road for a single line of traffic ③ a strip of track or water for one athlete or swimmer in a race

language NOUN ① the words we speak and write ② the words used in a particular country or by a particular group of people ③ a system of signs or symbols giving information, especially in computing

language laboratory NOUN a room equipped with audio equipment for learning a foreign language

languid ADJECTIVE lacking energy and moving slowly, sometimes in an elegant way

languish VERB ① to be forced to suffer miserable conditions for a long time ② to become weaker

lank ADJECTIVE lank hair is long and limp

lanky ADJECTIVE a lanky person is awkwardly thin and tall

lantern NOUN a transparent case for holding a light and shielding it from the wind

lanyard NOUN a short cord for fastening or holding something

lap NOUN ① the level place formed by the top of your legs when you are sitting down with your knees together ② going once round a racetrack ③ one section of a journey

lap VERB ① to overtake another competitor in a race to go one or more laps ahead ② a cat or other animal laps a liquid when it drinks it by scooping it up in its tongue ③ waves lap when they make a gentle splash on rocks or the shore

lapel (say la-**pel**) NOUN a flap folded back at the front edge of a coat or jacket

lapse NOUN ① a slight mistake or failure ② an amount of time that has passed

lapse VERB ① to pass or slip gradually into a state ② to be no

laptop NOUN a portable computer for use while travelling

lapwing NOUN a black and white bird with a crested head and a shrill cry

larch NOUN a tall deciduous tree that bears small cones

lard NOUN a white greasy substance prepared from pig fat and used in cooking

larder NOUN a cupboard or small room for storing food

large ADJECTIVE of more than the ordinary or average size; big

largely ADVERB to a great extent; mostly

lark NOUN ❶ a small sandy-brown bird; the skylark ❷ (*informal*) something amusing; a bit of fun
lark VERB ➤ **lark about** (*British*) (*informal*) to have fun playing jokes or tricks

larrikin NOUN (*Australian/NZ*) a young person who behaves in a wild and mischievous way

larva NOUN an insect in the first stage of its life, after it comes out of the egg

laryngitis NOUN inflammation of the larynx, causing hoarseness

larynx (say **la**-rinks) NOUN the part of your throat that contains the vocal cords

lasagne (say laz-**an**-ya) NOUN pasta in the form of flat sheets, usually cooked with minced meat and cheese sauce

laser NOUN a device that makes a very strong narrow beam of light

or other electromagnetic radiation

lash NOUN ❶ a stroke with a whip or stick ❷ the cord or cord-like part of a whip ❸ an eyelash
lash VERB ❶ to strike a person or animal with a whip or stick ❷ to hit something with great force ❸ to tie something tightly with a rope or cord

lashings PLURAL NOUN (*British*) (*informal*) plenty of food or drink

lass NOUN a girl or young woman

lasso NOUN a rope with a sliding noose at the end, used for catching cattle
lasso VERB to catch an animal with a lasso

last ADJECTIVE ❶ coming after all others; final ❷ latest; most recent ❸ least likely

last ADVERB at the end; after everything or everyone else

last VERB ❶ to continue; to go on existing or living or being usable ❷ to be enough for your needs

last NOUN ❶ a person or thing that is last ❷ a block of wood or metal shaped like a foot, used in making and repairing shoes

lasting ADJECTIVE able to last for a long time

lastly ADVERB in the last place; finally

last post NOUN a military bugle call sounded at sunset and at military funerals

last rites PLURAL NOUN a Christian ceremony given to a person who is close to death

latch NOUN a small bar fastening a door or gate, lifted by a lever or spring

latch VERB to fasten a door or gate with a latch

late ADJECTIVE & ADVERB ❶ after the usual or expected time ❷ near the end ❸ who has died recently

lately ADVERB recently

latent (say **lay**-tent) ADJECTIVE existing but not yet developed, active or visible

latent heat NOUN the heat needed to change a solid into a liquid or vapour, or a liquid into a vapour, without a change in temperature

later ADVERB after in time; afterwards

lateral ADJECTIVE ❶ to do with the side or sides of something ❷ sideways

latest ADJECTIVE very recent or new

latest NOUN the most recent or the newest thing or piece of news

latex NOUN the milky juice of various plants and trees, especially the rubber tree

lathe (say layth) NOUN a machine for holding and turning pieces of wood while they are being shaped

lather NOUN the thick foam you get when you mix soap with water

lather VERB ❶ to cover something with lather ❷ to form a lather

Latin NOUN the language of the ancient Romans

Latin America NOUN the parts of Central and South America where the main language is Spanish or Portuguese

latitude NOUN ❶ the distance of a place from the equator, measured in degrees ❷ freedom to choose

what you do or the way that you do it

latrine (say la-**treen**) NOUN a toilet in a camp or barracks

latter ADJECTIVE later or more recent Compare with **former**.

latterly ADVERB recently; not long ago

lattice NOUN a framework of crossed strips or bars with spaces between

laudable ADJECTIVE deserving praise

laugh VERB to make the sounds that show you are happy or think something is funny

laugh NOUN ❶ the sound of laughing ❷ (informal) something that is fun or amusing

laughable ADJECTIVE deserving to be laughed at

laughing stock NOUN a person or thing that is the object of ridicule and scorn

laughter NOUN laughing or the sound of laughing

launch VERB ❶ to send a ship from the land into the water ❷ to send a rocket or spacecraft into space ❸ to set a thing moving by throwing or pushing it ❹ to make a new product available for the first time ❺ to start something off

launch NOUN ❶ the launching of a ship or spacecraft ❷ a large motor boat

launch pad NOUN a platform from which a rocket is launched

launder VERB to wash and iron clothes etc.

launderette NOUN (British) a place fitted with washing machines that people pay to use

laundry NOUN ❶ a place where clothes, sheets, etc. are washed and ironed for customers ❷ clothes, sheets, etc. to be washed or sent to a laundry

laureate (say lorri-at) ADJECTIVE ➤ **Poet Laureate** a person appointed to write poems for national occasions

laurel NOUN an evergreen shrub with smooth shiny leaves

lava NOUN molten rock that flows from a volcano; the solid rock formed when it cools

lavatory NOUN ❶ a toilet ❷ a room containing a toilet

lavender NOUN ❶ a shrub with sweet-smelling purple flowers ❷ a light-purple colour

lavish ADJECTIVE ❶ generous ❷ plentiful

lavish VERB to give large or generous amounts of something

law NOUN ❶ a rule or set of rules that everyone must obey ❷ the profession of being a lawyer ❸ (informal) the police ❹ a scientific statement of something that always happens

law-abiding ADJECTIVE obeying the law

law court NOUN a room or building in which a judge or magistrate hears evidence and decides whether someone has broken the law

lawful ADJECTIVE allowed or accepted by the law

lawless ADJECTIVE ❶ without proper laws ❷ not obeying the law

lawn NOUN ❶ an area of closely-cut grass in a garden or park ❷ very fine cotton material

lawnmower NOUN a machine for cutting the grass of lawns

lawn tennis NOUN tennis played on an outdoor grass or hard court

lawsuit NOUN a dispute or claim that is brought to a law court to be settled

lawyer NOUN a person who is qualified to give advice in matters of law

lax ADJECTIVE slack; not strict enough

laxative NOUN a medicine that you take to empty your bowels

lay VERB lays, laying, laid ❶ to put something down in a particular place or way ❷ to lay a table is to arrange things on it ready for a meal ❸ to place blame or responsibility on someone ❹ to form or prepare something ❺ to lay an egg is to produce it

lay VERB past tense of **lie**

lay ADJECTIVE ❶ not belonging to the clergy ❷ not professionally qualified

lay NOUN (old use) a poem meant to be sung; a ballad

layabout NOUN (British) (informal) a person who lazily avoids working for a living

lay-by NOUN a place where vehicles can stop beside a main road

layer NOUN a single thickness or coating

layman, layperson NOUN ❶ a person who does not have specialized knowledge or training (e.g. as a doctor or lawyer) ❷ a person who is not ordained as a member of the clergy

layout *NOUN* the way in which the parts of something are arranged

laywoman *NOUN* ❶ a woman who does not have specialized knowledge or training (e.g. as a doctor or lawyer) ❷ a woman who is not ordained as a member of the clergy

laze *VERB* to spend time in a lazy way

lazy *ADJECTIVE* not wanting to work; doing little work

lea *NOUN* (*poetical use*) a meadow

leach *VERB* to remove a soluble substance from soil or rock by making water percolate through it

lead (say leed) *VERB* leads, leading, led ❶ to take or guide someone, especially by going in front ❷ to be winning in a race or contest; to be ahead ❸ to be in charge of a group of people ❹ to be a way or route ❺ to play the first card in a card game ❻ to live or experience a particular kind of life

lead (say leed) *NOUN* ❶ a leading place, part or position ❷ a good example or guidance for others to follow ❸ a clue to be followed ❹ a strap or cord for leading a dog or other animal ❺ an electrical wire attached to something

lead (say leed) *ADJECTIVE* the most important of a number or group

lead (say led) *NOUN* ❶ a soft heavy grey metal ❷ the writing substance (graphite) in a pencil

lead (say led) *ADJECTIVE* made of or like lead

leaden (say led-en) *ADJECTIVE*

❶ made of lead ❷ heavy and slow ❸ lead-coloured; dark grey

leader *NOUN* ❶ the person in charge of a group of people; a chief ❷ the person who is winning ❸ a newspaper article giving the editor's opinion

leadership *NOUN* being a leader; the ability to be a good leader

leaf *NOUN* leaves ❶ a flat, usually green, part of a plant, growing out from its stem, branch or root ❷ the paper forming one page of a book ❸ a very thin sheet of metal ❹ a flap that makes a table larger

leaf *VERB* ➤ **leaf through something** to turn the pages of a book, etc. quickly one by one

leaflet *NOUN* a piece of paper printed with information

league *NOUN* ❶ a group of teams who compete against each other for a championship ❷ a group of people or nations who agree to work together ❸ an old measure of distance, about 3 miles

leak *NOUN* ❶ a hole or crack through which liquid or gas accidentally escapes ❷ the revealing of secret information

leak *VERB* ❶ to get out or let something out through a leak ❷ to reveal secret information

leaky *ADJECTIVE* a leaky pipe or tap has a leak

lean *VERB* leans, leaning, leaned or leant ❶ to bend your body towards or over something ❷ to put something or be in a sloping position ❸ to rest against something ❹ to lean on someone is to rely or depend on them for help

lean ADJECTIVE ❶ lean meat has little or no fat ❷ a lean person or body is thin with little or no body fat

leaning NOUN a tendency or preference

leap VERB leaps, leaping, leaped or leapt ❶ to jump high or a long way ❷ to increase sharply in amount or value

leap NOUN ❶ a high or long jump ❷ a sudden increase in amount or value

leapfrog NOUN a game in which each player jumps with legs apart over another who is bending down

leap year NOUN a year with an extra day in it (29 February)

learn VERB learns, learning, learned or learnt ❶ to get knowledge or skill through study or training ❷ to find out about something

learned (say ler-nid) ADJECTIVE a learned person has gained a lot of knowledge through study

learner NOUN a person who is learning something, especially how to drive a car

learning NOUN knowledge you get by studying

lease NOUN an agreement to allow someone to use a building or land for a fixed period in return for payment

lease VERB to allow or obtain the use of something by lease

leash NOUN a dog's lead

least DETERMINER & ADVERB smallest in amount or degree; less than all the others

least PRONOUN the smallest amount or degree

leather NOUN material made from animal skins

leave VERB leaves, leaving, left ❶ to go away from a person or place ❷ to stop belonging to a group or working somewhere ❸ to allow something to stay where it is or as it is ❹ to go away without taking something ❺ to let someone deal with something ❻ to put something somewhere so that it can be collected or passed on later

leave NOUN ❶ permission ❷ official permission to be away from work; the time for which this permission lasts

leaven (say lev-en) NOUN a substance, especially yeast, used to make dough rise

leaven VERB to add leaven to dough

lectern NOUN a stand to hold a Bible or other large book or notes for reading

lecture NOUN ❶ a talk about a subject to an audience or a class ❷ a long serious talk to someone that warns them about something or tells them off

lecture VERB to give a lecture

led past tense of **lead**

ledge NOUN a narrow shelf

ledger NOUN an account book

lee NOUN the sheltered side or part of something, away from the wind

leech NOUN a small blood-sucking worm that lives in water

leek NOUN a long green and white vegetable of the onion family

leer VERB to look at someone in a lustful or unpleasant way

leeward ADJECTIVE on the lee side

leeway NOUN extra space or time available

left ADJECTIVE & ADVERB ❶ on or towards the west if you think of yourself as facing north ❷ in favour of socialist or radical views

left NOUN the left-hand side or part of something

left VERB past tense of **leave**

left-hand ADJECTIVE on the left side of something

left-handed ADJECTIVE using the left hand in preference to the right hand

leftovers PLURAL NOUN food not eaten at a meal

leg NOUN ❶ one of the limbs on a person's or animal's body on which they stand or move ❷ one of the parts of a pair of trousers that cover your leg ❸ each of the supports of a chair or other piece of furniture ❹ one part of a journey ❺ one of a pair of matches played between the same teams in a round of a competition

legacy NOUN ❶ something left to a person in a will ❷ a thing received from someone who did something before you or because of earlier events

legal ADJECTIVE ❶ allowed by the law ❷ to do with the law or lawyers

legalize (also **legalise**) VERB to make a thing legal

legate NOUN an official representative, especially of the Pope

legend NOUN ❶ an old story handed down from the past, which may or may not be true. Compare with **myth**. ❷ a very famous person

legendary ADJECTIVE ❶ to do with legends or happening in legends ❷ very famous or well known for a long time

leggings PLURAL NOUN ❶ tight-fitting stretchy trousers, worn by women ❷ protective outer coverings for each leg from knee to ankle

legible ADJECTIVE legible writing is clear enough to read

legion NOUN ❶ a division of the ancient Roman army ❷ a group of soldiers or former soldiers

legionnaire NOUN a member of an association of former soldiers

legionnaires' disease NOUN a serious form of pneumonia caused by bacteria

legislate VERB to make laws

legislation NOUN making laws; a set of laws passed by a parliament

legislative ADJECTIVE having the authority to make laws

legislature NOUN a country's parliament or law-making assembly

legitimate ADJECTIVE ❶ allowed by a law or rule ❷ (old use) a legitimate child is born of parents who are married to each other

leisure NOUN time that is free from work, when you can do what you like

leisurely ADJECTIVE done with plenty

of time; unhurried

lemming *NOUN* a small mouse-like animal of Arctic regions that migrates in large numbers and is said to run headlong into the sea and drown

lemon *NOUN* ❶ an oval yellow citrus fruit with a sour taste ❷ a pale yellow colour

lemonade *NOUN* a lemon-flavoured drink

lemur (say lee-mer) *NOUN* a monkey-like animal

lend *VERB* lends, lending, lent ❶ to allow a person to use something of yours for a short time ❷ to provide someone with money that they must repay over time, usually in return for payments (called **interest**) ❸ to give or add a quality

length *NOUN* ❶ how long something is ❷ a piece of cloth, rope or wire cut from a larger piece ❸ the distance of a swimming pool from one end to the other

lengthen *VERB* ❶ to make something longer ❷ to become longer

lengthways, lengthwise *ADVERB* from end to end; along the longest part

lengthy *ADJECTIVE* going on for a long time

lenient (say lee-nee-ent) *ADJECTIVE* not as strict as expected, especially when punishing someone

lens *NOUN* ❶ a curved piece of glass or plastic used to focus things ❷ the transparent part of the eye, immediately behind the pupil

Lent *NOUN* a period of about six weeks before Easter when some Christians give up something they enjoy

lent *past tense of* lend

lentil *NOUN* a kind of small bean

leopard (say lep-erd) *NOUN* a large spotted mammal of the cat family, also called a panther

leotard (say lee-o-tard) *NOUN* a close-fitting piece of clothing worn for dance, exercise and gymnastics

leper *NOUN* a person who has leprosy

leprechaun (say lep-rek-awn) *NOUN* in Irish folklore, an elf who looks like a little old man

leprosy *NOUN* an infectious disease that makes parts of the body waste away

lesbian *NOUN* a homosexual woman

less *DETERMINER & ADVERB* smaller in amount; not so much

less *PRONOUN* a smaller amount

less *PREPOSITION* minus; deducting

lessen *VERB* to make something less or to become less

lesser *ADJECTIVE* not so great as the other

lesson *NOUN* ❶ an amount of teaching given at one time ❷ something to be learnt by a pupil or student ❸ an example or experience from which you should learn ❹ a passage from the Bible read aloud as part of a Christian church service

lest *CONJUNCTION* (old use) so that something should not happen

let *VERB* lets, letting, let ❶ to allow

someone to do something **2** to allow something to happen and not prevent it **3** used to make a suggestion **4** to allow or cause a person or thing to come or go or pass **5** to allow someone to use a house or building in return for payment (**rent**)

lethal (say lee-thal) ADJECTIVE deadly; causing death

lethargy (say **leth**-er-jee) NOUN extreme lack of energy or interest in doing anything

letter NOUN **1** a symbol representing a sound used in speech **2** a written message, usually sent by post

letter box NOUN **1** a slot in a door, through which letters are delivered **2** a postbox

lettering NOUN letters drawn or painted

lettuce NOUN a garden plant with broad crisp leaves used in salads

leukaemia (say lew-**kee**-mee-a) NOUN a disease in which there are too many white corpuscles in the blood

level ADJECTIVE **1** flat or horizontal **2** at the same height or position as something else

level NOUN **1** height, depth or position **2** a standard or grade of achievement **3** a stage of a computer game that you reach **4** a level surface **5** a device that shows whether something is level

level VERB **1** to make something level or to become level **2** to aim a gun or missile **3** to direct an accusation at a person

level crossing NOUN (*British*)

a place where a road crosses a railway at the same level

lever NOUN **1** a bar that turns on a fixed point (the **fulcrum**) in order to lift something or force something open **2** a bar used as a handle to operate machinery

lever VERB to lift or move something by means of a lever

leverage NOUN **1** the force you need when you use a lever **2** influence over people

leveret NOUN a young hare

levitation NOUN rising into the air and floating there

levy VERB to collect a tax or other payment by the use of authority or force

levy NOUN an amount of money paid in tax

lewd ADJECTIVE indecent or crude

lexicography NOUN the writing of dictionaries

liability NOUN **1** being legally responsible for something **2** a debt or obligation **3** a disadvantage or handicap

liable ADJECTIVE **1** likely to do or suffer something **2** legally responsible for something

liaise (say lee-**ayz**) VERB to work closely with someone and keep them informed

liaison (say lee-**ay**-zon) NOUN **1** communication and cooperation between people or groups **2** a person who is a link or go-between **3** a romantic affair

liar NOUN a person who tells lies

libel (say **ly**-bel) NOUN an untrue written, printed or broadcast statement that damages a person's reputation. Compare with **slander**.

libel VERB to make a libel against someone

liberal ADJECTIVE ❶ tolerant of other people's point of view or behaviour ❷ supporting individual freedom and gradual political and social change ❸ giving or given freely and generously

liberal NOUN a person with liberal views

Liberal Democrat NOUN a member of the Liberal Democrat party in the UK, a political party favouring moderate reforms

liberate VERB to liberate a person or animal is to set them free

liberty NOUN the freedom to go where you want or do what you want

librarian NOUN a person in charge of or working in a library

library (say ly-bra-ree) NOUN ❶ a place where books are kept for people to use or borrow ❷ a collection of books, records, films, etc.

libretto NOUN the words of an opera or other long musical work

lice plural of **louse**

licence NOUN ❶ an official document allowing someone to do or use or own something ❷ special freedom to avoid the usual rules or customs

license VERB to give a licence to a person; to authorize someone to do something

lichen (say ly-ken) NOUN a dry-looking plant that grows on rocks, walls or trees

lick VERB ❶ to move your tongue over something ❷ a wave or flame licks a surface when it touches it lightly ❸ (informal) to defeat someone

lick NOUN ❶ licking something ❷ a small amount of paint

lid NOUN ❶ a cover for a box, pot or jar ❷ an eyelid

lido (say leed-oh) NOUN (British) a public open-air swimming pool or pleasure beach

lie VERB lies, lying, lay, lain ❶ to be or get in a flat or resting position ❷ to be or remain a certain way

lie VERB lies, lying, lied to say something that you know is untrue

lie NOUN something you say that you know is not true

liege, liege lord (say leej) NOUN (old use) a person who is entitled to receive feudal service or allegiance

lieu (say lew) NOUN ➤ in lieu instead

lieutenant (say lef-ten-ant) NOUN ❶ an officer in the army or navy ❷ a deputy or chief assistant

life NOUN lives ❶ the period between birth and death or the period that a person has been alive ❷ being alive and able to function and grow ❸ living things ❹ liveliness ❺ a biography ❻ the length of time that something exists or functions

lifebelt NOUN a ring of material that will float, used to support someone's body in water

lifeboat NOUN a boat for rescuing people at sea

lifebuoy NOUN a device to support someone's body in water

life cycle NOUN the series of changes in the life of a living thing

life form NOUN any living thing

lifeguard NOUN someone whose job is to rescue swimmers who are in difficulty

life jacket NOUN a jacket of material that will float, used to support someone's body in water

lifeless ADJECTIVE ❶ dead or appearing to be dead ❷ with no signs of life or living things

lifelike ADJECTIVE looking exactly like a real person or thing

lifelong ADJECTIVE continuing for the whole of someone's life

lifespan NOUN the length of someone's life

lifestyle NOUN the way of life of a person or a group of people

lifetime NOUN the time for which someone is alive

lift VERB ❶ to pick something up or move it to a higher position ❷ to rise or go upwards ❸ to remove or abolish something ❹ (informal) to steal something

lift NOUN ❶ a device in a building for taking people or goods from one floor or level to another ❷ a ride in someone else's vehicle ❸ a movement upwards

lift-off NOUN the vertical take-off of a rocket or spacecraft

ligament NOUN a piece of the tough flexible tissue that holds your bones together

light NOUN ❶ radiation that stimulates the sense of sight and makes things visible ❷ something that provides light, especially an electric lamp ❸ a flame

light ADJECTIVE ❶ full of light; not dark ❷ pale ❸ having little weight; not heavy ❹ small in amount or force; not severe ❺ needing little effort ❻ cheerful, not sad ❼ not serious or profound

light ADVERB ➤ **travel light** to travel without much luggage

light VERB lights, lighting, lit or lighted ❶ to start a thing burning or to begin to burn ❷ to provide light for something

lighten VERB ❶ to make something lighter in weight or less heavy; to become less heavy ❷ to make something brighter or less dark; to become less dark

lighter NOUN a device for lighting cigarettes etc.

light-hearted ADJECTIVE ❶ cheerful and free from worry ❷ not serious

lighthouse NOUN a tower with a bright light at the top to guide or warn ships

lighting NOUN lights or the way that a place is lit

lightly ADVERB ❶ gently, with very little force ❷ only a little; not much ❸ not seriously; without serious thought

lightning NOUN a flash of bright light produced by natural electricity during a thunderstorm

lightning conductor NOUN (British) a metal rod or wire fixed on a building to divert lightning into the earth

lightweight ADJECTIVE less than

A
B
C
D
E
F
G
H
I
J
K
L
M
N
O
P
Q
R
S
T
U
V
W
X
Y
Z

average weight

lightweight NOUN ❶ a person who is not heavy ❷ a boxer weighing between 57.1 and 59 kg

light year NOUN a unit of distance equal to the distance that light travels in one year (about 9.5 million million km)

like VERB ❶ to think a person or thing is pleasant or satisfactory; to enjoy doing something ❷ to wish to do something ❸ to click a button to show that you agree with or like something on a social media website

like PREPOSITION ❶ similar to; in the manner of ❷ in a suitable state for ❸ such as

like ADJECTIVE similar; having some or all of the qualities of another person or thing

like NOUN ❶ a similar person or thing ❷ a symbol on a social media website that shows that someone agrees with or likes something

likeable ADJECTIVE pleasant and easy to like

likelihood NOUN the chance of something happening; how likely something is to happen

likely ADJECTIVE ❶ probable; expected to happen or be true ❷ expected to be suitable or successful

liken VERB to compare one person or thing to another

likeness NOUN ❶ a similarity in appearance; a resemblance ❷ a portrait

likewise ADVERB similarly; in the same way

liking NOUN a feeling that you like something

lilac NOUN ❶ a bush with fragrant purple or white flowers ❷ pale purple

lilt NOUN a light pleasant rhythm in a voice or tune

lily NOUN a garden plant with trumpet-shaped flowers, growing from a bulb

limb NOUN ❶ a leg, arm or wing ❷ a large branch of a tree

limber VERB ➤ **limber up** to do exercises in preparation for a sport or athletic activity

limbo NOUN a West Indian dance in which you bend backwards to pass under a low bar

lime NOUN ❶ a green fruit like a small round lemon ❷ a drink made from lime juice ❸ a tree with yellow flowers ❹ a white chalky substance (calcium oxide) used in making cement and as a fertilizer

limelight NOUN ➤ **in the limelight** receiving a lot of publicity and attention

limerick NOUN a type of amusing poem with five lines

limestone NOUN a kind of rock from which lime (calcium oxide) is obtained

limit NOUN ❶ the greatest amount allowed ❷ a line, point or level where something ends

limit VERB to keep something within a limit

limitation NOUN a thing that stops someone or something from going beyond a certain point

limited ADJECTIVE kept within limits;

not great

limited company NOUN (*British*) a business company whose shareholders would have to pay only some of its debts

limousine (say lim-oo-zeen) NOUN a large luxurious car

limp VERB to walk with difficulty because of an injury to your leg or foot

limp NOUN a limping walk

limp ADJECTIVE ❶ not stiff or firm ❷ without strength or energy

limpet NOUN a small shellfish that attaches itself firmly to rocks

linchpin NOUN the person or thing that is vital to the success of something

line NOUN ❶ a long thin mark on paper or another surface ❷ a row or series of people or things; a row of words ❸ a length of rope, string or wire used for a special purpose ❹ a railway; a railway track ❺ a company operating a transport service of ships, aircraft or buses ❻ a way of doing things or behaving; a type of business ❼ a telephone connection ❽ several generations of a family

line VERB ❶ to mark something with lines ❷ to form something into a line or lines; to form a line along something ❸ to cover the inside of something with a different material

lineage (say lin-ee-ij) NOUN ancestry; a line of descendants from an ancestor

linear (say lin-ee-er) ADJECTIVE ❶ arranged in a line ❷ to do with a line or length

linen NOUN ❶ cloth made from flax ❷ shirts, sheets and tablecloths etc. (which were formerly made of linen)

liner NOUN a large passenger ship

linger VERB to stay for a long time, as if unwilling to leave; to be slow to leave

lingerie (say lan-zher-ee) NOUN women's underwear

lingo NOUN (*informal*) a foreign language

linguist NOUN an expert in languages or someone who can speak several languages well

linguistics NOUN the study of languages

liniment NOUN a lotion for rubbing on parts of the body that ache

lining NOUN a layer of material that covers the inside of something

link NOUN ❶ one of the rings or loops of a chain ❷ a connection or relationship ❸ a connection between documents on the Internet

link VERB ❶ to join things together; to connect people or things ❷ to link up to become connected

links NOUN & PLURAL NOUN a golf course, especially one near the sea

linnet NOUN a kind of finch

lino NOUN (*British*) (*informal*) linoleum

linocut NOUN a print made from a design cut into a block of thick linoleum

linoleum NOUN a stiff shiny floor covering

linseed NOUN the seed of flax, from

which oil is obtained

lint NOUN a soft material for covering wounds

lion NOUN a large strong flesh-eating animal of the cat family found in Africa and India

lioness NOUN a female lion

lip NOUN ❶ either of the two fleshy edges of the mouth ❷ the edge of something hollow, such as a cup or crater ❸ the pointed part at the top of a jug or saucepan from which you pour things

lip-read VERB to understand what a person says by watching the movements of their lips, not by hearing their voice

lipstick NOUN a stick of a waxy substance for colouring the lips

liqueur (say lik-yoor) NOUN a strong sweet alcoholic drink

liquid NOUN a substance like water or oil that flows freely but (unlike a gas) has a constant volume

liquid ADJECTIVE in the form of a liquid; flowing freely

liquidate VERB to close down a business and divide its value between its creditors

liquidize (also **liquidise**) VERB (British) to make something, especially food, into a liquid or pulp

liquor NOUN ❶ alcoholic drink ❷ juice produced in cooking; liquid in which food has been cooked

liquorice (say lick-er-iss) NOUN ❶ a black substance used in medicine and as a sweet ❷ the plant from whose root this substance is

obtained

lisp NOUN a fault in speech in which s and z are pronounced like th

lisp VERB to speak with a lisp

list NOUN ❶ a number of names, items or figures written or printed one after another ❷ leaning over to one side

list VERB ❶ to make a list of people or things ❷ a boat or ship lists when it leans over to one side

listen VERB to pay attention in order to hear something

listless ADJECTIVE too tired to be active or enthusiastic

lit past tense of **light** VERB

litany NOUN a formal prayer with fixed responses

literacy NOUN the ability to read and write

literal ADJECTIVE ❶ meaning exactly what is said, not metaphorical or exaggerated ❷ word for word

literally ADVERB really; exactly as stated

literary (say lit-er-er-i) ADJECTIVE to do with literature; interested in literature

literate ADJECTIVE able to read and write

literature NOUN books and other writings, especially those that are widely read and thought to be well written

lithe ADJECTIVE flexible and supple

litmus NOUN a blue substance that is turned red by acids and can be turned back to blue by alkalis

litmus paper NOUN paper stained with litmus

litre NOUN a measure of liquid, about 1¾ pints

litter NOUN ❶ rubbish or untidy things left lying about ❷ the young animals born to one mother at one time ❸ absorbent material put down on a tray for a cat to urinate and defecate in indoors ❹ a kind of stretcher

litter VERB to be scattered all over a place, making it untidy

little ADJECTIVE ❶ small in size or amount; not great or big ❷ short in time or distance

little DETERMINER & PRONOUN not much

little ADVERB not much; only slightly

liturgy NOUN a fixed form of public worship used in Christian churches

live (rhymes with *give*) VERB ❶ to have life; to be alive ❷ to have your home somewhere ❸ to pass your life in a certain way

live (rhymes with *hive*) ADJECTIVE ❶ alive ❷ a live wire or connection is connected to a source of electric current ❸ a live television programme is broadcast while it is actually happening, not from a recording ❹ a live coal is still burning

livelihood NOUN a way of earning money or providing enough food to support yourself

lively ADJECTIVE full of life, energy and excitement

liven VERB to make something lively or to become lively

liver NOUN ❶ a large organ of the body, found in your abdomen, that processes digested food and purifies the blood ❷ an animal's liver used as food

livery NOUN ❶ a uniform worn by male servants in a household ❷ the distinctive colours used by a railway, bus company or airline

livestock NOUN farm animals

live wire NOUN a person who is lively and full of energy

livid ADJECTIVE ❶ bluish-grey ❷ furiously angry

living ADJECTIVE alive now

living NOUN ❶ the way that a person lives ❷ a way of earning money or providing enough food to support yourself

living room NOUN a room for general use during the day

lizard NOUN a reptile with a rough or scaly skin, four legs and a long tail

llama (say *lah-ma*) NOUN a South American animal with woolly fur, like a camel but with no hump

lo EXCLAMATION (old use) see; behold

load NOUN ❶ something that is being carried ❷ the quantity that can be carried ❸ the total amount of electric current supplied ❹ (informal) a large amount

load VERB ❶ to put a load in or on something ❷ to load someone with something is to give them large amounts of it ❸ to load dice is to put a weight into them to make them land in a certain way ❹ to load a gun is to put a bullet or shell into it ❺ to load a camera is to put a film into it ❻ to enter programs or data into a computer

loaf NOUN loaves a shaped mass of bread baked in one piece

a
b
c
d
e
f
g
h
i
j
k
l
m
n
o
p
q
r
s
t
u
v
w
x
y
z

loaf VERB to spend time idly; to loiter or stand about

loam NOUN rich soil containing clay, sand and decayed leaves

loan NOUN something lent, especially money

loan VERB to lend something

loath (rhymes with *both*) ADJECTIVE unwilling to do something

loathe (rhymes with *clothe*) VERB to feel great hatred and disgust for someone or something

loathsome ADJECTIVE making you feel great hatred and disgust; repulsive

lob VERB to throw, hit or kick a ball high into the air, especially in a high arc

lob NOUN a lobbed ball in tennis or football

lobby NOUN ❶ an entrance hall ❷ a group of people who try to influence politicians or officials or persuade them of something

lobby VERB to try to persuade a politician or other person to support your cause, by speaking to them in person or writing letters

lobe NOUN ❶ a rounded fairly flat part of a leaf or an organ of the body ❷ the rounded soft part at the bottom of your ear

lobster NOUN a large shellfish with eight legs and two long claws

local ADJECTIVE belonging to a particular place or a small area

local NOUN (informal) ❶ someone who lives in a particular district ❷ the pub nearest to a person's home

local anaesthetic NOUN an anaesthetic affecting only the part of the body where it is applied

local government NOUN the system of administration of a town or county by people elected by those who live there

locality NOUN a place and the area that surrounds it

localized (also **localised**) ADJECTIVE restricted to a particular place

locate VERB to discover where something is

location NOUN the place where something is situated

loch NOUN a lake in Scotland

lock NOUN ❶ a fastening that is opened with a key or other device ❷ a section of a canal or river fitted with gates and sluices so that boats can be raised or lowered to the level beyond each gate ❸ the distance that a vehicle's front wheels can turn ❹ a wrestling hold that keeps an opponent's arm or leg from moving ❺ a clump of hair

lock VERB ❶ to fasten something by means of a lock ❷ to put or keep something in a safe place that can be fastened with a lock ❸ to become fixed in one place; to jam

locker NOUN a small cupboard for keeping things safe, often in a changing room

locket NOUN a small ornamental case for holding a portrait or lock of hair, worn on a chain round the neck

locks PLURAL NOUN the hair on a person's head

locksmith NOUN a person whose

job is to make and mend locks

locomotive NOUN a railway engine

locus (say **loh**-kus) NOUN (in mathematics) the path traced by a moving point or made by points placed in a certain way

locust NOUN a kind of grasshopper that travels in large swarms which eat all the plants in an area

lodestone NOUN a kind of stone that can be used as a magnet

lodge NOUN ❶ a small house, especially at the gates of a park ❷ a porter's room at the entrance to a college or other building ❸ a beaver's or otter's lair

lodge VERB ❶ to stay somewhere as a lodger ❷ to provide a person with somewhere to live temporarily ❸ to become stuck or caught somewhere

lodger NOUN (chiefly British) a person who pays to live in another person's house

lodgings PLURAL NOUN a room or rooms, not in a hotel, rented for living in

loft NOUN a room or storage space under the roof of a house or barn

lofty ADJECTIVE ❶ high or tall ❷ a lofty aim or ambition is a noble one that deserves praise ❸ a lofty attitude or manner is a very arrogant one

log NOUN ❶ a large piece of a tree that has fallen or been cut down; a piece cut off this ❷ a detailed record kept of a voyage or flight

log VERB to enter facts in a log

logarithm NOUN one of a series of numbers set out in tables which

make it possible to do sums by adding and subtracting instead of multiplying and dividing

logbook NOUN ❶ a book in which a log of a voyage is kept ❷ the registration document of a motor vehicle

log cabin NOUN a hut built of logs

loggerheads PLURAL NOUN ➤ at loggerheads disagreeing or quarrelling

logic NOUN ❶ reasoning; a system or method of reasoning ❷ the principles used in designing a computer

logical ADJECTIVE using logic or worked out by logic; reasonable or sensible

login NOUN the process of starting to use a computer system; the name or password you use to do this

logo (say **loh**-goh or **log**-oh) NOUN a printed symbol used by a business company as its emblem

loin NOUN the side and back of the body between the ribs and the hip bone

loincloth NOUN a piece of cloth wrapped round the hips, worn by men in some hot countries as their only piece of clothing

loiter VERB to stand about idly for no obvious reason

loll VERB ❶ to lean lazily against something ❷ to hang loosely

lollipop NOUN a large round hard sweet on a stick

lollipop woman, lollipop man NOUN an official who uses a circular sign on a stick to signal traffic to stop so that children can cross a road

lolly NOUN (*informal*) ❶ a lollipop or an ice lolly ❷ money

lone ADJECTIVE solitary; on its own

lonely ADJECTIVE ❶ sad because you are on your own or have no friends ❷ far from inhabited places; not often visited or used

long ADJECTIVE ❶ measuring a lot from one end to the other ❷ taking a lot of time ❸ having a certain length

long ADVERB ❶ for a long time ❷ at a long time before or after ❸ throughout a time

long VERB to want something very much

long-distance ADJECTIVE travelling or covering a long distance

long division NOUN dividing one number by another and writing down all the calculations

longevity (say lon-jev-it-ee) NOUN long life

longhand NOUN ordinary writing, contrasted with shorthand or typing

longing NOUN a strong desire for something or someone

longitude NOUN the distance east or west, measured in degrees, from the Greenwich meridian

longitudinal ADJECTIVE ❶ to do with longitude ❷ to do with length; measured lengthways

long jump NOUN an athletic contest in which competitors jump as far as possible along the ground in one leap

long-range ADJECTIVE covering a

long distance or period of time

longship NOUN a long narrow warship, with oars and a sail, used by the Vikings

long-sighted ADJECTIVE (*chiefly British*) able to see distant things clearly but not things close to you

long-suffering ADJECTIVE putting up with things patiently

long-term ADJECTIVE to do with or happening over a long period of time

long wave NOUN a radio wave of a wavelength above one kilometre and a frequency less than 300 kilohertz

long-winded ADJECTIVE talking or writing at too great a length and therefore boring

loo NOUN (*British*) (*informal*) a toilet

loofah NOUN a rough sponge made from a dried gourd

look VERB ❶ to use your eyes; to turn your eyes in a particular direction ❷ to face in a particular direction ❸ to have a certain appearance; to seem a certain way

look NOUN ❶ the act of looking; a gaze or glance ❷ the expression on a person's face ❸ an appearance or general impression

lookalike NOUN someone who looks very like a famous person

looking glass NOUN (*old use*) a glass mirror

lookout NOUN ❶ looking out or watching for something ❷ a place from which you can keep watch ❸ a person whose job is to keep watch ❹ (*informal*) a person's own fault or concern

loom VERB to appear suddenly; to seem large or close and threatening

loom NOUN a machine for weaving cloth

loony ADJECTIVE (informal) mad or crazy

loop NOUN the shape made by a curve crossing itself; a piece of string, ribbon or wire made into this shape

loop VERB ❶ to make string etc. into a loop ❷ to enclose something in a loop

loophole NOUN ❶ a way of avoiding a law, rule or promise without actually breaking it ❷ a narrow opening in the wall of a castle, for shooting arrows through

loose ADJECTIVE ❶ not tight or firmly fixed ❷ not tied up or shut in ❸ not packed in a box or packet ❹ not exact

loose VERB ❶ to fire an arrow, bullet, etc. ❷ to loosen something ❸ to untie or release someone or something

loose-leaf ADJECTIVE with each sheet of paper separate and able to be removed

loosely ADVERB not tightly or firmly

loosen VERB ❶ to make something loose or looser ❷ to become loose

loot NOUN stolen things; goods taken from an enemy

loot VERB ❶ to rob a place violently, especially during a war or riot ❷ to take something as loot

lop VERB to lop a branch or twig is to cut it off from a tree or bush

lope VERB to run with a long bounding stride

lopsided ADJECTIVE with one side lower or smaller than the other

lord NOUN ❶ a nobleman, especially one who is allowed to use the title 'Lord' in front of his name ❷ a master or ruler

lord VERB ➤ **lord it over someone** to behave in a superior or domineering way towards someone

lordly ADJECTIVE ❶ to do with a lord ❷ proud or haughty

Lord Mayor NOUN the title of the mayor of some large cities

lordship NOUN a title used in speaking to or about a man of the rank of 'Lord'

lore NOUN a set of traditional facts or beliefs about something

lorry NOUN (British) a large strong motor vehicle for carrying heavy goods or troops

lose VERB loses, losing, lost ❶ to be without something that you once had, especially because you cannot find it ❷ to fail to keep or obtain something ❸ to be defeated in a contest or argument ❹ to cause the loss of something ❺ a clock or watch loses time if it shows a time that is earlier than the correct one

loser NOUN ❶ a person who is defeated ❷ (informal) a person who is never successful

loss NOUN ❶ losing something ❷ something that has been lost

lost past tense and past participle of lose

lost ADJECTIVE ❶ not knowing where you are or not able to find your way ❷ missing or strayed

357

lot NOUN ❶ a large number or amount ❷ something for sale at an auction ❸ a piece of land ❹ a person's fate or situation in life

loth ADJECTIVE a different spelling of **loath**

lotion NOUN a liquid for putting on the skin

lottery NOUN a way of raising money by selling numbered tickets and giving prizes to people who hold winning numbers, which are chosen by a method depending on chance

lotto NOUN a game like bingo

lotus NOUN a kind of tropical water lily

loud ADJECTIVE ❶ easily heard; producing a lot of noise ❷ unpleasantly bright; gaudy

loudspeaker NOUN a device that changes electrical signals into sound, for reproducing music or voices

lounge NOUN a sitting room

lounge VERB to sit or stand in a lazy and relaxed way

louse NOUN **lice** a small insect that lives as a parasite on animals or plants

lousy ADJECTIVE ❶ full of lice ❷ (informal) very bad or unpleasant

lout NOUN a bad-mannered man

lovable ADJECTIVE easy to love

love NOUN ❶ great liking or affection ❷ sexual affection or passion ❸ a loved person; a sweetheart ❹ a score of nil in tennis

love VERB ❶ to feel love for a person ❷ to like something very much

love affair NOUN a romantic or sexual relationship between two people in love

loveless ADJECTIVE without love

lovelorn ADJECTIVE pining with love, especially when abandoned by a lover

lovely ADJECTIVE ❶ beautiful ❷ very pleasant or enjoyable

lover NOUN ❶ someone who loves something ❷ a person who someone is having a sexual relationship with but is not married to

lovesick ADJECTIVE longing for someone you love, especially someone who does not love you

loving ADJECTIVE feeling or showing love or affection

low ADJECTIVE ❶ only reaching a short way up; not high ❷ below average in importance, quality or amount ❸ unhappy ❹ not high-pitched; not loud

low ADVERB at or to a low level or position

low VERB to moo like a cow

lower ADJECTIVE & ADVERB less high

lower VERB to make something lower or move it down

lower case NOUN small letters, not capitals

lowlands PLURAL NOUN low-lying country

lowly ADJECTIVE low in importance or rank; humble

loyal ADJECTIVE always firmly supporting your friends, group or country

loyalist NOUN a person who is loyal to the government during a revolt

loyalty NOUN ❶ being loyal ❷ a strong feeling that you want to be loyal to someone

lozenge NOUN ❶ a small flavoured tablet, especially one containing medicine ❷ a diamond-shaped design

Ltd. ABBREVIATION limited (used after the name of a company)

lubricant NOUN oil or grease for lubricating machinery

lubricate VERB to oil or grease something so that it moves smoothly

lucid ADJECTIVE ❶ clear and easy to understand ❷ thinking clearly; not confused in your mind

luck NOUN ❶ the way things happen by chance without being planned ❷ good fortune

luckily ADVERB by a lucky chance; fortunately

luckless ADJECTIVE unlucky

lucky ADJECTIVE having, bringing or resulting from good luck

lucrative (say loo-kra-tiv) ADJECTIVE profitable; earning you a lot of money

ludicrous ADJECTIVE ridiculous or laughable

ludo NOUN (British) a game played with dice and counters on a board

lug VERB to drag or carry something heavy

lug NOUN ❶ an ear-like part on an object, by which it may be carried or fixed ❷ (informal) an ear

luggage NOUN suitcases and bags for holding things to take on a journey

lugubrious (say lug-oo-bree-us) ADJECTIVE gloomy or mournful

lukewarm ADJECTIVE ❶ only slightly warm; tepid ❷ not very enthusiastic

lull VERB ❶ to soothe or calm someone; to send someone to sleep ❷ to give someone a false feeling of being safe

lull NOUN a short period of quiet or inactivity

lullaby NOUN a song that you sing to send a baby to sleep

lumbago NOUN pain in the muscles of the lower back

lumber NOUN ❶ unwanted furniture or other goods; junk ❷ (North American) timber

lumber VERB ❶ to move in a heavy clumsy way ❷ to leave someone with an unwanted or unpleasant task

lumberjack NOUN a person whose job is to cut or carry timber

luminous ADJECTIVE glowing in the dark

lump NOUN ❶ a solid piece of something ❷ a swelling

lump VERB to lump things together is to put or treat them in a group because you regard them as alike in some way

lump sum NOUN a single payment, especially one covering a number of items

lunacy NOUN insanity or great foolishness

lunar ADJECTIVE to do with the moon

lunar month NOUN the period between new moons; four weeks

lunatic NOUN an insane person

lunch NOUN a meal eaten in the middle of the day

luncheon NOUN (formal) lunch

lung NOUN either of the two parts of the body, in your chest, used in breathing

lunge VERB to thrust your body forward suddenly

lunge NOUN a sudden forward movement

lupin NOUN a garden plant with tall spikes of flowers

lurch VERB ① to stagger; to lean suddenly to one side ② if you heart or stomach lurches, you have a sudden feeling of fear or excitement

lurch NOUN a sudden staggering or leaning movement

lure VERB to tempt a person or animal into a trap; to entice someone

lure NOUN the attractive qualities of something

lurid (say lewr-id) ADJECTIVE ① in very bright colours; gaudy ② sensational and shocking

lurk VERB to wait where you cannot be seen

luscious (say lush-us) ADJECTIVE tasting delicious

lush ADJECTIVE growing thickly and strongly

lust NOUN powerful desire, especially sexual desire

lust VERB to have a powerful desire for a person or thing

lustre NOUN brightness or brilliance

lusty ADJECTIVE strong and vigorous

lute NOUN a stringed musical instrument with a pear-shaped body, popular in the 14th-17th centuries

luxuriant ADJECTIVE growing thickly and strongly

luxurious ADJECTIVE full of luxury; expensive and comfortable

luxury NOUN ① something expensive that you enjoy but do not really need ② expensive and comfortable surroundings

Lycra NOUN (trademark) a thin stretchy material used especially for sports clothing

lying present participle of lie

lymph (say limf) NOUN a colourless fluid from the flesh or organs of the body, containing white blood cells

lynch VERB to join together to execute someone without a proper trial, especially by hanging them

lynx NOUN a wild animal like a very large cat with thick fur and very sharp sight

lyre NOUN an ancient musical instrument like a small harp

lyric (say li-rik) NOUN ① a short poem that expresses the poet's feelings ② lyrics are the words of a popular song

lyrical ADJECTIVE ① like a song ② expressing poetic feelings ③ expressing yourself enthusiastically

A B C D E F G H I J K L M N O P Q R S T U V W X Y Z

Mm

MA *ABBREVIATION* Master of Arts

ma *NOUN* (*informal*) mother

mac *NOUN* (*British*) (*informal*) a raincoat

macabre (say mak-**ahbr**) *ADJECTIVE* gruesome; strange and horrible

macadam *NOUN* layers of broken stone rolled flat to make a firm road surface

macaroni *NOUN* pasta in the form of short narrow tubes

macaroon *NOUN* a small sweet cake or biscuit made with ground almonds

macaw (say ma-**kaw**) *NOUN* a brightly coloured parrot from Central and South America

mace *NOUN* an ornamental staff carried or placed in front of an official

machete (say mash-**et-ee**) *NOUN* a broad heavy knife used as a tool or weapon

machine *NOUN* a piece of equipment made of moving parts that work together to do a job

machine gun *NOUN* a gun that can keep firing bullets quickly one after another

machine-readable *ADJECTIVE* machine-readable data is in a form that a computer can process

machinery *NOUN* ❶ machines ❷ the moving parts of a machine ❸ an organized system for doing something

macho (say **mach**-oh) *ADJECTIVE* showing off masculine strength

mackerel *NOUN* a sea fish used as food

mad *ADJECTIVE* ❶ having something wrong with the mind; insane ❷ extremely foolish ❸ very keen ❹ (*informal*) very excited or annoyed

madam *NOUN* a word used when speaking politely to a woman

mad cow disease *NOUN* BSE

madden *VERB* to make a person mad or angry

maddening *ADJECTIVE* annoying

madly *ADVERB* extremely; very much

madonna *NOUN* a picture or statue of the Virgin Mary

madrigal *NOUN* a song for several voices singing different parts together

maestro (say **my**-stroh) *NOUN* a master, especially a musician

mafia *NOUN* ❶ a large organization of criminals in Italy, Sicily and the United States of America ❷ any group of people who act together in a sinister way

magazine *NOUN* ❶ a paper-covered publication that comes out regularly, with articles, stories or features by several writers ❷ the part of a gun that holds the cartridges ❸ a store for weapons and ammunition or for explosives ❹ a device that holds film for a camera or slides for a projector

magenta (say ma-**jen**-ta) *NOUN* a colour between bright red and purple

maggot *NOUN* the larva of some kinds of fly

Magi (say **mayj**-eye) *PLURAL NOUN*

the 'wise men' from the East who brought offerings to the infant Jesus at Bethlehem

magic NOUN **1** the art of making impossible things happen by a mysterious or supernatural power **2** mysterious tricks performed for entertainment **3** a mysterious and enchanting quality

magic ADJECTIVE **1** used in or using magic **2** having a special or mysterious quality.

magical 1 to do with magic or using magic **2** wonderful or marvellous

magician NOUN **1** a person who does magic tricks **2** a wizard

magistrate NOUN an official who hears and judges minor cases in a local court

magma NOUN a molten substance beneath the earth's crust

magnanimous (say mag-**nan**-im-us) ADJECTIVE generous and forgiving, not petty-minded

magnate NOUN a wealthy influential person, especially in business

magnesia NOUN a white powder that is a compound of magnesium, used in medicine

magnesium NOUN a silvery-white metal that burns with a very bright flame

magnet NOUN a piece of iron or steel that can attract iron and that points north and south when it is hung up

magnetic ADJECTIVE **1** having or using the powers of a magnet **2** having the power to attract

people

magnetic tape NOUN a plastic strip coated with a magnetic substance, for recording sound or pictures or storing computer data

magnetism NOUN **1** the properties and effects of magnetic substances **2** great personal charm and attraction

magnetize (also **magnetise**) VERB to make something into a magnet

magneto (say mag-**neet**-oh) NOUN a small electric generator using magnets

magnificent ADJECTIVE **1** looking grand or splendid **2** very good; excellent

magnify VERB **1** to make something look bigger than it really is, as a lens or microscope does **2** to exaggerate something

magnifying glass NOUN a lens that magnifies things

magnitude NOUN the magnitude of something is how large or important it is

magnolia NOUN a tree with large white or pale-pink flowers

magpie NOUN a noisy bird with black and white feathers, related to the crow

maharajah NOUN the title of certain Indian princes

mahogany NOUN a hard brown wood

maid NOUN **1** a female servant **2** (old use) a girl

maiden NOUN (old use) a girl

maiden ADJECTIVE **1** a maiden aunt is one who is not married **2** a ship's maiden voyage is its first voyage after being built

maiden name NOUN a woman's family name before she marries

maiden over NOUN a cricket over in which no runs are scored

mail NOUN ❶ letters and parcels sent by post ❷ email; an email ❸ armour made of metal rings joined together

mail VERB to send something by post or by email

mailing list NOUN a list of names and addresses of people to whom an organization sends information from time to time

mail order NOUN a system for buying and selling goods by post

maim VERB to injure a person so badly that part of their body is damaged for life

main ADJECTIVE largest or most important

main NOUN ❶ the main pipe or cable in a public system carrying water, gas, or (usually called **mains**) electricity to a building ❷ (*old use*) the seas

main clause NOUN a clause that can be used as a complete sentence. Compare with **subordinate clause**.

mainframe NOUN a large powerful computer that a lot of people can use at the same time

mainland NOUN the main part of a country or continent, not the islands round it

mainly ADVERB chiefly or mostly

mainstay NOUN the chief support or main part

mainstream NOUN the most widely accepted ideas or opinions about something

maintain VERB ❶ to make something continue at the same standard or level ❷ to keep a thing in good condition ❸ to keep saying that something is true ❹ to provide money for a person to live on

maintenance NOUN ❶ maintaining or keeping something in good condition ❷ money for food and clothing ❸ money to be paid by a husband or wife to the other partner after a divorce

maize NOUN (*British*) a tall kind of corn with large seeds on cobs

majestic ADJECTIVE ❶ stately and dignified ❷ very impressive

majesty NOUN ❶ the title of a king or queen ❷ being majestic

major ADJECTIVE ❶ greater; very important or serious ❷ of the musical scale that has a semitone after the 3rd and 7th notes. Compare with **minor**.

major NOUN an army officer ranking next above a captain

major VERB (*North American & Australian/NZ*) to specialize in a particular subject at college or university

majority NOUN ❶ the greatest part of a group of people or things. Compare with **minority**. ❷ the amount by which the winner in an election beats the loser ❸ the age at which a person becomes an adult according to the law, now usually 18

make VERB makes, making, made

① to bring something into existence, especially by putting things together **②** to cause something to happen **③** to gain or earn an amount of money **④** to achieve or reach something **⑤** to estimate or reckon something **⑥** to result in or add up to something **⑦** to perform an action **⑧** to arrange something for use **⑨** to cause someone to be successful or happy

make NOUN a brand of goods; something made by a particular firm

make-believe NOUN pretending or imagining things

make-over NOUN changes in your make-up, hairstyle and the way you dress to make you look and feel more attractive

maker NOUN the person or firm that has made something

makeshift ADJECTIVE used for the time being because you have nothing better

make-up NOUN **①** creams and powders put on your face to make it look more attractive or different **②** the way something is made up **③** a person's character

malady NOUN an illness or disease

malapropism NOUN a comical confusion of words, e.g. using *hooligan* instead of *hurricane*

malaria NOUN a feverish disease spread by mosquitoes

male ADJECTIVE of the sex that reproduces by fertilizing egg cells produced by the female

male NOUN a male person, animal or plant

male chauvinist NOUN a man who thinks that women are not as good as men

malevolent (say ma-lev-ol-ent) ADJECTIVE showing a desire to harm other people

malfunction NOUN faulty functioning

malfunction VERB to fail to work properly

malice NOUN a desire to harm other people; spite

malicious ADJECTIVE intending to do harm

malign (say mal-y'n) ADJECTIVE **①** harmful and sinister **②** showing malice

malign VERB to say unpleasant and untrue things about someone

malignant ADJECTIVE **①** a malignant tumour is one that is growing uncontrollably **②** full of malice

malinger VERB to pretend to be ill in order to avoid work

mall (say mal or mawl) NOUN a large covered shopping centre

mallard NOUN a kind of wild duck of North America, Europe and parts of Asia

malleable ADJECTIVE **①** able to be pressed or hammered into shape **②** easy to influence

mallet NOUN **①** a large hammer, usually made of wood **②** an implement with a long handle, used in croquet or polo for striking the ball

malnutrition NOUN bad health because you do not have enough food or the right kind of food

malt NOUN dried barley used in

brewing, making vinegar, etc.

maltreat VERB to ill-treat a person or animal

mammal NOUN any animal of which the female gives birth to live babies which are fed with milk from her own body

mammoth NOUN an extinct elephant with a hairy skin and curved tusks

mammoth ADJECTIVE huge

man NOUN men ❶ a grown-up male human being ❷ an individual person ❸ people in general; mankind ❹ a piece used in chess or some other board game

man VERB to provide a place or machine with the people to run or work it

manacle NOUN a fetter or handcuff

manacle VERB to put manacles on someone

manage VERB ❶ to succeed in doing or dealing with something difficult ❷ to be in charge of a business or part of it or a group of people

manageable ADJECTIVE not too big or too difficult to deal with

management NOUN ❶ managing something ❷ managers; the people in charge of a business

manager NOUN a person who manages something

manageress NOUN (*British*) a woman manager, especially of a shop or hotel

mandarin NOUN ❶ an important official ❷ a kind of small orange

mandate NOUN authority given to someone to carry out a certain

task or policy

mandatory ADJECTIVE obligatory or compulsory

mandible NOUN ❶ a jaw, especially the lower one ❷ either part of a bird's beak or the similar part in insects etc.

mandolin NOUN a musical instrument rather like a guitar

mane NOUN the long hair on a horse's or lion's neck

manfully ADVERB using a lot of effort in a brave or determined way

manganese NOUN a hard brittle metal

manger NOUN a trough in a stable for horses or cattle to feed from

mangle VERB to damage something by crushing or cutting it roughly

mango NOUN a tropical fruit with yellow pulp

mangrove NOUN a tropical tree growing in mud and swamps, with many tangled roots above the ground

manhandle VERB to handle or push a person or thing roughly

manhole NOUN a space or opening, usually with a cover, by which a person can get into a sewer or boiler etc. to inspect or repair it

manhood NOUN ❶ the condition of being a man ❷ manly qualities

mania NOUN ❶ violent madness ❷ a great enthusiasm for something

maniac NOUN a person who acts in a wild or violent way

manic ADJECTIVE ❶ to do with or

suffering from mania ❷ (*informal*) full of excited activity or nervous energy

manicure *NOUN* care and treatment of the hands and nails

manifest *ADJECTIVE* clear and obvious

manifest *VERB* to manifest a feeling or sign is to show it clearly

manifestation *NOUN* a sign that something is happening

manifesto *NOUN* a public statement of a group's or person's policy or principles

manipulate *VERB* ❶ to handle or arrange something skilfully ❷ to get someone to do what you want by treating them cleverly

mankind *NOUN* human beings in general

manly *ADJECTIVE* ❶ suitable for a man ❷ brave and strong

manner *NOUN* ❶ the way something happens or is done ❷ a person's way of behaving

mannerism *NOUN* a person's own particular gesture or way of speaking

manners *PLURAL NOUN* how a person behaves with other people; politeness

manoeuvre (say man-oo-ver) *NOUN* a difficult or skilful or cunning action

manoeuvre *VERB* ❶ to move something skilfully into position ❷ to move carefully and skilfully

man-of-war *NOUN* a warship

manor *NOUN* (*British*) ❶ a manor house ❷ the land belonging to a manor house

manor house *NOUN* (*British*) a large important house in the country

manpower *NOUN* the number of people who are working or needed or available for work on something

mansion *NOUN* a large stately house

manslaughter *NOUN* the crime of killing a person unlawfully but without meaning to

mantelpiece *NOUN* a shelf above a fireplace

mantle *NOUN* ❶ a cloak ❷ a covering

mantra *NOUN* a word or phrase that is constantly repeated to help people meditate, originally in Hinduism and Buddhism

manual *ADJECTIVE* worked by or done with the hands

manual *NOUN* a handbook or book of instructions

manufacture *VERB* to make things in large quantities using machines

manufacture *NOUN* the process of making things in large quantities using machines

manufacturer *NOUN* a business that manufactures things

manure *NOUN* animal dung added to the soil as fertilizer

manuscript *NOUN* something written or typed but not printed

Manx *ADJECTIVE* to do with the Isle of Man

many *DETERMINER* ❶ great in number; numerous ❷ used to talk about the size of a number

many *PRONOUN* a large number of people or things

Maori (rhymes with *flowery*) *NOUN*

1 a member of the people who were living in New Zealand before European settlers arrived **2** their language

map NOUN a diagram of part or all of the earth's surface or of the sky

map VERB to make a map of an area

maple NOUN a tree with broad leaves

maple syrup NOUN a sweet substance made from the sap of some kinds of maple

mar VERB to spoil something

marathon NOUN a long-distance running race, especially one covering 26 miles 385 yards (42.195 km)

marauding ADJECTIVE a marauding army or pack of animals goes about attacking people or stealing things

marble NOUN **1** a small glass ball used in games **2** a kind of limestone polished and used in sculpture or building

March NOUN the third month of the year

march VERB **1** to walk with regular steps **2** to make someone walk somewhere

march NOUN **1** a large group of people marching, sometimes to protest about something **2** a journey by marching **3** music suitable for marching to

marchioness NOUN the wife or widow of a marquis

mare NOUN a female horse or donkey

margarine (say mar-ja-**reen**) NOUN a substance used like butter, made

from animal or vegetable fats

margin NOUN **1** an edge or border **2** the blank space between the edge of a page and the writing or pictures on it **3** the difference between two scores or prices etc.

marginal ADJECTIVE **1** very slight **2** in a margin

marginally ADVERB very slightly; by a small amount

marginal seat NOUN a constituency where an MP was elected with only a small majority and may be defeated in the next election

marigold NOUN a yellow or orange garden flower

marijuana (say ma-ri-**hwah**-na) NOUN a drug made from hemp

marina NOUN a harbour for yachts, motor boats, etc.

marinade NOUN a flavoured liquid in which meat or fish is soaked before being cooked

marinate VERB to soak meat or fish in a marinade

marine (say ma-**reen**) ADJECTIVE to do with the sea; living in the sea

marine NOUN a member of the troops who are trained to serve at sea as well as on land

mariner (say **ma**-rin-er) NOUN a sailor

marionette NOUN a puppet that you work by strings or wires

marital ADJECTIVE to do with marriage

maritime ADJECTIVE **1** to do with the sea or ships **2** found near the sea

marjoram NOUN a herb with a mild flavour, used in cooking

mark NOUN ❶ a spot, dot, line or stain on something ❷ a number or letter put on a piece of work to show how good it is ❸ a distinguishing feature ❹ a sign or symbol ❺ a target ❻ a unit of money used in Germany before the introduction of the euro

mark VERB ❶ to put a mark on something ❷ to give a mark to a piece of work ❸ to keep close to an opposing player in football etc. ❹ to pay attention to something

marked ADJECTIVE clear or noticeable

marker NOUN a thing that shows the position of something

market NOUN ❶ a place where things are bought and sold, usually from stalls in the open air ❷ a demand for goods

market VERB to offer things for sale

marketing NOUN the branch of business concerned with advertising and selling the product

marketplace NOUN the place in a town where a market is held or used to be held

market research NOUN the study of what people need or want to buy

marksman, markswoman NOUN an expert in shooting at a target

marmalade NOUN jam made from oranges, lemons or other citrus fruit

maroon VERB to abandon someone in a deserted place that they cannot leave

maroon NOUN dark red

marquee (say mar-**kee**) NOUN a large tent used for a party or exhibition

marquis NOUN a nobleman ranking next above an earl

marriage NOUN ❶ the legal relationship between a husband and wife or a similar legal relationship between any couple ❷ a wedding

marrow NOUN ❶ a large gourd eaten as a vegetable ❷ the soft substance inside bones

marry VERB ❶ to marry someone is to be legally joined in marriage with them ❷ to marry two people is to perform a marriage ceremony

marsh NOUN a low-lying area of very wet ground

marshal NOUN ❶ an official who helps to organize or control a large public event ❷ an army officer of very high rank ❸ a police official in the USA

marshal VERB ❶ to gather things together and arrange them neatly ❷ to control or organize a large group of people

marshmallow NOUN a soft spongy sweet, usually pink or white

marsupial (say mar-**soo**-pee-al) NOUN an animal such as a kangaroo, wallaby or koala. The female has a pouch on the front of its body in which its babies are carried.

martial ADJECTIVE to do with war; warlike

martial arts PLURAL NOUN fighting sports, such as judo and karate

martial law NOUN government

368

of a country by the armed forces
during a crisis

martin NOUN a bird rather like a
swallow

martinet NOUN a very strict person

martyr NOUN a person who is killed
or made to suffer because of their
beliefs, especially religious beliefs

martyr VERB to kill someone or
make them suffer as a martyr

marvel NOUN a wonderful thing

marvel VERB to be filled with
wonder or astonishment by
something

marvellous ADJECTIVE extremely
good; wonderful

Marxism NOUN the Communist
theories of the German writer Karl
Marx (1818–83)

marzipan NOUN a soft sweet food
made of ground almonds, eggs
and sugar

mascara NOUN a cosmetic for
darkening the eyelashes

mascot NOUN a person, animal or
object that is believed to bring
good luck

masculine ADJECTIVE ❶ to do with
or like men; thought to be suitable
for a man ❷ belonging to the
class of words (in some languages)
which includes the words referring
to men

mash VERB to crush something into
a soft mass

mash NOUN ❶ a soft mixture
of cooked grain or bran etc.
❷ (*informal*) mashed potatoes

mask NOUN a covering that you
wear over your face to disguise or
protect it

mask VERB ❶ to cover your face
with a mask ❷ to disguise or
conceal something

mason NOUN a person who builds or
works with stone

masonry NOUN ❶ the parts of a
building that are made of stone
❷ a mason's work

masquerade NOUN a pretence

masquerade VERB to pretend to be
something

Mass NOUN the Communion service
in a Roman Catholic church

mass NOUN ❶ a large amount of
something ❷ a heap or other
collection of matter ❸ (*in science*)
the quantity of physical matter
that a thing contains

mass ADJECTIVE involving a large
number of people

mass VERB to collect into a mass

massacre NOUN the deliberate and
brutal killing of a large number
of people

massacre VERB to kill a large
number of people deliberately

massage (say **mas**-ahzh) VERB to
rub and press the body to make it
less stiff or less painful

massage NOUN massaging
someone's body

massive ADJECTIVE large and heavy;
huge

mass media PLURAL NOUN the
main media of news information,
especially newspapers and
broadcasting

mass production NOUN
manufacturing goods in large
quantities

mast NOUN a tall pole that holds up

a
b
c
d
e
f
g
h
i
j
k
l
m
n
o
p
q
r
s
t
u
v
w
x
y
z

a ship's sails or a flag or an aerial

master NOUN ❶ a man who is in charge of something ❷ a person who is extremely skilled at doing something, such as a great artist or composer ❸ (*old use*) a male teacher ❹ something from which copies are made ❺ (*old use*) a title put before a boy's name

master VERB ❶ to master a subject or a skill is to learn it thoroughly ❷ to master a fear or difficulty is to control it ❸ to overcome someone

masterful ADJECTIVE having control; domineering

masterly ADJECTIVE very skilful

mastermind NOUN ❶ a very clever person ❷ the person who plans and organizes a scheme or crime

mastermind VERB to plan and organize a scheme or crime

Master of Arts NOUN a person who has taken the next degree after Bachelor of Arts

master of ceremonies NOUN a person who introduces the speakers at a formal event or the entertainers at a variety show

Master of Science NOUN a person who has taken the next degree after Bachelor of Science

masterpiece NOUN ❶ an excellent piece of work ❷ a person's best piece of work

mastery NOUN complete control or thorough knowledge or skill in something

mastiff NOUN a large kind of dog

masturbate VERB to get sexual pleasure by touching the genitals

mat NOUN ❶ a small carpet ❷ a doormat ❸ a small piece of material put on a table to protect the surface

matador NOUN a bullfighter who fights on foot

match NOUN ❶ a small thin stick with a head made of a substance that gives a flame when rubbed on something rough ❷ a game or contest between two teams or players ❸ one person or thing that is equal to or similar to another ❹ a marriage

match VERB ❶ to be equal or similar to another person or thing ❷ to go well with something so that they look good together ❸ to find something that is similar or corresponding ❹ to put teams or players together to compete against each other

matchbox NOUN a small box for matches

matchstick NOUN the thin wooden part of a match

mate NOUN ❶ a friend or companion ❷ each of a pair of birds or animals that produce young together ❸ an officer on a merchant ship ❹ checkmate in chess

mate VERB ❶ a pair of animals or birds mate when they come together in order to breed ❷ to mate a pair of animals is to bring them together in order to breed

material NOUN ❶ anything used for making something else ❷ cloth or fabric

material ADJECTIVE ❶ to do with possessions, money, etc. ❷ important or relevant

materialism NOUN the belief that possessions are very important

materialize (also **materialise**) VERB ❶ to become visible; to appear ❷ to become a fact; to happen

maternal ADJECTIVE ❶ to do with a mother ❷ motherly

maternity NOUN motherhood

maternity ADJECTIVE to do with having a baby

mathematical ADJECTIVE to do with or using mathematics

mathematician (say math-em-a-**tish**-an) NOUN an expert in mathematics

mathematics NOUN the study of numbers, measurements and shapes

maths NOUN (British) (informal) mathematics

matinee NOUN an afternoon performance at a theatre or cinema

matins NOUN the church service of morning prayer

matriarch (say **may**-tree-ark) NOUN a woman who is head of a family or tribe. Compare with **patriarch**.

matrimony NOUN marriage

matrix (say **may**-triks) NOUN matrices, (say **may**-tri-seez) ❶ (in mathematics) a set of quantities arranged in rows and columns ❷ a mould or framework in which something is made or allowed to develop

matron NOUN ❶ an older married woman ❷ a woman in charge of nursing in a school etc. or (formerly) of the nursing staff in a hospital

matt ADJECTIVE not shiny

matted ADJECTIVE matted hair or fur is tangled into a mass

matter NOUN ❶ something you can touch or see, not the spirit or mind or qualities etc. ❷ a substance ❸ things of a certain kind ❹ something you can think about or do ❺ a quantity

matter VERB to be important

matter-of-fact ADJECTIVE keeping to facts; not imaginative or emotional

matting NOUN rough material for covering floors

mattress NOUN soft or springy material in a fabric covering, used on or as a bed

mature ADJECTIVE ❶ fully grown or developed ❷ behaving in a sensible adult manner

mature VERB to become fully grown or developed

maturity NOUN ❶ being fully grown or developed ❷ behaving in a sensible adult manner

maudlin ADJECTIVE sentimental in a silly or tearful way

maul VERB to injure someone by violent handling or clawing

mausoleum (say maw-sol-**ee**-um) NOUN a magnificent tomb

mauve (say mohv) NOUN pale purple

maverick NOUN a person who belongs to a group but often disagrees with its beliefs or acts on his or her own

maxim NOUN a short saying giving a general truth or rule of behaviour, e.g. 'Waste not, want not'

maximize (also **maximise**) VERB to make something as great, large or effective as possible

maximum NOUN the greatest possible number or amount. (The opposite is **minimum**.)

maximum ADJECTIVE the greatest possible

May NOUN the fifth month of the year

may AUXILIARY VERB may, might used to express ❶ permission (*You may go now*) ❷ possibility (*It may be true*) ❸ wish (*Long may she reign*) ❹ uncertainty (*whoever it may be*)

maybe ADVERB perhaps; possibly

Mayday NOUN an international radio signal calling for help

mayfly NOUN an insect that lives for only a short time, in spring

mayhem NOUN violent confusion or damage

mayonnaise NOUN a creamy sauce made from eggs, oil, vinegar, etc., eaten with salad

mayor NOUN the person in charge of the council in a town or city

maypole NOUN a decorated pole round which people dance on 1 May

maze NOUN a network of paths, especially one designed as a puzzle in which to try and find your way

Mb ABBREVIATION megabyte(s)

MC ABBREVIATION master of ceremonies

MD ABBREVIATION Doctor of Medicine

ME NOUN (*British*) long-lasting fever, weakness and pain in the muscles following a viral infection

me PRONOUN the form of **I** used as the object of a verb or after a preposition

mead NOUN an alcoholic drink made from honey and water

meadow (say **med**-oh) NOUN a field of grass

meagre ADJECTIVE scanty in amount; barely enough

meal NOUN ❶ food served and eaten at one sitting ❷ coarsely-ground grain

mealie NOUN (*S. African*) a maize plant or cob

mealtime NOUN a regular time for having a meal

mealy-mouthed ADJECTIVE too polite or timid to say what you really mean

mean VERB means, meaning, meant (say ment) ❶ to have something as an equivalent or explanation; to have a certain meaning ❷ to intend to do something ❸ to be serious ❹ to show that something is likely ❺ to have something as a result

mean ADJECTIVE ❶ not generous; miserly ❷ unkind or spiteful ❸ poor in quality or appearance

mean NOUN a point or number midway between two extremes; the average of a set of numbers

mean ADJECTIVE midway between two points; average

meander (say mee-**an**-der) VERB ❶ a river or road that meanders has a lot of bends in it ❷ to walk

Sidebar letters: A B C D E F G H I J K L **M** N O P Q R S T U V W X Y Z or travel slowly or without any definite direction

meaning NOUN what something means

meaningful ADJECTIVE expressing an important meaning

meaningless ADJECTIVE with no meaning or purpose

means NOUN a way of achieving something or producing a result

means PLURAL NOUN money or other wealth

meantime NOUN ➤ **in the meantime** in the time between two events or while something else is happening

meanwhile ADVERB in the time between two events or while something else is happening

measles NOUN an infectious disease that causes small red spots on the skin

measly ADJECTIVE (*informal*) not adequate or generous

measure VERB ❶ to find the size, amount or extent of something by comparing it with a fixed unit or with an object of known size ❷ to be a certain size

measure NOUN ❶ a unit used for measuring ❷ a device used in measuring ❸ the size or quantity of something ❹ something done for a particular purpose

measurement NOUN ❶ the process of measuring something ❷ a size or amount found by measuring

meat NOUN animal flesh used as food

mecca NOUN a place which attracts people with a particular interest

mechanic NOUN a person who maintains or repairs machinery

mechanical ADJECTIVE ❶ to do with machines ❷ produced or worked by machines ❸ done or doing something without thinking about it

mechanically ADVERB without thinking about it

mechanics NOUN ❶ the study of movement and force ❷ the study or use of machines

mechanism NOUN ❶ the moving parts of a machine ❷ the way a machine works ❸ the process by which something is done

mechanized (also **mechanised**) ADJECTIVE equipped with machines

medal NOUN a piece of metal shaped like a coin, star or cross, given to a person for bravery or for achieving something

medallion NOUN a large medal, usually worn round the neck as an ornament

medallist NOUN a winner of a medal

meddle VERB ❶ to interfere in something without being asked ❷ to tinker with something

media *plural* of **medium** noun

median ADJECTIVE in the middle

median NOUN ❶ a median point or line ❷ (*in mathematics*) the middle number in a set of numbers that have been arranged in order. The median of 2, 3, 5, 8, 9, 14 and 15 is 8 ❸ a straight line passing from a point of a triangle to the centre of the opposite side

mediate VERB to negotiate between the opposing sides in a dispute

medical ADJECTIVE to do with the treatment of disease

medicated ADJECTIVE treated with a medicinal substance

medication NOUN ❶ a medicine ❷ treatment using medicine

medicinal (say med-**iss**-in-al) ADJECTIVE helping to cure an illness

medicine NOUN ❶ a substance, usually swallowed, used to try to cure a disease ❷ the study and treatment of diseases

medieval (say med-ee-**ee**-val) ADJECTIVE belonging to or to do with the Middle Ages

mediocre (say mee-dee-**oh**-ker) ADJECTIVE not very good; of only medium quality

meditate VERB ❶ to think deeply or seriously about something ❷ to think deeply in silence for religious reasons or to make your mind calm

Mediterranean ADJECTIVE to do with the Mediterranean Sea (which lies between Europe and Africa) or the countries round it

medium ADJECTIVE neither large nor small; average

medium NOUN ❶ media a thing in which something exists, moves or is expressed (see **media**) ❷ mediums a person who claims to be able to communicate with the dead

medium wave NOUN (*chiefly British*) a radio wave of a frequency between 300 kilohertz and 3 megahertz

medley NOUN ❶ an assortment or mixture of things ❷ a collection of songs or tunes played as a continuous piece

meek ADJECTIVE quiet and obedient

meet VERB meets, meeting, met ❶ to come together from different places ❷ to see someone for the first time and get to know them ❸ to go to a place and wait there for someone to arrive ❹ to touch, join or come into contact ❺ to meet the cost of something is to pay it ❻ to satisfy or fulfil something

meet NOUN a gathering of riders and hounds for a hunt

meeting NOUN ❶ a time when a number of people come together in order to discuss or decide something ❷ coming together

megabyte NOUN (*in computing*) a unit of information roughly equal to one million bytes

megalomaniac NOUN a person who has an exaggerated idea of their own importance

megaphone NOUN a funnel-shaped device for amplifying a person's voice

melancholy ADJECTIVE sad and gloomy

melancholy NOUN sadness or depression

melee (say **mel**-ay) NOUN a situation in which a lot of people are rushing or pushing each other in a confused way

mellow ADJECTIVE ❶ not harsh; soft and rich in flavour, colour or sound ❷ having become kinder and more sympathetic with age

mellow VERB ❶ to make something softer or less harsh or to become this ❷ a person mellows when they become kinder and more sympathetic with age

melodic ADJECTIVE to do with melody; pleasant to listen to

melodious ADJECTIVE like a melody; pleasant to listen to

melodrama NOUN a play full of dramatic excitement and strong emotion

melodramatic ADJECTIVE behaving in an exaggerated way that is full of emotion

melody NOUN a tune, especially one that is pleasant to listen to

melon NOUN a large sweet fruit with a yellow or green skin

melt VERB ① to make something liquid by heating it ② to become liquid by heating ③ to disappear slowly ④ to become softer

melting pot NOUN a place where people of many different races and cultures live and influence each other

member NOUN ① a person or thing that belongs to a particular society or group ② a part of something

Member of Parliament NOUN a person elected to represent the people of an area in Parliament

membership NOUN being a member of a particular society or group

membrane NOUN a thin skin or similar covering

memento NOUN a souvenir

memo (say mem-oh) NOUN a note from one person to another in the same firm

memoir (say mem-wahr) NOUN a

biography, especially one written by someone who knew the person

memoirs PLURAL NOUN an autobiography

memorable ADJECTIVE ① worth remembering ② easy to remember

memorandum NOUN memoranda or memorandums (formal) a memo

memorial NOUN something set up to remind people of a person or event

memorize (also **memorise**) VERB to learn something so that you can remember it exactly

memory NOUN ① the ability to remember things ② something that you remember from the past ③ the part of a computer where information is stored

menace NOUN ① a threat or danger ② a troublesome person or thing

menace VERB to threaten someone with harm or danger

menagerie NOUN a small zoo

mend VERB ① to repair something broken ② to make something better

mend NOUN ➤ on the mend getting better after an illness

menial (say meen-ee-al) ADJECTIVE needing little or no skill or thought

menial NOUN a person who does menial work; a servant

meningitis NOUN a disease causing inflammation of the membranes (meninges) round the brain and spinal cord

menopause NOUN the time of life when a woman gradually stops menstruating

a
b
c
d
e
f
g
h
i
j
k
l
m
n
o
p
q
r
s
t
u
v
w
x
y
z

menstruate VERB to bleed from the womb about once a month, as girls and women normally do from their teens until middle age

mental ADJECTIVE ❶ to do with or in the mind ❷ (*informal*) mad

mentality NOUN a person's mental ability or attitude

mentally ADVERB in your mind; to do with the mind

menthol NOUN a solid white peppermint-flavoured substance

mention VERB to speak or write about a person or thing briefly; to refer to a person or thing

mention NOUN an example of mentioning someone or something

mentor NOUN an experienced and trusted adviser

menu (say **men**-yoo) NOUN ❶ a list of the food available in a restaurant or served at a meal ❷ (*in computing*) a list of possible actions, shown on a screen, from which you choose what you want a computer to do

MEP ABBREVIATION Member of the European Parliament

mercenary ADJECTIVE interested only in the money you can get for the work you do

mercenary NOUN a soldier who fights for any army or country that will pay them

merchandise NOUN goods for sale

merchant NOUN a person involved in trade

merchant bank NOUN (*British*) a bank that gives loans and advice to businesses

merchant navy NOUN (*British*) the ships and sailors that carry goods for trade

merciful ADJECTIVE showing mercy

merciless ADJECTIVE showing no mercy; cruel

mercury NOUN a heavy silvery metal that is usually liquid, used in thermometers

mercy NOUN ❶ kindness or pity shown towards someone instead of harming them or punishing them ❷ something to be thankful for

mere ADJECTIVE not more than

mere NOUN (*British*) (*poetical use*) a lake

merely ADVERB only; simply

merest ADJECTIVE very small or slight

merge VERB when two or more things merge they combine together to form a single thing

merger NOUN the combining of two business companies into one

meridian NOUN a line on a map or globe from the North Pole to the South Pole. The meridian that passes through Greenwich is shown on maps as 0° longitude.

meringue (say mer-**ang**) NOUN a crisp cake made from egg white and sugar

merino NOUN a kind of sheep with fine soft wool

merit NOUN ❶ a quality that deserves praise ❷ excellence

merit VERB to deserve something

mermaid NOUN a mythical sea creature with a woman's body but with a fish's tail instead of legs

merriment NOUN happy talk, enjoyment and the sound of

people laughing

merry ADJECTIVE cheerful and lively

merry-go-round NOUN a roundabout at a fair

mesh NOUN ❶ the open spaces in a net, sieve or other criss-cross structure ❷ material made like a net

mesh VERB gears mesh when they fit together as they move

mesmerize (also **mesmerise**) VERB ❶ (old use) to hypnotize someone ❷ to fascinate or hold a person's attention completely

mess NOUN ❶ a dirty or untidy condition or thing ❷ a difficult or confused situation ❸ in the armed forces, a dining room

mess VERB ➤ **mess about** to behave stupidly or idly ➤ **mess something up** ❶ to make a thing dirty or untidy ❷ to bungle or ruin something ➤ **mess with something** to interfere or tinker with something

message NOUN ❶ a piece of information sent from one person to another ❷ the main theme or moral of a book, film, etc.

messenger NOUN a person who carries a message

Messiah (say mis-y-a) NOUN ❶ the saviour expected by the Jews ❷ Jesus Christ, who Christians believe was this saviour

Messrs (plural of **Mr**)

messy ADJECTIVE ❶ dirty and untidy ❷ difficult and complicated

metabolism (say mit-**ab**-ol-izm) NOUN the process by which food is built up into living material in a plant or animal or used to supply it with energy

metal NOUN a chemical substance, usually hard, that conducts heat and electricity and melts when it is heated. Gold, silver, copper, iron and uranium are metals.

metallic ADJECTIVE made of or like metal

metallurgy (say mit-**al**-er-jee) NOUN ❶ the study of metals ❷ the craft of making and using metals

metamorphic ADJECTIVE formed or changed by heat or pressure

metamorphosis (say met-a-**mor**-fo-sis) NOUN ❶ a complete change made by some living things, such as a caterpillar changing into a butterfly ❷ a change of form or character

metaphor NOUN using a word or phrase in a way that describes one thing as if it were something else, e.g. 'He was a little monkey' and 'Her heart leapt for joy'

metaphorical ADJECTIVE to do with or using metaphors

mete VERB ➤ **mete something out** to give someone a punishment or bad treatment

meteor (say **meet**-ee-er) NOUN a piece of rock or metal that moves through space and burns up when it enters the earth's atmosphere

meteoric (say meet-ee-o-rik) ADJECTIVE ❶ to do with meteors ❷ becoming very successful very rapidly

meteorite NOUN the remains of a meteor that has landed on the earth

meteorology NOUN the study of the conditions of the atmosphere, especially in order to forecast the weather

meter NOUN a device for measuring something, especially the amount of something used

methane (say mee-thayn) NOUN an inflammable gas produced by decaying matter

method NOUN ❶ a procedure or way of doing something ❷ good organization or orderly behaviour

methodical ADJECTIVE doing things in a careful and well-organized way

Methodist NOUN a member of a Christian religious group started by John and Charles Wesley in the 18th century

meths NOUN (British) (informal) methylated spirit

methylated spirit, spirits NOUN a liquid fuel made from alcohol

meticulous ADJECTIVE very careful and precise

metre NOUN ❶ a unit of length in the metric system, about 39½ inches ❷ rhythm in poetry

metric ADJECTIVE ❶ to do with the metric system ❷ to do with metre in poetry

metric system NOUN a measuring system based on decimal units (the metre, litre and gram)

metric ton NOUN 1,000 kilograms

metronome NOUN a device that makes a regular clicking noise to help you keep in time when practising music

metropolis NOUN the chief city of a country or region

metropolitan ADJECTIVE ❶ to do with a metropolis ❷ to do with a city and its suburbs

mettle NOUN courage or strength of character

mew VERB to make a cat's cry

mew NOUN a cat's cry

mews NOUN (British) a row of houses in a small street or square, converted from former stables

miaow (say mee-ow) VERB to make a cat's cry

miaow NOUN a cat's cry

mica NOUN a mineral substance used to make electrical insulators

mice plural of **mouse**

microbe NOUN a tiny organism that can only be seen with a microscope; a microorganism

microchip NOUN a very small piece of silicon etc. made to work like a complex wired electric circuit

microcomputer NOUN a small computer with a microprocessor as its central processing unit

microfiche NOUN a piece of film on which pages of information are photographed in greatly reduced size

microfilm NOUN a length of film on which written or printed material is photographed in greatly reduced size

micron NOUN a unit of measurement equal to one millionth of a metre

microorganism NOUN a microscopic creature, e.g. a bacterium or virus

microphone NOUN an electrical device that picks up sound waves for recording them or making them louder

microprocessor NOUN the central processing unit of a computer, consisting of one or more microchips

microscope NOUN an instrument with lenses that magnify tiny objects or details

microscopic ADJECTIVE ❶ extremely small; too small to be seen without the aid of a microscope ❷ to do with a microscope

microwave NOUN ❶ a very short electromagnetic wave ❷ a microwave oven

microwave VERB to cook food in a microwave oven

microwave oven NOUN an oven that uses microwaves to heat or cook food very quickly

mid ADJECTIVE ❶ in the middle of ❷ middle

midday NOUN the middle of the day; noon

middle NOUN ❶ the place or part of something that is at the same distance from all its sides or edges or from both its ends ❷ someone's waist

middle ADJECTIVE ❶ placed or happening in the middle ❷ moderate in size or rank etc.

middle-aged ADJECTIVE aged between about 45 and 65

Middle Ages NOUN the period in history from about AD 1000 to 1400

middle class, classes NOUN the class of people between the upper class and the working class, including business and professional people such as teachers, doctors and lawyers

Middle East NOUN the countries from Egypt to Iran inclusive

Middle English NOUN the English language from about 1150 to 1500

middle school NOUN a school for children aged from about 9 to 13

middling ADJECTIVE of medium size or quality

midge NOUN a small insect like a gnat

midget NOUN an extremely small person or thing

midland ADJECTIVE ❶ to do with the middle part of a country ❷ to do with the Midlands

Midlands PLURAL NOUN the central part of a country, especially the central counties of England

midnight NOUN twelve o'clock at night

midriff NOUN the front part of the body just above the waist

midst NOUN ➤ in the midst of in the middle of or surrounded by ➤ in our midst among us

midsummer NOUN the middle part of summer

Midsummer's Day NOUN 24 June

midway ADVERB halfway between two points

midwife NOUN a person trained to look after a woman who is giving birth to a baby

midwinter NOUN the middle part of winter

a
b
c
d
e
f
g
h
i
j
k
l
m
n
o
p
q
r
s
t
u
v
w
x
y
z

might NOUN great strength or power

might AUXILIARY VERB ❶ the past tense of may (*We told her she might go.*) ❷ used to express possibility (*It might be true.*)

mightily ADVERB ❶ very; very much ❷ with great strength or effort

mighty ADJECTIVE very strong or powerful

migraine (say *mee*-grayn or *my*-grayn) NOUN a severe kind of headache

migrant NOUN a person or animal that migrates or has migrated

migrate VERB ❶ to leave one place or country and settle in another ❷ birds and animals migrate when they move periodically from one area to another

migration NOUN moving in large numbers from one area to another

mike NOUN (*informal*) a microphone

mild ADJECTIVE ❶ not harsh or severe ❷ not great or extreme; slight ❸ gentle and kind ❹ not strongly flavoured ❺ mild weather is quite warm and pleasant

mildew NOUN a tiny fungus that forms a white coating on things kept in damp conditions

mildly ADVERB ❶ slightly ❷ in a gentle manner

mile NOUN a measure of distance equal to 1,760 yards (about 1.6 kilometres)

mileage NOUN the number of miles you have travelled

milestone NOUN a stone of a kind that used to be fixed beside a road to mark the distance between

towns ❷ an important stage or event in history or in a person's life

militant ADJECTIVE ❶ eager to fight ❷ forceful or aggressive

military ADJECTIVE to do with soldiers or the armed forces

militia (say mil-**ish**-a) NOUN a military force, especially one raised from civilians

milk NOUN ❶ a white liquid that female mammals produce in their bodies to feed their babies ❷ the milk of cows, used as food by human beings ❸ a milky liquid, e.g. that in a coconut

milk VERB to get the milk from a cow or other animal

milkman NOUN a man who delivers milk to customers' houses

milkshake NOUN a cold frothy drink made from milk whisked with sweet fruit flavouring

milk tooth NOUN one of the first set of teeth of a child or animal, which will be replaced by adult teeth

milky ADJECTIVE ❶ like milk; white ❷ made with a lot of milk

Milky Way NOUN the broad band of stars formed by our galaxy

mill NOUN ❶ machinery for grinding corn to make flour; a building containing this machinery ❷ a grinding machine ❸ a factory for processing certain materials

mill VERB ❶ to grind or crush something in a mill ❷ to cut markings round the edge of a coin

millennium NOUN millenniums a period of 1,000 years

miller NOUN a person who runs a

380

flour mill

millet NOUN a kind of cereal with tiny seeds

milligram NOUN one-thousandth of a gram

millilitre NOUN one-thousandth of a litre

millimetre NOUN one-thousandth of a metre

milliner NOUN a person who makes or sells women's hats

million NOUN & ADJECTIVE one thousand thousand (1,000,000)

millionaire NOUN a person who has at least a million pounds or dollars; an extremely rich person

millipede NOUN a small crawling creature like a centipede, with many legs

millstone NOUN either of a pair of large circular stones between which corn is ground

milometer NOUN (*British*) an instrument for measuring how far a vehicle has travelled

mime NOUN acting with movements of the body, not using words

mime VERB to use mime to act or express something

mimic VERB to imitate someone, especially to amuse people

mimic NOUN a person who is good at imitating others

minaret NOUN the tall tower of a mosque

mince VERB ❶ to cut meat or other food into very small pieces in a machine ❷ to walk in an affected way with short quick steps

mince NOUN (*British*) minced meat

mincemeat NOUN (*chiefly British*) a sweet mixture of currants, raisins, apple, etc. used in pies

mince pie NOUN (*chiefly British*) a pie containing mincemeat

mind NOUN ❶ the ability to think, feel, understand and remember, originating in the brain ❷ a person's thoughts, opinion or intention

mind VERB ❶ to look after a person or animal for a while ❷ to be careful about something ❸ to be sad or upset about something; to object to something

mindful ADJECTIVE taking thought or care

mindless ADJECTIVE done without thinking; stupid or pointless

mine POSSESSIVE PRONOUN belonging to me

mine NOUN ❶ a place where coal, metal or precious stones are dug out of the ground ❷ an explosive placed in or on the ground or in the sea to destroy people or things that come close to it

mine VERB ❶ to dig something from a mine ❷ to lay explosive mines in a place

minefield NOUN ❶ an area where explosive mines have been laid ❷ something with hidden dangers or problems

miner NOUN a person who works in a mine

mineral NOUN ❶ a substance that is formed naturally in rocks and in the ground, such as iron, salt and coal ❷ a cold fizzy non-alcoholic drink

mineralogy (say min-er-**al**-o-jee)

NOUN the study of minerals

mineral water NOUN water from a natural spring, containing mineral salts or gases

minestrone (say mini-**stroh**-nee) NOUN an Italian soup containing vegetables and pasta

mingle VERB to mix or blend with other things

miniature ADJECTIVE ❶ very small ❷ copying something on a very small scale

miniature NOUN ❶ a very small portrait ❷ a small-scale model

minibus NOUN a small bus, seating about ten people

minim NOUN a note in music, lasting twice as long as a crotchet (written ♩)

minimal ADJECTIVE very little; as little as possible

minimize (also **minimise**) VERB to make something as small as possible

minimum NOUN the lowest possible number or amount. (The opposite is **maximum**.)

minimum ADJECTIVE least or smallest

minion NOUN a very humble or obedient assistant or servant

minister NOUN ❶ a person in charge of a government department ❷ a member of the clergy

minister VERB to attend to people's needs

ministry NOUN ❶ a government department ❷ the work of the clergy

mink NOUN ❶ an animal rather like

a stoat ❷ this animal's valuable brown fur or a coat made from it

minnow NOUN a tiny freshwater fish

minor ADJECTIVE ❶ not very important, especially when compared to something else ❷ of the musical scale that has a semitone after the second note. Compare with **major**.

minor NOUN a person under the age of legal responsibility

minority NOUN ❶ the smallest part of a group of people or things ❷ a small group that is different from others. Compare with **majority**.

minstrel NOUN a travelling singer and musician in the Middle Ages

mint NOUN ❶ a plant with fragrant leaves that are used for flavouring things ❷ a sweet flavoured with peppermint ❸ the place where a country's coins are made

mint VERB to make coins by stamping metal

minuet NOUN a slow stately dance

minus PREPOSITION with the next number or thing subtracted

minus ADJECTIVE less than zero

minuscule ADJECTIVE extremely small

minute (say **min**-it) NOUN ❶ one-sixtieth of an hour ❷ a very short time; a moment ❸ one-sixtieth of a degree (used in measuring angles)

minute (say my-**newt**) ADJECTIVE ❶ very small ❷ very detailed

minutes PLURAL NOUN a written summary of what was said at a meeting

miracle NOUN ❶ a wonderful event

that seems to be impossible and is believed to have a supernatural or divine cause ❷ something fortunate and surprising

miraculous ADJECTIVE completely unexpected and very lucky

mirage (say mi-rahzh) NOUN an illusion; something that seems to be there but is not, especially when a lake seems to appear in a desert

mire NOUN ❶ a swamp ❷ deep mud

mirror NOUN a device or surface of reflecting material, usually glass

mirror VERB to reflect something in or like a mirror

mirth NOUN merriment or laughter

misapprehension NOUN a wrong idea or impression of something

misbehave VERB to behave badly

miscalculate VERB to calculate something incorrectly

miscarriage NOUN ❶ a woman has a miscarriage when she gives birth to a baby before it has developed enough to survive ❷ failure to achieve the right result

miscellaneous (say mis-el-ay-nee-us) ADJECTIVE of various kinds; mixed

miscellany (say mis-el-an-ee) NOUN a collection or mixture of different things

mischief NOUN ❶ naughty or troublesome behaviour ❷ trouble caused by this

mischievous ADJECTIVE liking to behave badly or cause trouble

misconception NOUN a wrong or mistaken idea

misconduct NOUN bad behaviour

by someone in a responsible position

misdeed NOUN a wrong or wicked act

misdemeanour NOUN an action which is wrong or illegal, but not very serious; a petty crime

miser NOUN a person who hoards money and spends as little as possible

miserable ADJECTIVE ❶ full of misery; very unhappy or uncomfortable ❷ unpleasant; making you feel depressed

misery NOUN ❶ great unhappiness or discomfort or suffering, especially lasting for a long time ❷ (informal) a person who is always unhappy or complaining

misfire VERB ❶ a gun or engine misfires when it fails to fire or start ❷ a plan or idea or joke misfires when it goes wrong or has the wrong effect

misfit NOUN a person who does not fit in well with other people or with their surroundings

misfortune NOUN ❶ bad luck ❷ an unlucky event or accident

misgiving NOUN a feeling of doubt, or slight fear or mistrust

misguided ADJECTIVE guided by mistaken ideas or beliefs

mishap (say mis-hap) NOUN an unlucky accident

misinterpret VERB to interpret something incorrectly

misjudge VERB to judge something wrongly; to form a wrong idea or opinion about someone or something

383

mislay VERB to lose something for a short time because you cannot remember where you put it

mislead VERB to give someone a wrong idea or impression deliberately

misplaced ADJECTIVE ❶ put in the wrong place ❷ inappropriate or unjustified

misprint NOUN a mistake in printing, such as a spelling mistake

mispronounce VERB to pronounce a word or name incorrectly

misquote VERB to quote someone or something incorrectly

misread VERB to read or interpret something incorrectly

Miss NOUN a title put before a girl's or unmarried woman's name

miss VERB ❶ to fail to hit, reach, catch, see, hear or find something ❷ to be sad because someone or something is not with you ❸ to miss a train, bus or plane is to arrive too late to catch it ❹ to miss a lesson or other activity is to fail to attend it ❺ to notice that something is not where it should be

miss NOUN missing something

misshapen ADJECTIVE distorted or badly shaped

missile NOUN ❶ a weapon that is fired a long distance and explodes when it hits its target ❷ an object that is thrown at someone in order to hurt them

missing ADJECTIVE ❶ lost; not in the proper place ❷ absent

mission NOUN ❶ an important job that someone is sent to do or feels

they must do ❷ a place or building where missionaries work ❸ a military or scientific expedition

missionary NOUN a person who is sent to another country to spread a religious faith

misspell VERB to spell a word wrongly

mist NOUN ❶ damp cloudy air near the ground ❷ condensed water vapour on a window, mirror, etc.

mist VERB to become covered with mist

mistake NOUN ❶ something done wrongly ❷ an incorrect opinion

mistake VERB mistakes, mistaking, mistook, mistaken ❶ to choose or identify a person or thing wrongly ❷ to misunderstand something

mistaken ADJECTIVE ❶ incorrect ❷ having an incorrect opinion

mister NOUN (informal) a form of address to a man

mistletoe NOUN a plant with white berries that grows as a parasite on trees

mistreat VERB to treat a person or thing in a cruel or unkind way

mistress NOUN ❶ a woman who is in charge of something ❷ a woman teacher ❸ the woman owner of a dog or other animal ❹ a woman who is a man's lover but not his wife

mistrust VERB to feel no trust in someone or something

misty ADJECTIVE ❶ full of mist ❷ not clear or distinct ❸ misty eyes are full of tears

misunderstand VERB to get a wrong idea or impression of

something

misunderstanding NOUN a situation in which someone gets a wrong idea or impression of something

misuse (say mis-**yooz**) VERB ❶ to use something incorrectly ❷ to treat someone badly

misuse (say mis-**yooss**) NOUN using something incorrectly

mite NOUN ❶ a tiny spider-like creature that lives on plants, animals, carpets, etc. ❷ a small child

mitigate VERB to make a thing less intense or less severe

mitigating circumstances PLURAL NOUN facts that may partially excuse wrongdoing

mitre NOUN ❶ the tall tapering hat that a bishop wears ❷ a joint of two pieces of wood or cloth with their ends tapered so that together they form a right angle

mitten NOUN a kind of glove without separate parts for the fingers

mix VERB ❶ to put different things together so that they make a single substance or thing; to blend or combine things ❷ to get together with other people

mix NOUN a mixture

mixed ADJECTIVE ❶ containing two or more kinds of things or people ❷ for both sexes

mixed farming NOUN farming of both crops and animals

mixture NOUN something made of different things mixed together

mix-up NOUN a confusion or

misunderstanding

mnemonic (say nim-**on**-ik) NOUN a verse or saying that helps you to remember something

moan VERB ❶ to make a long low sound of pain or suffering ❷ to complain or grumble

moan NOUN ❶ a long low sound of pain or suffering ❷ a complaint or grumble

moat NOUN a deep wide ditch round a castle, usually filled with water

mob NOUN a large disorderly crowd

mob VERB people mob someone when they crowd round them

mobile ADJECTIVE able to move or be moved or carried easily

mobile NOUN ❶ a mobile phone ❷ a decoration for hanging up so that its parts move in currents of air

mobile phone NOUN a phone you can carry around with you

mobilize (also **mobilise**) VERB to assemble people or things for a particular purpose, especially for war

moccasin NOUN a soft leather shoe

mock VERB ❶ to make fun of a person or thing ❷ to imitate someone or something to make people laugh

mock ADJECTIVE ❶ imitation, not real ❷ a mock exam is one done as a practice before the real one

mockery NOUN ❶ ridicule or contempt ❷ a ridiculous imitation

mock-up NOUN a model of something, made in order to test or study it

modal verb NOUN a verb such as

can, may or *will* that is used with another verb to express possibility, permission, intention, etc.

mode NOUN ❶ the way a thing is done; a type of something ❷ one of the ways in which a machine can work ❸ what is fashionable

model NOUN ❶ a copy of an object, usually on a smaller scale ❷ a particular design ❸ a person who poses for an artist or displays clothes by wearing them ❹ a person or thing that is worth copying

model VERB ❶ to make a model of something; to make something out of wood or clay ❷ to design or plan something using another thing as an example ❸ to work as an artist's model or a fashion model

modem (say moh-dem) NOUN a device that links a computer to a telephone line for transmitting data

moderate (say mod-er-at) ADJECTIVE ❶ medium; not too little and not too much ❷ not extreme or unreasonable

moderate (say mod-er-ayt) VERB to become or make something less strong or extreme

moderation NOUN being moderate

modern ADJECTIVE ❶ belonging to the present or recent times ❷ in fashion now

modernize (also **modernise**) VERB to make a thing more modern

modest ADJECTIVE ❶ not boasting about how good you are ❷ quite small in size or amount ❸ dressing or behaving in a decent or shy way

modification NOUN a slight change in something

modify VERB ❶ to change something slightly ❷ to describe a word or limit its meaning

modulate VERB ❶ to vary the pitch or tone of your voice or a sound ❷ to alter an electronic wave to allow signals to be sent

module NOUN ❶ a separate section or part of something larger, such as a spacecraft or building ❷ a unit or section of a course of study

mogul (say moh-gul) NOUN (*informal*) an important or influential person

mohair NOUN fine silky wool from an angora goat

moist ADJECTIVE slightly wet

moisten VERB to make something moist

moisture NOUN water in tiny drops in the air or on a surface

moisturizer (also **moisturiser**) NOUN a cream used to make the skin less dry

molar NOUN any of the wide teeth at the back of the jaw, used in chewing

molasses NOUN dark syrup from raw sugar

mole NOUN ❶ a small furry animal that burrows under the ground ❷ a spy working within an organization and passing information to another organization or country ❸ a small dark spot on skin

molecular (say mo-lek-yoo-ler) ADJECTIVE to do with molecules

molecule NOUN the smallest part

into which a substance can be divided without changing its chemical nature; a group of atoms

molehill NOUN a small pile of earth thrown up by a burrowing mole

molest VERB ❶ to annoy or pester someone ❷ to illegally touch or attack someone in a sexual way

mollify VERB to make a person feel less angry or upset

mollusc NOUN any of a group of animals including snails, slugs and mussels, with soft bodies, no backbones, and, in some cases, external shells

molten ADJECTIVE melted; made liquid by great heat

moment NOUN ❶ a very short time ❷ a particular time

momentary ADJECTIVE lasting for only a moment

momentous (say mo-**ment**-us) ADJECTIVE very important

momentum NOUN ❶ the ability something has to keep developing or increasing ❷ the ability an object has to keep moving as a result of the speed it already has ❸ (*in science*) the quantity of motion of a moving object, measured as its mass multiplied by its velocity

monarch NOUN a king, queen, emperor or empress ruling a country

monarchy NOUN ❶ a country ruled by a monarch ❷ government by a monarch

monastery NOUN a building where monks live and work

monastic ADJECTIVE to do with monks or monasteries

Monday NOUN the day of the week following Sunday

monetary ADJECTIVE to do with money

money NOUN ❶ coins and banknotes ❷ wealth or riches

mongoose NOUN a small tropical animal rather like a stoat, that can kill snakes

mongrel (say **mung**-rel) NOUN a dog of mixed breeds

monitor NOUN ❶ a device for watching or testing how something is working ❷ a screen that displays data and images produced by a computer ❸ a pupil who is given a special responsibility in a school

monitor VERB to regularly watch or test what is happening with something

monk NOUN a member of a community of men who live according to the rules of a religious organization. Compare with **nun**.

monkey NOUN ❶ an animal with long arms, hands with thumbs and often a tail ❷ a mischievous person, especially a child

monocle NOUN a lens worn over one eye, like half of a pair of glasses

monogram NOUN a design made up of a letter or letters, especially a person's initials

monolith NOUN a large single upright block of stone

monologue NOUN a long speech by one person

monopolize (also **monopolise**)

VERB to take the whole of something for yourself

monopoly NOUN ❶ complete control by a single company over selling a product or supplying a service ❷ complete possession, control or use of something by one group

monorail NOUN a railway that uses a single rail, not a pair of rails

monosyllable NOUN a word with only one syllable

monotone NOUN a level unchanging tone of voice in speaking or singing

monotonous ADJECTIVE boring because it does not change

monotony NOUN being always the same and therefore dull and boring

monoxide NOUN an oxide with one atom of oxygen

monsoon NOUN ❶ a strong wind in and near the Indian Ocean, bringing heavy rain in summer ❷ the rainy season brought by this wind

monster NOUN ❶ a large frightening creature ❷ a huge thing ❸ a wicked or cruel person

monster ADJECTIVE very large; huge

monstrosity NOUN a monstrous thing

monstrous ADJECTIVE ❶ like a monster; huge ❷ very shocking or outrageous

montage (say **mon**-tahzh) NOUN a picture, film, or other work of art made by putting together separate pieces or pieces from different works

month NOUN each of the twelve parts into which a year is divided

monthly ADJECTIVE & ADVERB happening or done once a month

monument NOUN a statue, building or column put up to remind people of some person or event

monumental ADJECTIVE ❶ built as a monument ❷ very large or important

moo VERB to make the low deep sound of a cow

moo NOUN the low deep sound a cow makes

mood NOUN the way someone feels

moody ADJECTIVE ❶ gloomy or sullen ❷ having sudden changes of mood for no apparent reason

moon NOUN ❶ the natural satellite of the earth that can be seen in the sky at night ❷ a satellite of any planet

moon VERB to go about in a dreamy way, often because you are in love

moonlight NOUN the light from the moon

moor NOUN (chiefly British) an area of rough land covered with heather, bracken and bushes

moor VERB to fasten a boat to a fixed object with a rope or cable

moorhen NOUN a small waterbird

mooring NOUN a place where a boat can be moored

moorland NOUN (chiefly British) land that consists of moors

moose NOUN moose a North American elk

moot ADJECTIVE ➤ a moot point a question that is undecided or debatable

mop NOUN ❶ a bunch or pad of soft material fastened on the end of a stick, used for cleaning floors etc. ❷ a thick mass of hair

mop VERB to clean or wipe something with a mop or sponge

mope VERB to be miserable and not interested in doing anything

moped (say moh-ped) NOUN a kind of small motorcycle that can be pedalled

moral ADJECTIVE ❶ to do with what is right and wrong in behaviour ❷ good or virtuous

moral NOUN a lesson in right behaviour taught by a story or event

morale (say mor-ahl) NOUN the level of confidence and good spirits in a person or group of people

moralize (also **moralise**) VERB to talk or write about right and wrong behaviour

morals PLURAL NOUN standards of behaviour

morbid ADJECTIVE ❶ thinking about gloomy or unpleasant things such as death ❷ (in medicine) unhealthy

more DETERMINER (comparative of **much** and **many**) greater in amount or degree

more PRONOUN a greater amount

more ADVERB ❶ to a greater extent ❷ again

moreover ADVERB besides; in addition to what has been said

Mormon NOUN a member of a religious group founded in the USA

morn NOUN (poetical use) morning

morning NOUN the early part of the day, before noon or before lunchtime

moron NOUN (informal) a very stupid person

morose (say mo-rohss) ADJECTIVE bad-tempered and miserable

morpheme NOUN the smallest unit of meaning that a word can be divided into, e.g. go and -ing in the word going

morphine (say mor-feen) NOUN a drug made from opium, used to lessen pain

morris dance NOUN a traditional English dance performed in costume by men with ribbons and bells

morrow NOUN (poetical use) the following day

Morse code NOUN a signalling code using short and long sounds or flashes of light (dots and dashes) to represent letters

morsel NOUN a small piece of food

mortal ADJECTIVE ❶ not living for ever ❷ causing death; fatal ❸ deadly or extreme

mortal NOUN a human being, as compared to a god or immortal spirit

mortality NOUN ❶ the state of being mortal and bound to die ❷ the number of people who die over a period of time

mortar NOUN ❶ a mixture of sand, cement and water used in building to stick bricks together ❷ a hard bowl in which substances are pounded with a pestle ❸ a short cannon for firing shells at a high angle

389

mortar board NOUN an academic cap with a stiff square top

mortgage (say mor-gij) NOUN an arrangement to borrow money to buy a house, with the house as security for the loan

mortgage VERB to take out a loan, with your house as security

mortify VERB to humiliate someone or make them feel very ashamed

mortuary NOUN a place where dead bodies are kept before being buried or cremated

mosaic (say mo-**zay**-ik) NOUN a picture or design made from small coloured pieces of stone or glass

mosque (say mosk) NOUN a building where Muslims worship

mosquito NOUN mosquitoes a kind of gnat that sucks blood

moss NOUN a plant that grows in damp places and has no flowers

most DETERMINER (superlative of much and many)

most PRONOUN the greatest amount

most ADVERB ❶ to the greatest extent; more than any other ❷ very or extremely

mostly ADVERB mainly; in most ways

motel NOUN a hotel for people who are travelling by car, with space for parking cars near the rooms

moth NOUN an insect rather like a butterfly, that usually flies at night

mother NOUN a female parent

mother VERB to look after someone in a motherly way

mother-in-law NOUN the mother of a married person's husband or wife

motherly ADJECTIVE kind and gentle like a mother

mother-of-pearl NOUN a pearly substance lining the shells of mussels etc.

motif (say moh-**teef**) NOUN a repeated design or theme

motion NOUN ❶ a way of moving; movement ❷ a formal suggestion at a meeting that people discuss and vote on

motion VERB to signal to someone with a gesture

motionless ADJECTIVE not moving

motivate VERB ❶ to give a person a motive or reason to do something ❷ to make a person determined to achieve something

motive NOUN what makes a person do something

motive ADJECTIVE producing movement

motley ADJECTIVE made up of various sorts of things or people that do not seem to belong together

motor NOUN a machine providing power to drive machinery etc.; an engine

motor ADJECTIVE having a motor; to do with vehicles that have motors

motor VERB to travel by car

motorbike NOUN a motorcycle

motorcade NOUN a procession of cars

motorcycle NOUN a two-wheeled road vehicle with an engine

motorist NOUN a person who drives a car

motorized (also **motorised**) ADJECTIVE equipped with a motor or with motor vehicles

motor neuron disease NOUN a disease of the nerves that control movement, so that the muscles get weaker and weaker until the person dies

motorway NOUN a wide road for fast long-distance traffic

mottled ADJECTIVE marked with spots or patches of colour

motto NOUN ① a short saying used as a guide for behaviour ② a short verse or riddle found inside a cracker

mould NOUN ① a hollow container of a particular shape, in which a liquid or soft substance is put to set into this shape ② a fine furry growth of very small fungi

mould VERB ① to make something have a particular shape ② to strongly influence how someone develops

mouldy ADJECTIVE covered with mould

moult VERB to shed feathers, hair or skin while a new growth forms

mound NOUN ① a pile of earth or stones etc. ② a small hill

mount VERB ① to go up something ② to get on a horse or bicycle ③ to increase in amount ④ to mount a picture or photograph is to put it in a frame or album in order to display it ⑤ to organize something

mount NOUN ① a mountain ② something on which an object is mounted ③ a horse for riding

mountain NOUN ① a very high hill ② a large heap, pile, or quantity

mountaineer NOUN a person who climbs mountains

mountainous ADJECTIVE ① having many mountains ② huge

mounted ADJECTIVE on horseback

mourn VERB to be sad, especially because someone has died

mournful ADJECTIVE sad and sorrowful

mouse NOUN mice ① a small animal with a long thin tail and a pointed nose ② (in computing) a small device which you move around on a mat to control the movements of a cursor on a computer screen

mousetrap NOUN a trap for catching and killing mice

moussaka NOUN a dish of minced meat, aubergine, etc., with a cheese sauce

mousse (say mooss) NOUN ① a creamy pudding flavoured with fruit or chocolate ② a frothy creamy substance put on the hair so that it can be styled more easily

moustache (say mus-tahsh) NOUN a strip of hair that a man grows above his upper lip

mouth NOUN ① the opening in your face that you use for eating and speaking ② the place where a river enters the sea ③ an opening or outlet

mouth VERB to form words carefully with your lips, especially without saying them aloud

mouthful NOUN an amount of food you put in your mouth

mouth organ NOUN (British) a small musical instrument that you play by blowing and sucking while passing it along your lips

mouthpiece NOUN the part of a musical instrument or other device that you put to your mouth

movable ADJECTIVE able to be moved

move VERB ① to go or take something from one place to another; to change a person's or thing's position ② to affect a person's feelings ③ to put forward a formal suggestion (a **motion**) to be discussed and voted on at a meeting

move NOUN ① a movement or action ② a player's turn to move a piece in a game such as chess

movement NOUN ① moving or being moved ② a group of people working together to achieve something ③ (*in music*) one of the main divisions of a symphony or other long musical work

movie NOUN (*North American*) (*informal*) a cinema film

moving ADJECTIVE making someone feel strong emotion, especially sorrow or pity

mow VERB mows, mowing, mowed, mown to cut down grass or cereal crops

mozzarella NOUN a kind of Italian cheese used in cooking, originally made from buffalo's milk

MP ABBREVIATION Member of Parliament

Mr (say **mist**-er) NOUN a title put before a man's name

Mrs (say **mis**-iz) NOUN a title put before a married woman's name

MS ABBREVIATION multiple sclerosis

Ms (say miz) NOUN a title put before a woman's name, regardless of whether she is married or not

MSc ABBREVIATION Master of Science

MSP ABBREVIATION Member of the Scottish Parliament

Mt ABBREVIATION mount or mountain

much ADJECTIVE existing in a large amount

much PRONOUN a large amount of something

much ADVERB ① greatly or considerably ② approximately

muck NOUN ① farmyard manure ② (*informal*) dirt or filth

muck VERB ➤ **muck about** (*informal*) to mess about ➤ **muck something out** to clean out the place where an animal is kept ➤ **muck something up** (*informal*) ① to make something dirty ② to spoil or make a mess of something

mucky ADJECTIVE dirty or filthy

mucous (say **mew**-kus) ADJECTIVE ① like mucus ② covered with mucus

mucus (say **mew**-kus) NOUN the moist sticky substance on the inner surface of the throat etc.

mud NOUN wet soft earth

muddle VERB ① to jumble or mix things up ② to confuse things in your mind

muddle NOUN confusion or disorder

muddy ADJECTIVE full of or covered with mud

mudguard NOUN a curved cover over the top part of a bicycle wheel to protect the rider from the mud and water thrown up by the wheel

muesli (say **mooz**-lee) NOUN (*chiefly British*) a breakfast food made of mixed cereals, dried fruit and nuts

muezzin (say moo-ez-in) NOUN a Muslim crier who calls the hours of prayer from a minaret

muff NOUN a short tube-shaped piece of warm material into which the hands are pushed from opposite ends

muff VERB (*informal*) to bungle something

muffin NOUN ❶ a flat bun eaten toasted and buttered ❷ a small sponge cake, usually containing fruit, chocolate chips, etc.

muffle VERB ❶ to cover or wrap something to protect it or keep it warm ❷ to deaden the sound of something

muffler NOUN a warm scarf

mug NOUN ❶ a kind of large straight-sided cup ❷ (*British*) (*informal*) a fool; a person who is easily fooled or cheated ❸ (*informal*) a person's face

mug VERB to attack and rob someone in the street

muggy ADJECTIVE muggy weather is unpleasantly warm and damp

mulberry NOUN a purple or white fruit rather like a blackberry

mule NOUN an animal that is the offspring of a donkey and a mare, known for being stubborn

mull VERB ➤ mull something over to think about something carefully

mulled ADJECTIVE mulled wine is heated with sugar and spices

mullet NOUN a kind of fish used as food

multi- PREFIX many (as in *multicoloured* = with many colours)

multicultural ADJECTIVE made up of people of many different races, religions and cultures

multimedia ADJECTIVE using more than one medium of communication

multimedia NOUN a computer program with sound and still and moving images linked to the text

multimillionaire NOUN a person with a fortune of several million pounds or dollars

multinational NOUN a large business company which works in several countries

multiple ADJECTIVE having many parts or elements

multiple NOUN a number that contains another number (a factor) an exact amount of times with no remainder

multiple sclerosis NOUN a disease of the nervous system which makes a person unable to control their movements and may affect their sight

multiplex NOUN a large cinema complex that has many screens

multiplication NOUN the process of multiplying one number by another

multiplicity NOUN a great variety or large number

multiply VERB ❶ to add a number to itself a given quantity of times ($5 \times 4 = 20$). ❷ to make things many or to become many; to increase

multiracial ADJECTIVE consisting of people of many different races

multitude NOUN a very large

number of people or things

mum NOUN (British) (informal) mother

mum ADJECTIVE (informal) saying nothing

mumble VERB to speak indistinctly so that you are not easy to hear

mumbo-jumbo NOUN (informal) talk or ceremony that has no real meaning

mummy NOUN ❶ (British) (informal) mother ❷ in ancient Egypt, a corpse wrapped in cloth and treated with oils etc. before being buried so that it does not decay

mumps NOUN an infectious disease that makes the neck swell painfully

munch VERB to chew food steadily and often noisily

mundane ADJECTIVE ordinary, not exciting

municipal (say mew-**nis**-ip-al) ADJECTIVE to do with a town or city that has its own local government

munitions PLURAL NOUN military weapons, ammunition and equipment

mural NOUN a large picture painted on a wall

murder VERB to kill a person unlawfully and deliberately

murder NOUN the murdering of someone

murderous ADJECTIVE likely to murder someone or looking as though you might

murky ADJECTIVE dark and gloomy

murmur VERB ❶ to speak in a soft voice ❷ to make a low continuous sound

murmur NOUN a sound of soft voices

muscle NOUN ❶ a band or bundle of fibrous tissue that can contract and relax and so produce movement in parts of the body ❷ the power of muscles; strength

muscular ADJECTIVE ❶ to do with the muscles ❷ having well-developed muscles

muse VERB ❶ to think deeply about something; to ponder ❷ to say something to yourself in a thoughtful way

museum NOUN a place where interesting, old or valuable objects are displayed for people to see

mush NOUN a soft thick mass

mushroom NOUN an edible fungus with a stem and a dome-shaped top

mushroom VERB to grow or appear suddenly in large numbers

mushy ADJECTIVE ❶ soft and thick, like mush ❷ too emotional or sentimental

music NOUN ❶ a pattern of pleasant or interesting sounds made by instruments or by the voice ❷ printed or written symbols which stand for musical sounds

musical ADJECTIVE ❶ to do with music ❷ producing music ❸ good at music or interested in it

musical NOUN a play or film containing a lot of songs

musician NOUN someone who plays a musical instrument

musk NOUN a strong-smelling substance used in perfumes

musket NOUN a kind of gun with

a long barrel, used in the past by soldiers

musketeer NOUN a soldier armed with a musket

Muslim NOUN someone who follows the religion of Islam

muslin NOUN very thin cotton cloth

mussel NOUN a black shellfish

must AUXILIARY VERB used to show ❶ that someone has to do something or that it is necessary that something happens (*I must go home soon.*) ❷ that something is certain (*You must be joking!*)

mustard NOUN a yellow paste or powder used to give food a hot taste

muster VERB ❶ to find as much of something as you can ❷ to gather people together in one place; to assemble

muster NOUN an assembly of people or things

musty ADJECTIVE smelling or tasting mouldy or stale

mutant NOUN a living creature that is different from others of the same type because of changes in its genes

mutation NOUN a change in the form of a living creature because of changes in its genes

mute ADJECTIVE ❶ silent; not speaking or able to speak ❷ not pronounced

mute NOUN ❶ a person who cannot speak ❷ a device fitted to a musical instrument to deaden its sound

muted ADJECTIVE quiet; not strongly expressed

mutilate VERB to damage something by breaking or cutting off part of it

mutineer NOUN a person who takes part in a mutiny

mutinous ADJECTIVE taking part in a mutiny; refusing to obey orders

mutiny NOUN rebellion against authority, especially refusal by soldiers or sailors to obey orders

mutiny VERB to take part in a mutiny

mutter VERB ❶ to speak in a low voice ❷ to grumble

mutton NOUN meat from a sheep

mutual (say **mew**-tew-al) ADJECTIVE ❶ given or done to each other ❷ shared by two or more people

muzzle NOUN ❶ an animal's nose and mouth ❷ a cover put over an animal's nose and mouth so that it cannot bite ❸ the open end of a gun

muzzle VERB ❶ to put a muzzle on an animal ❷ to silence someone; to prevent a person from expressing opinions

my DETERMINER belonging to me

myriad (say **mirri**-ad) ADJECTIVE very many; countless

myriad NOUN a huge number of people or things

myrrh (say mer) NOUN a substance used in perfumes, incense, and medicine

myself PRONOUN I or me and nobody else. The word is used to refer back to the subject of a sentence (e.g. *I have hurt myself.*) or for emphasis (e.g. *I myself will not be coming.*).

mysterious ADJECTIVE full of

mystery; puzzling

mystery NOUN something that cannot be explained or understood; something puzzling

mystic NOUN a person who seeks to obtain spiritual contact with God by deep religious meditation

mystic ADJECTIVE mystical

mystical ADJECTIVE having spiritual powers or qualities that are difficult to understand or explain

mystify VERB to puzzle or bewilder someone

myth (say mith) NOUN ❶ an old story containing ideas about ancient times or about supernatural beings. Compare with legend. ❷ an untrue story or belief

mythical ADJECTIVE ❶ imaginary; found only in myths ❷ to do with myths

mythological ADJECTIVE to do with myths

mythology NOUN myths or the study of myths

myxomatosis (say miks-om-at-oh-sis) NOUN a disease that kills rabbits

Nn

N. ABBREVIATION ❶ north ❷ northern

nab VERB (informal) to catch or arrest someone; to seize or grab something

nag VERB ❶ to pester a person by keeping on criticizing, complaining or asking for things ❷ to keep on hurting or bothering you

nag NOUN (informal) a horse

nail NOUN ❶ the hard covering over the end of a finger or toe ❷ a small sharp piece of metal hammered in to fasten pieces of wood together

nail VERB ❶ to fasten something with a nail or nails ❷ (informal) to catch or arrest someone

naive (say nah-**eev**) ADJECTIVE showing a lack of experience or good judgement; innocent and trusting

naked ADJECTIVE ❶ without any clothes or coverings on ❷ obvious; not hidden

naked eye NOUN the eye when it is not helped by a telescope, binoculars or microscope

name NOUN ❶ the word or words by which a person, animal, place or thing is known ❷ a person's reputation

name VERB ❶ to give a name to a person or thing ❷ to say what someone or something is called ❸ to say what you want something to be

nameless ADJECTIVE ❶ without a name ❷ not named or identified

namely ADVERB that is to say

namesake NOUN a person or thing with the same name as another

nanny NOUN ❶ a person, usually a woman, who looks after young children ❷ (informal) grandmother

nanny goat NOUN a female goat. Compare with billy goat.

nap NOUN a short sleep

napalm (say **nay**-pahm) NOUN a substance made of petrol, used in some incendiary bombs

nape NOUN the back part of your neck

napkin NOUN ❶ a piece of cloth or paper used at meals to protect your clothes or for wiping your lips or fingers ❷ (old use) a nappy

nappy NOUN (British) a piece of cloth or other fabric put round a baby's bottom

narcissus NOUN a garden flower like a daffodil

narcotic NOUN a drug that makes a person sleepy or unconscious

narrate VERB to tell a story or give an account of something

narrative NOUN a spoken or written account of something

narrator NOUN the person who is telling a story

narrow ADJECTIVE ❶ not wide or broad ❷ uncomfortably close; with only a small margin of error or safety

narrow VERB to make something narrower or to become narrower

narrowly ADVERB only by a small amount

narrow-minded ADJECTIVE not willing to accept other people's beliefs and ways

nasal ADJECTIVE ❶ to do with the nose ❷ sounding as if the breath comes out through the nose

nasturtium (say na-**ster**-shum) NOUN a garden plant with round leaves and red, yellow or orange flowers

nasty ADJECTIVE ❶ horrid or unpleasant ❷ cruel or unkind

nation NOUN a large community of people most of whom have the same ancestors, language, history and customs and who usually live in the same part of the world under one government

national ADJECTIVE to do with or belonging to a nation or country

national NOUN a citizen of a particular country

national anthem NOUN a nation's official song, which is played or sung on important occasions

national curriculum NOUN the subjects that must be taught by state schools in England and Wales

nationalist NOUN ❶ a person who is very patriotic ❷ a person who wants their country to be independent and not to form part of another country

nationality NOUN the condition of belonging to a particular nation

nationalize (also **nationalise**) VERB to put an industry or business under the ownership or control of the state

national park NOUN an area of natural beauty which is protected by the government and which the public may visit

nationwide ADJECTIVE & ADVERB over the whole of a country

native NOUN a person born in a particular place

native ADJECTIVE ❶ your native country or city is the place where you were born ❷ your native language is the language that you first learned to speak ❸ grown or originating in a particular place ❹ that you have naturally without having to learn it

Native American NOUN one of the original inhabitants of North and South America

nativity NOUN a person's birth

natter VERB (*informal*) to chat informally

natural ADJECTIVE ❶ produced or done by nature, not by people or machines ❷ normal; not surprising ❸ having a quality or ability that you were born with ❹ a natural note is neither sharp nor flat

natural NOUN ❶ a person who is naturally good at something ❷ a natural note in music; a sign (♮) that shows this

natural gas NOUN gas found underground or under the sea, not made from coal

natural history NOUN the study of plants and animals

naturalist NOUN an expert in natural history

naturally ADVERB ❶ in a natural way ❷ as you would expect

natural science NOUN the study of physics, chemistry and biology

natural selection NOUN Charles Darwin's theory that only the plants and animals best suited to their surroundings will survive and breed

nature NOUN ❶ everything in the world that was not made by people, such as plants and animals ❷ the qualities and characteristics of a person or thing ❸ a kind or sort of thing

nature reserve NOUN an area of land which is managed in a way that preserves the wild animals and plants that live there

nature trail NOUN a path in a country area with signs telling you about the plants and animals that live there

naughty ADJECTIVE ❶ badly behaved or disobedient ❷ slightly rude or indecent

nausea (say naw-zee-a) NOUN a feeling of sickness or disgust

nauseous ADJECTIVE feeling that you are going to be sick; sickening

nautical ADJECTIVE to do with ships or sailors

nautical mile NOUN a measure of distance used at sea, equal to 2,025 yards (1.852 kilometres)

naval ADJECTIVE to do with a navy

nave NOUN the main central part of a church (the other parts are the chancel, aisles and transepts)

navel NOUN the small hollow in the centre of the abdomen, where the umbilical cord was attached

navigable ADJECTIVE suitable for ships and boats to sail in

navigate VERB ❶ to sail in or through a river or sea etc. ❷ to make sure that a ship, aircraft or vehicle is going in the right direction ❸ to find your way around a website

navvy NOUN (*British*) a labourer digging a road, railway or canal

navy NOUN ❶ a country's warships and the people trained to use them ❷ (also **navy blue**) a very dark blue, the colour of naval uniform

nay ADVERB (*old use*) no

Nazi (say nah-tsee) NOUN a member

398

of the National Socialist Party in Germany in Hitler's time, with Fascist beliefs

NB ABBREVIATION take note that

NE ABBREVIATION ❶ north-east ❷ north-eastern

Neanderthal (say nee-**an**-der-tahl) NOUN an early type of human who lived in Europe during the Stone Age

near ADVERB & ADJECTIVE not far away

near PREPOSITION not far away from

near VERB to come close to something

nearby ADJECTIVE near; not far away

nearly ADVERB almost; not quite

neat ADJECTIVE ❶ arranged carefully; tidy and in order ❷ clever or skilful ❸ drunk without anything added ❹ (North American) (informal) excellent

neatly ADVERB ❶ in a tidy or carefully arranged way ❷ in a clever or skilful way

nebula NOUN nebulae a bright or dark patch in the sky, caused by a distant galaxy or a cloud of dust or gas

necessarily ADVERB in a way that cannot be avoided

necessary ADJECTIVE needed for something; essential

necessitate VERB to make a thing necessary

necessity NOUN ❶ need; great importance ❷ something necessary

neck NOUN ❶ the part of the body that joins the head to the shoulders ❷ the part of a piece of clothing round your neck

❸ a narrow part of something, especially of a bottle

necklace NOUN a piece of jewellery worn round the neck

necktie NOUN a strip of material worn passing under the collar of a shirt and knotted in front

nectar NOUN ❶ a sweet liquid collected by bees from flowers ❷ a delicious drink

nectarine NOUN a kind of peach with a thin smooth skin

née (say nay) ADJECTIVE born, used to give a married woman's maiden name

need VERB needs, needing, needed ❶ to be without something you should have; to require something ❷ (as an auxiliary verb) to have to do something

need NOUN ❶ something needed; a necessary thing ❷ a situation where something is necessary ❸ great poverty or hardship

needle NOUN ❶ a very thin pointed piece of steel used in sewing ❷ either of a pair of metal, plastic or bamboo rods used in knitting ❸ a thin spike on a tree or plant ❹ the pointer of a meter or compass

needlework NOUN sewing or embroidery

needy ADJECTIVE very poor; lacking things necessary for life

ne'er ADVERB (poetical use) never

negate VERB ❶ to make something ineffective ❷ to disprove or deny something

negative ADJECTIVE ❶ that says 'no' ❷ looking only at the bad aspects

399

of a situation ❸ showing no sign of what is being tested for ❹ less than zero; minus ❺ to do with the kind of electric charge carried by electrons

negative NOUN ❶ a negative statement ❷ a photograph or film with the dark parts light and the light parts dark, from which a positive print (with the dark and light or colours correct) can be made

neglect VERB ❶ to fail to look after or pay attention to a person or thing ❷ to fail or forget to do something

neglect NOUN neglecting or being neglected

negligence NOUN lack of proper care or attention; carelessness

negligible ADJECTIVE not big enough or important enough to be worth bothering about

negotiable ADJECTIVE able to be changed after being discussed

negotiate VERB ❶ to bargain or discuss something with others in order to reach an agreement ❷ to arrange something after discussion ❸ to get over or past an obstacle or difficulty

negotiation NOUN negotiations are discussions people have to reach an agreement about something

neigh VERB to make the high-pitched cry of a horse

neigh NOUN the high-pitched cry of a horse

neighbour NOUN someone who lives next door or near to you

neighbourhood NOUN ❶ the surrounding district or area ❷ a

part of a town where people live

neighbouring ADJECTIVE near each other

neighbourly ADVERB friendly and helpful to people who live near you

neither (say ny-ther or nee-ther) DETERMINER & PRONOUN not either

neither ADVERB CONJUNCTION
➤ neither ... nor not one thing and not the other

Neolithic (say nee-o-lith-ik) ADJECTIVE belonging to the later part of the Stone Age

neon NOUN a gas that glows when electricity passes through it, used in glass tubes to make illuminated signs

nephew NOUN the son of a person's brother or sister

nerve NOUN ❶ any of the fibres in your body that carry messages to and from your brain, so that parts of your body can feel and move ❷ courage and calmness in a dangerous situation ❸ cheek or impudence

nerve VERB to give someone the courage to do something

nerve-racking ADJECTIVE making you feel anxious or stressed

nervous ADJECTIVE ❶ anxious about something or afraid of something ❷ easily worried or frightened ❸ to do with the nerves

nervous breakdown NOUN a state of severe depression and anxiety, making it difficult to cope with life

nervous system NOUN the system, consisting of the brain, spinal cord and nerves, which sends electrical messages from one part of your body to another

nervy ADJECTIVE nervous or anxious

nest NOUN ❶ a structure or place in which a bird lays its eggs and feeds its young ❷ a place where some small creatures, especially mice and wasps, live ❸ a set of similar things that fit inside each other

nest VERB ❶ to have or make a nest ❷ to fit inside something

nest egg NOUN a sum of money saved up for future use

nestle VERB ❶ to curl up comfortably or put something in a comfortable position ❷ to be in a sheltered position

nestling NOUN a bird that is too young to leave the nest

net NOUN ❶ material made of pieces of thread, cord or wire joined together in a criss-cross pattern with holes between ❷ something made of this

net ADJECTIVE remaining when nothing more is to be deducted. Compare with **gross**.

net VERB ❶ to catch something with a net; to kick a ball into a net ❷ to gain or produce an amount as a net profit

netball NOUN a game in which two teams try to throw a ball into a high net hanging from a ring

nether ADJECTIVE lower

netting NOUN a piece of net

nettle NOUN a wild plant with leaves that sting when they are touched

nettle VERB to annoy someone

network NOUN ❶ a net-like arrangement or pattern of

intersecting lines or parts ❷ an organization with many connecting parts that work together ❸ a group of radio or television stations which broadcast the same programmes ❹ a set of computers which are linked to each other

neurology NOUN the study of nerves and their diseases

neuron, neurone NOUN a cell that is part of the nervous system and sends messages to and from your brain

neurotic (say newr-ot-ik) ADJECTIVE always very worried about something

neuter ADJECTIVE in some languages, belonging to the class of words which are neither masculine nor feminine, such as *Fenster* in German

neuter VERB to remove an animal's sex organs so that it cannot breed

neutral ADJECTIVE ❶ not supporting either side in a war or quarrel ❷ not very distinctive ❸ neither acid nor alkaline

neutral NOUN ❶ a neutral person or country ❷ a gear that is not connected to the driving parts of an engine

neutralize (also **neutralise**) VERB ❶ to stop something from having any effect ❷ to make a substance chemically neutral

neutron NOUN a particle of matter with no electric charge

never ADVERB ❶ at no time; not ever ❷ not at all

nevertheless ADVERB in spite of this; although this is a fact

new ADJECTIVE ❶ not existing before; just made, invented, discovered or received ❷ fresh; not used before ❸ different or changed

new ADVERB recently

New Age ADJECTIVE to do with a way of living and thinking that includes belief in astrology and alternative medicine and concern for environmental and spiritual matters rather than possessions

newborn ADJECTIVE recently born

newcomer NOUN a person who has arrived recently

newfangled ADJECTIVE disliked because it is new in method or style

newly ADVERB recently

new moon NOUN the moon at the beginning of its cycle, when only a thin crescent can be seen

news NOUN ❶ information about recent events or a broadcast report of this ❷ a piece of new information

newsagent NOUN (British) a shopkeeper who sells newspapers

newsflash NOUN a short news broadcast which interrupts a programme because something important has happened

newsgroup NOUN a place on the Internet where people discuss a particular subject and exchange information about it

newsletter NOUN a short, informal report sent regularly to members of an organization

newspaper NOUN ❶ a daily or weekly publication on large sheets of paper, containing news reports, reviews and articles ❷ the sheets of paper forming a newspaper

newt NOUN a small animal rather like a lizard, that lives near or in water

newton NOUN a unit for measuring force

New Year's Day NOUN the first day of the year, which in the modern Western calendar is 1 January

next ADJECTIVE nearest; coming immediately after

next ADVERB ❶ after this; then ❷ in the next place in order

next door ADVERB & ADJECTIVE in the next house or building

NGO ABBREVIATION non-governmental organization (a charity or association that is independent of government or business)

nib NOUN the pointed metal part of a pen

nibble VERB to eat something by taking small, quick or gentle bites

nice ADJECTIVE ❶ kind and friendly ❷ pleasant or enjoyable ❸ precise or careful

nicety (say ny-sit-ee) NOUN ❶ a small detail or difference pointed out ❷ precision or accuracy

niche (say nich or neesh) NOUN ❶ a small recess, especially in a wall ❷ a suitable place or position

nick NOUN ❶ a small cut or notch ❷ (informal) a police station or prison

nick VERB ❶ to make a nick in something ❷ (informal) to steal something ❹ (*informal*) to arrest someone

nickel NOUN ❶ a silvery-white metal ❷ (*North American*) a 5-cent coin

nickname NOUN an informal name given to a person instead of his or her real name

nicotine NOUN a poisonous substance found in tobacco

niece NOUN the daughter of a person's brother or sister

niggle VERB to be a small but constant worry

nigh ADVERB & PREPOSITION (*poetical use*) near or nearly

night NOUN ❶ the dark hours between sunset and sunrise ❷ a particular night or evening

nightcap NOUN ❶ (*old use*) a knitted cap worn in bed ❷ a drink, especially an alcoholic one, which you have before going to bed

nightclub NOUN a place that is open at night where people go to drink and dance

nightdress NOUN a loose dress that girls or women wear in bed

nightfall NOUN the coming of darkness at the end of the day

nightie NOUN (*informal*) a nightdress

nightingale NOUN a small brown bird that sings sweetly

nightlife NOUN the places of entertainment that you can go to at night

nightly ADJECTIVE & ADVERB happening every night

nightmare NOUN ❶ a frightening

dream ❷ an unpleasant experience

nil NOUN nothing or nought

nimble ADJECTIVE able to move quickly and easily; agile

nine NOUN & ADJECTIVE the number 9

ninepins NOUN the game of skittles played with nine objects

nineteen NOUN & ADJECTIVE the number 19

ninety NOUN & ADJECTIVE the number 90

ninth ADJECTIVE & NOUN ❶ next after eighth ❷ one of nine equal parts of a thing

nip VERB ❶ to pinch or bite someone quickly ❷ (*informal*) to go somewhere quickly

nip NOUN ❶ a quick pinch or bite ❷ sharp coldness ❸ a small drink of a spirit

nipper NOUN (*informal*) a young child

nipple NOUN the small part that sticks out at the front of a person's breast, from which babies suck milk

nippy ADJECTIVE (*informal*) ❶ quick or nimble ❷ rather cold

nirvana NOUN in Buddhism and Hinduism, the highest state of knowledge and understanding, achieved by meditation

nit NOUN a parasitic insect or its egg, found in people's hair

nit-picking NOUN pointing out very small faults or mistakes

nitrate NOUN ❶ a chemical compound containing nitrogen ❷ potassium or sodium nitrate, used as a fertilizer

nitric acid (say **ny**-trik) NOUN a very strong colourless acid containing nitrogen

nitrogen (say **ny**-tro-jen) NOUN a gas that makes up about four-fifths of the air

no DETERMINER not any

no EXCLAMATION used to deny or refuse something

no ADVERB not at all

No., no. ABBREVIATION number

nobility NOUN ❶ being noble ❷ the aristocracy

noble ADJECTIVE ❶ of high social rank; aristocratic ❷ having a very good character or qualities ❸ stately or impressive

noble NOUN a person of high social rank

nobleman, noblewoman NOUN a man or woman of high social rank

nobody PRONOUN no person; no one

nobody NOUN (informal) an unimportant person

nocturnal ADJECTIVE ❶ happening at night ❷ active at night

nod VERB to move your head up and down, especially as a way of agreeing with someone or as a greeting

nod NOUN a movement of your head up and down

node NOUN a small round swelling

noise NOUN a sound, especially one that is loud or unpleasant

noisy ADJECTIVE making a lot of noise or full of noise

nomad NOUN a member of a tribe that moves from place to place looking for pasture for their animals

nomadic ADJECTIVE moving from place to place

no man's land NOUN an area that does not belong to anybody, especially the land between opposing armies

nom de plume NOUN a name used by a writer instead of their real name; a pseudonym

nominal ADJECTIVE ❶ in name only ❷ small or insignificant

nominate VERB to formally suggest that someone should be a candidate in an election or should be given a job or award

nominee NOUN a person who is nominated

non- PREFIX not (as in non-stop)

nonchalant (say **non**-shal-ant) ADJECTIVE calm and casual; showing no anxiety or excitement

non-committal ADJECTIVE not saying what you think or what you plan to do

Nonconformist NOUN a member of a Protestant Church (e.g. Baptist, Methodist) that does not conform to all the customs of the Church of England

nondescript ADJECTIVE having no special or distinctive qualities and therefore difficult to describe

none PRONOUN ❶ not any ❷ no one

none ADVERB not at all

nonentity (say non-**en**-tit-ee) NOUN an unimportant person

nonetheless ADVERB in spite of this; although this is a fact

non-existent ADJECTIVE not existing or unreal

non-fiction NOUN writings that are not fiction; books about real people and things and true events

non-flammable ADJECTIVE not able to be set on fire

nonplussed ADJECTIVE puzzled or confused

nonsense NOUN ❶ words put together in a way that does not mean anything ❷ stupid ideas or behaviour

non-stop ADJECTIVE & ADVERB ❶ not stopping ❷ not stopping between two main stations

noodles PLURAL NOUN pasta made in narrow strips, used in soups and stir-fries

nook NOUN a small sheltered place or corner

noon NOUN twelve o'clock midday

no one PRONOUN no person; nobody

noose NOUN a loop in a rope that gets smaller when the rope is pulled

nor CONJUNCTION and not

norm NOUN ❶ a standard or average type, amount or level ❷ normal or expected behaviour

normal ADJECTIVE ❶ usual or ordinary ❷ natural and healthy; not suffering from an illness

normally ADVERB ❶ usually ❷ in the usual way

Norman NOUN a member of the people of Normandy in northern France, who conquered England in 1066

north NOUN ❶ the direction to the left of a person who faces east ❷ the northern part of a country, city or other area

north ADJECTIVE & ADVERB towards or in the north; coming from the north

north-east NOUN, ADJECTIVE & ADVERB midway between north and east

northward ADJECTIVE & ADVERB towards the north

north-west NOUN, ADJECTIVE & ADVERB midway between north and west

Nos., nos. plural of No. or no

nose NOUN ❶ the part of the face that is used for breathing and for smelling things ❷ the front end or part of something

nose VERB to go forward cautiously

nosebag NOUN a bag containing fodder, for hanging on a horse's head

nosedive NOUN a steep downward dive, especially by an aircraft

nostalgia (say nos-tal-ja) NOUN a feeling of pleasure, mixed with sadness, when you remember happy times in the past

nostril NOUN either of the two openings in the nose

nosy ADJECTIVE (informal) always wanting to know other people's business

not ADVERB used to change the meaning of something to its opposite or absence

notable ADJECTIVE worth noticing; remarkable or famous

notation NOUN a system of symbols representing numbers, quantities or musical notes

notch NOUN a small V-shape cut

notch into a surface

notch VERB to cut a notch or notches in a surface

note NOUN ❶ something written down as a reminder or as a comment or explanation ❷ a short letter ❸ a banknote ❹ a single sound in music ❺ any of the keys on a piano or other keyboard instrument ❻ a sound or quality that indicates something

note VERB ❶ to make a note about something; to write something down ❷ to notice or pay attention to something

notebook NOUN ❶ a book with blank pages on which to write notes ❷ a small computer that you can carry around with you

noted ADJECTIVE famous, especially for a particular reason

notepaper NOUN paper for writing letters

nothing PRONOUN ❶ no thing; not anything ❷ no amount; nought

nothing ADVERB not at all; in no way

notice NOUN ❶ something written or printed and displayed for people to see ❷ attention ❸ warning that something is going to happen ❹ a formal announcement that you are about to end an agreement or leave a job at a specified time

notice VERB to see or become aware of something

noticeable ADJECTIVE easily seen or noticed

noticeboard NOUN (British) a board on which notices may be displayed

notify VERB to tell someone about something formally or officially

notion NOUN an idea, especially one that is vague or incorrect

notorious ADJECTIVE well known for something bad

notwithstanding PREPOSITION in spite of

nougat (say noo-gah) NOUN a chewy sweet made from nuts, sugar or honey and egg white

nought (say nawt) NOUN (British) the figure 0

noun NOUN a word that stands for a person, place or thing. **Common nouns** are words such as boy, dog, river, sport, table, which are used of a whole kind of people or things; **proper nouns** are words such as Jennifer, Thames and London which name a particular person or thing.

nourish VERB to keep a person, animal or plant alive and well by means of food

nourishment NOUN food that a person, animal or plant needs to stay alive and well

nova (say noh-va) NOUN a star that suddenly becomes much brighter for a short time

novel NOUN a story that fills a whole book

novel ADJECTIVE of a new and unusual kind

novelist NOUN a person who writes novels

novelty NOUN ❶ the quality of being new, different and interesting ❷ something new and unusual ❸ a cheap toy or ornament

November NOUN the eleventh

month of the year

novice NOUN ❶ a beginner ❷ a person preparing to be a monk or nun

now ADVERB ❶ at the present time; this moment ❷ by this time ❸ immediately ❹ I wonder or I am telling you

now CONJUNCTION as a result of or at the same time as something

nowadays ADVERB at the present time, as contrasted with years ago

nowhere ADVERB not anywhere; in or to no place

noxious ADJECTIVE unpleasant and harmful

nozzle NOUN the spout of a hose, pipe or tube

nuclear ADJECTIVE ❶ to do with a nucleus, especially of an atom ❷ using the energy that is created by reactions in the nuclei of atoms

nucleus NOUN nuclei ❶ the central part of an atom or biological cell ❷ the part in the centre of something, round which other things are grouped

nude ADJECTIVE not wearing any clothes; naked

nude NOUN a painting or sculpture of a naked human figure

nudge VERB ❶ to poke a person gently with your elbow ❷ to push something slightly or gradually

nudge NOUN a slight push or poke

nugget NOUN ❶ a rough lump of something, especially gold, found in the earth ❷ a small but valuable fact

nuisance NOUN a person or thing that is annoying or causes trouble

null ADJECTIVE ➤ **null and void** not legally valid

numb ADJECTIVE not able to feel anything

numb VERB to make you unable to feel anything

number NOUN ❶ a symbol or word that tells you how many of something there are; a numeral or figure ❷ a series of numbers given to a thing to identify it ❸ a quantity of people or things ❹ one issue of a magazine or newspaper ❺ a song or piece of music

number VERB ❶ to give something a number or mark it with a number ❷ to amount to a certain figure

numeracy NOUN a good basic knowledge of mathematics

numeral NOUN a symbol that represents a certain number; a figure

numerator NOUN the number above the line in a fraction, showing how many parts are to be taken, e.g. 2 in ⅔. Compare with **denominator**.

numerical (say new-**merri**-kal) ADJECTIVE to do with or consisting of numbers

numerous ADJECTIVE many; lots of

nun NOUN a member of a community of women who live according to the rules of a religious organization. Compare with **monk**.

nunnery NOUN a convent

nuptial ADJECTIVE to do with marriage or a wedding

nuptials PLURAL NOUN a wedding

nurse NOUN ❶ a person trained to look after people who are ill or injured ❷ a woman employed to look after young children

nurse VERB ❶ to look after someone who is ill or injured ❷ to take care of an injury or illness ❸ to feed a baby at the breast ❹ to have a feeling for a long time ❺ to hold something carefully in your hands

nursemaid NOUN a young woman employed to look after young children

nursery NOUN ❶ a place where young children are looked after or play ❷ a place where young plants are grown and usually for sale

nursery rhyme NOUN a simple rhyme or song of the kind that young children like

nursery school NOUN a school for children below primary school age

nursing home NOUN a small hospital or home for invalids

nurture VERB ❶ to take care of and educate a young child while he or she is growing ❷ to help something to grow or develop ❸ to cherish an idea or hope

nurture NOUN a child's upbringing and education

nut NOUN ❶ a fruit with a hard shell ❷ a kernel ❸ a small piece of metal with a hole in the middle, for screwing onto a bolt ❹ (informal) the head ❺ (informal) a mad or eccentric person

nutcrackers PLURAL NOUN pincers for cracking nuts

nutmeg NOUN the hard seed of a tropical tree, grated and used in cooking

nutrient (say **new-tree-ent**) NOUN a substance that is needed to keep a plant or animal alive and to help it grow

nutrition (say new-**trish**-on) NOUN the food that you eat and the way that it affects your health; nourishment

nutritious (say new-**trish**-us) ADJECTIVE nutritious food has substances in it that help you to stay healthy

nuts ADJECTIVE (informal) mad or eccentric

nutshell NOUN the shell of a nut

nutty ADJECTIVE ❶ tasting of nuts or full of nuts ❷ (informal) slightly crazy

nuzzle VERB to rub gently against someone with the nose or face

NW ABBREVIATION ❶ north-west ❷ north-western

nylon NOUN a synthetic, strong, lightweight cloth or fibre

nymph (say nimf) NOUN ❶ in myths, a young goddess living in the sea or woods etc. ❷ the immature form of insects such as the dragonfly

Oo

O EXCLAMATION oh

oaf NOUN a stupid or clumsy man

oak NOUN a large deciduous tree with seeds called acorns

oar NOUN a pole with a flat blade at one end, used for rowing a boat

oasis (say oh-**ay**-sis) NOUN oases a fertile place in a desert, with a spring or well of water

oath NOUN ❶ a solemn promise to do something or that something is true, sometimes appealing to God as witness ❷ a swear word

oatmeal NOUN ground oats, used to make porridge or in baking

oats PLURAL NOUN a cereal used to make food for animals and for people

obedient ADJECTIVE doing what you are told; willing to obey

obelisk NOUN a tall pillar set up as a monument

obese (say o-beess) ADJECTIVE very fat; overweight

obesity (say o-beess-it-ee) NOUN being too fat in a way that is unhealthy

obey VERB to do what you are told to do

obituary NOUN an announcement in a newspaper of a person's death, often with a short account of their life

object (say ob-jikt) NOUN ❶ something solid that can be seen or touched ❷ a purpose or intention ❸ a person or thing to which some action or feeling is directed ❹ (in grammar) the word or words naming the person or thing that is affected by the action of a verb or preposition, e.g. him in The dog bit him. and I threw the ball to him.

object (say ob-jekt) VERB to say that you are not in favour of something or do not agree

objection NOUN ❶ objecting to something ❷ a reason for objecting

objectionable ADJECTIVE unpleasant or nasty

objective NOUN what you are trying to reach or do; an aim

objective ADJECTIVE ❶ not influenced by personal feelings or opinions Compare with subjective. ❷ having real existence outside someone's mind

obligation NOUN ❶ being obliged to do something ❷ what you are obliged to do; a duty

obligatory (say ob-lig-a-ter-ee) ADJECTIVE something is obligatory when you must do it because of a law or rule

oblige VERB ❶ to force someone to do something ❷ to help someone by doing what they ask

obliging ADJECTIVE polite and helpful

oblique (say ob-leek) ADJECTIVE ❶ slanting ❷ not saying something straightforwardly

obliterate VERB to remove all traces of something by destroying it completely or covering it up

oblivion NOUN ❶ being forgotten ❷ being unconscious

oblivious ADJECTIVE completely unaware of what is happening around you

oblong ADJECTIVE rectangular in shape and longer than it is wide

oblong NOUN a rectangular shape that is longer than it is wide

obnoxious ADJECTIVE very unpleasant or offensive

oboe NOUN a high-pitched woodwind instrument

a
b
c
d
e
f
g
h
i
j
k
l
m
n
o
p
q
r
s
t
u
v
w
x
y
z

obscene (say ob-**seen**) *ADJECTIVE* indecent in a very offensive way

obscure *ADJECTIVE* ❶ difficult to see or to understand; not clear ❷ not well known

obscure *VERB* to make a thing difficult to see or to understand

obscurity *NOUN* ❶ being not well known ❷ the quality of being difficult to understand

obsequious (say ob-**seek**-wee-us) *ADJECTIVE* showing too much respect or too willing to obey or serve someone

observance *NOUN* obeying or keeping a law, custom or religious festival

observant *ADJECTIVE* quick at observing or noticing things

observation *NOUN* ❶ noticing or watching something carefully ❷ a comment or remark

observatory *NOUN* a building with telescopes and other instruments for observing the stars or weather

observe *VERB* ❶ to see and notice something ❷ to watch something carefully ❸ to obey a law or rule ❹ to keep or celebrate a custom or religious festival ❺ to make a remark

obsessed *ADJECTIVE* to be obsessed with something is to be continually thinking about it

obsession *NOUN* something you cannot stop thinking about

obsessive *ADJECTIVE* showing that a person thinks too much about something in a way that is not normal

obsolete *ADJECTIVE* not used any

more; out of date

obstacle *NOUN* something that stands in the way or makes it difficult to do something

obstetrics *NOUN* the branch of medicine and surgery that deals with the birth of babies

obstinate *ADJECTIVE* ❶ refusing to change your ideas or ways, even though they may be wrong ❷ difficult to overcome or remove

obstruct *VERB* to stop a person or thing from getting past; to hinder the progress of something

obstruction *NOUN* ❶ obstructing something ❷ something that obstructs or hinders progress

obtain *VERB* to get or be given something

obtrusive *ADJECTIVE* unpleasantly noticeable

obtuse *ADJECTIVE* slow to understand something

obtuse angle *NOUN* an angle of more than 90° but less than 180°. Compare with **acute angle**.

obverse *NOUN* the side of a coin or medal showing the head or chief design (the other side is the reverse)

obvious *ADJECTIVE* easy to see or understand

obviously *ADVERB* it is obvious that; clearly

occasion *NOUN* ❶ the time when something happens ❷ a special event ❸ a suitable time or opportunity

occasion *VERB* (formal) to cause something to happen

occasional *ADJECTIVE* ❶ happening

from time to time but not regularly or frequently ❷ for special occasions

occasionally ADVERB sometimes, but not often

occult ADJECTIVE to do with the supernatural or magic

occupant NOUN someone who is in a place or building

occupation NOUN ❶ a person's job or profession ❷ something you do to pass your time ❸ capturing a country by military force

occupational ADJECTIVE caused by an occupation

occupational therapy NOUN creative work designed to help people to recover from certain illnesses

occupy VERB ❶ to live or work in a place or building; to inhabit somewhere ❷ to fill a space or position ❸ to keep someone busy or interested ❹ to capture a country by force and place troops there

occur VERB ❶ to happen or take place ❷ to exist or be found somewhere ❸ to come into a person's mind

occurrence NOUN ❶ something that happens; an incident or event ❷ occurring

ocean NOUN the seas that surround the continents of the earth, especially one of the large named areas of this

ocelot (say oss-il-ot) NOUN a leopard-like animal of Central and South America

ochre (say oh-ker) NOUN ❶ a

yellow, red or brownish mineral used as a pigment ❷ pale brownish-yellow

o'clock ADVERB used after the number of the hour when you are saying what time it is

octagon NOUN a flat shape with eight sides and eight angles

octave NOUN the interval of eight steps between one musical note and the next note of the same name above or below it

octet NOUN a group of eight instruments or singers

October NOUN the tenth month of the year

octogenarian NOUN a person aged between 80 and 89

octopus NOUN octopuses a sea creature with eight long tentacles

oculist NOUN a doctor who treats diseases of the eye

odd ADJECTIVE ❶ strange or unusual ❷ an odd number is one that cannot be divided exactly by two Compare with **even**. ❸ left over from a pair or set ❹ of various kinds; not regular

oddity NOUN a strange person or thing

oddly ADVERB ❶ strangely ❷ surprisingly

oddments PLURAL NOUN scraps or pieces left over from a larger piece or set

odds PLURAL NOUN ❶ the chances that a certain thing will happen ❷ the proportion of money that you will win if a bet is successful

ode NOUN a poem addressed to a person or thing

odious (say oh-dee-us) ADJECTIVE extremely unpleasant; hateful

odour NOUN a smell, especially an unpleasant one

odyssey (say od-iss-ee) NOUN a long adventurous journey

oesophagus (say ee-sof-a-gus) NOUN the tube leading from the throat to the stomach; the gullet

oestrogen (say ees-tro-jen) NOUN a hormone which develops and maintains female sexual and physical characteristics

of PREPOSITION ❶ belonging to ❷ concerning; about ❸ made from ❹ from

off PREPOSITION ❶ not on; away or down from ❷ not taking or wanting ❸ deducted from

off ADVERB ❶ away or down from something ❷ not working or happening ❸ to the end; completely ❹ as regards money or supplies ❺ food that is off is beginning to go bad ❻ behind or at the side of a stage

offal NOUN the organs of an animal, such as liver and kidneys, sold as food

off-colour ADJECTIVE slightly unwell

offence NOUN ❶ a crime or something illegal ❷ a feeling of annoyance or resentment

offend VERB ❶ to cause offence to someone; to hurt a person's feelings ❷ to commit a crime or do something wrong

offensive ADJECTIVE ❶ causing offence; insulting ❷ disgusting ❸ used for attacking

offensive NOUN a forceful attack or campaign

offer VERB ❶ to hold something out or present it so that people can accept it if they want to ❷ to say that you are willing to do or give something or to pay a certain amount

offer NOUN ❶ offering something ❷ an amount of money offered ❸ a specially reduced price

offering NOUN something that is offered

offhand ADJECTIVE rather casual and rude, without thought or consideration

offhand ADVERB without previous thought or preparation

office NOUN ❶ a room or building where people work, usually sitting at desks ❷ a place where people can go for tickets, information or some other service ❸ a government department ❹ an important job or position

officer NOUN ❶ a person who is in charge of others, especially in the armed forces ❷ a member of the police force ❸ an official

official ADJECTIVE ❶ approved or done by someone with authority ❷ done as part of your job or position

official NOUN a person who holds a position of authority

officially ADVERB ❶ publicly and by someone in a position of authority ❷ according to a set of rules

officiate VERB to be in charge of a meeting or event

officious ADJECTIVE too ready to give orders; bossy

offing NOUN ➤ in the offing likely to happen soon

off-licence NOUN (British) a shop with a licence to sell alcoholic drinks to be drunk away from the shop

off-putting ADJECTIVE making you less keen on something

offset VERB offsets, offsetting, offset to cancel out or make up for something

offshoot NOUN ❶ a side shoot on a plant ❷ a by-product

offshore ADJECTIVE ❶ in the sea some distance from the shore ❷ from the land towards the sea

offside ADJECTIVE & ADVERB a player in football or other sports is offside when they are in a position where the rules do not allow them to play the ball

offspring NOUN a person's child or children; the young of an animal

oft ADVERB (old use) often

often ADVERB many times; in many cases

ogle VERB to stare at someone whom you find attractive

ogre NOUN ❶ a cruel giant in fairy tales and legends ❷ a terrifying person

oh EXCLAMATION ❶ a cry of pain, surprise or delight ❷ used for emphasis

ohm NOUN a unit of electrical resistance

oil NOUN ❶ a thick slippery liquid that will not dissolve in water ❷ a kind of petroleum used as fuel ❸ oil paint

oil VERB to put oil on something, especially to make it work smoothly

oilfield NOUN an area where oil is found in the ground or under the sea

oil paint NOUN paint made with oil

oil painting NOUN a painting done with oil paints

oil rig NOUN a structure set up to support the equipment for drilling for oil

oilskin NOUN cloth made waterproof by treatment with oil

oil well NOUN a hole drilled in the ground or under the sea to get oil

oily ADJECTIVE ❶ containing or like oil; covered with or soaked with oil ❷ behaving in an insincerely polite way

ointment NOUN a cream or slippery paste for putting on sore skin and cuts

OK, okay ADVERB & ADJECTIVE (informal) all right

old ADJECTIVE ❶ having lived for a long time ❷ made or existing from a long time ago ❸ of a particular age ❹ former or original

old age NOUN the time when a person is old

olden ADJECTIVE of former times

Old English NOUN the English language from about 700 to 1150, also called Anglo-Saxon

old-fashioned ADJECTIVE of the kind that was usual a long time ago; no longer fashionable

Old Norse NOUN the language spoken by the Vikings, the ancestor

a b c d e f g h i j k l m n o p q r s t u v w x y z

olive NOUN ❶ an evergreen tree with a small bitter fruit ❷ this fruit, from which an oil (*olive oil*) is made ❸ a shade of green like an unripe olive

olive branch NOUN something you do or offer that shows you want to make peace

Olympic Games, Olympics PLURAL NOUN a series of international sports contests held every four years in a different part of the world

ombudsman NOUN an official whose job is to investigate complaints against government organizations

omega (say oh-meg-a) NOUN the last letter of the Greek alphabet, equivalent to Roman o

omelette NOUN eggs beaten together and cooked in a pan, often with a filling

omen NOUN an event regarded as a sign of what is going to happen

ominous ADJECTIVE suggesting that trouble is coming

omission NOUN ❶ something that has been missed out or not done ❷ missing something out or failing to do it

omit VERB ❶ to miss something out ❷ to fail to do something

omnibus NOUN ❶ a book containing several stories or books that were previously published separately ❷ a single edition of several radio or television programmes previously broadcast separately ❸ (*old use*) a bus

omnipotent ADJECTIVE having unlimited power or very great power

omniscient (say om-**niss**-ee-ent) ADJECTIVE knowing everything

omnivore (say **om**-niv-or) NOUN an animal that feeds on both plants and the flesh of other animals. Compare with **carnivore, herbivore**.

omnivorous (say om-**niv**-er-us) ADJECTIVE an omnivorous animal feeds on both plants and the flesh of other animals. Compare with **carnivorous, herbivorous**.

on PREPOSITION ❶ supported by, covering or attached to something ❷ during; at the time of ❸ close to; towards ❹ by reason of ❺ concerning; about ❻ in a state of; using or showing

on ADVERB ❶ so that it is on something ❷ further forward ❸ working; in action

once ADVERB ❶ for one time or on one occasion only ❷ at an earlier time; formerly

once CONJUNCTION as soon as

oncoming ADJECTIVE approaching or coming towards you

one ADJECTIVE ❶ single; only ❷ identical; the same ❸ a certain

one NOUN ❶ the smallest whole number, 1 ❷ a person or thing alone

one PRONOUN ❶ a person or thing previously mentioned ❷ a person; any person

onerous (say **ohn**-er-us or **on**-er-us) ADJECTIVE difficult to bear or do

one-sided ADJECTIVE ❶ with one side or person in a contest or conversation being much stronger or doing a lot more than the other ❷ showing only one point of view in an unfair way

one-way ADJECTIVE where traffic is allowed to travel in one direction only

ongoing ADJECTIVE continuing to exist or be in progress

onion NOUN a round vegetable with a strong flavour

online ADJECTIVE & ADVERB connected to a computer or to the Internet

onlooker NOUN a spectator

only ADJECTIVE being the one person or thing of a kind; sole

only ADVERB ❶ no more than; and that is all ❷ nothing other than

only CONJUNCTION but then; however

onomatopoeia (say on-om-at-o-**pee**-a) NOUN forming or using words that sound like the thing they stand for, e.g. *cuckoo, plop, sizzle*

onrush NOUN a surging rush forward

onset NOUN ❶ the beginning of something ❷ the first part of a syllable, e.g. *d* in *dog*

onshore ADJECTIVE from the sea towards the land

onslaught NOUN a fierce attack

onto, on to PREPOSITION to a position on

onward ADVERB & ADJECTIVE going forward; further on

onyx NOUN a stone rather like marble, with different colours in layers

ooze VERB ❶ to flow or trickle out

of something slowly ❷ a wound, crack or other opening oozes when liquid flows out of it slowly

ooze NOUN mud at the bottom of a river or sea

opal NOUN a kind of stone with a rainbow sheen

opaque (say o-**payk**) ADJECTIVE not able to be seen through; not transparent or translucent

open ADJECTIVE ❶ allowing people or things to go in and out; not closed or fastened ❷ not covered or blocked up ❸ spread out; unfolded ❹ not limited or restricted ❺ letting in visitors or customers ❻ with wide empty spaces ❼ honest and frank; not secret or secretive ❽ not decided ❾ willing or likely to receive something

open VERB ❶ to make something open or more open ❷ to become open or more open ❸ to begin; to start something ❹ a shop or office opens when it starts business for the day

opener NOUN a device for opening a bottle or can

opening NOUN ❶ a space or gap; a place where something opens ❷ the beginning of something ❸ an opportunity, especially for a job

openly ADVERB without trying to hide anything

open-minded ADJECTIVE ready to listen to other people's ideas and opinions; not having fixed ideas

opera NOUN ❶ a play in which all or most of the words are sung to music; works of this kind ❷ *plural*

a b c d e f g h i j k l m n o p q r s t u v w x y z

of opus

operate VERB ❶ to make a machine work ❷ to work or be in action ❸ to perform a surgical operation on someone

operatic ADJECTIVE to do with opera

operating system NOUN the software that controls a computer's basic functions

operation NOUN ❶ something done to the body by a surgeon to take away or repair a part of it ❷ a carefully planned activity involving a lot of people ❸ a piece of work performed by a machine

operative ADJECTIVE ❶ working or functioning ❷ to do with surgical operations

operator NOUN a person who works something, especially a telephone switchboard or exchange

operetta NOUN a short opera on a light or humorous theme

ophthalmic (say off-**thal**-mik) ADJECTIVE to do with or for your eyes

ophthalmic optician NOUN (British) a person who is qualified to test people's eyesight and prescribe glasses and contact lenses

opinion NOUN what you think of something; a belief or judgement

opinionated ADJECTIVE having strong opinions and holding them whatever anybody says

opinion poll NOUN an estimate of what people think, made by questioning a sample of them

opium NOUN a powerful drug made from the juice of certain poppies, used in the past in medicine

opossum NOUN a small furry marsupial that lives in trees, with different kinds in America and Australia

opponent NOUN a person or group opposing another in a contest or war

opportune ADJECTIVE ❶ an opportune time is convenient or suitable for a purpose ❷ done or happening at a suitable time

opportunity NOUN a good chance to do a particular thing

oppose VERB to argue or fight against someone or something; to resist something

opposite ADJECTIVE ❶ placed on the other or further side; facing ❷ moving away from or towards each other ❸ completely different

opposite NOUN an opposite person or thing

opposite ADVERB in an opposite position or direction

opposite PREPOSITION opposite to

opposition NOUN ❶ opposing something; resistance ❷ the people who oppose something

oppress VERB ❶ to govern or treat someone cruelly or unjustly ❷ to weigh someone down with worry or sadness

oppression NOUN governing or treating people cruelly or unjustly

oppressive ADJECTIVE ❶ cruel or harsh ❷ worrying and difficult to bear ❸ oppressive weather is unpleasantly hot and humid

opt VERB to choose something

optic ADJECTIVE to do with your eyes or sight

optical ADJECTIVE to do with sight; aiding sight

optical illusion NOUN a deceptive appearance that makes you think you see something that is not really there

optician NOUN a person who tests people's eyesight and makes or sells glasses and contact lenses

optics NOUN the study of sight and of light as connected with this

optimist NOUN a person who expects that things will turn out well. Compare with pessimist.

optimistic ADJECTIVE expecting things to turn out well

optimum ADJECTIVE best; most favourable

option NOUN ❶ the right or power to choose something ❷ something chosen or that may be chosen

optional ADJECTIVE that you can choose, not compulsory

opulent ADJECTIVE wealthy or luxurious

opus (say oh-pus) NOUN a numbered musical composition

or CONJUNCTION used to show that there is a choice or an alternative

oracle NOUN ❶ a shrine where the ancient Greeks consulted one of their gods for advice or a prophecy ❷ a wise or knowledgeable adviser

oral ADJECTIVE ❶ spoken, not written ❷ to do with or using your mouth

oral NOUN a spoken examination or test

orange NOUN ❶ a round juicy citrus fruit with reddish-yellow peel ❷ a reddish-yellow colour

orange ADJECTIVE reddish-yellow in colour

orangutan NOUN a large ape of Borneo and Sumatra

orator NOUN a person who is good at making speeches in public

oratorio NOUN a piece of music for voices and an orchestra, usually on a religious subject

oratory NOUN ❶ the art of making speeches in public ❷ eloquent speech

orb NOUN a sphere or globe

orbit NOUN ❶ the curved path taken by something moving round a planet, moon or star ❷ the range of someone's influence or control

orbit VERB to move in an orbit round something

orchard NOUN a piece of ground planted with fruit trees

orchestra NOUN a large group of people playing various musical instruments together

orchestrate VERB ❶ to compose or arrange music for an orchestra ❷ to coordinate things deliberately

orchid NOUN a kind of plant with brightly coloured, often unevenly shaped, flowers

ordain VERB ❶ to make a person a member of the clergy in the Christian Church ❷ to declare or order something by law

ordeal NOUN a difficult or horrific experience

order NOUN ❶ a command to do something ❷ a request for something to be supplied ❸ the way things are arranged ❹ a neat

a
b
c
d
e
f
g
h
i
j
k
l
m
n
o
p
q
r
s
t
u
v
w
x
y
z

arrangement, with everything in the right place **⑤** a situation in which people are behaving properly and obeying the rules **⑥** a kind or sort of thing **⑦** a group of monks or nuns who live by certain religious rules

order VERB **①** to command someone to do something **②** to ask for something to be supplied to you **③** to put something into order; to arrange things neatly

orderly ADJECTIVE **①** arranged neatly or well **②** well-behaved and obedient

orderly NOUN **①** an assistant in a hospital **②** a soldier whose job is to assist an officer

ordinal number NOUN a number that shows its position in a series, e.g. first, fifth, twentieth, etc. Compare with **cardinal number**.

ordinarily ADVERB usually or normally

ordinary ADJECTIVE normal or usual; not special

ordination NOUN ordaining someone or being ordained, as a member of the Christian clergy

Ordnance Survey NOUN an official survey organization that makes detailed maps of the British Isles

ore NOUN rock with metal or other useful substances in it

oregano (say o-ri-**gah**-noh) NOUN the dried leaves of wild marjoram used as a herb in cooking

organ NOUN **①** a musical instrument from which sounds are produced by air forced through pipes, played by keys and pedals

② a part of the body with a particular function

organdie NOUN a kind of thin fabric, usually stiffened

organic ADJECTIVE **①** to do with or formed from living things **②** organic food is grown or produced without using chemical fertilizers or pesticides **③** to do with the organs of the body

organism NOUN a living thing; an individual animal or plant

organist NOUN a person who plays the organ

organization (also **organisation**) NOUN **①** an organized group of people, such as a business, charity or government department **②** the organizing of something

organize (also **organise**) VERB **①** to plan and prepare something **②** to put things in order **③** to form people into a group to work together

orgasm NOUN the moment during sexual activity when feelings of sexual pleasure are at their strongest

Orient NOUN the countries of the East, especially east Asia

orient VERB to orientate something

oriental ADJECTIVE (old use) to do with the countries east of the Mediterranean Sea, especially China and Japan

orientate VERB (chiefly British) **①** to place something or face in a certain direction **②** to get your bearings

orienteering NOUN the sport of finding your way across rough country with a map and compass

origami (say o-rig-**ah**-mee) NOUN the art of folding paper into decorative shapes

origin NOUN ❶ the start of something; the point or cause from which something began ❷ a person's family background ❸ the point where two or more axes on a graph meet

original ADJECTIVE ❶ existing from the start; earliest ❷ new and interesting; different from others of its type ❸ producing new ideas; inventive ❹ made or created first, before copies

original NOUN a document, painting or other work which was the first one made and is not a copy

originality NOUN the quality of being new and interesting

originally ADVERB at first, before anything changed

originate VERB ❶ to have its origin; to begin to happen or appear ❷ to create something

ornament NOUN an object you display or wear as a decoration

ornament VERB to decorate something with beautiful things

ornamental ADJECTIVE used as an ornament; decorative rather than useful

ornate ADJECTIVE elaborately decorated

ornithology NOUN the study of birds

orphan NOUN a child whose parents are dead

orphanage NOUN a home for orphans

orthodox ADJECTIVE ❶ holding beliefs that are correct or generally accepted ❷ conventional or normal

Orthodox Church NOUN the Christian Churches of eastern Europe

orthopaedics (say orth-o-pee-diks) NOUN the treatment of deformities and injuries to bones and muscles

oscillate VERB to keep moving to and fro; to vibrate

osmosis NOUN the passing of fluid through a porous partition into another more concentrated fluid

ostensible ADJECTIVE apparently true, but actually concealing the true reason

ostentatious ADJECTIVE making a showy display of something to impress people

osteopath NOUN a person who treats certain diseases by pressing and moving a patient's bones and muscles

ostracize (also **ostracise**) VERB to exclude someone from your group and completely ignore them

ostrich NOUN a large long-legged African bird that can run very fast but cannot fly. It is said to bury its head in the sand when pursued, in the belief that it then cannot be seen.

other ADJECTIVE ❶ different; not the same ❷ remaining ❸ additional ❹ just recent or past

other PRONOUN the other person or thing

otherwise ADVERB ❶ if things

otter NOUN a fish-eating animal with webbed feet, a flat tail and thick brown fur, living near water

ought AUXILIARY VERB used with other words to show ❶ what you should or must do ❷ what is likely to happen

ounce NOUN ❶ a unit of weight equal to ¹⁄₁₆ of a pound (about 28 grams) ❷ a tiny amount

our DETERMINER belonging to us

ours POSSESSIVE PRONOUN belonging to us

ourselves PRONOUN we or us and nobody else. The word is used to refer back to the subject of a sentence (e.g. *We blame ourselves.*) or for emphasis (e.g. *We made all the costumes ourselves.*).

oust VERB to drive someone out from a position or office

out ADVERB ❶ away from or not in a particular place or position or state; not at home ❷ into the open; into existence or sight ❸ no longer burning or shining ❹ in error ❺ to or at an end; completely ❻ loudly or boldly ❼ no longer batting in cricket

out-and-out ADJECTIVE thorough or complete

outback NOUN the remote inland districts of Australia

outboard motor NOUN a motor fitted to the outside of a boat's stern

outbreak NOUN the start of something unpleasant, such as a disease or war

outburst NOUN a sudden bursting out of anger or laughter

outcast NOUN a person who has been rejected by family, friends or society

outcome NOUN the result of what happens or has happened

outcrop NOUN a large piece of rock from a lower level that sticks out on the surface of the ground

outcry NOUN a strong protest

outdated ADJECTIVE out of date

outdo VERB to do better than another person

outdoor ADJECTIVE done or used outdoors

outdoors ADVERB in the open air

outer ADJECTIVE outside or external; nearer to the outside

outermost ADJECTIVE nearest to the outside; furthest from the centre

outer space NOUN the universe beyond the earth's atmosphere

outfit NOUN ❶ a set of clothes worn together ❷ a set of equipment ❸ (*informal*) a team or organization

outflow NOUN ❶ flowing out; what flows out ❷ a pipe for liquid flowing out

outgoing ADJECTIVE ❶ soon to leave or retire from office ❷ sociable and friendly

outgoings PLURAL NOUN what you have to spend; expenditure

outgrow VERB ❶ to grow out of clothes or habits ❷ to grow faster or larger than another person or thing

outgrowth NOUN something that

grows out of another thing

outhouse NOUN a small building, such as a shed or barn, that belongs to a house but is separate from it

outing NOUN a journey for pleasure

outlandish ADJECTIVE looking or sounding strange or foreign

outlast VERB to last longer than something else

outlaw NOUN a robber or bandit who is hiding to avoid being caught and is not protected by the law

outlaw VERB to make something illegal

outlay NOUN the amount of money spent on something

outlet NOUN ❶ a way for something to get out ❷ a way of expressing strong feelings ❸ a place from which goods are sold or distributed

outline NOUN ❶ a line round the outside of something, showing its boundary or shape ❷ a summary

outline VERB ❶ to make an outline of something ❷ to summarize something

outlive VERB to live or last longer than another person or thing

outlook NOUN ❶ a view on which people look out ❷ a person's mental attitude to something ❸ what seems likely to happen in the future

outlying ADJECTIVE far from the centre; remote

outmanoeuvre VERB to use skill or cunning to gain an advantage over someone

outmoded ADJECTIVE out of date

outnumber VERB to be greater in number than another group

outpatient NOUN a person who visits a hospital for treatment but does not stay there

outpost NOUN a small town or camp that is in a remote place

output NOUN ❶ the amount produced, especially by a factory or business ❷ the information or results produced by a computer

outrage NOUN ❶ a strong feeling of shock and anger ❷ something that shocks people by being very wicked or cruel

outrage VERB to shock and anger people greatly

outrageous ADJECTIVE making people feel very angry or shocked

outrider NOUN a person riding on a motorcycle as an escort or guard

outright ADVERB ❶ completely; not gradually ❷ frankly

outright ADJECTIVE thorough or complete

outrun VERB to run faster or further than someone else

outset NOUN ➤ at or from the outset at or from the beginning of something

outside NOUN the outer side, surface or part of something

outside ADJECTIVE ❶ on or coming from the outside ❷ remote or slight

outside ADVERB on or to the outside; outdoors

outside PREPOSITION on or to the outside of

outside broadcast NOUN

(*British*) a broadcast made where something is happening and not in a studio

outsider NOUN ❶ a person who does not belong to a certain group ❷ a horse or person that people think has no chance of winning a race or competition

outsize ADJECTIVE much larger than average

outskirts PLURAL NOUN the parts of a town or city on its outside edge, furthest from the centre

outspoken ADJECTIVE speaking or spoken very frankly

outspread ADJECTIVE spread out

outstanding ADJECTIVE ❶ extremely good or distinguished ❷ an outstanding debt or bill is not yet paid or dealt with

outstretched ADJECTIVE reaching out as far as possible

outstrip VERB ❶ to run faster or further than someone else ❷ to achieve more or be more successful, than someone else

outward ADJECTIVE ❶ going outwards ❷ on the outside

outwardly ADVERB on the surface; for people to see

outwards ADVERB (*British*) towards the outside

outweigh VERB to be greater in weight or importance than something else

outwit VERB to deceive or defeat someone by being clever or crafty

ova *plural* of **ovum**

oval ADJECTIVE shaped like an O, rounded and longer than it is broad

oval NOUN an oval shape

ovary NOUN ❶ either of the two organs in which ova or egg-cells are produced in a woman's or female animal's body ❷ part of the pistil in a plant, from which fruit is formed

ovation NOUN enthusiastic applause

oven NOUN a closed space in which things are cooked or heated

over PREPOSITION ❶ above; higher than ❷ more than ❸ concerning; about ❹ across the top of; on or to the other side of ❺ during ❻ being better than

over ADVERB ❶ out and down from the top or edge; from an upright position ❷ so that a different side shows ❸ at or to a place; across ❹ remaining; still available ❺ all through; thoroughly ❻ at an end

over NOUN a series of six balls bowled in cricket

over- PREFIX too much; too (as in *over-anxious*)

overact VERB an actor overacts when they act their part in an exaggerated manner

overall ADJECTIVE including everything; total

overall ADVERB taken as a whole

overall NOUN a type of coat worn over other clothes to protect them when working

overalls PLURAL NOUN a piece of clothing, like a shirt and trousers combined, worn over other clothes to protect them

overarm ADJECTIVE & ADVERB (*chiefly British*) with your arm lifted above shoulder level and coming down in front of your body

overawed *ADJECTIVE* so impressed by something that you feel nervous or frightened

overbalance *VERB* (*chiefly British*) to lose balance and fall over

overbearing *ADJECTIVE* trying to control other people in an unpleasant way

overboard *ADVERB* over the side of a ship into the water

overcast *ADJECTIVE* covered with cloud

overcoat *NOUN* a warm outdoor coat

overcome *VERB* ❶ to find a way of dealing with a problem or difficulty ❷ to win a victory over someone; to defeat someone

overcrowded *ADJECTIVE* an overcrowded place or vehicle has too many people crammed into it

overdo *VERB* overdoes, overdoing, overdid, overdone ❶ to do something too much ❷ to cook food for too long

overdose *NOUN* too large a dose of a drug

overdose *VERB* to take an overdose

overdraft *NOUN* the amount by which a bank account is overdrawn

overdraw *VERB* to draw more money from a bank account than the amount you have in it

overdrive *NOUN* ➤ go into overdrive to start being very active

overdue *ADJECTIVE* late; not paid or arrived by the proper time

overestimate *VERB* to estimate something too highly

overflow *VERB* to flow over the edge or limits of something

overflow *NOUN* ❶ an amount of something that overflows ❷ an outlet for excess liquid

overgrown *ADJECTIVE* covered with weeds or unwanted plants

overhang *VERB* to jut out over something

overhang *NOUN* a part of a building that juts out

overhaul *VERB* ❶ to examine something thoroughly and repair it if necessary ❷ to overtake someone or something

overhaul *NOUN* an examination and repair of something

overhead *ADJECTIVE & ADVERB* ❶ above the level of your head ❷ in the sky

overheads *PLURAL NOUN* the expenses of running a business

overhear *VERB* to hear something accidentally or without the speaker intending you to hear it

overjoyed *ADJECTIVE* filled with great joy

overland *ADJECTIVE & ADVERB* travelling over the land, not by sea or air

overlap *VERB* ❶ two things overlap when one lies across part of the other ❷ events overlap when they happen partly at the same time

overlay *VERB* to cover something with a layer; to lie on top of something

overlay *NOUN* a thing laid over another

overleaf *ADVERB* on the other side of the page

overload VERB ① to put too great a load on someone or something

overlook VERB ① to fail to notice or consider something ② to overlook a mistake or offence is to ignore it or decide not to punish it ③ to have a view of a place from above

overly ADVERB too; excessively

overnight ADJECTIVE & ADVERB of or during a night

overpower VERB ① to defeat someone by being stronger than they are ② to affect you very strongly

overpowering ADJECTIVE very strong or powerful

overrate VERB to have too high an opinion of something

overreach VERB ➤ overreach yourself to fail through being too ambitious

override VERB ① to be more important than something ② to stop an automatic process and control it yourself ③ to overrule someone or something

overriding ADJECTIVE more important than anything else

overrule VERB to reject a suggestion or decision by using your authority

overrun VERB ① to spread all over a place in large numbers ② to go on for longer than it should

overseas ADVERB across or beyond the sea; abroad

overseas ADJECTIVE from abroad; foreign

oversee VERB to watch over people working to make sure things are done properly

overshadow VERB ① to cast a shadow over something ② to make a person or thing seem unimportant in comparison

overshoot VERB to go beyond a target or limit

oversight NOUN a mistake you make by not noticing something

oversleep VERB to sleep for longer than you intended

overspill NOUN ① what spills over ② the extra population of a town, who take homes in nearby districts

overstep VERB to go beyond a limit

overt ADJECTIVE done or shown openly

overtake VERB ① to pass a moving vehicle or person ② to affect you without warning

overtax VERB ① to tax people too heavily ② to put too heavy a burden or strain on someone

overthrow VERB to remove a ruler or government from power by force

overthrow NOUN ① overthrowing a ruler or government ② throwing a ball too far

overtime NOUN time spent working outside the normal hours; payment for this

overtone NOUN a feeling or quality that is suggested but not expressed directly

overture NOUN ① a piece of music written as an introduction to an opera or ballet ② a friendly attempt to start a discussion or relationship

overturn VERB ① to turn over or upside down or to make something do this ❷ to reverse a legal decision

overview NOUN a general outline of a subject or situation that gives the main ideas without explaining all the details

overweight ADJECTIVE too heavy or fat

overwhelm VERB ❶ to have a strong emotional effect on someone ❷ to defeat someone completely ❸ to come in such large numbers that you cannot deal with them

overwhelming ADJECTIVE extremely great or strong

overwork VERB ❶ to work too hard or to make someone work too hard ❷ to use something too often

overwork NOUN working too hard

overwrought ADJECTIVE very upset and nervous or worried

ovoid ADJECTIVE egg-shaped

ovulate VERB to produce an ovum from an ovary

ovum (say oh-vum) NOUN ova a female cell that can develop into a new individual when it is fertilized

owe VERB ❶ to have a duty to pay or give something to someone, especially money ❷ to have something because of the action of another person or thing

owing to PREPOSITION because of; caused by

owl NOUN a bird of prey with large eyes and a short beak, usually flying at night

own ADJECTIVE belonging to yourself or itself

own VERB to have something as your property

owner NOUN the person who owns something

own goal NOUN a goal scored by a member of a team against their own side

ox NOUN oxen a male animal of the cattle family kept for its meat and for pulling carts

oxide NOUN a compound of oxygen and one other element

oxidize (also **oxidise**) VERB ❶ to combine or to cause a substance to combine, with oxygen ❷ to coat something with an oxide

oxtail NOUN meat from the tail of a cow, used to make soup or stew

oxygen NOUN a colourless odourless tasteless gas that exists in the air and is essential for living things

oxymoron (say oksi-**mor**-on) NOUN putting together words which seem to contradict one another, e.g. bitter-sweet, living death

oyster NOUN a kind of shellfish whose shell sometimes contains a pearl

ozone NOUN a form of oxygen with a sharp smell

ozone layer NOUN a layer of ozone high in the atmosphere, which protects the earth from harmful amounts of the sun's radiation

Pp

p ABBREVIATION penny or pence

p. ABBREVIATION page

pa NOUN (informal) father

pace NOUN ❶ one step in walking or running ❷ the speed at which someone moves or something happens

pace VERB ❶ to walk with slow or regular steps ❷ to measure a distance in paces

pacemaker NOUN ❶ a person who sets the pace for someone else in a race ❷ an electrical device for keeping the heart beating

pacific (say pa-**sif**-ik) ADJECTIVE peaceful; making or loving peace

pacifist (say **pas**-if-ist) NOUN a person who believes that war is always wrong

pacify VERB to calm a person down

pack NOUN ❶ a bundle or collection of things wrapped or tied together ❷ a set of playing cards (usually 52) ❸ a bag carried on your back ❹ a large amount ❺ a group of hounds, wolves or other animals that hunt together ❻ a group of Brownies or Cub Scouts

pack VERB ❶ to put things into a suitcase, bag or box in order to move or store them ❷ to crowd together and fill a place

package NOUN ❶ a parcel or packet ❷ a number of things offered or accepted together

package holiday NOUN a holiday with all the travel and accommodation arranged and included in the price

packaging NOUN the container and wrapping in which something is sold

packed ADJECTIVE ❶ a room or space is packed when it is crowded with people ❷ full of something

packet NOUN a small box or bag in which something is sold

pack ice NOUN a mass of pieces of ice floating in the sea

pact NOUN an agreement or treaty

pad NOUN ❶ a set of sheets of paper fastened together at one edge ❷ a soft thick mass of material, used to protect or stuff something ❸ a piece of soft material worn to protect your leg in cricket and other games ❹ the soft fleshy part under an animal's foot or the end of a finger or toe ❺ a flat surface from which rockets are launched or where helicopters take off and land

pad VERB ❶ to walk softly ❷ to put a pad on or in something

padding NOUN material used to pad things

paddle NOUN ❶ a short oar with a broad blade; something shaped like this ❷ (British) walking about with bare feet in shallow water

paddle VERB ❶ (British) to walk about with bare feet in shallow water ❷ to move a boat along with a paddle or paddles; to row gently

paddock NOUN a small field where horses are kept

paddy NOUN a field where rice is grown

padlock NOUN a lock with a metal loop that passes through a ring or chain

padlock VERB to lock something with a padlock

padre (say **pah**-dray) NOUN (informal) a chaplain in the armed forces

paediatrics (say peed-ee-at-riks) NOUN the study of children's diseases

pagan (say **pay**-gan) NOUN ❶ a person who believes in a religion which is not one of the chief religions of the world ❷ a follower of a modern religion based on reverence for nature

page NOUN ❶ a piece of paper that is part of a book, magazine or newspaper; one side of this ❷ the information that you can see on a computer screen at any one time ❸ a boy or man employed to go on errands or be an attendant ❹ a young boy attending a bride at a wedding

pageant NOUN ❶ a play or entertainment about historical events and people ❷ a procession of people in costume as an entertainment

pagoda (say pag-**oh**-da) NOUN a Buddhist tower or a Hindu temple shaped like a pyramid, in India and the Far East

paid past tense of pay

pail NOUN a bucket

pain NOUN ❶ an unpleasant feeling caused by injury or disease ❷ suffering in the mind

pain VERB to cause suffering or distress to someone

painful ADJECTIVE causing pain

painfully ADVERB ❶ extremely ❷ in a way that causes pain

painkiller NOUN a medicine or drug that reduces pain

painless ADJECTIVE not causing any pain

painstaking ADJECTIVE very careful and thorough

paint NOUN a liquid substance put on something to colour it

paint VERB ❶ to put paint on something ❷ to make a picture with paints

paintbrush NOUN a brush you use for painting with

painter NOUN a person who paints

painting NOUN ❶ a painted picture ❷ using paints to make a picture

pair NOUN ❶ a set of two things or people ❷ something made of two joined parts

pair VERB to put two things together as a pair

pal NOUN (informal) a friend

palace NOUN a grand building where a king, queen or other important person lives

Palaeolithic (say pal-ee-o-**lith**-ik) ADJECTIVE belonging to the early part of the Stone Age

palaeontology (say pal-ee-on-**tol**-o-jee) NOUN the study of fossils

palatable ADJECTIVE tasting pleasant

palate NOUN ❶ the roof of your mouth ❷ a person's sense of taste

pale ADJECTIVE ❶ almost white ❷ without much colour or brightness

palette NOUN a board on which an artist mixes colours ready for use

palindrome NOUN a word or phrase that reads the same backwards as forwards, e.g. radar or Madam, I'm Adam

paling NOUN a fence made of

wooden posts or railings; one of its posts

pall (say pawl) NOUN ❶ a cloth spread over a coffin ❷ a thick dark cloud of something

pall VERB to become uninteresting or boring after a time

pallbearer NOUN a person helping to carry the coffin at a funeral

pallet NOUN ❶ a mattress stuffed with straw ❷ a hard narrow bed ❸ a large platform for carrying goods that are being stacked, especially one that can be lifted by a forklift truck

pallid ADJECTIVE pale, especially because of illness

pallor NOUN paleness in a person's face, especially because of illness

palm NOUN ❶ the inner part of the hand, between the fingers and the wrist ❷ a palm tree

palm VERB to pick something up secretly and hide it in the palm of your hand

palmistry NOUN fortune-telling by looking at the creases in the palm of a person's hand

palm tree NOUN a tropical tree with large leaves and no branches

palpable ADJECTIVE ❶ able to be touched or felt ❷ obvious

palsy (say **pawl**-zee) NOUN (old use) paralysis with tremors

paltry (say **pol**-tree) ADJECTIVE very small and almost worthless

pampas NOUN wide grassy plains in South America

pampas grass NOUN a tall grass with long feathery flowers

pamper VERB to take care of

someone very well and make them feel as comfortable as possible

pamphlet NOUN a leaflet or booklet giving information on a subject

pan NOUN ❶ a wide container with a flat base, used for cooking ❷ something shaped like this ❸ the bowl of a lavatory

panacea (say pan-a-**see**-a) NOUN a cure for all kinds of diseases or troubles

panache (say pan-**ash**) NOUN a confident stylish manner

panama NOUN a hat made of a fine straw-like material

pancake NOUN a thin round cake of batter fried on both sides

pancreas (say **pan**-kree-as) NOUN a gland near the stomach, producing insulin and digestive juices

panda NOUN a large bear-like black-and-white animal found in China

pandemonium NOUN uproar and complete confusion

pander VERB ➤ **pander to someone** to let someone have whatever they want even though you know it is not right

pane NOUN a sheet of glass in a window

panel NOUN ❶ a long flat piece of wood, metal, etc. that is part of a door, wall or piece of furniture ❷ a flat board with controls or instruments on it ❸ a group of people chosen to discuss or decide something

pang NOUN a sudden sharp feeling of pain or emotion

panic NOUN sudden uncontrollable fear that stops you from thinking clearly

panic VERB to be filled with panic

pannier NOUN a large bag or basket hung on one side of a bicycle, motorcycle or horse

panorama NOUN a view or picture of a wide area

pansy NOUN a small brightly coloured garden flower with velvety petals

pant VERB to take short quick breaths, usually after running or working hard

panther NOUN a leopard, especially a black one

panties PLURAL NOUN (*informal*) short knickers

pantomime NOUN a Christmas entertainment, usually based on a fairy tale

pantry NOUN a small room for storing food and crockery

pants PLURAL NOUN ❶ (*informal*) underpants or knickers ❷ (*North American*) trousers

pap NOUN ❶ soft food suitable for babies ❷ trivial entertainment; nonsense

papa NOUN (*old use*) father

papacy (*say* **pay**-pa-see) NOUN the position of pope

papal (*say* **pay**-pal) ADJECTIVE to do with the pope

paparazzi (*say* **pap**-a-rat-si) PLURAL NOUN photographers who pursue famous people to get photographs of them

paper NOUN ❶ a substance made in thin sheets from wood, rags, etc. and used for writing, printing, or

drawing on or for wrapping things ❷ a newspaper ❸ wallpaper ❹ a set of examination questions ❺ papers are official documents

paper VERB to cover a wall or room with wallpaper

paperback NOUN a book with a thin flexible cover

paperweight NOUN a small heavy object used for holding down loose papers

paperwork NOUN all the writing of reports and keeping of records that someone has to do as part of their job

papier mâché (*say* pap-yay **mash**-ay) NOUN paper made into pulp and moulded to make models, ornaments, etc.

paprika (*say* **pap**-rik-a) NOUN a powdered spice made from red pepper

papyrus (*say* pap-y-rus) NOUN ❶ a kind of paper made from the stems of a plant like a reed, used in ancient Egypt ❷ a document written on this paper

par NOUN the number of strokes in golf that a good player should normally take for a particular hole or course

parable NOUN a story told to teach people something, especially one of those told by Jesus Christ

parabola (*say* pa-**rab**-ol-a) NOUN a curve like the path of an object thrown up into the air and falling down again

parachute NOUN an umbrella-like device on which people or things can fall slowly to the ground from

a
b
c
d
e
f
g
h
i
j
k
l
m
n
o
p
q
r
s
t
u
v
w
x
y
z

an aircraft

parachute VERB to fall or drop something by means of a parachute

parade NOUN ❶ a line of people or vehicles moving forward through a place as a celebration ❷ an assembly of soldiers for inspection or drill ❸ a public square or row of shops

parade VERB ❶ to move forward through a place as a celebration ❷ soldiers parade when they assemble for inspection or drill

paradise NOUN ❶ heaven or, in the Bible, the Garden of Eden ❷ a place that seems perfect

paradox NOUN a statement that seems to contradict itself but which contains a truth, e.g. 'More haste, less speed'

paraffin NOUN a kind of oil used as fuel

paragliding NOUN the sport of gliding through the air while being supported by a wide parachute

paragon NOUN a person or thing that seems to be perfect

paragraph NOUN one or more sentences on a single subject, forming a section of a piece of writing and beginning on a new line, usually slightly in from the margin of the page

parakeet NOUN a kind of small parrot

parallax NOUN what seems to be a change in the position of something when you look at it from a different place

parallel ADJECTIVE ❶ parallel lines

run side by side and the same distance apart from each other for their whole length, like railway lines ❷ similar or corresponding

parallel NOUN ❶ something similar or corresponding ❷ a comparison ❸ a line that is parallel to another ❹ a line of latitude

parallel VERB to find or be a parallel to something

parallelogram NOUN a four-sided figure with its opposite sides equal and parallel

paralyse VERB ❶ to cause paralysis in a person or part of the body ❷ to be paralysed with fear or emotion is to be so affected by it that you cannot move or do anything

paralysis NOUN being unable to move, especially because of a disease or an injury to the nerves

paramedic NOUN a person who is trained to do medical work, especially emergency first aid, but is not a fully qualified doctor

paramilitary ADJECTIVE organized like a military force but not part of the armed services

paramount ADJECTIVE more important than anything else

paranoia NOUN ❶ a mental illness in which a person has delusions or suspects and distrusts people ❷ an unjustified suspicion and mistrust of others

paranoid ADJECTIVE suffering from paranoia

paranormal ADJECTIVE beyond what is normal and can be rationally explained: supernatural

parapet NOUN a low wall along the edge of a balcony, bridge or roof

paraphernalia NOUN numerous pieces of equipment or belongings

paraphrase VERB to give the meaning of something by using different words

paraplegia NOUN paralysis of the lower half of the body

parasite NOUN an animal or plant that lives in or on another, from which it gets its food

parasol NOUN a lightweight umbrella used to shade yourself from the sun

paratroops PLURAL NOUN troops trained to be dropped from aircraft by parachute

parboil VERB to boil food until it is partly cooked

parcel NOUN something wrapped up to be sent by post or carried

parcel VERB ❶ to wrap something up as a parcel ❷ to divide something into portions

parched ADJECTIVE very dry or thirsty

parchment NOUN a kind of heavy paper, originally made from animal skins

pardon NOUN ❶ forgiveness ❷ the cancelling of a punishment

pardon VERB ❶ to forgive or excuse someone ❷ to cancel a person's punishment

pardon EXCLAMATION (also **I beg your pardon** or **pardon me**) used to mean 'I didn't hear or understand what you said.' or 'I apologize.'

pare (say pair) VERB ❶ to trim

something by cutting away the edges ❷ to reduce something gradually

parent NOUN ❶ a father or mother; an animal or plant that has produced others of its kind ❷ something that produces others of the same type

parentage NOUN who your parents are

parental (say pa-**rent**-al) ADJECTIVE to do with parents

parenthesis (say pa-**ren**-thi-sis) NOUN parentheses ❶ something extra that is put into a sentence, usually between brackets or dashes ❷ either of the pair of brackets (like these) used to mark off words from the rest of a sentence

parenthood NOUN being a parent

pariah (say pa-**ry**-a) NOUN an outcast

parish NOUN in the Christian Church, a district with its own church

park NOUN ❶ a large open area with grass and trees for public use ❷ an area of grassland or woodland belonging to a country house

park VERB to leave a vehicle somewhere for a time

parka NOUN a warm jacket with a hood attached

Parkinson's disease NOUN a disease that makes a person's arms and legs shake and the muscles become stiff

parley VERB to hold a discussion with an opponent or enemy in order to reach an agreement

parliament NOUN the assembly

that makes a country's laws

parlour NOUN (*old use*) a sitting room

parochial (say per-**oh**-kee-al) ADJECTIVE ❶ to do with a church parish ❷ having a narrow point of view; interested only in your own local area

parody NOUN an amusing imitation of the style of a writer, composer, literary work, etc.

parody VERB to make or be a parody of a person or thing

parole NOUN the release of a prisoner before the end of their sentence on the condition that they behave well

parrot NOUN a brightly-coloured tropical bird with a curved beak that can learn to repeat words or sounds

parry VERB ❶ to turn aside an opponent's weapon or blow by using your own to block it ❷ to avoid an awkward question skilfully

parse VERB to state what is the grammatical form and function of a word or words in a sentence

parsley NOUN a plant with crinkled green leaves used to flavour and decorate food

parsnip NOUN a plant with a pointed pale-yellow root used as a vegetable

parson NOUN a member of the Church of England clergy, especially a rector or vicar

parsonage NOUN a parson's house

part NOUN ❶ some but not all of a thing or number of things;

anything that belongs to something bigger ❷ the character played by an actor or actress ❸ the words spoken by a character in a play ❹ how much a person or thing is involved in something ❺ one side in an agreement or in a dispute or quarrel

part VERB ❶ two people part when they leave each other ❷ to move apart or to make people or things move apart

partake VERB ❶ to eat or drink something ❷ to take part in something

partial ADJECTIVE ❶ not complete or total ❷ favouring one side more than the other; biased or unfair

partially ADVERB partly; not completely

participant NOUN a person who takes part in something

participate VERB to take part in something or have a share in it

participle NOUN a word formed from a verb (e.g. *gone, going; guided, guiding*) and used with an auxiliary verb to form certain tenses (e.g. *It has gone. It is going.*) or the passive (e.g. *We were guided to our seats.*) or as an adjective (e.g. *a guided missile; a guiding light*). The **past participle** (e.g. *gone, guided*) describes a completed action or past condition. The **present participle** (which ends in *-ing*) describes a continuing action or condition.

particle NOUN a very small piece or amount of something

particular ADJECTIVE ❶ only this one and no other; individual

❷ special or exceptional
❸ wanting something to be exactly right; difficult to please

particular NOUN a detail or single fact

particularly ADVERB especially; more than usual or more than the rest

parting NOUN ❶ leaving or separation ❷ a line where hair is combed away in different directions

partisan NOUN ❶ a strong supporter of a party or group ❷ a member of an armed group fighting secretly against an army that has taken control of its country

partisan ADJECTIVE strongly supporting a particular cause

partition NOUN ❶ a thin wall that divides a room or space ❷ dividing a country or territory into separate parts

partition VERB ❶ to divide something into separate parts ❷ to divide a room or space with a partition

partly ADVERB to some extent but not completely

partner NOUN ❶ one of a pair of people who do something together, such as dancing or playing a game ❷ a person who jointly owns a business with one or more other people ❸ the person that someone is married to, in a civil partnership with or is having a sexual relationship with

partner VERB to be a person's partner

partnership NOUN ❶ being a partner with someone, especially in business ❷ a business owned by two or more people

part of speech NOUN any of the groups into which words are divided in grammar (noun, pronoun, determiner, adjective, verb, adverb, preposition, conjunction, exclamation)

partook past tense of partake

partridge NOUN a game bird with brown feathers

part-time ADJECTIVE & ADVERB working for only some of the normal hours

party NOUN ❶ a gathering of people to enjoy themselves ❷ a group working or travelling together ❸ an organized group of people with similar political beliefs ❹ a person who is involved in a legal agreement or dispute

pass VERB ❶ to go or move in a certain direction ❷ to go past something ❸ to move something in a certain direction ❹ to give or transfer something to another person ❺ in ball games, to kick or throw the ball to another player of your own side ❻ to be successful in a test or examination ❼ to approve or accept something ❽ to spend time doing something ❾ to happen or go by ❿ to come to an end or no longer be there ⓫ to pass a remark or comment is to make it ⓬ in a game, quiz, etc., to let your turn go by or choose not to answer

pass NOUN ❶ passing something ❷ a success in an examination ❸ in ball games, kicking or

433

throwing the ball to another player on the same side ❹ a permit to go in or out of a place ❺ a route through a gap in a range of mountains

passable ADJECTIVE ❶ satisfactory but not especially good ❷ able to be passed

passage NOUN ❶ a way through something; a corridor ❷ a journey by sea or air ❸ a section of a piece of writing or music ❹ going by or passing

passageway NOUN a passage or way through, especially between buildings

passé (say **pas**-say) ADJECTIVE no longer fashionable

passenger NOUN a person who is driven or carried in a car, train, ship or aircraft

passer-by NOUN a person who happens to be going past something

passion NOUN ❶ strong emotion ❷ a great enthusiasm for something

passionate ADJECTIVE full of passion or strong feeling

passive ADJECTIVE ❶ not resisting or fighting against something ❷ acted upon and not active ❸ (in grammar) describing the form of a verb when the subject of the verb receives the action, e.g. was hit in 'She was hit on the head'. See also **active**.

passive smoking NOUN breathing in other people's cigarette smoke, thought of as a health risk

Passover NOUN a Jewish religious festival commemorating the freeing of the Jews from slavery in Egypt

passport NOUN an official document that allows you to travel abroad

password NOUN ❶ a secret word or phrase that you need to know in order to be allowed into a place ❷ a word you need to key in to gain access to a computer system or interface

past ADJECTIVE of the time gone by

past NOUN ❶ the time gone by ❷ (in grammar) the tense of a verb used to describe an action that happened at a time before now, e.g. took is the past tense of take

past PREPOSITION ❶ beyond a certain place ❷ after a certain time

pasta NOUN an Italian food consisting of a dried paste made from flour and shaped into macaroni, spaghetti, lasagne, etc.

paste NOUN ❶ a soft, moist and sticky substance ❷ a glue, especially for paper ❸ a soft edible mixture

paste VERB ❶ to stick something onto a surface by using paste ❷ to coat something with paste

pastel NOUN ❶ a crayon that is like chalk ❷ a light delicate colour

pasteurize (also **pasteurise**) VERB to purify milk by heating and then cooling it

pastille NOUN a small flavoured sweet that you suck

pastime NOUN something you do to make time pass pleasantly; a hobby or game

pastor NOUN a member of the clergy who is in charge of a church or congregation

pastoral ADJECTIVE ❶ to do with country life ❷ to do with a pastor or a pastor's duties

pastry NOUN ❶ dough made with flour, fat and water, rolled flat and baked ❷ something made of pastry

pasture NOUN land covered with grass that cattle, sheep or horses can eat

pasture VERB to put animals to graze in a pasture

pasty (say pas-tee) NOUN (British) a folded pastry case with a filling of meat and vegetables

pasty (say pay-stee) ADJECTIVE looking pale and unhealthy

pat VERB to tap something gently with the open hand or with something flat

pat NOUN ❶ a patting movement or sound ❷ a small piece of butter

patch NOUN ❶ a piece of material put over a hole or damaged place ❷ an area that is different from its surroundings ❸ a piece of ground ❹ a small area or piece of something

patch VERB to put a patch on something

patchwork NOUN ❶ needlework in which small pieces of different cloth are sewn edge to edge ❷ a collection of different things making up a whole

patchy ADJECTIVE occurring in some areas but not others; uneven

pate NOUN (old use) the top of a person's head

pâté (say pat-ay) NOUN paste made of meat or fish

patent (say pat-ent or pay-tent) NOUN the official right given to an inventor to make or sell their invention and to prevent other people from copying it

patent (say pay-tent) ADJECTIVE ❶ protected by a patent ❷ very clear or obvious

patent VERB to get a patent for an idea or invention

patent leather NOUN glossy leather

patently ADVERB clearly or obviously

paternal ADJECTIVE ❶ to do with a father ❷ fatherly

path NOUN ❶ a narrow way along which people or animals can walk ❷ a line along which a person or thing moves ❸ a course of action

pathetic ADJECTIVE ❶ making you feel pity or sympathy ❷ poor, weak or useless

pathology NOUN the study of diseases of the body

pathos (say pay-thoss) NOUN a quality of making people feel pity or sympathy

patience NOUN ❶ being patient ❷ a card game for one person

patient ADJECTIVE able to wait for a long time or put up with trouble or inconvenience without getting anxious or angry

patient NOUN a person who is receiving treatment from a doctor or dentist

patio NOUN a paved area beside a house

435

patriarch (say **pay**-tree-ark) NOUN
❶ a man who is head of a family or tribe. Compare with matriarch.
❷ a bishop of high rank in the Orthodox Christian churches

patriot (say *pay*-tree-ot or *pat*-ree-ot) NOUN a person who loves their country and supports it loyally

patriotic ADJECTIVE loving your country and supporting it loyally

patrol VERB to walk or travel regularly over an area in order to guard it and see that all is well

patrol NOUN ❶ a patrolling group of people, ships, aircraft, etc. ❷ a group of Scouts or Guides

patron (say **pay**-tron) NOUN
❶ someone who supports a person or cause with money or encouragement ❷ a regular customer

patronage (say *pat*-ron-ij) NOUN support given by a patron

patronize (also **patronise**) (say *pat*-ron-yz) VERB ❶ to be a regular customer of a particular shop, restaurant, etc. ❷ to talk to someone in a way that shows you think they are stupid or inferior to you

patron saint NOUN a saint who is thought to protect a particular place or activity

patter NOUN ❶ a series of light tapping sounds ❷ the quick talk of a comedian, conjuror, salesperson, etc.

patter VERB to make light tapping sounds

pattern NOUN ❶ a repeated arrangement of lines, shapes or colours ❷ a thing to be copied in order to make something ❸ the regular way in which something happens

paunch NOUN a large belly

pauper NOUN a person who is very poor

pause NOUN a temporary stop in speaking or doing something

pause VERB ❶ to stop speaking or doing something for a short time before starting again ❷ to temporarily interrupt the playing of a piece of music, film, computer game, etc.

pave VERB to lay a hard surface on a road or path

pavement NOUN (*British*) a paved path along the side of a street

pavilion NOUN ❶ a building at a sports ground for players and spectators to use ❷ an ornamental building or shelter used for dances, concerts or exhibitions

paw NOUN the foot of an animal that has claws

paw VERB to touch or scrape something with a hand or foot

pawn NOUN ❶ the least valuable piece in chess ❷ a person whose actions are controlled by someone else

pawn VERB to leave something with a pawnbroker in exchange for money

pawnbroker NOUN a shopkeeper who lends money to people in return for objects that they leave and which are sold if the money is not paid back

pawpaw NOUN an orange-coloured

tropical fruit used as food

pay VERB pays, paying, paid ❶ to give money in return for goods or services ❷ to give what is owed ❸ to be profitable or worthwhile ❹ to give or express something ❺ to suffer a penalty for something you have done ❻ to let out a rope by loosening it gradually

pay NOUN salary or wages

payable ADJECTIVE that must be paid

payment NOUN ❶ paying someone or being paid for something ❷ an amount of money paid

PC ABBREVIATION ❶ personal computer ❷ police constable

PE ABBREVIATION physical education

pea NOUN the small round green seed of a climbing plant, growing inside a pod and used as a vegetable; the plant bearing these pods

peace NOUN ❶ a time when there is no war, violence or disorder ❷ quietness and calm

peaceable ADJECTIVE fond of peace; not quarrelsome or warlike

peaceful ADJECTIVE ❶ quiet and calm ❷ not involving violence

peach NOUN ❶ a round soft juicy fruit with a pinkish or yellowish skin and a large stone ❷ (informal) a thing of great quality

peacock NOUN a large male bird with a long brightly coloured tail that it can spread out like a fan

peak NOUN ❶ a pointed top of a mountain ❷ the highest or most intense part of something ❸ the part of a cap that sticks out in front

peak VERB to reach the highest point or value

peaky ADJECTIVE (British) looking pale and ill

peal NOUN ❶ the loud ringing of a bell or set of bells ❷ a loud burst of thunder or laughter

peal VERB bells peal when they ring loudly

peanut NOUN a small round nut that grows in a pod in the ground

peanut butter NOUN roasted peanuts crushed into a paste

pear NOUN a juicy fruit that gets narrower near the stalk

pearl NOUN a small shiny white ball found in the shells of some oysters and used as a jewel

pearl barley NOUN grains of barley made small by grinding

peasant NOUN a person who belongs to a farming community, especially in poor areas of the world

peat NOUN rotted plant material that can be dug out of the ground and used as fuel or in gardening

pebble NOUN a small round stone found on a beach or in a river

peck VERB ❶ to bite at something quickly with the beak ❷ to kiss someone lightly on the cheek

peck NOUN ❶ a quick bite by a bird ❷ a light kiss on the cheek

peckish ADJECTIVE (British) (informal) hungry

pectoral ADJECTIVE to do with the chest or breast

peculiar ADJECTIVE ❶ strange or unusual ❷ belonging to a

437

particular person, place or thing; restricted ❹ special

peculiarity NOUN a strange or distinctive feature or habit

pecuniary ADJECTIVE (*formal*) to do with money

pedal NOUN a lever that you press with your foot to operate a bicycle, car or machine or to play certain musical instruments

pedal VERB to use a pedal; to move or work something, especially a bicycle, by means of pedals

pedant NOUN a pedantic person

pedantic ADJECTIVE too concerned with minor details or with sticking strictly to formal rules

peddle VERB ❶ to go from house to house selling goods ❷ to sell illegal drugs ❸ to try to get people to accept an idea or way of life

pedestal NOUN the raised base on which a statue or pillar stands

pedestrian NOUN a person who is walking

pedestrian ADJECTIVE ordinary and dull

pedestrian crossing NOUN (*British*) a place where pedestrians can cross the road safely

pedigree NOUN a list of a person's or animal's ancestors, especially to show how well an animal has been bred

pedlar NOUN (*chiefly British*) a person who goes from house to house selling small things

peek VERB to have a quick or sly look at something

peek NOUN a quick or sly look

peel NOUN the skin of certain fruits

and vegetables

peel VERB ❶ to remove the peel or covering from something ❷ to come off in strips or layers ❸ to lose a covering or skin

peelings PLURAL NOUN strips of skin peeled from potatoes etc.

peep VERB ❶ to look quickly or secretly ❷ to look through a narrow opening ❸ to come slowly or briefly into view

peep NOUN a quick look

peephole NOUN a small hole in a door or wall that you can look through

peer VERB to look at something closely or with difficulty

peer NOUN ❶ your peers are the people who are the same age or status as you ❷ a member of the nobility

peerage NOUN ❶ peers ❷ the rank of peer

peer group NOUN a group of people of roughly the same age or status

peerless ADJECTIVE without an equal; better than the others

peer pressure NOUN the pressure to do what others in your peer group do

peeved ADJECTIVE (*informal*) annoyed or irritated

peevish ADJECTIVE irritable or bad-tempered

peg NOUN a piece of wood or metal or plastic for fastening things together or for hanging things on

peg VERB to fix something with pegs

peke NOUN (*informal*) a Pekinese

Pekinese, Pekingese NOUN a small

kind of dog with short legs, a flat
face and long silky hair

pelican NOUN a large bird with a
pouch in its long beak for storing
fish

pelican crossing NOUN (British) a
place where pedestrians can cross
a street safely by operating lights
that signal traffic to stop

pellet NOUN a tiny ball of metal,
food, paper, etc.

pell-mell ADVERB & ADJECTIVE in a
hasty uncontrolled way

pelmet NOUN an ornamental strip of
wood or material above a window,
used to conceal a curtain rail

pelt VERB ❶ to throw a lot of things
at someone ❷ to run fast ❸ to
rain very hard

pelt NOUN an animal skin, especially
with the fur still on it

pelvis NOUN the round framework
of bones at the lower end of the
spine

pen NOUN ❶ an instrument with
a point for writing with ink ❷ an
enclosure for sheep, cattle, pigs
or other farm animals ❸ a female
swan. Compare with cob.

pen VERB ❶ to shut animals into a
pen or other enclosed space ❷ to
write something

penal (say **peen**-al) ADJECTIVE to do
with the punishment of criminals,
especially in prisons

penalize (also **penalise**) VERB to
punish someone or make them
suffer a disadvantage

penalty NOUN ❶ a punishment for
breaking a rule or law ❷ a point or
advantage given to one side in a

game when a member of the other
side has broken a rule, e.g. a free
kick at goal in football

penance NOUN a punishment that
you willingly suffer to show that
you regret something wrong that
you have done

pence PLURAL NOUN see penny

penchant (say **pahn**-shahn) NOUN a
special liking for something

pencil NOUN an instrument for
drawing or writing, made of a thin
stick of graphite or coloured chalk
enclosed in a cylinder of wood
or metal

pencil VERB to write or mark
something with a pencil

pendant NOUN an ornament worn
hanging on a cord or chain round
the neck

pending ADJECTIVE ❶ waiting to
be decided or settled ❷ about
to happen

pending PREPOSITION while waiting
for; until

pendulum NOUN a weight hung so
that it can swing from side to side,
especially in the works of a clock

penetrate VERB to make or find a
way through or into something

penetrating ADJECTIVE ❶ showing
great insight or understanding
❷ clearly heard above other
sounds

penfriend NOUN a friend, usually in
another country, who you write to
without meeting

penguin NOUN an Antarctic seabird
that cannot fly but uses its wings
as flippers for swimming

penicillin NOUN an antibiotic

obtained from mould

peninsula *NOUN* a piece of land that is almost surrounded by water

penis (say **peen**-iss) *NOUN* the part of the body with which a male urinates and has sexual intercourse

penitent *ADJECTIVE* sorry for having done something wrong

penknife *NOUN* a small folding knife

pen name *NOUN* a name used by an author instead of their real name

pennant *NOUN* a long pointed flag

penniless *ADJECTIVE* having no money; very poor

penny *NOUN* ❶ a British coin worth ¹⁄₁₀₀ of a pound ❷ a former coin worth ½ of a shilling

pension *NOUN* an income consisting of regular payments made to someone who is retired, widowed or disabled

pension *VERB* to pension someone off is to make them retire and pay them a pension

pensioner *NOUN* a person who receives a pension

pensive *ADJECTIVE* deep in thought

pentagon *NOUN* a flat shape with five sides and five angles

pentameter *NOUN* a line of verse with five rhythmic beats

pentathlon *NOUN* an athletic contest consisting of five events

penthouse *NOUN* an expensive flat at the top of a tall building

pent-up *ADJECTIVE* pent-up feelings are ones that you hold inside and do not express

penultimate *ADJECTIVE* last but one

peony *NOUN* a plant with large round red, pink or white flowers

people *PLURAL NOUN* human beings; persons

people *NOUN* a community or nation

people *VERB* to fill a place with people; to populate a place

pep *NOUN* (*informal*) vigour or energy

pepper *NOUN* ❶ a hot-tasting powder used to flavour food ❷ a bright green, red or yellow vegetable

pepper *VERB* ❶ to sprinkle something with pepper ❷ to pelt an area with many small objects

peppercorn *NOUN* the dried black berry from which pepper is made

peppermint *NOUN* ❶ a kind of mint used for flavouring ❷ a sweet flavoured with this mint

pepperoni *NOUN* beef and pork sausage seasoned with pepper

pep talk *NOUN* (*informal*) a talk given to someone to encourage them

per *PREPOSITION* for each

per annum *ADVERB* for each year; yearly

per capita (say **kap**-it-a) *ADVERB & ADJECTIVE* for each person

perceive *VERB* to see, notice or understand something

per cent *ADVERB* for or in every hundred

percentage *NOUN* an amount or rate expressed as a proportion of 100

perceptible *ADJECTIVE* able to be seen or noticed

perception NOUN ❶ the ability to notice or understand something ❷ receiving information through the senses, especially the sense of sight

perceptive ADJECTIVE quick to notice or understand things

perch NOUN ❶ a place where a bird sits or rests ❷ a seat high up ❸ an edible freshwater fish

perch VERB ❶ to rest on a perch or place something on a perch ❷ to sit on the edge of something or somewhere high or narrow

percolate VERB to flow through small holes or spaces

percolator NOUN a pot for making coffee, in which boiling water percolates through coffee grounds

percussion NOUN ❶ musical instruments that you play by hitting them or shaking them, such as drums and cymbals ❷ the striking of one thing against another

peregrine NOUN a kind of falcon

perennial ADJECTIVE lasting for a long time; happening again and again

perennial NOUN a plant that lives for many years

perfect (say **per**-fikt) ADJECTIVE ❶ so good that it cannot be made any better ❷ complete ❸ the perfect tense of a verb shows a completed action, e.g. He has arrived.

perfect (say per-**fekt**) VERB to make a thing perfect

perfection NOUN being perfect

perfectionist NOUN a person who is only satisfied if something is done perfectly

perfectly ADVERB ❶ completely ❷ without any faults

perforate VERB ❶ to make tiny holes in something, especially so that it can be torn off easily ❷ to pierce a surface

perforation NOUN perforations are the tiny holes made in something so that it can be torn off easily

perform VERB ❶ to do something in front of an audience ❷ to do or carry out something

performance NOUN ❶ a form of entertainment presented to an audience ❷ the way in which someone does something or the standard they reach

performer NOUN a person who performs an entertainment in front of an audience

perfume NOUN ❶ a pleasant smell ❷ a pleasant-smelling liquid that you put on your skin

perfume VERB to give a sweet smell to something

perfunctory ADJECTIVE done without much care or interest

pergola NOUN an arch formed by climbing plants growing over trellis-work

perhaps ADVERB it may be; possibly

peril NOUN great danger

perilous ADJECTIVE very dangerous

perimeter NOUN ❶ the outer edge or boundary of something ❷ the distance round the edge

period NOUN ❶ a length of time ❷ the time allowed for a lesson in school ❸ the time when a woman

A

or girl menstruates ❹ a full stop

B

periodic ADJECTIVE occurring at regular intervals

C

periodical NOUN a magazine published at regular intervals (e.g. monthly)

D

E

periodic table NOUN a table in which the chemical elements are arranged in order of increasing atomic number

F

G

peripheral ADJECTIVE ❶ of minor importance ❷ at the edge or boundary

H

I

periphery (say per-**if**-er-ee) NOUN the part at the edge or boundary

J

periscope NOUN a device with a tube and mirrors with which a person in a trench or submarine etc. can see things that are otherwise out of sight

K

L

M

perish VERB ❶ to die or be destroyed ❷ to rot

N

O

perishable ADJECTIVE perishable food is likely to go off quickly

perished ADJECTIVE (informal) feeling very cold

Q

periwinkle NOUN ❶ a trailing plant with blue or white flowers ❷ a winkle (a kind of edible shellfish)

R

S

perjury NOUN telling a lie while you are on oath to speak the truth in a law court

T

U

perk VERB ➤ **perk up** to become more cheerful or lively

V

perk NOUN (informal) something extra given to a worker

W

X

perky ADJECTIVE lively and cheerful

Y

perm NOUN treatment of the hair to give it long-lasting waves or curls

Z

permafrost NOUN a permanently frozen layer of soil in polar regions

permanent ADJECTIVE lasting for always or for a very long time

permeable ADJECTIVE allowing liquid or gas to pass through it

permeate VERB to spread into every part of a thing or place

permission NOUN the right to do something, given by someone else

permit (say per-**mit**) VERB to allow someone to do something or allow something to be done

permit (say **per**-mit) NOUN written or printed permission to do something or go somewhere

permutation NOUN ❶ changing the order of a set of things ❷ a changed order

pernicious ADJECTIVE very harmful

peroxide NOUN a chemical used for bleaching hair

perpendicular ADJECTIVE upright; at a right angle (90°) to a line or surface

perpetrate VERB to commit a crime or serious error

perpetual ADJECTIVE lasting for a long time; continual

perpetuate VERB to cause something to continue or be remembered for a long time

perplex VERB to bewilder or puzzle someone

perplexed ADJECTIVE confused because you cannot understand something

perplexity NOUN a puzzled and confused state of mind

persecute VERB to be continually cruel to someone, especially because you disagree with their beliefs

persevere VERB to go on doing something even though it is difficult

Persian ADJECTIVE to do with Persia, a country in the Middle East now called Iran, or its people or language

Persian NOUN the language of Persia. The modern form of the Persian language is called Farsi.

persist VERB ❶ to continue to do something firmly or obstinately ❷ to continue to exist for a long time

persistent ADJECTIVE ❶ continuing or constant ❷ determined to continue doing something and refusing to give up

person NOUN people or persons ❶ a human being; a man, woman, or child ❷ (*in grammar*) any of the three groups of personal pronouns and forms taken by verbs. The **first person** (= *I, me, we, us*) refers to the person or people speaking; the **second person** (= *you*) refers to the person or people spoken to; the **third person** (= *he, him, she, her, it, they, them*) refers to the person or thing referred to or the people or things spoken about.

personal ADJECTIVE ❶ to do with, belonging to or done by a particular person ❷ private ❸ criticizing a person's appearance, character or private affairs

personal computer NOUN a small computer designed to be used by one person at a time

personality NOUN ❶ a person's character ❷ a well-known person

personally ADVERB ❶ in person; being actually there ❷ as far as I am concerned

personify VERB ❶ to represent a quality or idea as if it were a person ❷ to be a perfect example of something

personnel NOUN the people employed by a firm or other large organization

perspective NOUN ❶ the impression of depth and space in a picture or scene ❷ a person's point of view

Perspex NOUN (*trademark*) a tough transparent plastic used instead of glass

perspiration NOUN moisture given off by the body through the pores of the skin; sweat

perspire VERB to sweat

persuade VERB to make someone believe or agree to do something

persuasion NOUN persuading someone to believe or agree to do something

persuasive ADJECTIVE able to make someone believe or agree to do something

pertain VERB to be relevant to something

pertinent ADJECTIVE relevant to what you are talking about

perturbed ADJECTIVE worried or anxious

pervade VERB to spread all through something

perverse ADJECTIVE obstinately

doing something different from what is reasonable or expected

pervert (say per-**vert**) VERB ❶ to turn something from the right course of action ❷ to make a person behave in a wrong or unacceptable way

pervert (say **per**-vert) NOUN a person whose sexual behaviour is thought to be unnatural or unacceptable

Pesach (say **pay**-sahk) NOUN the Passover festival

pessimist NOUN a person who expects that things will turn out badly. Compare with **optimist**.

pessimistic ADJECTIVE expecting things to turn out badly

pest NOUN ❶ a destructive insect or animal, such as a locust or a mouse ❷ an annoying person or thing

pester VERB to keep annoying someone by frequent questions or requests

pesticide NOUN a substance for killing harmful insects and other pests

pestilence NOUN a deadly epidemic

pestle NOUN a tool with a heavy rounded end for pounding substances in a mortar

pet NOUN ❶ a tame animal kept at home for companionship and pleasure ❷ a person treated as a favourite

pet ADJECTIVE favourite or particular

pet VERB to stroke a person or animal affectionately

petal NOUN one of the separate coloured outer parts of a flower

peter VERB ► peter out to become

gradually less and come to an end

petition NOUN a formal request for something, especially a written one signed by many people

petition VERB to request something by a petition

petrel NOUN a kind of seabird

petrify VERB ❶ to make someone so terrified that they cannot move ❷ to turn something to stone

petrochemical NOUN a chemical substance obtained from petroleum or natural gas

petrol NOUN (British) a liquid made from petroleum, used as fuel for engines

petroleum NOUN an oil found underground that is refined to make fuel (e.g. petrol or paraffin) or for use in dry-cleaning etc.

petticoat NOUN a woman's or girl's dress-length piece of underwear worn under a skirt or dress

petty ADJECTIVE ❶ unimportant or trivial ❷ mean and small-minded

petty cash NOUN cash kept by an office for small payments

petty officer NOUN a non-commissioned officer in the navy

petulant ADJECTIVE irritable or bad-tempered, especially in a childish way

petunia NOUN a garden plant with funnel-shaped flowers

pew NOUN a long wooden seat, usually fixed in rows, in a church

pewter NOUN a grey alloy of tin and lead

pH NOUN a measure of the acidity or alkalinity of a solution. Pure water has a pH of 7, acids have a pH between 0 and 7 and alkalis have a pH between 7 and 14.

phantom NOUN ❶ a ghost ❷ something that does not really exist

Pharaoh (say **fair**-oh) NOUN the title of the king of ancient Egypt

pharmaceutical (say farm-as-**yoot**-ik-al) ADJECTIVE to do with medicinal drugs or with pharmacy

pharmacist NOUN a person who is trained to prepare and sell medicines

pharmacy NOUN ❶ a shop where medicines are prepared and sold ❷ the job of preparing medicines

phase NOUN a stage in the progress or development of something

phase VERB to do something in stages, not all at once

PhD ABBREVIATION Doctor of Philosophy; a university degree awarded to someone who has done advanced research in their subject

pheasant (say **fez**-ant) NOUN a game bird with a long tail

phenomenal ADJECTIVE amazing or remarkable

phenomenon NOUN phenomena an event or fact, especially one that is remarkable or interesting

phial NOUN a small glass bottle

philanderer NOUN a man who has many casual affairs with women

philanthropist NOUN a rich person who generously gives money to people who need it

philanthropy NOUN concern for your fellow human beings, especially as shown by kind and generous acts that benefit large numbers of people

philately (say fil-**at**-il-ee) NOUN collecting postage stamps

philistine (say **fil**-ist-yn) NOUN a person who does not like or understand art, literature, music, etc.

philosopher NOUN an expert in philosophy

philosophical ADJECTIVE ❶ to do with philosophy ❷ calm and not upset after a misfortune or disappointment

philosophy NOUN ❶ the study of truths about life, knowledge, morals, etc. ❷ a set of ideas or principles or beliefs

phlegm (say flem) NOUN thick mucus that forms in the throat and lungs when you have a bad cold

phlegmatic (say fleg-**mat**-ik) ADJECTIVE not easily excited or worried

phobia (say **foh**-bee-a) NOUN a great or abnormal fear of something

phoenix (say **feen**-iks) NOUN a mythical bird that was said to burn itself to death in a fire and be born again from the ashes

phone NOUN a telephone

phone VERB to telephone someone

phone-in NOUN (British) a radio or television programme in which people telephone the studio and take part in a discussion

phoneme NOUN a distinct unit of sound that distinguishes one word from another, e.g. *p*, *b*, *d* and *t* in *pad*, *pat*, *bad* and *bat*

a
b
c
d
e
f
g
h
i
j
k
l
m
n
o
p
q
r
s
t
u
v
w
x
y
z

phonetic (say fon-**et**-ik) ADJECTIVE
① to do with speech sounds
② representing speech sounds

phoney ADJECTIVE (*informal*) sham; not genuine

phonic ADJECTIVE to do with speech sounds

phonics NOUN a method of teaching reading by relating sounds to letters of the alphabet

phosphate NOUN a substance containing phosphorus, especially an artificial fertilizer

phosphorescent (say fos-fer-**ess**-ent) ADJECTIVE glowing in the dark; luminous

phosphorus NOUN a chemical substance that glows in the dark

photo NOUN (*informal*) a photograph

photocopier NOUN a machine that makes photocopies

photocopy NOUN a copy of a document or page made by photographing it on special paper

photocopy VERB to make a photocopy of a document or page

photoelectric ADJECTIVE using the electrical effects of light

photograph NOUN a picture made using a camera

photograph VERB to take a photograph of a person or thing

photographer NOUN a person who takes photographs

photography NOUN taking photographs

photosynthesis NOUN the process by which green plants use sunlight to turn carbon dioxide and water into complex substances, giving

off oxygen

phrase NOUN ① a group of words that form a unit in a sentence or clause, e.g. *in the garden* in 'The Queen was in the garden.' ② a short section of a tune

phrase VERB ① to put something into words ② to divide music into phrases

phrase book NOUN a book which lists useful words and expressions in a foreign language, with their translations

physical ADJECTIVE ① to do with the body rather than the mind or feelings ② to do with things that you can touch or see ③ to do with physics ④ physical geography is the study of natural features of the Earth's surface, such as mountains and volcanoes

physical education, physical training NOUN exercises and sports done to keep the body healthy

physically ADVERB in a way that is connected with the body rather than the mind or feelings

physician NOUN a doctor, especially one who is not a surgeon

physicist (say **fiz**-i-sist) NOUN an expert in physics

physics (say **fiz**-iks) NOUN the study of the properties of matter and energy (e.g. heat, light, sound and movement)

physiology (say fiz-ee-**ol**-o-jee) NOUN the study of the body and its parts and how they function

physiotherapy (say fiz-ee-o-th'**erra**-pee) NOUN (*British*) the treatment of a disease or injury by physical methods such as massage and exercise

physique (say fiz-**eek**) NOUN a person's build

pi NOUN the symbol (π) of the ratio of the circumference of a circle to its diameter. The value of pi is approximately 3.14159.

pianist NOUN a person who plays the piano

piano NOUN a large musical instrument with a row of black and white keys on a keyboard

piccolo NOUN a small high-pitched flute

pick VERB ❶ to pull a flower or fruit away from its plant ❷ to choose something from a group ❸ to pull bits off or out of something ❹ to open a lock by using something pointed, not with a key

pick NOUN ❶ a choice ❷ the best of a group ❸ a pickaxe ❹ a plectrum

pickaxe NOUN a heavy pointed tool with a long handle, used for breaking up hard ground or concrete

picket NOUN ❶ a striker or group of strikers who try to persuade other people not to go into a place of work during a strike ❷ a pointed post as part of a fence

picket VERB to stand outside a place of work to try to persuade other people not to go in during a strike

pickle NOUN ❶ a strong-tasting food made of pickled vegetables ❷ (*informal*) a difficulty or mess

pickle VERB to preserve food in vinegar or salt water

pickpocket NOUN a thief who steals from people's pockets or bags

pick-up NOUN an open truck for carrying small loads

picnic NOUN a meal eaten in the open air away from home

picnic VERB to have a picnic

Pict NOUN a member of an ancient people of north Britain

pictogram NOUN a picture or symbol that stands for a word or phrase

pictorial ADJECTIVE with or using pictures

picture NOUN ❶ a representation of a person or thing made by painting, drawing or photography ❷ a film at the cinema ❸ how something seems; an impression

picture VERB ❶ to show someone or something in a picture ❷ to imagine a person or thing

picturesque ADJECTIVE ❶ forming an attractive scene ❷ vivid and expressive

pidgin NOUN a simplified form of a language, especially English, Dutch or Portuguese, including words from a local language, used by people who do not speak the same language

pie NOUN a baked dish of meat, fish or fruit covered with pastry

piebald ADJECTIVE with patches of black and white

piece NOUN ❶ a part or portion of something; a fragment ❷ a separate thing or example ❸ something written, composed or painted ❹ one of the objects used to play a game on a board

⑤ a coin

piece VERB to put different parts together to make something

piecemeal ADJECTIVE & ADVERB done or made one piece at a time

pie chart NOUN a diagram in the form of a circle divided into sectors to represent the way in which a quantity is divided up

pier NOUN **①** a long structure built out into the sea for people to walk on **②** a pillar supporting a bridge or arch

pierce VERB **①** to make a hole through something **②** to be suddenly seen or heard

piercing ADJECTIVE **①** very loud and high-pitched **②** penetrating; very strong

piety NOUN being very religious and devout

piffle NOUN (informal) nonsense

pig NOUN **①** a fat animal with short legs and a blunt snout, kept for its meat **②** (informal) someone greedy, dirty or unpleasant

pigeon NOUN **①** a bird with a fat body and a small head **②** (informal) a person's business or responsibility

pigeon-hole NOUN a small compartment for holding letters, messages or papers for someone to collect

pigeon-hole VERB to decide that a person belongs to a particular category

piggyback NOUN a ride on someone else's back or shoulders

piggy bank NOUN a money box made in the shape of a hollow pig

pig-headed ADJECTIVE stubborn or obstinate

piglet NOUN a young pig

pigment NOUN **①** a substance that colours skin or other tissue in animals and plants **②** a substance that gives colour to paint, inks and dyes

pigsty NOUN **①** a partly covered pen for pigs **②** a filthy room or house

pigtail NOUN a plait of hair worn hanging at the back of the head

pike NOUN **①** a heavy spear **②** a large freshwater fish

pilau (say pi-low) NOUN an Indian dish of spiced rice with meat and vegetables

pilchard NOUN a small sea fish

pile NOUN **①** a number of things on top of one another **②** (informal) a large quantity; a lot of money **③** a large impressive building **④** a heavy beam made of metal, concrete or timber driven into the ground to support something **⑤** a raised surface on fabric, made of upright threads

pile VERB to put things into a pile; to make a pile

pile-up NOUN a road accident that involves a number of vehicles

pilfer VERB to steal things of little value

pilgrim NOUN a person who travels to a holy place for religious reasons

pilgrimage NOUN a journey to a holy place

pill NOUN a small solid piece of medicine for swallowing

pillage VERB to carry off goods

using force, especially in a war; to plunder a place

pillar NOUN a tall stone or wooden post

pillar box NOUN a postbox standing in a street

pillion NOUN a seat behind the driver on a motorcycle

pillory NOUN a wooden framework with holes for a person's head and hands, in which offenders were formerly made to stand and be ridiculed by the public as a punishment

pillory VERB to expose a person to public ridicule and scorn

pillow NOUN a cushion for a person's head to rest on, especially in bed

pillow VERB to rest the head on something soft

pillowcase NOUN a cloth cover for a pillow

pilot NOUN ❶ a person who works the controls for flying an aircraft ❷ a person qualified to steer a ship in and out of a port or through a difficult stretch of water

pilot VERB ❶ to be pilot of an aircraft or ship ❷ to guide or steer someone

pilot ADJECTIVE testing on a small scale how something will work

pilot light NOUN a small flame that lights a larger burner on a gas cooker or boiler

pimp NOUN a man who gets clients for prostitutes and lives off their earnings

pimpernel (say **pimp**-er-nel) NOUN a plant with small red, blue or

white flowers that close in cloudy weather

pimple NOUN a small round raised spot on the skin

PIN ABBREVIATION personal identification number; a number that you need to key in when you use a cash machine or bank card

pin NOUN ❶ a short thin piece of metal with a sharp point and a rounded head, used to fasten pieces of material or paper together ❷ a pointed device for fixing or marking something

pin VERB ❶ to fasten something with a pin or pins ❷ to hold someone firmly so that they cannot move ❸ to fix blame or responsibility on someone

pinafore NOUN an apron like a dress without sleeves, worn over clothes to keep them clean

pinball NOUN a game in which you shoot small metal balls across a special table and score points when they strike special pins

pincer NOUN the claw of a shellfish such as a lobster

pincers PLURAL NOUN a tool with two parts that are pressed together for gripping and holding things

pinch VERB ❶ to squeeze something tightly or painfully between two things, especially between the finger and thumb ❷ (informal) to steal something

pinch NOUN ❶ a pinching movement ❷ the amount that can be held between the tips of your thumb and forefinger

pincushion NOUN a small pad into which you stick pins to keep them ready for use

pine NOUN an evergreen tree with needle-shaped leaves

pine VERB ❶ to feel an intense longing for someone or something ❷ to become weak through longing for someone or something

pineapple NOUN a large tropical fruit with a tough prickly skin and yellow flesh

ping NOUN a short sharp ringing sound

ping VERB to make a sharp ringing sound

ping-pong NOUN table tennis

pinion NOUN ❶ a bird's wing, especially the outer end ❷ a small cogwheel that fits into another or into a rod (called a **rack**)

pinion VERB ❶ to clip a bird's wings to prevent it from flying ❷ to hold or fasten someone's arms or legs in order to prevent them from moving

pink ADJECTIVE pale red

pink NOUN ❶ a pink colour ❷ a garden plant with fragrant flowers, often pink or white

pinnacle NOUN ❶ a pointed ornament on a roof ❷ a high pointed piece of rock ❸ the highest point of something

pinpoint ADJECTIVE exact or precise

pinpoint VERB to find or identify something precisely

pinstripe NOUN one of the very narrow stripes that form a pattern in cloth

pint NOUN a measure for liquids, equal to one-eighth of a gallon (or 0.57 of a litre)

pin-up NOUN (*informal*) a picture of an attractive or famous person for pinning on a wall

pioneer NOUN one of the first people to go to a place or do or study something

pioneer VERB to be one of the first people to go to a place or do something

pious ADJECTIVE very religious or devout

pip NOUN ❶ a small hard seed of an apple, pear, orange or other fruit ❷ (*British*) one of the stars on the shoulder of an army officer's uniform ❸ (*British*) a short high-pitched sound

pip VERB (*British*) (*informal*) to defeat someone by a small amount

pipe NOUN ❶ a tube through which water, gas or oil can flow from one place to another ❷ a short narrow tube with a bowl at one end for burning tobacco for smoking ❸ a tube forming a musical instrument or part of one

pipe VERB ❶ to send something along pipes ❷ to transmit music or other sound by wire or cable ❸ to play music on a pipe or the bagpipes ❹ to decorate a cake with thin lines of icing, cream, etc.

pipe dream NOUN an impossible wish

pipeline NOUN a pipe for carrying oil, water or gas over a long distance

piper NOUN a person who plays a pipe or bagpipes

pipette NOUN a small glass tube used in a laboratory, usually filled by suction

piping NOUN ❶ pipes; a length of pipe ❷ a decorative line of icing, cream, etc. on a cake or other dish ❸ a long, narrow pipe-like line decorating clothing, upholstery, etc.

piping ADJECTIVE shrill

pipit NOUN a small songbird

pique (say peek) NOUN a feeling of hurt pride

pique VERB to be piqued is to feel irritated or annoyed

piracy NOUN ❶ the crime of attacking ships in order to steal from them ❷ the crime of illegally making and selling copies of books, DVDs, computer programs, etc.

piranha NOUN a South American freshwater fish that has sharp teeth and eats flesh

pirate NOUN ❶ a person on a ship who attacks and robs other ships at sea ❷ someone who copies books, DVDs, computer programs, etc. in order to sell them illegally

pirouette (say pir-oo-et) NOUN a spinning movement of the body made while balanced on the point of the toe or on one foot

pirouette VERB to perform a pirouette

pistachio NOUN a nut with an edible green kernel

pistil NOUN the part of a flower that produces the seed, consisting of the ovary, style and stigma

pistol NOUN a small handgun

piston NOUN a disc or cylinder that fits inside a tube in which it moves up and down as part of an engine or pump

pit NOUN ❶ a deep hole ❷ a hollow ❸ a coal mine ❹ the part of a race circuit where racing cars are refuelled and repaired during a race

pit VERB ❶ to make holes or hollows in something ❷ to put someone in competition with someone else

pit bull terrier NOUN a small strong and fierce breed of dog

pitch NOUN ❶ a piece of ground marked out for cricket, football or another game ❷ how high or low a voice or a musical note is ❸ intensity or strength ❹ the steepness of a slope ❺ a black sticky substance rather like tar

pitch VERB ❶ to throw or fling something ❷ to set up a tent or camp ❸ to fall heavily forward ❹ a ship pitches when it moves up and down on a rough sea ❺ to set something at a particular level ❻ a bowled ball in cricket pitches when it strikes the ground

pitch-black, pitch-dark ADJECTIVE completely black or dark

pitchblende NOUN a mineral ore (uranium oxide) from which radium is obtained

pitched battle NOUN a battle between armies in prepared positions

pitcher NOUN a large jug

pitchfork NOUN a large fork with two prongs, used for lifting hay

pitfall NOUN a hidden danger or difficulty

pith NOUN the spongy substance in the stems of certain plants or lining the rind of oranges or other fruits

a
b
c
d
e
f
g
h
i
j
k
l
m
n
o
p
q
r
s
t
u
v
w
x
y
z

pithy ADJECTIVE ❶ like pith; containing much pith ❷ short and full of meaning

pitiful ADJECTIVE making you feel pity

pitiless ADJECTIVE showing no pity; harsh or cruel

pitta NOUN a kind of flat thick bread with a hollow inside

pittance NOUN a very small allowance of money

pity NOUN ❶ the feeling of being sorry because someone is in pain or trouble ❷ a cause for regret

pity VERB to feel pity for someone

pivot NOUN a point or part on which something turns or balances

pivot VERB to turn or balance on a pivot

pivotal ADJECTIVE of great importance, because other things depend on it

pixel (say **piks**-el) NOUN one of the tiny dots on a computer display screen from which the image is formed

pixie NOUN a small fairy or elf

pizza (say **peets**-a) NOUN an Italian food that consists of a layer of dough baked with a savoury topping

pizzicato (say pits-i-**kah**-toh) ADJECTIVE & ADVERB (in music) plucking the strings of a musical instrument such as a violin

placard NOUN a poster or notice, especially one carried at a demonstration

placate VERB to make someone feel calmer and less angry

place NOUN ❶ a particular part of space, especially where something belongs; an area or position ❷ a city, town or village ❸ a position in a race or competition ❹ a seat ❺ a job; employment ❻ a building; a home ❼ a role or function ❽ a point in a series of things

place VERB to put something in a particular place

placebo (say plas-**ee**-boh) NOUN a harmless substance given as if it were a medicine, usually to reassure a patient

placenta NOUN a piece of body tissue that forms in the womb during pregnancy and supplies the foetus with nourishment

placid ADJECTIVE calm and peaceful; not easily made anxious or upset

plagiarize (also **plagiarise**) (say **play**-jeer-yz) VERB to take someone else's writings or ideas and use them as if they were your own

plague NOUN ❶ a dangerous illness that spreads very quickly ❷ a large number of pests

plague VERB to keep causing someone trouble

plaice NOUN a flat edible sea fish

plaid (say plad) NOUN cloth with a tartan or similar pattern

plain ADJECTIVE ❶ simple; not decorated or elaborate ❷ not pretty or beautiful ❸ easy to see or hear or understand ❹ frank and straightforward

plain NOUN a large area of flat country

plain clothes NOUN civilian clothes worn instead of a uniform, e.g. by police

plainly ADVERB ❶ clearly or obviously ❷ simply

plaintiff NOUN the person who brings a complaint against someone else to a law court. Compare with **defendant**.

plaintive ADJECTIVE sounding sad

plait (say plat) VERB to weave three or more strands of hair or rope to form one length

plait NOUN a length of hair or rope that has been plaited

plan NOUN ❶ a way of doing something that you think out in advance ❷ a drawing showing how the parts of something are arranged ❸ a map of a town or district

plan VERB ❶ to think out in advance how you are going to do something ❷ to intend or expect to do something

plane NOUN ❶ an aeroplane ❷ a tool for making wood smooth by scraping its surface ❸ a flat or level surface ❹ a tall tree with broad leaves

plane VERB to smooth wood with a plane

plane ADJECTIVE flat or level

planet NOUN one of the large bodies in space that move in an orbit round the sun or another star

planetary ADJECTIVE to do with planets

plank NOUN a long flat piece of wood

plankton NOUN microscopic plants and animals that float in the sea and lakes

plant NOUN ❶ a living thing that cannot move, makes its food from chemical substances and usually has a stem, leaves and roots. Flowers, trees and shrubs are plants. ❷ a small plant, not a tree or shrub ❸ a factory or its equipment ❹ (informal) something deliberately placed for other people to find, usually to mislead people or cause trouble

plant VERB ❶ to put something in soil for growing ❷ to put something firmly in place ❸ to place something where it will be found, usually to mislead people or cause trouble

plantain (say plan-tin) NOUN ❶ a tropical tree and fruit resembling the banana ❷ a wild plant with broad flat leaves, bearing seeds that are used as food for cage birds

plantation NOUN ❶ a large area of land where a crop such as cotton, tobacco or tea is planted ❷ a group of planted trees

plaque (say plak) NOUN ❶ a flat piece of metal or porcelain fixed on a wall as an ornament or memorial ❷ a filmy substance that forms on teeth and gums, where bacteria can live

plasma NOUN the colourless liquid part of blood, carrying the corpuscles

plaster NOUN ❶ a small covering put over the skin around a cut or wound to protect it ❷ a mixture of lime, sand and water etc. for covering walls and ceilings ❸ plaster of Paris or a cast made of this to hold broken bones in place

plaster VERB ① to cover a wall or other surface with plaster ② to cover something thickly

plaster of Paris NOUN a white paste used for making moulds or for casts round a broken leg or arm

plastic NOUN a strong, light synthetic substance that can be moulded into a permanent shape

plastic ADJECTIVE ① made of plastic ② soft and easy to mould

plastic surgery NOUN surgery to repair or replace damaged skin or to improve the appearance of someone's face or body

plate NOUN ① an almost flat usually circular object from which food is eaten or served ② a thin flat sheet of metal, glass or other hard material ③ an illustration on special paper in a book

plate VERB ① to coat metal with a thin layer of gold, silver, tin, etc. ② to cover something with sheets of metal

plateau (say plat-oh) NOUN a flat area of high land

platform NOUN ① a flat raised area along the side of a line at a railway station, where passengers get on and off trains ② a flat surface that is above the level of the ground or floor, especially one from which someone speaks to an audience

platinum NOUN a valuable silver-coloured metal that does not tarnish

platitude NOUN a trite or insincere remark that people often use

platoon NOUN a small group of soldiers

platter NOUN a flat dish or plate

platypus NOUN an Australian animal with a beak like that of a duck, that lays eggs like a bird but is a mammal and suckles its young

plaudits PLURAL NOUN applause; expressions of approval

plausible ADJECTIVE seeming likely to be true; reasonable

play VERB ① to take part in a game, sport or other amusement ② to make music with a musical instrument ③ to put a CD, DVD, etc. into a machine and listen to it or watch it ④ to perform a part in a play or film

play NOUN ① a story acted on a stage or on radio or television ② doing things for fun or amusement ③ the playing of a game or sport

playback NOUN playing back something that has been recorded

player NOUN ① a person who plays a game or sport ② a person who plays a musical instrument ③ a machine for playing recorded sound or pictures

playful ADJECTIVE ① wanting to play; full of fun ② done in fun; not serious

playground NOUN a piece of ground for children to play on

playgroup NOUN (British) a group of very young children who play together regularly, supervised by adults

playing card NOUN each of a set of cards (usually 52) used for playing games

playing field NOUN a field used for

outdoor games

playmate *NOUN* a person you play games with

play-off *NOUN* an extra match that is played between teams with equal scores to decide who the winner is

playtime *NOUN* the time when young schoolchildren go out to play

playwright *NOUN* a person who writes plays; a dramatist

PLC, plc *ABBREVIATION* (*British*) public limited company

plea *NOUN* ❶ a request or appeal ❷ a formal statement of 'guilty' or 'not guilty' made in a law court by someone accused of a crime

plead *VERB* pleads, pleading, pleaded ❶ to beg someone to do something ❷ to state formally in a law court that you are guilty or not guilty of a crime ❸ to give something as an excuse

pleasant *ADJECTIVE* pleasing; giving pleasure

please *VERB* ❶ to make a person feel satisfied or glad ❷ used to make a request or an order polite

pleased *ADJECTIVE* happy or satisfied about something

pleasurable *ADJECTIVE* causing pleasure; enjoyable

pleasure *NOUN* ❶ a feeling of satisfaction or gladness; enjoyment ❷ something that pleases you

pleat *NOUN* a flat fold made by doubling cloth upon itself

plectrum *NOUN* a small piece of metal, plastic or bone for plucking the strings of a musical instrument

plentiful *ADJECTIVE* available in large amounts

plenty *NOUN* quite enough; as much as is needed or wanted

plenty *ADVERB* (*informal*) quite or fully

plethora *NOUN* too large a quantity of something

pliable *ADJECTIVE* ❶ easy to bend; flexible ❷ easy to influence or control

pliers *PLURAL NOUN* pincers that have jaws with flat surfaces for gripping things

plight *NOUN* a dangerous or difficult situation

plight *VERB* (*old use*) to pledge devotion or loyalty

plimsoll *NOUN* (*British*) a canvas sports shoe with a rubber sole

Plimsoll line *NOUN* a mark on a ship's side showing how deeply it may legally go down in the water when loaded

plinth *NOUN* a block or slab forming the base of a column or a support for a statue or vase

plod *VERB* ❶ to walk slowly and heavily ❷ to work slowly but steadily

plonk *NOUN* (*British*) (*informal*) cheap wine

plonk *VERB* (*informal, chiefly British*) to put something down carelessly or heavily

plop *NOUN* the sound of something dropping into water

plop *VERB* to fall into liquid with a plop

plot *NOUN* ❶ a secret plan by a group of people to do something illegal or wrong ❷ the story in a play, novel or film ❸ a small piece of land

plot VERB ❶ to make a secret plan to do something ❷ to make a chart or graph of something

plotter NOUN someone who takes part in a plot

plough NOUN a farming implement for turning the soil over, in preparation for planting seeds

plough VERB ❶ to turn over soil with a plough ❷ to plough through something is to read all of it with great effort or difficulty

plover (say pluv-er) NOUN a kind of wading bird

ploy NOUN a cunning trick or deception you use to get what you want

pluck VERB ❶ to pick a flower or fruit ❷ to pull the feathers off a bird ❸ to pull something up or out ❹ to pull a string (e.g. on a guitar) and let it go again

pluck NOUN courage or spirit

plucky ADJECTIVE brave or spirited

plug NOUN ❶ something used to stop up a hole ❷ a device that fits into a socket to connect a piece of electrical equipment to a supply of electricity ❸ (informal) a piece of publicity for something

plug VERB ❶ to stop up a hole ❷ (informal) to publicize something

plum NOUN ❶ a soft juicy fruit with a pointed stone in the middle ❷ a reddish purple colour

plum ADJECTIVE (informal) that is the best of its kind

plumage (say ploom-ij) NOUN a

bird's feathers

plumb VERB ❶ to investigate something mysterious in order to understand it ❷ (British) to fit a room or building with a plumbing system

plumb ADJECTIVE exactly upright or vertical

plumb ADVERB (informal) exactly or precisely

plumber NOUN a person who fits and mends plumbing

plumbing NOUN ❶ the water pipes, water tanks and drainage pipes in a building ❷ the work of a plumber

plumb line NOUN a cord with a weight on the end, used to find how deep something is or whether a wall etc. is vertical

plume NOUN ❶ a large feather ❷ a thin column of something that rises in the air

plummet VERB ❶ to drop downwards quickly ❷ to decrease rapidly in value

plump ADJECTIVE having a full, rounded shape; slightly fat

plump VERB to plump up a cushion or pillow is to shake it to give it a rounded shape

plunder VERB to rob a person or place using force, especially during a war

plunder NOUN ❶ plundering a person or place ❷ goods that have been plundered

plunge VERB ❶ to jump or dive into water with force ❷ to push something forcefully into something ❸ to fall or go downwards suddenly ❹ to force someone or something into an unpleasant situation

plunge NOUN a sudden fall or dive

plunger NOUN a rubber cup on a handle used for clearing blocked pipes

plural NOUN the form of a noun or verb used when it stands for more than one person or thing Compare with **singular**.

plural ADJECTIVE in the plural; meaning more than one

plus PREPOSITION with the next number or thing added

plus ADJECTIVE ❶ being a grade slightly higher ❷ more than zero

plush NOUN a thick velvety cloth used in furnishings

plush ADJECTIVE smart and expensive

plutonium NOUN a radioactive substance used in nuclear weapons and reactors

ply VERB ❶ to keep offering something to someone ❷ to ply a trade is to work at it as your regular job ❸ to go regularly back and forth

ply NOUN ❶ a thickness or layer of wood or cloth etc. ❷ a strand in yarn

plywood NOUN strong thin board made of layers of wood glued together

PM ABBREVIATION Prime Minister

p.m. ABBREVIATION after 12 o'clock midday

pneumatic (say new-**mat**-ik) ADJECTIVE filled with or worked by compressed air

pneumonia (say new-**moh**-nee-a) NOUN a serious illness caused by inflammation of one or both lungs

poach VERB ❶ to cook an egg (removed from its shell) in or over boiling water ❷ to cook fish or fruit in a small amount of liquid ❸ to steal game or fish from someone else's land or water ❹ to take something unfairly

poacher NOUN a person who steals game or fish from someone else's land or water

pocket NOUN ❶ a small bag-shaped part of a piece of clothing, for carrying things in ❷ a person's supply of money ❸ a small isolated area of something

pocket ADJECTIVE small enough to carry in your pocket

pocket VERB to put something into a pocket

pocket money NOUN (British) money given to a child to spend

pockmark NOUN a scar or mark left on the skin by a disease

pod NOUN a long seed container of the kind found on a pea or bean plant

podcast NOUN a digital recording, especially of a radio programme, that you can download from the Internet to a computer or portable media player

podgy ADJECTIVE (British) (informal) short and fat

podium (say **poh**-dee-um) NOUN a small platform on which a music conductor or someone making a speech stands

poem NOUN a piece of writing arranged in short lines, usually with a particular rhythm and sometimes with rhymes

poet NOUN a person who writes poetry

poetic ADJECTIVE to do with poetry or like poetry

poetry NOUN poems or the writing of poems

poignant (say poin-yant) ADJECTIVE having a strong effect on your feelings and making you feel sad

point NOUN ① the narrow or sharp end of something ② a dot ③ a single mark in a game or quiz ④ a particular place or time ⑤ something that someone says during a discussion ⑥ a detail or characteristic ⑦ the important or essential idea ⑧ purpose or value ⑨ an electrical socket ⑩ a device for changing a train from one track to another

point VERB ① to show where something is, especially by holding out your finger towards it ② to aim or direct something at a person or thing ③ to fill in the parts between bricks with mortar or cement

point-blank ADJECTIVE ① aimed or fired from close to the target ② direct and straightforward

point-blank ADVERB in a point-blank manner

pointed ADJECTIVE ① with a point at the end ② clearly directed at a particular person, especially to criticize them

pointer NOUN ① a stick, rod or mark used to point at something ② a dog that points with its muzzle towards birds that it scents ③ an indication or hint

pointless ADJECTIVE without a point; with no purpose

point of view NOUN ① a way of looking at something or thinking about it ② the way that a writer chooses to tell a story, e.g. by telling it through the experiences of one of the characters

poise NOUN a dignified self-confident manner

poise VERB to balance something or keep it steady

poised ADJECTIVE ① not moving but ready to move ② dignified and self-confident

poison NOUN a substance that can harm or kill a living thing if swallowed or absorbed into the body

poison VERB ① to give poison to someone; to kill someone with poison ② to put poison in something ③ to spoil or have a bad effect on something

poisonous ADJECTIVE ① causing death or illness if swallowed or absorbed into the body ② producing poison

poke VERB ① to prod or jab something with your finger or a pointed object ② to push something out or forward; to stick out ③ to search in a casual way

poke NOUN a poking movement; a prod

poker NOUN ① a stiff metal rod for poking a fire ② a card game in which players bet on who has the best cards

poky ADJECTIVE small and cramped

polar ADJECTIVE to do with or near the North Pole or South Pole

polar bear NOUN a white bear living in Arctic regions

pole NOUN ❶ a long slender rounded piece of wood or metal ❷ a point on the earth's surface that is as far north (**North Pole**) or as far south (**South Pole**) as possible ❸ either of the ends of a magnet ❹ either terminal of an electric cell or battery

polecat NOUN an animal of the weasel family with an unpleasant smell

pole star NOUN the star above the North Pole

pole vault NOUN an athletic contest in which competitors jump over a high bar with the help of a long flexible pole

police NOUN the people whose job is to catch criminals and make sure that people obey the law

police VERB to keep order in a place by means of police

policeman NOUN a male police officer

police officer NOUN a member of the police

policewoman NOUN a female police officer

policy NOUN ❶ the aims or plan of action of a person or group ❷ a document stating the terms of a contract of insurance

polio NOUN a disease that can cause paralysis

polish VERB ❶ to make a thing smooth and shiny by rubbing ❷ to make a thing better by making corrections and alterations

polish NOUN ❶ a substance used in polishing ❷ polishing a surface ❸ elegance of manner

polite ADJECTIVE having good manners; showing respect to other people

political ADJECTIVE connected with the governing of a country or region

politician NOUN a person who is involved in politics

politics NOUN political matters; the business of governing a country or region

polka NOUN a lively dance for couples

poll (say pole) NOUN ❶ voting at an election or the votes cast ❷ an opinion poll

poll VERB ❶ to receive a certain number of votes in an election ❷ to ask members of the public their opinion on a subject

pollen NOUN a fine yellow powder produced by the anthers of flowers, containing male cells for fertilizing other flowers

pollinate VERB to fertilize a plant with pollen

pollutant NOUN something that pollutes

pollute VERB to make the air, rivers, etc. dirty or impure

pollution NOUN making the air, rivers, etc. dirty or impure

polo NOUN a game rather like hockey, with players on horseback using long mallets

polo neck NOUN (British) a high round turned-over collar

poltergeist NOUN a ghost or spirit

that throws things about noisily

polyester NOUN a synthetic material, used to make clothing

polygon NOUN a flat shape with many sides. Hexagons and octagons are polygons.

polyhedron NOUN a solid shape with many sides

polymer NOUN a substance with a molecule structure consisting of a large number of simple molecules combined

polyp (say pol-ip) NOUN ❶ a tiny creature with a tube-shaped body ❷ a small abnormal growth

polystyrene NOUN a kind of plastic used for insulating or packing things

polythene NOUN (British) a lightweight plastic used to make bags or wrappings

pomegranate NOUN a tropical fruit with many seeds

pommel NOUN ❶ a knob on the handle of a sword ❷ the raised part at the front of a saddle

pomp NOUN the ceremonial splendour that is traditional on important public occasions

pompom NOUN a ball of coloured threads used as a decoration

pompous ADJECTIVE speaking or behaving in a grand way that shows you think too much of your own importance

pond NOUN a small lake

ponder VERB to think deeply and seriously about something

ponderous ADJECTIVE ❶ heavy and awkward ❷ slow, dull and too serious

pong (British) (informal) NOUN an unpleasant smell

pong VERB to have an unpleasant smell

pontoon NOUN ❶ a boat or float used to support a bridge (a **pontoon** bridge) over a river ❷ (British) a card game in which players try to get cards whose value totals 21

pony NOUN a small horse

ponytail NOUN a bunch of long hair tied at the back of the head

pony-trekking NOUN (British) travelling across country on a pony for pleasure

poodle NOUN a dog with thick curly hair

pool NOUN ❶ a pond ❷ a puddle ❸ a swimming pool ❹ a group of things shared by several people ❺ a game similar to snooker but played on a smaller table

pool VERB to put money or things together for sharing

poor ADJECTIVE ❶ with very little money ❷ not good; inadequate ❸ unfortunate; deserving pity

poorly ADVERB in a poor way

poorly ADJECTIVE (British) rather ill

pop NOUN ❶ modern popular music ❷ a small explosive sound ❸ a fizzy drink

pop VERB ❶ (informal) to go quickly or put something somewhere quickly ❷ to make a pop

popcorn NOUN maize heated to burst and form fluffy balls

Pope NOUN the leader of the Roman Catholic Church

popgun NOUN a toy gun that shoots a cork or pellet with a popping sound

poplar NOUN a tall slender tree

poppadam, poppadom NOUN a thin crisp biscuit made of lentil flour, eaten with Indian food

poppy NOUN a plant with large red flowers

populace NOUN the general public

popular ADJECTIVE ❶ liked or enjoyed by many people ❷ held or believed by many people ❸ intended for the general public

popularity NOUN being liked or enjoyed by a lot of people

popularize (also **popularise**) VERB to make a thing known and liked by a lot of people

popularly ADVERB by many people; generally

populate VERB to fill a place with people; to inhabit a country

population NOUN the people who live in a district or country; the total number of these people

porcelain NOUN the finest kind of china

porch NOUN a shelter outside the entrance to a building

porcupine NOUN a small animal covered with long prickles

pore NOUN a tiny opening on your skin through which moisture can pass in or out

pore VERB ➤ **pore over something** to study something with close attention

pork NOUN meat from a pig

pornography (say porn-**og**-ra-fee) NOUN pictures, magazines and films that show naked people and sexual acts in a way that is intended to be sexually exciting and that many people find offensive

porous ADJECTIVE allowing liquid or air to pass through

porpoise (say **por**-pus) NOUN a sea animal rather like a small whale

porridge NOUN a food made by boiling oatmeal to a thick paste

port NOUN ❶ a harbour ❷ a city or town with a harbour ❸ the left-hand side of a ship or aircraft when you are facing forward. Compare with **starboard**. ❹ a strong red Portuguese wine

portable ADJECTIVE able to be carried easily

portal NOUN ❶ a doorway or gateway ❷ a website with information on a particular subject and links to other websites

portcullis NOUN a strong heavy vertical grating that can be lowered to block the gateway to a castle

portent NOUN an omen; a sign that something will happen

porter NOUN ❶ a person whose job is to carry luggage or other goods ❷ (British) a person whose job is to look after the entrance to a large building

portfolio NOUN ❶ a case for holding documents or drawings ❷ a government minister's special responsibility ❸ a collection of examples of art or photography work that you have done

porthole NOUN a small window in the side of a ship or aircraft

portion NOUN a part or share given to someone

portion VERB to divide something into portions

portly ADJECTIVE rather fat

portmanteau (say port-**mant**-oh) NOUN a large travelling bag that opens into two equal parts

portmanteau word NOUN a word made from the sounds and meanings of two others, e.g. *motel* (from *motor* + *hotel*)

portrait NOUN ❶ a picture of a person ❷ a description in words or on film

portray VERB ❶ to make a picture of a person or scene ❷ to describe or show a person or thing in a certain way

pose NOUN ❶ a position in which someone stands or sits for a portrait or photograph ❷ a way of behaving that someone adopts to give a particular impression

pose VERB ❶ to take up a pose ❷ to put someone into a pose ❸ to pretend to be someone ❹ to pose a question or problem is to present it

poser NOUN ❶ a puzzling question or problem ❷ a person who behaves in a showy or unnatural way in order to impress other people

posh ADJECTIVE (*informal*) ❶ very smart; high-class ❷ upper-class

position NOUN ❶ the place where something is or should be ❷ the way a person or thing is placed or arranged ❸ a person's place in a race or competition ❹ a situation or condition ❺ paid employment; a job

position VERB to place a person or thing in a certain position

positive ADJECTIVE ❶ definite or certain ❷ agreeing or saying 'yes' ❸ looking at the best or most hopeful aspects of a situation ❹ showing signs of what is being tested for ❺ greater than zero ❻ to do with the kind of electric charge that lacks electrons ❼ the positive form of an adjective or adverb is its simplest form, not the comparative or superlative

positive NOUN a photograph or film in which the light and dark parts or colours appear as in the thing photographed or filmed. Compare with **negative**.

positively ADVERB ❶ really; extremely ❷ in a positive way

positron NOUN a particle of matter with a positive electric charge

posse (say **poss**-ee) NOUN a group of people, especially one put together to help a sheriff

possess VERB ❶ to have or own something ❷ to control someone's thoughts or behaviour

possessed ADJECTIVE seeming to be controlled by strong emotion or an evil spirit

possession NOUN ❶ something you own ❷ having or owning something

possessive ADJECTIVE ❶ wanting to possess and keep things for yourself ❷ (*in grammar*) showing what or whom something belongs to

possibility NOUN ❶ being possible ❷ something that may happen or be the case

possible ADJECTIVE that can exist, happen, be done or be used

possibly ADVERB ❶ in any way ❷ perhaps

possum NOUN an opossum

post NOUN ❶ an upright piece of wood, concrete or metal fixed in the ground ❷ the starting point or finishing point of a race ❸ the collecting and delivering of letters and parcels ❹ letters and parcels sent or delivered ❺ a message sent to an Internet site; a piece of writing on a blog ❻ a position of paid employment; a job ❼ the place where someone is on duty

post VERB ❶ to put up a notice or poster to announce something ❷ to send a message to an Internet site; to display information online ❸ to put a letter or parcel into a postbox for collection ❹ to send someone to go and work somewhere; to place someone on duty

post- PREFIX after (as in post-war)

postage NOUN the charge for sending something by post

postage stamp NOUN a stamp for sticking on letters and parcels to be posted, showing the amount paid

postal ADJECTIVE to do with or by the post

postal order NOUN (British) a document bought from a post office which can be sent by post

and exchanged for money by the person receiving it

postbox NOUN a box into which letters are put for collection

postcard NOUN a card for sending messages by post without an envelope

postcode NOUN (British) a group of letters and numbers included in an address to help in sorting the post

poster NOUN a large sheet of paper announcing or advertising something, for display in a public place

posterior NOUN a person's bottom

posterity NOUN future generations of people

postgraduate ADJECTIVE to do with studies carried on after taking a first university degree

postgraduate NOUN a person who continues studying or doing research after taking a first university degree

post-haste ADVERB with great speed or haste

posthumous (say poss-tew-mus) ADJECTIVE coming or happening after a person's death

postman NOUN (British) a person who delivers or collects post

postmark NOUN an official mark put on something sent by post to show where and when it was posted

post-mortem NOUN an examination of a dead body to discover the cause of death

post office NOUN ❶ a building or room where postal business is carried on ❷ the national

a b c d e f g h i j k l m n o p q r s t u v w x y z

organization responsible for postal services

postpone *VERB* to arrange for something to take place later than was originally planned

postscript *NOUN* something extra added at the end of a letter (after the writer's signature) or at the end of a book

posture *NOUN* the position in which you hold your body when you stand, sit or walk

post-war *ADJECTIVE* happening in the period after a war

posy *NOUN* a small bunch of flowers

pot *NOUN* ❶ a deep round container ❷ a flowerpot ❸ (*informal*) the drug cannabis

pot *VERB* ❶ to pot a plant is to plant it in a flowerpot ❷ to pot a ball in a game such as snooker or pool is to knock it into a pocket

potash *NOUN* potassium carbonate

potassium *NOUN* a soft silvery-white metal substance that is essential for living things

potato *NOUN* potatoes a round white vegetable with a brown or red skin that grows underground

potent (say poh-tent) *ADJECTIVE* having great power or effect

potential (say po-ten-shal) *ADJECTIVE* capable of happening or being used or developed

potential *NOUN* ❶ the ability of a person or thing to develop or succeed in the future ❷ the voltage between two points

potentially *ADVERB* as a possibility in the future

pothole *NOUN* ❶ a deep natural hole in the ground ❷ a hole in a road

potholing *NOUN* exploring underground caves by climbing down potholes

potion *NOUN* a drink containing medicine or poison or having magical powers

potpourri (say poh-poor-ee) *NOUN* a scented mixture of dried petals and spices

pot shot *NOUN* a shot aimed casually at something

potted *ADJECTIVE* ❶ shortened or abridged ❷ preserved in a pot

potter *NOUN* a person who makes pottery

potter *VERB* to spend time doing little jobs in a relaxed or leisurely way

pottery *NOUN* ❶ cups, plates, ornaments, etc. made of baked clay ❷ the craft of making these things ❸ a place where a potter works

potty *ADJECTIVE* (*British*) (*informal*) mad or foolish

potty *NOUN* (*informal*) a small bowl used by a young child instead of a toilet

pouch *NOUN* ❶ a small bag ❷ a fold of skin in which a kangaroo etc. keeps its young ❸ something shaped like a bag

poultice *NOUN* a soft hot dressing put on a sore or inflamed place

poultry *NOUN* chickens, geese, turkeys and other birds kept for their eggs and meat

pounce *VERB* to jump or swoop down quickly on something and grab it

pound NOUN ❶ a unit of money, in Britain equal to 100 pence ❷ a unit of weight equal to 16 ounces or about 454 grams ❸ a place where stray animals are taken ❹ a public enclosure for vehicles officially removed

pound VERB ❶ to hit something repeatedly ❷ to run or go heavily ❸ your heart pounds when it beats very fast and hard

pour VERB ❶ to make a liquid flow steadily out of a container ❷ to flow in a large amount ❸ to rain heavily ❹ to come or go in large amounts

pout VERB to push out your lips when you are annoyed or sulking

poverty NOUN ❶ being poor ❷ a lack or scarcity

POW ABBREVIATION prisoner of war

powder NOUN ❶ a mass of fine dry particles of something ❷ make-up in the form of powder ❸ gunpowder

powder VERB to put powder on something

powdered ADJECTIVE dried and made into a powder

powder room NOUN a women's toilet in a public building

powdery ADJECTIVE like powder

power NOUN ❶ strength or energy ❷ the ability to do something ❸ control over other people ❹ political control of a country ❺ a powerful country, person or organization ❻ mechanical or electrical energy; the electricity supply ❼ (in science) the rate of doing work, measured in watts or horsepower ❽ (in mathematics)

the product of a number multiplied by itself a given number of times

power VERB to supply power to a vehicle or machine

powerboat NOUN a powerful motor boat

powerful ADJECTIVE ❶ having great power, strength or influence ❷ having a strong effect

powerless ADJECTIVE not able to act or control things

power station NOUN a building where electricity is produced

pp. ABBREVIATION pages

practicable ADJECTIVE able to be done

practical ADJECTIVE ❶ able to do or make useful things ❷ likely to be useful or effective ❸ actually doing something, rather than just learning or thinking about it

practical NOUN (British) a lesson or examination in which you actually do or make something rather than reading or writing about it

practical joke NOUN a trick played on someone

practically ADVERB ❶ almost ❷ in a practical way

practice NOUN ❶ doing something repeatedly in order to become better at it ❷ actually doing something rather than thinking or talking about it ❸ the professional business of a doctor, dentist, lawyer, etc. ❹ a habit or custom

practise VERB ❶ to do something repeatedly in order to become better at it ❷ to practise an activity or custom is to do it regularly ❸ to work as a doctor,

lawyer or other professional person

practised ADJECTIVE experienced or expert

practitioner NOUN a professional worker, especially a doctor

prairie NOUN a large area of flat grass-covered land in North America

praise VERB ❶ to say that someone or something is very good or has done well ❷ to honour God in words

praise NOUN words that praise someone or something

praiseworthy ADJECTIVE deserving praise

pram NOUN (British) a four-wheeled carriage for a baby, pushed by a person walking

prance VERB to move about in a lively or happy way

prank NOUN a trick played on someone for mischief; a practical joke

prattle VERB to chatter like a young child

prawn NOUN an edible shellfish like a large shrimp

pray VERB ❶ to talk to God to give thanks or ask for help ❷ to hope very strongly for something

pray ADVERB (formal) please

prayer NOUN praying; words used in praying

pre- PREFIX before (as in pre-war)

preach VERB to give a talk about religion or about right and wrong

preacher NOUN a person who preaches

preamble NOUN the introduction to a speech or book or document

precarious (say pri-kair-ee-us) ADJECTIVE not very safe or secure

precaution NOUN something you do to prevent future trouble or danger

precede VERB to come or go before something else

precedence (say press-i-dens) NOUN the right of something to be put first because it is more important

precedent (say press-i-dent) NOUN a previous case that is taken as an example or guide to be followed

precinct (say pree-sinkt) NOUN ❶ a part of a town where traffic is not allowed ❷ the precincts of a place are the buildings and land around it

precious ADJECTIVE ❶ very valuable ❷ greatly loved

precious ADVERB (informal) very

precipice NOUN a very steep place, such as the face of a cliff

precipitate VERB ❶ to make something happen suddenly or soon ❷ to throw or send something down; to make something fall

precipitate NOUN a solid substance that has been separated chemically from a solution

precipitate ADJECTIVE hurried or hasty

precipitation NOUN the amount of rain, snow or hail that falls during a period of time

precis (say pray-see) NOUN a summary

precise ADJECTIVE ❶ clear and accurate ❷ exact

precisely ADVERB exactly

precision NOUN being exact and accurate

preclude VERB to prevent something from happening

precocious (say prik-**oh**-shus) ADJECTIVE a precocious child is very advanced or developed for their age

precursor NOUN something that was an earlier form of something that came later; a forerunner

predator (say **pred**-a-ter) NOUN an animal that hunts or preys upon others

predecessor (say **pree**-dis-ess-er) NOUN an earlier person or thing, e.g. an ancestor or the former holder of a job

predicament (say prid-**ik**-a-ment) NOUN a difficult or unpleasant situation

predict VERB to say what will happen in the future; to foretell or prophesy a future event

predictable ADJECTIVE ❶ able to be predicted ❷ always behaving in the same way

prediction NOUN saying what will happen; what someone thinks will happen

predominant ADJECTIVE greatest in size or most noticeable or most important

predominate VERB to be the greatest in number or the most important

preen VERB a bird preens its feathers when it smooths them

with its beak

prefab NOUN (*informal*) a prefabricated building

prefabricated ADJECTIVE made in sections ready to be assembled on a site

preface (say **pref**-as) NOUN an introduction at the beginning of a book or speech

prefect NOUN ❶ a senior pupil in a school, given authority to help to keep order ❷ a regional official in France, Japan and other countries

prefer VERB to like one person or thing more than another

preferable (say **pref**-er-a-bul) ADJECTIVE something is preferable to something else when it is better or you like it more

preference NOUN a liking for one thing rather than another; something you prefer

preferential (say pref-er-**en**-shal) ADJECTIVE better than other people get

prefix NOUN a word or syllable joined to the front of a word to change or add to its meaning, as in *dis*order, *out*stretched, *un*happy

pregnancy NOUN being pregnant

pregnant ADJECTIVE ❶ a woman is pregnant when she has a baby developing in the womb ❷ a pregnant pause or silence is one full of meaning or significance

prehensile ADJECTIVE an animal's foot or tail is called prehensile when it is able to grasp things

prehistoric ADJECTIVE belonging to very ancient times, before written records of events were made

a
b
c
d
e
f
g
h
i
j
k
l
m
n
o
p
q
r
s
t
u
v
w
x
y
z

prejudice NOUN a strong unreasonable feeling of not liking or trusting someone

prelate (say **prel**-at) NOUN an important member of the clergy

preliminary ADJECTIVE coming before something and preparing for it

prelude NOUN ❶ a thing that introduces or leads up to something else ❷ a short piece of music, especially one that introduces a longer piece

premature ADJECTIVE too early; coming before the usual or proper time

premier (say **prem**-ee-er) ADJECTIVE best or most important

premier NOUN a prime minister or other head of government

premiere (say prem-**yair**) NOUN the first public performance of a play or film

premise (say **prem**-iss) NOUN a statement used as the basis for a piece of reasoning

premises PLURAL NOUN a building and its grounds

premium NOUN ❶ an amount of money paid regularly to an insurance company ❷ an extra charge or payment

premonition NOUN a feeling that something bad is about to happen

preoccupation NOUN something you think or worry about all the time

preoccupied ADJECTIVE thinking or worrying about something so much that you cannot pay attention to anything else

preparation NOUN ❶ getting something ready ❷ something done in order to get ready for an event or activity ❸ a mixture to be used as a medicine or cosmetic

preparatory ADJECTIVE preparing for something

preparatory school NOUN a school that prepares pupils for a higher school

prepare VERB to get ready or to make something ready

prepared ADJECTIVE ready and able to deal with something

preposition NOUN a word used with a noun or pronoun to show place, position, time or means, e.g. *at* home, *in* the hall, *on* Sunday, *by* train

prepossessing ADJECTIVE attractive

preposterous ADJECTIVE completely absurd or ridiculous

prerogative NOUN a right or privilege that belongs to one person or group

Presbyterian (say prez-bit-**eer**-ee-an) NOUN a member of a Christian Church governed by elders who are all of equal rank, especially the national Church of Scotland

pre-school ADJECTIVE to do with the time before a child is old enough to go to school

prescribe VERB ❶ to advise a person to use a particular medicine or treatment ❷ to say what should be done

prescription NOUN a doctor's written order for a medicine or the medicine itself

presence NOUN ❶ being present in a place ❷ a person's impressive appearance or manner

presence of mind NOUN the ability to act quickly and sensibly in an emergency

present (say **prez**-ent) ADJECTIVE ❶ in a particular place ❷ belonging or referring to what is happening now; existing now

present (say **prez**-ent) NOUN ❶ the time now ❷ (in grammar) the tense of a verb used to describe an action that is happening now, e.g. *likes* in He likes swimming. ❸ something you give or receive as a gift

present (say pri-**zent**) VERB ❶ to give something, especially with a ceremony ❷ to introduce someone to another person; to introduce a radio or television programme to an audience ❸ to put on a play or other entertainment ❹ to show or reveal something ❺ to cause or provide something

presentable ADJECTIVE fit to be presented to other people; looking good

presentation NOUN ❶ a talk showing or demonstrating something ❷ a ceremony in which someone is given a gift or prize ❸ the way in which work is written or set out

presenter NOUN (British) someone who introduces the different parts of a radio or television programme

presently ADVERB ❶ soon; after a short time ❷ now

preservative NOUN a substance added to food to preserve it

preserve VERB to keep something safe or in good condition

preserve NOUN ❶ jam made with preserved fruit ❷ an activity that belongs to a particular person or group

preside VERB to be in charge of a meeting or other occasion

presidency NOUN the job of being president or the period of time that someone is president

president NOUN ❶ the person in charge of a club, society or council etc. ❷ the head of a country that is a republic

press VERB ❶ to put weight or force steadily on something; to squeeze something ❷ to make clothes smooth by ironing them ❸ to urge someone or make demands of them

press NOUN ❶ pushing something firmly ❷ a device for pressing things ❸ a machine for printing things ❹ a firm that prints or publishes books or magazines ❺ newspapers and journalists

press conference NOUN a meeting when a famous or important person answers questions from a group of journalists

press-gang NOUN (historical) a group of men whose job was to force people to serve in the army or navy

pressing ADJECTIVE needing immediate action; urgent

press-up NOUN (British) an exercise in which you lie face downwards and press down with your hands to lift your body

pressure NOUN ❶ continuous

pressing ❷ the force with which something presses ❸ the force of the atmosphere on the earth's surface ❹ an influence that persuades or forces you to do something

pressure cooker NOUN a large air-tight pan used for cooking food quickly under steam pressure

pressure group NOUN an organized group that tries to influence public policy on a particular issue

pressurize (also **pressurise**) VERB ❶ to keep a compartment at the same air pressure all the time ❷ to try to force a person to do something

prestige (say pres-**teej**) NOUN great respect that something has gained for being important, successful or of high quality

prestigious ADJECTIVE respected for being important, successful or of high quality

presumably ADVERB I imagine; I suppose

presume VERB ❶ to suppose something or assume that it is true ❷ to dare to do something which you have no right to do

presumptuous ADJECTIVE too bold or confident

pretence NOUN an attempt to pretend that something is true

pretend VERB ❶ to behave as if something is true or real when you know that it is not, in order to deceive people ❷ to imagine that something is true as part of a game ❸ to claim that something

is the case

pretender NOUN a person who claims a throne or title

pretension NOUN ❶ a doubtful claim ❷ pretentious or showy behaviour

pretentious ADJECTIVE trying to impress people by appearing more serious or important than you really are

pretext NOUN a reason put forward to conceal the true reason

pretty ADJECTIVE attractive in a delicate way

pretty ADVERB quite; fairly

prevail VERB ❶ to be the most frequent or general ❷ to be successful or victorious

prevalent (say **prev**-a-lent) ADJECTIVE most frequent or common; widespread

prevent VERB ❶ to stop something from happening ❷ to stop a person from doing something

preventive, preventative ADJECTIVE intended to help prevent something

preview NOUN a showing of a film or play before it is shown to the general public

previous ADJECTIVE coming before this; preceding

previously ADVERB before the present time; earlier

prey (say pray) NOUN an animal that is hunted or killed by another for food

prey VERB ➤ **prey on something** to hunt and kill an animal for food ➤ **prey on your mind** to worry you constantly

price NOUN ❶ the amount of money for which something is bought or sold ❷ what you have to give or do in order to achieve something

price VERB to decide the price of something

priceless ADJECTIVE ❶ very valuable ❷ (*informal*) very amusing

prick VERB ❶ to make a tiny hole in something ❷ to hurt someone with a pin or needle etc.

prick NOUN a pricking feeling

prickle NOUN ❶ a small thorn ❷ a sharp spine on a hedgehog or cactus etc. ❸ a feeling that a lot of small sharp points are sticking into your skin

prickle VERB to feel as though a lot of small sharp points are sticking into your skin; to cause this feeling

prickly ADJECTIVE ❶ covered in prickles or feeling like prickles ❷ irritable or bad-tempered

pride NOUN ❶ a feeling of deep pleasure or satisfaction when you have done something well ❷ something that makes you feel proud ❸ dignity or self-respect ❹ too high an opinion of yourself ❺ a group of lions

pride VERB ➤ **pride yourself on something** to be proud of something

priest NOUN ❶ a member of the clergy in certain Christian Churches ❷ a person who performs religious ceremonies in a non-Christian religion

priestess NOUN a female priest in a non-Christian religion

prig NOUN a self-righteous person

prim ADJECTIVE always behaving in a formal and correct manner and easily shocked by anything rude

primarily (say pry-mer-il-ee or pry-**me**-ril-ee) ADVERB more than anything else; mainly

primary ADJECTIVE first or most important. Compare with **secondary**.

primary colour NOUN one of the colours from which all others can be made by mixing (red, yellow and blue for paint; red, green and violet for light)

primary school NOUN (*British*) a school for the first stage of a child's education

primate (say pry-mat) NOUN ❶ an animal of the group that includes human beings, apes and monkeys ❷ an archbishop

prime ADJECTIVE ❶ chief or most important ❷ of the best quality

prime NOUN the best time or stage of something

prime VERB ❶ to prepare something for use or action ❷ to put a coat of liquid on something to prepare it for painting ❸ to give someone information in order to prepare them for something

prime minister NOUN the leader of a government

prime number NOUN a number (e.g. 2, 3, 5, 7, 11) that can be divided exactly only by itself and one

primer NOUN ❶ a liquid for priming a surface ❷ a textbook dealing with the first or simplest stages of a subject

primeval (say pry-mee-val)

a
b
c
d
e
f
h
i
j
k
l
m
n
o
p
q
r
s
t
u
v
w
x
y
z

primitive ADJECTIVE belonging to the earliest times of the world

primitive ADJECTIVE ❶ at an early stage of civilization ❷ at an early stage of development; not complicated or sophisticated

primrose NOUN a pale-yellow flower that blooms in spring

prince NOUN ❶ the son of a king or queen ❷ a man or boy in a royal family

princess NOUN ❶ the daughter of a king or queen ❷ a woman or girl in a royal family ❸ the wife of a prince

principal ADJECTIVE chief or most important

principal NOUN the head of a college or school

principality NOUN a country ruled by a prince

principally ADVERB chiefly or mainly

principle NOUN ❶ a general truth, belief or rule ❷ a rule of conduct based on what a person believes is right

print VERB ❶ to put words or pictures on paper by using a machine ❷ to write with letters that are not joined together ❸ to press a mark or design on a surface ❹ to make a picture from the negative of a photograph

print NOUN ❶ printed lettering or words ❷ a mark made by something pressing on a surface ❸ a printed picture, photograph or design

printed circuit NOUN an electric circuit made by pressing thin metal strips onto a board

printer NOUN ❶ a machine that prints on paper from data in a computer ❷ someone who prints books or newspapers

printout NOUN information produced in printed form by a computer

prior ADJECTIVE coming before or earlier

prior NOUN a monk who is the head of a religious house or order

prioritize (also **prioritise**) VERB to put tasks in order of importance, so that you can deal with the most important first

priority NOUN ❶ something that is more urgent or important than other things and needs to be dealt with first ❷ the right to go first or be dealt with before other things

priory NOUN a religious house governed by a prior or prioress

prise VERB to force or lever something out or open

prism (say prizm) NOUN ❶ (in mathematics) a solid shape with ends that are triangles or polygons which are equal and parallel ❷ a glass prism that breaks up light into the colours of the rainbow

prison NOUN a place where criminals are kept as a punishment

prisoner NOUN ❶ a person kept in prison ❷ a person who has been captured and kept somewhere

prisoner of war NOUN a person captured and imprisoned by the enemy in a war

pristine ADJECTIVE in its original condition; unspoilt

privacy (say **priv**-a-see) NOUN being

A B C D E F G H I J K L M N O P Q R S T U V W X Y Z

able to be alone without other people watching you or knowing what you are doing

private ADJECTIVE ❶ belonging to a particular person or group ❷ meant to be kept secret; confidential ❸ quiet and secluded ❹ not holding public office ❺ independent or commercial; not run by the government

private NOUN a soldier of the lowest rank

privet NOUN an evergreen shrub with small leaves, used to make hedges

privilege NOUN a special right, advantage or opportunity given to one person or group

privileged ADJECTIVE having an advantage or opportunity that most people do not have

privy ADJECTIVE ➤ be privy to something to be allowed to know about something secret

privy NOUN (old use) an outside toilet

prize NOUN ❶ an award given to someone who wins a game or competition or who does very good work ❷ something of great value that is worth trying to obtain

prize VERB to value something greatly

pro NOUN (informal) a professional

pro- PREFIX in favour of or supporting something (as in pro-British)

probability NOUN ❶ how likely it is that something will happen ❷ something that is likely to happen

probable ADJECTIVE likely to happen or be true

probably ADVERB almost certainly

probation NOUN a period of time at the start of a new job when a person is tested to see if they are suitable

probation officer NOUN an official who supervises the behaviour of a convicted criminal who is not in prison

probe NOUN ❶ a long thin instrument used to look closely at something such as a wound ❷ an unmanned spacecraft used for exploring ❸ an investigation

probe VERB ❶ to ask questions in order to find out hidden information ❷ to explore or look closely at something, especially with a probe

problem NOUN ❶ something that causes trouble or is difficult to deal with ❷ a question that you have to solve by thinking about it

proboscis (say pro-**boss**-iss) NOUN ❶ a long flexible snout ❷ an insect's long mouthpart

procedure NOUN a fixed or special way of doing something

proceed VERB ❶ to go forward or onward ❷ to continue; to go on to do something

proceedings PLURAL NOUN ❶ things that happen, especially at a formal meeting or ceremony ❷ a lawsuit

proceeds PLURAL NOUN the money made from a sale or event

process (say **proh**-sess) NOUN a series of actions for making or doing something

process (say **proh**-sess) VERB to put something through a manufacturing or other process

process (say pro-**sess**) VERB to go in procession

procession NOUN a number of people or vehicles moving steadily forward following each other

processor NOUN ❶ a machine that processes things ❷ the part of a computer that controls all its operations

proclaim VERB to announce something officially or publicly

proclamation NOUN a public or official announcement

procrastinate VERB to put off doing something

procure VERB to obtain or acquire something

prod VERB ❶ to poke something or someone with your finger or a pointed object ❷ to encourage or remind someone to do something

prodigal ADJECTIVE wasteful or extravagant

prodigious ADJECTIVE remarkably large or impressive

prodigy NOUN ❶ a child or young person with wonderful abilities ❷ a wonderful thing

produce (say pro-**dewss**) VERB ❶ to make or create something; to bring something into existence ❷ to bring something out so that it can be seen ❸ to organize the performance of a play, making of a film, etc. ❹ to extend a line further

produce (say **prod**-yewss) NOUN things that have been produced or grown, especially by farmers

producer NOUN ❶ a person, company or country that makes or grows something ❷ someone who produces a play, film, etc.

product NOUN ❶ something made or produced for sale ❷ the result of multiplying two numbers. Compare with **quotient**.

production NOUN ❶ the process of making or creating something, especially in large quantities ❷ the amount produced ❸ a version of a play, opera or other show

productive ADJECTIVE ❶ producing a lot of things ❷ producing good results; useful

profane ADJECTIVE showing disrespect for religion; blasphemous

profane VERB to treat something, especially religion, with disrespect

profanity NOUN words or language that show disrespect for religion

profess VERB ❶ to claim to have or do something ❷ to declare or express something

profession NOUN ❶ an occupation that needs special education and training, such as medicine or law ❷ a declaration

professional ADJECTIVE ❶ to do with a profession ❷ doing a certain kind of work as a full-time job for payment, not as an amateur ❸ done with a high standard of skill

professional NOUN ❶ a person who has been trained in a profession ❷ a person who does something to earn money, not as an amateur

professor NOUN a university teacher of the highest rank

proffer VERB to offer something

proficient ADJECTIVE able to do something well because of training or practice; skilled

profile NOUN ❶ a side view of a person's face ❷ a short description of a person's character or career

profit NOUN ❶ the extra money obtained by selling something for more than it cost to buy or make ❷ an advantage gained by doing something

profit VERB to gain an advantage or benefit from something

profitable ADJECTIVE making a profit

profound ADJECTIVE ❶ very deep or intense ❷ showing or needing great knowledge, understanding or thought

profuse ADJECTIVE given or produced in large amounts

profusion NOUN a very large quantity of something

prognosis (say prog-**noh**-sis) NOUN a forecast or prediction, especially about how a disease will develop

program NOUN a series of coded instructions for a computer to carry out

program VERB to put instructions into a computer by means of a program

programme NOUN ❶ a show, play or talk on radio or television ❷ a list of planned events ❸ a leaflet or pamphlet giving details of a

play, concert, football match, etc.

programmer NOUN a person whose job is to write computer programs

progress (say **proh**-gress) NOUN ❶ forward movement ❷ development or improvement

progress (say pro-**gress**) VERB ❶ to move forward or continue ❷ to develop or improve

progressive ADJECTIVE ❶ moving forward or developing steadily ❷ in favour of political or social reforms ❸ a progressive disease is one that becomes gradually more severe

prohibit VERB to forbid or ban something

prohibitive ADJECTIVE prices and costs are prohibitive when they are too high for most people to be able to afford

project (say **proj**-ekt) NOUN ❶ the task of finding out as much as you can about something and writing about it ❷ a plan or scheme

project (say pro-**jekt**) VERB ❶ to stick out ❷ to show a film or picture on a screen ❸ to project your voice is to speak loudly and clearly so that it carries a long way ❹ to give people a particular impression

projectile NOUN something fired from a gun or thrown; a missile

projection NOUN ❶ a part of something that sticks out ❷ showing a film or picture on a screen with a projector

projectionist NOUN a person who works a projector

projector NOUN a machine for

showing films or photographs on a screen

proletariat (say proh-lit-**air**-ee-at) NOUN working people

prolific ADJECTIVE producing a lot

prologue (say proh-log) NOUN an introduction to a poem, play or story

prolong VERB to make something last longer

prolonged ADJECTIVE continuing for a long time

prom NOUN (informal) ❶ a formal dance for secondary school students ❷ a promenade ❸ a promenade concert

promenade (say prom-in-**ahd**) NOUN ❶ a place suitable for walking, especially beside the seashore ❷ a leisurely walk

promenade VERB to take a leisurely walk

promenade concert a concert where part of the audience stands in an area without seating

prominence NOUN being important or well known

prominent ADJECTIVE ❶ easy to see or notice ❷ sticking out ❸ important

promise NOUN ❶ a statement that you will definitely do or not do something ❷ signs of future success or good results

promise VERB to make a promise

promising ADJECTIVE likely to be good or successful

promontory NOUN a piece of high land that sticks out into a sea or lake

promote VERB ❶ to move a person

to a more senior or more important job or position ❷ a sports team is promoted when it moves to a higher division or league ❸ to help the progress of something ❹ to publicize or advertise a product in order to sell it

promotion NOUN ❶ a move to a higher position or more important job ❷ when a sports team moves to a higher division or league ❸ a piece of publicity or advertising ❹ helping the progress of something

prompt ADJECTIVE ❶ without delay ❷ punctual

prompt ADVERB (British) exactly at that time

prompt VERB ❶ to cause or encourage a person to do something ❷ to remind an actor or speaker of words when they have forgotten them

promptly ADVERB ❶ without delay; immediately ❷ punctually

prone ADJECTIVE lying face downwards

prong NOUN one of the spikes on a fork

pronoun NOUN a word used instead of a noun: **demonstrative pronouns** are this, that, these, those; **interrogative pronouns** are who?, what?, which?, etc.; **personal pronouns** are I, me, we, us, you, he, him, she, her, it, they, them, etc.; **possessive pronouns** are mine, yours, theirs, etc.; **reflexive pronouns** are myself, yourself, etc.; **relative pronouns** are who, what, which, that, etc.

pronounce VERB ❶ to say a sound

or word in a particular way ❷ to declare something formally

pronounced ADJECTIVE very noticeable

pronouncement NOUN a formal public statement

pronunciation NOUN the way a word is pronounced

proof NOUN ❶ a fact or thing that shows something is true ❷ a printed copy of a book or photograph made for checking before other copies are printed

proof ADJECTIVE able to resist something or not be affected by it

prop NOUN ❶ a support, especially one made of a long piece of wood or metal ❷ an object or piece of furniture used on a theatre stage or in a film

prop VERB to support something by leaning it against something else

propaganda NOUN false or exaggerated information that is spread around to make people believe something

propagate VERB ❶ to grow new plants from an original plant ❷ to spread an idea or belief to a lot of people

propel VERB to push something forward

propeller NOUN a device with blades that spin round to drive an aircraft or ship

propensity NOUN a tendency to behave in a particular way

proper ADJECTIVE ❶ suitable or right ❷ respectable or socially acceptable ❸ (*informal*) complete or thorough

proper fraction NOUN a fraction that is less than 1, with the numerator less than the denominator, e.g.⅓

properly ADVERB in a correct or suitable way

proper noun NOUN the name of an individual person or thing, e.g. *Mary, London, Spain*, usually written with a capital first letter

property NOUN ❶ a thing or things that a person owns ❷ a building with the land belonging to it ❸ a quality or characteristic

prophecy NOUN ❶ a statement that says what will happen in the future ❷ the power to say what will happen in the future

prophesy VERB to say what you think will happen in the future

prophet NOUN ❶ a person who makes prophecies ❷ a religious teacher who is believed to be inspired by God

prophetic ADJECTIVE saying or showing what will happen in the future

proportion NOUN ❶ a part or share of a whole thing ❷ the proportion of one thing to another is how much there is of one compared to the other ❸ the correct relationship in size, amount or importance between two things

proportional, proportionate ADJECTIVE in proportion; according to a ratio

proportional representation NOUN a system in which each political party has a number of Members of Parliament in

proposal NOUN ❶ a plan that has been suggested ❷ when someone asks another person to marry them

propose VERB ❶ to suggest an idea or plan ❷ to plan or intend to do something ❸ to ask a person to marry you

proposition NOUN ❶ a suggestion or offer ❷ a statement ❸ a problem or task

propound VERB to put forward an idea for consideration

proprietary (say pro-**pry**-it-er-ee) ADJECTIVE ❶ made or sold by one firm; branded ❷ to do with an owner or ownership

proprietor NOUN the owner of a shop or business

propulsion NOUN propelling something or driving it forward

prosaic ADJECTIVE plain or dull and ordinary

proscribe VERB to forbid something by law

prose NOUN writing that is not in verse

prosecute VERB ❶ to make someone go to a law court to be tried for a crime ❷ (formal) to continue doing something

prosecution NOUN ❶ the process of prosecuting someone ❷ the lawyers who try to show that someone is guilty of a crime in a court of law

prospect NOUN ❶ a possibility or expectation of something ❷ a wide view

prospect (say pro-**spekt**) VERB to explore an area in search of gold or some other mineral

prospective ADJECTIVE expected to be or to happen; possible

prospectus NOUN a booklet describing and advertising a school, business company, etc.

prosper VERB to be successful or do well

prosperity NOUN being successful or rich

prosperous ADJECTIVE successful or rich

prostitute NOUN a person who takes part in sexual acts for payment

prostrate ADJECTIVE lying face downwards

prostrate VERB ➤ **prostrate yourself** to lie flat on the ground face down, usually in submission ➤ **prostration** NOUN

protagonist NOUN ❶ the main character in a play ❷ one of the main people involved in a situation

protect VERB to keep someone or something safe from harm or damage

protection NOUN keeping someone or something safe from harm or damage

protective ADJECTIVE ❶ that prevents a person or thing from being harmed or damaged ❷ wanting to keep someone or something safe

protectorate NOUN a country that is under the official protection of a stronger country

protégé (say **prot**-ezh-ay) NOUN

478

someone who is helped and supported by an older or more experienced person

protein *NOUN* a substance that is found in all living things and is an essential part of the food of animals

protest (say **proh**-test) *NOUN* a statement or action showing that you disapprove of something

protest (say pro-**test**) *VERB* ❶ to make a protest ❷ to declare something firmly

Protestant *NOUN* a member of any of the western Christian Churches separated from the Roman Catholic Church

protocol *NOUN* the correct or official procedure for behaving in certain formal situations

proton *NOUN* a particle of matter with a positive electric charge

prototype *NOUN* the first model of something, from which others are copied or developed

protracted *ADJECTIVE* lasting longer than usual or expected

protractor *NOUN* a device for measuring angles, usually a semicircle marked off in degrees

protrude *VERB* to stick out from somewhere

proud *ADJECTIVE* ❶ very pleased with yourself or with someone else who has done well ❷ causing pride ❸ full of self-respect and independence ❹ having too high an opinion of yourself

prove *VERB* proves, proving, proved ❶ to show that something is true ❷ to turn out a certain way

proven (say **proh**-ven) *ADJECTIVE* that has been shown to be true

proverb *NOUN* a short well-known saying that states a truth, e.g. 'Many hands make light work.'

proverbial *ADJECTIVE* ❶ referred to in a proverb ❷ familiar or well known

provide *VERB* ❶ to make something available; to supply something ❷ to prepare for something that might happen

provided *CONJUNCTION* on condition that; only if

providence *NOUN* ❶ being careful and providing for the future ❷ God's or nature's care and protection

provider *NOUN* a person or thing that provides something

providing *CONJUNCTION* on condition that; only if

province *NOUN* ❶ a section of a country ❷ the area of a person's special knowledge or responsibility

provincial (say pro-**vin**-shul) *ADJECTIVE* ❶ to do with the provinces ❷ culturally limited or narrow-minded

provision *NOUN* ❶ providing something ❷ a statement in a legal document

provisional *ADJECTIVE* arranged or agreed on for the time being but possibly to be changed later

provisions *PLURAL NOUN* supplies of food and drink

provocation *NOUN* something done or said deliberately to annoy someone

provocative *ADJECTIVE* ❶ likely to

make someone angry ❷ intended to make someone feel sexual desire

provoke VERB ❶ to deliberately make a person angry ❷ to cause or give rise to something

prow NOUN the front end of a ship

prowess NOUN great ability or skill

prowl VERB to move about quietly or cautiously, like a hunter

prowl NOUN ➤ **on the prowl** moving about quietly or cautiously, hunting or looking for something ➤ **prowler** NOUN

proximity NOUN nearness

proxy NOUN a person authorized to represent or act for another person

prude NOUN a person who is easily shocked

prudent ADJECTIVE sensible and careful; not taking risks

prune NOUN a dried plum

prune VERB to cut off unwanted parts of a tree or bush

pry VERB to look into or ask about someone else's private business

PS ABBREVIATION postscript (used when you add something at the end of a letter)

psalm (say sahm) NOUN a religious song, especially one from the Book of Psalms in the Bible

pseudonym NOUN a name used by a writer instead of their real name

PSHE ABBREVIATION personal, social and health education (as a school subject)

psychedelic ADJECTIVE having vivid colours and patterns

psychiatrist (say sy-**ky**-a-trist) NOUN a doctor who treats mental illnesses

psychic (say sy-kik) ADJECTIVE ❶ appearing to have supernatural powers, especially being able to predict the future or read people's minds ❷ supernatural

psychoanalysis NOUN investigation of a person's mental processes, especially in psychotherapy

psychological ADJECTIVE ❶ to do with the mind or how it works ❷ to do with psychology

psychology NOUN the study of the mind and how it works

psychotherapy NOUN treatment of mental illness by psychological methods

PT ABBREVIATION (British) physical training

PTA ABBREVIATION parent-teacher association; an organization that arranges discussions between teachers and parents about school business and raises money for the school

pterodactyl (say te-ro-**dak**-til) NOUN an extinct flying reptile

PTO ABBREVIATION please turn over (put at the end of a page of writing when there is more writing on the next page)

pub NOUN (British) a building licensed to serve alcoholic drinks to the public

puberty (say **pew**-ber-tee) NOUN the time when a young person is developing physically into an adult

pubic (say **pew**-bik) ADJECTIVE to do with the lower front part of the abdomen

public ADJECTIVE ❶ belonging to

everyone or able to be used by everyone ❷ to do with people in general

public NOUN people in general

publican NOUN (*British*) the person in charge of a pub

publication NOUN ❶ publishing ❷ a published book, newspaper or magazine

public house NOUN (*British*) (*formal*) a pub

publicity NOUN information or advertising that makes people know about something

publicize (also **publicise**) VERB to bring something to people's attention; to advertise something

public school NOUN ❶ in England, a private secondary school that charges fees ❷ in Scotland and the USA, a school run by a local authority or by the state

publish VERB ❶ to produce a book, magazine, etc. and sell it to the public ❷ to make something available for people to read online ❸ to make something known publicly

publisher NOUN a person or company that publishes books, magazines, etc.

puce NOUN a dark red or brownish-purple colour

puck NOUN a hard rubber disc used in ice hockey

pucker VERB to form into wrinkles or to make something do this

pudding NOUN (*chiefly British*) ❶ the sweet course of a meal ❷ a food made in a soft mass, especially in a mixture of flour and

other ingredients

puddle NOUN a shallow patch of liquid, especially of rainwater on a road

pudgy ADJECTIVE short and fat

puerile (say *pew*-er-yl) ADJECTIVE silly and childish

puff NOUN ❶ a short blowing of breath, wind, smoke or steam ❷ a soft pad for putting powder on the skin ❸ a cake of very light pastry filled with cream

puff VERB ❶ to blow out puffs of smoke or steam ❷ to pant or breathe with difficulty ❸ to inflate or swell something

puffin NOUN a seabird with a large striped beak

puffy ADJECTIVE puffed out or swollen

pug NOUN a small dog with a flat face like a bulldog

puke VERB (*informal*) to vomit

pull VERB ❶ to hold something and make it come towards you ❷ to move something along behind you ❸ to move with an effort

pull NOUN a pulling movement

pullet NOUN a young hen

pulley NOUN a wheel with a rope, chain or belt over it, used for lifting or moving heavy things

pullover NOUN a knitted piece of clothing for the top half of the body

pulmonary (say *pul*-mon-er-ee) ADJECTIVE to do with the lungs

pulp NOUN ❶ the soft moist part of fruit ❷ any soft moist mass

pulpit NOUN a small enclosed

platform for the preacher in a church or chapel

pulsate VERB to move or shake with strong regular movements

pulse NOUN ❶ the rhythmical movement of the arteries as blood is pumped through them by the beating of the heart ❷ a throb ❸ the edible seed of peas, beans, lentils, etc.

pulse VERB to move or flow with strong regular movements; to throb

pulverize (also **pulverise**) VERB to crush something into powder

puma (say pew-ma) NOUN a large brown cat of western America, also called a cougar or mountain lion

pumice NOUN a kind of porous stone used for rubbing stains from the skin or as powder for polishing things

pummel VERB to keep on hitting something

pump NOUN ❶ a device that pushes air or liquid into or out of something or along pipes ❷ a canvas sports shoe with a rubber sole

pump VERB ❶ to move air or liquid into or out of something with a pump ❷ (*informal*) to question a person to obtain information

pumpkin NOUN a very large round fruit with a hard orange skin

pun NOUN a joking use of a word sounding the same as another or having more than one meaning, e.g. 'Deciding where to bury him was a *grave* decision.'

punch VERB ❶ to hit someone

with your fist ❷ to make a hole in something

punch NOUN ❶ a hit with a fist ❷ a device for making holes in paper, metal, leather, etc. ❸ a drink made by mixing wine or spirits and fruit juice in a bowl

punchline NOUN words that give the climax of a joke or story

punch-up NOUN (*British*) (*informal*) a fight

punctual ADJECTIVE arriving exactly on time; not late

punctuate VERB ❶ to put punctuation marks into a piece of writing ❷ to be punctuated by something is to be frequently interrupted by it

punctuation NOUN marks such as commas, full stops and brackets put into a piece of writing to make it easier to read

puncture NOUN a small hole made by something sharp, especially in a tyre

puncture VERB to make a small hole in something

pundit NOUN a person who is an expert on a subject and is asked for their opinions

pungent (say pun-jent) ADJECTIVE ❶ having a strong taste or smell ❷ pungent remarks are sharp and effective

punish VERB to make a person suffer because they have done something wrong

punishment NOUN something a person suffers because they have done something wrong

punk NOUN ❶ (also **punk rock**) a

loud aggressive style of rock music ② a person who likes this music

punnet NOUN (British) a small container for soft fruit such as strawberries

punt NOUN a flat-bottomed boat moved by pushing a pole against the bottom of a river while standing in the punt

punt VERB ① to move a punt along with a pole ② to kick a football after dropping it from your hands and before it touches the ground

punter NOUN ① a person who lays a bet ② (informal) a customer

puny (say pew-nee) ADJECTIVE very small and weak

pup NOUN ① a puppy ② a young seal

pupa (say pew-pa) NOUN an insect at the stage of development between a larva and an adult insect; a chrysalis

pupil NOUN ① someone who is being taught by a teacher, especially at school ② the opening in the centre of the eye

puppet NOUN ① a kind of doll that can be made to move by fitting it over your hand or working it by strings or wires ② a person whose actions are controlled by someone else

puppy NOUN a young dog

purchase VERB to buy something

purchase NOUN ① something you have bought ② buying something ③ a firm hold or grip

purdah NOUN the practice in some Muslim and Hindu societies of keeping women from the sight of men or strangers

pure ADJECTIVE ① not mixed with anything else ② clean and clear ③ free from evil or sin ④ mere; nothing but

purée (say pewr-ay) NOUN fruit or vegetables made into pulp

purely ADVERB only or simply

purgatory NOUN ① a state of temporary suffering ② in Roman Catholic belief, a place in which souls are purified by punishment before they can enter heaven

purge VERB to get rid of unwanted people or things

purge NOUN an act of purging

purify VERB to make something pure, especially by removing dirty or harmful substances from it

Puritan NOUN a Protestant in the 16th and 17th centuries who wanted simpler religious ceremonies and strict moral behaviour

puritan NOUN a person with very strict morals

purity NOUN being pure

purple NOUN a deep reddish-blue colour

purport (say per-port) VERB to claim to be something or someone

purport (say per-port) NOUN the general meaning of something

purpose NOUN ① what you intend to do; a plan or aim ② determination

purposeful ADJECTIVE determined and having a definite plan or aim

purposely ADVERB on purpose

purr VERB ① a cat purrs when it

makes a low murmuring sound to show it is pleased ❷ to make a low continuous sound ❸ to speak in a low and gentle voice

purr NOUN a purring sound

purse NOUN a small pouch for carrying money

purse VERB to draw your lips tightly together, especially to show disapproval

purser NOUN a ship's officer in charge of accounts

pursue VERB ❶ to chase someone in order to catch them ❷ to continue with something; to work at something

pursuit NOUN ❶ chasing someone ❷ a regular activity

purveyor NOUN a person or company that sells or supplies something

pus NOUN a thick yellowish substance produced in boils or other sore or infected places on your body

push VERB ❶ to make a thing go away from you by using force on it ❷ to press something ❸ to move yourself by using force ❹ to try to force someone to do or use something; to urge someone

push NOUN a pushing movement or effort

pushchair NOUN (British) a folding chair on wheels, for pushing a child along

pusher NOUN a person who sells illegal drugs

pushy ADJECTIVE determined to get what you want, in an unpleasant way

puss NOUN (informal, chiefly British) a cat

pussy NOUN (informal) a cat

pussy willow NOUN a willow with furry catkins

put VERB puts, putting, put ❶ to move a person or thing to a place or position ❷ to make a person or thing do or experience something or be in a certain condition ❸ to express something in words

putt VERB to hit a golf ball gently towards the hole

putt NOUN hitting a golf ball gently towards the hole

putter NOUN a golf club used to putt the ball

putty NOUN a soft paste that sets hard, used for fitting the glass in a window frame

puzzle NOUN ❶ a difficult question or problem ❷ a game or toy that sets a problem to solve or a difficult task to complete

puzzle VERB ❶ to give someone a problem that is hard to understand ❷ to think hard about something in order to understand or explain it

puzzlement NOUN a feeling of being confused because you do not understand something

PVC ABBREVIATION polyvinyl chloride, a plastic used to make clothing, pipes, flooring, etc.

pygmy (say **pig**-mee) NOUN ❶ a very small person or thing ❷ a member of certain unusually short peoples of equatorial Africa

pyjamas PLURAL NOUN a loose jacket and trousers that you wear in bed

pylon NOUN a tall framework made

of strips of steel, supporting electric cables

pyramid NOUN ① a structure with a square base and with sloping sides that meet in a point at the top ② an ancient Egyptian royal tomb shaped like this

pyre NOUN a pile of wood for burning a dead body as part of a funeral ceremony

python NOUN a large snake that kills its prey by coiling round and crushing it

Qq

QED ABBREVIATION *quod erat demonstrandum* (Latin, = which was the thing that had to be proved)

quack VERB to make the harsh cry of a duck

quack NOUN ① the harsh cry made by a duck ② a person who falsely claims to have medical skill or have remedies to cure diseases

quad (say kwod) NOUN ① a quadrangle ② a quadruplet

quadrangle NOUN a rectangular courtyard with large buildings round it

quadrant NOUN a quarter of a circle

quadratic equation NOUN an equation that involves quantities or variables raised to the power of two, but no higher than two

quadrilateral NOUN a flat geometric shape with four sides

quadruped NOUN an animal with four feet

quadruple ADJECTIVE ① four times as much or as many ② having four parts

quadruple VERB to become or make something, four times as much or as many

quadruplet NOUN each of four children born to the same mother at one time

quaff (say kwof) VERB to drink a lot of something

quagmire NOUN a bog or marsh

quail NOUN a bird related to the partridge

quail VERB to feel or show fear

quaint ADJECTIVE attractively odd or old-fashioned

quake VERB to tremble or shake because you are afraid

quake NOUN an earthquake

Quaker NOUN a member of a religious group called the Society of Friends, founded by George Fox in the 17th century

qualification NOUN ① a skill or ability that makes someone suitable for a job ② an exam that you have passed or a course of study that you have completed ③ something that limits the meaning of a remark or statement or makes it less extreme

qualify VERB ① to become able to do something through having certain qualities or training or by passing an exam or to make someone able to do this ② to qualify for a competition is to reach a high enough standard to take part in it ③ to make a remark or statement less extreme or to limit its meaning ④ an adjective

485

a b c d e f g h i j k l m n o p q r s t u v w x y z

A B C D E F G H I J K L M N O P Q R S T U V W X Y Z

qualifies a noun when it describes it or adds meaning to it

quality NOUN ❶ how good or bad something is ❷ a characteristic; something that is special in a person or thing

qualm (say kwahm) NOUN a feeling of worry that what you are doing may not be right

quandary NOUN a difficult situation where you are uncertain what to do

quantity NOUN ❶ how much of something there is or the number of things there are ❷ a large amount

quantum leap, quantum jump NOUN a sudden large increase or advance

quarantine NOUN keeping a person or animal isolated in case they have a disease which could spread to others

quarrel NOUN an angry argument

quarrel VERB to argue fiercely with someone

quarrelsome ADJECTIVE often quarrelling with people

quarry NOUN ❶ an open place where stone or slate is dug or cut out of the ground ❷ an animal or person that is being hunted or pursued

quarry VERB to dig or cut stone or slate from a quarry

quart NOUN a measure for liquids, equal to two pints (or 1.136 litres)

quarter NOUN ❶ each of four equal parts into which a thing is or can be divided ❷ three months, one-fourth of a year ❸ a district

or region

quarter VERB ❶ to divide something into quarters ❷ to put soldiers into lodgings

quarter-final NOUN each of the matches or rounds before a semi-final, in which there are eight contestants or teams

quarterly ADJECTIVE & ADVERB happening or produced once in every three months

quarterly NOUN a quarterly magazine

quarters PLURAL NOUN rooms where soldiers or servants live; lodgings

quartet NOUN ❶ a group of four musicians ❷ a piece of music for four musicians ❸ a set of four people or things

quartz NOUN a hard mineral, often in crystal form

quash VERB to cancel or annul a decision or verdict

quatrain NOUN a stanza with four lines

quaver VERB to speak unsteadily because you are afraid or nervous

quaver NOUN ❶ a quavering sound ❷ a note in music (♪) lasting half as long as a crotchet

quay (say kee) NOUN a landing place where ships can be tied up for loading and unloading; a wharf

quayside NOUN the area around a quay

queasy ADJECTIVE feeling slightly sick

queen NOUN ❶ a woman who is the ruler of a country through inheriting the position ❷ the wife of a king ❸ a female bee

queen mother NOUN a title given to the widow of a king who has died and who is the mother of the present king or queen

queer ADJECTIVE ① strange or odd ② slightly ill or faint

quell VERB ① to crush a rebellion by force ② to stop yourself from feeling fear, anger etc.

quench VERB ① to satisfy your thirst by drinking ② to put out a fire or flame

query (say **kweer-ee**) NOUN a question asking for information or expressing doubt about something

query VERB to question whether something is true or correct

quest NOUN a long search for something

question NOUN ① a sentence asking something ② a problem or subject that needs to be discussed or dealt with ③ doubt about something

question VERB ① to ask someone questions ② to say that you are doubtful about something

questionable ADJECTIVE causing doubt; not certainly true or honest or advisable

question mark NOUN the punctuation mark (?) placed after a question

questionnaire NOUN a written set of questions asked to provide information for a survey

queue (say **kew**) NOUN a line of people or vehicles waiting for something

queue VERB to wait in a queue

quibble NOUN a trivial complaint or objection

quibble VERB to make trivial complaints or objections

quiche (say **keesh**) NOUN an open tart with a savoury filling

quick ADJECTIVE ① taking only a short time to do something ② done in a short time ③ able to notice or learn or think quickly

quick ADVERB quickly

quicken VERB ① to make something quicker ② to become quicker

quickly ADVERB fast; in a short time

quicksand NOUN an area of loose wet deep sand that sucks in anything resting or falling on top of it

quid NOUN (British) (informal) £1

quiet ADJECTIVE ① silent; not saying anything ② with little sound; not loud or noisy ③ calm and peaceful; without disturbance ④ quiet colours are soft and not bright

quiet NOUN a time when it is calm and there is no noise

quieten VERB (chiefly British) to become quiet or to make a person or thing quiet

quietly ADVERB ① without making much noise ② in a quiet voice ③ without attracting much attention

quiff NOUN (chiefly British) an upright tuft of hair

quill NOUN ① a large feather ② a pen made from a large feather ③ one of the spines on a porcupine or hedgehog

quilt NOUN a cover for a bed filled with soft padding

quilt VERB to line material with padding and fix it with lines of stitching

quin NOUN (British) (informal) a quintuplet

quince NOUN a hard pear-shaped fruit used for making jam

quinine (say kwin-**een**) NOUN a bitter-tasting medicine used to cure malaria

quintet NOUN ❶ a group of five musicians ❷ a piece of music for five musicians

quintuplet NOUN each of five children born to the same mother at one time

quip NOUN a witty remark

quip VERB to make a witty remark

quirk NOUN ❶ a peculiarity of a person's behaviour ❷ a trick of fate

quit VERB quits, quitting, quitted or quit ❶ to leave or abandon a place or job ❷ (informal) to stop doing something

quite ADVERB ❶ completely or entirely ❷ rather or fairly; to some extent

quits ADJECTIVE people are quits when they are even or equal again and neither owes the other anything or has an advantage over them

quiver VERB to tremble

quiver NOUN ❶ a container for arrows ❷ a trembling movement

quiz NOUN a series of questions, especially as an entertainment or competition

quiz VERB to ask someone a lot of questions

quizzical ADJECTIVE seeming to be asking a question, especially in an amused way

quoit (say koit) NOUN a ring thrown at a peg in the game of **quoits**

quota NOUN a fixed or limited amount or share that is allowed or expected

quotation NOUN ❶ something quoted ❷ a statement of how much a piece of work will cost

quotation marks PLURAL NOUN inverted commas (" " or ' ') used to mark direct speech or a quotation

quote VERB ❶ to repeat words that were first written or spoken by someone else ❷ to mention an example of something to support what you are saying ❸ to state the price of goods or services that you can supply

quote NOUN a quotation

quotient (say **kwoh**-shent) NOUN the result of dividing one number by another. Compare with **product**.

Qur'an NOUN another spelling of **Koran**

Rr

rabbi (say **rab**-eye) NOUN a Jewish religious leader

rabbit NOUN a furry animal with long ears that digs burrows

rabble NOUN a noisy or disorderly crowd or mob

rabid (say **rab**-id) ADJECTIVE

1 extreme or fanatical **2** suffering from rabies

rabies (say ray-beez) NOUN a fatal disease that affects dogs and other mammals and can be passed to humans by the bite of an infected animal

raccoon NOUN a North American animal with a bushy, striped tail and greyish-brown fur

race NOUN **1** a sports contest in which the fastest competitor wins **2** a competition to be the first to reach a particular place or to do something **3** a very large group of people thought to have the same ancestors and with physical characteristics (e.g. colour of skin and hair, shape of eyes and nose) that differ from those of other groups **4** racial origin

race VERB **1** to compete in a race **2** to move very fast

racecourse NOUN a place where horse races are run

racehorse NOUN a horse bred or kept for racing

race relations NOUN relationships between people of different races in the same country

racetrack NOUN a track for horse or vehicle races

racial (say ray-shul) ADJECTIVE to do with a particular race or based on race

racism (say ray-sizm) NOUN **1** discrimination against or hostility towards people of other races **2** belief that a particular race of people is better than others

rack NOUN **1** a framework used as

a shelf or container **2** an ancient device for torturing people by stretching them **3** a bar or rail with cogs into which the cogs of a gear or wheel fit

rack VERB to be racked with physical or mental pain is to be tormented by it

racket NOUN **1** a bat with strings stretched across a frame, used in tennis, badminton and squash **2** a loud noise or din **3** a dishonest or illegal business

racoon NOUN a different spelling of raccoon

racquet NOUN a different spelling of racket

racy ADJECTIVE lively and slightly shocking in style

radar NOUN a system or apparatus that uses radio waves to show on a screen the position of ships, planes, etc. that cannot be seen because of distance or poor visibility

radial ADJECTIVE **1** to do with rays or radii **2** having spokes or lines that radiate from a central point

radiant ADJECTIVE **1** radiating light or heat **2** transmitted by radiation **3** looking very bright and happy

radiate VERB **1** to send out light, heat or other energy in rays **2** to give out a strong feeling or quality **3** to spread out from a central point like the spokes of a wheel

radiation NOUN **1** light, heat or other energy given out by something **2** the energy or particles sent out by a radioactive substance **3** the process of radiating light, heat or other energy

radiator NOUN ❶ a device that gives out heat, especially a metal case that is heated electrically or through which steam or hot water flows ❷ a device that cools the engine of a motor vehicle

radical ADJECTIVE ❶ basic and thorough; going right to the root of something ❷ wanting to make great social or political reforms

radical NOUN a person who wants to make great social or political reforms

radicchio (say ra-dee-ki-oh) NOUN a kind of chicory with dark red leaves

radio NOUN ❶ the process of sending and receiving sound or pictures by means of electromagnetic waves ❷ an apparatus for receiving radio programmes or for sending or receiving radio messages ❸ sound broadcasting

radio VERB to send a message to someone by radio

radioactive ADJECTIVE having atoms that break up spontaneously and send out radiation which produces electrical and chemical effects and penetrates things

radiocarbon dating NOUN carbon dating

radiography NOUN the production of X-ray photographs

radiology NOUN the study of X-rays and similar radiation, especially in treating diseases

radio telescope NOUN an instrument that can detect radio waves from space

radiotherapy NOUN the use of radioactive substances in treating diseases such as cancer

radish NOUN a small hard round red vegetable with a hot taste, eaten raw in salads

radium NOUN a radioactive substance found in pitchblende, often used in radiotherapy

radius NOUN radii or radiuses ❶ a straight line from the centre of a circle to the circumference; the length of this line ❷ a range or distance from a central point

radon NOUN a radioactive gas used in radiotherapy

raffia NOUN soft fibre from the leaves of a kind of palm tree, used for making mats and baskets

raffle NOUN a way of raising money, usually for a charity, by selling numbered tickets, some of which win prizes

raffle VERB to offer something as a prize in a raffle

raft NOUN ❶ a flat floating structure made of wood etc., used as a boat ❷ a large number or amount of things

rafter NOUN any of the long sloping pieces of wood that hold up a roof

rag NOUN ❶ an old or torn piece of cloth ❷ a piece of ragtime music ❸ (*British*) a series of entertainments and activities held by students to collect money for charity

rag VERB (*informal*) to tease someone

rage NOUN great or violent anger

rage VERB ❶ to be very angry ❷ to continue violently or with great force

ragged (say **rag**-id) ADJECTIVE ❶ torn or frayed ❷ wearing torn clothes ❸ not smooth or controlled

ragtime NOUN a kind of jazz music played on the piano

raid NOUN ❶ a sudden attack ❷ a surprise visit by police to arrest people or seize illegal goods

raid VERB to make a raid on a place

rail NOUN ❶ a level or sloping bar for hanging things on or forming part of a fence or banisters ❷ a long metal bar forming part of a railway track

rail VERB to complain angrily or bitterly about something

railings PLURAL NOUN a fence made of metal bars

railway NOUN (British) ❶ the parallel metal bars that trains travel on ❷ a system of transport using rails

rain NOUN drops of water that fall from the sky

rain VERB ❶ it is raining when rain is falling ❷ to come down in large amounts ❸ to send something down in large amounts

rainbow NOUN an arch of all the colours of the spectrum formed in the sky when the sun shines through rain

raincoat NOUN a waterproof coat

raindrop NOUN a single drop of rain

rainfall NOUN the amount of rain that falls in a particular place or time

rainforest NOUN a dense tropical forest in an area of very heavy rainfall

rainy ADJECTIVE having a lot of rainfall

raise VERB ❶ to move something to a higher place or an upright position ❷ to increase the amount or level of something ❸ to succeed in collecting an amount of money ❹ to bring up young children or animals ❺ to mention or put something forward for people to think about ❻ to raise a laugh or smile is to make people laugh or smile ❼ to raise your voice is to speak more loudly

raisin NOUN a dried grape

Raj (say rahj) NOUN the period of Indian history when the country was ruled by Britain

raja, rajah NOUN an Indian king or prince.

rake NOUN ❶ a gardening tool with a row of short spikes fixed to a long handle ❷ (old use) a man who lives an irresponsible and immoral life

rake VERB ❶ to gather or smooth something with a rake ❷ to search through something

rakish (say ray-kish) ADJECTIVE jaunty and dashing in appearance

rally NOUN ❶ a large meeting to support something or share an interest ❷ a competition to test skill in driving ❸ an exchange of strokes in tennis, squash, etc. before a point is won

rally VERB ❶ to bring people together for a united effort ❷ to come together to help or support someone ③ to improve or become stronger after an illness or setback

RAM *ABBREVIATION (in computing)* random-access memory, with contents that can be retrieved or stored directly without having to read through items already stored

ram *NOUN* ① a male sheep ② a part of a machine that is used for hitting something very hard

ram *VERB* ① to push one thing hard against another ② to crash into another vehicle

Ramadan *NOUN* the ninth month of the Muslim year, when Muslims do not eat or drink between sunrise and sunset

ramble *NOUN* a long walk in the countryside

ramble *VERB* ① to go for a ramble; to wander ② to talk a lot without keeping to the subject

rambling *ADJECTIVE* ① confused and wandering from one subject to another ② growing or spreading in many directions

ramifications *PLURAL NOUN* the many effects of a plan or action

ramp *NOUN* a slope joining two different levels

rampage *VERB* to rush about wildly or destructively

rampant *ADJECTIVE* ① growing or spreading uncontrollably ② (said about an animal on coats of arms) standing upright on a hind leg

rampart *NOUN* a wide bank of earth built as a fortification or a wall on top of this

ramshackle *ADJECTIVE* badly made and rickety

ranch *NOUN* a large cattle farm in North America

rancid *ADJECTIVE* smelling or tasting unpleasant like stale fat

rancour (say rank-er) *NOUN* bitter resentment or ill will

random *NOUN* ➤ at random using no particular order or method

random *ADJECTIVE* done or taken at random

range *NOUN* ① a set of different things of the same type ② the limits between which something varies ③ the distance that a gun can shoot, an aircraft can travel or a sound can be heard ④ a place with targets for shooting practice ⑤ a line or series of mountains or hills ⑥ a kitchen fireplace with ovens

range *VERB* ① to exist or vary between two limits ② to arrange things in a certain way ③ to wander or move over a wide area

Ranger *NOUN* a senior Guide

ranger *NOUN* someone who looks after or patrols a park or forest

rank *NOUN* ① a position in a series of different levels ② a line of people or things ③ a place where taxis stand to wait for customers

rank *VERB* ① to have a certain rank or place ② to put things in order according to their rank

rank *ADJECTIVE* ① smelling very unpleasant ② unmistakably bad; complete ③ growing too thickly and coarsely

rankle *VERB* to cause lasting annoyance or resentment

ransack *VERB* ① to search a place thoroughly or roughly ② to rob or pillage a place

ransom NOUN money that has to be paid for a prisoner to be set free

ransom VERB ❶ to free someone by paying a ransom ❷ to get a ransom for someone

rant VERB to speak or shout loudly and angrily

rant NOUN a spell of ranting

rap VERB ❶ to knock quickly and loudly ❷ to speak words rapidly in rhythm to a strong musical beat ❸ (*informal*) to criticize someone strongly

rap NOUN ❶ a rapping movement or sound ❷ a type of pop music in which you speak words rapidly in rhythm to a strong musical beat

rape NOUN ❶ the crime of forcing someone to have sexual intercourse when they do not want to ❷ a plant with bright yellow flowers, grown as food for sheep and for its seed from which oil is obtained

rape VERB to force someone to have sexual intercourse

rapid ADJECTIVE moving or happening very quickly; swift

rapids PLURAL NOUN part of a river where the water flows very quickly

rapier NOUN a thin lightweight sword

rapport (say rap-**or**) NOUN a friendly and understanding relationship between people

rapt ADJECTIVE so interested and absorbed in something that you do not notice anything else

rapture NOUN very great joy or delight

rare ADJECTIVE ❶ unusual; not often found or happening ❷ meat is rare when it is lightly cooked so that the inside is still red

rarefied ADJECTIVE ❶ rarefied air is thin and below normal pressure ❷ remote from everyday life

rarely ADVERB not very often

rarity NOUN ❶ rareness ❷ something uncommon; a thing valued because it is rare

rascal NOUN a dishonest or mischievous person

rash ADJECTIVE doing something or done without thinking of the possible risks or effects

rash NOUN ❶ an outbreak of red spots or patches on the skin ❷ a number of unwelcome events happening in a short time

rasher NOUN a slice of bacon

rasp NOUN ❶ a file with sharp points on its surface ❷ a rough grating sound

rasp VERB ❶ to say something in a rough unpleasant voice ❷ to make a rough grating sound or effect ❸ to scrape something roughly

raspberry NOUN a small soft red fruit

Rastafarian NOUN a member of a religious group that started in Jamaica

rat NOUN ❶ an animal like a large mouse ❷ an unpleasant or treacherous person

ratchet NOUN a row of notches on a bar or wheel in which a device catches to prevent it running backwards

rate NOUN ❶ how fast or how often

something happens **②** a charge, cost or value **③** quality or standard

rate VERB **①** to say how good you think something is **②** to regard something in a certain way

rates PLURAL NOUN a local tax paid by owners of commercial land and buildings

rather ADVERB **①** slightly or quite **②** you would rather do one thing than another thing if you would prefer to do it **③** more exactly; instead of **④** (informal) definitely, yes

ratify VERB to confirm or agree to something officially

rating NOUN **①** the way something is rated **②** a sailor who is not an officer

ratio (say ray-shee-oh) NOUN **①** the relationship between two numbers, showing how many times one number goes into the other **②** proportion (= two measures of flour to one measure of butter)

ration NOUN **①** a fixed amount allowed to one person **②** rations are a fixed daily amount of food given to a soldier or member of an expedition

ration VERB to share something out in fixed amounts

rational ADJECTIVE **①** reasonable or sensible; based on reason **②** able to reason and make sensible decisions

rationalize (also **rationalise**) VERB **①** to make a thing logical and consistent **②** to justify something by inventing a reasonable explanation for it **③** to make a company or industry more efficient by reorganizing it

rattle VERB **①** to make a series of short sharp hard sounds **②** to move quickly with a rattling noise **③** to make a person feel nervous or flustered

rattle NOUN **①** a rattling sound **②** a device or baby's toy that rattles

rattlesnake NOUN a poisonous American snake with a tail that rattles

raucous (say raw-kus) ADJECTIVE sounding loud and harsh

ravage VERB to do great damage to something; to devastate a place or thing

ravages PLURAL NOUN damaging effects

rave VERB **①** to talk wildly or angrily or madly **②** to talk enthusiastically about something

rave NOUN (informal) a large party or event with dancing to loud fast electronic music

raven NOUN a large black bird, related to the crow

ravenous ADJECTIVE very hungry

ravine (say ra-veen) NOUN a deep narrow gorge or valley

ravings PLURAL NOUN wild talk that makes no sense

ravioli NOUN small squares of pasta filled with meat and served with a sauce

ravishing ADJECTIVE very beautiful

raw ADJECTIVE **①** not cooked **②** in the natural state; not yet processed **③** without much experience **④** with the skin removed **⑤** cold and damp

raw material NOUN natural

substances used in industry

ray *NOUN* ❶ a thin line of light, heat or other radiation ❷ each of a set of lines or parts extending from a centre ❸ a trace of something ❹ a large sea fish with a flat body and a long tail

rayon *NOUN* a synthetic fibre or cloth made from cellulose

raze *VERB* to destroy a building or town completely

razor *NOUN* a device with a very sharp blade, especially one used for shaving

RC *ABBREVIATION* Roman Catholic

re- *PREFIX* again (as in *rebuild*)

reach *VERB* ❶ to go as far as a place or point; to arrive at a place or thing ❷ to stretch out your hand to get or touch something ❸ to succeed in achieving something

reach *NOUN* ❶ the distance a person or thing can reach ❷ a distance you can easily travel

react *VERB* ❶ to respond to something; to have a reaction ❷ to undergo a chemical change

reaction *NOUN* ❶ an effect or feeling produced in one person or thing by another ❷ a chemical change caused when substances act upon each other

reactor *NOUN* an apparatus for producing nuclear power in a controlled way

read *VERB* reads, reading, read (say red) ❶ to look at something written or printed and understand it or say it aloud ❷ a computer reads data when it copies, searches or extracts it ❸ to show a

particular number or amount ❹ to study a subject at university

readable *ADJECTIVE* ❶ easy or enjoyable to read ❷ clear and able to be read

reader *NOUN* ❶ a person who reads ❷ a device that reads or displays data ❸ a book that helps someone learn to read

readership *NOUN* the readers of a newspaper or magazine; the number of these

readily (say red-il-ee) *ADVERB* ❶ willingly or eagerly ❷ easily; without any difficulty

readiness *NOUN* ❶ being ready or prepared for something ❷ being willing to do something

reading *NOUN* ❶ the activity of reading books and other forms of writing ❷ the figure shown on a meter, gauge or other instrument ❸ a gathering of people at which something is read aloud

ready *ADJECTIVE* ❶ fully prepared to do something; completed and able to be used ❷ willing to do something ❸ quick and clever

ready *ADVERB* beforehand

ready-made *ADJECTIVE* made already and so able to be used or served immediately

real *ADJECTIVE* ❶ actually existing, not imaginary ❷ actual or true ❸ genuine; not an imitation

real estate *NOUN* (*North American*) property consisting of land and buildings

realism *NOUN* seeing or showing things as they really are

realistic *ADJECTIVE* ❶ true to life

a
b
c
d
e
f
g
h
i
j
k
l
m
n
o
p
q
r
s
t
u
v
w
x
y
z

② seeing things as they really are

reality NOUN **①** what is real **②** something real

reality TV NOUN television shows that are based on real people, not actors, in real situations

realization (also **realisation**) NOUN realizing something

realize (also **realise**) VERB **①** to be fully aware of something; to accept something as true **②** to make a hope or plan happen **③** to obtain money in exchange for something by selling it

really ADVERB **①** truly or in fact **②** very

realm (say relm) NOUN **①** a kingdom **②** an area of knowledge or interest

reams PLURAL NOUN a large quantity of writing or information

reap VERB **①** to cut down and gather corn when it is ripe **②** to gain something as the result of something you have done

reappear VERB to appear again

rear NOUN the back part of something

rear ADJECTIVE placed or found at the back

rear VERB **①** to care for and bring up young children or animals **②** a horse rears when it rises up on its hind legs so that its front legs are in the air **③** to rise up over you

rearguard NOUN troops protecting the rear of an army

rearrange VERB to arrange something in a different way or order

reason NOUN **①** a cause or explanation of something; why

something happens **②** reasoning; common sense

reason VERB **①** to use your ability to think and draw conclusions **②** to try to persuade someone by giving reasons

reasonable ADJECTIVE **①** ready to use or listen to reason; sensible or logical **②** fair or moderate; not expensive **③** acceptable or fairly good

reasonably ADVERB **①** in a reasonable way; sensibly **②** fairly or quite

reassure VERB to restore someone's confidence by removing doubts and fears

rebel (say rib-el) VERB to refuse to obey someone in authority, especially the government; to fight against the rulers of your own country

rebel (say reb-el) NOUN **①** someone who rejects accepted standards of behaviour **②** someone who fights against their country's government because they want things to change

rebellion NOUN **①** rebelling against authority **②** organized armed resistance to the government; a revolt

rebellious ADJECTIVE often refusing to obey authority; likely to rebel

rebirth NOUN a return to life or activity; a revival of something

rebound VERB to bounce back after hitting something

rebound NOUN ➤ **on the rebound** to hit a ball on the rebound is to hit it when it has bounced up or back

rebuff *NOUN* an unkind refusal; a snub

rebuff *VERB* to give someone a rebuff

rebuild *VERB* to build something again after it has been destroyed

rebuke *VERB* to speak severely to a person who has done wrong

rebuke *NOUN* a sharp or severe criticism

recall *VERB* ① to remember something from the past ② to tell a person to come back ③ to ask for a product to be returned because it is faulty

recall *NOUN* ① the ability to remember; remembering something ② an order for a person to return or for a thing to be returned

recap *VERB* (*informal*) to summarize what has been said

recapture *VERB* ① to catch a person or animal that has escaped ② to take back a place that was taken from you ③ to bring or get back a mood or feeling

recede *VERB* ① to move back or away ② to become less strong or severe ③ a man's hair is receding when he starts to go bald at the front of his head

receipt (say ris-**eet**) *NOUN* ① a written statement that money has been paid or something has been received ② receiving something

receive *VERB* ① to take or get something that is given or sent to you ② to experience something ③ to react to something in a certain way ④ to greet a guest or visitor

receiver *NOUN* ① a person or thing that receives something ② a radio or television set that receives broadcasts ③ the part of a telephone that receives the sound and that you hold to your ear ④ an official who takes charge of a bankrupt person's property ⑤ a person who buys and sells stolen goods

recent *ADJECTIVE* happening or made or done a short time ago

recently *ADVERB* not long ago

receptacle *NOUN* something for holding or containing what is put into it

reception *NOUN* ① the type of welcome that a person or thing receives ② a formal party to receive guests ③ a place in a hotel or office where visitors are greeted and registered ④ the first class in an infant school ⑤ the quality of television or radio signals

receptionist *NOUN* a person whose job is to greet and deal with visitors, clients or patients

recess (say ris-**ess**) *NOUN* ① a section of a wall that is set back from the main part; an alcove ② a time when work or business is stopped for a while

recession *NOUN* a reduction in a country's trade or prosperity

recharge *VERB* to put more electrical power into a battery

recipe (say **ress**-ip-ee) *NOUN* a list of ingredients and instructions for preparing or cooking food

recipient *NOUN* a person who receives something

reciprocal (say ris-**ip**-rok-al) ADJECTIVE given or done in return for the same thing that is given to or done for you; mutual

reciprocal NOUN a reversed fraction

reciprocate VERB to behave or feel towards someone in the same way as they behave or feel towards you; to do the same thing in return

recital NOUN ❶ reciting something ❷ a musical entertainment given by one performer or group

recite VERB to say a poem or other piece of writing aloud from memory

reckless ADJECTIVE rash; ignoring risk or danger

reckon VERB ❶ to have something as an opinion; to think or believe something ❷ to calculate an amount or total

reclaim VERB ❶ to claim or get something back ❷ to reclaim land is to make it suitable for farming or building on again by clearing or draining it

recline VERB to lean or lie back

recluse NOUN a person who lives alone and avoids mixing with people

recognition NOUN recognizing someone or something

recognize (also **recognise**) VERB ❶ to know who someone is or what something is because you have seen that person or thing before ❷ to realize or admit something ❸ to accept something as genuine, valid or lawful

recoil VERB ❶ to move back suddenly in shock or disgust ❷ a gun recoils when it jerks backwards when it is fired

recollect VERB to remember something

recollection NOUN ❶ being able to remember something ❷ something you remember

recommend VERB ❶ to suggest something because you think it is good or suitable ❷ to advise someone to do something

recommendation NOUN ❶ saying that something is good and should be tried or used ❷ a statement about what should be done

reconcile VERB ❶ to be reconciled with someone is to become friendly with them again after quarrelling or fighting with them ❷ to be reconciled to something is to be persuaded to put up with it ❸ to make things agree

reconnaissance (say rik-**on**-i-sans) NOUN an exploration of an area, especially in order to gather information about it for military purposes

reconsider VERB to consider something again and perhaps change an earlier decision

reconstruct VERB ❶ to construct or build something again ❷ to create or act out past events again

record (say **rek**-ord) NOUN ❶ information kept in a permanent form, e.g. in writing or stored on a computer ❷ the best performance in a sport etc. or the most remarkable event of its kind ❸ what is known about a person's past life or career ❹ a disc on which sound has been recorded

record (say **rek**-ord) ADJECTIVE best, highest or most extreme recorded up to now

record (say rik-**ord**) VERB ❶ to keep information by writing it down or storing it on a computer ❷ to store sounds or scenes (e.g. television pictures) using electronic equipment so that you can play or show them later

recorder NOUN ❶ a kind of flute held downwards from the player's mouth ❷ a person or thing that records something

record player NOUN a machine that plays records

recount VERB ❶ (say ri-**kownt**) to give an account of something ❷ (say ree-**kownt**) to count something again

recount (say ree-**kownt**) NOUN counting something again, especially votes in an election

recoup (say ri-**koop**) VERB to recover the cost of an investment or of a loss

recourse NOUN a source of help

recover VERB ❶ to get well again after being ill or weak ❷ to get something back again after losing it

recovery NOUN ❶ getting well again after being ill or weak ❷ getting something back again after losing it

recreation NOUN ❶ enjoying yourself and relaxing when you are not working ❷ a game or hobby that is an enjoyable activity

recrimination NOUN an accusation made against a person who has

criticized or blamed you

recruit NOUN ❶ a person who has just joined the armed forces ❷ a new member of a society, company or other group

recruit VERB ❶ to get someone to join something you belong to ❷ to get someone to join the armed forces

rectangle NOUN a shape with four straight sides and four right angles

rectify VERB to correct a mistake or put something right

rector NOUN a member of the Church of England clergy in charge of a parish

rectum NOUN the last part of the large intestine, ending at the anus

recuperate VERB to get better after an illness

recur VERB to happen again or keep on happening

recurring decimal NOUN (in mathematics) a decimal fraction in which a digit or group of digits is repeated indefinitely, e.g. 0.666 …

recycle VERB to convert waste material into a form in which it can be used again

red ADJECTIVE ❶ of the colour of blood or a colour rather like this ❷ red hair or fur is of a reddish brown colour ❸ having communist or socialist views

red NOUN ❶ a red colour ❷ a communist or socialist

red deer NOUN a kind of large deer with a reddish-brown coat, found in Europe and Asia

redden VERB to become red; to blush

a b c d e f g h i j k l m n o p q r s t u v w x y z

redeem VERB ❶ to make up for faults ❷ to get something back by paying for it or handing over a voucher ❸ to save a person from damnation, as in some religions

redevelop VERB to develop a place or area in a different way

red-handed ADJECTIVE ➤ **catch someone red-handed** to catch someone while they are actually committing a crime or doing something wrong

redhead NOUN a person with reddish hair

red herring NOUN something that draws attention away from the main subject; a misleading clue

red-hot ADJECTIVE very hot; so hot that it has turned red

red meat NOUN meat, such as beef, lamb or mutton, which is red when raw

redolent (say **red**-ol-ent) ADJECTIVE ❶ smelling strongly of something ❷ strongly suggesting or reminding you of something

redress VERB to correct something that is unfair or wrong

redress NOUN compensation for something wrong that has been done

red tape NOUN all the rules and forms that make it difficult to get official business done quickly

reduce VERB ❶ to make something smaller or less ❷ to become smaller or less ❸ to force someone into a condition or situation

reduction NOUN ❶ when something becomes smaller or less ❷ the amount by which a thing

is reduced

redundant ADJECTIVE ❶ no longer needed ❷ someone is made redundant when they lose their job because it is no longer needed

reed NOUN ❶ a tall plant that grows in water or marshy ground ❷ a thin strip that vibrates to make the sound in a clarinet, saxophone, oboe, etc.

reedy ADJECTIVE ❶ full of reeds ❷ a reedy voice has a thin high tone like a reed instrument

reef NOUN a ridge of rock, coral or sand, especially one near the surface of the sea

reef VERB to shorten a sail by drawing in a strip (called a **reef**) at the top or bottom to reduce the area exposed to the wind

reek VERB to smell strongly or unpleasantly

reek NOUN a strong unpleasant smell

reel NOUN ❶ a round device on which cotton, thread or film is wound ❷ a lively Scottish dance or the music for this

reel VERB ❶ to wind something onto or off a reel ❷ to stagger ❸ to feel dizzy or confused

re-elect VERB to elect someone again

re-enter VERB to enter a place or contest again

ref NOUN (informal) a referee

refectory NOUN the dining room of a college or monastery etc.

refer VERB ❶ to refer to someone or something is to mention them or speak about them ❷ to refer to a dictionary or other source of information is to look in it so that you can find something out **③** to refer a question or problem to someone else is to pass it on to them to deal with

referee NOUN the person who has the job of seeing that people keep to the rules of a game

referee VERB to act as a referee

reference NOUN **①** a mention of something **②** a direction to a book or page or file where information can be found **③** a letter from a previous employer describing someone's abilities and qualities

reference book NOUN a book (such as a dictionary or encyclopedia) that gives information about a subject

reference library NOUN a library where books can be used but not taken away

referendum NOUN a vote on a particular question by all the people of a country

refill VERB to fill something again

refill NOUN a container holding a substance which is used to refill something

refine VERB **①** to remove impurities from a substance **②** to improve something, especially by making small changes

refined ADJECTIVE **①** made pure by having other substances taken out of it **②** polite, educated and well-mannered

refinement NOUN **①** good manners and polite behaviour **②** something added to improve a thing

refinery NOUN a factory for refining something

reflect VERB **①** to send back light, heat or sound from a surface **②** to form an image of something as a mirror does **③** to think deeply or carefully about something **④** to be a sign of something or to make it clear

reflection NOUN **①** an image you can see in a mirror or other reflecting surface **②** reflecting light **③** a spell of thinking about something

reflective ADJECTIVE **①** reflecting light or heat **②** suggesting or showing serious thought

reflex NOUN a movement or action that you do without any conscious thought

reflex angle NOUN an angle of more than 180°

reflexive pronoun NOUN (in grammar) any of the pronouns *myself, herself, himself,* etc. (as in 'She cut *herself*.'), which refer back to the subject of the verb

reflexive verb NOUN a verb where the subject and the object are the same person or thing, as in 'She cut *herself*.', 'The cat *washed itself*.'

reform VERB **①** to make changes in something in order to improve it **②** to give up a criminal or immoral lifestyle or to make someone do this

reform NOUN **①** reform is changing something in order to improve it **②** a reform is a change made in order to improve something

Reformation NOUN the Reformation was a religious

movement in Europe in the 16th century intended to reform certain teachings and practices of the Roman Catholic Church, which resulted in the establishment of the Reformed or Protestant Churches

reformer NOUN someone who makes reforms

refract VERB to bend a ray of light at the point where it enters water or glass at an angle

refrain VERB to stop yourself from doing something

refrain NOUN the chorus of a song

refresh VERB to make someone feel less tired or less hot and full of energy again

refresher course NOUN a training course to bring people's knowledge up to date

refreshing ADJECTIVE ❶ producing new strength or energy ❷ pleasantly different or unusual

refreshment NOUN ❶ food and drink ❷ the state of feeling strong and energetic again

refreshments PLURAL NOUN drinks and snacks provided at an event

refrigerate VERB to make food or drink extremely cold, especially in order to preserve it and keep it fresh

refrigerator NOUN a cabinet in which food or drink is stored at a very low temperature

refuel VERB to supply a ship or aircraft with more fuel

refuge NOUN a place where a person can go to be safe from danger

refugee NOUN a person who has been forced to leave their home or country and live somewhere else, e.g. because of war or persecution or famine

refund VERB to pay money back

refund NOUN money that is paid back to you

refurbish VERB to redecorate a room or building and make repairs to it

refusal NOUN saying that you are unwilling to do or give or accept something

refuse (say ri-fewz) VERB to say that you are unwilling to do, give or accept something

refuse (say ref-yooss) NOUN rubbish or waste material

refute VERB to prove that a person or statement is wrong

regain VERB to get something back after losing it

regal (say ree-gal) ADJECTIVE ❶ by or to do with a monarch ❷ dignified and splendid; fit for a king or queen

regalia (say rig-ayl-i-a) PLURAL NOUN the emblems of royalty or rank

regard VERB ❶ to think of a person or thing in a certain way; to consider someone or something to be ❷ to look closely at someone or something

regard NOUN ❶ consideration or heed ❷ respect

regarding PREPOSITION concerning; about

regardless ADVERB without considering something; in spite of something

regards PLURAL NOUN kind wishes you send in a message

regatta NOUN a meeting for boat or yacht races

regenerate VERB to give new life or strength to something

regent NOUN a person appointed to rule a country while the monarch is too young or unable to rule

reggae (say reg-ay) NOUN a West Indian style of music with a strong beat

regime (say ray-zh eem) NOUN a system of government or organization

regiment NOUN an army unit, usually divided into battalions or companies

region NOUN ❶ a part of a country or of the world ❷ an area of someone's body

regional ADJECTIVE belonging to a particular region

register NOUN ❶ an official list of names or items ❷ a book in which information about school attendances is recorded ❸ the range of a voice or musical instrument

register VERB ❶ to list names or items in a register ❷ to indicate or show something ❸ to make an impression on someone's mind ❹ to pay extra for a letter or parcel to be sent with special care

register office NOUN an office where marriages are performed and records of births, marriages and deaths are kept

registrar NOUN an official whose job is to keep written records or registers

registration NOUN putting someone's name on an official list

registration number NOUN a series of letters and numbers identifying a motor vehicle

registry NOUN a place where registers are kept

registry office NOUN a register office

regret NOUN a feeling of sorrow or disappointment about something that has happened or been done

regret VERB to feel sorry or disappointed about something

regretful ADJECTIVE feeling sorry or disappointed about something

regrettable ADJECTIVE that you are sorry about and wish had not happened

regular ADJECTIVE ❶ always happening or doing something at certain times ❷ even or symmetrical ❸ normal, standard or correct ❹ belonging to a country's permanent armed forces

regularly ADVERB ❶ at regular times or intervals ❷ often

regulate VERB ❶ to control something by using laws or rules ❷ to control the way a machine works

regulation NOUN ❶ a rule or law ❷ regulating something

regurgitate VERB to bring swallowed food up again into the mouth

rehearsal NOUN practising something before you perform it in front of an audience

rehearse VERB to practise

something before performing it in front of an audience

reign VERB ❶ to rule a country as king or queen ❷ to be supreme; to be the most noticeable or important thing

reign NOUN ❶ the time when someone is king or queen

rein NOUN ❶ a strap used by a rider to guide a horse ❷ a harness used to guide a very young child while walking

reincarnation NOUN the belief that after death the soul is born again in a new body

reindeer NOUN a kind of deer that lives in Arctic regions

reinforce VERB ❶ to strengthen something by adding extra people or supports ❷ to strengthen or support an idea or feeling

reinforcement NOUN ❶ making something stronger ❷ a thing that strengthens something

reinforcements PLURAL NOUN extra troops sent to strengthen a military force

reinstate VERB to put a person or thing back into a previous position

reiterate VERB to say something again or repeatedly

reject (say ri-jekt) VERB ❶ to refuse to accept a person or thing ❷ to throw away or discard something

reject (say ree-jekt) NOUN a person or thing that is rejected, especially because of being faulty or poorly made

rejoice VERB to feel or show great joy

rejoin VERB to join someone or

something again after leaving them

rejuvenate VERB to make a person seem young again

relapse VERB ❶ to return to a previous condition ❷ to become worse after improving

relate VERB ❶ to tell a story or give an account of something ❷ things relate to each other when there is a link or connection between them ❸ to make a connection between one thing and another ❹ to understand someone and get on well with them

related ADJECTIVE ❶ belonging to the same family ❷ connected or linked

relation NOUN ❶ a relative ❷ the way one thing is related to another

relationship NOUN ❶ how people or things are related ❷ how people get on with each other ❸ a loving or sexual friendship between two people

relative NOUN a person who is related to another

relative ADJECTIVE connected or compared with something; compared with the average

relative density NOUN the ratio of the density of a substance to that of a standard substance (usually water for liquids and air for gases)

relatively ADVERB to a fairly large degree when compared with other things

relative pronoun NOUN a word used instead of a noun to introduce a clause that gives more information about the noun. The relative pronouns are *what, who, whom, whose, which* and *that*.

relax *VERB* ❶ to rest or stop working ❷ to become less anxious or worried ❸ to make a rule less strict or severe ❹ to make a limb or muscle less stiff or tense

relay (say ri-**lay**) *VERB* to pass on a message or broadcast

relay (say **re**-lay) *NOUN* ❶ a fresh group taking the place of another ❷ a relay race ❸ a device for relaying a broadcast

relay race *NOUN* a race between teams in which each person covers part of the distance

release *VERB* ❶ to set someone or something free or unfasten them ❷ to let a thing fall or fly or go out ❸ to make information available ❹ to make a film or recording available to the public

release *NOUN* ❶ being released ❷ something released, such as a new film or recording ❸ a device that unfastens something

relegate *VERB* ❶ a sports team is relegated when it goes down into a lower division of a league ❷ to put something into a lower group or position than before

relent *VERB* to finally agree to something that you had refused; to become less severe

relentless *ADJECTIVE* not stopping or letting up

relevant *ADJECTIVE* connected with what is being discussed or dealt with. (The opposite is **irrelevant**.)

reliable *ADJECTIVE* able to be relied on or trusted

relic *NOUN* something that has survived from an earlier time

relief *NOUN* ❶ a good feeling you get because something unpleasant has stopped or is not going to happen ❷ the ending or lessening of pain, trouble or suffering ❸ something that gives relief or help ❹ help given to people in need ❺ a person who takes over a turn of duty when another finishes ❻ a method of making a map or design that stands out from a flat surface

relief map *NOUN* a map that shows hills and valleys by shading or moulding

relieve *VERB* to make an unpleasant feeling or situation stop or get better

relieved *ADJECTIVE* feeling happy because something unpleasant has stopped or has not happened

religion *NOUN* ❶ what people believe about God or gods and how they worship ❷ a particular system of beliefs and worship

religious *ADJECTIVE* ❶ to do with religion ❷ believing firmly in a religion and taking part in its customs

religiously *ADVERB* very carefully or regularly

relinquish *VERB* to give something up; to let something go

relish *NOUN* ❶ great enjoyment ❷ a tasty sauce or pickle that adds flavour to plainer food

relish *VERB* to enjoy something greatly; to look forward to something with great pleasure

a
b
c
d
e
f
g
h
i
j
k
l
m
n
o
p
q
r
s
t
u
v
w
x
y
z

relive *VERB* to remember something that happened very vividly, as though it was happening again

relocate *VERB* to move to a new place or to make someone or something do this

reluctant *ADJECTIVE* not willing or not keen to do something

rely *VERB* ❶ to rely on someone is to trust them to help or support you ❷ to rely on something is to need it for a particular purpose

remain *VERB* ❶ to be left after other parts have gone or been dealt with ❷ to continue to be in the same place or condition; to stay

remainder *NOUN* ❶ the remaining part of people or things ❷ the number left after subtraction or division

remains *PLURAL NOUN* ❶ all that is left over after other parts have been removed or destroyed ❷ ancient ruins or objects that have survived to the present day ❸ a dead body

remand *VERB* to send a prisoner back into custody while further evidence is being gathered

remark *NOUN* something you say; a comment

remark *VERB* to make a remark; to say something

remarkable *ADJECTIVE* unusual or extraordinary in a way that people notice

remedial *ADJECTIVE* ❶ helping to cure an illness or deficiency ❷ (*old use*) to do with the teaching of school students who are not doing

as well as expected

remedy *NOUN* something that cures or relieves a disease or that puts a matter right

remedy *VERB* to be a remedy for something; to put something right

remember *VERB* ❶ to keep something in your mind ❷ to bring something back into your mind

remembrance *NOUN* you do something in remembrance of someone or something when you do it as a way of remembering them

remind *VERB* ❶ to help or make a person remember something ❷ to make a person think of something because of being similar

reminder *NOUN* ❶ a thing that reminds you of something ❷ a letter sent to remind you to pay a bill

reminiscences *PLURAL NOUN* a person's memories of their past life

reminiscent *ADJECTIVE* reminding you of something

remission *NOUN* ❶ a period during which a serious illness improves for a time ❷ the reduction of a prison sentence, especially for good behaviour while in prison

remit *VERB* ❶ to reduce or cancel a punishment or debt ❷ to send money in payment

remittance *NOUN* ❶ sending money ❷ the amount of money sent

remnant *NOUN* a part or piece left over from something

remorse *NOUN* deep regret for something wrong you have done

remorseless ADJECTIVE relentless; not stopping or ending

remote ADJECTIVE ❶ far away in place or time ❷ far away from where most people live; isolated ❸ unlikely or slight

remote NOUN a remote control device

remote control NOUN ❶ controlling something from a distance, usually by electricity or radio ❷ a device for doing this

remotely ADVERB ❶ to a very slight degree; slightly ❷ from a distance

removable ADJECTIVE able to be removed

removal NOUN removing or moving something

remove VERB ❶ to take something away or take it off ❷ to get rid of something

Renaissance (say ren-**ay**-sans) NOUN the revival of classical styles of art and literature in Europe in the 14th-16th centuries

renal (say **reen**-al) ADJECTIVE to do with the kidneys

rename VERB to give a new name to a person or thing

render VERB ❶ to cause a person or thing to become something ❷ to give or perform something

rendezvous (say **rond**-ay-voo) NOUN ❶ a meeting with someone at an agreed time and place ❷ a place arranged for this

rendition NOUN the way a piece of music, a poem or a dramatic role is performed

renew VERB ❶ to replace a thing with something new or arrange

for it to be valid for a further period ❷ to begin or make or give something again

renewable ADJECTIVE able to be renewed

renewable resource NOUN a resource (such as power from the sun, wind or waves) that can never be used up or which can be renewed

renounce VERB to give up or reject something

renovate VERB to repair an old building and make it look new

renown NOUN great fame

renowned ADJECTIVE famous

rent NOUN ❶ a regular payment for the use of something, especially a house that belongs to another person ❷ a torn place; a split

rent VERB ❶ to have or allow the use of something in return for rent ❷ past tense of **rend**

rental NOUN ❶ the amount paid as rent ❷ renting something

renunciation NOUN renouncing something

reorganize (also **reorganise**) VERB to change the way in which something is organized

repair VERB ❶ to put something into good condition after it has been damaged or broken ❷ (formal) to repair to a place is to go there

repair NOUN ❶ repairing something ❷ a place where something has been mended

repartee NOUN witty replies and remarks

repay VERB ❶ to pay back money

a
b
c
d
e
f
g
h
i
j
k
l
m
n
o
p
q
r
s
t
u
v
w
x
y
z

A

that you owe ② to do something
for someone in return for kindness
or help

B **repeal** VERB to cancel a law
officially

D **repeat** VERB ① to say or do the
same thing again ② to tell another
person about something told
to you

F **repeat** NOUN ① the action of
repeating something ② something
that is repeated

H **repeatedly** ADVERB many times;
again and again

I **repel** VERB ① to drive someone
back or away ② to push something
away from itself by means of
a physical force ③ to disgust
someone

M **repellent** ADJECTIVE causing a
strong feeling of disgust

N **repellent** NOUN a chemical
substance used to keep something
away

P **repent** VERB to be sorry for what
you have done

Q **repercussion** NOUN a consequence
or effect of an event or action

R **repertoire** (say rep-er-twahr)
NOUN a stock of songs or plays etc.
that a person or company knows
and can perform

U **repetition** NOUN ① repeating
something ② something repeated

V **repetitive** ADJECTIVE involving too
much repetition

W **replace** VERB ① to put a thing back
where it was before ② to take the
place of another person or thing
③ to put a new or different thing
in place of something

replacement NOUN ① a person
or thing that takes the place of
another ② when a person or thing
is replaced by another

replay NOUN ① a sports match
played again after a draw ② the
playing or showing again of a
recording

replay VERB ① to play a match
again ② to play back a recording

replenish VERB to make something
full again by replacing what has
been used

replica NOUN an exact copy

reply NOUN something you say
or write to deal with a question,
letter, etc.; an answer

reply VERB to give a reply to
someone; to answer

report VERB ① to describe
something that has happened or
that you have done or studied
② to make an official complaint or
accusation against someone ③ to
go and tell someone that you have
arrived or are ready for work

report NOUN ① a description or
account of something ② a regular
statement of how someone has
worked or behaved, e.g. at school
③ an explosive sound

reported speech NOUN indirect
speech

reporter NOUN a person whose job
is to collect and report news for
a newspaper, radio or television
programme, etc.

repose NOUN calm, rest or sleep

repose VERB to rest or lie
somewhere

repossess VERB to take something
back because it has not been

paid for

represent VERB ❶ to help someone by speaking or doing something on their behalf ❷ to symbolize or stand for something ❸ to be an example or equivalent of something ❹ to show a person or thing in a picture or play etc. ❺ to describe a person or thing in a particular way

representation NOUN ❶ a thing that shows or describes something ❷ being represented by someone or something

representative NOUN a person or thing that represents another or others

representative ADJECTIVE ❶ representing others ❷ typical of a group

repress VERB ❶ to control or hold back a feeling ❷ to control or restrain people by force

reprieve NOUN postponement or cancellation of a punishment, especially the death penalty

reprieve VERB to give a reprieve to someone

reprimand NOUN a telling-off, especially a formal or official one

reprimand VERB to scold someone or tell them off

reprisal NOUN an act of revenge

reproach VERB to tell someone you are upset and disappointed by something they have done

reproach NOUN blame or criticism

reproduce VERB ❶ to cause something to be seen or heard or happen again ❷ to make a copy of something ❸ animals, people and plants reproduce when they produce offspring

reproduction NOUN ❶ a copy of something, especially a work of art ❷ the process of producing offspring

reproductive ADJECTIVE to do with reproduction

reproof NOUN something you say to someone when you do not approve of what they have done

reprove VERB to tell someone that you do not approve of something that they have done

reptile NOUN a cold-blooded animal that has a backbone and very short legs or no legs at all, e.g. a snake, lizard, crocodile or tortoise

republic NOUN a country that has a president, especially one who is elected. Compare with **monarchy**.

Republican NOUN a supporter of the Republican Party in the USA

repudiate VERB to reject or deny a suggestion or accusation

repulse VERB ❶ to drive back an attacking force ❷ to reject an offer firmly ❸ to make someone feel disgust

repulsion NOUN ❶ a feeling of disgust ❷ repelling or repulsing something

repulsive ADJECTIVE ❶ disgusting or revolting ❷ repelling things

reputable (say **rep**-yoo-ta-bul) ADJECTIVE having a good reputation; respected

reputation NOUN what most people say or think about a person or thing

repute NOUN reputation

reputed *ADJECTIVE* said or thought to be something

request *VERB* ① to ask for a thing ② to ask a person to do something

request *NOUN* ① asking for something ② a thing asked for

requiem (say **rek**-wee-em) *NOUN* ① a special Mass for someone who has died ② music for the words of this

require *VERB* ① to need something ② to officially demand or order something; to make someone do something

requirement *NOUN* what is required; a need

requisite (say **rek**-wiz-it) *ADJECTIVE* required or needed for something

requisite *NOUN* a thing needed for something

requisition *VERB* to take something over for official use

rescue *VERB* to save a person or thing from danger or harm; to free someone from captivity

rescue *NOUN* the action of rescuing a person or thing

research *NOUN* careful study or investigation to discover facts or information

research (say ri-**serch**) *VERB* to carry out research into something

resemblance *NOUN* likeness or similarity

resemble *VERB* to be or look like another person or thing

resent *VERB* to feel bitter and angry about something done or said to you

resentful *ADJECTIVE* feeling bitter and angry about something done

or said to you

reservation *NOUN* ① reserving something ② something reserved ③ an area of land kept for a special purpose ④ a doubt or feeling of unease ⑤ a limit on how far you agree with something; a doubt or condition

reserve *VERB* to keep or order something for a particular person or a special use in the future

reserve *NOUN* ① a person or thing kept ready to be used if necessary ② an extra player chosen in case a substitute is needed in a team ③ an area of land kept for a special purpose ④ shyness; being reserved

reserved *ADJECTIVE* ① kept for someone's use ② shy or unwilling to show your feelings

reservoir (say **rez**-er-vwar) *NOUN* a place where water is stored, especially an artificial lake

reshuffle *NOUN* a rearrangement, especially an exchange of jobs between members of a group

reside *VERB* to live in a particular place

residence *NOUN* ① a place where a person lives ② living in a particular place

resident *NOUN* ① a person living in a particular place ② a person staying in a hotel

resident *ADJECTIVE* living in a particular place

residential *ADJECTIVE* ① containing people's homes ② providing accommodation

residue *NOUN* what remains or is left over

resign VERB to give up your job or position

resignation NOUN ❶ accepting a difficulty without complaining ❷ resigning a job or position; a letter saying you wish to do this

resilient ADJECTIVE able to recover quickly from illness or trouble

resin NOUN a sticky substance that comes from plants or is manufactured, used in varnish, plastics, etc.

resist VERB ❶ to oppose or refuse to accept something; to fight or act against something ❷ to stop yourself having or doing something

resistance NOUN ❶ resisting something ❷ the ability of a substance to hinder the flow of electricity

resistant ADJECTIVE ❶ not affected or damaged by something ❷ not willing to accept something

resistor NOUN a device that increases the resistance to an electric current

resit NOUN (British) an examination that you sit again because you did not do well enough the first time

resolute ADJECTIVE showing great determination

resolution NOUN ❶ being resolute; great determination ❷ something you have resolved to do ❸ a formal decision made by a committee ❹ the solving of a problem ❺ the last part of a story where we find out how the story comes to an end and how difficulties are sorted out

resolve VERB ❶ to decide something firmly or formally ❷ to solve or settle a problem ❸ to overcome doubts or disagreements

resolve NOUN great determination to do something

resonant ADJECTIVE ❶ resounding or echoing ❷ suggesting or bringing to mind a feeling or memory

resonate VERB to make a deep continuing sound; to echo

resort VERB to turn to or make use of something, especially when everything else has failed

resort NOUN a place where people go for relaxation or a holiday

resound VERB to fill a place with sound; to echo

resounding ADJECTIVE ❶ loud and echoing ❷ very great; outstanding

resource NOUN ❶ something that can be used; an asset ❷ a person's resources are their natural qualities and abilities

resourceful ADJECTIVE clever at finding ways of doing things

respect NOUN ❶ admiration for a person's or thing's good qualities ❷ politeness or consideration ❸ a detail or aspect

respect VERB to have respect for a person or thing

respectable ADJECTIVE ❶ having good manners and character; decent ❷ fairly good; adequate

respectful ADJECTIVE showing respect

respecting PREPOSITION concerning; to do with

respective ADJECTIVE belonging to

each one of several

respectively ADVERB in the same order as the people or things already mentioned

respiration NOUN breathing

respirator NOUN ❶ a device that fits over a person's nose and mouth to purify air before it is breathed ❷ an apparatus for giving artificial respiration

respire VERB to breathe

respite NOUN a short break from something unpleasant or difficult

respond VERB ❶ to reply ❷ to act in answer to, or because of, something; to react ❸ to show a good reaction to something

respondent NOUN the person answering

response NOUN ❶ a reply or answer ❷ a reaction to something

responsibility NOUN ❶ being responsible ❷ something for which a person is responsible

responsible ADJECTIVE ❶ looking after a person or thing and having to take the blame if something goes wrong ❷ reliable and trustworthy ❸ with important duties ❹ causing something

responsive ADJECTIVE responding well or quickly to something

rest NOUN ❶ a time of sleep or freedom from work as a way of regaining strength ❷ a support, especially on a piece of furniture ❸ an interval of silence between notes in music

rest VERB ❶ to have a rest; to be still ❷ to allow a part of your body to rest ❸ to lean or place

something so it is supported; to be supported ❹ to stop moving and stay in one place ❺ to be left without further investigation

restaurant NOUN a place where you can buy a meal and eat it

restful ADJECTIVE giving rest or a feeling of rest

restless ADJECTIVE unable to rest or keep still

restoration NOUN returning something to its original condition

restore VERB ❶ to put something back to its original place or condition ❷ to clean and repair a work of art or building so that it looks as good as it did originally

restrain VERB to hold a person or thing back; to keep a person or animal under control

restraint NOUN ❶ a limit or control on something ❷ calm and controlled behaviour

restrict VERB to keep someone or something within certain limits

restriction NOUN a rule or situation that limits what you can do

result NOUN ❶ a thing that happens because something else has happened; an effect or consequence ❷ the score or situation at the end of a game, competition or race ❸ the answer to a sum or calculation

result VERB ❶ to happen as a result ❷ to have something as a particular result

resume VERB ❶ to begin something again after stopping for a while ❷ to take or occupy something again

résumé (say **rez**-yoo-may) NOUN a summary

resurrect VERB to bring something back into use or existence

resurrection NOUN ❶ coming back to life after being dead ❷ the revival of something

resuscitate VERB to revive a person who has become unconscious or stopped breathing

retail VERB to sell goods to the general public

retail NOUN selling goods to the general public. Compare with **wholesale**.

retain VERB ❶ to continue to have something; to keep something in your possession or memory ❷ to hold something in place

retainer NOUN ❶ a sum of money regularly paid to someone so that they will work for you when needed ❷ a servant who has worked for a person or family for a long time

retake VERB to take a test or examination again

retake NOUN ❶ a test or examination taken again ❷ a scene filmed again

retaliate VERB to repay an injury or insult with a similar one; to attack someone in return for a similar attack

retard VERB to slow down or delay the progress or development of something

retch VERB to strain your throat as if you are being sick

retention NOUN retaining or keeping something

retentive ADJECTIVE able to retain facts and remember things easily

reticent (say **ret**-i-sent) ADJECTIVE not willing to tell people what you feel or think

retina NOUN a layer of membrane at the back of the eyeball, sensitive to light

retinue NOUN a group of people accompanying an important person

retire VERB ❶ to give up your regular work because you have reached a certain age ❷ to go to bed ❸ to leave a place and go somewhere more private

retired ADJECTIVE no longer working

retirement NOUN the time when someone gives up regular work

retiring ADJECTIVE shy; avoiding company

retort NOUN ❶ a quick, witty or angry reply ❷ a glass bottle with a long downward-bent neck, used in distilling liquids

retort VERB to make a quick, witty or angry reply

retrace VERB to go back over the route that you have just taken

retract VERB ❶ to pull something back or in ❷ to withdraw a statement or accusation

retreat VERB to go back after being defeated or to avoid danger or difficulty

retreat NOUN ❶ retreating ❷ a quiet place to which someone can go to relax

retribution NOUN a deserved punishment

retrieve VERB ❶ to bring or

get something back ② **to find
information stored in a computer**
③ **to rescue or save a situation**

retriever NOUN a kind of dog
originally trained to find and bring
back birds and animals that have
been shot

retrospect NOUN ➤ **in retrospect**
when you look back at what has
happened

retrospective ADJECTIVE ① looking
back on the past ② applying to the
past as well as the future

return VERB ① to come back or go
back ② to bring, give, put or send
something back

return NOUN ① returning to a place
② giving or sending something
back ③ profit ④ a return ticket

return match NOUN a second
match played between the same
teams

return ticket NOUN a ticket for a
journey to a place and back again

reunify VERB to make a divided
country into one again

reunion NOUN ① a meeting of
people who have not met for some
time ② coming together again
after being apart

reunite VERB to come together
again or bring people together
again after a period of separation

reuse (say ree-yooz) VERB to use
something again

reuse (say ree-yooss) NOUN using
something again

rev VERB (informal) to make an
engine run quickly, especially when
starting

rev NOUN (informal) a revolution of
an engine

Rev. ABBREVIATION Reverend

reveal VERB ① to make something
known ② to show something that
was hidden

reveille (say riv-al-ee) NOUN a
military waking signal sounded on
a bugle or drums

revel VERB ① to take great delight
in something ② to enjoy yourself
with others in a lively and noisy
celebration

revelation NOUN ① something
revealed, especially something
surprising ② revealing something

revelry NOUN ① revelling ② lively
and noisy celebration

revels PLURAL NOUN lively and noisy
celebrations

revenge NOUN harming someone
in return for harm that they have
done to you

revenge VERB to take revenge on
someone

revenue NOUN ① a country's
income from taxes etc., used
for paying public expenses ② a
company's income

reverberate VERB to be repeated as
an echo; to resound

revere (say riv-eer) VERB to respect
or admire someone deeply

reverence NOUN a feeling of awe
and deep or religious respect

Reverend NOUN the title of a
member of the clergy

reverent ADJECTIVE feeling or
showing reverence

reversal NOUN ① a change to an

opposite direction, position or course of action ❷ a piece of bad luck or misfortune

reverse ADJECTIVE ❶ facing or moving in the opposite direction ❷ opposite in character or order

reverse NOUN ❶ the opposite of something ❷ the reverse side or face of something ❸ a piece of misfortune ❹ the reverse gear of a vehicle

reverse VERB ❶ to turn something upside down or the other way round ❷ to change round the usual order, position or function of two things ❸ to drive a vehicle backwards ❹ to cancel a decision; to change an opinion to the opposite one

reverse gear NOUN a gear that allows a vehicle to be driven backwards

revert VERB to return to a former state, habit or subject

review NOUN ❶ an inspection or survey of something ❷ a published description and opinion of a book, film, play, etc.

review VERB ❶ to write a review of a book, film, play, etc. ❷ to reconsider a matter or decision ❸ to inspect or survey something

revise VERB ❶ to go over work that you have already done, especially in preparing for an examination ❷ to correct or change something

revision NOUN ❶ a change in something in order to correct or improve it ❷ going over work that you have already done, especially in preparing for an examination

revival NOUN ❶ an improvement

in the condition or strength of something ❷ a renewal of interest or popularity

revive VERB ❶ to bring someone or something back to life, strength or use ❷ to restore interest in or the popularity of something

revoke VERB to withdraw or cancel a decree, licence or right

revolt VERB ❶ to disgust someone ❷ to take part in a rebellion

revolt NOUN a rebellion

revolting ADJECTIVE disgusting or horrible

revolution NOUN ❶ a rebellion that overthrows the government ❷ a complete or drastic change ❸ a movement around something; one complete turn of a wheel or engine

revolutionary ADJECTIVE ❶ involving a great change ❷ to do with a political revolution

revolutionary NOUN a person who supports a political revolution

revolutionize (also **revolutionise**) VERB to make a great change in something

revolve VERB ❶ to turn in a circle round a central point or make something do this ❷ to have something as the most important element

revolver NOUN a pistol with a revolving mechanism that can be fired a number of times without reloading

revue NOUN an entertainment consisting of songs and sketches, often about current events

revulsion NOUN a feeling of strong disgust

a b c d e f g h i j k l m n o p q r s t u v w x y z

A

reward NOUN ❶ something given in return for something good you have done ❷ a sum of money offered for help in catching a criminal or finding lost property

reward VERB to give a reward to someone

rewarding ADJECTIVE giving satisfaction and a feeling of achievement

rewind VERB to wind a cassette or videotape back to or towards the beginning

rewrite VERB to write something again or differently

rhapsody (say **rap**-so-dee) NOUN ❶ a statement of great delight about something ❷ a romantic piece of music

rhetoric (say **ret**-er-ik) NOUN ❶ the art of using words impressively, especially in public speaking ❷ language that is used for its impressive effect but is not sincere or meaningful

rhetorical question NOUN a question that you ask for dramatic effect without expecting to get an answer, e.g. 'Who cares?' (= nobody cares)

rheumatism NOUN a disease that causes pain and stiffness in joints and muscles

rhino NOUN (informal) a rhinoceros

rhinoceros NOUN a large heavy animal with a horn or two horns on its nose

rhizome NOUN a thick underground stem which produces roots and new plants

rhododendron NOUN an evergreen shrub with large clusters of trumpet-shaped flowers

rhomboid NOUN a shape with four straight sides, with only the opposite sides and angles equal to each other

rhombus NOUN a shape with four equal sides but no right angles, like the diamond on playing cards

rhubarb NOUN a plant with thick reddish stalks that are used as fruit

rhyme NOUN ❶ a similar sound in the endings of words, e.g. bat/fat/mat, batter/fatter/matter ❷ a poem with rhymes ❸ a word that rhymes with another

rhyme VERB ❶ to form a rhyme ❷ to have rhymes

rhythm NOUN a regular pattern of beats, sounds or movements

rhythmic ADJECTIVE having a regular pattern of beats, sounds or movements

rib NOUN ❶ each of the curved bones round the chest ❷ a curved part that looks like a rib or supports something

ribbon NOUN ❶ a narrow strip of silk, nylon or other material, used for decoration or for tying something ❷ a long narrow strip of inked material used in some printers and typewriters

rice NOUN a cereal plant grown in flooded fields in hot countries or its seeds

rich ADJECTIVE ❶ having a lot of money or property; wealthy ❷ having a large supply of something ❸ a rich colour, sound or smell is pleasantly deep or strong **④** rich food contains a lot of fat, butter or eggs **⑤** expensive or luxurious

riches NOUN *PLURAL* great wealth

richly ADVERB **①** in a rich or luxurious way **②** fully or thoroughly

Richter scale NOUN a scale (from 0–10) used to show the force of an earthquake

rick NOUN a large neat stack of hay or straw

rick VERB (*British*) to sprain or wrench your neck or back

rickets NOUN a disease caused by lack of vitamin D, causing deformed bones

rickety ADJECTIVE poorly made and likely to break or fall down

rickshaw NOUN a two-wheeled carriage pulled by one or more people, used in the Far East

ricochet (say rik-osh-ay) VERB to bounce away from a surface after hitting it

ricotta NOUN a kind of soft Italian cheese made from sheep's milk

rid VERB rids, ridding, rid to make a person or place free from something unwanted

riddle NOUN a puzzling question, especially as a joke

riddle VERB to make a lot of holes in something

ride VERB rides, riding, rode, ridden **①** to sit on a horse, bicycle, etc. and control it as it carries you along **②** to travel in a car, bus, train, etc. **③** to float or be supported on something

ride NOUN **①** a journey on a horse, bicycle, etc. or in a vehicle **②** a roundabout etc. that you ride on at a fair or amusement park

rider NOUN **①** a person who rides something, especially a horse **②** an extra comment or statement

ridge NOUN **①** a long narrow part higher than the rest of something **②** a long narrow range of hills or mountains

ridicule VERB to make fun of a person or thing

ridicule NOUN unkind words or behaviour that make a person or thing look ridiculous

ridiculous ADJECTIVE so silly or foolish that it makes people laugh or despise it

rife ADJECTIVE widespread; happening frequently

rifle NOUN a long gun with spiral grooves (called *rifling*) inside the barrel that make the bullet spin and so travel more accurately

rifle VERB to search quickly through a place in order to find or steal something

rift NOUN **①** a crack or split in something **②** a disagreement that separates friends

rift valley NOUN a steep-sided valley formed where the land has sunk

rig VERB **①** to fit a ship with ropes, spars, sails, etc. **②** to arrange the result of an election or contest dishonestly

rig NOUN **①** a framework supporting the machinery for drilling an oil well **②** the way a ship's masts and sails etc. are arranged ③ (*informal*) an outfit of clothes

rigging NOUN the ropes etc. that support a ship's mast and sails

right ADJECTIVE ① on or towards the east if you think of yourself as facing north ② correct; true ③ morally good; fair or just ④ conservative; not in favour of socialist reforms

right ADVERB ① on or towards the right ② straight; directly ③ all the way; completely ④ exactly ⑤ correctly or appropriately

right NOUN ① the right-hand side or part of something ② what is morally good or fair or just ③ something that people are allowed to do or have

right VERB ① to make a thing upright ② to put something right

right angle NOUN an angle of 90°

righteous ADJECTIVE doing what is right; virtuous

rightful ADJECTIVE deserved or proper

right-hand ADJECTIVE on the right side of something

right-handed ADJECTIVE using the right hand in preference to the left hand

right-hand man NOUN the person you depend on the most to help you in your work

rightly ADVERB correctly or justifiably

right-minded ADJECTIVE having ideas and opinions which are sensible and morally good

right of way NOUN ① a public path across private land ② the right

of one vehicle to pass or cross a junction before another

rigid ADJECTIVE ① stiff or firm; not bending easily ② strict and difficult to change

rigmarole NOUN ① a long rambling statement ② a complicated procedure

rigor mortis (say ri-ger **mor**-tis) NOUN stiffening of the body after death

rigorous ADJECTIVE ① strict or severe ② careful and thorough

rigour NOUN ① doing something carefully with great attention to detail ② strictness or severity ③ harshness of weather or conditions

rile VERB (*informal*) to annoy or irritate someone

rill NOUN a very small stream

rim NOUN the outer edge of a cup, wheel or other round object

rind NOUN the tough skin on bacon, cheese or fruit

ring NOUN ① a circle; a circular band ② a thin circular piece of metal you wear on a finger ③ the space where a circus performs ④ a square area in which a boxing match or wrestling match takes place ⑤ the act or sound of ringing

ring VERB rings, ringing, rang, rung ① to telephone someone ② to cause a bell to sound ③ to make a loud clear sound like that of a bell ④ to be filled with sound

ring VERB rings, ringing, ringed ① to put a ring round something ② to surround something

ringleader NOUN a person who leads others in rebellion, mischief or crime

ringlet NOUN a tube-shaped curl of hair

ringmaster NOUN the person in charge of a performance in a circus ring

ring road NOUN (British) a road that runs around the edge of a town so that traffic does not have to go through the centre

ringtone NOUN the sound your mobile phone makes when it receives a call

ringworm NOUN a fungal skin infection that causes itchy circular patches, especially on the scalp

rink NOUN a place made for skating

rinse VERB ❶ to wash something in clean water to remove soap ❷ to wash something lightly

rinse NOUN ❶ rinsing ❷ a liquid for colouring the hair

riot NOUN wild or violent behaviour by a crowd of people in a public place

riot VERB to take part in a riot

riot gear NOUN protective clothing, helmets, shields, etc. worn or carried by the police or army dealing with a riot

riotous ADJECTIVE ❶ noisy and uncontrolled; boisterous ❷ disorderly or unruly

RIP ABBREVIATION may he or she (or they) rest in peace

rip VERB ❶ to tear something roughly ❷ to become torn ❸ to remove something quickly by pulling hard ❹ to rush along

rip NOUN a torn place

ripe ADJECTIVE ❶ ready to be harvested or eaten ❷ ready and suitable

ripen VERB to become ripe or to make something ripe

rip-off NOUN (informal) something that costs a lot more than it should

ripple NOUN ❶ a small wave or series of waves ❷ a gentle sound that rises and falls

ripple VERB to form ripples

rise VERB rise, rising, rose, risen ❶ to go upwards ❷ to increase ❸ to get up from lying, sitting or kneeling ❹ to get out of bed ❺ to rebel ❻ bread or cake rises when it swells up by the action of yeast ❼ a river rises when it begins its course ❽ wind rises when it begins to blow more strongly

rise NOUN ❶ the action of rising; an upward movement ❷ an increase in amount or in wages ❸ an upward slope

rising NOUN a revolt against a government

risk NOUN a chance that something bad will happen

risk VERB ❶ to take the chance of damaging or losing something ❷ to accept the risk of something unpleasant happening

risky ADJECTIVE full of risk

risotto NOUN an Italian dish of rice cooked with vegetables and, usually, meat

rissole NOUN (British) a fried cake of minced meat or fish

rite NOUN a religious ceremony; a solemn ritual

ritual NOUN the series of actions used in a religious or other ceremony

ritual ADJECTIVE done as part of a ritual

rival NOUN a person or thing that competes with another or tries to do the same thing

rival VERB to be as good as another person or thing

rivalry NOUN competition between people or groups

river NOUN a large stream of water flowing in a natural channel

rivet NOUN a strong nail or bolt for holding pieces of metal together. The end opposite the head is flattened to form another head when it is in place.

rivet VERB ① to fasten something with rivets ② to hold someone still ③ to hold someone's attention completely

riveting ADJECTIVE so fascinating that it holds your attention completely

rivulet NOUN a small stream

roach NOUN a small freshwater fish

road NOUN ① a level way with a hard surface made for traffic to travel on ② a way or course

roadblock NOUN a barrier across a road, set up by the police or army to stop and check vehicles

road rage NOUN aggressive or violent behaviour by a driver towards other drivers

roadway NOUN the middle part of the road, used by traffic

roam VERB to wander widely

roan ADJECTIVE a roan horse has a brown or black coat with many white hairs

roar NOUN ① a loud deep sound like that made by a lion ② loud laughter

roar VERB ① to make a roar ② to laugh loudly

roast VERB ① to cook meat etc. in an oven or over a fire ② to be roasting is to feel very hot

roast ADJECTIVE cooked by roasting

roast NOUN a piece of meat that has been roasted

rob VERB ① to steal something from a person or place, often using force ② to prevent someone from having something that they should have

robber NOUN a person who steals from a place, often using force

robbery NOUN the crime of stealing from a place, often using force

robe NOUN a long loose piece of clothing, especially one worn in ceremonies

robe VERB to dress someone in a robe or ceremonial robes

robin NOUN a small brown bird with a red breast

robot NOUN ① a machine that looks or acts like a person ② a machine operated by remote control ③ (S. African) a set of traffic lights

robotic ADJECTIVE to do with robots; like a robot

robust ADJECTIVE strong and healthy

rock NOUN ① a large stone or boulder ② the hard part of the earth's crust, under the soil ③ a hard sweet usually shaped like a stick and sold at the seaside

❹ rock music ❺ a rocking movement

rock VERB ❶ to move gently backwards and forwards or from side to side; to make something do this ❷ to shake someone or something violently ❸ to shock or upset someone

rock and roll, rock 'n' roll NOUN a kind of popular dance music with a strong beat, originating in the 1950s

rock-bottom ADJECTIVE at the lowest level

rocker NOUN ❶ a curved support for a chair or cradle ❷ a rocking chair

rockery NOUN a mound or bank in a garden, where plants are made to grow between large rocks

rocket NOUN ❶ a firework that shoots high into the air ❷ a tube-shaped structure that is pushed up into the air by burning gases, used to send up a missile or a spacecraft

rocket VERB to move quickly upwards or away

rocking chair NOUN a chair that can be rocked by a person sitting in it

rocking horse NOUN a model of a horse that can be rocked by a child sitting on it

rock music NOUN popular music with a heavy beat

rocky ADJECTIVE ❶ covered with or made of rocks ❷ unsteady or unstable

rod NOUN ❶ a long thin stick or bar ❷ a stick with a line attached for fishing

rodent NOUN an animal that has large front teeth for gnawing things. Rats, mice and squirrels are rodents

rodeo (say roh-**day**-oh) NOUN a display of cowboys' skill in riding wild horses, controlling cattle, etc.

roe NOUN ❶ a mass of eggs or reproductive cells in a fish's body ❷ a kind of small deer of Europe and Asia. The male is called a **roebuck**.

rogue NOUN ❶ a dishonest person ❷ a mischievous but likeable person

rogue ADJECTIVE behaving in a way that is different from the rest and causing trouble

roguish ADJECTIVE playful and mischievous

role NOUN ❶ an actor's part in a play or film ❷ someone's or something's purpose or function

role model NOUN a person looked up to by others as an example of how to behave

roll VERB ❶ to move along by turning over and over, like a ball or wheel; to make something do this ❷ to form something into the shape of a cylinder or ball ❸ to flatten something by rolling a rounded object over it ❹ a ship or boat rolls when it rocks from side to side ❺ to pass steadily ❻ thunder rolls when it makes a long rumbling sound

roll NOUN ❶ a cylinder made by rolling something up ❷ a small individual portion of bread baked in a rounded shape ❸ an official list of names ❹ a long vibrating or rumbling sound

roll-call NOUN the calling of a list of names to check that everyone is present

roller NOUN ❶ a cylinder used for flattening or spreading things or on which something is wound ❷ a long swelling sea wave

Rollerblade NOUN (*trademark*) a boot like an ice-skating boot, with a line of wheels in place of the skate, for rolling smoothly on hard ground

roller coaster NOUN a type of railway ride in fairgrounds and amusement parks with a series of alternate steep descents and ascents

roller skate NOUN a boot with small wheels fitted under it so that you can roll smoothly over the ground

rolling pin NOUN a heavy cylinder for rolling over pastry to flatten it

rolling stock NOUN the railway engines, carriages and wagons used on a railway

ROM ABBREVIATION read-only memory, a type of computer memory with contents that can be searched or copied but not changed

Roman ADJECTIVE to do with ancient or modern Rome or its people

Roman NOUN a person from ancient or modern Rome

Roman alphabet NOUN this alphabet, in which most European languages are written

Roman Catholic ADJECTIVE belonging to or to do with the Christian Church that has the Pope (bishop of Rome) as its head

Roman Catholic NOUN a member of this Church

romance (say ro-manss) NOUN ❶ tender feelings, experiences and qualities connected with love ❷ a love story ❸ a love affair ❹ mystery and excitement ❺ a medieval story about the adventures of heroes

Romance language NOUN any of the group of European languages descended from Latin, such as French, Italian and Spanish

Roman numerals PLURAL NOUN letters that represent numbers (I = 1, V = 5, X = 10, etc.), used by the ancient Romans. Compare with Arabic numerals.

romantic ADJECTIVE ❶ to do with love or romance ❷ sentimental or idealistic; not realistic or practical

Romany NOUN ❶ a member of a people who live in travelling communities; a gypsy ❷ the language of these people

romp VERB to play in a rough or lively way

rompers PLURAL NOUN a piece of clothing for a baby or young child, covering the body and legs

roof NOUN ❶ the part that covers the top of a building, shelter or vehicle ❷ the top inside surface of something

rook NOUN ❶ a black crow that nests in large groups ❷ a chess piece shaped like a castle

rookery NOUN ❶ a place where many rooks nest ❷ a breeding place for penguins or seals

room NOUN ❶ a part of a building with its own walls and ceiling ❷ enough space

roomy ADJECTIVE containing plenty of room; spacious

roost VERB birds roost when they perch or settle for sleep

roost NOUN a place where birds roost

rooster NOUN (North American) a cockerel

root NOUN ❶ the part of a plant that grows under the ground and absorbs water and nourishment from the soil ❷ a source or basis of something ❸ a number which, when multiplied by itself a particular number of times, produces another number

root VERB ❶ to take root in the ground; to cause something to take root ❷ to fix someone firmly in one place ❸ to search for something by moving things ❹ a pig or other animal roots when it turns up ground in search of food

rope NOUN a strong thick cord made of twisted strands of fibre

rope VERB to fasten something with a rope

rosary NOUN a string of beads for keeping count of a set of prayers as they are said

rose NOUN ❶ a scented flower with a long thorny stem; the bush this flower grows on ❷ a deep pink colour ❸ a sprinkling nozzle with many holes, e.g. on a watering can or hosepipe

rose VERB past tense of **rise**

rosemary NOUN an evergreen shrub with fragrant leaves, used in cooking

rosette NOUN a large circular badge or ornament, made of ribbon

Rosh Hashanah, Rosh Hashana NOUN the Jewish New Year festival

roster NOUN a list showing people's turns to be on duty

rostrum NOUN a platform for one person, e.g. for giving a speech or conducting an orchestra

rosy ADJECTIVE ❶ deep pink ❷ hopeful or cheerful

rot VERB to go soft or bad and become useless; to decay

rot NOUN ❶ rotting or decay ❷ (informal) nonsense

rota (say roh-ta) NOUN a list of people to do things or of things to be done in turn

rotate VERB ❶ to turn or spin in circles round a central point; to revolve ❷ to happen or make something happen in a fixed order; to take turns at doing something

rotation NOUN ❶ movement in circles round a central point ❷ happening or making things happen in a certain order

rote NOUN ➤ by rote by repeating something again and again, but without full understanding of its meaning

rotor NOUN a rotating part of a machine or helicopter

rotten ADJECTIVE ❶ rotted or decayed ❷ (informal) very bad or unpleasant

Rottweiler NOUN a breed of powerful black-and-tan dog, sometimes used as a guard dog

rouble (say roo-bul) NOUN the unit

of money in Russia

rouge (say roozh) NOUN a reddish cosmetic for colouring the cheeks

rough ADJECTIVE ❶ not smooth or level; uneven ❷ not gentle or careful; violent ❸ not exact or detailed ❹ rough sea or weather is wild and stormy ❺ difficult and unpleasant

rough VERB ➤ rough it to do without ordinary comforts ➤ rough something out to draw or plan something without including all the details ➤ rough someone up (informal) to beat someone up

roughage NOUN fibre in food, which helps digestion

roughen VERB to make something rough

roughly ADVERB ❶ approximately; not exactly ❷ in a rough way; not gently

roulette (say roo-let) NOUN a gambling game where players bet on where the ball on a revolving wheel will come to rest

round ADJECTIVE ❶ shaped like a circle, ball or cylinder; curved ❷ full or complete ❸ a round number is expressed to the nearest whole number or the nearest ten, hundred, etc.

round ADVERB (chiefly British) ❶ in a circle or curve; surrounding something ❷ in every direction or to every person ❸ in a new direction ❹ from place to place ❺ to someone's house or place of work

round PREPOSITION (chiefly British) ❶ on all sides of ❷ in a curve or

circle at an even distance from ❸ to all parts of a place ❹ on or to the further side of a place

round NOUN ❶ a series of visits made by a doctor, postman, etc. ❷ one section or stage in a competition ❸ the playing of all the holes on a golf course ❹ a shot or series of shots from a gun; ammunition for this ❺ (British) a whole slice of bread; a sandwich made with two slices of bread ❻ a song in which people sing the same words but start at different times ❼ a set of drinks bought for all the members of a group

round VERB to travel round something

roundabout NOUN ❶ a road junction where traffic has to pass round a circular structure in the road ❷ a circular revolving ride in a playground or at a funfair

roundabout ADJECTIVE indirect; not using the shortest way of going or of saying or doing something

rounded ADJECTIVE round in shape

rounders NOUN a game in which players try to hit a ball and run round a circuit

Roundhead NOUN a supporter of the Parliamentary party in the English Civil War (1642-9)

roundly ADVERB thoroughly or severely

round-the-clock ADJECTIVE lasting or happening all day and all night

round trip NOUN a trip to one or more places and back to where you started

round-up NOUN ❶ a gathering up of cattle or people ❷ a summary

roundworm NOUN a kind of worm that lives as a parasite in the intestines of animals and birds

rouse VERB ① to wake someone up ② to make someone excited, angry or active

rousing ADJECTIVE exciting and powerful

rout VERB to defeat an enemy completely and force them to retreat

rout NOUN a complete defeat; a disorderly retreat of defeated troops

route (say root) NOUN the way you have to go to get to a place

router (say roo-ter) NOUN a device that connects computer networks and sends information between them

routine (say roo-teen) NOUN ① a regular or fixed way of doing things ② a set sequence in a performance

rove VERB to roam or wander

row (rhymes with go) NOUN a line of people or things

row (rhymes with go) VERB to make a boat move by using oars

row (rhymes with cow) NOUN (British) ① a loud noise or uproar ② a quarrel or noisy argument

row (rhymes with cow) VERB (British) to have a noisy argument

rowan (say roh-an) NOUN a tree that bears hanging bunches of red berries

rowdy ADJECTIVE noisy and disorderly

rower NOUN a person who rows a boat

rowing boat NOUN (British) a small boat that you move forward by using oars

royal ADJECTIVE to do with a king or queen

Royalist NOUN a supporter of the monarchy in the English Civil War (1642-9)

royalist NOUN a person who supports the idea of a monarchy

royalty NOUN ① being royal ② a royal person or royal people ③ a payment made to an author or composer for each copy of a work sold or for each performance

RSVP ABBREVIATION please reply (often written at the end of an invitation)

rub VERB to move something backwards and forwards while pressing it on something else

rub NOUN rubbing something

rubber NOUN ① a strong elastic substance used for making tyres, balls, hoses, etc. ② a piece of rubber for rubbing out pencil or ink marks

rubber plant NOUN ① a tall evergreen plant with tough shiny leaves, often grown as a house plant ② a rubber tree

rubber tree NOUN a tropical tree from which rubber is obtained

rubbish NOUN (chiefly British) ① things that are not wanted and are to be thrown away ② nonsense; something of very poor quality

rubbish ADJECTIVE (British) (informal) very poor in quality

rubble NOUN broken pieces of brick

or stone

rubella NOUN an infectious disease which causes a red rash and which can damage a baby if the mother catches it early in pregnancy

rubric NOUN a set of instructions at the beginning of an official document or an examination paper

ruby NOUN a red jewel

ruby wedding NOUN a couple's fortieth wedding anniversary

ruck VERB cloth rucks up when it forms untidy creases or folds

rucksack NOUN a bag with shoulder straps for carrying on your back

rudder NOUN a hinged upright piece at the back of a ship or aircraft, used for steering

ruddy ADJECTIVE a ruddy complexion is red and healthy-looking

rude ADJECTIVE ❶ impolite or bad-mannered ❷ to do with sex or the body in a way that might offend people; indecent ❸ roughly made ❹ unexpected and unpleasant

rudimentary ADJECTIVE ❶ very basic or simple ❷ not fully developed

rudiments (say rood-i-ments) PLURAL NOUN the elementary principles of a subject

rueful ADJECTIVE showing sad regret

ruff NOUN ❶ a starched pleated frill worn round the neck in the 16th century ❷ a collar-like ring of feathers or fur round a bird's or animal's neck

ruffian NOUN a rough or violent person

ruffle VERB ❶ to disturb the smoothness of a thing ❷ to upset or annoy someone

ruffle NOUN a gathered ornamental frill

rug NOUN ❶ a small carpet or thick mat for the floor ❷ a piece of thick fabric used as a blanket

rugby, rugby football NOUN a kind of football game using an oval ball that players may carry or kick

rugged (say rug-id) ADJECTIVE ❶ having a rough or uneven surface or outline ❷ strong and tough

ruin VERB to damage or spoil a thing so severely that it is useless or no longer enjoyable

ruin NOUN ❶ a building that is so badly damaged that it has almost fallen down ❷ severe damage or destruction to something

rule NOUN ❶ something that people have to obey ❷ ruling or governing ❸ a carpenter's ruler

rule VERB ❶ to govern or reign ❷ to make a decision ❸ to draw a straight line with a ruler or other straight edge

ruler NOUN ❶ a person who governs ❷ a strip of wood, metal or plastic with straight edges, used for measuring and drawing straight lines

ruling NOUN a judgement or decision

rum NOUN a strong alcoholic drink made from sugar or molasses

rumble VERB to make a deep heavy continuous sound

rumble NOUN a deep heavy continuous sound

ruminant *NOUN* an animal that chews the cud (see **cud**), such as cattle, sheep, deer, etc.

rummage *VERB* to turn things over or move them about while looking for something

rummy *NOUN* a card game in which players try to form sets or sequences of cards

rumour *NOUN* news or information that spreads to a lot of people but may not be true

rumour *VERB* ➤ **be rumoured** to be spread as a rumour

rump *NOUN* the hind part of an animal

rumple *VERB* to make something untidy or no longer smooth

rump steak *NOUN* a piece of meat from the rump of a cow

rumpus *NOUN* (*informal*) an uproar; an angry protest

run *VERB* runs, running, ran, run **1** to move with quick steps so that both or all feet leave the ground at each stride **2** to go or travel; to flow **3** to move something over or through a thing **4** to produce a flow of liquid **5** to work or function **6** to start or use a computer program **7** to manage or organize something **8** to compete in a contest or election **9** to extend **10** to last or continue for a certain amount of time **11** to take a person somewhere in a vehicle

run *NOUN* **1** the action of running; a time spent running **2** a point scored in cricket or baseball **3** a continuous series of events **4** an enclosure for animals **5** a series of

damaged stitches in a pair of tights or stockings **6** a track

runaway *NOUN* someone who has run away

runaway *ADJECTIVE* **1** having run away or out of control **2** won easily

rundown *ADJECTIVE* **1** tired and in bad health **2** in bad condition

rung *NOUN* one of the crossbars on a ladder

rung *VERB* past participle of **ring** *VERB*

runner *NOUN* **1** a person or animal that runs, especially in a race **2** a stem that grows away from a plant and roots itself **3** a rod or strip on which something slides; each of the long strips under a sledge **4** a long narrow strip of carpet or covering

runner bean *NOUN* (*British*) a kind of climbing bean with long green pods which are eaten

runner-up *NOUN* someone who comes second in a race or competition

running *present participle* of **run** ➤ **in the running** competing and with a chance of winning

running *ADJECTIVE* continuous or consecutive; without an interval

runny *ADJECTIVE* **1** flowing like liquid **2** producing a flow of liquid

run-of-the-mill *ADJECTIVE* ordinary, not special

runway *NOUN* a long hard surface on which aircraft take off and land

rupee *NOUN* the unit of money in India and Pakistan

rupture *VERB* to break or burst

a
b
c
d
e
f
g
h
i
j
k
l
m
n
o
p
q
r
s
t
u
v
w
x
y
z

suddenly or to cause something to do this

rural ADJECTIVE to do with or belonging to the countryside

ruse NOUN a deception or trick

rush VERB ❶ to move or do something quickly; to hurry ❷ to take someone to a place very quickly ❸ to make someone hurry ❹ to attack or capture someone by dashing forward suddenly

rush NOUN ❶ a hurry ❷ a sudden quick movement ❸ a sudden great demand for something ❹ a plant with a thin stem that grows in marshy places

rush hour NOUN the time when traffic is busiest

rusk NOUN (chiefly British) a kind of hard dry biscuit for babies to chew

rust NOUN ❶ a red or brown substance that forms on iron or steel exposed to damp and corrodes it ❷ a reddish-brown colour

rust VERB to make something rusty or to become rusty

rustic ADJECTIVE ❶ to do with life in the countryside; rural ❷ made of rough timber or branches

rustle VERB ❶ to make a sound like dry leaves moving or paper being crumpled ❷ (North American) to steal horses or cattle

rustle NOUN a rustling sound

rusty ADJECTIVE ❶ coated with rust ❷ weakened by lack of use or practice

rut NOUN ❶ a deep track made by wheels in soft ground ❷ a settled and usually dull way of life

ruthless ADJECTIVE determined to get what you want and not caring if you hurt other people

rye NOUN a cereal used to make flour and whisky

Ss

S. ABBREVIATION ❶ south ❷ southern

sabbath NOUN a weekly day for rest and prayer, Saturday for Jews, Sunday for Christians

sable NOUN ❶ a kind of dark fur ❷ (poetical use) black

sabotage NOUN deliberately damaging machinery or equipment to hinder an enemy or large organization

sabotage VERB to deliberately damage something by an act of sabotage

saboteur NOUN a person who carries out sabotage

sabre NOUN ❶ a heavy sword with a curved blade ❷ a light fencing sword

sac NOUN a bag-shaped part in an animal or plant

saccharin (say **sak**-er-in) NOUN a very sweet substance used as a substitute for sugar

saccharine (say **sak**-er-een) ADJECTIVE unpleasantly sweet or sentimental

sachet (say **sash**-ay) NOUN a small sealed packet or bag containing a small amount of shampoo, sugar, etc.

sack NOUN a large bag made of strong material

sack VERB ❶ to dismiss someone from a job ❷ (old use) to plunder and destroy a captured town

sacrament NOUN an important Christian religious ceremony such as baptism or Holy Communion

sacred ADJECTIVE holy; to do with God or a god

sacrifice NOUN ❶ giving up a thing you value, so that something good may happen ❷ killing an animal or person as an offering to a god ❸ a thing sacrificed

sacrifice VERB ❶ to give something up so that something good may happen ❷ to kill an animal or person as an offering to a god

sacrilege (say sak-ril-ij) NOUN disrespect or damage to something people think of as sacred or valuable

sad ADJECTIVE unhappy; showing or causing sorrow

sadden VERB to make a person sad

saddle NOUN ❶ a seat for putting on the back of a horse or other animal ❷ the seat of a bicycle ❸ a ridge of high land between two peaks

saddle VERB to put a saddle on a horse or other animal for riding

sadist (say say-dist) NOUN a person who enjoys hurting or humiliating other people

sadly ADVERB ❶ in a sad way ❷ unfortunately

safari NOUN an expedition to watch or hunt wild animals

safari park NOUN a large park where wild animals can roam around freely and visitors can watch them from their cars

safe ADJECTIVE ❶ not in danger ❷ not dangerous

safe NOUN a strong cupboard or box in which valuables can be locked away safely

safeguard NOUN something that protects against possible dangers

safeguard VERB to protect something from danger

safely ADVERB ❶ without harm or danger ❷ without risk

safe sex NOUN sexual activity in which precautions, such as using a condom, are taken to prevent the spread of infections

safety NOUN being safe; freedom from danger, harm or risk

safety pin NOUN a U-shaped pin with a clip fastening over the point

saffron NOUN ❶ a deep yellow spice used to colour or flavour food, made from the dried stigmas of a crocus ❷ a deep yellow colour

sag VERB ❶ to go down in the middle because something heavy is pressing on it ❷ to hang down loosely; to droop

saga (say sah-ga) NOUN a long story with many episodes or adventures

sage NOUN ❶ a kind of herb used in cooking and formerly used in medicine ❷ a wise and respected person

sage ADJECTIVE wise and experienced

sago NOUN a starchy white food used to make puddings

said past tense of say

sail NOUN ❶ a large piece of strong cloth attached to a mast to catch the wind and make a ship or boat

529

move ❷ a short voyage ❸ an arm of a windmill

sail VERB ❶ to travel in a ship or boat ❷ to start out on a voyage ❸ to control a ship or boat ❹ to move quickly and smoothly

sailboard NOUN a flat board with a mast and sail, used in windsurfing

sailor NOUN a person who sails; a member of a ship's crew or of a navy

saint NOUN a holy or very good person

sake NOUN ➤ **for the sake of something** in order to get or achieve something ➤ **for someone's sake** in order to help or please someone

salad NOUN a mixture of vegetables eaten raw or cold

salamander NOUN a lizard-like amphibian

salami NOUN a spiced sausage, originally made in Italy

salary NOUN a regular wage, usually for a year's work, paid in monthly instalments

sale NOUN ❶ the selling of something ❷ a time when things are sold at reduced prices

salesperson NOUN a person employed to sell goods

salient (say **say**-lee-ent) ADJECTIVE most noticeable or important

saline ADJECTIVE containing salt

saliva NOUN the natural liquid in a person's or animal's mouth

salivate (say **sal**-iv-ayt) VERB to form saliva, especially a large amount

sallow ADJECTIVE sallow skin is slightly yellow

sally NOUN ❶ a lively or witty remark ❷ a sudden attack by an enemy

sally VERB ➤ **sally forth** or **out** to set out in a determined way

salmon (say **sam**-on) NOUN a large edible fish with pink flesh

salmonella (say sal-mon-**el**-a) NOUN a bacterium that can cause food poisoning

salon NOUN ❶ a large elegant room ❷ a room or shop where customers go for hair or beauty treatment

saloon NOUN ❶ a car with a hard roof and a separate boot ❷ a place where alcoholic drinks are bought and drunk, especially a comfortable bar in a pub

salsa NOUN ❶ a hot spicy sauce ❷ a kind of modern Latin American dance music; a dance to this

salt NOUN ❶ sodium chloride, the white substance that gives sea water its taste and is used for flavouring food ❷ a chemical compound of a metal and an acid

salt VERB to flavour or preserve food with salt

salt cellar NOUN a small dish or perforated pot holding salt for use at meals

salts PLURAL NOUN a substance that looks like salt

salty ADJECTIVE containing or tasting of salt

salute VERB ❶ to raise your right hand to your forehead as a sign of respect, especially in the armed forces ❷ to greet someone ❸ to say that you respect or admire something

salute NOUN ❶ the act of saluting ❷ the firing of guns as a sign of respect

salvage VERB to save or rescue something such as a damaged ship's cargo so that it can be used again

salvation NOUN ❶ in Christian teaching, being saved by God from the power of evil ❷ something that rescues a person from danger or disaster

salve NOUN ❶ a soothing ointment ❷ something that soothes

salve VERB ➤ **salve your conscience** to make you feel less guilty about something

salver NOUN a small metal tray

salvo NOUN firing a number of guns at the same time

same ADJECTIVE ❶ of one kind, exactly alike or equal ❷ not changing; not different

samosa NOUN a triangular fried pastry case filled with spicy meat or vegetables

sampan NOUN a small flat-bottomed boat used in China

sample NOUN a small amount that shows what something is like

sample VERB ❶ to take a sample of something ❷ to try part of something

sampler NOUN a piece of embroidery worked in various stitches to show skill in needlework

samurai (say **sam**-oor-eye) NOUN a member of an ancient Japanese warrior class

sanction NOUN ❶ action taken against a nation that is considered to have broken an international law ❷ a penalty for disobeying a law ❸ official permission or approval for something

sanction VERB to officially permit or authorize something

sanctity NOUN being sacred; holiness

sanctuary NOUN ❶ a safe place where people can be protected; a refuge ❷ an area where wildlife is protected ❸ a sacred place; the part of a church where the altar stands

sanctum NOUN a person's private room

sand NOUN the tiny grains of rock that cover the ground on beaches, river beds and deserts

sand VERB to smooth or polish a surface with sandpaper or some other rough material

sandal NOUN a lightweight shoe with straps over the foot

sandalwood NOUN a scented wood from a tropical tree

sandbag NOUN a bag filled with sand, used to build defences against flood water or bullets

sandbank NOUN a bank of sand under water

sandpaper NOUN strong paper coated with sand or a similar substance, rubbed on rough surfaces to make them smooth

sands PLURAL NOUN a beach or sandy area

sandstone NOUN rock made of

compressed sand

sandwich NOUN two or more slices of bread with a filling (e.g. of meat or cheese) between them

sandwich VERB to put a person or thing in a narrow space between two others

sandwich course NOUN (*British*) a college or university course which includes periods in industry or business

sandy ADJECTIVE ❶ like sand ❷ covered with sand ❸ yellowish-red

sane ADJECTIVE ❶ having a healthy mind; not mad ❷ sensible or reasonable

sanguine (say **sang**-gwin) ADJECTIVE cheerful and optimistic

sanitary ADJECTIVE ❶ free from germs and dirt; hygienic ❷ to do with sanitation

sanitary towel NOUN an absorbent pad worn by women to absorb blood during menstruation

sanitation NOUN arrangements for drainage and the disposal of sewage

sanity NOUN being sane; sensible behaviour

Sanskrit NOUN the ancient and sacred language of the Hindus in India

sap NOUN the liquid inside a plant, carrying food to all its parts

sap VERB to sap someone's strength or energy is to use it up or weaken it gradually

sapling NOUN a young tree

sapphire NOUN a bright-blue jewel

Saracen NOUN an Arab or Muslim

of the time of the Crusades

sarcasm NOUN being sarcastic

sarcastic ADJECTIVE saying the opposite of what you mean in order to insult someone or make fun of them

sarcophagus NOUN a stone coffin, often decorated with carvings

sardine NOUN a small sea fish, usually sold in tins, packed tightly in oil

sari NOUN a length of cloth worn wrapped round the body as a dress, especially by Indian women and girls

sarong NOUN a large piece of cloth worn around the body, originally in SE Asia

sash NOUN a strip of cloth worn round the waist or over one shoulder

sash window NOUN a window that slides up and down

SAT ABBREVIATION standard assessment task

satanic (say sa-**tan**-ik) ADJECTIVE to do with or like Satan, the Devil in Jewish and Christian teaching

satchel NOUN a bag you wear on the shoulder or the back, especially for carrying books to and from school

sate VERB to satisfy an appetite or desire fully

satellite NOUN ❶ a spacecraft put in orbit round a planet to collect information or transmit communications signals ❷ a moon moving in an orbit round a planet

satellite dish NOUN a bowl-shaped aerial for receiving broadcasting signals transmitted by satellite

satellite television NOUN television broadcasting in which the signals are transmitted by means of a communications satellite

satin NOUN a silky material that is shiny on one side

satire NOUN ❶ the use of humour or exaggeration to show what is bad or weak about a person or thing, especially the government ❷ a play, poem or other piece of writing that does this

satirical ADJECTIVE using satire to mock or show the faults of a person or thing

satisfaction NOUN ❶ the feeling of pleasure you have when you achieve something or get what you need or want ❷ giving someone what they need or want

satisfactory ADJECTIVE good enough; acceptable

satisfy VERB ❶ to give someone what they need or want ❷ to make someone feel certain; to convince someone ❸ to fulfil or achieve something

satsuma NOUN a kind of mandarin orange originally grown in Japan

saturate VERB ❶ to make a thing thoroughly wet ❷ to make a place or thing take in as much as possible of something

Saturday NOUN the day of the week following Friday

satyr (say **sat**-er) NOUN in Greek myths, a woodland god with a man's body and a goat's ears, tail and legs

sauce NOUN ❶ a thick liquid served with food to add flavour ❷ (informal) being cheeky; impudence

saucepan NOUN a metal cooking pan with a handle at the side

saucer NOUN a small curved plate for a cup to stand on

saucy ADJECTIVE rude or cheeky

sauerkraut (say **sour**-krowt) NOUN chopped and pickled cabbage, originally made in Germany

sauna NOUN a room filled with steam where people sit and sweat a lot, used as a kind of bath

saunter VERB to walk slowly and casually

sausage NOUN a tube of skin or plastic stuffed with minced meat and other filling

savage ADJECTIVE wild and fierce; cruel

savage NOUN ❶ a savage person ❷ (old use) a member of a people thought of as primitive or uncivilized

savage VERB an animal savages a person or another animal when it attacks them and bites or scratches them fiercely

savannah, savanna NOUN a grassy plain in a hot country, with few or no trees

save VERB ❶ to keep a person or thing safe; to free a person or thing from danger or harm ❷ to keep something, especially money, so that it can be used later ❸ to avoid wasting something ❹ (in computing) to keep data by storing it in the computer's memory or on a disk ⑤ to stop a goal being scored

save NOUN preventing a goal from being scored

save PREPOSITION (*formal*) except

savings PLURAL NOUN your savings are the money that you have saved

saviour NOUN a person who saves someone

savour VERB ① to enjoy the taste or smell of something ② to enjoy a feeling or experience

savour NOUN the taste or smell of something

savoury ADJECTIVE ① tasty but not sweet ② having an appetizing taste or smell

savoury NOUN (*chiefly British*) a savoury dish

saw NOUN a tool with a zigzag edge for cutting wood or metal etc.

saw VERB saws, sawing, sawed, sawn ① to cut something with a saw ② to move something backwards and forwards as if you were using a saw

saw VERB past tense of **see**

sawdust NOUN powder that comes from wood cut by a saw

sawmill NOUN a mill where timber is cut into planks etc. by machinery

Saxon NOUN ① a member of a people who came from Europe and occupied parts of England in the 5th-6th centuries ② an Anglo-Saxon

saxophone NOUN a brass wind instrument with a reed in the mouthpiece

say VERB says, saying, said ① to speak or express something

in words ② to give an opinion ③ to show something or give information

say NOUN ➤ **have a say** to be able to give your opinion or help decide something

saying NOUN a well-known phrase or proverb that gives advice or says something true about life

scab NOUN a hard crust that forms over a cut or graze while it is healing

scabbard NOUN the sheath of a sword or dagger

scabies (say skay-beez) NOUN a contagious skin disease with severe itching, caused by a parasite

scaffold NOUN a platform on which criminals are executed

scaffolding NOUN a structure of poles or tubes and planks making platforms for workers to stand on while building or repairing a house

scald VERB ① to burn yourself with very hot liquid or steam ② to heat milk until it is nearly boiling

scald NOUN a burn from very hot liquid or steam

scale NOUN ① a series of units, degrees or qualities for measuring something ② a series of musical notes going up or down in a fixed pattern ③ the relationship between the size of something on a map or model and the actual size of the thing in the real world ④ the relative size or importance of something ⑤ each of the thin overlapping parts on the outside of fish, snakes, etc.; a thin flake or part like this ⑥ a hard substance formed in a kettle or boiler by hard water or on teeth

scale VERB ❶ to climb to the top of something steep ❷ to remove scales or scale from something

scale model NOUN a model of something, made to scale

scalene (say skay-leen) ADJECTIVE a scalene triangle has unequal sides

scales PLURAL NOUN a device for weighing things

scallop NOUN ❶ a shellfish with two hinged fan-shaped shells ❷ each curve in an ornamental wavy border

scalp NOUN the skin on the top of the head

scalp VERB to cut or tear the scalp from a person

scalpel NOUN a small knife with a thin, sharp blade, used by a surgeon or artist

scaly ADJECTIVE covered in scales or scale

scam NOUN (informal) a dishonest scheme or a swindle

scamper VERB to run quickly with short light steps

scampi PLURAL NOUN large prawns eaten in batter or breadcrumbs

scan VERB ❶ to look at every part of something ❷ to glance at something ❸ poetry scans when it is correct in rhythm ❹ to use a scanner to read data from something into a computer ❺ to sweep a radar or electronic beam over an area to examine it or in search of something

scan NOUN ❶ scanning something ❷ an examination using a scanner

scandal NOUN ❶ something

shameful or disgraceful ❷ gossip about people's faults and wrongdoing

scandalize (also **scandalise**) VERB to shock a person by something considered shameful or disgraceful

scandalous ADJECTIVE shocking or disgraceful

Scandinavian ADJECTIVE from or to do with the countries of Scandinavia (Norway, Sweden and Denmark and sometimes also Finland and Iceland)

scanner NOUN ❶ a machine that examines things by means of light or other rays ❷ a machine that converts printed text, pictures, etc. into a form that can be put into a computer

scant ADJECTIVE barely enough or adequate

scanty ADJECTIVE small in amount or extent; meagre

scapegoat NOUN a person who is made to bear the blame or punishment for what others have done

scar NOUN ❶ the mark left by a cut or burn after it has healed ❷ a lasting effect left by an unpleasant experience

scar VERB to make a scar or scars on skin

scarab NOUN an ancient Egyptian ornament or symbol carved in the shape of a beetle

scarce ADJECTIVE not enough to supply people

scarcely ADVERB only just; only with difficulty

scare VERB to frighten someone

scare NOUN ❶ a fright ❷ a sudden widespread sense of alarm about something

scarecrow NOUN a figure of a person dressed in old clothes, put in a field to frighten birds away from crops

scared ADJECTIVE frightened or afraid

scaremonger NOUN a person who spreads scare stories

scarf NOUN scarves a strip of material that you wear round your neck or head

scarlet ADJECTIVE & NOUN bright red

scarlet fever NOUN an infectious fever producing a scarlet rash

scarper VERB (British) (informal) to run away or leave in a hurry

scary ADJECTIVE (informal) frightening

scathing (say skay th-ing) ADJECTIVE severely criticizing a person or thing

scatter VERB ❶ to throw or send things in all directions ❷ to run or leave quickly in all directions

scatterbrain NOUN a careless forgetful person

scattered ADJECTIVE spread over a large area or happening several times over a period of time

scattering NOUN a small number of things spread over an area

scavenge VERB ❶ to search in rubbish for useful things ❷ a bird or animal scavenges when it searches for decaying flesh as food

scenario NOUN ❶ a summary of the plot of a play or story ❷ an imagined series of events or set of circumstances

scene NOUN ❶ the place where something has happened ❷ a part of a play or film ❸ a view someone sees ❹ an angry or noisy outburst ❺ stage scenery ❻ an area of activity

scenery NOUN ❶ the natural features of a landscape ❷ things put on a stage to make it look like a place

scenic ADJECTIVE having fine natural scenery

scent NOUN ❶ a pleasant smell ❷ a liquid perfume ❸ an animal's smell that other animals can detect

scent VERB ❶ to discover something by its scent ❷ to give something a pleasant smell ❸ to feel that something is about to happen

sceptic (say skep-tik) NOUN a sceptical person

sceptical (say skep-tik-al) ADJECTIVE doubting whether something is true; not believing things easily

sceptre NOUN a rod carried by a king or queen as a symbol of power

schedule (say shed-yool) NOUN a programme or timetable of things that will happen or have to be done

schedule VERB to arrange something for a certain time

scheme NOUN a plan of what to do

scheme VERB to make secret plans; to plot

schism (say skizm or sizm) NOUN the splitting of a group into two opposing sections because they disagree about something important

schizophrenia (say skid-zo-**free**-nee-a) NOUN a kind of mental illness in which people cannot relate their thoughts and feelings to reality

scholar NOUN ❶ a person who has studied a subject thoroughly ❷ a person who has been awarded a scholarship

scholarly ADJECTIVE showing knowledge and learning

scholarship NOUN ❶ a grant of money given to someone to help to pay for their education ❷ serious study of an academic subject and the knowledge you get

scholastic ADJECTIVE to do with schools or education; academic

school NOUN ❶ a place where teaching is done, especially of pupils aged 5-18 ❷ the pupils in a school ❸ the time when teaching takes place in a school ❹ a group of people who have the same beliefs or style of work ❺ a large group of fish, whales or dolphins

school VERB to teach or train a person or animal

schoolchild NOUN a child who goes to school

schooling NOUN education at a school

schoolteacher NOUN a person who teaches in a school

schooner (say **skoon**-er) NOUN ❶ a sailing ship with two or more masts ❷ a tall glass for serving sherry

science (say **sy**-ens) NOUN ❶ the study of the physical world by means of observation and experiment ❷ a branch of this, such as chemistry, physics or biology

science fiction NOUN stories about imaginary scientific discoveries or space travel and life on other planets, often set in the future

science park NOUN an area set up for industries using science or for organizations doing scientific research

scientific ADJECTIVE ❶ to do with science or scientists ❷ studying things in an organized, logical way and testing ideas carefully

scientist NOUN ❶ an expert in science ❷ someone who uses scientific methods

scimitar (say **sim**-it-ar) NOUN a curved oriental sword

scintillating ADJECTIVE ❶ sparkling ❷ lively and witty

scissors PLURAL NOUN a cutting instrument used with one hand, with two blades joined so that they can close against each other

scoff VERB ❶ to laugh or speak in a mocking way about something you think is silly ❷ (informal) to eat something greedily or to eat it all up

scold VERB to speak angrily to someone because they have done wrong; to tell someone off

scone (say skon or skohn) NOUN a soft flat cake, usually eaten with butter

scoop NOUN ❶ a kind of deep spoon for serving ice cream etc. ❷ an amount picked up with a scoop ❸ a deep shovel for lifting grain, sugar, etc. ❹ an important piece

a
b
c
d
e
f
g
h
i
j
k
l
m
n
o
p
q
r
s
t
u
v
w
x
z

scoop *VERB* ❶ to lift or hollow something out with a scoop, spoon or the palm of your hand ❷ to lift something with a broad sweeping movement

scoot *VERB* ❶ to make a bicycle or scooter move along by sitting or standing on it and pushing it along with one foot ❷ (*informal*) to run or go away quickly

scooter *NOUN* ❶ a kind of motorcycle with small wheels ❷ a board with wheels and a long handle, which you ride on by scooting

scope *NOUN* ❶ opportunity or possibility for something ❷ the range or extent of a subject

scorch *VERB* to make something go brown by burning it slightly

scorching *ADJECTIVE* (*informal*) very hot

score *NOUN* ❶ the number of points or goals made in a game; a result ❷ (*old use*) twenty ❸ written or printed music

score *VERB* ❶ to get a point or goal in a game ❷ to keep a count of the score in a game ❸ to cut or mark a line on a surface with something sharp ❹ to write out a musical score

scorer *NOUN* ❶ a person who scores a goal or point ❷ a person who keeps a count of the score in a game

scores *PLURAL NOUN* many; a large number

scorn *NOUN* contempt or lack of respect for someone

scorn *VERB* ❶ to treat someone with contempt ❷ to refuse something because you are too proud

scornful *ADJECTIVE* feeling or showing scorn

scorpion *NOUN* an animal that looks like a tiny lobster, with a poisonous sting in its curved tail

Scot *NOUN* a person who comes from Scotland

scotch *NOUN* whisky made in Scotland

scotch *VERB* to put an end to an idea or rumour

scot-free *ADJECTIVE* avoiding the punishment that is deserved

Scots *ADJECTIVE* from or belonging to Scotland

Scots *NOUN* the form of English used in Scotland

Scottish *ADJECTIVE* to do with or belonging to Scotland

scoundrel *NOUN* a wicked or dishonest person

scour *VERB* ❶ to search a place thoroughly ❷ to rub something until it is clean and bright ❸ to clear a channel or pipe by the force of water flowing through it

scourge (say skerj) *NOUN* ❶ a whip for flogging people ❷ something that causes a lot of suffering or trouble

Scout *NOUN* a member of the Scout Association, an organization for boys

scout *NOUN* someone sent out ahead of a group to collect information

scout VERB to search an area thoroughly

scowl NOUN a bad-tempered frown

scowl VERB to have an angry or bad-tempered look

scrabble VERB ① to scratch or claw at something with the hands or feet ② to move your fingers quickly, trying to find or get hold of something

scraggy ADJECTIVE thin and bony

scram VERB (informal) go away!

scramble VERB ① to move quickly and awkwardly ② to struggle to do or get something ③ military aircraft or their crew scramble when they take off quickly to go into action ④ to cook eggs by mixing them up and heating them in a pan ⑤ to alter a radio or telephone signal so that it cannot be used without a decoding device

scramble NOUN ① a climb or walk over rough ground ② a struggle to do or get something ③ a motorcycle race over rough country

scrap NOUN ① a small piece of something ② unwanted metal or paper that can be used again ③ (informal) a fight or argument

scrap VERB ① to get rid of something that is not wanted any more ② (informal) to fight or quarrel

scrape VERB ① to remove something from a surface by moving a sharp edge across it ② to damage or hurt something by rubbing it against something rough or hard ③ to make a harsh sound by rubbing against

something rough or hard ④ to get something by great effort or care

scrape NOUN ① a scraping movement or sound ② a mark made by scraping something ③ (informal) an awkward situation caused by mischief or foolishness

scrappy ADJECTIVE done carelessly or untidily

scratch VERB ① to mark or cut the surface of a thing with something sharp ② to rub the skin with fingernails or claws because it itches ③ to make a noise by rubbing a surface with something sharp

scratch NOUN ① a mark made by scratching ② the action of scratching

scratch card NOUN a card you buy as part of a lottery and scratch off part of the surface to see whether you have won a prize

scrawl NOUN untidy handwriting

scrawl VERB to write in a scrawl

scrawny ADJECTIVE thin and bony

scream NOUN ① a loud cry of pain, fear, anger or excitement ② a loud piercing sound ③ (informal) a very amusing person or thing

scream VERB to let out a scream

screech NOUN a harsh high-pitched scream or sound

screech VERB to make a harsh high-pitched scream or sound

screed NOUN a very long piece of writing

screen NOUN ① a surface on which films or television pictures or computer data are shown ② a movable panel used to hide, protect or divide something ③ a

539

vehicle's windscreen

screen VERB ❶ to show a film or television pictures on a screen ❷ to protect, hide or divide something with a screen ❸ to carry out tests on someone to find out if they have a disease ❹ to check whether a person is suitable for a job

screenplay NOUN the script of a film, with instructions about how scenes should be acted and filmed

screw NOUN ❶ a metal pin with a spiral ridge (the thread) round it, holding things together by being twisted in ❷ a twisting movement ❸ a propeller, especially for a ship or motor boat

screw VERB ❶ to fasten something with a screw or screws ❷ to fit or turn something by twisting

screwdriver NOUN a tool for turning screws

scribble VERB ❶ to write something quickly or untidily or carelessly ❷ to make meaningless marks

scribe NOUN a person who made copies of writings before printing was invented

scrimp VERB to spend as little money as possible on the things you need so that you can save it for something else

script NOUN ❶ handwriting ❷ the text of a play, film or broadcast

scripture NOUN ❶ sacred writings ❷ the Christian writings in the Bible

scroll NOUN ❶ a roll of paper or parchment used for writing on ❷ a spiral design

scroll VERB to move the display on a computer screen up or down to see what comes before or after it

scrotum (say **skroh**-tum) NOUN the pouch of skin behind the penis, containing the testicles

scrounge VERB to get something without paying for it

scrub VERB ❶ to clean something with water by rubbing it hard, especially with a brush ❷ (informal) to cancel something

scrub NOUN ❶ scrubbing something ❷ low trees and bushes ❸ land covered with these

scrubby ADJECTIVE ❶ scrubby trees and bushes are small and not fully developed ❷ scrubby land is covered with low bushes and trees

scruff NOUN the back of the neck

scruffy ADJECTIVE shabby and untidy

scrum NOUN ❶ (also **scrummage**) a group of players from each side in rugby football who push against each other and try to win the ball with their feet ❷ a crowd pushing against each other

scrumptious ADJECTIVE (informal) delicious

scrunch VERB ❶ to make a loud crunching sound ❷ to squeeze or crumple something into a smaller shape

scrunchy, scrunchie NOUN a band of elastic covered in fabric, used to tie up your hair

scruple NOUN a feeling of doubt or hesitation when your conscience tells you that an action would be wrong

scruple VERB ① to have scruples about something

scrupulous ADJECTIVE ① very careful about paying attention to every detail ② strictly honest or honourable

scrutinize (also **scrutinise**) VERB to look at or examine something carefully

scrutiny NOUN a careful look at or examination of something

scuba diving NOUN swimming underwater using a tank of air strapped to your back

scuff VERB ① to drag your feet while walking ② to mark your shoes by scraping your feet on something

scuffle NOUN a confused fight or struggle

scuffle VERB to take part in a scuffle

scull NOUN a small or lightweight oar

scull VERB to row with sculls

scullery NOUN a room for washing dishes and other kitchen work

sculpt VERB to carve something; to make sculptures

sculptor NOUN a person who makes sculptures

sculpture NOUN ① a figure or object that is carved or shaped out of a hard material such as stone, clay or metal ② the art of making sculptures

scum NOUN ① froth or dirt on top of a liquid ② worthless people

scupper NOUN an opening in a ship's side to let water drain away

scupper VERB ① to sink a ship deliberately ② (*informal*) to wreck something or make it fail

scurry VERB to run quickly with short steps

scurvy NOUN a disease caused by lack of vitamin C from not eating enough fruit and vegetables

scuttle VERB ① to run with short quick steps; to hurry away ② to sink a ship deliberately by letting water into it

scuttle NOUN ① a bucket or container for coal in a house ② a small opening with a lid in a ship's deck or side

scythe NOUN a tool with a long curved blade for cutting grass or corn

scythe VERB to cut something with a scythe

SE ABBREVIATION ① south-east ② south-eastern

sea NOUN ① the salt water that covers most of the earth's surface ② a large area of salt water; a large lake ③ a large area of something

sea anemone NOUN a sea creature with short tentacles round its mouth

seabed NOUN the bottom of the sea

seabird NOUN a bird that lives close to the sea and gets its food from it

sea breeze NOUN a breeze blowing from the sea onto the land

seafaring ADJECTIVE & NOUN working or travelling on the sea

seafood NOUN fish or shellfish from the sea eaten as food

seagull NOUN a seabird with long

a
b
c
d
e
f
g
h
i
j
k
l
m
n
o
p
q
r
s
t
u
v
w
x
y
z

A wings

sea horse NOUN a small fish that swims upright, with a head rather like a horse's head

seal NOUN ❶ a sea mammal with thick fur or bristles, that breeds on land ❷ something designed to close an opening and prevent air or liquid from getting in or out ❸ a piece of metal with an engraved design for pressing on a soft substance to leave an impression ❹ this impression, especially one made on a piece of wax ❺ a small decorative sticker

seal VERB ❶ to close something by sticking two parts together ❷ to close or cover something securely so that no air or liquid can get in or out ❸ to settle or decide something

sea level NOUN the level of the sea halfway between high and low tide

sealing wax NOUN a substance that is soft when heated but hardens when cooled, used for marking or closing something with a seal

sea lion NOUN a kind of large seal that lives in the Pacific Ocean

seam NOUN ❶ the line of stitches where two edges of cloth join ❷ a layer of coal in the ground

seaman NOUN a sailor

seamanship NOUN skill in sailing a boat or ship

seance (say say-ahns) NOUN a meeting at which people try to make contact with the spirits of dead people

seaplane NOUN an aeroplane that can land and take off from

water

seaport NOUN a port on the coast

sear VERB to scorch or burn the surface of something

search VERB ❶ to look very carefully in a place in order to find something ❷ to examine the clothes and body of a person to see if something is hidden there

search NOUN ❶ a very careful look for someone or something ❷ looking for information in a computer database or on the Internet

search engine NOUN (in computing) a computer program that allows you to search the Internet for information

searching ADJECTIVE examining closely and thoroughly

searchlight NOUN a light with a strong beam that can be turned in any direction

search warrant NOUN an official document giving the police permission to search private property

searing ADJECTIVE a searing pain is sharp and burning

seascape NOUN a picture or view of the sea

seashore NOUN the land close to the sea

seasick ADJECTIVE sick because of the movement of a ship

seaside NOUN a place by the sea where people go for holidays

season NOUN ❶ each of the four main parts of the year (spring, summer, autumn, winter) ❷ the time of year when something happens

season VERB ① to give extra flavour to food by adding salt, pepper, herbs or spices ② to dry and treat timber to make it ready for use

seasonable ADJECTIVE suitable for the time of year

seasonal ADJECTIVE ① for or to do with a season ② done or happening only at certain times of year

seasoning NOUN a substance used to season food

season ticket NOUN a ticket that you can use as often as you like throughout a period of time

seat NOUN ① a thing made or used for sitting on ② a place as a member of a council, committee or parliament ③ a person's bottom; the part of a skirt or trousers covering this ④ the place where something is based or located

seat VERB ① to place someone in or on a seat ② to have seats for a certain number of people

seat belt NOUN a strap to hold a person securely in a seat

seating NOUN ① the seats in a place ② the arrangement of seats

sea urchin NOUN a sea animal with a spherical shell covered in sharp spikes

seaward ADJECTIVE & ADVERB towards the sea

seaweed NOUN a plant or plants that grow in the sea

seaworthy ADJECTIVE a ship is seaworthy when it is fit for a sea voyage

secateurs PLURAL NOUN clippers held in the hand for pruning plants

secluded ADJECTIVE quiet and sheltered from view

second ADJECTIVE ① next after the first ② another

second NOUN ① a person or thing that is second ② an attendant of a fighter in a boxing match or duel ③ one-sixtieth of a minute of time or of a degree used in measuring angles ④ (*informal*) a short time

second VERB ① to support a proposal that someone else has put forward ② to act as a fighter's second ③ (say sik-**ond**) (*British*) to transfer (a person temporarily to another job or department

secondary ADJECTIVE ① coming after or from something ② less important. Compare with **primary**.

secondary colour NOUN a colour made by mixing two primary colours

secondary school NOUN a school for children of more than about 11 years old

second-hand ADJECTIVE ① bought or used after someone else has owned it ② selling used goods

secondly ADVERB in the second place; as the second thing

second nature NOUN behaviour that has become automatic or a habit

second-rate ADJECTIVE inferior; not very good

seconds PLURAL NOUN ① goods that are not of the best quality, sold at a reduced price ② a second helping of food at a meal

second sight NOUN the ability to

foresee the future

secrecy NOUN being secret; keeping things secret

secret ADJECTIVE ❶ that must not be told or shown to other people ❷ not known by everyone ❸ working secretly

secret NOUN ❶ something secret ❷ a way of achieving something that is not widely known

secret agent NOUN a spy acting for a country

secretary (say sek-rit-ree) NOUN ❶ a person whose job is to help with letters, keep files, answer the telephone and make business arrangements for a person or organization ❷ the person in a club or society who whose job is to keep records and write letters ❸ the head of a government department

secrete (say sik-reet) VERB ❶ to hide something ❷ to produce a substance in the body

secretion NOUN a substance that is secreted

secretive (say seek-ritiv) ADJECTIVE liking or trying to keep things secret

secretly ADVERB without other people knowing

secret police NOUN a police force which works in secret for political purposes, not to deal with crime

secret service NOUN a government department responsible for espionage

sect NOUN a group of people whose beliefs differ from those of others in the same religion

sectarian (say sek-**air**-ee-an) ADJECTIVE to do with disagreements between different religious groups

section NOUN ❶ one of the parts that something is divided into ❷ a cross-section

sector NOUN ❶ one part of an area ❷ a part of something ❸ (in mathematics) a section of a circle between two lines drawn from its centre to its circumference

secular ADJECTIVE not connected with religion at all

secure ADJECTIVE ❶ well locked or protected ❷ firmly fixed and certain not to slip ❸ feeling safe and confident and not worried ❹ certain or reliable

secure VERB ❶ to make a thing secure ❷ to fasten something firmly ❸ to obtain or achieve something

security NOUN ❶ being secure or safe; safety ❷ precautions against theft, spying or terrorism ❸ something you give as a guarantee that you will pay back a loan ❹ investments such as stocks and shares

security guard NOUN a person employed to guard a building or its contents against theft and vandalism

sedan chair NOUN an enclosed chair for one person, mounted on two horizontal poles and carried by two men, used in the 17th-18th centuries

sedate ADJECTIVE calm and dignified

sedate VERB to give a sedative to someone

sedative (say sed-a-tiv) NOUN a

medicine that makes a person calm or helps them sleep

sedentary (say **sed**-en-ter-ee) ADJECTIVE done sitting down

Seder NOUN in Judaism, a ritual and a ceremonial meal to mark the beginning of Passover

sedge NOUN a grass-like plant growing in marshes or near water

sediment NOUN fine particles of solid matter that float in liquid or sink to the bottom of it

sedimentary ADJECTIVE sedimentary rocks are formed from particles that have settled on a surface

seductive ADJECTIVE ❶ sexually attractive ❷ temptingly attractive

see VERB sees, seeing, saw, seen ❶ to use your eyes to notice or be aware of something ❷ to meet or visit someone ❸ to understand something ❹ to imagine or regard something in a certain way ❺ to consider something before deciding ❻ to make sure of something ❼ to check or discover something ❽ to escort or lead someone

see NOUN the district of which a bishop or archbishop is in charge

seed NOUN ❶ a tiny, hard part of a plant, capable of growing into a new plant ❷ a seeded player

seed VERB ❶ to plant or sprinkle seeds in something ❷ to name the best players and arrange for them not to play against each other in the early rounds of a tournament

seedling NOUN a very young plant growing from a seed

seedy ADJECTIVE shabby and not respectable

seeing CONJUNCTION considering

seek VERB seeks, seeking, sought ❶ to search for something ❷ to try to obtain or do something

seem VERB to give the impression of being something

seemingly ADVERB apparently, but perhaps not

seemly ADJECTIVE (old use) seemly talk or behaviour is proper or suitable

seep VERB to ooze slowly out or through something

seer NOUN a person who claims they can see into the future; a prophet

see-saw NOUN a plank balanced in the middle so that two people can sit, one on each end and make it go up and down

seethe VERB ❶ you are seething when you are very angry ❷ to be full of people or animals moving around ❸ to bubble and surge like water boiling

segment NOUN a part that is cut off or separates naturally from other parts

segregate VERB ❶ to separate people of different religions or races ❷ to isolate a person or thing

seismic (say **sy**-zmik) ADJECTIVE to do with earthquakes or other vibrations of the earth

seismograph (say **sy**-zmo-grahf) NOUN an instrument for measuring the strength of earthquakes

seize VERB ❶ to take hold of a person or thing suddenly or firmly ❷ to take control or possession

545

of something by force or by legal authority ❸ to take advantage of a chance or opportunity ❹ to have a sudden effect on someone

seizure NOUN ❶ seizing something ❷ a sudden fit, as in epilepsy or a heart attack

seldom ADVERB rarely; not often

select VERB to choose a person or thing carefully

select ADJECTIVE ❶ small and carefully chosen ❷ a select club or organization is exclusive and chooses its members carefully

selection NOUN ❶ selecting something or being selected ❷ a person or thing selected ❸ a group selected from a larger group ❹ a range of goods from which to choose

selective ADJECTIVE choosing or chosen carefully

self NOUN selves ❶ a person as an individual ❷ a person's particular nature

self-assured ADJECTIVE confident of your abilities

self-catering NOUN catering for yourself, instead of having meals provided

self-centred ADJECTIVE selfish; thinking about yourself too much

self-confident ADJECTIVE confident of your own abilities

self-conscious ADJECTIVE embarrassed or worried about how you look or what other people think of you

self-contained ADJECTIVE accommodation is self-contained when it is complete in itself and contains all the necessary facilities

self-control NOUN the ability to control your own behaviour or feelings

self-defence NOUN ❶ defending yourself against attack ❷ techniques for doing this

self-denial NOUN deliberately going without things you would like to have

self-determination NOUN a country's right to rule itself and choose its own government

self-employed ADJECTIVE working independently, not for an employer

self-esteem NOUN your own opinion of yourself and your own worth

self-evident ADJECTIVE obvious and not needing proof or explanation

selfie NOUN (informal) a photograph that you take of yourself, usually using a mobile phone, and send to a social media website

self-important ADJECTIVE having a high opinion of yourself; pompous

self-interest NOUN your own personal advantage

selfish ADJECTIVE doing what you want and not thinking of other people; keeping things for yourself

selfless ADJECTIVE thinking of other people rather than yourself; unselfish

self-made ADJECTIVE rich or successful because of your own efforts

self-pity NOUN too much sorrow and pity for yourself and your own problems

546

self-possessed ADJECTIVE calm and confident in a difficult situation

self-raising ADJECTIVE self-raising flour makes cakes rise without needing to have baking powder added

self-respect NOUN your own proper respect for yourself

self-righteous ADJECTIVE smugly sure that you are behaving virtuously

selfsame ADJECTIVE the very same

self-satisfied ADJECTIVE very pleased with yourself

self-seeking ADJECTIVE selfishly trying to benefit yourself

self-service ADJECTIVE where customers help themselves to things and pay a cashier for what they have taken

self-sufficient ADJECTIVE able to produce or provide what you need without help from others

self-willed ADJECTIVE obstinately doing what you want; stubborn

sell VERB sells, selling, sold ❶ to give something in exchange for money ❷ to have something available for people to buy ❸ to be on sale at a certain price
sell NOUN

sell-by date NOUN (British) a date, marked on the packaging of food, by which it must be sold

sell-out NOUN an entertainment, sporting event, etc. for which all the tickets have been sold

selves plural of self

semaphore NOUN a system of signalling by holding flags out with your arms in positions that indicate letters of the alphabet

semblance NOUN an outward appearance or apparent likeness

semen (say seem-en) NOUN a white liquid produced by males and containing sperm

semi NOUN (informal) a semi-detached house

semibreve NOUN (British) the longest musical note normally used (○), lasting four times as long as a crotchet

semicircle NOUN half a circle

semicolon NOUN a punctuation mark (;) used to separate two sentences or main clauses that are linked or of equal importance

semiconductor NOUN a substance that can conduct electricity but not as well as most metals do

semi-detached ADJECTIVE a semi-detached house is joined to another house on one side only

semi-final NOUN a match or round whose winner will take part in the final

seminar NOUN a meeting for advanced discussion and research on a subject

seminary NOUN a training college for priests or rabbis

semiquaver NOUN (British) a note in music (♪), equal in length to one quarter of a crotchet

Semitic (say sim-it-ik) ADJECTIVE to do with the Semites, the group of people that includes the Jews and Arabs

semitone NOUN (British) half a tone in music

a
b
c
d
e
f
g
h
i
j
k
l
m
n
o
p
q
r
s
t
u
v
w
x
y
z

547

semolina NOUN hard round grains of wheat used to make milk puddings and pasta

senate NOUN ❶ the governing council in ancient Rome ❷ the upper house of the parliament of the United States, France and certain other countries

senator NOUN a member of a senate

send VERB sends, sending, sent ❶ to make something go or be taken somewhere ❷ to tell someone to go somewhere ❸ to make a person or thing move quickly in a certain direction ❹ to affect someone in a certain way

senile (say seen-yl) ADJECTIVE weak or confused and forgetful because of old age

senior ADJECTIVE ❶ older than someone else ❷ higher in rank or importance ❸ for older children

senior NOUN ❶ a person who is older or higher in rank than you are ❷ a member of a senior school

senior citizen NOUN an elderly person, especially a pensioner

senna NOUN the dried pods or leaves of a tropical tree, used as a laxative

sensation NOUN ❶ a physical feeling ❷ great excitement or interest or something that causes this

sensational ADJECTIVE ❶ causing great excitement, interest or shock ❷ (informal) very good; wonderful

sense NOUN ❶ the ability to see, hear, smell, touch or taste things ❷ the ability to feel or appreciate something ❸ the power to think

or make wise decisions ❹ the meaning of a word or phrase

sense VERB ❶ to feel or be aware of something ❷ to detect or record something

senseless ADJECTIVE ❶ stupid; not showing good sense ❷ unconscious

sensibility NOUN sensitiveness or delicate feeling

sensible ADJECTIVE wise; having or showing good sense

sensitive ADJECTIVE ❶ easily affected or damaged by something ❷ easily hurt or offended ❸ considerate about other people's feelings ❹ needing to be deal with tactfully ❺ able to measure very small changes

sensor NOUN a device or instrument for detecting a physical property such as light, heat or sound

sensory ADJECTIVE ❶ to do with the senses ❷ receiving physical sensations

sensual ADJECTIVE ❶ to do with physical pleasure ❷ liking or suggesting physical or sexual pleasures

sensuous ADJECTIVE giving pleasure to the senses, especially by being beautiful or delicate

sentence NOUN ❶ a group of words that express a complete thought and form a statement, question, exclamation or command ❷ the punishment announced to a convicted person in a law court

sentence VERB to give someone a sentence in a law court

sentiment NOUN ❶ an attitude

or opinion ❷ a show of feeling or emotion; sentimentality

sentimental ADJECTIVE showing or making you feel tenderness, romantic feeling or foolish emotion

sentinel NOUN a guard or sentry

sentry NOUN a soldier guarding something

sepal NOUN each of the leaves forming the calyx of a bud

separate (say sep-er-at) ADJECTIVE ❶ apart; not joined to something else ❷ different; not connected

separate (say sep-er-ayt) VERB ❶ to make or keep people or things separate or to divide them ❷ to become separate ❸ to stop living together as a couple

separately ADVERB apart; not together

separation NOUN ❶ separating or being separated; time spent apart ❷ an agreement when a couple decide to stop living together

sepia NOUN reddish-brown, like the colour of early photographs

September NOUN the ninth month of the year

septet NOUN ❶ a group of seven musicians ❷ a piece of music for seven musicians

septic ADJECTIVE infected with harmful bacteria that cause pus to form

sepulchre (say sep-ul-ker) NOUN a tomb

sequel NOUN ❶ a book or film etc. that continues the story of an earlier one ❷ something that follows or results from an earlier

event

sequence NOUN ❶ the following of one thing after another; the order in which things happen ❷ a series of things

sequin NOUN a tiny bright disc sewn on clothes to decorate them

serenade NOUN a song or tune of a kind played by a man under his lover's window

serenade VERB to sing or play a serenade to someone

serendipity NOUN the ability to make pleasant or interesting discoveries by accident

serene ADJECTIVE calm and peaceful

serf NOUN a farm labourer who worked for a landowner in the Middle Ages and who was not allowed to leave

serge NOUN a kind of strong woven fabric

sergeant (say sar-jent) NOUN a soldier or police officer who is in charge of others

sergeant major NOUN a soldier who is two ranks higher than a sergeant

serial NOUN a story that is broadcast or published in separate parts over a period of time

serialize (also **serialise**) VERB to broadcast or publish a story as a serial

serial killer NOUN a person who commits a series of murders

serial number NOUN a number put onto an object by the manufacturers to distinguish it from other identical objects

series NOUN series ❶ a number of

things following or connected with each other **②** a number of separate radio or television programmes with the same characters or on the same subject **③** a number of games or matches between the same competitors

serious ADJECTIVE **①** a person or look is serious when they are solemn and thoughtful and not smiling **②** needing careful thought; important **③** sincere; not casual or light-hearted **④** causing anxiety, not trivial

seriously ADVERB in a serious way

sermon NOUN a talk given by a preacher, especially as part of a religious service

serpent NOUN a snake

serpentine ADJECTIVE twisting and curving like a snake

serrated ADJECTIVE having a notched edge

serum (say **seer**-um) NOUN **①** the thin pale-yellow liquid that remains from blood when the rest has clotted **②** this fluid used medically, usually for the antibodies it contains

servant NOUN a person whose job is to work or serve in someone else's house

serve VERB **①** to sell things to people in a shop **②** to give out food to people at a meal **③** to work for a person or organization or country **④** to spend time doing or suffering something **⑤** to be suitable for something **⑥** to start play in tennis etc. by hitting the ball

serve NOUN serving in tennis etc.

server NOUN **①** a person or thing that serves **②** (in computing) a computer or program that controls or supplies information to several computers connected to a network

service NOUN **①** working for a person, organization or country **②** something that helps people or supplies what they want **③** the army, navy or air force **④** a religious ceremony **⑤** providing people with goods, food, etc. **⑥** a set of dishes and plates for a meal **⑦** the checks and repairs that are needed to keep a vehicle or machine in working order **⑧** the action of serving in tennis or badminton

service VERB to repair or keep a vehicle or machine in working order

service industry NOUN an industry which sells a service, not goods

serviceman NOUN a man serving in the armed forces

services PLURAL NOUN an area beside a motorway with a garage, shop, restaurant, toilets, etc. for travellers to use

service station NOUN a place beside a road, where petrol and other services are available

servicewoman NOUN a woman serving in the armed forces

serviette NOUN (British) a piece of cloth or paper that you use to keep your clothes or hands clean at a meal

servile ADJECTIVE like a slave; too willing to serve or obey others

serving NOUN a helping of food

sesame NOUN an African plant whose seeds can be eaten or used to make an edible oil

session NOUN ❶ a time spent doing one thing ❷ a meeting or series of meetings

set VERB sets, setting, set ❶ to set something somewhere is to put it into position ❷ to set a date or time is to arrange or decide when something will happen ❸ to make something ready to work ❹ to become firm or hard ❺ to give someone a task or problem to deal with ❻ to make something happen ❼ the sun sets when it goes down below the horizon

set NOUN ❶ a group of people or things that belong together ❷ a radio or television receiver ❸ (British) a group of school students with the same level of ability in a particular subject ❹ (in mathematics) a collection of things that have a common property ❺ the scenery or stage for a play or film ❻ a group of games in a tennis match ❼ the way something is placed ❽ a badger's burrow

set ADJECTIVE ❶ fixed or arranged in advance ❷ ready or prepared to do something

setback NOUN something that stops progress or slows it down

set book NOUN a book that must be studied for a literature examination

set square NOUN (British) a device shaped like a right-angled triangle, used to draw straight lines and angles

settee NOUN (British) a long soft seat with a back and arms

setter NOUN a dog of a long-haired breed that can be trained to stand rigid when it scents game

set theory NOUN the branch of mathematics that deals with sets and the relations between them

setting NOUN ❶ the place and time in which a story happens ❷ the land surrounding something ❸ one of the positions of the controls of a machine ❹ a set of cutlery or crockery for one person at a meal ❺ music for the words of a song

settle VERB ❶ to arrange something; to decide or solve something ❷ to become calm or comfortable or orderly; to stop being restless ❸ to go and live somewhere ❹ to come to rest on something ❺ to pay a bill or debt

settle NOUN a long wooden seat with a high back and arms

settlement NOUN ❶ a small number of people or houses established in a new area ❷ an agreement to end an argument

settler NOUN one of the first people to settle in a new country; a pioneer or colonist

set-up NOUN (informal) the way something is organized or arranged

seven NOUN & ADJECTIVE the number 7

seventeen NOUN & ADJECTIVE the number 17

seventy NOUN & ADJECTIVE the number 70

sever VERB to cut or break

a
b
c
d
e
f
g
h
i
j
k
l
m
n
o
p
q
r
s
t
u
v
w
x
y
z

something off

several DETERMINER & PRONOUN more than two but not many

severe ADJECTIVE ❶ strict; not gentle or kind ❷ extremely bad or serious ❸ intense or forceful ❹ very plain

sew VERB sews, sewing, sewed, sewn or sewed ❶ to join things together by using a needle and thread ❷ to work with a needle and thread or with a sewing machine

sewage (say soo-ij) NOUN liquid waste matter carried away in drains

sewer (say soo-er) NOUN a large underground drain for carrying away sewage

sewing machine NOUN a machine for sewing things

sex NOUN ❶ each of the two groups (*male* and *female*) into which people and animals are divided ❷ sexual activity, especially sexual intercourse

sexism NOUN the unfair or offensive treatment of people of a particular sex, especially women

sexist NOUN a person who treats people of a particular sex, especially women, in an unfair or offensive way

sexist ADJECTIVE offensive to people of a particular sex, especially women

sextant NOUN an instrument for measuring the angle of the sun and stars, used for finding your position when navigating

sextet NOUN ❶ a group of six

musicians ❷ a piece of music for six musicians

sextuplet NOUN each of six children born to the same mother at one time

sexual ADJECTIVE ❶ to do with sex ❷ to do with the difference between males and females ❸ sexual reproduction happens by the fusion of male and female cells

sexual intercourse NOUN an intimate physical act between two people, especially one in which a man puts his penis into the woman's vagina, to express love, for pleasure or to conceive a child

sexy ADJECTIVE (*informal*) ❶ sexually attractive ❷ concerned with sex

SF ABBREVIATION science fiction

shabby ADJECTIVE ❶ in a poor or worn-out condition ❷ poorly dressed ❸ unfair or dishonourable

shack NOUN a roughly-built hut

shackle NOUN an iron ring for fastening a prisoner's wrist or ankle to something

shackle VERB ❶ to put shackles on a prisoner ❷ to be shackled by something is to be restricted or limited by it

shade NOUN ❶ slight darkness produced where something blocks the sun's light ❷ a device that reduces or shuts out bright light ❸ a colour; how light or dark a colour is ❹ a slight difference ❺ (*poetical use*) a ghost

shade VERB ❶ to shelter something from bright light ❷ to make part of a drawing darker than the rest ❸ to move gradually from one state or quality to another

shadow NOUN ❶ the dark shape that falls on a surface when something is between the surface and a light ❷ an area of shade ❸ a slight trace

shadow VERB ❶ to cast a shadow on something ❷ to follow a person secretly

Shadow Cabinet NOUN (British) members of the Opposition in Parliament who each have responsibility for a particular area of policy

shadowy ADJECTIVE ❶ dark and full of shadows ❷ difficult to see because there is not much light

shady ADJECTIVE ❶ giving shade ❷ in the shade ❸ not completely honest or legal

shaft NOUN ❶ a long slender rod or straight part ❷ a ray of light ❸ a deep narrow hole

shaggy ADJECTIVE ❶ having long rough hair or fibre ❷ rough, thick and untidy

shah NOUN the title of the former ruler of Iran

shake VERB shakes, shaking, shook, shaken ❶ to move something quickly up and down or from side to side ❷ to move in this way ❸ to shock or upset someone ❹ to tremble or seem to be unsteady

shake NOUN ❶ a quick movement up and down or from side to side ❷ (informal) a milkshake

shaky ADJECTIVE unsteady or wobbly

shale NOUN a kind of stone that splits easily into layers

shall AUXILIARY VERB ❶ used, especially with I and we, to refer to the future ❷ used with I and we in questions when making a suggestion or offer or asking for advice

shallot NOUN a kind of small onion

shallow ADJECTIVE ❶ not deep ❷ not capable of deep feelings

shallows PLURAL NOUN a shallow part of a stretch of water

sham NOUN something that is not genuine; a pretence

sham ADJECTIVE not real or genuine, but intended to seem so

sham VERB to pretend or fake something

shamble VERB to walk in a lazy or awkward way, dragging your feet along the ground

shambles NOUN a scene of great disorder or confusion

shame NOUN ❶ a feeling of great sorrow or guilt because you have done something wrong ❷ dishonour or disgrace ❸ something you regret; a pity

shame VERB to make a person feel ashamed

shamefaced ADJECTIVE looking ashamed

shameful ADJECTIVE causing shame; disgraceful

shameless ADJECTIVE feeling or showing no shame

shampoo NOUN ❶ a liquid substance for washing the hair ❷ a substance for cleaning a carpet etc. or washing a car ❸ a wash with shampoo

shampoo VERB to wash or clean something with a shampoo

shamrock NOUN a plant rather

like clover, the national emblem of Ireland

shandy NOUN (*British*) a mixture of beer and lemonade or some other soft drink

shank NOUN ① the leg, especially the part from knee to ankle ② a long narrow part

shanty NOUN ① a shack ② a sailors' song with a chorus

shanty town NOUN a settlement consisting of shanties

shape NOUN ① what a thing's outline looks like ② something that has a definite or regular form, such as a square, circle or triangle ③ a person's physical condition ④ the general form or condition of something

shape VERB to make something into a particular shape

shaped ADJECTIVE having a particular shape

shapeless ADJECTIVE having no definite shape

shapely ADJECTIVE having an attractive shape

share NOUN ① a part given to one person or thing out of something that is being divided ② each of the equal parts into which the ownership of a business company is divided, giving the person who holds it the right to receive a portion (a **dividend**) of the company's profits

share VERB ① to give portions of something to two or more people ② to have, use or experience something jointly with others

shareholder NOUN a person who owns shares in a company

shareware NOUN computer software which is given away or which you can use free of charge

shark NOUN ① a large sea fish with sharp teeth ② a person who exploits or cheats people

sharp ADJECTIVE ① with an edge or point that can cut or make holes ② quick at noticing or learning things ③ changing direction suddenly; not gradual ④ forceful or severe ⑤ distinct and easy to see clearly ⑥ loud and shrill ⑦ slightly sour ⑧ (*in music*) one semitone higher than the natural note

sharp ADVERB ① with a sudden change of direction ② punctually or precisely ③ (*in music*) above the correct pitch

sharp NOUN (*in music*) a note one semitone higher than the natural note; the sign (#) that indicates this

sharpen VERB to make something sharp or to become sharp

sharply ADVERB ① suddenly and by a large amount ② in a critical or severe way

sharpshooter NOUN a person who is skilled at shooting a gun

shatter VERB ① to break violently into small pieces or to make something do this ② to destroy something ③ to upset someone greatly

shattered ADJECTIVE (*informal*) completely exhausted

shave VERB ① to scrape growing hair off the skin with a razor ② to cut or scrape a thin slice off

something

shave NOUN the act of shaving the face

shaven ADJECTIVE with all the hair shaved off

shavings PLURAL NOUN thin strips shaved off a piece of wood or metal

shawl NOUN a large piece of material worn round the shoulders or head or wrapped round a baby

she PRONOUN the female person or animal being talked about

sheaf NOUN **1** a bundle of papers or other objects held together **2** a bundle of corn stalks tied together after reaping

shear VERB shears, shearing, sheared, sheared or, in sense 1, shorn **1** to cut the wool off a sheep **2** to break because of a sideways or twisting force

shears PLURAL NOUN a cutting tool shaped like a very large pair of scissors and worked with both hands

sheath NOUN **1** a cover for the blade of a knife or sword **2** a close-fitting cover **3** a condom

sheathe VERB **1** to put something into a sheath **2** to put a close covering on something

shed NOUN a simply-made building used for storing things, sheltering animals or as a workshop

shed VERB sheds, shedding, shed **1** to let something fall or flow **2** to shed light is to give it out **3** to get rid of people or things

sheen NOUN a shine or gloss on a surface

sheep NOUN sheep an animal that eats grass and has a thick fleecy coat, kept in flocks for its wool and its meat

sheepdog NOUN a dog trained to guard and herd sheep

sheepish ADJECTIVE embarrassed or shamefaced because you have done something silly

sheer ADJECTIVE **1** complete or thorough **2** vertical, with almost no slope **3** sheer material is very thin and transparent

sheer VERB to swerve or move sharply away

sheet NOUN **1** a large piece of lightweight material used on a bed in pairs for a person to sleep between **2** a whole flat piece of paper, glass or metal **3** a wide area of water, ice or flame **4** a rope or chain fastening a sail

sheikh (say shayk) NOUN the leader of an Arab tribe or village

shelf NOUN shelves **1** a flat piece of wood, metal or glass fixed to a wall or in a piece of furniture so that things can be placed on it **2** a flat level surface that sticks out from a cliff or under the sea

shelf life NOUN the length of time something can be kept in a shop before it becomes too old to sell

shell NOUN **1** the hard outer covering of an egg or nut or of an animal such as a snail, crab or tortoise **2** the walls or framework of a building, ship or other large structure **3** a metal case filled with explosive, fired from a large gun

shell VERB ❶ to take something out of its shell ❷ to fire explosive shells at something

shellfish NOUN a sea animal that has a shell

shelter NOUN ❶ a place or structure that protects people from rain, wind or danger ❷ protection from the weather or from danger

shelter VERB ❶ to find a shelter somewhere ❷ to provide someone with shelter ❸ to protect or cover a person or thing

shelve VERB ❶ to put things on a shelf or shelves ❷ to postpone or reject a plan or piece of work ❸ to slope

shepherd NOUN a person whose job is to look after sheep

shepherd VERB to guide or direct people

shepherdess NOUN (now usually poetical) a woman whose job is to look after sheep

shepherd's pie NOUN a dish of minced beef or lamb under a layer of mashed potato

sherbet NOUN a fizzy sweet powder or drink

sheriff NOUN the chief law officer of a county, whose duties vary in different countries

sherry NOUN a kind of strong wine

shield NOUN ❶ a large piece of metal or wood carried to protect the body in fighting ❷ a model of a triangular shield used as a trophy ❸ a protection from harm

shield VERB to protect a person or thing from harm or from being discovered

shift VERB ❶ to move, or move something, from one position or place to another ❷ an opinion or situation shifts when it changes slightly

shift NOUN ❶ a change of position or condition ❷ a group of workers who start work as another group finishes; the time when they work ❸ a straight dress with no waist

shifty ADJECTIVE looking dishonest or as if you are hiding something

Shiite (say shee-eyt) NOUN a member of one of the two main branches of Islam, based on the teachings of Muhammad and regarding his son-in-law Ali as his successor. Compare with Sunni.

shilling NOUN a former British coin, equal to 5p

shilly-shally VERB to be unable to make up your mind

shimmer VERB to shine with a quivering light

shimmer NOUN a quivering light

shin NOUN the front of your leg between your knee and your ankle

shin VERB to climb up or down something vertical by using the arms and legs

shine VERB shines, shining, shone or, in sense 3, shined ❶ to give out or reflect light; to be bright ❷ to aim a light somewhere ❸ to polish shoes or a surface ❹ to be very good at something

shine NOUN ❶ brightness on a surface ❷ a polish

shingle NOUN pebbles on a beach

shingles NOUN a disease caused by the chicken pox virus, producing a painful rash

556

Shinto *NOUN* a Japanese religion which includes worship of ancestors and nature

shiny *ADJECTIVE* shining or glossy

ship *NOUN* a large boat, especially one that goes to sea

ship *VERB* to transport goods, especially by ship

shipment *NOUN* ❶ the process of shipping goods ❷ the amount shipped

shipping *NOUN* ❶ all the ships of a country ❷ the business of transporting goods by ship

shipshape *ADJECTIVE* in good order; tidy

shipwreck *NOUN* ❶ the wrecking of a ship by storm or accident ❷ the remains of a wrecked ship

shipwrecked *ADJECTIVE* someone is shipwrecked when they are left somewhere after their ship has been wrecked at sea

shipyard *NOUN* a place where ships are built or repaired

shire *NOUN* a county

shire horse *NOUN* a kind of large, strong horse used for ploughing or pulling carts

shirk *VERB* to avoid a task or duty selfishly or unfairly

shirt *NOUN* a piece of clothing you wear on the top half of the body, made of light material and with a collar and sleeves

shiver *VERB* to tremble with cold or fear

shiver *NOUN* the act of shivering

shivery *ADJECTIVE* shaking with cold, illness or fear

shoal *NOUN* ❶ a large number of fish swimming together ❷ an underwater sandbank

shock *NOUN* ❶ a sudden unpleasant surprise ❷ a serious medical condition of great weakness caused by damage to the body ❸ the effect of a violent shake or knock ❹ an effect caused by electric current passing through the body ❺ a bushy mass of hair

shock *VERB* ❶ to give someone a shock; to surprise or upset a person greatly ❷ to make someone feel disgusted or offended

shocking *ADJECTIVE* ❶ horrifying or disgusting ❷ (*informal*) very bad

shock wave *NOUN* a sharp change in pressure in the air around an explosion or an object moving very quickly

shod *past tense of* shoe

shoddy *ADJECTIVE* of poor quality; badly made or done

shoe *NOUN* ❶ a strong covering for the foot ❷ a horseshoe ❸ something shaped or used like a shoe

shoe *VERB* shoes, shoeing, shod to fit a horse with a horseshoe

shoehorn *NOUN* a curved piece of stiff material for easing your heel into the back of a shoe

shoelace *NOUN* a cord for lacing up and fastening a shoe

shoestring *NOUN* ➤ on a shoestring using only a small amount of money

shoo *EXCLAMATION* a word used to frighten animals away

shoo VERB to frighten or drive away an animal or person

shoot VERB shoots, shooting, shot ① to fire a gun or missile ② to hurt or kill a person or animal by shooting ③ to move at great speed ④ to kick or hit a ball at a goal ⑤ to film or photograph something ⑥ to slide the bolt of a door into or out of its fastening ⑦ to shoot someone a glance is to look at them sharply

shoot NOUN ① a young branch or new growth of a plant ② an expedition for shooting animals

shooting star NOUN a meteor

shop NOUN ① a building or room where goods or services are on sale to the public ② a workshop

shop VERB ① to visit shops in order to buy things ② to buy things

shop floor NOUN (British) ① the workers in a factory, not the managers ② the place where they work

shopkeeper NOUN a person who owns or manages a shop

shoplifter NOUN a person who steals goods from a shop after entering as a customer

shopping NOUN ① buying goods in shops ② the goods bought

shop-soiled ADJECTIVE (British) dirty, faded or slightly damaged through being displayed in a shop

shop steward NOUN a trade-union official who represents a group of fellow workers

shore NOUN the land along the edge of a sea or of a lake

shore VERB to prop something up with a piece of wood or other support

shorn past participle of **shear**

shorn ADJECTIVE with hair cut very short

short ADJECTIVE ① not long; not lasting long ② not tall ③ not enough; not having enough of something ④ speaking to someone in a bad-tempered and impatient way ⑤ short pastry is rich and crumbly because it contains a lot of fat

short ADVERB suddenly

shortage NOUN there is a shortage of something when there is not enough of it

shortbread NOUN a rich sweet biscuit, made with butter

shortcake NOUN ① shortbread ② a light cake usually served with fruit

short circuit NOUN a fault in an electrical circuit in which current flows along a shorter route than the normal one

short-circuit VERB to have or cause a short circuit

shortcoming NOUN a fault or failure to reach a good standard

short cut NOUN a route or method that is quicker than the usual one

shorten VERB to make something shorter or to become shorter

shortfall NOUN a shortage; an amount lower than needed or expected

shorthand NOUN a set of special signs for writing words down as quickly as people say them

short-handed ADJECTIVE not having

enough workers or helpers

shortlist NOUN a list of the most suitable people or things, from which a final choice will be made

shortlist VERB to put someone on a shortlist

shortly ADVERB ❶ in a short time; soon ❷ in an impatient and angry way

shorts PLURAL NOUN trousers with legs that do not reach to the knee

short-sighted ADJECTIVE (British) ❶ unable to see things clearly when they are further away ❷ not thinking enough about what may happen in the future

short-tempered ADJECTIVE easily becoming angry

short-term ADJECTIVE to do with or happening over a short period of time

short wave NOUN a radio wave of a wavelength between 10 and 100 metres and a frequency of about 3 to 30 megahertz

shot NOUN ❶ the firing of a gun or missile or the sound this makes ❷ lead pellets for firing from small guns ❸ a person judged by skill in shooting ❹ a hit or stroke in a game with a ball, such as football, tennis, golf or snooker ❺ a heavy metal ball thrown as a sport ❻ a photograph or a filmed scene ❼ an attempt to do something ❽ an injection of a drug or vaccine

shot ADJECTIVE shot fabric is woven so that different colours show at different angles

shot VERB past tense of **shoot**

shotgun NOUN a gun for firing small lead pellets at close range

shot put NOUN an athletic contest in which competitors throw a heavy metal ball

should AUXILIARY VERB ❶ used to say what someone ought to do ❷ used to say what someone expects ❸ used to say what might happen ❹ used with *I* and *we* to make a polite statement (*I should like to come.*) or in a conditional clause (*If they had supported us we should have won.*)

shoulder NOUN the part of your body between your neck and your arm

shoulder VERB ❶ to take something on your shoulder or shoulders ❷ to push something with your shoulder ❸ to accept responsibility or blame for something

shoulder blade NOUN either of the two large flat bones at the top of your back

shout NOUN a loud cry or call

shout VERB to give a shout; to speak or call very loudly

shove VERB to push something roughly

shove NOUN a rough push

shovel NOUN a tool like a spade with the sides turned up, used for lifting coal, earth, snow, etc.

shovel VERB ❶ to move or clear things with a shovel ❷ to scoop or push something roughly

show VERB shows, showing, showed, shown ❶ to allow or cause something to be seen ❷ to make a person understand something; to explain or demonstrate something ❸ to guide or lead someone to a place

❹ to treat someone in a certain way **❺** to be visible **❻** to prove your ability to someone

show NOUN **❶** an entertainment **❷** a display or exhibition **❸** (*informal*) something that happens or is done

show business NOUN the entertainment industry; the theatre, films, radio and television

showcase NOUN **❶** a glass case for displaying something in a shop, museum or gallery **❷** an event that is designed to present someone's good qualities or abilities attractively

showdown NOUN a final test or confrontation

shower NOUN **❶** a brief fall of rain or snow **❷** a lot of small things coming or falling like rain **❸** a device or cabinet for spraying water to wash a person's body; a wash in this

shower VERB **❶** to fall or drop things like rain **❷** to give someone a lot of things **❸** to wash under a shower

showery ADJECTIVE raining often in showers

showjumping NOUN a competition in which riders make their horses jump over fences and other obstacles, with penalty points for errors

showman NOUN **❶** a person who presents entertainments **❷** someone who is good at entertaining and getting a lot of attention

show-off NOUN (*informal*) a person who tries to impress people

boastfully

showpiece NOUN a fine example of something for people to see and admire

showroom NOUN a large room where goods are displayed for people to look at

showy ADJECTIVE likely to attract attention; brightly or highly decorated

shrapnel NOUN pieces of metal scattered from an exploding shell

shred NOUN **❶** a tiny piece torn or cut off something **❷** a very small amount of something

shred VERB to tear or cut something into shreds

shrew NOUN **❶** a small mouse-like animal **❷** (*old use*) a bad-tempered woman who is constantly scolding people

shrewd ADJECTIVE clever and showing good judgement

shriek NOUN a shrill cry or scream

shriek VERB to give a shriek

shrift NOUN ➤ **give someone short shrift** to give someone little attention or sympathy

shrill ADJECTIVE sounding very high and piercing

shrimp NOUN a small shellfish, pink when boiled

shrine NOUN an altar, chapel or other sacred place

shrink VERB shrinks, shrinking, shrank, shrunk **❶** to become smaller **❷** to make something smaller, especially by washing it **❸** to move back or away because you are frightened or shocked **❹** to avoid doing something unpleasant or difficult

shrivel VERB to become dry and wrinkled or to make something like this

shroud NOUN ❶ a cloth in which a dead body is wrapped ❷ each of a set of ropes supporting a ship's mast

shroud VERB ❶ to wrap a dead body in a shroud ❷ to cover or conceal something

Shrove Tuesday NOUN the day before Lent begins, when people eat pancakes

shrub NOUN a woody plant smaller than a tree; a bush

shrubbery NOUN an area planted with shrubs

shrug VERB to raise your shoulders slightly as a sign that you do not care or do not know about something

shrug NOUN a gesture of shrugging the shoulders

shrunken ADJECTIVE having shrunk; small and shrivelled

shudder VERB ❶ to shiver violently with horror, fear or cold ❷ to make a strong shaking movement

shudder NOUN a strong shivering or shaking movement

shuffle VERB ❶ to walk without lifting your feet from the ground ❷ to move your body or feet around because you are uncomfortable or nervous ❸ to mix up playing cards by sliding them over each other several times ❹ to move things around

shuffle NOUN the act of shuffling

shun VERB to deliberately avoid

or keep away from someone or something

shunt VERB ❶ to move a train or wagons onto another track ❷ to divert something or someone to a less important place or position

shut VERB shuts, shutting, shut ❶ to move a door, window, lid or cover so that it blocks an opening ❷ to become closed ❸ to bring or fold parts together

shut ADJECTIVE closed

shutter NOUN ❶ a panel or screen that can be closed over a window ❷ the device in a camera that opens and closes to let light fall on the film

shuttle NOUN ❶ a train, bus or aircraft that makes frequent short journeys between two points ❷ a space shuttle ❸ the part of a loom that carries the thread from side to side

shuttle VERB to move or travel continuously between two places

shuttlecock NOUN a small rounded piece of cork or plastic with a crown of feathers, struck to and fro by players in badminton

shy ADJECTIVE afraid to meet or talk to other people; timid

shy VERB ❶ to jump or move suddenly in alarm ❷ to throw a stone or other object

shy NOUN a throw

SI NOUN an internationally recognized system of metric units of measurement, including the metre and kilogram

Siamese cat NOUN a cat with short pale fur with darker face, ears, tail and feet

561

sibling NOUN a brother or sister

sibyl NOUN a prophetess in ancient Greece or Rome

sick ADJECTIVE ① ill; physically or mentally unwell ② vomiting or likely to vomit ③ disgusted, angry or anxious ④ making fun of death, disability or misfortune in an unpleasant way

sicken VERB ① to make someone feel upset or disgusted ② to start feeling ill

sickle NOUN a tool with a narrow curved blade, used for cutting crops or grass

sickle-cell anaemia NOUN a severe form of anaemia which is passed on in the genes and which causes pain in the joints, fever, jaundice and sometimes death

sickly ADJECTIVE ① often ill; unhealthy ② making people feel sick ③ weak or sentimental

sickness NOUN ① illness ② a disease ③ vomiting

side NOUN ① a surface, especially one joining the top and bottom of something ② a line that forms part of the boundary of a triangle, square, etc. ③ either of the two halves into which something can be divided by a line down its centre ④ one of the surfaces of something except the top, bottom, front or back ⑤ the part near the edge and away from the centre ⑥ the right or left part of your body, especially from under your arm to the top of your leg ⑦ the place or region next to a person or thing ⑧ one aspect or view of something ⑨ one of two groups or

teams who oppose each other

side ADJECTIVE at or on a side

side VERB ➤ **side with someone** to take a person's side in an argument

sideboard NOUN a long piece of furniture with drawers and cupboards and a flat top

sideburns PLURAL NOUN the strips of hair growing on each side of a man's face in front of his ears

sidecar NOUN a small compartment for a passenger, fixed to the side of a motorcycle

side effect NOUN an effect, especially an unpleasant one, that a medicine has on you as well as the effect intended

sideline NOUN ① something that you do in addition to your main work or activity ② each of the lines on the two long sides of a sports pitch

sidelong ADJECTIVE towards one side; sideways

sideshow NOUN a small entertainment forming part of a large one, e.g. at a fair

sidetrack VERB to take someone's attention away from the main subject or problem

sidewalk NOUN (North American) a pavement

sideways ADVERB & ADJECTIVE ① to or from one side ② with one side facing forwards

siding NOUN a short railway line by the side of a main line

sidle VERB to walk in a shy or nervous manner

siege NOUN the surrounding of a place in order to capture it or force someone to surrender

siesta (say see-**est**-a) NOUN an afternoon rest, especially in a hot country

sieve (say siv) NOUN a device made of mesh or perforated metal or plastic, used to separate the smaller or soft parts of something from the larger or hard parts

sieve VERB to put something through a sieve

sift VERB ① to pass a fine or powdery substance through a sieve in order to remove any lumps ② to examine and analyse facts or evidence carefully

sigh NOUN a sound made by breathing out heavily when you are sad, tired or relieved

sigh VERB to make a sigh

sight NOUN ① the ability to see ② a view or glimpse ③ a thing that can be seen or is worth seeing ④ something silly or ridiculous to look at ⑤ a device looked through to help aim a gun or telescope

sight VERB ① to see or observe something ② to aim a gun or telescope

sighted ADJECTIVE able to see; not blind

sightless ADJECTIVE blind

sight-reading NOUN playing or singing music at sight, without preparation

sightseeing NOUN visiting interesting places in a town as a tourist

sign NOUN ① something that shows that a thing exists ② a mark or symbol that stands for something

③ a board or notice that tells or shows people something ④ an action or movement giving information or a command ⑤ any of the twelve divisions of the zodiac, represented by a symbol

sign VERB ① to make a sign or signal ② to write your signature on something; to accept a contract or agreement by doing this ③ to give someone a contract for a job, especially in a professional sport ④ to use signing

signal NOUN ① a device, gesture or sound that gives information or a command ② a message made up of such things ③ a sequence of electrical impulses or radio waves

signal VERB to give someone a signal

signal ADJECTIVE remarkable or striking

signal box NOUN (British) a building from which railway signals and points are controlled

signature NOUN ① the form in which a person writes their own name ② (in music) a set of sharps and flats after the clef in a score, showing the key the music is written in (the key signature) or the sign, often a fraction such as ¾ (the time signature), showing the number of beats in the bar and their rhythm

signature tune NOUN (British) a special tune always used to announce a particular programme or performer on television or radio

signet ring NOUN a ring with a person's initials or a design engraved on it

significance NOUN the meaning or importance of something

significant ADJECTIVE ❶ having a meaning; full of meaning ❷ important

signify VERB ❶ to be a sign or symbol of something; to mean something ❷ to indicate something ❸ to be important; to matter

signing, sign language NOUN a way of communicating by using movements of your hands instead of sounds, used mainly by deaf people

signpost NOUN a sign at a road junction showing the names and distances of the places that each road leads to

Sikh (say seek) NOUN a follower of Sikhism

Sikhism (say seek-izm) NOUN a religion founded in Punjab in the 15th century by Guru Nanak and based on belief in one God

silage NOUN fodder made from green crops stored in a silo

silence NOUN ❶ absence of sound ❷ not speaking

silence VERB to make a person or thing silent

silencer NOUN a device for reducing the sound made by a gun or a vehicle's exhaust system

silent ADJECTIVE ❶ without any sound ❷ not speaking

silhouette (say sil-oo-et) NOUN ❶ a dark shadow seen against a light background ❷ a portrait of a person in profile, showing the shape and outline only in solid black

silhouette VERB to show an outline as a silhouette

silica NOUN a hard white mineral that is a compound of silicon, used to make glass

silicon NOUN a substance found in many rocks, used in making microchips

silicone NOUN a compound of silicon used in paints, varnish and lubricants

silk NOUN ❶ a fine soft thread or cloth made from the fibre produced by silkworms for making their cocoons ❷ a length of silk thread used for embroidery

silken ADJECTIVE made of silk

silkworm NOUN the caterpillar of a kind of moth, which feeds on mulberry leaves and spins itself a cocoon

silky ADJECTIVE soft, smooth and shiny like silk

sill NOUN a strip of stone, wood or metal underneath a window or door

silly ADJECTIVE foolish or unwise

silo (say sy-loh) NOUN ❶ a pit or tower for storing green crops (see silage) or corn or cement ❷ an underground place for storing a missile ready for firing

silt NOUN fine sand and mud that is laid down by a river or the sea

silt VERB ➤ **silt up** to become blocked with silt

silver NOUN ❶ a shiny white precious metal ❷ the colour of silver ❸ coins or objects made of silver or silver-coloured metal

❹ a silver medal, usually given as second prize

silver ADJECTIVE **❶** made of silver **❷** coloured like silver

silver VERB **❶** to make something silvery or to become silvery

silver wedding NOUN a couple's 25th wedding anniversary

silvery ADJECTIVE shiny like silver or silver in colour

SIM card NOUN a small piece of plastic inside a mobile phone that stores information about the person using the phone

similar ADJECTIVE **❶** nearly the same as another person or thing; of the same kind **❷** (in mathematics) having the same shape but not the same size

similarity NOUN **❶** the quality of being alike **❷** a feature that makes one thing like another

simile (say **sim**-il-ee) NOUN a way of describing something by comparing it with something else, e.g. He is as strong as a horse. and We ran like the wind.

simmer VERB to boil very gently over a low heat

simper VERB to smile in a silly and annoying way

simple ADJECTIVE **❶** easy to answer or solve **❷** not complicated or elaborate **❸** plain, not showy **❹** without much sense or intelligence

simple-minded ADJECTIVE naive or foolish

simplicity NOUN the quality of being simple

simplify VERB to make a thing simple or easy to understand

simply ADVERB **❶** in a simple way **❷** without doubt; completely **❸** only or merely

simulate VERB **❶** to reproduce the appearance or conditions of something **❷** to pretend to have a certain feeling

simulator NOUN a machine or device for simulating actual conditions or events, often used for training

simultaneous (say sim-ul-**tay**-nee-us) ADJECTIVE happening at the same time

sin NOUN **❶** the breaking of a religious or moral law **❷** a very bad action

sin VERB to commit a sin

since CONJUNCTION **❶** from the time when **❷** because

since PREPOSITION from a certain time

since ADVERB between then and now

sincere ADJECTIVE you are being sincere when you mean what you say and express your true feelings

sine NOUN in a right-angled triangle, the ratio of the length of a side opposite one of the acute angles to the length of the hypotenuse. Compare with **cosine**.

sinew NOUN strong tissue that connects a muscle to a bone

sinewy ADJECTIVE slim, muscular and strong

sinful ADJECTIVE **❶** guilty of sin **❷** bad or wicked

sing VERB sings, singing, sang, sung **❶** to make musical sounds with your voice **❷** to perform a song

singe (say sinj) VERB to burn something slightly

singer NOUN a person who sings or whose job is singing

single ADJECTIVE ❶ one only; not double or multiple ❷ suitable for one person ❸ distinct or separate ❹ not married ❺ for the journey to a place but not back again

single NOUN ❶ a single person or thing ❷ a single ticket ❸ a record with one short piece of music on it

single VERB ➤ **single someone out** to pick someone out or distinguish them from other people

single file ➤ **in single file** in a line, one behind the other

single-handed ADJECTIVE by your own efforts; without any help

single-minded ADJECTIVE with your mind set on one purpose only

single parent NOUN a person bringing up a child or children without a partner

singlet NOUN a man's vest or similar piece of clothing worn under or instead of a shirt

singly ADVERB in ones; one by one

singsong ADJECTIVE having a monotonous tone or rhythm

singsong NOUN ❶ informal singing by a gathering of people ❷ a singsong tone

singular NOUN the form of a noun or verb used when it stands for only one person or thing Compare with **plural**.

singular ADJECTIVE ❶ in the singular; meaning only one ❷ uncommon or extraordinary

sinister ADJECTIVE ❶ looking or seeming evil or harmful ❷ wicked; intending to do harm

sink VERB sinks, sinking, sank, sunk ❶ to fall under the surface of water or to the bottom of the sea or to make something do this ❷ to go or fall slowly downwards ❸ to push something sharp deeply into something ❹ to dig or drill a hole or well ❺ to invest money in something

sink NOUN a fixed basin with a tap or taps to supply water, especially one in a kitchen

sinuous ADJECTIVE with many bends or curves

sinus (say sy-nus) NOUN a hollow part in the bones of the skull, connected with the nose

sip VERB to drink something in small mouthfuls

sip NOUN a small amount of a drink that you take into your mouth

siphon NOUN ❶ a pipe or tube in the form of an upside-down U, arranged so that liquid is forced up it and down to a lower level ❷ a bottle containing soda water which is released through a tube

siphon VERB to draw out liquid through a siphon

sir NOUN ❶ a word used when speaking or writing politely to a man ❷ the title given to a knight or baronet

sire NOUN a word formerly used when speaking to a king

sire VERB to be the male parent of a horse or dog

siren NOUN ❶ a device that makes a long loud sound as a signal ❷ a dangerously attractive woman

sirloin NOUN beef from the upper part of the loin

sirocco NOUN a hot dry wind that reaches Italy from Africa

sisal (say **sy**-sal) NOUN fibre from a tropical plant, used for making ropes

sissy NOUN a timid or cowardly person

sister NOUN ❶ a daughter of the same parents as another person ❷ a female friend or associate ❸ a nun ❹ a senior hospital nurse, especially one in charge of a ward

sisterhood NOUN ❶ companionship and mutual support between women ❷ a society or association of women

sister-in-law NOUN the sister of a married person's husband or wife; the wife of a person's brother

sit VERB sits, sitting, sat ❶ to rest on your bottom, as you do when you are on a chair ❷ to put someone in a sitting position ❸ to be situated or positioned in a certain place ❹ to take a test or examination ❺ a parliament or law court sits when it has assembled for business ❻ to act as a babysitter

sitar NOUN an Indian musical instrument that is like a guitar

sitcom NOUN (*informal*) a situation comedy

site NOUN the place where something happens or happened or is built or positioned

site VERB to site something somewhere is to locate or build it there

sit-in NOUN a protest in which people sit down in a public place and refuse to move

sitter NOUN ❶ a person who poses for a portrait ❷ a person who looks after children, pets or a house while the owners are away

sitting NOUN ❶ the time when people are served a meal ❷ the time when a parliament or committee is conducting business

sitting room NOUN (*chiefly British*) a room with comfortable chairs for sitting in

situated ADJECTIVE in a particular place or situation

situation NOUN ❶ a state of affairs at a certain time; the way things are ❷ a position of a building or town, with its surroundings ❸ a job

situation comedy NOUN a comedy series on radio or television, based on how characters react to unusual or comic situations

six NOUN & ADJECTIVE the number 6

sixteen NOUN & ADJECTIVE the number 16

sixth form NOUN (*British*) a form for students aged 16-18 in a secondary school

sixth sense NOUN the ability to know something by instinct rather than by using any of the five senses; intuition

sixty NOUN & ADJECTIVE the number 60

size NOUN ❶ the measurements or extent of something ❷ any of the series of standard measurements in which certain things are made ❸ a gluey substance used to glaze or stiffen paper or cloth

size VERB ❶ to arrange things according to their size ❷ to treat something with size

sizeable ADJECTIVE large or fairly large

sizzle VERB to make a crackling or hissing sound

sjambok (say sham-bok) NOUN (S. African) a strong whip originally made from the skin of a rhinoceros

skate NOUN ❶ a boot with a steel blade attached to the sole, used for sliding smoothly over ice ❷ a roller skate ❸ a large flat edible sea fish

skate VERB to move around on skates

skateboard NOUN a small board with wheels, used for standing and riding on as a sport

skeleton NOUN ❶ the framework of bones in a person's or animal's body ❷ a framework, e.g. of a building

sketch NOUN ❶ a rough drawing or painting ❷ a short account of something ❸ a short amusing play

sketch VERB to make a sketch

sketchy ADJECTIVE rough and not detailed or careful

skew, skewed ADJECTIVE slanting; not straight or level

skewer NOUN a long pin pushed through meat to hold it together while it is being cooked

skewer VERB to fix or pierce something with a skewer or pin

ski (say skee) NOUN each of a pair of long narrow strips of wood, metal or plastic fixed under the feet for moving quickly over snow

ski VERB to travel on skis

skid VERB to slide accidentally, especially in a vehicle

skid NOUN ❶ a skidding movement ❷ a runner on a helicopter, for use in landing

skier NOUN a person who skis

ski jump NOUN a steep slope with a sharp drop where it levels out at the bottom, for skiers to jump off as a sport

skilful ADJECTIVE having or showing great skill

skill NOUN ❶ the ability to do something well ❷ an ability that you need in order to do something

skilled ADJECTIVE ❶ skilful; highly trained or experienced ❷ skilled work needs particular skills or special training

skim VERB ❶ to remove something from the surface of a liquid; to take the cream off milk ❷ to move quickly over a surface, almost touching it ❸ to read something quickly

skimmed milk NOUN milk that has had the cream removed

skimp VERB to supply or use less than is needed

skimpy ADJECTIVE skimpy clothes do not cover much of the body

skin NOUN ❶ the flexible outer covering of a person's or animal's body ❷ an outer layer or covering, e.g. of a fruit ❸ a skin-like film formed on the surface of a liquid

skin VERB to take the skin off something

skin diving NOUN swimming under water with flippers and breathing apparatus but without a diving suit

skinhead NOUN a youth with very closely cropped hair

skinny ADJECTIVE very thin

skip VERB ❶ to move along lightly, especially by hopping on each foot in turn ❷ to jump with a skipping rope ❸ to go quickly from one subject to another ❹ to miss something out

skip NOUN ❶ a skipping movement ❷ a large open-topped metal container for taking away builders' rubbish

skipper NOUN (informal) the captain of a ship or team

skipping rope NOUN (British) a rope, usually with a handle at each end, that you swing over your head and under your feet as you jump

skirmish NOUN a short rough fight

skirmish VERB to take part in a skirmish

skirt NOUN ❶ a piece of clothing for a woman or girl that hangs down from the waist ❷ the part of a dress below the waist

skirt VERB to go round the edge of something

skirting, skirting board NOUN (British) a narrow board round the wall of a room, close to the floor

skittish ADJECTIVE frisky; lively and excitable

skittle NOUN a wooden or plastic bottle-shaped object that people try to knock down by bowling a ball in the game of **skittles**

skive VERB (British) (informal) to

dodge work

skulk VERB to move around or wait somewhere secretly, usually when you are planning to do something bad

skull NOUN the framework of bones in your head

skullcap NOUN a small close-fitting cap worn on the top of the head

skunk NOUN a North American animal with black and white fur that can spray a bad-smelling fluid

sky NOUN the space above the earth, appearing blue in daylight on fine days

skydiving NOUN the sport of jumping from an aeroplane and performing manoeuvres before opening your parachute

skylark NOUN a lark that sings while it hovers high in the air

skylight NOUN a window in a roof

skyline NOUN the outline of land or buildings seen against the sky

skyscraper NOUN a very tall building

slab NOUN a thick flat piece of something

slack ADJECTIVE ❶ not pulled tight ❷ not busy or working hard

slack NOUN the slack part of a rope or line

slack VERB to avoid work; to be lazy

slacken VERB ❶ to loosen something or to become loose ❷ to become or make something slower or less busy

slacks PLURAL NOUN trousers for informal occasions

slag NOUN waste material separated

slag heap NOUN (*British*) a mound of waste matter from a mine

slain past participle of slay

slake VERB to slake your thirst is to quench it

slalom NOUN a ski race down a zigzag course

slam VERB ❶ to shut or make something shut loudly ❷ to hit something with great force

slam NOUN the act or sound of slamming

slander NOUN a spoken statement that damages a person's reputation and is untrue. Compare with libel.

slander VERB to make a slander against someone

slang NOUN words that are used very informally to add vividness or humour to what is said, especially those used only by a particular group of people

slant VERB ❶ to slope or lean ❷ to present news or information from a particular point of view

slant NOUN ❶ a sloping or leaning position ❷ a way of presenting news or information from a particular point of view

slap VERB ❶ to hit someone with the palm of the hand or with something flat ❷ to put something somewhere forcefully or carelessly

slap NOUN slapping someone

slapdash ADJECTIVE hasty and careless

slapstick NOUN comedy with people hitting each other, falling over and throwing things

slash VERB ❶ to make large cuts in something ❷ to cut or strike something with a long sweeping movement ❸ to reduce something greatly

slash NOUN ❶ a slashing cut ❷ a slanting line (/) used in writing and printing

slat NOUN each of the thin strips of wood, metal or plastic arranged so that they overlap and form a screen, e.g. in a venetian blind

slate NOUN ❶ a kind of grey rock that is easily split into flat plates ❷ a piece of this rock used in covering a roof or (in the past) for writing on

slate VERB ❶ to cover a roof with slates ❷ (*informal*) to criticize a person or thing severely

slaughter VERB ❶ to kill an animal for food ❷ to kill people or animals ruthlessly or in great numbers

slaughter NOUN the killing of a lot of people or animals

slaughterhouse NOUN a place where animals are killed for food

slave NOUN a person who is owned by someone else and has to work for them without being paid

slave VERB to work very hard

slave-driver NOUN a person who makes others work very hard

slaver (say slav-er or slay-ver) VERB to have saliva flowing from the mouth

slavery NOUN ❶ being a slave ❷ the system of having slaves

slay VERB slays, slaying, slew, slain (*old or poetical use*) to kill someone

sled NOUN (*North American*) a sledge

sledge NOUN (*British*) a vehicle for travelling over snow, with strips of metal or wood instead of wheels

sledgehammer NOUN a very large heavy hammer

sleek ADJECTIVE smooth and shiny

sleep NOUN ❶ the condition of rest in which your eyes are closed, your body is relaxed and your mind is unconscious ❷ a time when you are resting like this

sleep VERB sleeps, sleeping, slept to have a sleep

sleeper NOUN ❶ someone who is asleep ❷ each of the wooden or concrete beams on which the rails of a railway rest ❸ a railway carriage with beds or berths for passengers to sleep in; a place in this

sleeping bag NOUN a padded bag to sleep in, especially when you are camping

sleepless ADJECTIVE without sleep or unable to sleep

sleepover NOUN a night spent away from home, after a party

sleepwalker NOUN a person who walks about while they are asleep

sleepy ADJECTIVE ❶ feeling a need or wish to sleep ❷ quiet and lacking activity

sleet NOUN a mixture of rain and snow or hail

sleeve NOUN ❶ the part of a piece of clothing that covers your arm ❷ the cover of a record

sleeveless ADJECTIVE without sleeves

sleigh (say slay) NOUN a large sledge

pulled by horses

sleight of hand (say slight) NOUN skilful movements of your hand that other people cannot see, especially when doing conjuring tricks

slender ADJECTIVE ❶ slim and graceful ❷ slight or small

sleuth (say slooth) NOUN a detective

slew past tense of **slay**

slice NOUN ❶ a thin flat piece cut off something ❷ a portion of something

slice VERB ❶ to cut something into slices ❷ to cut something from a larger piece ❸ to cut something cleanly

slick ADJECTIVE ❶ done quickly and cleverly, without obvious effort ❷ clever at persuading people but not sincere ❸ smooth and slippery

slick NOUN ❶ a large patch of oil floating on water ❷ a slippery place

slide VERB slides, sliding, slid ❶ to move smoothly over a flat or slippery surface or to make something do this ❷ to move somewhere quietly or secretly

slide NOUN ❶ a sliding movement ❷ a structure for children to play on, with a smooth slope for sliding down ❸ a photograph that can be projected on a screen ❹ a small glass plate on which you can place things to examine them under a microscope ❺ a fastener to keep your hair tidy

slight ADJECTIVE very small; not serious or important

slight VERB to insult a person by treating them without respect

571

slight NOUN an insult

slightly ADVERB to a small degree; a little

slim ADJECTIVE ❶ thin and graceful ❷ small; hardly enough

slim VERB (British) to try to make yourself thinner, especially by dieting

slime NOUN unpleasant wet slippery stuff

slimy ADJECTIVE ❶ covered in slime ❷ pretending to be friendly in a way that is not sincere

sling NOUN ❶ a piece of cloth tied round your neck to support an injured arm ❷ a looped strap used to throw a stone

sling VERB slings, slinging, slung ❶ to hang something up or support it so that it hangs loosely ❷ (informal) to throw something roughly or carelessly

slink VERB slinks, slinking, slunk to move in a stealthy or guilty way

slip VERB ❶ to slide accidentally; to lose your balance by sliding ❷ to move somewhere quickly and quietly ❸ to slip something somewhere is to put it there quickly without being seen ❹ to escape from something

slip NOUN ❶ an accidental slide or fall ❷ a small mistake ❸ a small piece of paper ❹ a piece of women's underwear like a thin dress or skirt ❺ a pillowcase

slipper NOUN a soft comfortable shoe to wear indoors

slippery ADJECTIVE smooth or wet so that it is difficult to stand on or hold

slip road NOUN (British) a road by which you enter or leave a motorway

slipshod ADJECTIVE a slipshod piece of work is careless or badly done

slipstream NOUN a current of air driven backward as an aircraft or vehicle moves forward very fast

slit NOUN a narrow straight cut or opening

slit VERB slits, slitting, slit to make a slit or slits in something

slither VERB ❶ to move along the ground like a snake ❷ to slip or slide unsteadily

sliver (say sliv-er) NOUN a thin strip of something hard or brittle, such as wood or glass

slob NOUN (informal) a careless, untidy, lazy person

slobber VERB to have saliva coming out of your mouth

sloe NOUN the small dark plum-like fruit of blackthorn

slog VERB ❶ to work hard ❷ to walk with effort ❸ to hit something hard

slog NOUN a piece of hard work or effort

slogan NOUN a short catchy phrase used to advertise something or to sum up an idea

slop VERB ❶ to spill liquid over the edge of its container ❷ liquid slops when it spills in this way

slope VERB to be at an angle so that it is higher at one end than the other; to lean to one side

slope NOUN ❶ a surface or piece of land that slopes ❷ the amount by which something slopes

sloppy ADJECTIVE ❶ liquid and splashing easily ❷ careless or badly done ❸ too sentimental or romantic

slops PLURAL NOUN ❶ waste food fed to animals ❷ dirty water or liquid waste matter

slosh VERB (informal) ❶ to splash in a messy way ❷ to pour or splash liquid carelessly

slot NOUN a narrow opening to put things in

slot VERB to put something into a place where it fits

sloth (rhymes with both) NOUN ❶ laziness ❷ a South American animal that lives in trees and moves very slowly

slot machine NOUN a machine worked by putting a coin in the slot

slouch VERB to stand, sit or move in a lazy awkward way, with your shoulders and head bent forward

slough (say sluf) VERB to shed a layer of dead skin

slough (rhymes with cow) NOUN a swamp or marshy place

slovenly (say sluv-en-lee) ADJECTIVE careless or untidy

slow ADJECTIVE ❶ not quick; taking more time than is usual ❷ showing a time earlier than the correct time ❸ not clever; not able to understand quickly or easily

slow ADVERB slowly; at a slow rate

slow VERB ❶ to go more slowly ❷ to make something go more slowly

slowly ADVERB at a slow rate or speed

slow motion NOUN movement in a film or on television which has been slowed down

slow-worm NOUN a small European legless lizard that looks like a snake and gives birth to live young

sludge NOUN thick mud

slug NOUN ❶ a small slimy animal like a snail without a shell ❷ a pellet for firing from a gun

sluggish ADJECTIVE slow-moving; not alert or lively

sluice (say slooss) NOUN ❶ a sluice gate ❷ a channel carrying off water

sluice VERB to wash something with a flow of water

sluice gate NOUN a sliding barrier for controlling a flow of water

slum NOUN an area of dirty and overcrowded houses in a city

slumber NOUN peaceful sleep

slumber VERB to sleep peacefully

slump VERB to fall or sit down heavily or suddenly

slump NOUN a sudden great fall in prices or trade

slur VERB ❶ to pronounce words indistinctly by running the sounds together ❷ to mark notes in music with a slur

slur NOUN ❶ a slurred sound ❷ an unfair comment or insult that harms a person's reputation ❸ a curved line placed over notes in music to show that they are to be sung or played smoothly without a break

slurp VERB to eat or drink something with a loud sucking sound

slurp NOUN a loud sucking sound

slush NOUN ❶ partly melted snow on the ground ❷ very sentimental talk or writing

sly ADJECTIVE ❶ unpleasantly cunning or secret ❷ mischievous and knowing

slyly ADVERB in a sly way

smack NOUN ❶ a hard slap with your hand ❷ a loud sharp sound of a thing hitting something ❸ a loud kiss ❹ (*informal*) a hard hit or blow ❺ a slight flavour or trace of something ❻ (*British*) a small sailing boat used for fishing

smack VERB ❶ to slap someone with your hand, especially as a punishment ❷ to hit something hard ❸ to have a slight flavour or trace of something

smack ADVERB (*informal*) forcefully or directly

small ADJECTIVE ❶ not large; less than the usual size ❷ not important or significant

small hours PLURAL NOUN the early hours of the morning, after midnight

small-minded ADJECTIVE not willing to change your opinions or think about what is really important; petty

smallpox NOUN a serious contagious disease that causes a fever and produces spots that leave permanent scars on the skin

small print NOUN (*British*) the details of a contract, especially if they are in very small letters or difficult to understand

small talk NOUN conversation about unimportant things

smarmy ADJECTIVE (*informal*) flattering someone or being too polite to them in a way that seems false

smart ADJECTIVE ❶ neat and elegant; dressed well ❷ clever or shrewd ❸ forceful and brisk ❹ fashionable and expensive ❺ controlled by a computer

smart VERB ❶ to feel a stinging pain ❷ to feel upset about a criticism or failure

smart card NOUN a small plastic card on which information is stored in electronic form

smarten VERB to make a person or thing smarter or to become smarter

smartly ADVERB ❶ to be smartly dressed is to be well dressed in neat clothes ❷ quickly and suddenly

smartphone NOUN a mobile phone that also works as a computer

smash VERB ❶ to break noisily into pieces or make something break in this way ❷ to hit something or move with great force ❸ to strike the ball forcefully downwards in tennis and other games ❹ to destroy or defeat someone completely

smash NOUN ❶ the action or sound of smashing ❷ a collision between vehicles ❸ (*informal*) a smash hit

smash hit NOUN (*informal*) a very successful song or show

smashing ADJECTIVE (*British*) (*informal*) excellent

smattering NOUN a slight knowledge of a subject or a foreign language

smear VERB ❶ to rub something greasy or sticky or dirty on a surface ❷ to try to damage someone's reputation

smear NOUN ❶ a dirty or greasy mark made by smearing ❷ material smeared on a slide to be examined under a microscope ❸ a smear test

smell VERB smells, smelling, smelt or smelled ❶ to be aware of something by means of your nose ❷ to give out a smell

smell NOUN ❶ something you can smell; a quality in something that makes people able to smell it ❷ an unpleasant quality of this kind ❸ the ability to smell things

smelly ADJECTIVE having an unpleasant smell

smelt VERB to melt ore to get the metal it contains

smile NOUN an expression on your face that shows you are pleased or amused, with your lips stretched and turning upwards at the ends

smile VERB to give a smile

smirk NOUN a self-satisfied smile

smirk VERB to give a smirk

smith NOUN a person who makes things out of metal, especially a blacksmith

smithereens PLURAL NOUN small fragments

smithy NOUN a blacksmith's workshop

smock NOUN ❶ an overall shaped like a long loose shirt ❷ a loose top worn by a pregnant woman

smog NOUN a mixture of smoke and fog

smoke NOUN ❶ the mixture of gas and solid particles given off by a burning substance ❷ a time spent smoking a cigarette

smoke VERB ❶ to give out smoke ❷ someone is smoking when they have a lit cigarette between their lips and are drawing its smoke into their mouth ❸ to preserve meat or fish by treating it with smoke

smokescreen NOUN ❶ a mass of smoke used to hide the movement of troops ❷ something that conceals what is happening

smoky ADJECTIVE ❶ full of or producing smoke ❷ like smoke

smooth ADJECTIVE ❶ having a surface without any lumps, wrinkles or roughness ❷ a smooth liquid or mixture has no lumps in it ❸ moving without bumps or jolts ❹ not harsh ❺ without problems or difficulties

smooth VERB to make something smooth and flat

smoothly ADVERB ❶ in an even and steady way ❷ without any problems or difficulties

smother VERB ❶ to cover someone's face so that they cannot breathe ❷ to put out a fire by covering it ❸ to cover something thickly ❹ to hold back or conceal something

smoulder VERB ❶ to burn slowly without a flame ❷ to feel an emotion strongly without showing it

smudge NOUN a dirty mark made by rubbing something

smudge VERB to make a smudge on something or to become smudged

a b c d e f g h i j k l m n o p q r s t u v w x y z

smug ADJECTIVE too pleased with your own good fortune or abilities

smuggle VERB ❶ to bring something into a country secretly or illegally ❷ to take something secretly into or out of a place

snack NOUN ❶ a small meal ❷ food eaten between meals

snack bar NOUN a small cafe where snacks are sold

snag NOUN ❶ an unexpected difficulty ❷ a sharp or jagged part sticking out from something

snag VERB to catch something you are wearing on something sharp

snail NOUN a small animal with a soft body and a shell

snail's pace NOUN a very slow pace

snake NOUN a reptile with a long narrow body and no legs

snake VERB to move or go in long twisting curves

snap VERB ❶ to break suddenly or with a sharp sound or to make something do this ❷ an animal snaps when it bites suddenly or quickly ❸ to say something quickly and angrily ❹ to move something into a certain position with a sharp noise ❺ to take a quick photograph of something

snap NOUN ❶ the action or sound of snapping ❷ an informal photograph ❸ a card game in which players shout 'Snap!' when they see two similar cards

snap ADJECTIVE made or done very quickly or suddenly

snapdragon NOUN a plant with flowers that have a mouth-like opening

snappy ADJECTIVE ❶ snapping at people ❷ quick and lively

snapshot NOUN an informal photograph that you take quickly

snare NOUN ❶ a trap for catching birds or small animals ❷ something that attracts someone but is a trap or a danger

snare VERB to catch a bird or animal in a snare

snarl VERB ❶ to growl angrily ❷ to speak in a bad-tempered way

snarl NOUN a snarling sound

snatch VERB ❶ to grab or take something quickly ❷ to quickly make use of time or a chance

snatch NOUN ❶ a short and incomplete part of a song or conversation ❷ an act of snatching something

sneak VERB sneaks, sneaking, sneaked ❶ to move somewhere quietly and secretly ❷ (informal) to take something secretly ❸ (informal) to tell tales about someone

sneak NOUN (informal) a person who tells tales

sneakers PLURAL NOUN (North American) soft-soled shoes

sneaky ADJECTIVE dishonest or deceitful

sneer VERB to show contempt for someone by the way you speak or the expression on your face

sneer NOUN the expression on someone's face when they sneer

sneeze VERB to send out air suddenly and uncontrollably through your nose and mouth in order to get rid of something irritating the nostrils

sneeze NOUN the action or sound of sneezing

snide ADJECTIVE sneering in a sly way

sniff VERB ❶ to make a sound by drawing air in through your nose ❷ to smell something

sniff NOUN the act or sound of sniffing

sniffle VERB to keep sniffing because you have a cold or are crying

sniffle NOUN the act or sound of sniffling

snigger VERB (*British*) to laugh quietly and slyly

snigger NOUN (*British*) a quiet sly laugh

snip VERB to cut something with scissors or shears in small quick cuts

snip NOUN an act of snipping something

snipe NOUN a marsh bird with a long beak

snipe VERB ❶ to shoot at people from a hiding place ❷ to attack someone with sly critical remarks

snippet NOUN a small piece of news or information

snivel VERB to cry or complain in a whining way

snob NOUN a person who despises those who have not got wealth, power or particular tastes or interests

snooker NOUN a game played with long sticks (called *cues*) and 22 balls on a special cloth-covered table

snoop VERB to look around a place secretly in order to find something out

snooty ADJECTIVE (*informal*) haughty and contemptuous

snooze (*informal*) NOUN a short sleep

snooze VERB to have a short sleep

snore VERB to breathe noisily while you are sleeping

snore NOUN noisy breathing while you are sleeping

snorkel NOUN a tube through which a person swimming under water can take in air

snort VERB to make a rough sound by breathing forcefully through your nose

snort NOUN a snorting noise

snout NOUN an animal's snout is the front part sticking out from its head, with its nose and jaws

snow NOUN frozen drops of water that fall from the sky in small white flakes

snow VERB it is snowing when snow is falling

snowball NOUN snow pressed into a ball for throwing

snowball VERB to grow quickly in size or intensity

snow-blindness NOUN temporary blindness caused by the glare of light reflected by snow

snowdrift NOUN a large heap or bank of snow piled up by the wind

snowdrop NOUN a small white flower that blooms in early spring

snowflake NOUN a flake of snow

snowline NOUN the level above which snow never melts

snowman NOUN a figure made of snow

A B C D E F G H I J K L M N O P Q R S T U V W X Y Z

snowplough NOUN a vehicle or device for clearing roads of snow

snowshoe NOUN a frame rather like a tennis racket for walking on soft snow

snowstorm NOUN a storm in which snow falls

snowy ADJECTIVE ❶ with snow falling ❷ covered with snow ❸ pure white

snub VERB to treat someone rudely, especially by ignoring them

snub NOUN an insulting remark or unfriendly treatment

snub-nosed ADJECTIVE having a short turned-up nose

snuff NOUN powdered tobacco for taking into the nose by sniffing

snuff VERB to put out a candle by covering or pinching the flame

snuffle VERB to sniff in a noisy way

snuffle NOUN the sound of snuffling

snug ADJECTIVE ❶ warm and cosy ❷ fitting closely or tightly

snuggle VERB to curl up in a warm comfortable place

so ADVERB ❶ in this way; to such an extent ❷ very ❸ also; too

so CONJUNCTION for that reason

soak VERB to make a person or thing very wet or leave them in water

so-and-so NOUN a person whose name you do not know or do not need to say

soap NOUN ❶ a substance you use with water for washing and cleaning things ❷ a soap opera

soap VERB to put soap on something

soap opera NOUN a television serial about the day-to-day lives of a group of people

soar VERB ❶ to rise or fly high in the air ❷ to increase very quickly

sob VERB to make a gasping sound when crying

sob NOUN a sound of sobbing

sober ADJECTIVE ❶ not drunk ❷ serious and calm ❸ not bright or showy

sober VERB to become sober again or to make someone sober

sob story NOUN an account of someone's experiences, told to get your help or sympathy

so-called ADJECTIVE named in what may be the wrong way

soccer NOUN football (Association football, not rugby or American football)

sociable ADJECTIVE friendly and liking to be with other people

social ADJECTIVE ❶ to do with people meeting one another in their spare time ❷ to do with life in a community ❸ living in groups, not alone ❹ liking to be with other people

socialism NOUN a political system where wealth is shared equally between people and the main industries and resources are controlled by the state. Compare with **capitalism**.

socialist NOUN a person who believes in socialism

socialize (also **socialise**) VERB to meet other people socially

social media NOUN websites and computer programs that people use to communicate on the Internet using mobile phones, computers, etc.

social security NOUN money and other assistance provided by the government for those in need through being unemployed, ill or disabled

social services PLURAL NOUN welfare services provided by the government, for example care for vulnerable children and adults

social worker NOUN a person trained to help people in a community who have family or money problems

society NOUN ❶ a community; people living together in a group or nation ❷ a group of people organized for a particular purpose ❸ company or companionship

sociology (say soh-see-ol-o-jee) NOUN the study of human society and social behaviour

sock NOUN a piece of clothing that covers your foot and the lower part of your leg

sock VERB (informal) to hit or punch someone hard

socket NOUN ❶ a hollow into which something fits ❷ a device into which an electric plug or bulb is put to make a connection

sod NOUN a piece of turf

soda NOUN ❶ a substance made from sodium, such as baking soda ❷ soda water ❸ (North American) a sweet fizzy drink

soda water NOUN water made fizzy with carbon dioxide, used in drinks

sodden ADJECTIVE made very wet

sodium NOUN a soft white metal

sodium bicarbonate NOUN a soluble white powder used in fire extinguishers and fizzy drinks and to make cakes rise; baking soda

sodium carbonate NOUN white powder or crystals used to clean things; washing soda

sofa NOUN a long soft seat with a back and arms

soft ADJECTIVE ❶ not hard or firm; easily pressed or cut into a new shape ❷ smooth, not rough or stiff ❸ gentle and not loud ❹ not bright or harsh ❺ soft drugs are not likely to be addictive ❻ soft water is free of minerals that prevent soap from making much lather

soft drink NOUN a cold drink that is not alcoholic

soften VERB ❶ to make something soft or to become soft ❷ to become kinder or more friendly

soft-hearted ADJECTIVE sympathetic and easily moved

softly ADVERB ❶ in a gentle way ❷ quietly

software NOUN computer programs and data, which are not part of the machinery of a computer. Compare with **hardware**.

softwood NOUN wood from pine trees or other conifers

soggy ADJECTIVE very wet and heavy

soil NOUN ❶ the loose earth in which plants grow ❷ a nation's territory

soil VERB to make something dirty

solace (say sol-as) NOUN something that makes you feel better when you are unhappy or disappointed

solar ADJECTIVE from or to do with the sun

solar panel NOUN a panel designed to catch the sun's rays and use their energy for heating or to make electricity

solar power NOUN electricity or other forms of power that come from the sun's rays

solar system NOUN the sun and the planets that revolve round it

solder NOUN a soft alloy that is melted to join pieces of metal together

solder VERB to join two pieces of metal together with solder

soldier NOUN a member of an army

sole NOUN ① the bottom surface of a foot or shoe ② a flat edible sea fish

sole VERB to put a new sole on a shoe

sole ADJECTIVE single or only

solely ADVERB only; involving nothing or nobody else

solemn ADJECTIVE ① not smiling or cheerful ② dignified or formal

sol-fa NOUN a system of syllables (*doh, ray, me, fah, so, la, te*) used to represent the notes of the musical scale

solicit VERB to ask for or try to obtain something

solicitor NOUN a lawyer who advises clients, prepares legal documents and represents clients in the lower courts

solid ADJECTIVE ① not hollow; with no space inside ② keeping its shape; not liquid or gas ③ continuous ④ firm or strongly made; not flimsy ⑤ strong and dependable

solid NOUN ① a solid thing ② a shape that has three dimensions (length, width and height or depth)

solidarity NOUN unity and support between people sharing opinions and interests

solidify VERB to become solid

solids PLURAL NOUN solid food; food that is not liquid

soliloquy (say sol-**il**-ok-wee) NOUN a speech in a play in which a person speaks their thoughts aloud when alone or without addressing anyone else

solitaire NOUN ① a game for one person, in which marbles are moved on a special board until only one is left ② a diamond or other precious stone set by itself

solitary ADJECTIVE ① alone, without other people ② single; by itself

solitary confinement NOUN a form of punishment in which a prisoner is kept alone in a cell and not allowed to see other people

solitude NOUN being solitary or alone

solo NOUN something sung, played, danced or done by one person alone

solo ADJECTIVE & ADVERB done alone; by yourself

soloist NOUN a person who plays, sings or performs a solo

solstice (say sol-stiss) NOUN either of the two times in each year when the sun is at its furthest point north or south of the equator

soluble ADJECTIVE ① a soluble substance is able to be dissolved ② a soluble problem or puzzle is able to be solved

solution NOUN ❶ the answer to a problem or puzzle ❷ a liquid in which something is dissolved

solve VERB to find the answer to a problem or puzzle

solvent NOUN a liquid used for dissolving something

solvent ADJECTIVE having enough money to pay all your debts

sombre ADJECTIVE ❶ dark in colour ❷ gloomy or serious

sombrero (say som-**brair**-oh) NOUN a hat with a very wide brim

some DETERMINER ❶ a few or a little ❷ an unknown person or thing ❸ about

some PRONOUN a certain number or amount that is less than the whole

somebody PRONOUN ❶ some person; someone ❷ an important or impressive person

somehow ADVERB in some way or for some reason

someone PRONOUN some person; somebody

somersault NOUN a movement in which you turn head over heels before landing on your feet

somersault VERB to perform a somersault

something PRONOUN some thing; a thing which you cannot or do not want to name

sometime ADVERB at some point in time

sometimes ADVERB at some times but not always

somewhat ADVERB to some extent

somewhere ADVERB in or to some place

son NOUN a boy or man who is someone's child

sonar NOUN a system for finding objects under water by the reflection of sound waves

sonata NOUN a piece of music for one instrument or two, in several movements

song NOUN ❶ a tune with words for singing ❷ a bird's song is the musical sounds it makes ❸ singing

songbird NOUN a bird that sings sweetly

sonic ADJECTIVE to do with sound or sound waves

sonic boom NOUN a loud noise caused by the shock wave of an aircraft travelling faster than the speed of sound

son-in-law NOUN a daughter's husband

sonnet NOUN a kind of poem with 14 lines

sonny NOUN (*informal*) boy or young man

soon ADVERB ❶ in a short time from now ❷ not long after something ❸ early or quickly

soot NOUN the black powder left by smoke in a chimney or on a building

soothe VERB ❶ to make someone calmer or less upset ❷ to make a part of the body or a feeling feel less painful

soothing ADJECTIVE that soothes someone or something

soothsayer NOUN a prophet

sop NOUN something unimportant

you give to a troublesome person to make them feel better

sop *VERB* ➤ **sop something up** to soak up liquid with a sponge

sophisticated *ADJECTIVE* ❶ a sophisticated person has refined or cultured tastes and is experienced about life ❷ complicated and advanced

sopping *ADJECTIVE* very wet; drenched

soppy *ADJECTIVE* (*British*) (*informal*) sentimental in a silly way

soprano *NOUN* a woman, girl or boy with a high singing voice

sorcerer *NOUN* a person who can perform magic

sorceress *NOUN* a woman who can perform magic

sorcery *NOUN* magic or witchcraft

sordid *ADJECTIVE* ❶ dirty and nasty ❷ dishonourable or immoral

sore *ADJECTIVE* ❶ painful or smarting ❷ (*informal*) annoyed or offended ❸ serious or upsetting

sore *NOUN* a sore place on your body

sorely *ADVERB* seriously; very

sorrel *NOUN* ❶ a herb with sharp-tasting leaves ❷ a reddish-brown horse

sorrow *NOUN* ❶ sadness or regret caused by loss or disappointment ❷ something that causes this

sorrow *VERB* to feel sorrow; to grieve

sorrowful *ADJECTIVE* feeling or showing great sadness

sorry *ADJECTIVE* ❶ feeling regret for something you have done and wanting to apologize ❷ feeling

pity or sympathy for someone ❸ wretched or unattractive

sort *NOUN* ❶ a group of things or people that are similar; a kind or variety ❷ (*in computing*) putting data in a particular order

sort *VERB* to arrange things in groups according to their size or type

sortie *NOUN* ❶ an attack by troops coming out of a besieged place ❷ an attacking expedition by a military aircraft

SOS *NOUN* an urgent appeal for help

sought *past tense* of seek

soul *NOUN* ❶ the invisible part of a person that some people believe goes on living after the body has died ❷ a person's mind and emotions ❸ a person ❹ a kind of popular music that developed from gospel music

soulful *ADJECTIVE* having or showing deep feeling

sound *NOUN* ❶ vibrations that travel through the air and can be detected by the ear; the sensation they produce ❷ sound reproduced in a film or recording ❸ a mental impression you get from something ❹ a narrow stretch of water connecting two seas; a strait

sound *VERB* ❶ to make a sound ❷ to make a sound with something ❸ to give a certain impression when heard ❹ to test something by noting the sounds you can hear from it ❺ to test the depth of water beneath a ship

sound *ADJECTIVE* ❶ in good condition; not damaged ❷ healthy; not diseased

❸ reasonable or correct ❹ reliable or secure ❺ thorough or deep

sound barrier NOUN the resistance of the air to objects moving at speeds near the speed of sound

sound bite NOUN a very short part of a speech or statement broadcast on radio or television because it seems to sum up the person's opinion in a few words

sound effects PLURAL NOUN sounds produced artificially to make a play, film, etc. seem more realistic

soundly ADVERB deeply or thoroughly

soundtrack NOUN the sound or music that goes with a cinema film

soup NOUN a liquid food made from meat, fish or vegetables

sour ADJECTIVE ❶ tasting sharp like vinegar or lemons ❷ stale and unpleasant; not fresh ❸ bad-tempered and unfriendly

sour VERB to become sour or to make something sour

source NOUN ❶ the place where something comes from ❷ the starting point of a river

sour grapes PLURAL NOUN pretending that something you want is no good because you know you cannot have it

south NOUN ❶ the direction to the right of a person who faces west ❷ the southern part of a country, city or other area

south ADJECTIVE & ADVERB towards or in the south; coming from the south

south-east NOUN, ADJECTIVE & ADVERB midway between south and east

southward ADJECTIVE & ADVERB towards the south

south-west NOUN, ADJECTIVE & ADVERB midway between south and west

souvenir (say soo-ven-eer) NOUN something that you keep to remind you of a person, place or event

sou'wester NOUN a waterproof hat with a wide flap at the back

sovereign NOUN ❶ a king or queen who is the ruler of a country; a monarch ❷ an old British gold coin, originally worth £1

sovereign ADJECTIVE ❶ supreme ❷ a sovereign state is independent and runs its own affairs

sovereignty NOUN the power a country has to govern itself and make its own laws

sow (rhymes with go) VERB sows, sowing, sowed, sown or sowed ❶ to put seeds into the ground so that they will grow into plants ❷ to cause feelings or ideas to develop

sow (rhymes with cow) NOUN a female pig

soya bean NOUN a kind of bean from which edible oil and flour are made

soy sauce, soya sauce NOUN a Chinese or Japanese sauce made from fermented soya beans

spa NOUN a health resort where there is a spring of water containing mineral salts

space NOUN ❶ the whole area outside the earth, where the stars and planets are ❷ an area or volume ③ an empty area; a gap ④ an interval of time

space VERB to arrange things so that there are spaces between them

spacecraft NOUN a vehicle for travelling in outer space

spaceman NOUN a male astronaut

spaceship NOUN a spacecraft, especially one carrying people

space shuttle NOUN a spacecraft that can travel into space and land like a plane when it returns to earth

space station NOUN a satellite which orbits the earth and is used as a base by scientists and astronauts

space walk NOUN moving about or walking by an astronaut outside the spacecraft

spacewoman NOUN a female astronaut

spacious ADJECTIVE providing a lot of space; roomy

spade NOUN ① a tool with a long handle and a wide blade for digging ② a playing card with black shapes like upside-down hearts on it, each with a short stem

spaghetti NOUN pasta made in long thin sticks, which soften into strings when you cook them

span NOUN ① the length from end to end or across something ② the part between two uprights of an arch or bridge ③ the length of a period of time ④ the distance from the tip of your thumb to the tip of your little finger when your hand is spread out

span VERB to reach from one side or end to the other

spangle NOUN a small piece of glittering material

spaniel NOUN a kind of dog with long ears and silky fur

spank VERB to smack a person on the bottom as a punishment

spanner NOUN (*British*) a tool for gripping and turning a nut or bolt

spar NOUN a strong pole used for a mast or boom on a ship

spar VERB ① to practise boxing ② to argue with someone, often in a friendly way

spare VERB ① to afford to give or do without something ② to be merciful towards someone; to not kill, hurt or harm a person or thing ③ to avoid making a person suffer something ④ to use or treat something economically

spare ADJECTIVE ① not used but kept ready in case it is needed; extra ② thin or lean

spare NOUN a spare thing or part

spare time NOUN time not needed for work

sparing (say *spair*-ing) ADJECTIVE careful or economical; not wasteful

spark NOUN ① a tiny glowing piece of something hot ② a flash produced electrically ③ a trace of something

spark VERB ① to give off a spark or sparks ② to cause something

sparkle VERB ① to shine with tiny flashes of light ② to show brilliant wit or liveliness

sparkle NOUN ① a lot of tiny flashes of light ② liveliness

sparkler NOUN a hand-held firework that gives off sparks

sparkling wine NOUN a bubbly wine

sparrow NOUN a small brown bird

sparse ADJECTIVE thinly scattered; small in number or amount

spartan ADJECTIVE simple and without comfort or luxuries

spasm NOUN ① a sudden involuntary movement of a muscle ② a sudden brief burst of something

spasmodic ADJECTIVE ① happening or done at irregular intervals ② to do with or caused by a spasm

spat past tense of spit

spat NOUN a short gaiter

spate NOUN ① a lot of things coming one after another ② a sudden flood in a river

spatial ADJECTIVE to do with space

spatter VERB ① to scatter something wet in small drops ② to splash someone or something

spatter NOUN a small amount of something in small drops

spatula NOUN a tool like a knife with a broad blunt flexible blade, used for spreading or mixing things

spawn NOUN ① the eggs of fish, frogs, toads or shellfish ② the thread-like matter from which fungi grow

spawn VERB ① to produce spawn ② to be produced from spawn ③ to produce something in large numbers

spay VERB to sterilize a female animal by removing the ovaries

speak VERB speaks, speaking, spoke, spoken ① to say something; to talk ② to talk or be able to talk in a foreign language

speaker NOUN ① a person who is speaking ② someone who makes a speech ③ the part of a radio, CD player, computer, etc. that the sound comes out of

spear NOUN a weapon for throwing or stabbing, with a long shaft and a pointed tip

spear VERB to pierce something with a spear or with something pointed

spearhead VERB to lead a campaign or attack

spearmint NOUN mint used in cookery and for flavouring chewing gum

special ADJECTIVE ① not ordinary or usual; exceptional ② meant for a particular person or purpose

special effects PLURAL NOUN illusions created for films or television by using props, trick photography or computer images

specialist NOUN an expert in one subject

speciality NOUN ① something in which a person specializes ② a special product, especially a food

specialize (also **specialise**) VERB to give particular attention or study to one subject or thing

specially ADVERB ① in a special way ② for a special purpose

special needs PLURAL NOUN educational requirements resulting from learning difficulties, physical disability or emotional and behavioural difficulties

species (say **spee**-shiz) NOUN species ① a group of animals or plants that have the same features and can breed with each other ② a kind or sort

specific ADJECTIVE ① definite or precise ② to do with a particular thing

specifically ADVERB ① clearly and precisely ② in a special way or for a special purpose

specification NOUN a detailed description of how to make or do something

specific gravity NOUN relative density

specify VERB to name or list things precisely

specimen NOUN ① a sample of something ② an example

speck NOUN ① a tiny piece of something ② a tiny mark or spot

speckle NOUN a small spot or mark

speckled ADJECTIVE covered with small spots or marks

specs PLURAL NOUN (informal) spectacles

spectacle NOUN ① an impressive sight or display ② a ridiculous sight

spectacles PLURAL NOUN (British) a pair of glasses

spectacular ADJECTIVE very impressive to see

spectator NOUN a person who watches a game, show or other event

spectre NOUN a ghost

spectrum NOUN ① the bands of colours seen in a rainbow ② a wide range of things or ideas

speculate VERB ① to form opinions without having any definite evidence ② to invest in stocks or property in the hope of making a profit but with the risk of loss

sped past tense of speed

speech NOUN ① the ability to speak or a person's way of speaking ② a talk to an audience ③ a group of lines spoken by a character in a play

speechless ADJECTIVE too surprised or emotional to be able to say anything

speech marks PLURAL NOUN punctuation marks " " or ' ' used to show that someone is speaking; inverted commas

speed NOUN ① a measure of the time in which something moves or happens ② being quick or fast

speed VERB speeds, speeding, sped (in senses 2 and 3 speeded) ① to go quickly ② to drive faster than the legal limit

speedboat NOUN a fast motor boat

speed limit NOUN the maximum speed at which vehicles may legally travel on a particular road

speedometer NOUN a device in a vehicle, showing its speed

speedway NOUN a track for motorcycle racing

speedwell NOUN a wild plant with small blue flowers

speedy ADJECTIVE quick or swift

spell VERB spells, spelling, spelled

or **spelt** ❶ to put letters in the right order to make a word or words ❷ a set of letters spell a word when they form it ❸ to have something as a result

spell NOUN ❶ a period of time ❷ a period of a certain work or activity ❸ a set of words that is supposed to have magical power

spellbound ADJECTIVE with your attention completely held as if by magic

spellchecker, spellcheck NOUN a computer program that you use to check your writing to see if your spelling is correct

spelling NOUN ❶ the way a word is spelled ❷ how well someone can spell

spend VERB spends, spending, spent ❶ to use money to pay for things ❷ to use up time, energy or effort in doing something ❸ to pass time doing something

spendthrift NOUN a person who spends money extravagantly and wastefully

sperm NOUN the male cell that fuses with an ovum to produce offspring

spew VERB ❶ to vomit ❷ to send out something unpleasant in a stream

sphere NOUN ❶ a perfectly round solid shape; the shape of a ball ❷ a field of interest, activity or knowledge

spherical ADJECTIVE having the shape of a sphere

sphinx NOUN a stone statue with the body of a lion and a human head, especially the huge one

(almost 5,000 years old) in Egypt

spice NOUN ❶ a strong-tasting substance used to flavour food, often made from dried parts of plants ❷ something that adds interest or excitement

spice VERB ❶ to flavour food with spices ❷ to make something more interesting or exciting

spick and span ADJECTIVE neat and clean

spicy ADJECTIVE spicy food tastes strongly of spices

spider NOUN a small animal with eight legs that spins webs to catch insects on which it feeds

spike NOUN a pointed piece of metal; a sharp point

spike VERB to pierce something with a spike

spiky ADJECTIVE full of spikes or sharp points

spill VERB spills, spilling, spilt or spilled ❶ to let something fall out of a container ❷ to fall out of a container

spill NOUN ❶ spilling; something spilt ❷ a fall from a horse or bicycle

spin VERB spins, spinning, spun ❶ to turn round and round quickly or to make something do this ❷ to make raw wool or cotton into threads by pulling and twisting its fibres ❸ a spider or silkworm spins a web or cocoon when it forms one out of threads from its body

spin NOUN ❶ a spinning movement ❷ a short outing in a car

spinach NOUN a vegetable with dark green leaves

spinal ADJECTIVE to do with the spine

spinal cord NOUN the thick cord of nerves enclosed in the spine, that carries messages to and from the brain

spindle NOUN ❶ a thin rod on which you wind thread ❷ a pin or bar that turns round or on which something turns

spindly ADJECTIVE thin and long or tall

spin doctor NOUN a person whose job is to make information or events seem favourable to their employer, usually a politician or political party

spin drier NOUN a machine in which washed clothes are spun to remove excess water

spindrift NOUN spray blown along the surface of the sea

spine NOUN ❶ the line of bones down the middle of your back ❷ a sharp point on an animal or plant ❸ the back part of a book where the pages are joined together

spine-chilling ADJECTIVE frightening and exciting

spineless ADJECTIVE ❶ without a backbone ❷ lacking in determination or strength of character

spinning wheel NOUN a household device for spinning wool or cotton into thread

spin-off NOUN something extra produced while making something else

spinster NOUN an insulting word for a woman who has not married, especially an older woman

spiny ADJECTIVE covered with spines; prickly

spiral ADJECTIVE going round and round a central point and becoming gradually closer to it or further from it; twisting continually round a central line or cylinder

spiral NOUN a spiral line or course

spiral VERB ❶ to move in a spiral ❷ to increase or decrease continuously and quickly

spire NOUN a tall pointed part on top of a church tower

spirit NOUN ❶ a person's mood or mind and feelings ❷ the part of a person that is thought to survive death; a person's soul ❸ a ghost or a supernatural being ❹ courage or liveliness ❺ a kind of quality in something ❻ a strong distilled alcoholic drink

spirit VERB to carry off a person or thing quickly and secretly

spirited ADJECTIVE brave; self-confident and lively

spirit level NOUN a device consisting of a tube of liquid with an air bubble in it, used to find out whether something is level

spiritual ADJECTIVE ❶ to do with the human soul; not physical ❷ to do with religious beliefs

spiritual NOUN a religious folk song, originally sung by black Christians in America

spit VERB spits, spitting, spat or spit ❶ to send out drops of liquid forcibly from your mouth ❷ to force something out of your mouth ❸ to rain lightly

spit NOUN ❶ saliva or spittle ❷ a long thin metal spike put through meat to hold it while it is being roasted ❸ a narrow strip of land sticking out into the sea

spite NOUN a desire to hurt or annoy someone

spite VERB to hurt or annoy someone from spite

spiteful ADJECTIVE behaving unkindly in order to hurt or annoy someone

spitfire NOUN a fiery-tempered person

spitting image NOUN an exact likeness

spittle NOUN saliva, especially when it is spat out

splash VERB ❶ to make liquid fly about in drops ❷ liquid splashes when it flies about in drops ❸ to make a person or thing wet by splashing

splash NOUN ❶ the action, sound or mark of splashing ❷ a bright patch of colour or light

splatter VERB to splash over something

splay VERB to spread wide apart or make something do this

spleen NOUN an organ of the body, close to the stomach, that helps to keep the blood in good condition

splendid ADJECTIVE ❶ magnificent; full of splendour ❷ excellent; very fine

splendour NOUN a brilliant display or appearance

splice VERB ❶ to join pieces of rope or wire by twisting their strands together ❷ to join pieces of film,

tape or wood by overlapping the ends

splint NOUN a straight piece of wood or metal tied to a broken arm or leg to hold it firm

splinter NOUN a thin sharp piece of wood, glass or stone broken off a larger piece

splinter VERB to break into splinters

split VERB splits, splitting, split ❶ to break apart, especially along the length of something ❷ to divide something into parts ❸ to divide something among people

split NOUN ❶ the splitting or dividing of something ❷ a crack or tear in something, where it has split

split second NOUN a very brief moment of time; an instant

split-second ADJECTIVE ❶ done very quickly ❷ very precise

splodge NOUN a dirty mark or stain

splutter VERB ❶ to make a quick series of spitting or coughing sounds ❷ to speak quickly and in a confused way

spoil VERB spoils, spoiling, spoilt or spoiled ❶ to damage something and make it useless or unsatisfactory ❷ to make someone selfish by always letting them have what they want ❸ to treat someone kindly

spoils PLURAL NOUN plunder or other things gained by a victor

spoilsport NOUN a person who spoils other people's enjoyment of things

spoke past tense of speak

spoke NOUN each of the bars or rods that go from the centre of a wheel to its rim

spokesman NOUN a spokesperson, especially a man

spokesperson NOUN a person who speaks on behalf of a group of people

spokeswoman NOUN a female spokesperson

sponge NOUN ❶ a sea creature with a soft porous body ❷ the skeleton of this creature or a piece of a similar substance, used for washing or padding things ❸ a soft lightweight cake or pudding

sponge VERB ❶ to wipe or wash something with a wet sponge ❷ to get money or food off other people without giving anything in return

spongy ADJECTIVE soft and absorbent, like a sponge

sponsor NOUN ❶ a person or organization that provides money for an arts or sports event or for a broadcast in return for advertising ❷ someone who gives money to a charity in return for something achieved by another person

sponsor VERB to be a sponsor for a person or thing

spontaneous (say spon-**tay**-nee-us) ADJECTIVE happening or done naturally; not forced or suggested by someone else

spoof NOUN an amusing imitation of a film, television programme, etc.

spook NOUN (informal) a ghost

spooky ADJECTIVE (informal) strange and frightening; haunted by ghosts

spool NOUN a rod or cylinder on which something is wound

spoon NOUN a small device with a rounded bowl on a handle, used for lifting food to your mouth or for stirring or measuring things

spoon VERB to take or lift something with a spoon

spoonerism NOUN an accidental swapping round of the initial letters of two words, e.g. by saying a boiled sprat instead of a spoiled brat

spoon-feed VERB ❶ to feed a baby or invalid with a spoon ❷ to provide someone with so much help or information that they do not have to make any effort

spoonful NOUN as much as a spoon will hold

spoor NOUN the track left by an animal

sporadic ADJECTIVE happening or found at irregular intervals; scattered

spore NOUN a tiny reproductive cell of a plant such as a fungus or fern

sporran NOUN a pouch worn in front of a kilt

sport NOUN ❶ a game or activity that exercises your body, especially a game you play outdoors ❷ games of this kind ❸ (informal) a person who behaves well when they are defeated or teased

sport VERB ❶ to wear something in a showy way ❷ (old use) to play; to amuse yourself

sporting ADJECTIVE ❶ connected with sport; interested in sport ❷ behaving fairly and generously

sports car NOUN an open low-built fast car

sports jacket NOUN a man's jacket for informal wear (not part of a suit)

sportsman NOUN a man who takes part in sport

sportsmanship NOUN sporting behaviour; behaving fairly and generously to rivals

sportswoman NOUN a woman who takes part in sport

spot NOUN ❶ a small round mark ❷ a pimple on your skin ❸ a small amount of something ❹ a place ❺ a drop

spot VERB ❶ to notice or recognize someone or something ❷ to watch for certain things and take note of them, as a hobby

spot check NOUN a check, usually without warning, on one of a group of people or things

spotless ADJECTIVE perfectly clean

spotlight NOUN ❶ a strong light that can shine on one small area ❷ the centre of public attention

spotted ADJECTIVE marked or decorated with spots

spotty ADJECTIVE marked with spots

spouse NOUN a person's husband or wife

spout NOUN ❶ a pipe or similar opening from which liquid can pour ❷ a jet of liquid

spout VERB ❶ to come out as a jet of liquid ❷ (informal) to speak for a long time

sprain VERB to injure a joint by twisting it

sprain NOUN an injury by spraining

sprat NOUN a small edible fish

sprawl VERB ❶ to sit or lie with your arms and legs spread out loosely ❷ to spread out loosely or untidily

sprawl NOUN something that spreads over a large area in an untidy way

spray VERB to scatter tiny drops of liquid over something

spray NOUN ❶ tiny drops of liquid sent through the air ❷ a device for spraying liquid ❸ a liquid for spraying ❹ a single shoot with its leaves and flowers ❺ a small bunch of flowers

spread VERB spreads, spreading, spread ❶ to open or stretch something out to its full size ❷ to make something cover a surface ❸ to become longer or wider ❹ to become or make something more widely known or distributed

spread NOUN ❶ a paste for spreading on bread ❷ the action or result of spreading ❸ a thing's breadth or extent ❹ (informal) a large or grand meal

spreadeagled ADJECTIVE with arms and legs stretched out

spreadsheet NOUN a computer program that allows you to set out tables of figures and to do complex calculations

spree NOUN a short time you spend doing something you enjoy

sprig NOUN a small branch or shoot

sprightly ADJECTIVE lively and full of energy

spring VERB springs, springing, sprang, sprung ❶ to jump or move quickly or suddenly ❷ to grow or come from something

① to produce something without warning

spring NOUN **①** the season of the year when most plants begin to grow **②** a coil of wire or metal that goes back to its original shape when you bend or squeeze it and let it go **③** a sudden upward movement **④** a place where water comes up naturally from the ground

springboard NOUN a springy board from which people jump in diving and gymnastics

springbok NOUN a South African gazelle

spring-clean VERB to clean a house thoroughly in springtime

spring onion NOUN (British) a small onion with a long green stem, eaten raw in salads

spring roll NOUN a Chinese pancake filled with vegetables and (sometimes) meat and fried until crisp

springtime NOUN the season of spring

springy ADJECTIVE able to spring back easily after being bent or squeezed

sprinkle VERB to make tiny drops or pieces fall on something

sprinkling NOUN a few here and there; a small amount

sprint VERB to run very fast for a short distance

sprint NOUN a short fast race

sprite NOUN an elf, fairy or goblin

sprout VERB to start to grow; to put out shoots

sprout NOUN **①** a shoot of a plant **②** a Brussels sprout

spruce NOUN a kind of fir tree

spruce ADJECTIVE neat and smart

spruce VERB to smarten someone or something

spry ADJECTIVE active, nimble and lively

spud NOUN (informal) a potato

spur NOUN **①** a sharp device worn on the heel of a rider's boot to urge a horse to go faster **②** something shaped like a spur, such as a hard spike on the back of a cock's leg **③** something that encourages you to do something **④** a ridge that sticks out from a mountain

spur VERB **①** to urge someone on or encourage them to do something **②** to use spurs to make a horse go faster

spurn VERB to refuse to accept something

spurt VERB to gush out

spurt NOUN **①** a sudden gush **②** a sudden increase in speed or effort

sputter VERB **①** to make a quick series of spitting or popping sounds **②** to speak quickly and in a confused way

spy NOUN someone who works secretly for one country, person, etc. to find out things about another

spy VERB **①** to be a spy **②** to keep watch secretly **③** to see or notice something

squabble VERB to quarrel or bicker

squabble NOUN a minor quarrel or argument

squad NOUN a small group of people

working or being trained together

squadron NOUN part of an army, navy or air force

squalid ADJECTIVE dirty and unpleasant

squall NOUN ① a sudden storm or gust of wind ② a baby's loud cry

squall VERB a baby squalls when it cries loudly

squalor NOUN dirty and unpleasant conditions

squander VERB to spend money or time wastefully

square NOUN ① a flat shape with four equal sides and four right angles ② an area in a town or city, surrounded by buildings ③ the result of multiplying a number by itself

square ADJECTIVE ① having the shape of a square ② forming a right angle ③ equal or even ④ used to give the length of each side of a square shape or object ⑤ used to give a measurement of an area

square VERB ① to make a thing have straight edges and right angles ② to multiply a number by itself ③ to square with something is to match it or agree with it ④ to settle or pay a bill or debt

squarely ADVERB directly or exactly

square meal NOUN a good satisfying meal

square root NOUN the number that gives a particular number if it is multiplied by itself

squash VERB ① to press something so that it becomes flat or out of shape ② to force something into

a small space; to pack something tightly ③ to stop something from developing

squash NOUN ① a lot of people forced into a small space ② a fruit-flavoured soft drink ③ a game played with rackets and a soft ball in a special indoor court ④ a kind of gourd used as a vegetable

squat VERB ① to sit back on your heels; to crouch ② to live in an unoccupied building without permission

squat NOUN an unoccupied building that people are living in without permission

squat ADJECTIVE short and fat

squawk VERB to make a loud harsh cry

squawk NOUN a loud harsh cry

squeak VERB to make a short high-pitched cry or sound

squeak NOUN a short high-pitched cry or sound

squeal VERB to make a long shrill cry or sound

squeal NOUN a long shrill cry or sound

squeamish ADJECTIVE easily disgusted or shocked

squeeze VERB ① to press something from opposite sides, especially to get liquid out of it ② to force your way into or through a place

squeeze NOUN ① the action of squeezing ② a drop of liquid squeezed out ③ a tight fit ④ a time when money is difficult to get or borrow

squelch VERB to make a sound like someone treading in thick mud

squelch NOUN a squelching sound

squib NOUN a small firework that hisses and then explodes

squid NOUN a sea animal with eight short tentacles and two long ones

squiggle NOUN a short curly line

squint VERB ❶ to peer at something or look at it with half-shut eyes ❷ to have eyes that look in different directions at the same time

squint NOUN a fault in someone's eyesight that makes them squint

squire NOUN ❶ the man who owns most of the land in a country parish or district ❷ a young nobleman in the Middle Ages who served a knight

squirm VERB to wriggle about, especially when you feel embarrassed or awkward

squirrel NOUN a small animal with a bushy tail and red or grey fur, living in trees

squirt VERB to send liquid out in a jet or to come out like this

squirt NOUN a jet of liquid

St., St ABBREVIATION ❶ Saint ❷ Street

stab VERB to pierce or wound someone with something sharp

stab NOUN ❶ the action of stabbing ❷ a sudden sharp pain ❸ (informal) an attempt

stability NOUN being stable or steady

stabilize (also **stabilise**) VERB to make something stable or to become stable

stabilizer (also **stabiliser**) NOUN a device for keeping a vehicle or ship steady

stable ADJECTIVE ❶ steady and firmly fixed or balanced ❷ not likely to change or end suddenly ❸ sensible and dependable

stable NOUN a building where horses are kept

stable VERB to keep a horse in a stable

staccato ADVERB & ADJECTIVE (in music) played with each note short and separate

stack NOUN ❶ a neat pile ❷ a haystack ❸ (informal) a large amount ❹ a single tall chimney; a group of small chimneys

stack VERB to pile things up

stadium NOUN a sports ground surrounded by seats for spectators

staff NOUN ❶ the people who work in an office, shop, etc. ❷ the teachers in a school or college ❸ a stick or pole used as a weapon or support or as a symbol of authority ❹ a set of five horizontal lines on which music is written

staff VERB to provide a place or organization with a staff of people

stag NOUN a male deer

stage NOUN ❶ a platform for performances in a theatre or hall ❷ a point or part of a process or journey

stage VERB ❶ to present a performance on a stage ❷ to organize an event

stagecoach NOUN a horse-drawn coach of a kind that used to run regularly from one point to another along the same route

stage fright NOUN fear or nervousness before or while performing to an audience

stage-manage VERB ❶ to be stage manager of a performance ❷ to organize and control an event so that it has a particular effect

stage manager NOUN the person in charge of the scenery, lighting, sound, etc. during a stage performance

stagger VERB ❶ to walk unsteadily ❷ to amaze or shock someone ❸ to arrange things so that they do not all happen at the same time

staggering ADJECTIVE very surprising and almost unbelievable

stagnant ADJECTIVE ❶ not flowing ❷ not active or developing

staid ADJECTIVE steady and serious in manner

stain NOUN ❶ a dirty mark that is difficult to remove ❷ a blemish on someone's character or past record ❸ a liquid used for staining things

stain VERB ❶ to make a stain on something ❷ to colour material or wood with a liquid that sinks into the surface

stained glass NOUN pieces of coloured glass held together in a lead framework to make a picture or pattern

stainless ADJECTIVE without a stain

stainless steel NOUN steel that does not rust easily

stair NOUN each of the fixed steps in a series that lead from one level or floor to another in a building

staircase NOUN a set of stairs

stairway NOUN a staircase

stairwell NOUN the space going up through a building, which contains the stairs

stake NOUN ❶ a thick pointed stick to be driven into the ground ❷ the post to which people used to be tied for execution by being burnt alive ❸ an amount of money bet on something ❹ an investment that gives a person a share or interest in a business

stake VERB ❶ to fasten, support or mark something out with stakes ❷ to bet or risk money on an event

stalactite NOUN a stony spike hanging like an icicle from the roof of a cave

stalagmite NOUN a stony spike standing like a pillar on the floor of a cave

stale ADJECTIVE ❶ no longer fresh ❷ bored and lacking new ideas because you have been doing something for too long

stalemate NOUN ❶ a drawn position in chess when a player cannot make a move without putting the king in check ❷ a deadlock; a situation in which neither side in an argument will give way

stalk NOUN a stem of a plant or fruit

stalk VERB ❶ to track or hunt a person or animal stealthily ❷ to walk in a stiff or angry way

stall NOUN ❶ a table or counter from which things are sold ❷ a place for one animal in a stable or shed

stall VERB ❶ an engine or vehicle stalls when it stops suddenly because of lack of power ❷ to delay things or avoid giving an answer to give yourself more time

stallion NOUN a male horse

stalls PLURAL NOUN the seats in the lowest level of a theatre

stalwart ADJECTIVE strong and faithful

stamen NOUN the part of a flower that produces pollen

stamina NOUN the strength and energy you need to keep doing something for a long time

stammer VERB to keep repeating the same syllables when you speak

stammer NOUN a tendency to stammer

stamp NOUN ❶ a small piece of gummed paper with a special design on it; a postage stamp ❷ a small device for pressing words or marks on something; the words or marks made by this ❸ a distinctive characteristic

stamp VERB ❶ to bang your foot heavily on the ground ❷ to walk with loud heavy steps ❸ to stick a postage stamp on something ❹ to press a mark or design on something

stampede NOUN a sudden rush by animals or people

stampede VERB animals or people stampede when they rush fast and wildly

stance NOUN ❶ the way a person or animal stands ❷ a person's attitude to something

stand VERB stands, standing, stood ❶ to be on your feet without moving; to rise to your feet ❷ to put something in an upright position ❸ to be somewhere ❹ to stay there ❺ to be a candidate for election ❻ to be able to bear or tolerate something ❼ to provide

and pay for something

stand NOUN ❶ something made for putting things on ❷ a stall where things are sold or displayed ❸ a building at a sports ground with a roof and rows of seats for spectators ❹ a standing position ❺ when someone resists an attack or defends their opinion

standard NOUN ❶ how good something is ❷ a thing used to measure or judge something else ❸ a special flag

standard ADJECTIVE ❶ of the usual or average quality or kind ❷ regarded as the best and widely used

standard assessment task NOUN a standard test given to schoolchildren to assess their progress in one of the subjects of the national curriculum

Standard English NOUN the form of English widely accepted as the normal and correct form. It is taught in schools and spoken and written by educated people.

standardize (also **standardise**) VERB to make things be of a standard size or type

standard lamp NOUN (British) a lamp on an upright pole that stands on the floor

standard of living NOUN the level of comfort and wealth that a country or a person has

standby NOUN ❶ something or someone kept to be used if needed ❷ a system by which tickets for a play or an air flight can be bought cheaply at the last minute if there are any seats left

stand-in NOUN a deputy or substitute

standing NOUN ❶ a person's status or reputation ❷ the period for which something has existed

stand-offish ADJECTIVE cold and formal; not friendly

standpoint NOUN a way of thinking about something; a point of view

standstill NOUN a stop; an end to movement or activity

stanza NOUN a verse of poetry

staple NOUN ❶ a small piece of metal pushed through papers and clenched to fasten them together ❷ a U-shaped nail ❸ a basic or important food or product that people eat or use a lot

staple VERB to fasten pieces of paper together with a staple

staple ADJECTIVE main or usual

stapler NOUN a device for putting staples in paper

star NOUN ❶ a large mass of burning gas that is seen as a bright speck of light in the sky at night ❷ a shape with a number of points or rays sticking out from it; an asterisk ❸ an object or mark of this shape showing rank or quality ❹ a famous performer; one of the chief performers in a play, film or show

star VERB ❶ to be one of the main performers in a film or show ❷ to have someone as a main performer

starboard NOUN the right-hand side of a ship or aircraft when you are facing forward. Compare with port.

starch NOUN ❶ a white carbohydrate in bread, potatoes and other food ❷ a form of this substance used to stiffen clothes

starch VERB to stiffen something with starch

stardom NOUN being a star performer

stare VERB to look at something intensely

stare NOUN a long fixed look

starfish NOUN a sea animal shaped like a star with five points

stark ADJECTIVE ❶ complete or unmistakable ❷ desolate and bare

stark ADVERB completely or entirely

starling NOUN a noisy black or brown bird with speckled feathers

starred ADJECTIVE marked with an asterisk or star symbol

starry ADJECTIVE full of stars

starry-eyed ADJECTIVE made happy by foolish dreams or unrealistic hopes

start VERB ❶ to begin something or to make it begin ❷ to make an engine or machine begin running ❸ to begin a journey ❹ to make a sudden movement because of pain or surprise

start NOUN ❶ the beginning of something ❷ the place where a race starts ❸ an advantage that someone starts with ❹ a sudden movement of surprise or fear

starter NOUN ❶ a small amount of food served before the main course of a meal ❷ someone who starts a race

startle VERB to surprise or alarm a person or animal

starvation NOUN suffering or death

starve VERB ❶ to suffer or die from lack of food; to make someone do this ❷ to deprive someone of something they need

starving ADJECTIVE (*informal*) very hungry

stash VERB (*informal*) to store something safely in a secret place

state NOUN ❶ the quality of a person or thing or their circumstances; the way they are ❷ an organized community under one government or forming part of a republic ❸ a country's government ❹ (*informal*) an excited or upset condition

state VERB to say or write something clearly or formally

stately ADJECTIVE grand and dignified

stately home NOUN (*British*) a large and magnificent house belonging to an aristocratic family

statement NOUN ❶ words stating something ❷ a formal account of something that happened ❸ a printed report of a financial account

state school NOUN (*British*) a school which is funded by the government and which does not charge fees to pupils

statesman NOUN a person, especially a man, who is important or skilled in governing a country

stateswoman NOUN a woman who is important or skilled in governing a country

static ADJECTIVE not moving or changing

static electricity NOUN electricity that is present in something but does not flow as current

station NOUN ❶ a stopping place for trains or buses with platforms and buildings for passengers and goods ❷ a building equipped for people who serve the public or for certain activities ❸ a broadcasting company with its own frequency ❹ a place where a person stands ready to do something ❺ (*old use*) a person's position or rank ❻ (*Australian/NZ*) a large sheep or cattle farm

station VERB to put someone in a certain place for a purpose

stationary ADJECTIVE not moving

stationer NOUN a shopkeeper who sells stationery

stationery NOUN paper, envelopes, pens and other things used for writing

statistic NOUN a piece of information expressed as a number

statistics NOUN the study of information based on the numbers of things

statue NOUN a model made of stone or metal to look like a person or animal

statuette NOUN a small statue

stature NOUN ❶ a person's height ❷ the importance or reputation a person has because of their ability or achievements

status (say *stay*-tus) NOUN ❶ a person's or thing's position or rank in relation to others ❷ high rank or social position ❸ the category that a person or thing is put into ❹ a message on a social networking website that tells people what you are doing or thinking

status quo (say stay-tus **kwoh**) NOUN the state of affairs as it was before a change

status symbol NOUN something that you own because it shows off your wealth or position in society, rather than because you like it or need it

statute NOUN a law passed by a parliament

staunch ADJECTIVE firm and loyal

stave NOUN ❶ a set of five horizontal lines on which music is written ❷ each of the curved strips of wood forming the side of a cask or tub

stave VERB staves, staving, staved or stove to dent something or break a hole in it

stay VERB ❶ to continue to be in the same place or condition; to remain somewhere ❷ to spend time in a place as a visitor ❸ to keep something or someone back or in control

stay NOUN ❶ a time spent somewhere ❷ a postponement ❸ a support, especially a rope or wire holding up a mast or pole

stead NOUN ➤ in a person's or thing's stead instead of this person or thing ➤ stand a person in good stead to be very useful to someone

steadfast ADJECTIVE firm and not changing

steadily ADVERB in an even and regular way; gradually and continuously

steady ADJECTIVE ❶ not shaking or moving; firm ❷ regular or constant; continuing the same

steady VERB to make something steady or to become steady

steak NOUN a thick slice of meat (especially beef) or fish

steal VERB steals, stealing, stole, stolen ❶ to take and keep something that does not belong to you; to take something secretly or dishonestly ❷ to move secretly or without being noticed

stealth (say stelth) NOUN doing something in a quiet and secret way so that you are not noticed

stealthy (say stelth-ee) ADJECTIVE quiet and secret, so as not to be noticed

steam NOUN the gas or vapour that comes from boiling water; this used to drive machinery

steam VERB ❶ to give off steam ❷ to move somewhere by the power of steam ❸ to cook food with steam

steam engine NOUN an engine driven by steam

steamer NOUN ❶ a steamship ❷ a container in which things are steamed

steamroller NOUN a heavy vehicle with a large roller used to flatten surfaces when making roads

steamship NOUN a ship driven by steam

steed NOUN (old or poetical use) a horse

steel NOUN ❶ a strong metal made from iron and carbon ❷ a steel rod for sharpening knives

steel VERB ► **steel yourself** to find courage to face something difficult

steel band NOUN a West Indian band of musicians who play instruments made from oil drums

steel wool NOUN a mass of fine, sharp steel threads used for cleaning a surface or rubbing it smooth

steely ADJECTIVE ❶ like or to do with steel ❷ cold, hard and severe

steep ADJECTIVE ❶ sloping very sharply, not gradually ❷ (*informal*) unreasonably high

steep VERB to soak something thoroughly

steepen VERB to become steeper

steeple NOUN a church tower with a spire on top

steeplechase NOUN a race across country or over hedges or fences

steeplejack NOUN a person who climbs tall chimneys or steeples to do repairs

steer VERB to make a car, ship or bicycle etc. go in the direction you want; to guide something

steer NOUN a young castrated bull kept for its beef

steering wheel NOUN a wheel for steering a vehicle

stellar ADJECTIVE to do with a star or stars

stem NOUN ❶ the main central part of a tree, shrub or plant ❷ a thin part on which a leaf, flower or fruit is supported ❸ a thin upright part, e.g. the thin part of a wine glass between the bowl and the foot ❹ (*in grammar*) the main part

of a verb or other word, to which endings are attached

stem VERB to stop the flow of something

stench NOUN a very unpleasant smell

stencil NOUN a piece of card, metal or plastic with pieces cut out of it, used to produce a picture or design

stencil VERB to produce or decorate something with a stencil

step NOUN ❶ a movement made by lifting the foot and setting it down ❷ the sound of a person putting down their foot when walking or running ❸ each of the level surfaces on a stair or ladder for placing the foot ❹ each of a series of things done in some process or action

step VERB to tread or walk

stepbrother NOUN the son of one of your parents from an earlier or later marriage

stepchild NOUN a child that a person's husband or wife has from an earlier marriage

stepfather NOUN a man who is married to your mother but was not your natural father

stepladder NOUN a folding ladder with flat treads

stepmother NOUN a woman who is married to your father but was not your natural mother

steppe NOUN a grassy plain with few trees, especially in Russia

stepping stone NOUN ❶ each of a line of stones put into a shallow stream so that people can walk across ❷ a way of achieving something or a stage in achieving it

steps PLURAL NOUN a stepladder

stepsister NOUN the daughter of one of your parents from an earlier or later marriage

stereo ADJECTIVE stereophonic

stereo NOUN ❶ stereophonic sound or recording ❷ a stereophonic CD player, record player, etc.

stereophonic ADJECTIVE using sound that comes from two different directions to give a natural effect

stereotype NOUN a fixed image or idea of a type of person or thing that is widely held

sterile ADJECTIVE ❶ clean and free from germs ❷ not able to have children or reproduce

sterilize (also **sterilise**) VERB ❶ to make a thing free from germs, e.g. by heating it ❷ to make a person or animal unable to reproduce

sterling NOUN British money

sterling ADJECTIVE ❶ genuine ❷ excellent; of great worth

stern ADJECTIVE strict and severe; not smiling

stern NOUN the back part of a ship

steroid NOUN a substance of a kind that includes certain hormones and other natural secretions

stethoscope NOUN a device used by doctors for listening to sounds in a person's body, e.g. heartbeats and breathing

stew VERB to cook food slowly in liquid

stew NOUN a dish of meat and vegetables cooked slowly in liquid

steward NOUN ❶ a man whose job is to look after the passengers on a ship or aircraft ❷ an official who keeps order or looks after the arrangements at a large public event

stewardess NOUN a woman whose job is to look after the passengers on a ship or aircraft

stick NOUN ❶ a long thin piece of wood ❷ a walking stick ❸ the implement used to hit the ball in hockey, polo or other games ❹ a long thin piece of something

stick VERB sticks, sticking, stuck ❶ to push a thing into something ❷ to fix something by glue or as if by glue ❸ to become fixed and unable to move ❹ (informal) to bear something or put up with it

sticker NOUN a sticky label or sign for sticking on something

sticking plaster NOUN (British) a strip of sticky material for covering cuts

stick insect NOUN an insect with a long thin body and legs, which looks like a twig

stickleback NOUN a small fish with sharp spines on its back

stickler NOUN a person who insists on something

sticky ADJECTIVE ❶ able or likely to stick to things ❷ sticky weather is hot and humid, causing perspiration ❸ (informal) difficult or awkward

stiff ADJECTIVE ❶ not bending, moving or changing its shape easily ❷ not able to move or bend the body easily ❸ thick and hard to stir ❹ difficult ❺ formal in manner; not friendly ❻ severe or strong

stiffen VERB to become stiff or to make something stiff

stifle VERB ❶ to stop something happening or developing ❷ to make it difficult for someone to breathe because of heat or lack of fresh air

stigma NOUN ❶ a mark of disgrace; a stain on a reputation ❷ the part of a pistil that receives the pollen in pollination

stile NOUN an arrangement of steps or bars for people to climb over a fence

stiletto NOUN a dagger with a narrow blade

stiletto heel NOUN a high pointed shoe heel

still ADJECTIVE ❶ not moving ❷ silent ❸ not fizzy

still ADVERB ❶ without moving ❷ up to this or that time ❸ in a greater amount or degree ❹ nevertheless

still VERB to make something still

still NOUN ❶ a photograph of a scene from a cinema film ❷ an apparatus for distilling alcohol or other liquid

stillborn ADJECTIVE born dead

still life NOUN a painting of an arrangement of objects, especially fruit, flowers or ornaments

stilted ADJECTIVE stiffly formal

stilts PLURAL NOUN ❶ a pair of poles with supports for the feet so that the user can walk high above the ground ❷ posts for supporting a house built above marshy ground

stimulant NOUN a drug or substance that makes you feel more awake and active for a while

stimulate VERB ❶ to make someone excited or enthusiastic ❷ to encourage something to develop

stimulus NOUN stimuli something that encourages a thing to develop or produces a reaction

sting NOUN ❶ a sharp-pointed part of an animal or plant, often containing a poison, that can cause a wound ❷ a painful wound caused by this part

sting VERB stings, stinging, stung ❶ to wound or hurt someone with a sting ❷ to feel a sharp pain ❸ to make someone feel upset or hurt ❹ (informal) to cheat someone by charging them too much

stingray NOUN a fish with a flat body, fins like wings and a poisonous spine in its tail

stingy (say stin-jee) ADJECTIVE mean, not generous; giving or given in small amounts

stink NOUN ❶ an unpleasant smell ❷ (informal) an unpleasant fuss or protest

stink VERB stinks, stinking, stank or stunk to have an unpleasant smell

stint NOUN a fixed amount of work to be done

stint VERB to stint on something is to be sparing with it and not use much

stipulate VERB to insist on something as part of an agreement

stir VERB ❶ to mix a liquid or soft mixture by moving a spoon etc. round and round in it ❷ to move slightly or start to move after sleeping or being still ❸ to make someone feel a strong emotion

stir NOUN ❶ the action of stirring ❷ strong public feeling or excitement

stir-fry VERB to cook something by frying it quickly over a high heat while stirring and tossing it

stir-fry NOUN a dish cooked by stir-frying

stirring ADJECTIVE making people feel strong emotion

stirrup NOUN a metal part that hangs from each side of a horse's saddle and supports the rider's foot

stitch NOUN ❶ a loop of thread made in sewing or knitting ❷ a method of arranging the threads ❸ a sudden sharp pain in your side, caused by running

stitch VERB to sew or fasten something with stitches

stoat NOUN a kind of weasel, also called an ermine

stock NOUN ❶ a number of things kept ready to be sold or used ❷ farm animals; livestock ❸ the line of a person's ancestors ❹ a liquid used in cooking, made from the juices you get by stewing meat, fish or vegetables ❺ a number of shares in a company's capital ❻ the main stem of a tree or plant ❼ the base, holder or handle of an implement or weapon ❽ a garden flower with a sweet smell

stock VERB ❶ to keep a supply of goods to sell ❷ to provide a place with a stock of something

stockade NOUN a fence made of stakes

stockbroker NOUN a person who buys and sells stocks and shares for clients

stock car NOUN an ordinary car strengthened for use in races where deliberate bumping is allowed

stock exchange NOUN a country's central place for buying and selling stocks and shares

stocking NOUN a piece of clothing covering the foot and part or all of the leg

stock market NOUN ❶ a stock exchange ❷ the buying and selling of stocks and shares

stockpile NOUN a large stock of things kept in reserve

stocks PLURAL NOUN a wooden framework with holes for a seated person's legs, in which criminals were locked as a punishment

stocktaking NOUN the counting, listing and checking of the amount of stock held by a shop or business

stocky ADJECTIVE short and solidly built

stodgy ADJECTIVE (British) ❶ stodgy food is heavy and filling ❷ dull and boring

stoke VERB to put fuel in a furnace or on a fire

stole past tense of **steal**

stole NOUN a wide piece of material worn round the shoulders by women

stomach NOUN ❶ the part of your body where food starts to be digested ❷ the front part of your body that contains your stomach; your abdomen

stomach VERB ① to tolerate something or put up with it

stone NOUN ① a piece of rock ② stones or rock as material, e.g. for building ③ a jewel ④ the hard case round the kernel of plums, cherries, peaches, etc. ⑤ a unit of weight equal to 14 pounds (6.35 kg)

stone VERB ① to throw stones at someone ② to remove the stones from fruit

Stone Age NOUN the earliest period of human history, when tools and weapons were made of stone

stone circle NOUN a circle of large stones or boulders, put up in prehistoric times

stone-cold ADJECTIVE extremely cold

stoned ADJECTIVE (informal) under the influence of drugs or alcohol

stone-deaf ADJECTIVE completely deaf

stony ADJECTIVE ① full of stones ② hard like stone ③ unfriendly and not answering

stooge NOUN (informal) ① a comedian's assistant, used as a target for jokes ② an assistant who does dull or routine work

stool NOUN ① a movable seat without arms or a back ② a lump of faeces

stoop VERB ① to bend your body forwards and down ② to lower your standards of behaviour

stoop NOUN ① a way of standing or walking with your head and shoulders bent forwards ② (North American & S. African) a porch, small verandah or set of steps in front of a house

stop VERB ① to come to an end or bring something to an end; to no longer do something ② to be no longer moving or working ③ to prevent something happening or continuing ④ to fill a hole or gap ⑤ to stay somewhere for a short time

stop NOUN ① stopping; a pause or end ② a place where a bus or train regularly stops ③ a lever or knob that controls pitch in a wind instrument or allows organ pipes to sound

stopcock NOUN a valve controlling the flow of liquid or gas in a pipe

stoppage NOUN ① an interruption in the work of a factory or business ② a break in play during a game ③ a blockage in something

stopper NOUN a plug for closing a bottle or sealing a hole

stopwatch NOUN a watch that can be started and stopped when you wish, used for timing races

storage NOUN the storing of things

store NOUN ① a supply of things kept for future use ② a place where things are kept until they are needed ③ a shop, especially a large one ④ (North American) any shop

store VERB to keep things until they are needed

storey NOUN one whole floor of a building

stork NOUN a large bird with long legs and a long beak

storm NOUN ① a period of bad

weather with strong winds, rain or snow and often thunder and lightning **2** a violent attack or outburst

storm VERB **1** to move or behave violently or angrily **2** to suddenly attack and capture a place

stormy ADJECTIVE **1** having a storm or a lot of storms **2** loud and angry

story NOUN **1** an account of a real or imaginary event **2** the plot of a novel, play or film **3** (*informal*) a lie

stout ADJECTIVE **1** rather fat **2** thick and strong **3** brave and determined

stout NOUN a kind of dark beer

stove NOUN **1** a device containing an oven or ovens **2** a device for heating a room

stove VERB past tense of stave

stow VERB to pack or store something away

stowaway NOUN someone who stows away on a ship or aircraft

straddle VERB **1** to sit or stand with your legs either side of something **2** to be built across something

straggle VERB **1** to grow or spread in an untidy way **2** to walk too slowly and not keep up with the rest of a group

straight ADJECTIVE **1** going continuously in one direction; not curving or bending **2** level, horizontal or upright **3** tidy; in proper order **4** honest and frank

straight ADVERB **1** in a straight line or manner **2** directly; without delay

straightaway, straight away ADVERB immediately; at once

straighten VERB **1** to make something straight **2** to become straight; to stand up straight

straightforward ADJECTIVE **1** easy to understand or do, not complicated **2** honest and frank

strain VERB **1** to injure a part of your body by stretching or using it too much **2** to put a lot of pressure on something **3** to stretch something tightly **4** to make a great effort **5** to put something through a sieve or filter to separate liquid from solid matter

strain NOUN **1** the process or force of straining **2** an injury caused by straining **3** the effect on someone of too much work or worry **4** something that uses up strength, patience or resources **5** a part of a tune **6** a breed or variety of an animal, plant, etc.; a line of descent **7** an inherited characteristic

strainer NOUN a device for straining liquids

strait NOUN a narrow stretch of water connecting two seas

straitened ADJECTIVE > in straitened circumstances short of money

straitjacket NOUN a strong jacket-like piece of clothing put round a violent person to tie their arms

strait-laced ADJECTIVE very prim and proper

straits PLURAL NOUN a strait

strand NOUN **1** each of the threads

or wires twisted together to form a rope, yarn or cable ② a single thread or hair ③ an idea, theme or story that forms part of a whole

stranded ADJECTIVE ① left on sand or rocks in shallow water ② left in a difficult or lonely position

strange ADJECTIVE ① unusual or surprising ② not known or seen or experienced before

strangely ADVERB in a strange way

stranger NOUN ① a person you do not know ② a person who is in a place that they do not know

strangle VERB ① to kill someone by squeezing their throat to prevent them breathing ② to restrict something so that it does not develop

strangulation NOUN killing someone by strangling them

strap NOUN a flat strip of leather, cloth or plastic for fastening things or holding them in place

strap VERB to fasten or bind something with a strap or straps

strapping ADJECTIVE tall and healthy-looking

strata plural of **stratum**

stratagem NOUN a cunning method of achieving something; a plan or trick

strategic ADJECTIVE ① to do with strategy ② giving you an advantage

strategist NOUN an expert in strategy

strategy NOUN ① a plan or policy to achieve something ② the planning of a war or campaign. Compare with **tactics**.

stratosphere NOUN a layer of the atmosphere between about 10 and 60 kilometres above the earth's surface

stratum (say **strah**-tum) NOUN strata a layer or level

straw NOUN ① dry cut stalks of corn ② a narrow tube for drinking through

strawberry NOUN a small red juicy fruit, with its seeds on the outside

stray VERB to leave a group or proper place and wander; to become lost

stray ADJECTIVE ① that has strayed; wandering around lost ② found on its own, separated from the others

stray NOUN a stray dog or cat

streak NOUN ① a long thin line or mark ② a trace or sign of something ③ a spell of success or good fortune

streak VERB ① to mark something with streaks ② to move very quickly ③ to run naked in a public place for fun or to get attention

streaky bacon NOUN (British) bacon with alternate strips of lean and fat

stream NOUN ① water flowing in a channel; a brook or small river ② liquid flowing in one direction ③ a number of things moving in the same direction, such as traffic ④ a group in which children of similar ability are placed in a school

stream VERB ① to move in a strong fast flow ② to produce a stream of liquid ③ to arrange schoolchildren in streams according to their ability

streamer NOUN ① a long narrow ribbon or strip of paper

streamline VERB ① to give something a smooth shape that helps it to move easily through air or water ② to organize something so that it works more efficiently

street NOUN a road with houses beside it in a city or village

strength NOUN ① how strong a person or thing is; being strong ② an ability or good quality

strengthen VERB to become stronger or to make something stronger

strenuous ADJECTIVE needing or using great effort

stress NOUN ① a force that presses, pulls or twists something ② emphasis, especially the extra force with which you pronounce part of a word or phrase ③ worry and pressure caused by having too many problems or too much to do

stress VERB ① to pronounce part of a word or phrase with extra emphasis ② to emphasize a point or idea ③ to make someone suffer stress

stressed ADJECTIVE too anxious and tired to be able to relax

stressful ADJECTIVE causing worry and pressure

stretch VERB ① to pull something or be pulled so that it becomes longer or wider or larger ② to extend or be continuous ③ to push out your arms and legs as far as you can ④ to make use of all your ability or intelligence

stretch NOUN ① the action of stretching ② a continuous period of time or area of land or water

stretcher NOUN a framework for carrying a sick or injured person

strew VERB strews, strewing, strewed, strewn or strewed to scatter things over a surface

stricken ADJECTIVE overcome or strongly affected by an illness or a feeling such as grief or fear

strict ADJECTIVE ① demanding that people obey rules and behave well ② complete or exact

strictly ADVERB completely or exactly

stride VERB strides, striding, strode, stridden to walk with long steps

stride NOUN ① a long step when walking or running ② a step that helps you make progress

strident (say stry-dent) ADJECTIVE loud and harsh

strife NOUN conflict; fighting or quarrelling

strike VERB strikes, striking, struck ① to hit a person or thing ② to attack or afflict people suddenly ③ to make an impression on someone's mind ④ to light a match by rubbing it against a rough surface ⑤ to refuse to work as a protest against pay or conditions ⑥ to produce coins or medals by pressing or stamping metal ⑦ to sound or ring a number of times ⑧ to find gold or oil by digging or drilling ⑨ to go in a certain direction

strike NOUN ① a hit ② a military attack ③ refusing to work as a way

a b c d e f g h i j k l m n o p q r s t u v w x y z

A of making a protest ❹ a sudden
discovery of gold or oil

B **striker** NOUN ❶ a worker who is on
strike ❷ a football player whose

C main job is to try to score goals

D **striking** ADJECTIVE ❶ impressive
or attractive ❷ so unusual or

E interesting that you cannot help
noticing it

F **string** NOUN ❶ thin cord made of
twisted threads, used to fasten or

G tie things; a piece of this or similar

H material ❷ a piece of wire or cord
stretched and vibrated to produce

I sounds in a musical instrument
❸ a line or series of things

J
string VERB strings, stringing,

K strung ❶ to hang something on
a string ❷ to fit something with a

L string ❸ to thread pearls or beads
on a string ❹ to remove the tough

M fibre from beans

N **stringed** ADJECTIVE stringed
instruments are ones that have

O strings, especially members of the
violin family

P **stringent** (say **strin**-jent) ADJECTIVE

Q strict and precise

strings PLURAL NOUN the stringed

R instruments of an orchestra

S **stringy** ADJECTIVE ❶ long and thin,
like string ❷ containing tough

T fibres

strip VERB ❶ to take a covering or

U layer off something ❷ to undress

V ❸ to take something away from
someone as a punishment

W **strip** NOUN ❶ a long narrow piece

X or area ❷ the distinctive clothes
worn by a sports team while

Y playing

Z **strip cartoon** NOUN a series of

drawings telling a story

stripe NOUN ❶ a long narrow band
of colour ❷ a strip of cloth worn
on the sleeve of a uniform to show
the wearer's rank

striped, stripy ADJECTIVE marked
with a pattern of stripes

strip light NOUN (British) a
fluorescent lamp in the form of
a tube

stripling NOUN a youth

stripper NOUN ❶ a tool or
substance used for stripping
paint ❷ a person who performs
striptease

striptease NOUN an entertainment
in which a person slowly undresses

strive VERB strives, striving, strove,
striven ❶ to try hard to do or get
something

strobe NOUN (short for
stroboscope) a light that flashes
on and off continuously

stroke NOUN ❶ a movement of
the arm when hitting something,
swimming or rowing ❷ a style
of swimming ❸ a movement you
make when you are writing or
painting ❹ an action or effort
❺ the sound made by a clock
striking ❻ a sudden illness that
often causes paralysis ❼ an act of
stroking something

stroke VERB to move your hand
gently along something

stroll VERB to walk in a leisurely way

stroll NOUN a short leisurely walk

strong ADJECTIVE ❶ having great
power, energy or effect ❷ not
easy to break, damage or defeat
❸ great in intensity ❹ having a

lot of flavour or smell ⑤ having a
certain number of members

strong ADVERB ➤ be going strong
to be making good progress

stronghold NOUN ① a fortified
place ② an area where many
people live or think in a particular
way

strongly ADVERB ① in a strong way;
with strength ② very much

strong point NOUN a strength;
something that you are very
good at

strongroom NOUN a room designed
to protect valuable things from fire
and theft

strontium NOUN a soft silvery
metal

strove past tense of strive

structural ADJECTIVE to do with
the way that something is built or
constructed

structure NOUN ① something
that has been constructed or
built ② the way something is
constructed or organized

structure VERB to organize or
arrange something into a system
or pattern

struggle VERB ① to move your
arms and legs and wriggle fiercely
in trying to get free ② to try very
hard to do something difficult
③ to try to overcome an opponent
or a problem

struggle NOUN ① the act of
struggling ② a hard fight or great
effort

strum VERB to sound a guitar by
running your fingers across its
strings

strut VERB to walk proudly or stiffly

strut NOUN ① a bar of wood
or metal that strengthens a
framework ② a strutting walk

strychnine (say **strik**-neen) NOUN a
bitter poisonous substance

stub NOUN ① a short stump left
when the rest has been used
or worn down ② the part of a
ticket or cheque that you keep as
a record

stub VERB to bump your toe
painfully

stubble NOUN ① the short stalks
of corn left in the ground after
the harvest is cut ② short hairs
growing on a man's chin when he
has not shaved

stubborn ADJECTIVE ① determined
not to change your ideas or ways;
obstinate ② difficult to remove
or deal with

stucco NOUN plaster or cement
used for coating walls and ceilings,
often moulded into decorations

stuck past tense and past
participle of stick

stuck ADJECTIVE unable to move or
make progress

stuck-up ADJECTIVE (informal)
conceited or snobbish

stud NOUN ① a small curved
lump or knob ② a device like a
button on a stalk, used to fasten
a detachable collar to a shirt
③ a number of horses kept for
breeding; the place where they are
kept ④ a stallion

studded ADJECTIVE ① covered
with studs or other decorations
② scattered or sprinkled with
something

student NOUN a person who studies a subject, especially at a college or university

studied ADJECTIVE not natural but done with deliberate effort

studio NOUN ❶ the room where an artist or photographer works ❷ a place where cinema films are made ❸ a room from which radio or television broadcasts are made or recorded

studious ADJECTIVE spending a lot of time studying or reading

study VERB ❶ to spend time learning about something ❷ to look at something carefully

study NOUN ❶ the process of studying ❷ a subject studied; a piece of research ❸ a room used for studying or writing ❹ a piece of music for playing as an exercise ❺ a drawing done for practice or in preparation for another work

stuff NOUN ❶ a substance or material ❷ a group of things or belongings

stuff VERB ❶ to fill something tightly ❷ to fill something with stuffing ❸ to push a thing roughly into something ❹ (informal) to eat greedily

stuffing NOUN ❶ material used to fill the inside of something ❷ a savoury mixture put into meat or poultry before cooking

stuffy ADJECTIVE ❶ a stuffy room is badly ventilated, without enough fresh air ❷ with blocked breathing passages ❸ formal and boring

stumble VERB ❶ to trip and lose your balance ❷ to make a mistake or hesitate while you are speaking

or doing something

stumbling block NOUN an obstacle; something that causes difficulty

stump NOUN ❶ the bottom of a tree trunk left in the ground when the rest has fallen or been cut down ❷ something left when the main part is cut off or worn down ❸ each of the three upright sticks of a wicket in cricket

stump VERB ❶ to be too difficult or puzzling for someone ❷ to walk stiffly or noisily ❸ in cricket, to stump the person batting is to get them out by knocking the bails off the stumps while the person is standing out of the crease

stumpy ADJECTIVE short and thick

stun VERB ❶ to knock a person unconscious ❷ to daze or shock someone

stunning ADJECTIVE extremely beautiful or attractive

stunt NOUN ❶ something daring done as a performance or as part of the action of a film ❷ something unusual done to attract attention

stunt VERB to prevent a thing from growing or developing normally

stupendous ADJECTIVE amazing or tremendous

stupid ADJECTIVE ❶ not clever or thoughtful ❷ without reason or common sense

stupor (say stew-per) NOUN a state of being dazed or only partly conscious

sturdy ADJECTIVE strong and solid

sturgeon NOUN a large edible fish

stutter VERB to keep repeating the sounds at the beginning of words

stutter NOUN a tendency to stutter

sty NOUN ❶ a pigsty ❷ (also **stye**) a sore swelling on an eyelid

style NOUN ❶ the way something is done, made, said or written ❷ fashion or elegance ❸ the part of a pistil that supports the stigma in a plant

style VERB to design or arrange something, especially in a fashionable style

stylish ADJECTIVE fashionable and elegant

stylistic ADJECTIVE to do with the style of something

stylus NOUN the device like a needle that travels in the grooves of a record to produce the sound

suave (say swahv) ADJECTIVE polite in a charming and confident way

sub NOUN (informal) ❶ a submarine ❷ a subscription ❸ a substitute

sub-aqua ADJECTIVE to do with underwater sports, such as diving

subatomic ADJECTIVE ❶ smaller than an atom ❷ forming part of an atom

subconscious ADJECTIVE to do with mental processes of which we are not fully aware but which influence our actions

subconscious NOUN the hidden part of your mind that influences your actions without you being fully aware of it

subcontinent NOUN a large mass of land that forms part of a continent

subcontractor NOUN a person

or company hired by another company to do a particular part of their work

subdivide VERB to divide something again or into smaller parts

subdue VERB ❶ to overcome someone or bring them under control ❷ to make a person or animal quieter or gentler

subject NOUN ❶ the person or thing being talked or written about or dealt with ❷ something that is studied ❸ (in grammar) the word or words naming who or what does the action of a verb, e.g. 'The book' in The book fell off the table. ❹ someone who is ruled by a monarch or government

subject ADJECTIVE ruled by a monarch or government; not independent

subject (say sub-jekt) VERB ❶ to make a person or thing undergo something ❷ to bring a country under your control

subjective ADJECTIVE ❶ based on a person's own tastes, feelings or opinions. Compare with **objective**. ❷ existing only in a person's mind and not produced by things outside it

subjunctive NOUN the form of a verb used to indicate what is imagined or wished or possible. There are only a few cases where it is commonly used in English, e.g. 'were' in if I were you and 'save' in God save the Queen.

sublime ADJECTIVE ❶ noble or impressive ❷ extreme; not caring about the consequences

submarine NOUN a ship that can

611

travel under water

submarine ADJECTIVE under the sea

submerge VERB ❶ to go under water or to put something under water

submission NOUN ❶ submitting to someone ❷ something that you submit or offer for consideration

submissive ADJECTIVE willing to obey

submit VERB ❶ to give in to someone or agree to obey them ❷ to hand something in or offer it to be judged or considered

subordinate ADJECTIVE ❶ less important ❷ lower in rank

subordinate NOUN a person working under someone's authority or control

subordinate VERB to treat something as being less important than another thing

subordinate clause NOUN a clause which adds details to the main clause of the sentence, but cannot be used as a sentence by itself

sub-plot NOUN a secondary plot in a play, film or novel

subpoena (say sub-**peen**-a) NOUN an official document ordering a person to appear in a law court

subpoena VERB to summon someone by a subpoena

subscribe VERB ❶ to make a regular payment in order to be a member of a society or to receive a magazine or other service ❷ to apply to take part in something ❸ to contribute money to a project or charity ❹ to say that you agree with something

subscription NOUN money you pay

to subscribe to something

subsequent ADJECTIVE coming after something in time or order; later

subservient ADJECTIVE prepared to obey others without question

subside VERB ❶ to begin to sink into the ground ❷ to become less intense or quieter

subsidence (say sub-**sy**-dens or **sub**-sid-ens) NOUN the gradual sinking or caving in of an area of land

subsidiary less important; secondary

subsidiary NOUN a business company that is controlled by another larger company

subsidize (also **subsidise**) VERB to pay a subsidy to a person or firm

subsidy NOUN money paid to an industry that needs help or to keep down the price at which its goods or services are sold to the public

subsist VERB to manage to live with very little food or money

subsoil NOUN soil lying just below the surface layer

substance NOUN ❶ a solid or liquid material; what something is made of ❷ the main or essential part of something

substantial ADJECTIVE ❶ of great size, value or importance ❷ solidly built

substantially ADVERB mostly

substation NOUN a subsidiary station for distributing electric current

substitute NOUN a person or thing that acts or is used instead of another

substitute *VERB* to substitute one thing or person for another is to use the first one instead of the second

subterfuge *NOUN* a deception

subterranean *ADJECTIVE* underground

subtitle *NOUN* ❶ a secondary or additional title ❷ words shown on the screen during a film, e.g. to translate a foreign language

subtle (say **sut**-el) *ADJECTIVE* ❶ faint or delicate ❷ slight and difficult to detect or describe ❸ ingenious but not immediately obvious

subtotal *NOUN* the total of part of a group of figures

subtract *VERB* to subtract one number or amount from another is to take it away

subtraction *NOUN* the process of taking one number or amount from another

subtropical *ADJECTIVE* of regions that border on the tropics

suburb *NOUN* a district with houses that is outside the central part of a city

suburbia *NOUN* the suburbs of a city and the people who live there

subvert *VERB* to try to destroy or weaken something by attacking it secretly and in an indirect way

subway *NOUN* ❶ an underground passage for pedestrians ❷ (*North American*) an underground railway

succeed *VERB* ❶ to do or get what you wanted or intended ❷ to come after another person or thing ❸ to become the next holder of an office, especially the monarchy

success *NOUN* ❶ doing or getting what you wanted or intended ❷ a person or thing that does well

successful *ADJECTIVE* having success or being a success

succession *NOUN* ❶ a series of people or things following in order ❷ the process of following in order ❸ succeeding to the throne; the right of doing this

successive *ADJECTIVE* following one after another

successor *NOUN* a person or thing that comes after another and takes their place

succinct (say suk-**sinkt**) *ADJECTIVE* concise; expressed briefly

succulent *ADJECTIVE* ❶ juicy and tasty ❷ succulent plants have thick juicy leaves or stems

succumb (say suk-**um**) *VERB* to give way to something overpowering

such *DETERMINER* ❶ of the same kind; similar ❷ of the kind described ❸ so great or so much

such-and-such *DETERMINER* one in particular but you are not saying which

suchlike *PRONOUN* of that kind

suck *VERB* ❶ to take in liquid or air through almost-closed lips ❷ to squeeze something in your mouth by using your tongue ❸ to draw something in

suck *NOUN* the action of sucking

sucker *NOUN* ❶ a rubber or plastic cup that sticks to a surface by suction ❷ an organ on the body of an animal or insect that it uses to cling to a surface by suction ❸ a shoot coming up from a root or underground stem ❹ (*informal*) a

a b c d e f g h i j k l m n o p q r s t u v w x y z

person who is easily deceived

suckle VERB to feed on milk at the mother's breast or udder

sucrose NOUN the form of sugar that is obtained from sugar cane and sugar beet

suction NOUN ① the process of sucking ② producing a vacuum so that things are sucked into the empty space

sudden ADJECTIVE happening or done quickly and without warning

suddenly ADVERB quickly and without warning

sudoku (say soo-**doh**-koo) NOUN a puzzle in which you have to write the numbers 1 to 9 in a particular pattern in a grid of 81 squares

suds PLURAL NOUN froth on soapy water

sue VERB to start a lawsuit to claim money from someone

suede (say swayd) NOUN leather with one side rubbed to make it soft and velvety

suet NOUN hard fat from cattle and sheep, used in cooking

suffer VERB ① to feel pain or sadness ② to experience something bad ③ to become worse or be badly affected

sufferance NOUN ➤ on sufferance allowed but only reluctantly

suffering NOUN pain or misery

suffice VERB to be enough for someone's needs

sufficient ADJECTIVE enough; as much as is necessary

suffix NOUN a letter or set of letters joined to the end of a word

to make another word (e.g. in forget*ful*, lion*ess*, rust*y*) or a form of a verb (e.g. sing*ing*, wait*ed*)

suffocate VERB ① to suffer or die because you cannot breathe ② to make it difficult or impossible for someone to breathe

suffrage NOUN the right to vote in political elections

suffragette NOUN a woman who campaigned in the early 20th century for women to have the right to vote

suffuse VERB to spread through or over something

sugar NOUN a sweet food obtained from the juices of various plants, such as sugar cane or sugar beet

sugar VERB to add sugar to food or drink

suggest VERB ① to put forward an idea or plan for someone to consider ② to make an idea or possibility come into your mind

suggestion NOUN ① something that you mention to someone as an idea or possibility ② a slight amount or sign of something

suggestive ADJECTIVE making you think of something

suicide NOUN ① killing yourself deliberately ② a person who deliberately kills himself or herself

suit NOUN ① a matching jacket and trousers or a jacket and skirt, that are meant to be worn together ② a set of clothing for a particular activity ③ any of the four sets of cards (clubs, hearts, diamonds, spades) in a pack of playing cards ④ a lawsuit

suit VERB ❶ to be suitable or convenient for a person or thing ❷ a piece of clothing or hairstyle suits you when it looks good on you

suitable ADJECTIVE satisfactory or right for a particular person, purpose or occasion

suitcase NOUN a rectangular container for carrying clothes, usually with a hinged lid and a handle

suite (say sweet) NOUN ❶ a set of matching furniture ❷ a set of rooms in a hotel ❸ a set of short pieces of music

suitor NOUN a man who is courting a woman

sulk VERB to be silent and bad-tempered because you are not pleased

sulk NOUN a period of sulking

sulky ADJECTIVE silent and bad-tempered because you are not pleased

sullen ADJECTIVE sulking and gloomy

sully VERB to stain or spoil something; to blemish something

sulphur NOUN a yellow chemical used in industry and in medicine

sulphuric acid NOUN a strong colourless acid containing sulphur

sultan NOUN the ruler of certain Muslim countries

sultana NOUN a raisin without seeds

sultry ADJECTIVE hot and humid

sum NOUN ❶ a total ❷ a problem in arithmetic ❸ an amount of money

sum VERB ➤ **sum up** to give a summary at the end of a talk or discussion

summarize (also **summarise**) VERB to make or give a summary of something

summary NOUN a statement of the main points of something said or written

summary ADJECTIVE ❶ brief or concise ❷ done or given hastily, without delay

summer NOUN the warm season between spring and autumn

summer house NOUN a small building providing shade in a garden or park

summertime NOUN the season of summer

summit NOUN ❶ the top of a mountain or hill ❷ a meeting between the leaders of powerful countries

summon VERB ❶ to order someone to come or appear ❷ to call people together

summons NOUN a command to appear in a law court

sumptuous ADJECTIVE splendid and expensive-looking

sun NOUN ❶ the star round which the earth travels ❷ light and warmth from the sun ❸ any star in the universe round which planets travel

sun VERB ➤ **sun yourself** to sit or lie in the sunshine

sunbathe VERB to sit or lie in the sunshine to get a suntan

sunbeam NOUN a ray of the sun

sunbed NOUN (British) a bench that you lie on under a sunlamp

sunblock NOUN a cream or lotion that you put on your skin to

A
protect it from the sun's harmful rays

B

sunburn NOUN redness of the skin someone gets if they are in the sun for too long

C

D

sundae (say **sun**-day) NOUN a mixture of ice cream and fruit, nuts and cream

E

F

Sunday NOUN the day of the week between Saturday and Monday, thought of as either the first or the last day of the week

G

H

sundial NOUN a device that shows the time by a shadow on a dial

I

J

sundown NOUN (North American) sunset

K

sundry ADJECTIVE various or several

L

sunflower NOUN a very tall flower with golden petals round a dark centre

M

N

sunglasses PLURAL NOUN dark glasses you wear to protect your eyes from strong sunlight

O

sunken ADJECTIVE sunk deeply into a surface

P

Q

sunlamp NOUN a lamp which uses ultraviolet light to give people an artificial tan

R

S

sunlight NOUN light from the sun

sunlit ADJECTIVE lit by sunlight

T

Sunni NOUN a member of one of the two main branches of Islam, based on the teachings of Muhammad and regarding his father-in-law Abu Bakr as his successor; about 90% of Muslims are Sunnis. Compare with Shiite.

U

V

W

X

sunny ADJECTIVE ❶ full of sunshine ❷ cheerful

Y

Z

sunrise NOUN the rising of the

---

sun; dawn

sunscreen NOUN a cream or lotion that you put on your skin to protect it from the sun's harmful rays

sunset NOUN the setting of the sun

sunshade NOUN a parasol or other device to protect people from the sun

sunshine NOUN warmth and light that comes from the sun

sunspot NOUN a dark place on the sun's surface

sunstroke NOUN an illness caused by being in the sun too long

suntan NOUN a brown colour of the skin caused by the sun

sup VERB to drink liquid in sips or spoonfuls

super ADJECTIVE (informal) excellent or superb

superb ADJECTIVE magnificent or excellent

supercilious ADJECTIVE haughty and scornful

superficial ADJECTIVE ❶ on the surface ❷ not deep or thorough

superfluous (say soo-**per**-floo-us) ADJECTIVE more than is wanted; not necessary

superglue NOUN a kind of strong glue that sticks very quickly

superhuman ADJECTIVE ❶ beyond ordinary human ability ❷ higher than human; divine

superimpose VERB to place a thing on top of something else

superintend VERB to be in charge of someone or something

superintendent NOUN ❶ a

supervisor ② a police officer above the rank of inspector

superior ADJECTIVE ① higher in position or rank ② better than another person or thing ③ showing that you think you are better than other people

superior NOUN a person or thing that is superior to another

superiority NOUN ① being better than something else ② behaviour that shows that you think you are better than other people

superlative ADJECTIVE of the highest degree or quality

superlative NOUN the form of an adjective or adverb that expresses 'most'

superman NOUN a man with superhuman powers

supermarket NOUN a large self-service shop that sells food and other goods

supernatural ADJECTIVE not belonging to the natural world or having a natural explanation

superpower NOUN one of the most powerful nations of the world, such as the USA

supersede VERB to take the place of something

supersonic ADJECTIVE faster than the speed of sound

superstition NOUN a belief or action that is not based on reason or evidence, e.g. the belief that it is unlucky to walk under a ladder

superstitious ADJECTIVE believing in superstitions

superstore NOUN a very large supermarket selling a wide range

of goods

superstructure NOUN ① a structure that rests on something else ② a building as distinct from its foundations

supertanker NOUN a very large tanker

supervise VERB to be in charge of a person or thing and inspect what is done

superwoman NOUN a woman with superhuman powers

supper NOUN a meal eaten in the evening

supplant VERB to take the place of a person or thing that has been removed

supple ADJECTIVE able to bend easily; flexible, not stiff

supplement NOUN ① something added as an extra ② an extra section added to a book or newspaper

supplement VERB to add to something

supplementary ADJECTIVE added as an extra

supplication NOUN asking or begging humbly for something, especially when praying

supply VERB to give or sell or provide what is needed or wanted

supply NOUN ① an amount of something that is kept ready to be used when needed ② supplies are things like food, medicines or fuel needed by an army, expedition, etc. ③ the action of supplying something

supply teacher NOUN a teacher who takes the place of a regular

A

teacher when he or she is away

B

support VERB ❶ to hold something up so that it does not fall down ❷ to give help or encouragement to someone or something ❸ to like a particular sports team and want it do well ❹ to provide someone with the necessities of life

C

D

E

F

support NOUN ❶ the action of supporting ❷ a person or thing that supports

G

H

supporter NOUN a person who supports something, especially a sports team or political party

I

supportive ADJECTIVE giving help or support to someone in a difficult situation

J

K

suppose VERB ❶ to think that something is likely to happen or be true ❷ to assume something or consider it as a suggestion

L

M

N

supposedly ADVERB so people believe or think

O

suppress VERB ❶ to put an end to something using force or by authority ❷ to keep something from being known or seen

P

Q

R

supremacy (say soo-**prem**-asi) NOUN having more authority or power than anyone else

S

supreme ADJECTIVE ❶ most important or highest in rank ❷ very great

T

U

surcharge NOUN an extra charge

V

sure ADJECTIVE ❶ completely confident that you are right; feeling no doubt ❷ certain to happen or do something ❸ reliable; that you can be certain of ❹ steady and confident

W

X

Y

Z

sure ADVERB (informal) surely; certainly

surely ADVERB ❶ without doubt; certainly ❷ it must be true; I feel sure

surf NOUN the white foam of waves breaking on a rock or shore

surf VERB ❶ to go surfing ❷ to browse through the Internet

surface NOUN ❶ the outside of something ❷ any of the sides of an object, especially the top part ❸ an outward appearance

surface VERB ❶ to come up to the surface from under water ❷ to put a surface on a road or path

surface mail NOUN letters and packages carried by sea or over land, not by air

surfboard NOUN a board used in surfing

surfeit (say **ser**-fit) NOUN too much of something

surfer NOUN a person who goes surfing

surfing NOUN balancing yourself on a board that is carried to the shore on the waves

surge VERB ❶ to move forwards or upwards like waves ❷ to increase suddenly and powerfully

surge NOUN ❶ a sudden rush forward or upward ❷ a sudden increase in something, especially a strong feeling

surgeon NOUN a doctor who treats disease or injury by cutting or repairing the affected parts of the body

surgery NOUN ❶ the work of a surgeon ❷ the place where a doctor or dentist regularly gives advice and treatment to patients ❸ the time when patients can visit a doctor or dentist

surgical ADJECTIVE to do with a surgeon or surgery

surly ADJECTIVE bad-tempered and unfriendly

surmise VERB to guess or suspect something

surmise NOUN a guess

surmount VERB ❶ to overcome a difficulty ❷ to get over an obstacle ❸ to be on top of something

surname NOUN the name that you share with other members of your family

surpass VERB to do or be better than someone or something

surplus NOUN an amount left over after you have spent or used what you need

surplus ADJECTIVE more than you need

surprise NOUN ❶ something unexpected ❷ the feeling caused by something that was not expected

surprise VERB ❶ to be a surprise; to make someone feel surprise ❷ to come upon or attack someone unexpectedly

surprised ADJECTIVE feeling or showing surprise

surprising ADJECTIVE causing surprise

surreal ADJECTIVE strange and bizarre, like some dreams are

surrealism NOUN a style of painting that shows strange objects and

scenes like those seen in dreams and fantasies

surrender VERB ❶ to stop fighting and give yourself up to an enemy ❷ to hand something over to another person, especially when forced to do so

surrender NOUN when someone surrenders

surreptitious (say su-rep-**tish**-us) ADJECTIVE done secretly or quickly so other people will not notice

surrogate mother NOUN a woman who agrees to conceive and give birth to a baby for a woman who cannot have a baby herself

surround VERB to come or be all round a person or thing

surroundings PLURAL NOUN the conditions or area around a person or thing

surveillance (say ser-**vay**-lans) NOUN a close watch kept on a person or thing

survey (say **ser**-vay) NOUN ❶ a general look at something ❷ an inspection of an area or building

survey (say ser-**vay**) VERB ❶ to look carefully at the whole of something ❷ to make a survey of an area or building

survival NOUN ❶ surviving; the likelihood of surviving ❷ something that has survived from an earlier time

survive VERB ❶ to stay alive; to continue to exist ❷ to remain alive after an accident or disaster ❸ to continue living after someone has died

survivor NOUN a person who

survives, especially after an accident or disaster

susceptible (say sus-**ept**-ib-ul) ADJECTIVE likely to be affected by something

suspect (say sus-**pekt**) VERB ❶ to think that a person is not to be trusted or has committed a crime; to distrust someone ❷ to have a feeling that something is likely or possible

suspect (say **sus**-pekt) NOUN a person who is suspected of a crime or doing something wrong

suspect (say **sus**-pekt) ADJECTIVE possibly not true or not to be trusted

suspend VERB ❶ to hang something up ❷ to postpone something or stop it temporarily ❸ to remove a person from a job or position for a time ❹ to keep something from falling or sinking in air or liquid

suspender NOUN a fastener to hold up a sock or stocking by its top

suspense NOUN an anxious or uncertain feeling while waiting for something to happen or become known

suspension NOUN ❶ suspending something or someone ❷ the springs etc. in a vehicle that lessen the effect of rough road surfaces ❸ a liquid containing small pieces of solid material which do not dissolve

suspension bridge NOUN a bridge supported by cables

suspicion NOUN ❶ a feeling that someone has done something wrong or cannot be trusted ❷ a slight feeling that something is

likely or possible

suspicious ADJECTIVE ❶ making you suspect or distrust someone or something ❷ suspecting or distrusting someone or something

sustain VERB ❶ to keep something going ❷ to keep someone alive or healthy ❸ to experience or suffer something bad

sustainable ADJECTIVE ❶ using natural products and energy in a way that does not harm the environment ❷ able to be continued for a long time

sustenance NOUN food and drink; nourishment

SW ABBREVIATION ❶ south-west ❷ south-western

swab (say swob) NOUN ❶ a mop or pad for cleaning or wiping something; a small pad for cleaning a wound ❷ a specimen of fluid from the body taken on a swab for testing

swab VERB to clean or wipe something with a swab

swagger VERB to walk or behave in a conceited and confident way

swagger NOUN a way of walking or behaving that seems too confident

swallow VERB ❶ to make something go down your throat ❷ to believe something that ought not to be believed

swallow NOUN a small bird with a forked tail and pointed wings

swamp NOUN an area of soft, wet land; a marsh

swamp VERB ❶ to flood an area ❷ to overwhelm someone with a great mass or number of things

swan NOUN a large usually white swimming bird with a long neck

swansong NOUN a person's last performance or work

swap (*informal*) VERB to exchange one thing for another

swap NOUN ❶ an act of swapping ❷ something you swap for something else

swarm NOUN a large number of insects flying or moving about together

swarm VERB ❶ to gather or move in a swarm ❷ to be crowded with people

swarthy ADJECTIVE having a dark complexion

swashbuckling ADJECTIVE a swashbuckling film is full of daring adventures and sword-fighting, set in the past

swastika NOUN an ancient symbol formed by a cross with its ends bent at right angles, adopted by the Nazis as their sign

swat VERB to hit or crush a fly or other insect

swathe (say swawth) NOUN a broad strip or area

swathe (say swayth) VERB to wrap a person or thing in layers of bandages, paper or clothes

sway VERB ❶ to move or swing gently from side to side ❷ to influence or affect someone

swear VERB swears, swearing, swore, sworn ❶ to make a solemn promise ❷ to make someone promise something ❸ to use very rude or offensive words

swear word NOUN a word

considered rude or shocking, often used by someone who is angry

sweat (say swet) NOUN moisture given off by your body through the pores of your skin; perspiration

sweat VERB sweats, sweating, sweated to give off sweat; to perspire

sweater NOUN a jersey or pullover

sweatshirt NOUN a thick cotton jersey worn for sports or casual wear

sweaty ADJECTIVE covered or damp with sweat

swede NOUN a large kind of turnip with purple skin and yellow flesh

sweep VERB sweeps, sweeping, swept ❶ to clean or clear an area with a broom or brush ❷ to move or remove something quickly ❸ to go smoothly and quickly ❹ to travel quickly over an area

sweep NOUN ❶ the process of sweeping ❷ a sweeping movement ❸ a chimney sweep ❹ a sweepstake

sweeping ADJECTIVE general or wide-ranging

sweepstake NOUN a form of gambling on sporting events in which all the money staked is divided among the winners

sweet ADJECTIVE ❶ tasting as if it contains sugar; not bitter ❷ very pleasant ❸ charming or delightful

sweet NOUN ❶ a small shaped piece of sweet food made with sugar or chocolate ❷ a pudding; the sweet course in a meal ❸ a loved person

sweetcorn NOUN the juicy yellow seeds of maize

a
b
c
d
e
f
g
h
i
j
k
l
m
n
o
p
q
r
s
t
u
v
w
x
y
z

sweeten VERB to make something sweet

sweetheart NOUN a person you love very much

sweet pea NOUN a climbing plant with sweet-smelling flowers

sweet potato NOUN a root vegetable with reddish skin and sweet yellow flesh

swell VERB swells, swelling, swelled, swollen or swelled ❶ to become larger or to make something larger ❷ to increase in amount, volume or force

swell NOUN the rise and fall of the sea's surface

swell ADJECTIVE (informal) (North American) very good

swelling NOUN a swollen place on your body

sweltering ADJECTIVE uncomfortably hot

swerve VERB to turn to one side suddenly

swift ADJECTIVE happening or moving quickly

swift NOUN a small bird rather like a swallow

swig (informal) VERB to drink quickly, taking large mouthfuls

swig NOUN a large mouthful of a drink

swill VERB to pour water over or through something; to wash or rinse something

swill NOUN ❶ the process of swilling something ❷ a sloppy mixture of waste food given to pigs

swim VERB swims, swimming, swam, swum ❶ to move your body through the water; to be in the

water for pleasure ❷ to cross a stretch of water by swimming ❸ to be covered with or full of liquid ❹ to feel dizzy

swim NOUN a spell of swimming

swimmer NOUN a person who swims

swimming bath NOUN (British) a public swimming pool

swimming costume NOUN (British) the clothing a woman wears to go swimming; a bikini or swimsuit

swimming pool NOUN an artificial pool for swimming in

swimming trunks PLURAL NOUN shorts which a man wears to go swimming

swimsuit NOUN a one-piece swimming costume

swindle VERB to cheat a person of their money or possessions in business

swindle NOUN a trick to swindle someone

swine NOUN ❶ a pig ❷ a very unpleasant person ❸ (informal) a difficult thing

swing VERB swings, swinging, swung ❶ to move back and forth while hanging ❷ to move or turn in a curve ❸ to change from one opinion or mood to another

swing NOUN ❶ a swinging movement ❷ a seat hung on chains or ropes so that it can be moved backwards and forwards ❸ the amount by which votes or opinions change from one side to another ❹ a kind of jazz music

swipe VERB ❶ to hit a person

or thing with a swinging blow
② (*informal*) to steal something
③ to pass a credit card through
an electronic reading device when
making a payment **④** to move a
finger across a touchscreen

swipe NOUN an attempt to hit a
person or thing with a swinging
blow

swirl VERB to move round quickly
in circles

swirl NOUN a swirling movement

swish VERB to move with a hissing
or rushing sound

swish NOUN a swishing sound

swish ADJECTIVE (*British*) (*informal*)
smart and fashionable

switch NOUN **①** a device that you
press or turn to start or stop
something working, especially by
electricity **②** a change of opinion,
policy or methods **③** a mechanism
for moving the points on a railway
track **④** a flexible rod or whip

switch VERB **①** to turn something
on or off by means of a switch
② to change something suddenly
③ to replace a thing with
something else

switchboard NOUN a panel with
switches for making telephone
connections or operating electric
circuits; the staff operating a
switchboard

swivel VERB to turn round smoothly

swollen *past participle* of **swell**

swollen ADJECTIVE thicker or wider
than usual

swoon (*old use*) VERB to faint

swoon NOUN when someone faints

swoop VERB **①** to dive or come
down with a rushing movement

② to make a sudden attack or raid

swoop NOUN a sudden dive or
attack

swop VERB a different spelling
of **swap**

sword (say sord) NOUN a weapon
with a long pointed blade fixed in a
handle or hilt

swordfish NOUN a large sea fish
with a long sword-like upper jaw

sworn ADJECTIVE **①** sworn evidence
or testimony is given under oath
② sworn enemies are determined
to remain enemies

swot (*British*) (*informal*) VERB to
study hard

swot NOUN a person who swots

sycamore NOUN a tall tree with
winged seeds, often grown for
its timber

syllable NOUN a word or part of a
word that has one vowel sound
when you say it

syllabus NOUN syllabuses a list of
the subjects to be studied by a
class or for an examination

symbol NOUN **①** a thing used as
a sign to stand for something
② a mark or sign with a special
meaning (e.g. +, - and x, in
mathematics)

symbolic ADJECTIVE acting as a
symbol of something

symbolism NOUN the use of
symbols to stand for things

symbolize (also **symbolise**) VERB
to be a symbol of something

symmetrical ADJECTIVE able to be
divided into two halves which are
exactly the same but the opposite
way round

symmetry NOUN the quality of being symmetrical or well-proportioned

sympathetic ADJECTIVE feeling or showing sympathy or understanding for someone

sympathize (also **sympathise**) VERB to show or feel sympathy

sympathy NOUN ❶ the sharing or understanding of other people's feelings or opinions ❷ a feeling of pity or tenderness towards someone who is hurt, sad or in trouble

symphony NOUN a long piece of music for an orchestra

symptom NOUN a sign that a disease or condition exists

synagogue (say sin-a-gog) NOUN a place where Jews meet for worship

synchronize (also **synchronise**) (say sink-ron-yz) VERB ❶ to make things happen at the same time ❷ to make watches or clocks show the same time ❸ to happen at the same time

syncopated (say sink-o-payt-id) ADJECTIVE a piece of music is syncopated when the strong beats are played weak and the weak beats are played strong

syndicate NOUN ❶ a group of people or firms who work together in business ❷ a group of people who buy something together or who gamble together, sharing the cost and any gains

syndrome NOUN ❶ a set of symptoms ❷ a set of opinions or ways of behaving that are characteristic of a particular condition

synod (say sin-od) NOUN a council of senior members of the clergy

synonym (say sin-o-nim) NOUN a word that means the same or almost the same as another word

synopsis (say sin-op-sis) NOUN synopses a summary of a story or book

synthesis (say sin-thi-sis) NOUN syntheses combining different things to make something

synthesize (also **synthesise**) (say sin-thi-syz) VERB to make something by combining parts

synthesizer (also **synthesiser**) NOUN an electronic musical instrument that can make a large variety of sounds

synthetic ADJECTIVE artificially made; not natural

syringe NOUN a device for sucking in a liquid and squirting it out

syrup NOUN a thick sweet liquid

system NOUN ❶ a set of parts, things or ideas that are organized to work together ❷ a way of doing something

systematic ADJECTIVE done using a fixed plan or method; methodical

Tt

tab NOUN a small flap or strip that sticks out

tabby NOUN a grey or brown cat with dark stripes

tabernacle NOUN ❶ (in the Bible) the portable shrine used by the ancient Jews during their wanderings in the wilderness ❷ a meeting place for worship used by some groups of Christians

table NOUN ❶ a piece of furniture with a flat top supported on legs ❷ a list of facts or figures arranged in rows and columns ❸ a list of the results of multiplying a number by other numbers

table VERB to put forward a proposal for discussion at a meeting

tableau (say **tab**-loh) NOUN tableaux (say **tab**-lohz) a dramatic or attractive scene, especially one posed on a stage by a group of people who do not speak or move

tablecloth NOUN a cloth for covering a table, especially at meals

tablespoon NOUN a large spoon for serving food

tablet NOUN ❶ a pill ❷ a solid piece of soap ❸ a flat piece of stone or wood with words carved or written on it ❹ a small flat computer that you use by touching the screen

table tennis NOUN a game played on a table divided by a net, over which you hit a small ball with bats

tabloid NOUN a newspaper with pages that are half the size of larger newspapers

taboo ADJECTIVE not to be done, used or talked about

taboo NOUN a custom that you should avoid doing or talking about a particular thing because it might offend or embarrass other people

tacit (say **tas**-it) ADJECTIVE implied or understood without being put into words

taciturn (say **tas**-i-tern) ADJECTIVE saying very little

tack NOUN ❶ a short nail with a flat top ❷ the direction taken when tacking in sailing ❸ a course of action or policy ❹ riding equipment, such as harnesses and saddles

tack VERB ❶ to nail something down, especially a carpet, with tacks ❷ to sew material together with long stitches ❸ to sail a zigzag course to take advantage of what wind there is

tackle VERB ❶ to try to do something that needs doing ❷ to try to get the ball from someone else in a game of football, rugby or hockey ❸ to talk to someone about a difficult or awkward matter

tackle NOUN ❶ equipment, especially for fishing ❷ a set of ropes and pulleys ❸ tackling someone in football, rugby or hockey

tacky ADJECTIVE ❶ sticky or not quite dry ❷ (informal) showing poor taste or style; cheaply made

tact NOUN taking care not to offend or upset people by saying the wrong thing

tactful ADJECTIVE having or showing tact

tactical ADJECTIVE to do with tactics

tactics NOUN ❶ the methods you use to achieve something or gain an advantage ❷ the method of arranging military forces in battle or players in a team game

tactile ADJECTIVE to do with the

sense of touch

tactless ADJECTIVE having or showing a lack of tact

tadpole NOUN a young frog or toad that has developed from the egg and lives entirely in water

taffeta NOUN a stiff silky material, often used for dresses

tag NOUN ➊ a label tied on or stuck to something ➋ a metal or plastic point at the end of a shoelace ➌ a game in which one person chases the others

tag VERB ➊ to label something with a tag ➋ to add something as an extra thing ➌ to identify a person shown in a photograph on a social networking website

tail NOUN ➊ the part that sticks out from the rear end of the body of a bird, fish or animal ➋ the part at the end or rear of something, such as an aircraft

tail VERB ➊ to remove stalks from fruit or vegetables ➋ (informal) to follow someone closely without them seeing you

tailback NOUN a long line of traffic stretching back from an obstruction

tailless ADJECTIVE without a tail

tailor NOUN a person who makes men's clothes

tailor VERB ➊ to make or fit clothes ➋ to adapt or make something for a special purpose

tailor-made ADJECTIVE specially made or suited for a purpose

tails PLURAL NOUN ➊ the side of a coin opposite the head ➋ a man's formal jacket with two long pieces

hanging down at the back

taint NOUN a small amount of something bad or unpleasant that spoils something

taint VERB to spoil something with a taint

take VERB takes, taking, took, taken This word has many uses, including ➊ to get something into your hands, possession or control ➋ to carry, drive or lead a person or thing to a place ➌ to make use of something ➍ to have or do something ➎ to take an exam is to sit it ➏ to study or teach a subject ➐ to make an effort ➑ to experience a feeling ➒ to accept or put up with something ➓ to require something ⓫ to write something down ⓬ to use a camera to make a photograph ⓭ to subtract one number from another ⓮ to assume that something is true

takeaway NOUN ➊ a place that sells cooked meals for customers to take away ➋ a meal from such a place

take-off NOUN the act of an aircraft leaving the ground and becoming airborne

takeover NOUN the taking control of one business company by another

takings PLURAL NOUN money that has been received, especially by a shopkeeper

talcum powder NOUN a scented powder put on the skin to make it feel smooth and dry

tale NOUN a story

talent NOUN a natural ability to do

something well

talented ADJECTIVE having a natural ability to do something well

talisman NOUN an object that is supposed to bring good luck

talk VERB to speak or have a conversation

talk NOUN ① a conversation or discussion ② an informal lecture

talkative ADJECTIVE talking a lot

tall ADJECTIVE ① higher than the average ② measured from the bottom to the top

tallow NOUN animal fat used to make candles, soap, lubricants, etc.

tall story NOUN (*informal*) a story that is hard to believe

tally NOUN the total amount of a debt or score

tally VERB to match or agree with something else

Talmud NOUN the collection of writings that contain Jewish religious law

talon NOUN a strong claw, especially on a bird of prey

tambourine NOUN a circular musical instrument with metal discs fixed round it, so that it jingles when you tap or shake it

tame ADJECTIVE ① a tame animal is gentle and not afraid of people; not wild or dangerous ② not exciting; dull

tame VERB to make an animal become tame

Tamil NOUN ① a member of a people of southern India and Sri Lanka ② their language

tam-o'-shanter NOUN a round Scottish cap with a bobble in the

middle

tamper VERB ➤ **tamper with something** to interfere with something or make changes to it so that it will not work properly

tampon NOUN a plug of soft material that a woman puts into her vagina to absorb the blood during her period

tan NOUN ① brown colour in skin that has been exposed to sun; a suntan ② a light brown colour

tan VERB ① to turn your skin brown by exposing it to the sun ② to make an animal's skin into leather by treating it with chemicals

tandem NOUN a bicycle for two riders, one behind the other

tandoori NOUN a style of Indian cooking in which food is cooked in a clay oven (a **tandoor**)

tang NOUN a strong flavour or smell

tangent NOUN a straight line that touches the outside of a curve or circle

tangerine NOUN a kind of small orange

tangible ADJECTIVE ① able to be touched ② that can be clearly seen; real or definite

tangle VERB to twist things together or become twisted into a confused mass

tangle NOUN a twisted or muddled mass of hair, wires, etc.

tango NOUN a ballroom dance with gliding steps and sudden pauses

tank NOUN ① a large container for a liquid or gas ② a heavy armoured vehicle used in war

tankard NOUN a large mug for

a
b
c
d
e
f
g
h
i
j
k
l
m
n
o
p
q
r
s
t
u
v
w
x
y
z

drinking beer from, usually made of silver or pewter

tanker NOUN ❶ a large ship for carrying oil ❷ a large lorry for carrying a liquid

tanner NOUN a person who tans animal skins into leather

tannin NOUN a substance obtained from the bark or fruit of various trees (also found in tea), used in tanning and dyeing things

tantalize (also **tantalise**) VERB to tease or torment a person by showing them something good that they cannot have

tantamount ADJECTIVE to be tantamount to something is to be equivalent to it or virtually the same as it

tantrum NOUN an outburst of bad temper

tap NOUN ❶ a device for letting out liquid or gas in a controlled flow ❷ a quick light hit; the sound of this ❸ tap dancing

tap VERB ❶ to hit a person or thing quickly and lightly ❷ to obtain supplies or information from a source ❸ to fix a device to a telephone line so that you can overhear conversations on it

tap dancing NOUN dancing in shoes with metal caps that make sharp tapping sounds on the floor

tape NOUN ❶ a narrow strip of cloth, paper or plastic ❷ a narrow plastic strip coated with a magnetic substance and used for making recordings ❸ a tape recording ❹ a tape measure

tape VERB ❶ to fix, cover or surround something with tape

❷ to record something on magnetic tape

tape measure NOUN a long strip marked in centimetres or inches for measuring things

taper VERB to become thinner or narrower towards one end

taper NOUN a very thin candle, used for lighting things

tape recorder NOUN a machine for recording music or sound on magnetic tape and playing it back

tapestry NOUN a piece of strong cloth with pictures or patterns woven or embroidered on it

tapeworm NOUN a long flat worm that can live as a parasite in the intestines of people and animals

tapioca NOUN a starchy substance in hard white grains obtained from cassava, used for making milk puddings

tapir (say **tay**-per) NOUN a pig-like animal with a long flexible snout

tar NOUN a thick black liquid made from coal or wood and used in making roads

tar VERB to coat something with tar

tarantula NOUN a large kind of spider found in southern Europe and in tropical countries. Some species of tarantula have a poisonous bite.

tardy ADJECTIVE slow or late

target NOUN something that you aim at and try to hit or reach

target VERB to aim at something or have it as a target

tariff NOUN a list of prices or charges

tarmac NOUN ❶ a mixture of

tar and broken stone, used for making a hard surface on roads, paths, playgrounds, etc. ❷ an area surfaced with tarmac, especially on an airfield

tarnish VERB ❶ metal tarnishes when it becomes stained and less shiny ❷ to spoil or damage something

tarot card (rhymes with *barrow*) NOUN one of the cards in a special pack used for fortune-telling

tarpaulin NOUN a large sheet of waterproof canvas

tarragon NOUN a plant with leaves that are used to flavour salads and in cooking

tarry (say *tar-ee*) ADJECTIVE covered with or like tar

tarry (say *ta-ree*) VERB (old use) to stay for a while longer; to linger

tart NOUN ❶ a pie containing fruit or sweet filling ❷ a piece of pastry with jam etc. on top

tart ADJECTIVE ❶ sour-tasting ❷ sharp in manner

tartan NOUN a pattern with coloured stripes crossing each other, especially one that is used by a Scottish clan

tartar NOUN ❶ a hard chalky deposit that forms on teeth ❷ a person who is fierce or difficult to deal with

task NOUN a piece of work that needs to be done

task force NOUN a group specially organized for a particular task

taskmaster NOUN a person who gives other people a lot of work to do

tassel NOUN a bundle of threads tied together at the top and used to decorate something

taste VERB ❶ to take a small amount of food or drink to try its flavour ❷ to be able to notice or recognize flavours ❸ to have a certain flavour

taste NOUN ❶ the feeling caused in the tongue by something placed on it ❷ the ability to taste things ❸ the ability to enjoy beautiful things or to choose things that are of good quality or go together well ❹ a liking for something ❺ a very small amount of food or drink

tasteful ADJECTIVE showing good taste

tasteless ADJECTIVE ❶ having no flavour ❷ showing poor taste

tasty ADJECTIVE having a strong pleasant taste

tattered ADJECTIVE badly torn and ragged

tatters PLURAL NOUN rags; badly torn pieces

tattoo NOUN ❶ a picture or pattern marked on someone's skin by using a needle and dye ❷ a drumming or tapping sound ❸ an outdoor entertainment consisting of military music and marching

tattoo VERB to mark a person's skin with a tattoo

tatty ADJECTIVE shabby and worn

taunt VERB to jeer at or insult someone

taunt NOUN a taunting remark

taut ADJECTIVE stretched tightly

tautology NOUN saying the same thing again in different words, e.g. *You can get the book free for nothing.* (where *free* and *for nothing* mean the same)

tavern NOUN (old use) an inn or public house

tawdry ADJECTIVE cheap and gaudy

tawny ADJECTIVE brownish-yellow

tax NOUN ❶ money that people or business firms have to pay to the government, to be used for public purposes ❷ a strain or burden

tax VERB ❶ to put a tax on something ❷ to charge someone a tax ❸ to put a strain or burden on a person or thing ❹ (formal) to accuse someone of doing something wrong

taxation NOUN money that has to be paid as taxes

taxi NOUN a car with a driver that you can hire for journeys, usually with a meter to record the fare to be paid

taxi VERB an aircraft taxis when it moves slowly along the ground before taking off or after landing

taxidermist NOUN a person who prepares and stuffs the skins of animals in a lifelike form

taxpayer NOUN a person who pays tax

TB ABBREVIATION tuberculosis

tea NOUN ❶ a drink made by pouring hot water on the dried leaves of an evergreen shrub (the *tea plant*) ❷ these dried leaves ❸ a drink made with the leaves of other plants ❹ a meal in the afternoon or early evening

tea bag NOUN a small bag holding about a teaspoonful of tea

teacake NOUN (British) a kind of bun usually served toasted and buttered

teach VERB teaches, teaching, taught ❶ to give a person knowledge or skill; to train someone ❷ to give lessons in a subject ❸ to show someone what to do or avoid

teacher NOUN a person who teaches others, especially in a school

teaching NOUN things that are taught

tea cloth NOUN a tea towel

teacup NOUN a cup for drinking tea

teak NOUN the hard strong wood of an evergreen Asian tree

teal NOUN a kind of duck

team NOUN ❶ a set of players who form one side in certain games and sports ❷ a set of people working together ❸ two or more animals harnessed to pull a vehicle or a plough

team VERB ➤ team up with someone to join someone in order to do something together ➤ team someone with someone to put people together in a team

teamwork NOUN the ability of a team or group to work well together

teapot NOUN a pot with a lid and a handle, for making and pouring tea

tear (say teer) NOUN a drop of the water that comes from the eyes when a person cries

tear (say tair) VERB tears, tearing, tore, torn ❶ to make a split in something or pull it apart ❷ to pull or remove something with force ❸ to become torn ❹ to run or travel hurriedly

tear (say tair) NOUN a split made by tearing

teardrop NOUN a single tear

tearful ADJECTIVE in tears; crying easily

tear gas NOUN a gas that makes people's eyes water painfully, sometimes used by the police or army to control crowds

tease VERB ❶ to make fun of someone and say things to make them annoyed ❷ to pick threads apart into separate strands

tease NOUN a person who often teases others

teaser NOUN (informal) a difficult problem or puzzle

teaspoon NOUN a small spoon for stirring tea or measuring small amounts

teat NOUN ❶ one of the nipples on a female animal, through which the young suck milk ❷ the cap of a baby's feeding bottle

tea towel NOUN (chiefly British) a cloth for drying washed dishes and cutlery

tech (say tek) NOUN (informal) a technical college

technical ADJECTIVE ❶ to do with technology or the way things work ❷ to do with a particular subject and its methods ❸ using words that only people who know a lot about a subject will understand

technical college NOUN a college where technical and practical subjects are taught

technicality NOUN a small detail of the law or a process

technically ADVERB according to the strict facts or rules

technician NOUN a person whose job is to look after scientific equipment and do practical work in a laboratory

technique NOUN a method of doing something skilfully

technological ADJECTIVE to do with technology

technology NOUN the study of machinery, engineering and how things work

teddy bear NOUN a soft furry toy bear

tedious ADJECTIVE annoyingly slow or long; boring

tedium NOUN a dull or boring time or experience

tee NOUN ❶ the flat area from which golfers strike the ball at the start of play for each hole ❷ a small piece of wood or plastic on which a golf ball is placed for being struck

teem VERB ❶ to be full of something ❷ to rain very hard; to pour

teen ADJECTIVE & NOUN (informal) a teenager

teenage ADJECTIVE in your teens; to do with teenagers

teenaged ADJECTIVE in your teens

teenager NOUN a person in their teens

teens PLURAL NOUN the time of your life between the ages of 13 and 19

teeny ADJECTIVE (informal) tiny

631

tee-shirt NOUN a T-shirt

teeter VERB to stand or move unsteadily

teethe VERB a baby is teething when its first teeth are beginning to grow through the gums

teetotal ADJECTIVE never drinking alcohol

Teflon NOUN (*trademark*) a type of plastic used as a non-stick coating for pans

telecommunications PLURAL NOUN communications over long distances, e.g. by telephone, radio or television

telegram NOUN a message sent by telegraph

telegraph NOUN a way of sending messages by using electric current along wires or by radio

telepathy (say til-**ep**-ath-ee) NOUN communication of thoughts from one person's mind to another without speaking, writing or gestures

telephone NOUN a device or system using electric wires or radio to enable one person to speak to another who is some distance away

telephone VERB to speak to a person by telephone

telephonist (say til-**ef**-on-ist) NOUN (*British*) a person who operates a telephone switchboard

telescope NOUN an instrument using lenses to magnify distant objects

telescope VERB to become shorter or make something shorter, by sliding overlapping sections into each other

televise VERB to broadcast an event or programme by television

television NOUN ➊ a system using radio waves to reproduce a view of scenes or events on a screen ➋ an apparatus for receiving these pictures ➌ televised programmes

tell VERB tells, telling, told ➊ to make a thing known to someone, especially by words ➋ to say something ➌ to order or advise someone to do something ➍ to reveal a secret ➎ to be certain about something or recognize it ➏ to produce an effect

telling ADJECTIVE having a strong effect or meaning

tell-tale NOUN a person who tells tales

tell-tale ADJECTIVE revealing or indicating something that is supposed to be secret

telly NOUN (*British*) (*informal*) ➊ a television ➋ a television set

temerity (say tim-**erri**-tee) NOUN rashness or boldness

temp NOUN (*informal*) a secretary or other worker who works for short periods of time in different companies

temper NOUN ➊ a person's mood ➋ an angry mood

temper VERB ➊ to harden or strengthen metal by heating and cooling it ➋ to make something less severe or soften its effects

temperament NOUN a person's nature as shown in the way they usually behave

temperamental ADJECTIVE ➊ likely to become excitable or moody suddenly ② to do with a person's temperament

temperance NOUN ① drinking little or no alcohol ② the ability to control your behaviour; self-restraint

temperate ADJECTIVE a temperate climate is neither extremely hot nor extremely cold

temperature NOUN ① how hot or cold a person or thing is ② an abnormally high temperature of the body

tempest NOUN (old use) a violent storm

tempestuous ADJECTIVE stormy; full of commotion

template NOUN a thin sheet of shaped metal, plastic or card used as a guide for cutting or shaping things

temple NOUN ① a building where a god is worshipped ② the part of your head between your forehead and your ear

tempo NOUN ① the speed or rhythm of something ② the speed at which a piece of music is played

temporary ADJECTIVE lasting for a short time only; not permanent

tempt VERB ① to try to persuade or attract someone, especially into doing something wrong or unwise ② to be tempted to do something is to want to do it even though it may not be the right thing to do

temptation NOUN ① a feeling that you want to do something, even if you know it is wrong ② something that tempts you

tempting ADJECTIVE attractive in a

way that makes you want to do or have something

ten NOUN ADJECTIVE the number 10

tenacious (say ten-ay-shus) ADJECTIVE ① holding or clinging firmly to something ② obstinate and persistent

tenant NOUN a person who rents a house, building or land from a landlord

tend VERB ① to be likely to do something; to usually happen ② to look after something or someone

tendency NOUN the way a person or thing is likely to behave

tender ADJECTIVE ① easy to chew; not tough or hard ② easily hurt or damaged; delicate or sensitive ③ a tender part of your body is painful when touched ④ gentle and loving

tender VERB to offer something formally

tender NOUN ① a formal offer to supply goods or carry out work at a stated price ② a truck attached to a steam locomotive to carry its coal and water ③ a small boat carrying stores or passengers to and from a larger one

tendon NOUN a strong strip of tissue that joins muscle to bone

tendril NOUN ① a thread-like part by which a climbing plant clings to a support ② a thin curl of hair

tenement NOUN a large house or building divided into flats or rooms that are let to separate tenants

tenet (say ten-it) NOUN a firm belief held by a person or group

tenner NOUN (British) (informal) a ten-pound note; £10

tennis NOUN a game played with rackets and a ball on a court with a net across the middle

tenon NOUN a piece of wood shaped to fit into a mortise

tenor NOUN ❶ a male singer with a high voice ❷ the general meaning or drift of something

tenpin bowling NOUN a game in which players try to knock over ten skittles set up at the end of a track by rolling hard balls down it

tense NOUN the form of a verb that shows when something happens, e.g. he *came* (**past tense**), he *comes* or *is coming* (**present tense**)

tense ADJECTIVE ❶ tightly stretched ❷ nervous or worried and unable to relax ❸ making people tense

tense VERB to have muscles that have become hard and not relaxed

tension NOUN ❶ how tightly stretched a rope or wire is ❷ a feeling of anxiety or nervousness about something that is just about to happen ❸ voltage

tent NOUN a shelter made of canvas or cloth supported by upright poles

tentacle NOUN a long flexible part of the body of an animal such as an octopus, used for feeling or grasping things or for moving

tentative ADJECTIVE cautious; trying something out

tenterhooks PLURAL NOUN ➤ **on tenterhooks** tense and anxious about something that is going to happen

tenth ADJECTIVE & NOUN next after the ninth

tenuous ADJECTIVE very slight or thin

tepee (say tee-pee) NOUN a tent formerly used by Native Americans, made by fastening skins or mats over poles

tepid ADJECTIVE only slightly warm; lukewarm

term NOUN ❶ the period of weeks when a school or college is open ❷ a definite period ❸ a word or expression with a special meaning

term VERB to describe or name something by using a certain word or expression

terminal NOUN ❶ a building where passengers arrive or depart ❷ a place where a wire is connected in an electric circuit or battery ❸ a computer keyboard and screen used for sending data to or from the main computer

terminal ADJECTIVE a terminal illness is one that cannot be cured and that the person will die from

terminate VERB to end or stop or to make something end or stop

terminology NOUN the technical terms of a subject

terminus NOUN the last station on a railway or bus route

termite NOUN a small insect that eats wood and lives in large groups

terms PLURAL NOUN ❶ a relationship between people ❷ conditions offered or agreed, especially in a treaty or contract

tern NOUN a seabird with long wings

terrace NOUN ❶ a row of houses joined together ❷ a level area on a slope or hillside ❸ a paved area beside a house

terracotta NOUN ❶ a kind of pottery ❷ the brownish-red colour of flowerpots

terrain NOUN a stretch of land

terrapin NOUN an edible freshwater turtle of North America

terrestrial ADJECTIVE ❶ to do with the earth or land ❷ terrestrial television is broadcast by aerials on the ground rather than by satellite

terrible ADJECTIVE very bad; awful

terribly ADVERB ❶ very badly ❷ (informal) very; extremely

terrier NOUN a kind of small lively dog

terrific ADJECTIVE (informal) ❶ very great ❷ very good or excellent

terrify VERB to make a person or animal very frightened

territorial ADJECTIVE ❶ to do with or belonging to a country's territory ❷ a territorial animal or bird guards and defends an area of land it believes to be its own

territory NOUN ❶ an area of land, especially one that belongs to a country ❷ an area of land that an animal or bird thinks of as its own and defends against others

terror NOUN ❶ very great fear ❷ a terrifying person or thing

terrorist NOUN a person who uses violence for political purposes

terrorize (also **terrorise**) VERB to frighten someone by threatening them

terse ADJECTIVE using few words and not very friendly

tertiary (say ter-sher-ee) ADJECTIVE to do with the third stage of something; coming after secondary

tessellated ADJECTIVE decorated with shapes that fit together into a pattern without overlapping or leaving gaps

test NOUN ❶ a short examination ❷ a way of discovering the qualities, abilities or presence of a person or thing ❸ a test match

test VERB to carry out a test on a person or thing

testament NOUN ❶ a written statement ❷ either of the two main parts of the Bible, the Old Testament or the New Testament

testicle NOUN either of the two glands in the scrotum where semen is produced

testify VERB ❶ to give evidence or swear that something is true ❷ to be evidence or proof of something

testimonial NOUN ❶ a letter describing someone's abilities and character ❷ a gift presented to someone as a mark of respect

testimony NOUN evidence; what someone testifies

test match NOUN a cricket or rugby match between teams from different countries

testosterone (say test-ost-er-ohn) NOUN a male sex hormone

test tube NOUN a tube of thin glass with one end closed, used for experiments in chemistry

test-tube baby NOUN a baby that develops from an egg that has been fertilized outside the mother's body and then placed

testy ADJECTIVE easily annoyed; irritable

tetanus NOUN a disease that makes the muscles become stiff, caused by bacteria

tetchy ADJECTIVE easily annoyed; irritable

tête-à-tête (say tayt-ah-**tayt**) NOUN a private conversation between two people

tether VERB to tie up an animal so that it cannot move far

tether NOUN a rope for tethering an animal

tetrahedron NOUN a solid with four sides (i.e. a pyramid with a triangular base)

text NOUN ❶ the words of something written or printed ❷ a text message ❸ a sentence from the Bible used as the subject of a sermon in a Christian church

text VERB to send a text message to someone on a mobile phone

textbook NOUN a book that teaches you about a subject

textiles PLURAL NOUN kinds of cloth; fabrics

text message NOUN a written message sent on a mobile phone

texture NOUN the way that the surface of something feels when you touch it

thalidomide NOUN a medicinal drug that was found (in 1961) to cause babies to be born with deformed arms and legs

than CONJUNCTION & PREPOSITION compared with another person or thing

thank VERB to tell someone that you are grateful to them

thankful ADJECTIVE ❶ pleased and relieved ❷ showing thanks; grateful

thankfully ADVERB ❶ in a grateful way ❷ fortunately; luckily

thankless ADJECTIVE a thankless task is one that you are not likely to get thanked or rewarded for doing

thanks PLURAL NOUN ❶ words that thank someone; gratitude ❷ (informal) thank you

thanksgiving NOUN an expression of gratitude, especially to God

that DETERMINER & PRONOUN the one there

that ADVERB to such an extent

that RELATIVE PRONOUN which, who or whom

that CONJUNCTION used to introduce a wish, reason or result

thatch NOUN straw or reeds used to make a roof

thatch VERB to make a roof with thatch

thaw VERB to melt; to stop being frozen

thaw NOUN a period of warm weather that thaws ice and snow

the DETERMINER a particular one; that or those

theatre NOUN ❶ a building where people go to see plays or shows ❷ the writing, acting and producing of plays ❸ a special room where surgical operations are done

theatrical ADJECTIVE ❶ to do with plays or acting ❷ theatrical behaviour is exaggerated and done for showy effect

theatricals PLURAL NOUN performances of plays

thee PRONOUN (old use) you (referring to one person and used as the object of a verb or after a preposition)

theft NOUN stealing

their DETERMINER ❶ belonging to them ❷ (informal) belonging to a person

theirs POSSESSIVE PRONOUN belonging to them

them PRONOUN the form of they used as the object of a verb or after a preposition

theme NOUN ❶ the subject of a speech, piece of writing, discussion, etc. ❷ a melody

theme park NOUN an amusement park where the rides and attractions are based on a particular subject

theme tune NOUN a special tune always used to announce a particular programme or performer

themselves PRONOUN they or them and nobody else. The word is used to refer back to the subject of a sentence (e.g. They blame themselves.) or for emphasis (e.g. My grandparents built this house themselves.).

then ADVERB ❶ at that time ❷ after that; next ❸ in that case; therefore

thence ADVERB from that place

theology NOUN the study of religion

theorem NOUN a mathematical

statement that can be proved by reasoning

theoretical ADJECTIVE based on theory, not on practice or experience

theory NOUN ❶ an idea or set of ideas put forward to explain something ❷ the principles of a subject rather than its practice

therapeutic (say therra-**pew**-tik) ADJECTIVE helping to treat or cure a disease or illness

therapy NOUN a way of treating a physical or mental illness, especially without using surgery or artificial medicines

there ADVERB ❶ in or to that place ❷ used to call attention to something or to talk about it

thereabouts ADVERB near there

thereby ADVERB by that means; because of that

therefore ADVERB for that reason; and so

therm NOUN a unit for measuring heat, especially from gas

thermal ADJECTIVE ❶ to do with heat; worked by heat ❷ designed to keep you warm in cold weather

thermodynamics NOUN the science dealing with the relation between heat and other forms of energy

thermometer NOUN a device for measuring temperature

Thermos NOUN (trademark) a kind of vacuum flask

thermostat NOUN a piece of equipment that automatically keeps the temperature of a room or piece of equipment steady

thesaurus (say thi-**sor**-us) NOUN a kind of dictionary that lists words in groups that have similar meanings

these DETERMINER & PRONOUN plural of this

thesis NOUN theses ① a theory that someone has put forward ② a long essay written by a candidate for a university degree

they PRONOUN ① the people or things being talked about ② people in general ③ he or she; a person

they're (mainly spoken) they are

thick ADJECTIVE ① measuring a lot from one side to the other; broad or wide ② measuring from one side to the other ③ with a lot of things packed close together; dense ④ fairly stiff; not flowing easily ⑤ (informal) stupid

thicken VERB to become thicker or to make something thicker

thicket NOUN a number of shrubs and small trees growing close together

thickly ADVERB ① in thick pieces or in a deep layer ② with a lot of things packed close together

thickness NOUN how thick something is

thickset ADJECTIVE ① having a stocky or burly body ② with parts placed or growing close together

thief NOUN thieves a person who steals things

thieving NOUN stealing things

thieving ADJECTIVE behaving like a thief

thigh NOUN the part of your leg between your hip and your knee

thimble NOUN a small metal or plastic cap that you put on the end of your finger to protect it when you are sewing

thin ADJECTIVE ① measuring a small amount from one side to the other ② not fat ③ not dense or closely packed together ④ runny or watery

thin VERB to become less thick or to make something less thick

thine DETERMINER & POSSESSIVE PRONOUN (old use) yours (referring to one person)

thing NOUN an object; something which can be seen, touched or thought about

things PLURAL NOUN ① personal belongings ② events or circumstances

think VERB thinks, thinking, thought ① to use your mind ② to have something as an idea or opinion ③ to intend or plan to do something

think NOUN a time spent thinking about something

thinker NOUN a person who thinks about things, especially important subjects

thinly ADVERB ① in thin pieces or in a thin layer ② with only a few things or people spread over a place ③ in a way that is not sincere or enthusiastic

third ADJECTIVE next after the second

third NOUN ① the third person or thing ② one of three equal parts of something

Third World NOUN the poorest and underdeveloped countries of Asia, Africa and South America

thirst NOUN ① a feeling of dryness in your mouth and throat that makes you want to drink ② a strong desire for something

thirst VERB to have a strong desire for something

thirsty ADJECTIVE feeling that you need to drink

thirteen NOUN & ADJECTIVE the number 13

thirty NOUN & ADJECTIVE the number 30

this DETERMINER & PRONOUN the one here

this ADVERB to such an extent

thistle NOUN a prickly wild plant with purple, white or yellow flowers

thither ADVERB (old use) to that place

thong NOUN a narrow strip of leather used for fastening things

thorax NOUN the part of the body between the head or neck and the abdomen

thorn NOUN ① a small pointed growth on the stem of a plant ② a thorny tree or shrub

thorny ADJECTIVE ① having many thorns; prickly ② causing difficulty or disagreement

thorough ADJECTIVE ① done or doing things carefully and in detail ② complete in every way

thoroughbred ADJECTIVE bred of pure or pedigree stock

thoroughbred NOUN an animal of pure or pedigree stock

thoroughfare NOUN a public road or path that is open at both ends

thoroughly ADVERB ① completely; very much ② carefully and in detail

those DETERMINER & PRONOUN plural of that

thou PRONOUN (old use) you (referring to one person)

though CONJUNCTION in spite of the fact that; even if

though ADVERB however; all the same

thought past tense of think

thought NOUN ① something that you think; an idea or opinion ② the process of thinking

thoughtful ADJECTIVE ① thinking a lot ② thinking of other people and what they need or want; considerate

thoughtless ADJECTIVE ① careless; not thinking of what may happen ② not thinking of others; inconsiderate

thousand NOUN & ADJECTIVE the number 1,000

thrash VERB ① to beat someone with a stick or whip; to keep hitting someone very hard ② to defeat someone completely ③ to move about, or move a part of your body, violently

thread NOUN ① a thin length of any substance ② a length of spun cotton, wool or nylon used for making cloth or in sewing or knitting ③ the spiral ridge round a screw ④ a theme or idea running through a story or argument ⑤ a series of connected messages from an Internet discussion of a subject

thread VERB ① to put a thread through the eye of a needle ② to pass something long and thin through or round something ③ to put beads on a thread

threadbare ADJECTIVE threadbare cloth or clothing is old and worn thin with the threads showing

threat NOUN ① a warning that you will punish, hurt or harm a person or thing ② the possibility of trouble or danger ③ a person or thing causing danger

threaten VERB ① to make threats against someone ② to be a threat or danger to a person or thing

three NOUN & ADJECTIVE the number 3

three-dimensional ADJECTIVE having three dimensions (length, width and height or depth)

thresh VERB to beat corn in order to separate the grain from the husks

threshold NOUN ① a slab of stone or board forming the bottom of a doorway; the entrance ② the point at which something begins to happen or change

thrice ADVERB (old use) three times

thrift NOUN being careful with money and not spending too much

thrill NOUN a feeling of great excitement or pleasure

thrill VERB to give someone a feeling of great excitement or pleasure

thriller NOUN an exciting story or film, usually about crime or spying

thrilling ADJECTIVE very exciting

thrive VERB to prosper or grow

strongly

throat NOUN ① the tube in your neck that takes food and drink down into your body ② the front of your neck

throb VERB to beat or vibrate with a strong rhythm

throb NOUN a throbbing sound or feeling

throes PLURAL NOUN severe pangs of pain

thrombosis NOUN the formation of a clot of blood in the body

throne NOUN ① a special chair for a king or queen at ceremonies ② the position of being king or queen

throng NOUN a large crowd of people

throng VERB to go somewhere in large numbers

throttle NOUN a device that controls the flow of fuel to an engine; an accelerator

throttle VERB to strangle someone

through PREPOSITION ① from one end or side to the other end or side of ② during; throughout ③ by means of; because of ④ at the end of; having finished successfully

through ADVERB ① through something ② with a telephone connection made ③ finished

through ADJECTIVE ① going directly all the way to a destination ② a through road leads directly from one place to another

throughout PREPOSITION & ADVERB all the way through; from beginning to end

throve past tense of thrive

throw VERB throws, throwing,

threw, thrown ❶ to send a person or thing through the air **❷** to put something in a place carelessly or hastily **❸** to move part of your body quickly **❹** to put someone in a certain state **❺** to confuse or upset someone **❻** to move a switch or lever in order to operate it **❼** to shape a pot on a potter's wheel **❽** to hold a party

throw NOUN a throwing action or movement

thrum VERB to make a low regular sound

thrush NOUN **❶** a songbird with a speckled breast **❷** an infection causing tiny white patches in the mouth and throat

thrust VERB thrusts, thrusting, thrust to push something somewhere with a lot of force

thrust NOUN a hard push

thud NOUN the dull sound of a heavy knock or fall

thud VERB to fall with a thud; to make a thud

thug NOUN a rough and violent person

thumb NOUN the short thick finger set apart from the other four

thumb VERB to turn the pages of a book or magazine quickly with your thumb

thumbnail ADJECTIVE brief; giving only the main facts

thumbnail NOUN a very small picture on a computer screen which shows you what a larger picture looks like

thumbscrew NOUN a former instrument of torture for squeezing the thumb

thump VERB **❶** to hit or knock something heavily **❷** to punch someone **❸** to make a heavy dull sound; to thud **❹** to throb or beat strongly

thump NOUN an act or sound of thumping

thunder NOUN **❶** the loud noise that you hear with lightning during a storm **❷** a similar noise

thunder VERB **❶** to make the noise of thunder or a noise like thunder **❷** to speak loudly

thunderbolt NOUN a lightning flash thought of as a destructive missile

thunderous ADJECTIVE extremely loud

thunderstorm NOUN a storm with thunder and lightning

thunderstruck ADJECTIVE amazed or shocked

Thursday NOUN the day of the week following Wednesday

thus ADVERB **❶** in this way **❷** for this reason; therefore

thwart VERB to frustrate a plan or attempt; to prevent someone from achieving something

thy DETERMINER (old use) your (referring to one person)

thyme (say time) NOUN a herb with fragrant leaves

thyroid gland NOUN a large gland at the front of the neck

thyself PRONOUN (old use) yourself (referring to one person)

tiara (say tee-ar-a) NOUN a woman's jewelled crescent-shaped ornament worn like a crown

tic NOUN an unintentional twitch of a muscle, especially of the face

tick NOUN ❶ (*British*) a mark (✓) put next to something to show that it is correct or has been checked or done ❷ a regular clicking sound, especially the sound made by a clock or watch ❸ (*British*) (*informal*) a moment ❹ a bloodsucking insect

tick VERB ❶ (*British*) to mark something with a tick ❷ to make the sound of a tick

ticket NOUN ❶ a printed piece of paper or card that allows a person to travel on a bus or train, see a show, etc. ❷ a label showing a thing's price

tickle VERB ❶ to touch a person's skin lightly in order to produce a slight tingling feeling and make them laugh and wriggle ❷ a part of your body tickles when you have a slight tingling or itching feeling there ❸ to amuse or please someone

ticklish ADJECTIVE ❶ a ticklish person is likely to laugh or wriggle when they are tickled ❷ awkward or difficult

tidal ADJECTIVE to do with or affected by tides

tidal wave NOUN a huge sea wave

tiddler NOUN (*British*) (*informal*) a very small fish

tiddlywinks NOUN a game, playing by flicking a small counter into a cup by pressing on its edge with another counter

tide NOUN ❶ the regular rising and falling of the level of the sea, which usually happens twice a day ❷ (*old use*) a time or season

tide VERB ➤ **tide someone over** to give someone what they need, especially money, for a short time

tidings PLURAL NOUN (*formal*) news or information

tidy ADJECTIVE ❶ with everything in its right place; neat and orderly ❷ (*informal*) fairly large

tidy VERB to make a place tidy

tidy NOUN the act of tidying a place

tie VERB ❶ to fasten something with string, rope, ribbon, etc. ❷ to arrange something into a knot or bow ❸ to make the same score as another competitor

tie NOUN ❶ a strip of material worn passing under the collar of a shirt and knotted in front ❷ a result when two or more competitors have equal scores ❸ one of the matches in a competition ❹ a close connection or bond

tie-break, tie-breaker NOUN a way to decide the winner when competitors have tied, especially an additional question in a quiz or an additional game at the end of a set in tennis

tier (say teer) NOUN each of a series of rows or levels placed one above the other

tiff NOUN a slight quarrel

tiger NOUN a large wild animal of the cat family, with yellow and black stripes

tight ADJECTIVE ❶ fitting very closely ❷ firmly fastened ❸ fully stretched; tense ❹ in short supply ❺ mean or stingy ❻ severe or strict ❼ (*informal*) slightly drunk

tight ADVERB tightly or firmly

tighten VERB to make something

tighter or to become tighter

tightly ADVERB closely and firmly; in a tight manner

tightrope NOUN a tightly stretched rope high above the ground, for acrobats to perform on

tights PLURAL NOUN a piece of clothing that fits tightly over the feet, legs and lower part of the body

tigress NOUN a female tiger

tile NOUN a thin square piece of baked clay or other hard material, used in rows for covering roofs, walls or floors

tiled ADJECTIVE a tiled roof, wall or floor is covered with tiles

till PREPOSITION & CONJUNCTION until

till NOUN a drawer or box for money in a shop; a cash register

till VERB to plough land to prepare it for cultivating

tiller NOUN a handle used to turn a boat's rudder

tilt VERB to move or move something into a sloping position

tilt NOUN a sloping position

timber NOUN ❶ wood for building or making things ❷ a wooden beam

timbre (say tambr) NOUN the quality of a voice or musical sound

time NOUN ❶ a measure of the continuing existence of everything in years, months, days and other units ❷ what point in the day it is, as shown on a watch or clock ❸ a particular moment or period of things existing or happening ❹ an occasion ❺ a period that is suitable or available for something

❻ a system of measuring time ❼ (*in music*) rhythm depending on the number and stress of beats in the bar

time VERB ❶ to measure how long something takes ❷ to arrange when something is to happen

timeless ADJECTIVE not affected by the passage of time; eternal

time limit NOUN a fixed amount of time within which something must be done

timely ADJECTIVE happening at a suitable or useful time

timer NOUN a device for timing things

times PLURAL NOUN (*in mathematics*) multiplied by

time scale NOUN the length of time that something takes or that you need in order to do something

timetable NOUN a list showing the times when things happen, e.g. when buses or trains arrive and depart or when school lessons take place

timid ADJECTIVE nervous and easily frightened

timing NOUN ❶ the choice of time to do something ❷ the time when something happens

timpani PLURAL NOUN kettledrums

tin NOUN ❶ a silvery-white metal ❷ a metal container for preserving food

tin VERB to seal food in a tin to preserve it

tinder NOUN any dry substance that catches fire easily

tinge VERB ❶ to colour something slightly ❷ to add a slight amount

a
b
c
d
e
f
g
h
i
j
k
l
m
n
o
p
q
r
s
t
u
v
w
x
y
z

of another feeling

tinge NOUN ❶ a slight amount of a colour ❷ a slight amount of a feeling

tingle VERB to have a slight pricking or stinging feeling

tingle NOUN a tingling feeling

tinker NOUN (old use) a person travelling about mending pots and pans

tinker VERB to work at something casually, trying to improve or mend it

tinkle VERB to make a gentle ringing sound

tinkle NOUN a tinkling sound

tinny ADJECTIVE a tinny sound is unpleasantly thin and high-pitched

tinsel NOUN strips of glittering material used for decoration

tint NOUN a shade of colour, especially a pale one

tint VERB to colour something slightly

tiny ADJECTIVE very small

tip NOUN ❶ the part right at the top or end of something ❷ a small but useful piece of advice or information ❸ a small present of extra money given to someone who has served you ❹ a place where you can take rubbish and leave it ❺ a very untidy place

tip VERB ❶ to turn something upside down or tilt it ❷ to give a person a tip to thank them for a service ❸ to name someone as likely to win or succeed ❹ to be tipped with something is to have it right at the end ❺ to leave rubbish somewhere

tipsy ADJECTIVE slightly drunk

tiptoe VERB to walk on your toes very quietly or carefully

tip-top ADJECTIVE (informal) excellent; very best

tirade (say ty-**rayd**) NOUN a long angry or violent speech

tire VERB to make someone tired or to become tired

tired ADJECTIVE feeling that you need to sleep or rest

tireless ADJECTIVE having a lot of energy; not tiring easily

tiresome ADJECTIVE continually annoying

tiring ADJECTIVE making you tired

tissue NOUN ❶ tissue paper ❷ a paper handkerchief ❸ the substance forming any part of the body of an animal or plant

tissue paper NOUN very thin soft paper used for wrapping and packing things

tit NOUN a kind of small bird

titanic (say ty-**tan**-ik) ADJECTIVE huge

titanium NOUN a strong silver-grey metal used to make light alloys that do not corrode easily

titbit NOUN a nice little piece of something, e.g. of food, gossip or information

tithe NOUN one-tenth of a year's output from a farm etc., formerly paid as tax to support the clergy and church

title NOUN ❶ the name of a book, film, song, etc. ❷ a word used to show a person's rank or position, e.g. Dr, Lord, Mrs ❸ a championship in sport ❹ a legal

right to something, especially land or property

titled *ADJECTIVE* a titled person has a title as a noble

titter *VERB* to laugh quietly in a nervous or silly way

titter *NOUN* a quiet nervous or silly laugh

tittle-tattle *NOUN* gossip

TNT *ABBREVIATION* trinitrotoluene; a powerful explosive

to *PREPOSITION* ❶ used to show direction towards a place or position ❷ used to show the limit of something ❸ used for comparison ❹ used to show the person or thing that receives or is affected by something ❺ used before a verb to form an infinitive (*I want to see him.*) or to show purpose (*He does that to annoy us.*) or alone when the verb is understood (*We meant to go but forgot to.*)

to *ADVERB* to or in the proper or closed position or condition

toad *NOUN* a frog-like animal that lives mainly on land

toadstool *NOUN* a fungus (usually poisonous) with a round top on a stalk

toady *VERB* to flatter someone to make them want to help you

toast *VERB* ❶ to heat bread etc. to make it brown and crisp ❷ to warm something in front of a fire or grill ❸ to drink in honour of someone

toast *NOUN* ❶ toasted bread ❷ the call to drink in honour of someone; the person honoured in this way

toaster *NOUN* an electrical device for toasting bread

tobacco *NOUN* the dried leaves of certain plants prepared for smoking in cigarettes, cigars or pipes or for making snuff

toboggan *NOUN* a small sledge used for sliding downhill

today *NOUN* this present day

today *ADVERB* ❶ on this day ❷ nowadays

toddler *NOUN* a young child who has only recently learnt to walk

to-do *NOUN* a fuss or commotion

toe *NOUN* ❶ any of the separate parts (five in humans) at the end of each foot ❷ the part of a shoe, sock or stocking that covers the toes

toffee *NOUN* a sticky sweet made from heated butter and sugar

toga (say **toh**-ga) *NOUN* a long loose piece of clothing worn by men in ancient Rome

together *ADVERB* with another person or thing; with each other

toggle *NOUN* a short piece of wood, metal, etc. used like a button

toil *VERB* ❶ to work hard ❷ to move slowly and with difficulty

toil *NOUN* hard work

toilet *NOUN* ❶ a bowl-like object, connected by pipes to a drain, which you use to get rid of urine and faeces ❷ a room containing a toilet ❸ the process of washing, dressing and tidying yourself

toilet paper *NOUN* paper for cleaning yourself after you have used a toilet

token *NOUN* ❶ a piece of metal or

plastic that can be used instead of money ❷ a voucher or coupon that can be exchanged for goods ❸ a sign or signal of something

tolerable ADJECTIVE able to be put up with

tolerant ADJECTIVE willing to accept or put up with other people's behaviour and opinions even if you do not agree with them

tolerate VERB ❶ to allow something even if you do not approve of it ❷ to bear or put up with something unpleasant

toll (rhymes with *hole*) NOUN ❶ a charge made for using a road or bridge ❷ loss or damage caused by something

toll VERB to ring a bell slowly

tom, tomcat NOUN a male cat

tomahawk NOUN a small axe used by Native Americans

tomato NOUN tomatoes a soft round red or yellow fruit eaten as a vegetable

tomb (say *toom*) NOUN a place where someone is buried; a monument built over this

tombola NOUN (*British*) a kind of lottery

tomboy NOUN a girl who enjoys playing rough noisy games

tombstone NOUN a memorial stone set up over a grave

tome NOUN a large heavy book

tommy gun NOUN a small machine gun

tomorrow NOUN & ADVERB the day after today

tom-tom NOUN a drum beaten with the hands

ton NOUN ❶ a unit of weight equal to 2,240 pounds or about 1,016 kilograms ❷ a large amount ❸ (*informal*) a speed of 100 miles per hour

tonal ADJECTIVE to do with tone

tone NOUN ❶ a sound in music or of the voice ❷ each of the five larger intervals between notes in a musical scale (the smaller intervals are **semitones**) ❸ a shade of a colour ❹ the quality or character of something

tone VERB

tone-deaf ADJECTIVE not able to tell the difference between different musical notes

tongs PLURAL NOUN a tool with two arms joined at one end, used to pick up or hold things

tongue NOUN ❶ the long soft muscular part that moves about inside your mouth ❷ a language ❸ the leather flap on a shoe or boot underneath the laces ❹ a pointed flame

tongue-tied ADJECTIVE too shy to speak

tongue-twister NOUN something that is difficult to say quickly and correctly, e.g. 'She sells seashells.'

tonic NOUN ❶ a medicine etc. that makes a person healthier or stronger ❷ anything that makes a person more energetic or cheerful ❸ (also **tonic water**) a fizzy mineral water with a bitter taste, often mixed with gin ❹ the first note in a scale, providing the keynote in a piece of music

646

tonight *NOUN & ADVERB* this evening or night

tonnage *NOUN* the amount a ship or ships can carry, expressed in tons

tonne *NOUN* a metric ton (1,000 kilograms)

tonsil *NOUN* either of two small masses of soft flesh inside your throat

tonsillitis *NOUN* inflammation of the tonsils

too *ADVERB* ❶ also ❷ more than is wanted or allowed etc.

tool *NOUN* ❶ a device that helps you to do a particular job ❷ a thing used for a particular purpose

toolbar *NOUN* a row of symbols on a computer screen that show the different things that you can do with a particular program

toot *NOUN* a short sound produced by a horn

toot *VERB* to make a toot

tooth *NOUN* teeth ❶ one of the hard white bony parts that are rooted in your gums, used for biting and chewing things ❷ one of a row of sharp parts

toothache *NOUN* pain in your teeth or gums

toothbrush *NOUN* a long-handled brush for cleaning your teeth

toothpaste *NOUN* a paste for cleaning your teeth

toothpick *NOUN* a small pointed piece of wood or plastic for removing bits of food from between your teeth

toothy *ADJECTIVE* having large teeth or showing a lot of teeth

top *NOUN* ❶ the highest part of something ❷ the upper surface of something ❸ the covering or stopper of a bottle, jar, etc. ❹ a piece of clothing you wear on the upper part of your body ❺ a toy that can be made to spin on its point

top *ADJECTIVE* highest or most important

top *VERB* ❶ to put a top on something ❷ to be at the top of something ❸ to remove the top of something

topaz *NOUN* a kind of gem, often yellow

top hat *NOUN* a man's tall stiff black or grey hat worn with formal clothes

topic *NOUN* a subject to write, learn or talk about

topical *ADJECTIVE* to do with things that are happening or in the news now

topless *ADJECTIVE* not wearing any clothes on the top half of the body

topmost *ADJECTIVE* highest or tallest

topography (say top-**og**-ra-fee) *NOUN* the position of the rivers, mountains, roads, buildings, etc. in a place

topping *NOUN* food that is put on the top of a cake, dessert, pizza, etc.

topple *VERB* ❶ to fall over; to totter and fall ❷ to make something fall over ❸ to topple someone in power is to overthrow them

top secret *ADJECTIVE* extremely secret

topsy-turvy *ADVERB & ADJECTIVE*

a
b
c
d
e
f
g
h
i
j
k
l
m
n
o
p
q
r
s
t
u
v
w
x
y
z

upside down; muddled

Torah (say **tor**-uh) NOUN in Judaism, the law of God as given to Moses and recorded in the first five books of the Bible

torch NOUN ❶ a small electric lamp that you can carry in your hand ❷ a stick with burning material on the end, used as a light

toreador (say **tor**ree-a-dor) NOUN a bullfighter

torment VERB ❶ to make someone suffer greatly ❷ to tease or keep annoying someone

torment NOUN great suffering

torn past participle of tear VERB

tornado (say tor-**nay**-doh) NOUN a violent storm or whirlwind

torpedo NOUN torpedoes a long tube-shaped missile that can be fired under water to destroy ships

torpedo VERB to attack or destroy a ship with a torpedo

torrent NOUN ❶ a rushing stream; a great flow ❷ a heavy downpour of rain

torrential ADJECTIVE torrential rain pours down very heavily

torrid ADJECTIVE ❶ very hot and dry ❷ emotional and passionate

torso NOUN the trunk of the human body

tortilla NOUN in Mexican cookery, a flat cake made from flour or maize, often stuffed

tortoise NOUN a slow-moving animal with a shell over its body

tortoiseshell (say **tort**-a-shell) NOUN ❶ the mottled brown and yellow shell of certain turtles, used for making combs etc. ❷ a cat

or butterfly with mottled brown colouring

tortuous ADJECTIVE ❶ full of twists and turns ❷ complicated and not easy to follow

torture VERB ❶ to make a person feel great pain, especially so that they will give information ❷ to cause someone great emotional pain or worry

torture NOUN something done to torture a person; mental or physical suffering

torturous ADJECTIVE like torture; agonizing

Tory NOUN a member of the British Conservative Party

toss VERB ❶ to throw something, especially up into the air ❷ to spin a coin to decide something according to which side of it is upwards after it falls ❸ to move restlessly or unevenly from side to side

toss NOUN the act of tossing a coin or other object

toss-up NOUN ❶ the tossing of a coin ❷ an even chance

tot NOUN ❶ a small child ❷ (informal, chiefly British) a small amount of spirits

tot VERB ➤ to tot something up (informal, chiefly British) to add up figures or amounts

total ADJECTIVE ❶ including everything ❷ complete

total NOUN the amount you get by adding everything together

total VERB ❶ to add up the total ❷ to reach an amount as a total

totalitarian ADJECTIVE using a form of government where people are

not allowed to form rival political
parties

totally *ADVERB* completely

totem pole *NOUN* a pole carved or
painted by Native Americans with
the symbols (*totems*) of their tribes
or families

totter *VERB* to walk unsteadily; to
wobble

toucan (say *too-kan*) *NOUN* a
tropical American bird with a huge
brightly-coloured beak

touch *VERB* ❶ to put your hand
or fingers on something lightly
❷ two things touch when they
join together so that there is no
space between ❸ to come into
contact with something or hit it
gently ❹ to move or meddle with
something ❺ to reach a certain
point ❻ to affect someone's
feelings, e.g. by making them feel
sympathy

touch *NOUN* ❶ the action of
touching ❷ the ability to feel
things by touching them ❸ a small
thing that improves something
❹ communication with someone
❺ a special skill or style of
workmanship ❻ the part of a
football field outside the playing
area

touchdown *NOUN* the action of
touching down

touché (say *too-shay*) *EXCLAMATION*
used to acknowledge a true or
clever point made against you in
an argument

touching *ADJECTIVE* making you feel
sadness, pity or sympathy

touchline *NOUN* one of the lines
that mark the side of a sports pitch

touchscreen *NOUN* a screen on a
computer or phone which allows
you to interact with it by touching
areas on the screen

touchstone *NOUN* a test by which
the quality of something is judged

touchy *ADJECTIVE* easily offended

tough *ADJECTIVE* ❶ strong; difficult
to break or damage ❷ difficult to
chew ❸ able to stand hardship and
not easily hurt ❹ firm or severe
❺ difficult

toughen *VERB* to make someone
or something tough or to become
tough

tour *NOUN* a journey in which you
visit several places

tour *VERB* to make a tour

tourism *NOUN* the industry of
providing services for people on
holiday in a place

tourist *NOUN* a person who visits a
place for pleasure, especially when
on holiday

tournament *NOUN* a competition
in which there is a series of games
or contests

tourniquet (say *toor-nik-ay*)
NOUN a strip of material pulled
tightly round an arm or leg to stop
bleeding from an artery

tousle (say *towz-el*) *VERB* to ruffle
someone's hair

tout (rhymes with *scout*) *VERB* to try
to sell something or get business

tout *NOUN* a person who sells tickets
for a sports match, concert, etc. at
more than the original price

tow (rhymes with *go*) *VERB* to pull a
vehicle along behind you

tow *NOUN* an act of towing

towards, **toward** PREPOSITION ❶ in the direction of ❷ in relation to; regarding ❸ as a contribution to ❹ near; close to

towel NOUN a piece of absorbent cloth for drying things

tower NOUN a tall narrow building or part of a building

tower VERB to be very high; to be taller than others

tower block NOUN (British) a tall building containing offices or flats

town NOUN a place with many houses, shops, offices and other buildings

town hall NOUN a building with offices for the local council and usually a hall for public events

township NOUN in South Africa under apartheid, a town set aside for black people to live

towpath NOUN a path beside a canal or river, originally for use when a horse was towing a barge

toxic ADJECTIVE poisonous; caused by poison

toxin NOUN a poisonous substance, especially one formed in the body by germs

toy NOUN a thing to play with

toy ADJECTIVE ❶ made as a toy ❷ a toy dog is one belonging to a very small breed kept as a pet

toy VERB ► **toy with something** ❶ to think about an idea casually or idly ❷ to move something about without thinking about what you are doing

trace NOUN ❶ a mark or sign left by a person or thing ❷ a very small amount

trace VERB ❶ to copy a picture or map etc. by drawing over it on transparent paper ❷ to find a person or thing after following tracks or other evidence

track NOUN ❶ a mark or marks left by a moving person or thing ❷ a rough path made by being used ❸ a road or area of ground specially prepared for racing ❹ a set of rails for trains or trams to run on ❺ one of the songs or pieces of music on a CD, tape, etc. ❻ a continuous band round the wheels of a heavy vehicle such as a tank or tractor

track VERB ❶ to follow a person or animal by following the tracks they leave ❷ to follow or observe something as it moves

track events PLURAL NOUN athletic events that involve racing on a running track, as opposed to field events

track record NOUN a person's past achievements

track suit NOUN a warm loose suit of the kind worn by athletes before and after contests or for jogging

tract NOUN ❶ an area of land ❷ a series of connected parts along which something passes ❸ a pamphlet containing a short essay, especially about religion

traction NOUN ❶ pulling a load ❷ the ability of a vehicle to grip the ground ❸ a medical treatment in which an injured arm or leg is pulled gently for a long time by means of weights and pulleys

traction engine NOUN a steam or diesel engine for pulling a heavy load along a road or across a field etc.

tractor NOUN a motor vehicle for pulling farm machinery or other heavy loads

trade NOUN ❶ buying, selling or exchanging goods ❷ business of a particular kind; the people working in this ❸ a job or occupation, especially a skilled craft

trade VERB to buy, sell or exchange things

trademark NOUN a symbol or name that a firm puts on its products and that other firms are not allowed to use

trader NOUN a person who buys and sells things

tradesman NOUN a person employed in trade, especially one who sells or delivers goods

trade union NOUN a group of workers organized to help and protect workers in their own trade or industry

tradition NOUN ❶ the passing down of customs or beliefs from one generation to another ❷ a custom or belief passed on in this way

traditional ADJECTIVE ❶ passed down from one generation to another ❷ following older methods and ideas rather than modern ones

traffic NOUN ❶ vehicles, ships or aircraft moving along a route ❷ trading or dealing in drugs or other illegal goods

traffic VERB to deal in something illegal, especially drugs

traffic lights PLURAL NOUN coloured lights used as a signal to traffic at road junctions or roadworks

traffic warden NOUN (British) an official whose job is to make sure that vehicles are parked legally

tragedy NOUN ❶ a play with unhappy events or a sad ending ❷ a very sad or distressing event

tragic ADJECTIVE ❶ very sad or distressing ❷ to do with tragedies

trail NOUN ❶ a track or scent left behind by an animal ❷ a series of marks in a line behind by someone or something that has passed ❸ a path or track for walking through the countryside or a forest

trail VERB ❶ to follow the trail of an animal or person ❷ to be dragged along behind you; to drag something along behind you ❸ to follow someone more slowly or wearily ❹ to hang down or float loosely ❺ to become fainter

trailer NOUN ❶ a truck or other container pulled along by a vehicle ❷ a short piece from a film or television programme, shown in advance to advertise it

train NOUN ❶ a railway engine pulling a line of carriages or trucks that are linked together ❷ a number of people or animals moving in a line ❸ a series of things ❹ part of a long dress or robe that trails on the ground at the back

train VERB ❶ to give a person instruction or practice so that they become skilled ❷ to learn how to do a job ❸ to practise for a sporting event ❹ to make a plant grow in a particular direction ❺ to aim a gun, camera, etc.

trainee NOUN a person who is being trained

trainer NOUN ❶ a person who trains people or animals ❷ a soft rubber-soled shoe of the kind worn for running and sport

traipse VERB to walk wearily; to trudge a long distance

trait (say trayt) NOUN one of a person's characteristics

traitor NOUN a person who betrays their country or friends

trajectory NOUN the path taken by a moving object such as a bullet or rocket

tram NOUN a public passenger vehicle which runs on rails in the road

tramlines PLURAL NOUN ❶ rails for a tram ❷ the pair of parallel lines at the side of a tennis court

tramp NOUN ❶ a person without a home or job who walks from place to place ❷ a long walk ❸ the sound of heavy footsteps

tramp VERB ❶ to walk with heavy footsteps ❷ to walk for a long distance

trample VERB to tread heavily on something; to crush something by treading on it

trampoline NOUN a large piece of canvas joined to a frame by springs, used by gymnasts for jumping on

trance NOUN a dreamy or unconscious state rather like sleep

tranquil ADJECTIVE calm and quiet

tranquillity NOUN being calm and quiet

tranquillizer (also **tranquilliser**) NOUN a drug or medicine used to make a person feel calm

transaction NOUN a piece of business done between people

transatlantic ADJECTIVE across or on the other side of the Atlantic Ocean

transcend VERB to go beyond the usual limits of something

transcribe VERB to copy or write something out

transcript NOUN a written copy

transept NOUN the part that is at right angles to the nave in a cross-shaped church

transfer VERB ❶ to move a person or thing from one place to another ❷ to hand something over to someone else

transfer NOUN ❶ the transferring of a person or thing ❷ a picture or design that can be transferred onto another surface

transfixed ADJECTIVE unable to move because of fear or surprise

transform VERB to change the form, appearance or character of a person or thing to something quite different

transformation NOUN a complete change in the form, appearance or character of a person or thing

transformer NOUN a device used to change the voltage of an electric current

transfusion NOUN putting blood taken from one person into another person's body

transgress *VERB* to break a rule or law

transient *ADJECTIVE* not lasting or staying for long

transistor *NOUN* ❶ a tiny electronic device that controls a flow of electricity ❷ (also **transistor radio**) a portable radio that uses transistors

transit *NOUN* the process of travelling from one place to another

transition *NOUN* the process of changing from one state or form to another

transitive *ADJECTIVE* a transitive verb is one that is used with a direct object after it, e.g. *change* in *change your shoes* (but not in *change into dry shoes*). Compare with **intransitive**.

transitory *ADJECTIVE* existing for a time but not lasting

translate *VERB* to put something into another language

translation *NOUN* something translated from another language

translucent (say tranz-**loo**-sent) *ADJECTIVE* allowing light to shine through but not transparent

transmission *NOUN* ❶ transmitting something ❷ a broadcast ❸ the gears by which power is transmitted from the engine to the wheels of a vehicle

transmit *VERB* ❶ to send or pass something on from one person or place to another ❷ to send out a signal or broadcast

transmitter *NOUN* a device for transmitting radio or television signals

transom *NOUN* ❶ a horizontal bar of wood or stone dividing a window or separating a door from a window above it ❷ a small window above a door

transparency *NOUN* ❶ being transparent ❷ a transparent photograph that can be projected onto a screen

transparent *ADJECTIVE* able to be seen through

transpire *VERB* ❶ to become known; to turn out ❷ to happen ❸ plants transpire when they give off watery vapour from leaves etc.

transplant *VERB* ❶ to transfer an organ from the body of one person to another ❷ to remove a plant and put it to grow somewhere else

transplant *NOUN* ❶ the process of transplanting something ❷ something transplanted

transport *VERB* to take people, animals or things from one place to another

transport *NOUN* the process or means of transporting people, animals or things

transporter *NOUN* a heavy vehicle for transporting large objects, such as cars

transpose *VERB* ❶ to change the position or order of something ❷ to put a piece of music into a different key

transverse *ADJECTIVE* lying across something

transvestite *NOUN* a person who likes wearing clothes intended for someone of the opposite gender

a
b
c
d
e
f
g
h
i
j
k
l
m
n
o
p
q
r
s
t
u
v
w
x
y
z

trap NOUN **1** a device for catching and holding animals **2** a plan or trick for capturing, detecting or cheating someone **3** a two-wheeled carriage pulled by a horse **4** a bend in a pipe, filled with water to prevent gases from rising up from a drain

trap VERB **1** to catch or hold a person or animal in a trap **2** to be trapped is to be stuck in a dangerous place or difficult situation you cannot escape from **3** to trick someone into doing or saying something

trapdoor NOUN a door in a floor, ceiling or roof

trapeze NOUN a bar hanging from two ropes as a swing for acrobats

trapezium NOUN a quadrilateral in which two opposite sides are parallel and the other two are not

trapezoid NOUN a quadrilateral in which no sides are parallel

trapper NOUN someone who traps wild animals, especially for their fur

trappings PLURAL NOUN **1** the clothes or possessions that show your rank or position **2** an ornamental harness for a horse

trash NOUN rubbish or nonsense

trash can NOUN (*North American*) a dustbin

trauma (say *traw*-ma) NOUN a shock or upsetting experience that produces a lasting effect on a person's mind

traumatic ADJECTIVE a traumatic experience is very unpleasant and upsetting

travel VERB to go from one place to another

travel NOUN going on journeys

travel agent NOUN a person whose job is to arrange travel and holidays for people

traveller NOUN **1** a person who is travelling or who often travels **2** a gypsy or a person who does not settle in one place

traveller's cheque NOUN a cheque for a fixed amount of money that is sold by banks and that can be exchanged for money in foreign countries

traverse VERB to go across something, especially as part of a journey or expedition

travesty NOUN a bad or ridiculous form of something

trawl VERB to fish by dragging a large net along the seabed

trawler NOUN a boat used in trawling

tray NOUN **1** a flat piece of wood, metal or plastic, usually with raised edges, for carrying cups, plates, food, etc. **2** an open container for holding documents and letters in an office

treacherous ADJECTIVE **1** betraying someone; disloyal or unreliable **2** dangerous or unreliable

treachery NOUN doing something that betrays someone

treacle NOUN a thick sticky liquid produced when sugar is purified

tread VERB treads, treading, trod, trodden to walk on something or put your foot on it

tread NOUN ❶ a sound or way of walking ❷ the top surface of a stair; the part you put your foot on ❸ the part of a tyre that touches the ground

treadmill NOUN ❶ a wide mill wheel turned by the weight of people or animals treading on steps fixed round its edge ❷ monotonous routine work

treason NOUN betraying your country

treasure NOUN ❶ a store of precious metals or jewels ❷ a precious thing or person

treasure VERB to value greatly something that you have

treasure hunt NOUN a game in which people try to find a hidden object

treasurer NOUN a person in charge of the money of a club, society, etc.

treasure trove NOUN gold or silver etc. found hidden and with no known owner

treasury NOUN a place where money and valuables are kept

treat VERB ❶ to behave in a certain way towards a person or thing ❷ to deal with a subject ❸ to give medical care to a person or animal ❹ to put something through a chemical or other process ❺ to pay for someone else's food, drink or entertainment

treat NOUN ❶ something special that gives pleasure ❷ the process of treating someone to food, drink or entertainment

treatise NOUN a book or long essay on a subject

treatment NOUN ❶ the way you behave towards or deal with a person, animal or thing ❷ medical care

treaty NOUN a formal agreement between two or more countries

treble ADJECTIVE three times as much or as many

treble NOUN ❶ a treble amount ❷ a person with a high-pitched or soprano voice

treble VERB to make something, or to become, three times as much or as many

tree NOUN a tall plant with a single very thick hard stem or trunk that is usually without branches for some distance above the ground

trek NOUN a long walk or journey

trek VERB to go on a long walk or journey

trellis NOUN a framework with crossing bars of wood or metal to support climbing plants

tremble VERB to shake gently, especially because you are afraid

tremble NOUN a trembling movement or sound

tremendous ADJECTIVE ❶ very large; huge ❷ excellent

tremor NOUN ❶ a shaking or trembling movement ❷ a slight earthquake

tremulous ADJECTIVE trembling from nervousness or weakness

trench NOUN a long narrow hole cut in the ground

trend NOUN the general direction in which something is going or developing

trendy ADJECTIVE (informal)

a
b
c
d
e
f
h
i
j
k
l
m
n
o
p
q
r
s
t
u
v
w
x
y
z

fashionable; following the latest trends

trepidation NOUN fear and anxiety about something that may happen

trespass VERB ❶ to go on someone's land or property without their permission ❷ (old use) to do wrong; to sin

trespass NOUN (old use) wrongdoing; sin

tress NOUN a lock of hair

trestle NOUN each of a set of supports on which you place a board to form a table

triad (say try-ad) NOUN ❶ a group or set of three things ❷ a Chinese secret organization involved in crime

trial NOUN ❶ the process of examining the evidence in a law court to decide whether a person is guilty of a crime ❷ testing a thing to see how good it is or how well it works ❸ a test of qualities or ability ❹ an annoying person or thing; a hardship

triangle NOUN ❶ a flat shape with three sides and three angles ❷ a percussion instrument made from a metal rod bent into a triangle

triangular ADJECTIVE in the shape of a triangle

tribal ADJECTIVE to do with or belonging to a tribe

tribe NOUN ❶ a group of families living in one area as a community, ruled by a chief ❷ a set of people

tribulation NOUN great trouble or hardship

tribunal (say try-bew-nal) NOUN a committee appointed to hear

evidence and give judgements when there is a dispute

tribune NOUN an official chosen by the people in ancient Rome

tributary NOUN a river or stream that flows into a larger one or into a lake

tribute NOUN ❶ something said, done or given as a mark of respect or admiration for someone ❷ payment that one country or ruler had to pay to a more powerful one in the past

trice NOUN (old use) ➤ in a trice in a moment

triceps (say try-seps) NOUN the large muscle at the back of the upper arm

trick NOUN ❶ a crafty or deceitful action; a practical joke ❷ a skilful action, especially one done for entertainment ❸ the cards picked up by the winner after one round of a card game such as whist

trick VERB to deceive or cheat someone by a trick

trickery NOUN the use of tricks; deception

trickle VERB to flow or move slowly

trickle NOUN a slow gradual flow

trickster NOUN a person who tricks or cheats people

tricky ADJECTIVE ❶ difficult to do or deal with ❷ cunning or deceitful

tricolour (say trik-ol-er) NOUN a flag with three coloured stripes, e.g. the national flag of France or Ireland

tricycle NOUN a vehicle like a bicycle but with three wheels

trident NOUN a three-pronged

spear, carried by Neptune and Britannia as a symbol of their power over the sea

trifle NOUN ❶ a pudding made of sponge cake covered in custard, fruit and cream ❷ a very small amount ❸ something that has very little importance or value

trifle VERB to treat a person or thing without seriousness or respect

trifling ADJECTIVE small in value or importance

trigger NOUN a lever that is pulled to fire a gun

trigger VERB to make something happen, especially suddenly

trigonometry (say trig-on-**om**-it-ree) NOUN the calculation of distances and angles by using triangles

trilby NOUN (chiefly British) a man's soft felt hat

trill VERB ❶ to make a quivering musical sound ❷ to say something in a high cheerful voice

trill NOUN a quivering musical sound

trillion NOUN ❶ a million million ❷ (old use) a million million million

trilogy NOUN a group of three stories, poems or plays etc. about the same people or things

trim VERB ❶ to cut the edges or unwanted parts off something ❷ to decorate a piece of clothing by adding lace, ribbons, etc. ❸ to arrange sails to suit the wind

trim NOUN ❶ cutting or trimming ❷ lace, ribbons, etc. used to decorate something

trim ADJECTIVE neat and orderly

Trinity NOUN in Christianity, God regarded as three persons (Father, Son and Holy Spirit)

trinket NOUN a small ornament or piece of jewellery

trio NOUN ❶ a group of three people or things ❷ a group of three musicians or singers ❸ a piece of music for three musicians

trip VERB ❶ to catch your foot on something and fall; to make someone do this ❷ to move with quick light steps ❸ to operate a switch

trip NOUN ❶ a journey or outing ❷ the action of tripping; a stumble ❸ (informal) hallucinations caused by taking a drug

tripe NOUN ❶ part of an ox's stomach used as food ❷ (informal) rubbish or nonsense

triple ADJECTIVE ❶ consisting of three parts ❷ involving three people or groups ❸ three times as much or as many

triple VERB to make something, or to become, three times as much or as many

triple jump NOUN an athletic contest in which competitors try to jump as far as possible by doing a hop, step and jump

triplet NOUN each of three children or animals born to the same mother at one time

tripod (say try-pod) NOUN a stand with three legs, e.g. to support a camera or telescope

trite (rhymes with kite) ADJECTIVE worn out by constant repetition; hackneyed

triumph NOUN ❶ a great success or victory ❷ a feeling of joy at success or victory

triumph VERB ❶ to be successful or victorious ❷ to rejoice in success or victory

triumphant ADJECTIVE ❶ victorious in a battle or contest ❷ rejoicing over a victory or success

triumvirate NOUN a ruling group of three people

trivet NOUN an iron stand for a pot or kettle, placed over a fire

trivia PLURAL NOUN unimportant details or pieces of information

trivial ADJECTIVE small in value or importance

troll (rhymes with *hole*) NOUN ❶ in Scandinavian mythology, a supernatural being, either a giant or a friendly but mischievous dwarf ❷ a person who writes unpleasant comments on the Internet in order to annoy people

trolley NOUN ❶ a small table on wheels or castors, used for serving food and drink ❷ a basket on wheels, used in supermarkets

trombone NOUN a large brass musical instrument with a sliding tube

troop NOUN ❶ an organized group of soldiers, Scouts, etc. ❷ a number of people or animals moving along together

troop VERB to move along as a group or in large numbers

trooper NOUN a soldier in the cavalry or in an armoured unit

troops PLURAL NOUN soldiers

trophy NOUN ❶ a cup or other prize given for winning a competition ❷ something taken in war or hunting as a souvenir of success

tropic NOUN a line of latitude about 23½° north of the equator (**tropic of Cancer**) or 23½° south of the equator (**tropic of Capricorn**)

tropical ADJECTIVE to do with, or found in, the tropics

trot VERB ❶ a horse trots when it moves faster than when walking but more slowly than when cantering ❷ a person trots when they run gently with short steps

trot NOUN a trotting run

troth (rhymes with *both*) NOUN (*old use*) loyalty; a solemn promise

trotter NOUN a pig's foot used for food

troubadour (say **troo**-bad-oor) NOUN a poet and singer in southern France in the 11th-13th centuries

trouble NOUN ❶ a problem, difficulty or worry ❷ a cause of any of these

trouble VERB ❶ to cause trouble to someone ❷ to bother or disturb someone ❸ to make an effort to do something

troublemaker NOUN a person who often deliberately causes trouble

troublesome ADJECTIVE causing trouble or annoyance

trough (say trof) NOUN ❶ a long narrow open container, especially one holding water or food for animals ❷ a channel for liquid ❸ the low part between two waves or ridges ❹ a long region of low air pressure

trounce VERB to defeat someone

heavily

troupe (say troop) NOUN a company of actors or other performers

trousers PLURAL NOUN a piece of clothing worn over the lower half of your body, with a separate part for each leg

trout NOUN a freshwater fish that is caught as a sport and for food

trowel NOUN ❶ a small garden tool with a curved blade for lifting plants or scooping things ❷ a small tool with a flat blade for spreading mortar or cement

truant NOUN a child who stays away from school without permission

truce NOUN an agreement to stop fighting for a while

truck NOUN ❶ a lorry ❷ an open container on wheels for transporting loads; an open railway wagon ❸ an axle with wheels attached, fitted under a skateboard

truculent (say **truk**-yoo-lent) ADJECTIVE defiant and aggressive

trudge VERB to walk slowly and heavily

true ADJECTIVE ❶ representing what has really happened or exists ❷ genuine or proper; not false ❸ accurate or exact ❹ loyal or faithful

truffle NOUN ❶ a soft sweet made with chocolate ❷ a fungus that grows underground and is valued as food because of its rich flavour

truly ADVERB ❶ truthfully ❷ sincerely or genuinely ❸ (old use) loyally or faithfully

trump NOUN ❶ a playing card of a

suit that ranks above the others for one game or round of play ❷ (old use) a blast of a trumpet

trump VERB to beat a card by playing a trump

trumpet NOUN ❶ a metal wind instrument with a narrow tube that widens near the end ❷ something shaped like this

trumpet VERB ❶ an elephant trumpets when it makes a loud sound with its trunk ❷ to blow a trumpet ❸ to shout or announce something loudly

truncate VERB to shorten something by cutting off its beginning or end

truncheon NOUN (chiefly British) a short thick stick carried as a weapon by a police officer

trundle VERB to move something along heavily, especially on wheels, or to move like this

trunk NOUN ❶ the main stem of a tree ❷ an elephant's long flexible nose ❸ a large box with a hinged lid for transporting or storing clothes etc. ❹ the human body except for the head, arms and legs ❺ (North American) the boot of a car

trunks PLURAL NOUN shorts worn by men and boys for swimming, boxing, etc.

truss NOUN ❶ a framework of beams or bars supporting a roof or bridge ❷ a type of padded belt worn to support a hernia

truss VERB ❶ to tie up a person or thing securely ❷ to support a roof or bridge with trusses

trust VERB ❶ to believe that a

person or thing is good, truthful or reliable ❷ to let a person have or use something in the belief that they will look after it ❸ to hope or expect something

trust NOUN ❶ the belief that a person or thing can be trusted ❷ responsibility; being trusted ❸ a legal arrangement in which a person looks after money or property for someone else with instructions about how to use it

trustee NOUN a person who looks after money or property for someone else

trustworthy ADJECTIVE able to be trusted; reliable

trusty ADJECTIVE trustworthy or reliable

truth NOUN ❶ a true fact or statement ❷ the quality of being true

truthful ADJECTIVE ❶ telling the truth ❷ true

try VERB ❶ to make an effort to do something; to attempt something ❷ to test something by using or doing it ❸ to examine the evidence in a law court to decide whether a person is guilty of a crime ❹ to be a strain on something

try NOUN ❶ a go at trying something; an attempt ❷ in rugby, putting the ball down behind the opponents' goal line in order to score points

trying ADJECTIVE putting a strain on your patience; annoying

tsar (say zar) NOUN the title of the former ruler of Russia

tsetse fly (say **tet**-see) NOUN a

tropical African fly which has a bite that can cause sleeping sickness in people

T-shirt NOUN a short-sleeved shirt shaped like a T

tsunami NOUN a huge sea wave caused by an underwater earthquake

tub NOUN a round open container holding liquid, ice cream, soil for plants, etc.

tuba (say **tew**-ba) NOUN a large brass wind instrument that makes a deep sound

tubby ADJECTIVE short and fat

tube NOUN ❶ a long hollow piece of metal, plastic, rubber, glass, etc., especially for liquids or gases to pass along ❷ a long hollow container made of soft metal or plastic, for something soft ❸ the underground railway in London

tuber NOUN a short thick rounded root (e.g. of a dahlia) or underground stem (e.g. of a potato) that produces buds from which new plants will grow

tuberculosis NOUN a disease of people and animals, producing small swellings in parts of the body, especially in the lungs

tubing NOUN tubes; a length of tube

tubular ADJECTIVE shaped like a tube

tuck VERB ❶ to push a loose edge into something so that it is hidden or held in place ❷ to put something away in a small space

tuck NOUN ❶ a flat fold stitched in a piece of clothing ❷ (informal) food, especially sweets and cakes etc. that children enjoy

tucker NOUN (*informal*) (*Australian/NZ*) food

Tuesday NOUN the day of the week following Monday

tuft NOUN a bunch of threads, grass, hair or feathers growing or held close together

tug VERB ❶ to pull something hard or suddenly ❷ to tow a ship

tug NOUN ❶ a hard or sudden pull ❷ a small powerful boat used for towing others

tug of war NOUN a contest between two teams pulling a rope from opposite ends

tuition NOUN teaching, especially when given to one person or a small group

tulip NOUN a large cup-shaped flower on a tall stem growing from a bulb

tumble VERB ❶ to fall or roll over suddenly or clumsily ❷ to move or fall somewhere in an uncontrolled or untidy way

tumble NOUN a sudden fall or drop

tumble-drier NOUN a machine that dries washing by turning it over many times in heated air

tumbler NOUN ❶ a drinking glass with no stem or handle ❷ a part of a lock that is lifted when a key is turned to open it ❸ an acrobat

tummy NOUN (*informal*) your stomach

tumour (say **tew**-mer) NOUN an abnormal lump growing on or in the body

tumult (say **tew**-mult) NOUN an

uproar or state of noisy confusion and agitation

tumultuous (say tew-**mul**-tew-us) ADJECTIVE noisy and excited

tun NOUN a large cask or barrel

tuna (say **tew**-na) NOUN a large edible sea fish with pink flesh

tundra NOUN the vast level Arctic regions of Europe, Asia and America where there are no trees and the subsoil is always frozen

tune NOUN a short piece of music; a pleasant series of musical notes

tune VERB ❶ to put a musical instrument in tune ❷ to adjust a radio or television set to receive a certain channel ❸ to adjust an engine so that it runs smoothly

tuneful ADJECTIVE having a pleasant tune

tungsten NOUN a grey metal used to make a kind of steel

tunic NOUN ❶ a jacket worn as part of a uniform ❷ a piece of clothing without sleeves, reaching from the shoulders to the hips or knees

tunnel NOUN a passage made underground or through a hill

tunnel VERB to make a tunnel

turban NOUN a covering for the head made by wrapping a strip of cloth round a cap, worn especially by Muslims and Sikhs

turbine NOUN a machine or motor that is driven by a flow of water, steam or gas

turbojet NOUN a jet engine or aircraft with turbines

turbot NOUN a large flat edible sea fish

turbulence NOUN violent and

uneven movement of air or water

turbulent ADJECTIVE ❶ moving violently and unevenly ❷ involving much change and disagreement and sometimes violence

tureen NOUN a deep dish with a lid, from which soup is served at the table

turf NOUN ❶ short grass and the earth round its roots ❷ a piece of this cut from the ground

turf VERB to cover ground with turf

turgid (say ter-jid) ADJECTIVE pompous and boring

turkey NOUN a large bird kept for its meat

turmoil NOUN wild confusion or agitation

turn VERB ❶ to move round or take a new direction; to make something move in this way ❷ to change in appearance etc.; to become ❸ to make something change ❹ to move a switch or tap etc. to control something ❺ to pass a certain time ❻ to shape something on a lathe

turn NOUN ❶ the action of turning; a turning movement ❷ a change; the point where something turns ❸ a place where a road bends ❹ an opportunity or duty that comes to each person in succession ❺ a short performance in an entertainment ❻ (informal) an attack of illness; a nervous shock

turncoat NOUN a person who changes sides or changes what they believe

turning NOUN a place where one road meets another, forming a corner

turning point NOUN a point where an important change takes place

turnip NOUN a plant with a large round white root used as a vegetable

turnout NOUN the number of people who attend a meeting, vote at an election, etc.

turnover NOUN ❶ the amount of money received by a firm selling things ❷ the rate at which goods are sold or workers leave and are replaced ❸ a small pie made by folding pastry over fruit, jam, etc.

turnpike NOUN (old use) a road on which a toll was charged

turnstile NOUN a revolving gate that lets one person in at a time

turntable NOUN a circular revolving platform or support, e.g. for the record in a record player

turpentine NOUN a kind of oil used for thinning paint, cleaning paintbrushes, etc.

turps NOUN (informal) turpentine

turquoise NOUN ❶ a sky-blue or greenish-blue colour ❷ a bright blue jewel

turret NOUN ❶ a small tower on a castle or other building ❷ a revolving structure containing a gun

turtle NOUN a sea animal that looks like a tortoise

turtle-dove NOUN a wild dove

tusk NOUN a long pointed tooth that sticks out from the mouth of an elephant, walrus, etc.

tussle NOUN a struggle or conflict over something

tussle VERB to struggle or fight over something

tussock NOUN a tuft or clump of grass

tutor NOUN ❶ a private teacher, especially of one pupil or a small group ❷ a teacher of students in a college or university

tutorial NOUN a meeting in which students discuss a subject with their tutor

tutu (say **too**-too) NOUN a ballet dancer's short stiff frilled skirt

TV ABBREVIATION television

twaddle NOUN (informal) nonsense

twain NOUN & ADJECTIVE (old use) two

twang NOUN ❶ a sharp sound like that of a wire when plucked ❷ a nasal tone in a person's voice

twang VERB ❶ to make a sharp sound like that of a wire when plucked ❷ to play a guitar etc. by plucking its strings

tweak VERB to pinch and twist or pull something sharply

tweak NOUN a tweaking movement

tweed NOUN a thick rough woollen cloth, often woven of mixed colours

tweeds PLURAL NOUN clothes made of tweed

tweet NOUN ❶ the chirping sound made by a small bird ❷ a short message sent on the social network Twitter

tweet VERB ❶ a small bird tweets when it makes a chirping sound ❷ to send a message on the social network Twitter

tweezers PLURAL NOUN small pincers for picking up or pulling very

small things

twelve NOUN & ADJECTIVE the number 12

twenty NOUN & ADJECTIVE the number 20

twice ADVERB ❶ two times; on two occasions ❷ double the amount

twiddle VERB to turn something round or over and over in an idle way

twiddle NOUN a twiddling movement

twig NOUN a small shoot on a branch or stem of a tree or shrub

twig VERB (informal) to realize what something means

twilight NOUN dim light from the sky just after sunset or just before sunrise

twin NOUN ❶ either of two children or animals born to the same mother at one time ❷ either of two things that are exactly alike

twin VERB ❶ to put things together as a pair ❷ (British) if a town is twinned with a town in a different country, the two towns exchange visits and organize cultural events together

twine NOUN strong thin string

twine VERB to twist or wind one thing round another

twinge NOUN a sudden pain or unpleasant feeling

twinkle VERB ❶ to shine with tiny flashes of light; to sparkle ❷ your eyes twinkle when they look bright because you are happy or amused

twinkle NOUN ❶ a twinkling light ❷ a bright expression in your

663

eyes that shows you are happy or amused

twirl VERB ❶ to twist something round quickly ❷ to turn around in a circle

twirl NOUN a twirling movement

twist VERB ❶ to turn the ends of something in opposite directions ❷ to turn round or from side to side ❸ to bend something out of its proper shape ❹ to pass threads or strands round something or round each other ❺ to distort the meaning of what someone says

twist NOUN ❶ a twisting movement or action ❷ a strange or unexpected development in a story or series of events

twister NOUN (North American) a tornado

twit NOUN (informal, chiefly British) a silly or foolish person

twitch VERB to move suddenly with a slight jerk or to make something do this

twitch NOUN a twitching movement

twitter VERB birds twitter when they make quick chirping sounds

twitter NOUN a twittering sound

two NOUN & ADJECTIVE the number 2

two-dimensional ADJECTIVE having two dimensions (length and width); flat

two-faced ADJECTIVE insincere or deceitful

tycoon NOUN a rich and influential business person

tying present participle of tie

type NOUN ❶ a kind or sort ❷ letters or figures etc. designed for use in printing

type VERB to write something by using a keyboard

typecast VERB an actor is typecast when they are always given the same kind of role to play

typescript NOUN a typed copy of a text or document

typewriter NOUN a machine with keys that you press to print letters or figures etc. on a piece of paper

typhoid fever NOUN a serious infectious disease with fever, caused by harmful bacteria in food or water

typhoon NOUN a violent hurricane in the western Pacific or East Asian seas

typhus NOUN an infectious disease causing fever, weakness and a rash

typical ADJECTIVE ❶ having the usual characteristics or qualities of a particular type of person or thing ❷ as you would expect from a particular person or thing

typify (say **tip**-if-eye) VERB to be a typical example of something

typist NOUN a person who types, especially as their job

tyrannize (also **tyrannise**) (say **tirran**-yz) VERB to behave like a tyrant to people

tyrannosaurus NOUN a huge flesh-eating dinosaur that walked upright on its large hind legs

tyranny (say **tirran**-ee) NOUN ❶ government by a tyrant ❷ the way a tyrant behaves towards people

tyrant (say **ty**-rant) NOUN a person who rules cruelly and unjustly; someone who insists on being obeyed

tyre *NOUN* a covering of rubber fitted round a wheel to make it grip the road and run more smoothly

Uu

udder *NOUN* the bag-like part of a cow, ewe, female goat, etc. from which milk is taken

UFO *ABBREVIATION* unidentified flying object

ugly *ADJECTIVE* ❶ unpleasant to look at; not beautiful ❷ hostile and threatening

UHF *ABBREVIATION* ultra-high frequency (between 300 and 3000 megahertz)

UHT *ABBREVIATION* (*British*) ultra heat-treated; used to describe milk that has been treated at a very high temperature so that it will keep for a long time

UK *ABBREVIATION* United Kingdom

ukulele (say yoo-kul-**ay**-lee) *NOUN* a small guitar with four strings

ulcer *NOUN* a sore on the inside or outside of the body

ulterior *ADJECTIVE* beyond what is obvious or stated

ultimate *ADJECTIVE* furthest in a series of things; final

ultimately *ADVERB* in the end; finally

ultimatum (say ul-tim-**ay**-tum) *NOUN* a final demand or statement that, unless something is done by a certain time, action will be taken or war will be declared

ultra– *PREFIX* ❶ beyond (as in *ultraviolet*) ❷ extremely; excessively (as in *ultra-modern*)

ultramarine *NOUN* a deep bright blue

ultrasonic *ADJECTIVE* an ultrasonic sound is beyond the range of human hearing

ultrasound *NOUN* sound with an ultrasonic frequency, used in medical examinations

ultraviolet *ADJECTIVE* ultraviolet light rays are beyond the violet end of the spectrum and so not visible to the human eye

umber *NOUN* a kind of brown pigment

umbilical cord (say um-**bil**-ik-al) *NOUN* the tube through which a baby receives nourishment before it is born, connecting its body with the mother's womb

umbrage *NOUN* ➤ take umbrage to take offence

umbrella *NOUN* a circular piece of material stretched over a folding frame with a central stick or pole, which you open to protect yourself from rain

umlaut *NOUN* a mark (¨) placed over a vowel in German to indicate a change in its pronunciation

umpire *NOUN* a referee in cricket, tennis and some other games

umpire *VERB* to act as an umpire

un– *PREFIX* ❶ not (as in *uncertain*) ❷ used before a verb to reverse its action (as in *unlock* = release from being locked)

unable *ADJECTIVE* not able to do something

unaided ADJECTIVE without any help

unanimous (say yoo-**nan**-im-us) ADJECTIVE with everyone agreeing

unarmed ADJECTIVE without weapons

unassuming ADJECTIVE modest; not arrogant or pretentious

unavoidable ADJECTIVE not able to be avoided; bound to happen

unaware ADJECTIVE not aware; not knowing about something

unawares ADVERB unexpectedly; without warning

unbalanced ADJECTIVE ❶ not balanced ❷ slightly mad or mentally ill

unbearable ADJECTIVE so painful or unpleasant that you cannot bear or endure it

unbeatable ADJECTIVE unable to be defeated or improved on

unbeaten ADJECTIVE that has not been defeated or improved on

unbecoming ADJECTIVE ❶ not making a person look attractive ❷ not suitable or fitting

unbelievable ADJECTIVE ❶ difficult to believe ❷ amazing

unbend VERB unbends, unbending, unbent ❶ to change from a bent position; to straighten up ❷ to relax and become friendly

unblock VERB to remove an obstruction from something

unborn ADJECTIVE not yet born

unbridled ADJECTIVE not controlled or restrained

unbroken ADJECTIVE not broken or interrupted

unburden VERB to remove a burden

from the person carrying it

uncalled for ADJECTIVE not justified or necessary

uncanny ADJECTIVE strange or mysterious

uncertain ADJECTIVE ❶ not known certainly ❷ not sure or confident about something ❸ not reliable

uncertainly ADVERB without confidence; hesitantly

uncharitable ADJECTIVE making unkind judgements about people or actions

uncle NOUN the brother of your father or mother; your aunt's husband

unclear ADJECTIVE ❶ not clear or definite ❷ not certain about something

uncomfortable ADJECTIVE ❶ not comfortable ❷ uneasy or awkward about something

uncommon ADJECTIVE not common; unusual

uncompromising (say un-**komp**-ro-my-zing) ADJECTIVE not allowing a compromise; inflexible

unconcerned ADJECTIVE not caring about something; not worried

unconditional ADJECTIVE without any conditions; complete or absolute

unconscious ADJECTIVE ❶ not conscious ❷ not aware of things ❸ done without realizing it

uncontrollable ADJECTIVE unable to be controlled or stopped

uncooperative ADJECTIVE not cooperative

uncouth (say un-**kooth**) ADJECTIVE

rude and rough in manner

uncover VERB ❶ to remove the covering from something ❷ to discover or reveal something

undecided ADJECTIVE ❶ not yet settled; not certain ❷ not having made up your mind yet

undeniable ADJECTIVE impossible to deny; undoubtedly true

under PREPOSITION ❶ below or beneath ❷ less than ❸ governed or controlled by ❹ in the process of; undergoing ❺ making use of ❻ according to the rules of

under ADVERB in or to a lower place or level or condition

underarm ADJECTIVE & ADVERB ❶ moving the hand and arm forward and upwards ❷ in or for the armpit

undercarriage NOUN an aircraft's landing wheels and their supports

underclothes PLURAL NOUN underwear

undercover ADJECTIVE done or doing things secretly

undercurrent NOUN ❶ a current that is below the surface or below another current ❷ a feeling or influence that is hidden beneath the surface but whose effects are felt

undercut VERB to sell something for a lower price than someone else sells it

underdeveloped ADJECTIVE ❶ not fully developed or grown ❷ an underdeveloped country is poor and lacks modern industrial development

underdog NOUN a person or team in a contest that is expected to lose

underdone ADJECTIVE not thoroughly done; undercooked

underestimate VERB to make too low an estimate of a person or thing

underfoot ADVERB on the ground; under your feet

undergo VERB undergoes, undergoing, underwent, undergone to experience or go through something

undergraduate NOUN a student at a university who has not yet taken a degree

underground ADJECTIVE & ADVERB ❶ under the ground ❷ done or working in secret

underground NOUN a railway that runs through tunnels under the ground

undergrowth NOUN (British) bushes and other plants growing closely, especially under trees

underhand ADJECTIVE done or doing things in a sly or secret way

underlie VERB underlies, underlying, underlay, underlain ❶ to be the basis or explanation of something ❷ to be or lie under something

underline VERB ❶ to draw a line under something you have written ❷ to emphasize something or show it clearly

underlying ADJECTIVE ❶ forming the basis or explanation of something but not easy to notice ❷ lying under something

undermine VERB to weaken

a
b
c
d
e
f
g
h
i
j
k
l
m
n
o
p
q
r
s
t
u
v
w
x
y
z

something gradually

underneath PREPOSITION & ADVERB below or beneath

underpants PLURAL NOUN a piece of men's underwear covering the lower part of the body, worn under trousers

underpass NOUN a road that goes underneath another

underprivileged ADJECTIVE having a lower standard of living and fewer opportunities than most other people in society

underrate VERB to have too low an opinion of a person or thing

undersigned ADJECTIVE who has or have signed at the bottom of this document

undersized ADJECTIVE of less than the normal size

understand VERB understands, understanding, understood ① to know what something means or how it works or why it exists ② to know what someone is like and why they behave the way they do ③ to have heard or been told something ④ to take something for granted

understandable ADJECTIVE ① able to be understood ② reasonable or natural

understanding NOUN ① the power to understand or think; intelligence ② sympathy or tolerance ③ agreement in opinion or feeling

understanding ADJECTIVE sympathetic and helpful

understatement NOUN a statement that does not say

something strongly enough or give the complete truth

understudy NOUN an actor who learns a part in order to be able to play it if the usual actor is ill or absent

understudy VERB to be an understudy for an actor or part

undertake VERB ① to agree or promise to do something ② to take on a task or responsibility

undertaker NOUN a person whose job is to arrange funerals and burials or cremations

undertaking NOUN ① a job or task that is being undertaken ② a promise or guarantee ③ the business of an undertaker

undertone NOUN ① a low or quiet tone to someone's voice ② an underlying quality or feeling

underwater ADJECTIVE & ADVERB placed, used or done beneath the surface of water

underwear NOUN clothes you wear next to your skin, under other clothes

underweight ADJECTIVE not heavy enough

underwent past tense of undergo

underworld NOUN ① the people who are regularly involved in crime ② in myths and legends, the place for the spirits of the dead, under the earth

undesirable ADJECTIVE not wanted or liked

undeveloped ADJECTIVE not yet developed

undignified ADJECTIVE not dignified

undo VERB ① to unfasten or unwrap

something ❷ to cancel the effect of something

undoing NOUN ➤ **be someone's undoing** to be the cause of someone's ruin or failure

undoubted ADJECTIVE certain or definite; not regarded as doubtful

undoubtedly ADVERB definitely; without a doubt

undress VERB to take your clothes off

undue ADJECTIVE more than is necessary or reasonable

undulate VERB to move like a wave or waves; to have a wavy appearance

unduly ADVERB excessively; more than is reasonable

undying ADJECTIVE lasting forever

unearth VERB ❶ to dig something up; to uncover something by digging ❷ to find something by searching

unearthly ADJECTIVE ❶ unnatural; strange and frightening ❷ (informal) very early or inconvenient

uneasy ADJECTIVE ❶ worried or anxious ❷ uncomfortable

unemployed ADJECTIVE without a job

unemployment NOUN ❶ being without a job ❷ the number of people without a job

unending ADJECTIVE not coming to an end; endless

unequal ADJECTIVE ❶ not equal in amount, size or value ❷ not giving the same opportunities to everyone

unerring (say un-**er**-ing) ADJECTIVE making no mistake

uneven ADJECTIVE ❶ not level or regular ❷ not equally balanced

unexpected ADJECTIVE not expected; coming as a surprise

unexpectedly ADVERB when you are not expecting it

unfair ADJECTIVE not fair; unjust

unfaithful ADJECTIVE ❶ not faithful or loyal ❷ not sexually loyal to one partner

unfamiliar ADJECTIVE not familiar

unfasten VERB to open the fastenings of something

unfavourable ADJECTIVE not favourable or helpful

unfeeling ADJECTIVE not caring about other people's feelings; unsympathetic

unfit ADJECTIVE ❶ not in perfect health because you do not take enough exercise ❷ not suitable for something

unfold VERB ❶ to open something out or spread it out ❷ to become known gradually

unforeseen ADJECTIVE not foreseen; unexpected

unforgettable ADJECTIVE not likely to be forgotten

unforgivable ADJECTIVE not able to be forgiven

unfortunate ADJECTIVE ❶ unlucky ❷ that you feel sorry about; regrettable

unfortunately ADVERB in a way that is sad or disappointing

unfounded ADJECTIVE not based on facts

unfriendly ADJECTIVE not friendly

unfurl VERB to unroll something or spread it out

unfurnished ADJECTIVE without furniture

ungainly ADJECTIVE awkward-looking or clumsy

ungracious ADJECTIVE not kindly or courteous

ungrateful ADJECTIVE not grateful

unguarded ADJECTIVE ❶ without a guard or protection ❷ without thought or caution; indiscreet

unhappily ADVERB ❶ in an unhappy way ❷ unfortunately

unhappy ADJECTIVE ❶ not happy; sad ❷ not pleased or satisfied ❸ unfortunate or regrettable

unhealthy ADJECTIVE ❶ not in good health ❷ not good for you

unheard-of ADJECTIVE never known or done before; extraordinary

unhinge VERB to cause a person's mind to become unbalanced

unicorn NOUN a mythical animal that is like a horse with one long straight horn growing from its forehead

uniform NOUN special clothes showing that the wearer is a member of a certain school, army or organization

uniform ADJECTIVE always the same; not varying

uniformed ADJECTIVE wearing a uniform

unify VERB to join several things together into one thing; to unite things

uninhabited ADJECTIVE with nobody living there

unintentional ADJECTIVE not done deliberately

uninterested ADJECTIVE having or showing no interest in something

uninteresting ADJECTIVE not interesting

union NOUN ❶ the joining of things together ❷ a group of states or countries that have joined together to form one country or group ❸ a trade union

unionist NOUN ❶ a member of a trade union ❷ a person who wishes to unite one country with another

Union Jack NOUN the flag of the United Kingdom

unique (say yoo-**neek**) ADJECTIVE being the only one of its kind; unlike any other

unisex ADJECTIVE designed to be suitable for both sexes

unison NOUN ➤ in unison ❶ with all saying, singing or doing the same thing at the same time ❷ in agreement

unit NOUN ❶ an amount used as a standard in measuring or counting things ❷ a group of people who have a certain job within a larger organization ❸ a device or piece of furniture regarded as a single thing but forming part of a larger group or whole ❹ (in mathematics) any whole number less than 10

unite VERB ❶ to form several people or things into one group or thing ❷ people or things unite when they join together to do

something

United Kingdom NOUN Great Britain and Northern Ireland

unity NOUN ❶ being united or being in agreement ❷ something whole that is made up of parts

universal ADJECTIVE to do with, including or done by everyone or everything

universally ADVERB by everyone; everywhere

universe NOUN everything that exists, including the earth and living things and all the stars and planets

university NOUN a place where people go to study at an advanced level after leaving school

unjust ADJECTIVE not fair or just

unkempt ADJECTIVE looking untidy or neglected

unkind ADJECTIVE not kind; harsh

unknown ADJECTIVE not known or familiar

unlawful ADJECTIVE not allowed by the law or rules

unleaded ADJECTIVE unleaded petrol has no added lead

unleash VERB to let a strong feeling or force be released

unleavened (say un-**lev**-end) ADJECTIVE unleavened bread is made without yeast or other substances that would make it rise

unless CONJUNCTION except when; if ... not

unlike PREPOSITION not like

unlike ADJECTIVE not alike; different

unlikely ADJECTIVE not likely to happen or be true

unlimited ADJECTIVE not limited; very great or very many

unload VERB to remove the load of things carried by a ship, aircraft or vehicle

unlock VERB to open something by undoing a lock

unluckily ADVERB unfortunately; as a result of bad luck

unlucky ADJECTIVE not lucky; having or bringing bad luck

unmanageable ADJECTIVE difficult or impossible to control or deal with

unmarried ADJECTIVE not married

unmask VERB ❶ to remove a person's mask ❷ to reveal what a person or thing is really like

unmistakable ADJECTIVE that cannot be mistaken for another person or thing

unmitigated ADJECTIVE absolute

unnatural ADJECTIVE not natural or normal

unnecessary ADJECTIVE not necessary; more than is necessary

unnerve VERB to make someone lose courage or determination

unoccupied ADJECTIVE a building or room is unoccupied when nobody is using it or living in it

unofficial ADJECTIVE not official

unorthodox ADJECTIVE different from what is usual or generally accepted

unpack VERB to take things out of a suitcase, bag, box, etc.

unpaid ADJECTIVE ❶ not yet paid ❷ not receiving payment for work you do

unparalleled ADJECTIVE having no parallel or equal

unpick VERB to undo the stitching of something

unpleasant ADJECTIVE not pleasant; nasty

unpopular ADJECTIVE not liked or popular

unprecedented (say un-press-id-en-tid) ADJECTIVE that has never happened before

unprepared ADJECTIVE not prepared beforehand; not ready or equipped to deal with something

unprincipled ADJECTIVE without good moral principles; unscrupulous

unprofitable ADJECTIVE not producing a profit or advantage

unprotected ADJECTIVE ❶ not protected or kept safe ❷ used to describe sexual activity in which a condom is not used

unqualified ADJECTIVE ❶ not officially qualified to do something ❷ complete; not limited in any way

unravel VERB ❶ to disentangle things ❷ to undo something that is knitted ❸ to look into a problem or mystery and solve it

unready ADJECTIVE not ready; hesitating

unreal ADJECTIVE not real; existing only in the imagination

unrealistic ADJECTIVE not showing or accepting things as they really are

unreasonable ADJECTIVE ❶ not reasonable ❷ excessive or unjust

unrelieved ADJECTIVE without anything to vary it

unremitting ADJECTIVE never stopping or relaxing; persistent

unrequited (say un-ri-kwy-tid) ADJECTIVE unrequited love is not returned or rewarded

unreserved ADJECTIVE ❶ not reserved ❷ without restriction; complete

unrest NOUN trouble or rioting caused by people because they are angry and dissatisfied

unripe ADJECTIVE not yet ripe

unrivalled ADJECTIVE having no equal; better than all others

unroll VERB to open something that has been rolled up

unruly ADJECTIVE badly behaved and difficult to control

unsafe ADJECTIVE not safe; dangerous

unsavoury ADJECTIVE unpleasant or disgusting

unscathed ADJECTIVE not harmed or injured

unscrew VERB to undo or remove something by twisting it or by taking out screws

unscrupulous ADJECTIVE willing to do things that are dishonest or unfair in order to get what you want

unseat VERB to throw a person from horseback or from the seat on a bicycle

unseemly ADJECTIVE not proper or suitable; indecent

unseen ADJECTIVE not seen or noticed

unseen NOUN (British) a passage for translation without previous preparation

unselfish ADJECTIVE not selfish; not thinking only about yourself

unsettle VERB to make someone feel uneasy or anxious

unsettled ADJECTIVE ❶ not settled or calm ❷ unsettled weather is likely to change

unshakeable ADJECTIVE not able to be shaken or changed; strong and firm

unshaven ADJECTIVE an unshaven man has not shaved recently

unsightly ADJECTIVE not pleasant to look at; ugly

unskilled ADJECTIVE not having or not needing special skill or training

unsociable ADJECTIVE not sociable or friendly

unsolicited ADJECTIVE not asked for

unsound ADJECTIVE ❶ not reliable; not based on sound evidence or reasoning ❷ not firm or strong ❸ not healthy

unspeakable ADJECTIVE too bad or horrid to be described

unstable ADJECTIVE not stable; likely to change or become unbalanced

unsteady ADJECTIVE not steady; shaking or wobbling or likely to fall

unstuck ADJECTIVE ➤ come unstuck ❶ to stop sticking to something ❷ (informal) to fail or go wrong

unsuccessful ADJECTIVE not successful; failed

unsuitable ADJECTIVE not suitable or appropriate

unsung ADJECTIVE (formal) not famous or praised but deserving to be

unsure ADJECTIVE not confident or certain

unthinkable ADJECTIVE too bad or too unlikely to be worth considering

unthinking ADJECTIVE thoughtless; not thinking of other people

untidy ADJECTIVE messy and not tidy

untie VERB to undo something that has been tied or to free someone who has been tied up

until PREPOSITION & CONJUNCTION up to a particular time or event

untimely ADJECTIVE happening too soon or at an unsuitable time

unto PREPOSITION (old use) to

untold ADJECTIVE too much or too many to be counted

untoward ADJECTIVE inconvenient or unfortunate

untrue ADJECTIVE not true; false

untruth NOUN an untrue statement; a lie

unused ADJECTIVE ❶ (say un-**yoozd**) not yet used ❷ (say un-**yoost**) not familiar with something

unusual ADJECTIVE not usual; strange or exceptional

unusually ADVERB ❶ more than is usual ❷ in a way that is not normal or typical

unveil VERB ❶ to remove a veil or covering from something ❷ to reveal something new that has been kept hidden or secret

unwanted ADJECTIVE not wanted

unwarranted ADJECTIVE not justified or reasonable

unwary ADJECTIVE not cautious or careful about danger

unwelcome ADJECTIVE not welcome or wanted

unwell ADJECTIVE not in good health

unwieldy ADJECTIVE awkward to move or control because of its size, shape or weight

unwilling ADJECTIVE not willing to do something; reluctant

unwind VERB ① to unroll something ② (informal) to relax after you have been working hard

unwise ADJECTIVE not wise; foolish

unwitting ADJECTIVE ① not intended ② not realizing something

unworn ADJECTIVE not yet worn

unworthy ADJECTIVE not worthy or deserving

unwrap VERB to open something that is wrapped

unzip VERB to undo something that is zipped up

up ADVERB ① to or in a higher place or position or level ② so as to be in a standing or upright position ③ out of bed ④ completely ⑤ finished ⑥ (informal) happening

up PREPOSITION upwards through, along or into

up-and-coming ADJECTIVE (informal) likely to become successful

upbraid VERB (formal) to angrily tell someone off because they have done something wrong

upbringing NOUN your upbringing is the way you have been brought

up

update VERB to bring a thing up to date

update NOUN the version of something that has the most recent information

upgrade VERB ① to improve a machine by installing new parts in it ② to improve a piece of software by installing a newer version

upheaval NOUN a sudden violent change or disturbance

uphill ADVERB up a slope

uphill ADJECTIVE ① going up a slope ② difficult

uphold VERB to support or agree with a decision, opinion or belief

upholster VERB to put a soft padded covering on furniture

upholstery NOUN covers and padding for furniture

upkeep NOUN keeping something in good condition or the cost of this

uplands PLURAL NOUN the higher parts of a country or region

uplifting ADJECTIVE making you feel more cheerful or hopeful

upload VERB (in computing) to move data from your computer to a larger computer network or system so that it can be read by other users

upon PREPOSITION on

upper ADJECTIVE higher in place or rank

upper case NOUN capital letters

upper class NOUN the highest class in society, especially the aristocracy

uppermost ADJECTIVE highest in place or importance

uppermost ADVERB on or to the top or the highest place

upright ADJECTIVE ❶ standing straight up; vertical ❷ strictly honest or honourable

upright NOUN a post or rod placed upright, especially as a support

uprising NOUN a rebellion or revolt against the government

uproar NOUN an outburst of noise or excitement or anger

uproot VERB ❶ to remove a plant and its roots from the ground ❷ to make someone leave the place where they have lived for a long time

upset ADJECTIVE ❶ unhappy or anxious about something ❷ slightly ill

upset VERB upsets, upsetting, upset ❶ to make a person unhappy or anxious ❷ to disturb the normal working of something ❸ to overturn something or knock it over

upset NOUN ❶ a slight illness ❷ an unexpected result or setback

upshot NOUN the eventual outcome

upside down ADVERB & ADJECTIVE ❶ with the upper part underneath instead of on top ❷ in great disorder; very untidy

upstairs ADVERB & ADJECTIVE to or on a higher floor

upstart NOUN a person who has risen suddenly to a high position and who then behaves arrogantly

upstream ADJECTIVE & ADVERB in the direction from which a stream flows

uptake NOUN ➤ **quick on the uptake** quick to understand ➤ **slow on the uptake** slow to understand

uptight ADJECTIVE (*informal*) tense and nervous or annoyed

up-to-date ADJECTIVE ❶ modern or fashionable ❷ giving the most recent information

upward ADJECTIVE & ADVERB going towards what is higher

uranium NOUN a heavy radioactive grey metal used as a source of nuclear energy

urban ADJECTIVE to do with a town or city

urchin NOUN a rough and poorly dressed young boy

Urdu (say **oor**-doo) NOUN a language related to Hindi, spoken in northern India and Pakistan

urge VERB ❶ to try to persuade a person to do something ❷ to drive people or animals onward ❸ to recommend or advise something

urge NOUN a strong desire or wish

urgent ADJECTIVE needing to be done or dealt with immediately

urinal (say yoor-**ry**-nal) NOUN a bowl or trough fixed to the wall in a men's public toilet, for men to urinate into

urinate (say **yoor**-in-ayt) VERB to pass urine out of your body

urine (say **yoor**-in) NOUN waste liquid that collects in the bladder and is passed out of the body

urn NOUN ❶ a large metal container with a tap, in which water is heated ❷ a container shaped like a vase with a base, especially one for holding the ashes of a cremated person

US *ABBREVIATION* United States (of America)

us *PRONOUN* the form of we used when it is the object of a verb or after a preposition

USA *ABBREVIATION* United States of America

usable *ADJECTIVE* able to be used

usage *NOUN* ❶ use; the way something is used ❷ the way words are used in a language

use (say yooz) *VERB* to perform an action or job with something

use (say yooss) *NOUN* ❶ the action of using something; being used ❷ the purpose for which something is used ❸ the quality of being useful

used *ADJECTIVE* not new; second-hand

useful *ADJECTIVE* able to be used a lot or to do something that needs doing

useless *ADJECTIVE* ❶ not having any use; producing no effect ❷ (*informal*) not very good at something

user *NOUN* a person who uses something

user-friendly *ADJECTIVE* designed to be easy to use

username *NOUN* the name you use to log on to a computer system

usher *NOUN* a person who shows people to their seats in a cinema, theatre or church

usher *VERB* to lead someone in or out

usherette *NOUN* a woman who shows people to their seats in a cinema or theatre

USSR *ABBREVIATION* (*old use*) Union of Soviet Socialist Republics

usual *ADJECTIVE* as happens or is done or used often or at the time

usually *ADVERB* most of the time; normally

usurp (say yoo-**zerp**) *VERB* to take power or a position or right from someone wrongly or by force

utensil (say yoo-**ten**-sil) *NOUN* a tool or device, especially one you use in the house

uterus (say **yoo**-ter-us) *NOUN* the womb

utilitarian *ADJECTIVE* designed to be useful rather than decorative or luxurious; practical

utility *NOUN* ❶ the quality of being useful ❷ an organization that supplies water, gas, electricity, etc. to the community

utilize (also **utilise**) *VERB* to make use of something

utmost *ADJECTIVE* extreme or greatest

Utopia (say yoo-**toh**-pee-a) *NOUN* an imaginary place or state of things where everything is perfect

utter *VERB* to say something or make a sound with your mouth

utter *ADJECTIVE* complete or absolute

utterly *ADVERB* completely or totally

uttermost *ADJECTIVE & NOUN* extreme or greatest; utmost

U-turn *NOUN* ❶ a U-shaped turn made in a vehicle so that it then travels in the opposite direction ❷ a complete change of ideas or policy

Vv

vacancy NOUN ❶ a position or job that has not been filled ❷ an available room in a hotel or guest house

vacant ADJECTIVE ❶ empty; not filled or occupied ❷ not showing any expression; blank

vacate VERB to leave or give up a place or position

vacation (say vak-ay-shon) NOUN a holiday, especially between the terms at a university

vaccinate (say **vak**-sin-ayt) VERB to protect someone from a disease by injecting them with a vaccine

vaccine (say vak-seen) NOUN a substance used to give someone immunity against a disease

vacuum NOUN ❶ a completely empty space; a space without any air in it ❷ (informal) a vacuum cleaner

vacuum VERB to clean something using a vacuum cleaner

vacuum cleaner NOUN an electrical device that sucks up dust and dirt from the floor

vacuum flask NOUN (chiefly British) a container with double walls that have a vacuum between them, used for keeping liquids hot or cold

vagabond NOUN a person with no settled home or regular work; a vagrant

vagary (say **vay**-ger-ee) NOUN a change in something that is difficult to control or predict

vagina (say va-**jy**-na) NOUN the passage in a female body that leads from the vulva to the womb

vagrant (say **vay**-grant) NOUN a person with no settled home or regular work; a tramp

vague ADJECTIVE ❶ not definite or clear ❷ not thinking clearly or precisely

vaguely ADVERB ❶ in a way that is not definite or clear; slightly ❷ without thinking clearly

vain ADJECTIVE ❶ conceited, especially about how you look ❷ useless or unsuccessful

vale NOUN a valley

valency NOUN (in science) the power of an atom to combine with other atoms, measured by the number of hydrogen atoms it is capable of combining with

valentine NOUN ❶ a card sent on St Valentine's day (14 February) to the person you love ❷ the person you send this card to

valet (say **val**-ay or **val**-it) NOUN a man's servant who takes care of his clothes and appearance

valiant ADJECTIVE brave or courageous

valid ADJECTIVE ❶ legally able to be used or accepted ❷ valid reasoning is sound and logical

valley NOUN ❶ a long low area between hills ❷ an area through which a river flows

valour NOUN bravery, especially in battle

a
b
c
d
e
f
g
h
i
j
k
l
m
n
o
p
q
r
s
t
u
v
w
x
y
z

A
B
C
D
E
F
G
H
I
J
K
L
M
N
O
P
Q
R
S
T
U
V
W
X
Y
Z

valuable ADJECTIVE ❶ worth a lot of money ❷ very useful or important

valuables PLURAL NOUN valuable things

value NOUN ❶ the amount of money that something could be sold for ❷ how useful or important something is ❸ (*in mathematics*) the number or quantity represented by a figure

value VERB ❶ to think that something is important or worth having ❷ to work out how much something could be sold for

valve NOUN ❶ a device for controlling the flow of gas or liquid through a pipe or tube ❷ a structure in the heart or in a blood vessel allowing blood to flow in one direction only ❸ a device that controls the flow of electricity in old televisions and radios

vampire NOUN in stories, a dead creature that is supposed to leave its grave at night and suck blood from living people

van NOUN ❶ a covered vehicle for carrying goods ❷ (*British*) a railway carriage for luggage or goods or for the use of the guard

vandal NOUN a person who deliberately breaks or damages things, especially public property

vandalize (also **vandalise**) VERB to damage property deliberately

vane NOUN ❶ the blade of a propeller, sail of a windmill or other device that acts on or is moved by wind or water ❷ a weathervane

vanguard NOUN ❶ the leading part of an army or fleet ❷ the first people to adopt a fashion or idea

vanilla NOUN a flavouring obtained from the pods of a tropical plant

vanish VERB to disappear completely

vanity NOUN the quality of being too proud of your abilities or of how you look

vanquish VERB to defeat someone completely

vantage point NOUN a place from which you have a good view of something

vaporize (also **vaporise**) VERB to turn into vapour or to change something into vapour

vapour NOUN a visible gas to which some substances can be converted by heat; steam or mist

variable ADJECTIVE likely to vary; not staying the same

variable NOUN something that varies or can vary; a variable quantity

variance NOUN the amount by which things differ

variant NOUN a thing that is a slightly different form of something else

variant ADJECTIVE differing from something

variation NOUN ❶ varying; the amount by which something varies ❷ a different form of something

varicose ADJECTIVE varicose veins are permanently swollen

varied ADJECTIVE of different sorts; full of variety

variety ADJECTIVE ❶ a number of different kinds of the same thing ❷ a particular kind of something ❸ the quality of not always being the same; variation ❹ a form of entertainment made up of short performances of singing, dancing and comedy

various ADJECTIVE ❶ of several different kinds ❷ several

varnish NOUN a liquid that dries to form a hard shiny usually transparent coating

varnish VERB to coat something with varnish

vary VERB ❶ to keep changing ❷ to make changes to something ❸ to be different from one another

vase NOUN an open usually tall container for holding cut flowers or as an ornament

Vaseline NOUN (trademark) petroleum jelly for use as an ointment

vassal NOUN in feudal times, a man who was given land to live on in return for promising loyally to fight for the landowner

vast ADJECTIVE very great, especially in area

VAT ABBREVIATION value added tax; a tax on goods and services

vat NOUN a very large container for holding liquid

vaudeville (say vawd-vil) NOUN a kind of variety entertainment popular in the early 20th century

vault VERB to jump over something, especially while supporting yourself with your hands or with the help of a pole

vault NOUN ❶ a vaulting jump ❷ an arched roof ❸ an underground room used to store things ❹ a

room for storing money or valuables ❺ a burial chamber

vaulting horse NOUN a padded wooden block for vaulting over in gymnastics

VDU ABBREVIATION visual display unit; a monitor for a computer

veal NOUN meat from a calf

vector NOUN (in mathematics) a quantity that has size and direction, such as velocity (which is speed in a certain direction)

Veda (say vay-da or vee-da) NOUN the most ancient and sacred literature of the Hindus

veer VERB to swerve or change direction suddenly

vegan NOUN a person who does not eat or use any animal products

vegetable NOUN a plant that can be used as food

vegetarian NOUN a person who does not eat meat

vegetation NOUN plants that are growing

vehement (say vee-im-ent) ADJECTIVE showing strong feeling

vehicle NOUN a means of transporting people or goods, especially on land

veil NOUN a piece of thin material worn to cover a woman's face or head

veil VERB ❶ to cover something with a veil ❷ to partially conceal something

veiled ADJECTIVE partly hidden or disguised

vein NOUN ❶ any of the tubes that carry blood from all parts of the body to the heart. Compare with **artery**. ❷ a line or streak on a leaf, rock or insect's wing ❸ a long deposit of mineral or ore in the middle of a rock ❹ a mood or manner

veld (say velt) *NOUN* an area of open grassland in South Africa

vellum *NOUN* smooth parchment or writing paper

velocity *NOUN* speed in a given direction

velvet *NOUN* a woven material with very short soft furry fibres on one side

vendetta *NOUN* a long-lasting bitter quarrel; a feud

vending machine *NOUN* a slot machine from which you can obtain drinks, chocolate, etc.

vendor *NOUN* someone who is selling something, especially a house

veneer *NOUN* ❶ a thin layer of good wood covering the surface of a cheaper wood in furniture ❷ an outward show of some good quality

venerable *ADJECTIVE* worthy of respect or honour because of being so old

venerate *VERB* to honour someone with great respect or reverence

venetian blind *NOUN* a window blind consisting of horizontal strips that can be adjusted to let light in or shut it out

vengeance *NOUN* harming or punishing someone in return for something bad they have done to you; revenge

vengeful *ADJECTIVE* wanting to punish someone who has harmed you

venison *NOUN* the meat from a deer

Venn diagram *NOUN* (*in mathematics*) a diagram in which circles are used to show the relationships between different sets of things

venom *NOUN* ❶ the poisonous fluid produced by snakes, scorpions, etc. ❷ a feeling of bitter hatred for someone

vent *NOUN* an opening in something, especially to let out smoke or gas

vent *VERB* to express your feelings, especially anger, strongly

ventilate *VERB* to let air move freely in and out of a room or building

ventriloquist *NOUN* an entertainer who makes their voice sound as if it comes from another source

venture *NOUN* something you decide to do that is risky or adventurous

venture *VERB* to dare or be bold enough to do or say something or to go somewhere

venue (say **ven**-yoo) *NOUN* the place where an event such as a meeting, sports match or concert is held

veracity (say ver-**as**-it-ee) *NOUN* truth or being truthful

veranda *NOUN* a terrace with a roof along the side of a house

verb *NOUN* a word that shows what a person or thing is doing or what is happening, e.g. *bring, came, sing, were*

verbal *ADJECTIVE* ❶ spoken, not written ❷ to do with words or in the form of words

verbatim (say ver-**bay**-tim) ADVERB & ADJECTIVE in exactly the same words

verdict NOUN a judgement or decision made after considering something, especially one made by a jury

verdigris (say **verd**-i-grees) NOUN green rust on copper or brass

verge NOUN ❶ a strip of grass along the edge of a road or path ❷ to be on the verge of something is to be close to doing it

verge VERB ➤ verge on something to be nearly something

verger NOUN a person who is caretaker and attendant in a church

verify VERB to check or show that something is true or correct

veritable ADJECTIVE real; rightly named

vermicelli (say verm-i-**sel**-ee) NOUN pasta made in long thin threads

vermilion NOUN & ADJECTIVE bright red

vermin PLURAL NOUN animals or insects that damage crops or food or carry disease, such as rats and fleas

vernacular (say ver-**nak**-yoo-ler) NOUN the language of a country or district, as distinct from an official or formal language

vernal ADJECTIVE to do with the season of spring

verruca (say ver-**oo**-ka) NOUN a kind of wart on the sole of the foot

versatile ADJECTIVE able to do or be

used for many different things

verse NOUN ❶ writing arranged in short lines, usually with a particular rhythm and often with rhymes; poetry ❷ a group of lines forming a unit in a poem or song ❸ each of the short numbered sections of a chapter in the Bible

versed ADJECTIVE ➤ versed in something experienced or skilled in something

version NOUN ❶ a particular person's account of something that happened ❷ a different form of something ❸ a translation

versus PREPOSITION against; competing with

vertebra NOUN vertebrae each of the bones that form your backbone

vertebrate NOUN an animal that has a backbone. (The opposite is **invertebrate.**)

vertex NOUN (in mathematics) the highest point of a cone or triangle.

vertical ADJECTIVE going directly upwards, at right angles to something level or horizontal

vertigo NOUN a feeling of dizziness and loss of balance, especially when you are very high up

verve (say verv) NOUN enthusiasm and liveliness

very ADVERB ❶ to a great amount or intensity; extremely ❷ used to emphasize something

very ADJECTIVE ❶ exact or actual ❷ extreme

vespers NOUN a church service held in the evening

vessel NOUN ❶ a ship or boat ❷ a container, especially for liquid ❸ a tube carrying blood or other liquid in the body of an animal or plant

vest NOUN a piece of underwear you wear on the top half of your body

vested interest NOUN a strong reason for wanting something to happen, usually because you will benefit from it

vestibule NOUN ① an entrance hall or lobby ② a church porch

vestige NOUN a trace; a very small amount of something that is left after the rest has gone

vestment NOUN a ceremonial garment, especially one worn by the clergy or choir at a church service

vestry NOUN a room in a church where vestments are kept and where the clergy and choir put these on

vet NOUN (*chiefly British*) a person trained to give medical and surgical treatment to animals

vet VERB (*British*) to make a careful check of a person or thing, especially of someone's background before employing them

veteran NOUN a person who has long experience, especially in the armed forces

veterinary (say vet-rin-ree) ADJECTIVE to do with the medical and surgical treatment of animals

veto (say vee-toh) NOUN vetoes ① a refusal to let something happen ② the right to stop something from happening

veto VERB to refuse to let something happen

vex VERB to annoy someone or cause them worry

vexed question NOUN a problem that is difficult or much discussed

VHF ABBREVIATION very high frequency

via (say vy-a) PREPOSITION ① going through; by way of ② by means of; using

viable ADJECTIVE able to work or exist successfully

viaduct NOUN a long bridge, usually with many arches, carrying a road or railway over a valley or low ground

vial NOUN a small glass bottle

vibrant ADJECTIVE ① full of energy; lively ② vibrant colours are bright and strong

vibrate VERB to move very quickly from side to side and with small movements

vibration NOUN a continuous shaking movement that you can feel

vicar NOUN a member of the Church of England clergy who is in charge of a parish

vicarage NOUN the house of a vicar

vice NOUN ① an evil or bad habit; a bad fault ② evil or wickedness ③ a device for gripping something and holding it firmly while you work on it

vice– PREFIX ① authorized to act as a deputy or substitute (as in *vice-captain, vice-president*) ② next in rank to someone (as in *vice-admiral*)

vice versa ADVERB the other way round

vicinity NOUN the area near or round a place

vicious ADJECTIVE ① cruel and aggressive ② severe or violent

vicious circle NOUN a situation in which a problem produces an effect which in turn makes the problem worse

victim NOUN someone who is injured, killed, robbed, etc.

victor NOUN the winner of a battle or contest

Victorian ADJECTIVE belong to the time of Queen Victoria (1837-1901)

victorious ADJECTIVE that wins a victory

victory NOUN success won against an opponent in a battle, contest or game

video NOUN ① a system of recording moving pictures and sound, especially as a digital file ② a short film or recording that you can watch on a computer or mobile phone, especially over the Internet ③ a copy of a film or television programme that has been recorded

video VERB (chiefly British) to record something on video

video game NOUN a game in which you press electronic controls to move images on a screen

vie VERB to compete with someone; to carry on a rivalry

view NOUN ① what you can see from one place, e.g. beautiful scenery ② sight or range of vision ③ an opinion

view VERB ① to watch or look at something ② to consider or regard a person or thing in a certain way

viewer NOUN someone who views something, especially a television programme

viewpoint NOUN ① an opinion or point of view ② a place giving a good view

vigil (say vij-il) NOUN staying awake to keep watch or to pray

vigilant (say vij-il-ant) ADJECTIVE keeping careful watch for danger or difficulties

vigilante (say vij-il-an-tee) NOUN a member of a group who organize themselves, without authority, to try to prevent crime and disorder in their community

vigorous ADJECTIVE full of strength and energy

vigour NOUN strength and energy

Viking NOUN a Scandinavian trader and pirate in the 8th-11th centuries

vile ADJECTIVE ① extremely disgusting ② very bad or wicked

villa NOUN a house, especially a holiday home abroad

village NOUN a group of houses and other buildings in a country district, smaller than a town and usually having a church

villain NOUN a wicked person or a criminal

villein (say vil-an or vil-ayn) NOUN a tenant in feudal times

vim NOUN (informal) vigour and energy

vindicate VERB ① to clear a

person of blame or suspicion ② to prove something to be true or worthwhile

vindictive ADJECTIVE showing a desire for revenge; spiteful

vine NOUN a climbing or trailing plant whose fruit is the grape

vinegar NOUN a sour liquid used to flavour food or in pickling

vineyard (say vin-yard) NOUN an area of land where vines are grown to produce grapes for making wine

vintage NOUN ① all the grapes that are harvested in one season or the wine made from them ② the period from which something comes

vintage car NOUN (British) a car made between 1917 and 1930

vinyl NOUN a kind of plastic

viola (say vee-oh-la) NOUN a musical instrument like a violin but slightly larger and with a lower pitch

violate VERB ① to break an agreement, rule or law ② to treat a person or place with disrespect and violence

violence NOUN ① physical force that does harm or damage ② strength or intensity

violent ADJECTIVE ① using or involving violence ② strong or intense

violet NOUN ① a small plant that often has purple flowers ② a bluish-purple colour

violin NOUN a musical instrument with four strings, played with a bow

VIP ABBREVIATION very important person

viper NOUN a small poisonous snake

virgin NOUN a person who has never had sexual intercourse

virgin ADJECTIVE not yet touched or used

virtual ADJECTIVE ① being something in effect though not strictly in fact ② existing as a computer image and not physically

virtually ADVERB nearly or almost

virtual reality NOUN an image or environment produced by a computer that is so realistic that it seems to be part of the real world

virtue NOUN ① moral goodness; a particular form of this ② a good quality or advantage

virtuoso (say ver-tew-oh-soh) NOUN a person with outstanding skill, especially in singing or playing music

virtuous ADJECTIVE behaving in a morally good way

virus NOUN ① a very tiny living thing, smaller than a bacterium, that can cause disease ② a disease caused by a virus ③ a hidden set of instructions in a computer program that is designed to destroy data

visa (say vee-za) NOUN an official mark put on someone's passport by officials of a foreign country to show that the holder has permission to enter that country

viscount (say vy-kownt) NOUN a nobleman ranking below an earl and above a baron

viscous (say visk-us) ADJECTIVE thick and gluey, not pouring easily

visibility *NOUN* the distance you can see clearly

visible *ADJECTIVE* able to be seen or noticed

visibly *ADVERB* in a way that is easy to notice

vision *NOUN* ❶ the ability to see; sight ❷ something that you see in your imagination or in a dream ❸ the ability to make imaginative plans for the future ❹ a person or thing that is beautiful to see

visionary *ADJECTIVE* extremely imaginative or fanciful

visionary *NOUN* a person with extremely imaginative ideas and plans

visit *VERB* ❶ to go to see a person or place ❷ to stay somewhere for a while

visit *NOUN* ❶ going to see a person or place ❷ a short stay somewhere

visitation *NOUN* an official visit, especially to inspect something

visitor *NOUN* a person who is visiting or staying at a place

visor (say vy-zer) *NOUN* ❶ the part of a helmet that covers the face ❷ a shield to protect the eyes from bright light or sunshine

vista *NOUN* a long view

visual *ADJECTIVE* to do with or used in seeing; to do with sight

visual aid *NOUN* a picture, video or film used as an aid in teaching

visual display unit *NOUN* (British) a device that looks like a television screen and displays data being received from a computer or fed into it

visualize (also **visualise**) *VERB*
to form a mental picture of something

vital *ADJECTIVE* ❶ essential; very important ❷ connected with life; necessary for life to continue

vitality *NOUN* liveliness or energy

vitally *ADVERB* extremely

vitamin (say vit-a-min or vy-ta-min) *NOUN* any of a number of substances that are present in various foods and are essential to keep people and animals healthy

vitriol (say vit-ree-ol) *NOUN* savage criticism

vivacious (say viv-ay-shus) *ADJECTIVE* happy and lively

vivid *ADJECTIVE* ❶ bright and strong or clear ❷ active and lively

vivisection *NOUN* doing experiments on live animals as part of scientific research

vixen *NOUN* a female fox

vizier (say viz-eer) *NOUN* (historical) an important Muslim official

vocabulary *NOUN* ❶ all the words used in a particular subject or language ❷ the words known to an individual person

vocal *ADJECTIVE* to do with or using the voice

vocal cords *PLURAL NOUN* two strap-like membranes in the throat that can be made to vibrate and produce sounds

vocalist *NOUN* a singer, especially in a pop group

vocation *NOUN* ❶ a person's job or occupation ❷ a strong desire to do a particular kind of work or a feeling of being called by God to

a
b
c
d
e
f
g
h
i
j
k
l
m
n
o
p
q
r
s
t
u
v
w
x
y
z

do something

vocational ADJECTIVE teaching you the skills you need for a particular job or profession

vodka NOUN a strong alcoholic drink very popular in Russia

vogue NOUN the current fashion

voice NOUN ① the sounds that you make when you speak or sing ② the ability to speak or sing ③ someone expressing a particular opinion about something ④ the right to express an opinion or desire

voice VERB to say something clearly and strongly

voicemail NOUN a system for recording and storing phone messages for people to listen to later

void ADJECTIVE ① completely lacking something ② not legally valid

void NOUN an empty space or hole

volatile (say vol-a-tyl) ADJECTIVE ① evaporating quickly ② changing quickly from one mood to another

volcanic ADJECTIVE caused or produced by a volcano

volcano NOUN a mountain with an opening at the top from which lava, ashes and hot gases from below the earth's crust are or have been thrown out

vole NOUN a small animal rather like a rat

volition NOUN to do something of your own volition is to choose to do it

volley NOUN ① a number of bullets or shells fired at the same time ② in tennis and football, hitting or kicking the ball before it touches the ground

volley VERB to hit or kick the ball before it touches the ground

volleyball NOUN a game in which two teams hit a large ball to and fro over a net with their hands

volt NOUN a unit for measuring electric force

voltage NOUN electric force measured in volts

voluble ADJECTIVE talking very much

volume NOUN ① the amount of space filled by something ② an amount or quantity ③ the strength or power of sound ④ a book, especially one of a set

voluminous (say vol-yoo-min-us) ADJECTIVE ① bulky; large and full ② able to hold a lot

voluntary ADJECTIVE ① done or doing something because you want to do it, not because you have to do it ② unpaid

volunteer VERB ① to offer to do something of your own accord, without being asked or forced to ② to provide something willingly or freely without being asked for it

volunteer NOUN a person who volunteers to do something, e.g. to serve in the armed forces

voluptuous ADJECTIVE ① giving a luxurious feeling ② a woman is voluptuous when she has an attractively curved figure

vomit VERB ① to bring up food from the stomach and out through the mouth; to be sick

vomit NOUN food from the stomach brought back out through the mouth

voodoo NOUN a form of witchcraft and magical rites, especially in the West Indies

voracious (say vor-**ay**-shus) ADJECTIVE greedy; devouring things eagerly

vortex NOUN a whirlpool or whirlwind

vote VERB to show which person or thing you prefer by putting up your hand or making a mark on a piece of paper

vote NOUN ❶ the action of voting ❷ the right to vote

voter NOUN someone who votes, especially in an election

vouch VERB ➤ **vouch for something** to guarantee that something is true or certain

voucher NOUN a piece of paper showing that you are allowed to pay less for something or that you can get something in exchange

vouchsafe VERB (formal) to grant or offer something

vow NOUN a solemn promise

vow VERB to make a solemn promise to do something

vowel NOUN any of the letters a, e, i, o, u and sometimes y, which represent sounds in which breath comes out freely. Compare with **consonant**.

voyage NOUN a long journey on a ship or in a spacecraft

voyage VERB to make a voyage

vulgar ADJECTIVE rude; without good manners

vulgar fraction NOUN (British) a fraction shown by numbers above and below a line (e.g. ½, ¾), not a decimal fraction

vulnerable ADJECTIVE able to be hurt or harmed or attacked

vulture NOUN a large bird that feeds on dead animals

vulva NOUN the outer parts of the female genitals

vying present participle of **vie**

Ww

wacky ADJECTIVE (informal) crazy or silly

wad (say wod) NOUN a pad or bundle of soft material or banknotes, papers, etc.

wad VERB to pad something with soft material

waddle VERB to walk with short steps, swaying from side to side, as a duck does

waddle NOUN a waddling walk

wade VERB ❶ to walk through water or mud ❷ to read through something with effort because it is dull, difficult or long

wader NOUN ❶ (also **wading bird**) any bird with long legs that feeds in shallow water ❷ **waders** are long rubber boots that you wear for standing in water

wafer NOUN a kind of thin biscuit

wafer-thin ADJECTIVE very thin

waffle (say **wof**-el) NOUN ❶ a small cake made of batter and eaten hot ❷ talking or writing for a long time without saying anything

waffle VERB to talk or write for a long time without saying anything important or interesting

waft (say woft) VERB to float gently through the air

wag VERB ① a dog wags its tail when it moves it quickly from side to side because it is happy or excited ② you wag your finger when you move it up and down or from side to side

wag NOUN ① a wagging movement ② a person who makes jokes

wage NOUN (or **wages**) PLURAL NOUN a regular payment to someone in return for the work they do

wage VERB to carry on a war or campaign

wager (say **way**-jer) NOUN a bet

wager VERB to make a bet with someone

waggle VERB to move something quickly to and fro

wagon NOUN ① a cart with four wheels, pulled by a horse or an ox ② an open railway truck, e.g. for coal

wagtail NOUN a small bird with a long tail that it moves up and down

waif NOUN a homeless and helpless person, especially a child

wail VERB to make a long sad cry

wail NOUN a sound of wailing

wainscot, wainscoting NOUN wooden panelling on the wall of a room

waist NOUN the narrow part in the middle of your body

waistcoat NOUN (British) a short close-fitting jacket without sleeves, worn over a shirt and under a jacket

waistline NOUN the amount you measure around your waist, which indicates how fat or thin you are

wait VERB ① to stay somewhere or delay doing something until something happens ② to be left to be dealt with later ③ to be a waiter

wait NOUN an act or time of waiting

waiter NOUN a man who serves people with food and drink in a restaurant

waiting list NOUN a list of people waiting for something to become available

waiting room NOUN a room provided for people who are waiting for something

waitress NOUN a woman who serves people with food and drink in a restaurant

waive VERB to not insist on having something

wake VERB wakes, waking, woke, woken ① to stay sleeping ② to make someone stop sleeping

wake NOUN ① the track left on the water by a moving ship or boat ② currents of air left behind a moving aircraft ③ a party held after a funeral

wakeful ADJECTIVE unable to sleep

waken VERB to wake up or to wake someone up

walk VERB to move along on your feet at an ordinary speed

walk NOUN ① a journey on foot ② the way that someone walks ③ a path or route for walking

walkabout NOUN ❶ an informal stroll among a crowd by an important visitor ❷ (*Australian*) a journey through a remote area taken by an Australian Aboriginal wishing to experience a traditional way of life

walker NOUN someone who goes for a walk, especially a long one

walkie-talkie NOUN (*informal*) a small portable radio transmitter and receiver

walking stick NOUN a stick used as a support while walking

walk of life NOUN a person's occupation or social position

walkover NOUN an easy victory

wall NOUN ❶ a continuous upright structure, usually made of brick or stone, forming one of the sides of a building or room or supporting something or enclosing an area ❷ the outside part of something ❸ something that forms a barrier

wall VERB to block or surround something with a wall

wallaby NOUN a kind of small kangaroo

wallet NOUN a small flat folding case for holding banknotes, credit cards, documents, etc.

wallflower NOUN a garden plant with fragrant flowers, blooming in spring

wallop (*informal*) VERB to hit or beat someone

wallop NOUN a heavy blow or punch

wallow VERB ❶ to roll about in water or mud ❷ to get great pleasure by being surrounded by something

wallow NOUN an area of mud or shallow water where mammals go to wallow

wallpaper NOUN ❶ paper used to cover the inside walls of rooms ❷ the background pattern or picture that you choose to have on your computer screen

walnut NOUN ❶ an edible nut with a wrinkled surface ❷ the wood from the tree that bears this nut, used for making furniture

walrus NOUN a large Arctic sea animal with two long tusks

waltz NOUN a dance with three beats to a bar

waltz VERB to dance a waltz

wan (say wonn) ADJECTIVE ❶ pale from being ill or tired ❷ a wan smile is faint and without enthusiasm

wand NOUN a thin rod, especially one used by a magician or wizard

wander VERB ❶ to go about without trying to reach a particular place ❷ to leave the right path or direction; to stray ❸ to be distracted or move on to other things

wander NOUN a wandering journey

wane VERB the moon wanes when it shows a bright area that becomes gradually smaller after being full. (The opposite is wax.) ❷ to become less, smaller or weaker

wane NOUN ➤ on the wane becoming less or weaker

wangle VERB (*informal*) to get or arrange something by trickery or clever planning

want VERB ❶ to have a desire or wish for something ❷ to need something

want NOUN ❶ a wish to have something ❷ a lack or need of something

wanted ADJECTIVE a wanted person is a suspected criminal that the police wish to find or arrest

wanting ADJECTIVE lacking in what is needed or usual

wanton (say wonn-ton) ADJECTIVE done deliberately for no good reason

war NOUN ❶ fighting between nations or groups, especially using armed forces ❷ a serious struggle or effort against crime, disease, poverty, etc.

warble VERB to sing with a gentle trilling sound, as some birds do

warble NOUN a warbling song or sound

warbler NOUN a kind of small songbird

war crime NOUN a crime committed during a war that breaks international rules of war

ward NOUN ❶ a room with beds for patients in a hospital ❷ a child looked after by a guardian ❸ an area electing a councillor to represent it

ward VERB ➤ **ward something off** to keep something away

warden NOUN an official who is in charge of a hostel, college, etc. or who supervises something

warder NOUN (chiefly British) an official in charge of prisoners in a prison

wardrobe NOUN ❶ a cupboard to hang clothes in ❷ a stock of clothes or costumes

ware NOUN manufactured goods of a certain kind

warehouse NOUN a large building where goods are stored

warfare NOUN fighting a war

warhead NOUN the explosive head of a missile or torpedo

warlike ADJECTIVE ❶ fond of making war ❷ threatening war

warm ADJECTIVE ❶ fairly hot; not cold or cool ❷ keeping the body warm ❸ friendly or enthusiastic ❹ close to the right answer or to something hidden

warm VERB (also **warm up**) to make something warm or to become warm

warm-blooded ADJECTIVE a warm-blooded animal has blood that remains warm permanently

warmly ADVERB ❶ in warm clothes ❷ in a friendly or enthusiastic way

warmth NOUN ❶ being warm or keeping warm ❷ being friendly or enthusiastic

warn VERB to tell someone about a danger or difficulty that may affect them or about what they should do

warning NOUN something said or written to warn someone

warp (say worp) VERB ❶ to become bent or twisted out of shape, e.g. because of dampness; to bend or twist something in this way ❷ to distort a person's ideas or judgement

warp NOUN the lengthwise threads in weaving, crossed by the weft

warpath NOUN ➤ **on the warpath** angry and getting ready for a fight or argument

warrant NOUN a document that authorizes a person to do something (e.g. to search a place) or to receive something

warrant VERB ❶ to justify or deserve something ❷ to guarantee or bet that something will happen

warranty NOUN a guarantee

warren NOUN ❶ a piece of ground where there are many burrows in which rabbits live and breed ❷ a building or place with many winding passages

warring ADJECTIVE involved in a war

warrior NOUN a person who fights in battle; a soldier

warship NOUN a ship used in war

wart NOUN a small hard lump on the skin, caused by a virus

wartime NOUN a time of war

wary (say **wair-ee**) ADJECTIVE cautious about possible danger or difficulty

wash VERB ❶ to clean something with water or other liquid ❷ to be washable ❸ to flow against or over something ❹ to carry something along by a moving liquid ❺ (informal) to be believable or acceptable

wash NOUN ❶ the action of washing ❷ a quantity of clothes for washing ❸ the disturbed water behind a moving ship ❹ a thin coating of colour or paint

washbasin NOUN (chiefly British) a small sink for washing your hands and face

washer NOUN ❶ a small ring of rubber or metal placed between two surfaces (e.g. under a bolt or screw) to fit them tightly together ❷ a washing machine

washing NOUN clothes that need to be washed or have been washed

washing machine NOUN a machine for washing clothes

washing-up NOUN (British) washing the dishes and cutlery after a meal

wash-out NOUN (informal) a complete failure

wasp NOUN a stinging insect with black and yellow stripes round its body

wastage NOUN loss of something by waste

waste VERB ❶ to use more of something than you need or to use it without getting enough results ❷ to fail to use something

waste ADJECTIVE ❶ left over or thrown away because it is not wanted ❷ not used or usable

waste NOUN ❶ wasting a thing or not using it well ❷ things that are not wanted or not used ❸ an area of desert or frozen land

wasteful ADJECTIVE using more than is needed; producing waste

wasteland NOUN a barren or empty area of land

watch VERB ❶ to look at a person or thing for some time ❷ to be on guard or ready for something to happen ❸ to pay careful attention to something ❹ to take care of

A | something

watch NOUN watches ❶ a device like a small clock, usually worn on the wrist ❷ the action of watching ❸ a turn of being on duty in a ship

watchdog NOUN a dog kept to guard property

watchful ADJECTIVE watching closely; alert

watchman NOUN a person employed to look after an empty building at night

watchword NOUN a word or phrase that sums up a group's policy; a slogan

water NOUN ❶ a colourless odourless tasteless liquid that is a compound of hydrogen and oxygen ❷ a lake or sea ❸ the tide

water VERB ❶ to sprinkle or supply something with water ❷ to produce tears or saliva

watercolour NOUN ❶ paint made with pigment and water (not oil) ❷ a painting done with this kind of paint

watercress NOUN a kind of cress that grows in water

water cycle NOUN the process by which water falls to the ground as rain and snow, runs into rivers and lakes, flows into the sea, evaporates into the air and forms clouds and then falls to the ground again

waterfall NOUN a place where a river or stream flows over the edge of a cliff or large rock

watering can NOUN a container with a long spout, for watering plants

water lily NOUN a plant that grows in water, with broad floating leaves and large flowers

waterlogged ADJECTIVE waterlogged ground is so wet that it cannot soak up any more water

watermark NOUN ❶ a mark showing how high a river or tide rises or how low it falls ❷ a faint design in some kinds of paper that can be seen when the paper is held up to the light

watermelon NOUN a melon with a smooth green skin, red pulp and black seeds

watermill NOUN a mill worked by a waterwheel

water polo NOUN a game played by teams of swimmers with a ball like a football

waterproof ADJECTIVE that keeps out water

waterproof NOUN (British) a waterproof coat or jacket

watershed NOUN ❶ a turning point in the course of events ❷ a line of high land from which streams flow down on each side

waterskiing NOUN the sport of skimming over the surface of water on a pair of flat boards (**waterskis**) while being towed by a motor boat

waterspout NOUN a column of water formed when a whirlwind draws up a whirling mass of water from the sea

water table NOUN the level below which the ground is saturated with water

watertight ADJECTIVE ❶ made or fastened so that water cannot get in or out ❷ so carefully put together that it has no mistakes and cannot be proved to be untrue

waterway NOUN a river or canal that ships can travel on

waterwheel NOUN a large wheel turned by a flow of water, used to work machinery

waterworks PLURAL NOUN a place with pumping machinery for supplying water to a district

watery ADJECTIVE ❶ like water ❷ full of water or tears ❸ made weak or thin by too much water

watt NOUN a unit of electric power

wattage NOUN electric power measured in watts

wattle NOUN ❶ sticks and twigs woven together to make a fence or walls ❷ an Australian tree with golden flowers

wave NOUN ❶ a ridge moving along the surface of the sea or breaking on the shore ❷ a curling piece of hair ❸ (*in science*) the wave-like movement by which heat, light, sound or electricity etc. travels ❹ a sudden build-up of something ❺ the action of waving your hand

wave VERB ❶ to move your hand from side to side as a greeting or signal ❷ to move loosely from side to side or up and down, or to move something like this ❸ to make a thing wavy ❹ to be wavy

waveband NOUN a set of radio waves of similar length that are used for broadcasting radio programmes

wavelength NOUN ❶ the distance between corresponding points on

a sound wave or electromagnetic wave ❷ the length of a radio wave that a particular radio station uses to broadcast its programmes

waver VERB ❶ to be unsteady or to move unsteadily ❷ to begin to weaken ❸ to hesitate or be uncertain

wavy ADJECTIVE full of waves or curves

wax NOUN ❶ a soft substance that melts easily, used to make candles, crayons and polish ❷ beeswax

wax VERB ❶ to coat or polish something with wax ❷ the moon waxes when it shows a bright area that becomes gradually larger. (The opposite is wane.) ❸ to become stronger or more important ❹ to speak or write in a certain way

waxen ADJECTIVE ❶ made of wax ❷ like wax

waxwork NOUN a lifelike model of a person made in wax

way NOUN ❶ how something is done; a method or style ❷ a manner ❸ how to get somewhere; a route ❹ a direction or position ❺ a path or road leading from one place to another ❻ a distance in space or time ❼ a respect ❽ a condition or state

way ADVERB (*informal*) far

wayfarer NOUN a traveller, especially someone who is walking

waylay VERB to lie in wait for a person or people, especially in order to talk to them or rob them

▶ **wayside** NOUN ➤ fall by the wayside to fail to continue doing something

wayward ADJECTIVE disobedient; wilfully doing what you want

WC ABBREVIATION a toilet

we PRONOUN a word used by a person to refer to himself or herself and another or others

weak ADJECTIVE ❶ having little strength, power or energy ❷ easy to break, damage or defeat ❸ not great in intensity ❹ poor at doing something

weaken VERB to make something weaker or to become weaker

weakling NOUN a weak person or animal

weakly ADVERB without much strength or force

weakly ADJECTIVE sickly; not strong

weakness NOUN ❶ being weak ❷ a fault or something that you do not do well

weal NOUN a raised mark left on someone's flesh by a whip or blow

wealth NOUN ❶ a lot of money or property; riches ❷ a large quantity

wealthy ADJECTIVE having wealth; rich

wean VERB to get a baby used to taking food other than milk

weapon NOUN something used to harm or kill people in a battle or fight

weaponry NOUN weapons

wear VERB wears, wearing, wore, worn ❶ to have clothes, jewellery, etc. on your body ❷ to have a certain look on your face ❸ to damage something by rubbing or using it often; to become damaged in this way ❹ to last while being used

wear NOUN ❶ what you wear; clothes ❷ (also **wear and tear**) gradual damage done by rubbing or using something

wearisome ADJECTIVE causing weariness; tiring

weary ADJECTIVE ❶ worn out and tired ❷ tiring

weary VERB ❶ to make someone weary ❷ to grow tired of something

weasel NOUN a small fierce animal with a slender body and reddish-brown fur

weather NOUN the rain, snow, wind, sunshine etc. at a particular time or place

weather VERB ❶ to become worn or change colour because of the effects of the weather; to make something do this ❷ to come through a difficult time or experience successfully

weathercock, weathervane NOUN a pointer, often shaped like a cockerel, that turns in the wind and shows from which direction it is blowing

weave VERB weaves, weaving, wove, woven ❶ to make material or baskets by crossing threads or strips under and over each other ❷ to put a story together ❸ (past tense also **weaved**) to move from side to side to get round things in the way

weave NOUN a style of weaving

web NOUN ❶ a cobweb ❷ something complicated

webbed ADJECTIVE webbed feet have toes joined by pieces of skin, as ducks' and frogs' feet do

webcam *NOUN* a camera that is connected to a computer so that what it records can be seen on a website as it happens

weblog *NOUN* a blog

web page *NOUN* a document forming part of a website

website *NOUN* a place on the Internet where you can get information about a subject, company, etc.

wed *VERB* weds, wedding, wedded to marry someone

wedding *NOUN* the ceremony and celebration when a couple get married

wedge *NOUN* ❶ a piece of wood or metal that is thick at one end and thin at the other. It is pushed between things to force them apart or prevent something from moving. ❷ a wedge-shaped thing

wedge *VERB* ❶ to keep something in place with a wedge ❷ to pack things tightly together

wedlock *NOUN* the state of being married

Wednesday *NOUN* the day of the week following Tuesday

wee *ADJECTIVE* (*Scottish*) little or small

weed *NOUN* a wild plant that grows where it is not wanted

weed *VERB* to remove weeds from the ground

weedy *ADJECTIVE* ❶ full of weeds ❷ thin and weak

week *NOUN* ❶ a period of seven days, especially from Sunday to the following Saturday ❷ the part of the week that does not include the weekend

weekday *NOUN* a day other than Saturday or Sunday

weekend *NOUN* Saturday and Sunday

weekly *ADJECTIVE & ADVERB* happening or done once a week

weeny *ADJECTIVE* (*informal*) tiny

weep *VERB* weeps, weeping, wept ❶ to shed tears; to cry ❷ to ooze moisture in drops

weeping willow *NOUN* a willow tree that has drooping branches

weevil *NOUN* a kind of small beetle

weft *NOUN* the threads on a loom that are woven across the warp

weigh *VERB* ❶ to measure the weight of something ❷ to have a certain weight ❸ to be important or have influence

weight *NOUN* ❶ how heavy something is; the amount that something weighs ❷ a piece of metal of known weight, especially one used on scales to weigh things ❸ a heavy object, used to hold things down ❹ importance or influence

weight *VERB* to attach a weight to something

weightless *ADJECTIVE* having no weight, for example when travelling in space

weightlifting *NOUN* the sport or exercise of lifting heavy weights

weighty *ADJECTIVE* ❶ heavy ❷ serious and important

weir (say weer) *NOUN* a small dam across a river or canal to control the flow of water

a b c d e f g h i j k l m n o p q r s t u v w x y z

weird ADJECTIVE very strange or unnatural

welcome NOUN a greeting or reception, especially a kind or friendly one

welcome ADJECTIVE ❶ that you are glad to receive or see ❷ allowed or invited to do or take something

welcome VERB ❶ to show that you are pleased when a person arrives ❷ to be glad to receive or hear of something

weld VERB to join pieces of metal or plastic by heating and pressing or hammering them together

welfare NOUN people's health, happiness and comfort

welfare state NOUN a system in which a country's government provides money to pay for health care, social services, benefits, etc.

well ADVERB ❶ in a good or suitable way ❷ thoroughly; to a great extent ❸ probably or reasonably

well ADJECTIVE better, best ❶ in good health ❷ satisfactory; fine

well NOUN ❶ a deep hole dug to bring up water or oil from underground ❷ a deep space in a building, e.g. containing a staircase

well VERB to rise or flow up

well-being NOUN good health, happiness and comfort

wellies PLURAL NOUN (informal) wellingtons

wellingtons PLURAL NOUN rubber or plastic waterproof boots

well-known ADJECTIVE known by many people

well-mannered ADJECTIVE having good manners

well-meaning ADJECTIVE having good intentions

well-nigh ADVERB almost or nearly

well-read ADJECTIVE having read a lot of good books

well-to-do ADJECTIVE fairly rich

welt NOUN a raised mark left on someone's flesh by a whip or blow; a weal

welter NOUN a confused mixture; a jumble

wench NOUN (old use) a girl or young woman

wend VERB ➤ wend your way to go somewhere slowly or by an indirect route

werewolf NOUN in legends and stories, a person who changes into a wolf when the moon is full

west NOUN ❶ the direction where the sun sets, opposite east ❷ the western part of a country, city or other area

west ADJECTIVE & ADVERB towards or in the west; coming from the west

western ADJECTIVE of or in the west

western NOUN a film or story about cowboys or American Indians in western North America during the 19th and early 20th centuries

westward ADJECTIVE & ADVERB towards the west

wet ADJECTIVE ❶ soaked or covered in water or other liquid ❷ not yet dry ❸ rainy

wet VERB wets, wetting, wet or wetted to make something wet

wet suit NOUN a close-fitting rubber suit, worn by skin divers and windsurfers to keep them warm and dry

whack (*informal*) VERB to hit someone or something hard

whack NOUN a hard hit or blow

whale NOUN a very large sea mammal

whaler NOUN a person or ship that hunts whales

whaling NOUN hunting whales

wharf (say worf) NOUN a quay where ships are loaded and unloaded

what DETERMINER ❶ used to ask the amount or kind of something ❷ used to say how strange or great a person or thing is

what PRONOUN ❶ what thing or things ❷ the thing that

whatever PRONOUN ❶ anything or everything ❷ no matter what

whatever DETERMINER of any kind or amount

whatever ADVERB at all

whatsoever ADVERB at all

wheat NOUN a cereal plant from which flour is made

wheedle VERB to persuade someone to do something by coaxing or flattering them

wheel NOUN ❶ a round device that turns on a shaft that passes through its centre ❷ a steering wheel ❸ a horizontal revolving disc on which clay is made into a pot

wheel VERB ❶ to push a bicycle or trolley etc. along on its wheels ❷ to move or fly in a wide circle or curve

wheelbarrow NOUN a small cart with one wheel at the front and legs at the back, pushed by handles

wheelchair NOUN a chair on wheels, used by a person who cannot walk

wheel clamp NOUN (*British*) a device that can be locked around a vehicle's wheel to stop it from moving, used especially on cars that have been parked illegally

wheelie NOUN (*informal*) the stunt of riding a bicycle or motorcycle for a short distance with the front wheel off the ground

wheelie bin NOUN (*British*) a large dustbin on wheels

wheeze VERB to make a hoarse whistling sound as you breathe

wheeze NOUN the sound of wheezing

welk NOUN a shellfish that looks like a snail

whelp NOUN a young dog; a pup

when ADVERB at what time; at which time

when CONJUNCTION ❶ at the time that ❷ although; considering that

whence ADVERB (*formal*) from where; from which

whenever CONJUNCTION at whatever time; every time

where ADVERB & CONJUNCTION in or to what place or that place

where PRONOUN ❶ what place ❷ the place that

whereabouts ADVERB in or near what place

whereabouts PLURAL NOUN the place where something is

whereas CONJUNCTION but in contrast

whereby ADVERB by which; by means of which

A B C D E F G H I J K L M N O P Q R S T U V W X Y Z

whereupon CONJUNCTION after which; and then

wherever ADVERB in or to whatever place; no matter where

whet VERB to sharpen a blade or edge by rubbing it against a stone

whether CONJUNCTION used to show a doubt or choice between two possibilities; if

whetstone NOUN a shaped stone for sharpening tools

whey (say way) NOUN the watery liquid left when milk forms curds

which DETERMINER what particular

which PRONOUN ❶ what person or thing ❷ the person or thing referred to

whichever PRONOUN & DETERMINER no matter which; any which

whiff NOUN a slight smell of something

Whig NOUN a member of a political party in the 17th-19th centuries, opposed to the Tories

while CONJUNCTION ❶ during the time that; as long as ❷ although; but

while NOUN a period of time

while VERB ➤ **while away time** to pass time in a leisurely way

whilst CONJUNCTION during the time that; while

whim NOUN a sudden wish to do or have something

whimper VERB to cry or whine softly

whimper NOUN a sound of whimpering

whimsical ADJECTIVE slightly odd and playful

whine VERB ❶ to make a long high miserable cry or a shrill sound ❷ to complain in a petty or feeble way

whine NOUN a whining sound or cry

whinge VERB (British) (informal) to grumble persistently

whinny VERB a horse whinnies when it neighs gently or happily

whinny NOUN a gentle neigh

whip NOUN a cord or strip of leather fixed to a handle and used for hitting people or animals

whip VERB ❶ to beat a person or animal with a whip ❷ to beat cream until it becomes thick ❸ (informal) to steal something

whippet NOUN a small dog rather like a greyhound, used for racing

whirl VERB to turn or spin very quickly or to make something do this

whirl NOUN a quick turn or spin

whirlpool NOUN a whirling current of water, often drawing floating objects towards its centre

whirlwind NOUN a strong wind that whirls round a central point

whirr VERB to make a continuous buzzing sound

whirr NOUN a continuous buzzing sound

whisk VERB ❶ to move or brush something away quickly and lightly ❷ to take a person somewhere very quickly ❸ to beat eggs, etc. until they are frothy

whisk NOUN ❶ a kitchen tool used for whisking things ❷ a whisking movement

whisker NOUN ❶ whiskers are the long stiff hairs growing near the mouth of a cat ❷ a man's whiskers are the hair growing on his face, especially on his cheeks

whisky NOUN a strong alcoholic drink

whisper VERB ❶ to speak very softly ❷ to talk secretly; to spread a rumour

whisper NOUN ❶ a whispering tone of voice ❷ a rumour

whist NOUN a card game usually for four people

whistle VERB ❶ to make a shrill or musical sound by blowing through your lips ❷ to make a shrill sound

whistle NOUN ❶ a whistling sound ❷ a device that makes a shrill sound when air or steam is blown through it

whit NOUN the least possible amount

white NOUN ❶ the very lightest colour, like snow or salt ❷ the transparent substance (albumen) round the yolk of an egg, which turns white when it is cooked ❸ a person with light-coloured skin

white ADJECTIVE ❶ of the colour white ❷ having light-coloured skin ❸ very pale from the effects of illness, fear or worry ❹ white coffee is made with milk

whitebait NOUN a small silvery-white fish

white elephant NOUN a useless possession, especially one that is expensive to keep

white-hot ADJECTIVE extremely hot; so hot that heated metal looks white

white lie NOUN a harmless or trivial

lie that you tell in order to avoid hurting someone's feelings

whiten VERB to become white or to make something white

whitewash NOUN ❶ a white liquid containing lime or powdered chalk, used for painting walls and ceilings ❷ concealing mistakes or other unpleasant facts so that someone will not be punished

whitewash VERB to coat a wall or ceiling with whitewash

whither ADVERB (old use) to what place

whiting NOUN a small edible sea fish with white flesh

whittle VERB to shape wood by trimming thin slices off the surface

whizz, whiz VERB to move very quickly, often making a sound like something rushing through the air

who PRONOUN ❶ which person or people ❷ the particular person or people

whoa EXCLAMATION a command to a horse to stop or stand still

whoever PRONOUN ❶ any or every person who ❷ no matter who

whole ADJECTIVE ❶ complete; all of ❷ not broken or cut; in one piece

whole NOUN ❶ the full amount ❷ a complete thing

wholefood NOUN (British) food that has been processed as little as possible

wholehearted ADJECTIVE given without doubts or reservations

wholemeal ADJECTIVE (British) made from the whole grain of wheat

whole number NOUN a number without fractions

a
b
c
d
e
f
g
h
i
j
k
l
m
n
o
p
q
r
s
t
u
v
w
x
y
z

wholesale NOUN the business of selling goods in large quantities to be resold by others. Compare with retail.

wholesale ADJECTIVE & ADVERB ❶ on a large scale; including everybody or everything ❷ in the wholesale trade

wholesome ADJECTIVE healthy and good for you

wholly ADVERB completely or entirely

whom PRONOUN the form of who used when it is the object of a verb or comes after a preposition, as in *the boy whom I saw* or *to whom we spoke*

whoop (say woop) NOUN a loud cry of excitement

whoop VERB to give a whoop

whoopee EXCLAMATION a cry of joy

whooping cough (say hoop-ing) NOUN an infectious disease that causes spasms of coughing and gasping for breath

whopper NOUN (informal) ❶ something very large ❷ a blatant lie

whopping ADJECTIVE (informal) very large or remarkable

whorl NOUN ❶ a coil or curved shape ❷ a ring of leaves or petals

who's (mainly spoken) who is; who has

whose DETERMINER belonging to what person or persons; of whom; of which

why ADVERB for what reason or purpose; the particular reason on account of which

wick NOUN ❶ the string that goes

through the middle of a candle and is lit ❷ the strip of material that you light in a lamp or heater that uses oil

wicked ADJECTIVE ❶ morally bad or cruel ❷ mischievous ❸ (informal) excellent; very good

wicker NOUN thin canes or twigs woven together to make baskets, fences or furniture

wicket NOUN ❶ a set of three stumps and two bails used in cricket ❷ the strip of ground between the wickets

wicketkeeper NOUN the fielder in cricket who stands behind the batsman's wicket

wide ADJECTIVE ❶ measuring a lot from side to side; not narrow ❷ measuring from side to side ❸ covering a great range ❹ fully open ❺ missing the target

wide ADVERB ❶ to the full extent; far apart ❷ missing the target ❸ over a large area

widely ADVERB commonly; among many people

widen VERB to make something wider or to become wider

widespread ADJECTIVE existing in many places or over a wide area

widow NOUN a woman whose husband has died

widowed ADJECTIVE made a widow or widower

widower NOUN a man whose wife has died

width NOUN ❶ how wide something is ❷ the distance of a swimming pool from one side to the other

wield VERB ❶ to hold and use a

weapon or tool ② to have and use power or influence

wife *NOUN* wives the woman someone is married to

wi-fi *NOUN* the system for connecting computers, mobile phones, etc. to the Internet without using wires

wig *NOUN* a covering made of real or artificial hair, worn on the head

wiggle *VERB* to move something from side to side

wiggle *NOUN* a wiggling movement

wigwam *NOUN* a tent formerly used by Native Americans, made by fastening skins or mats over poles

wild *ADJECTIVE* ① wild animals and plants live or grow in their natural state and are not looked after by people ② wild land is in its natural state and has not been changed by people ③ not controlled; very violent or excited ④ very foolish or unreasonable ⑤ a wild guess has not been thought about carefully and is unlikely to be correct

wild *NOUN* ① the wild is the natural environment in which animals live ② the wilds are remote areas far from towns and cities

wildebeest *NOUN* a gnu

wilderness *NOUN* an area of natural land which is wild and uncultivated

wildfire *NOUN* ➤ spread like wildfire to spread or become known over a large area very fast

wildlife *NOUN* wild animals in their natural setting

wildly *ADVERB* ① in a way that is not controlled ② extremely; very

Wild West *NOUN* the western states of the USA during the period when the first Europeans were settling there and there was not much law and order

wiles *PLURAL NOUN* clever tricks that someone uses to get what they want

wilful *ADJECTIVE* ① obstinately determined to do what you want ② done deliberately

will *AUXILIARY VERB* used to talk about what will happen in the future and in questions or promises

will *NOUN* ① the mental power to decide and control what you do ② a desire; a chosen decision ③ determination to do something ④ a legal document saying what is to be done with someone's possessions when they die

will *VERB* wills, willing, willed to use your will power to try to influence something

willing *ADJECTIVE* ready and happy to do what is wanted

will-o'-the-wisp *NOUN* ① a flickering spot of light seen on marshy ground ② something that is impossible to achieve

willow *NOUN* a tree or shrub with flexible branches, usually growing near water

will power *NOUN* strength of mind to control what you do

willy-nilly *ADVERB* ① whether you want to or not ② without planning; haphazardly

wilt *VERB* ① a flower or plant wilts when it loses freshness and droops ② to lose your strength or energy

wily (say **wy-lee**) *ADJECTIVE* cunning

or crafty

wimp NOUN (*informal*) a weak or timid person

win VERB wins, winning, won ❶ to defeat your opponents in a game, contest or battle ❷ to get or achieve something by a victory or by using effort or skill ❸ to gain someone's favour or support

win NOUN a victory in a game or contest

wince VERB to make a slight movement because you are in pain or embarrassed

winch NOUN a device for lifting or pulling things, using a rope or cable that winds onto a revolving drum or wheel

winch VERB to lift or pull something with a winch

wind (rhymes with *tinned*) NOUN ❶ a current of air ❷ gas in the stomach or intestines that makes you feel uncomfortable ❸ the breath that you need to do something, e.g. for running or speaking ❹ the wind instruments of an orchestra

wind (rhymes with *tinned*) VERB winds, winding, winded to make a person out of breath

wind (rhymes with *find*) VERB winds, winding, wound ❶ to have a lot of bends or curves ❷ to wrap or twist a thing round something else ❸ to move something up or down by turning a handle ❹ (also **wind up**) to make a clock or watch work by tightening its spring

windbag NOUN (*informal*) a person who talks too much

windfall NOUN ❶ a piece of

unexpected good luck, especially a sum of money ❷ a fruit blown off a tree by the wind

wind farm NOUN a group of windmills or wind turbines for producing electricity

wind instrument NOUN a musical instrument played by blowing, e.g. a trumpet or flute

windlass NOUN a machine for pulling or lifting things (e.g. a bucket from a well), with a rope or cable that is wound round an axle by turning a handle

windmill NOUN a mill worked by the wind turning its sails

window NOUN ❶ an opening in a wall or roof or in the side of a vehicle to let in light and air, usually filled with glass ❷ (*in computing*) a framed area on a computer screen used for a particular purpose

window-shopping NOUN looking at things in shop windows but not buying anything

windpipe NOUN the tube by which air passes from the throat to the lungs

windscreen NOUN (*British*) the glass in the window at the front of a motor vehicle

windshield NOUN (*North American*) a windscreen

windsurfing NOUN the sport of surfing on a board that has a sail fixed to it

wind turbine NOUN a large modern windmill used for producing electricity

windward ADJECTIVE facing the

wind

windy ADJECTIVE with much wind

wine NOUN ① an alcoholic drink made from grapes or other plants ② a dark red colour

wing NOUN ① one of the pair of parts of a bird, bat or insect, that it uses for flying ② one of the pair of long flat parts that stick out from the side of an aircraft and support it while it flies ③ a part of a large building that extends from the main part ④ the part of a motor vehicle's body above a wheel ⑤ a player whose place is at one of the far ends of the forward line in football or hockey ⑥ a section of a political party, with more extreme opinions than the others

wing VERB ① to fly somewhere ② to wound a bird in the wing or a person in the arm

winged ADJECTIVE having wings

wingspan NOUN the length between the two wing tips of a bird or aircraft

wink VERB ① to close and open your eye quickly, especially as a signal to someone ② a light winks when it flickers or twinkles

wink NOUN ① the action of winking ② a very short period of sleep

winkle NOUN a kind of edible shellfish

winkle VERB ➤ **winkle something out** (chiefly British) to get information from someone with difficulty

winner NOUN ① a person, team or animal that wins something ② something very successful

winning ADJECTIVE attractive and charming

winnings PLURAL NOUN the money someone wins in a game or by gambling

winnow VERB to toss or fan grain so that the loose dry outer part is blown away

winter NOUN the coldest season of the year, between autumn and spring

winter VERB to spend the winter somewhere

wintry ADJECTIVE ① wintry weather is cold, like winter ② a wintry smile is cold and unfriendly

wipe VERB ① to dry or clean something by rubbing it ② to remove something by rubbing it

wipe NOUN the action of wiping

wiper NOUN a device for wiping something, especially on a vehicle's windscreen

wire NOUN ① a strand or thin flexible rod of metal ② a piece of wire used to carry electric current ③ a fence made from wire

wire VERB ① to fit or connect something with wires to carry electric current ② to fasten or strengthen something with wire

wireless ADJECTIVE able to send and receive signals without using wires

wireless NOUN (old use) a radio set

wiring NOUN the system of wires carrying electricity in a building or in a device

wiry ADJECTIVE ① a wiry person is lean and strong ② wiry hair is tough and stiff

wisdom NOUN ① being wise ② wise sayings or writings

wisdom tooth NOUN a molar tooth that may grow at the back of the jaw of a person aged about 20 or more

wise ADJECTIVE ❶ able to make sensible decisions and give good advice because of the experience and knowledge that you have ❷ sensible and showing good judgement

wish VERB ❶ to feel or say that you would like to have or do something or would like something to happen ❷ to say that you hope someone will get something

wish NOUN ❶ something you wish for; a desire ❷ the action of wishing

wishbone NOUN a forked bone between the neck and breast of a chicken or other bird

wishful thinking NOUN belief in something based on what you would like, not on the facts

wisp NOUN ❶ a few strands of hair or bits of straw etc. ❷ a small streak of smoke or cloud

wisteria, wistaria (say wist-**eer**-ee-a or wist-**air**-ee-a) NOUN a climbing plant with hanging blue, purple or white flowers

wistful ADJECTIVE sadly longing for something

wit NOUN ❶ the ability to think quickly and clearly and make good decisions ❷ a clever kind of humour ❸ a witty person

witch NOUN a person, especially a woman, who is thought to have magic powers

witchcraft NOUN the use of magic,

especially for evil purposes

witch doctor NOUN a magician who belongs to a tribe and is believed to use magic to heal people

with PREPOSITION used to indicate ❶ being in the company or care of someone ❷ having or wearing something ❸ using something ❹ because of something ❺ feeling or showing something ❻ towards or concerning something ❼ against someone or something

withdraw VERB withdraws, withdrawing, withdrew, withdrawn ❶ to take something away or take it back ❷ to go away from a place or stop taking part in something

withdrawal NOUN ❶ withdrawing something ❷ an amount of money taken out of an account ❸ the process of stopping taking drugs to which you are addicted, often with unpleasant reactions

withdrawn ADJECTIVE very shy or reserved

wither VERB ❶ a plant withers when it shrivels or wilts ❷ to become weaker then disappear

withering ADJECTIVE scornful or sarcastic

withers PLURAL NOUN the ridge between a horse's shoulder blades

withhold VERB withholds, withholding, withheld to refuse to give something to someone

within PREPOSITION & ADVERB inside; not beyond something

without PREPOSITION ❶ not having or using ❷ free from ❸ (old use) outside

withstand VERB withstands, withstanding, withstood to resist something or put up with it successfully

witness NOUN ❶ a person who sees or hears something happen ❷ a person who gives evidence in a law court

witness VERB ❶ to be a witness of something ❷ to sign a document to confirm that it is genuine

witted ADJECTIVE having wits of a certain kind

witticism NOUN a witty remark

witty ADJECTIVE clever and amusing; full of wit

wizard NOUN ❶ a man with magic powers; a magician ❷ a person with amazing abilities

wizardry NOUN ❶ the clever and impressive things that a person or thing can do ❷ the powers that a wizard has

wizened (say wiz-end) ADJECTIVE full of wrinkles

wobble VERB to move unsteadily from side to side or to make something do this

wobble NOUN a wobbling movement

wobbly ADJECTIVE moving unsteadily from side to side

woe NOUN ❶ great sorrow ❷ someone's woes are their troubles and misfortunes

woebegone ADJECTIVE looking unhappy

woeful ADJECTIVE ❶ very sad; full of woe ❷ very bad; disgraceful

wok NOUN a Chinese cooking pan

shaped like a large bowl

wolf NOUN wolves a fierce wild animal of the dog family, often hunting in packs

wolf VERB to eat something greedily

woman NOUN women a grown-up female human being

womanhood NOUN the condition of being a woman

womanly ADJECTIVE having qualities that are thought to be typical of women

womb (say woom) NOUN the hollow organ in a female's body where babies develop before they are born

wombat NOUN an Australian animal rather like a small bear

wonder VERB ❶ to feel that you want to know something; to try to decide about something ❷ to feel great surprise and admiration

wonder NOUN ❶ a feeling of surprise and admiration ❷ something that fills you with surprise and admiration; a marvel

wonderful ADJECTIVE marvellous or excellent

wonderment NOUN a feeling of wonder

wondrous ADJECTIVE (old use) wonderful; marvellous

wont (say wohnt) ADJECTIVE (old use) accustomed; used to doing something

wont NOUN a habit or custom

won't (mainly spoken) will not

woo VERB (old use) ❶ to try to win the love of a woman ❷ to seek someone's favour or support

wood NOUN ❶ the substance that

trees are made of **②** many trees growing close together

woodcut NOUN an engraving made on wood; a print made from this

wooded ADJECTIVE covered with growing trees

wooden ADJECTIVE **①** made of wood **②** stiff and showing no expression or liveliness

woodland NOUN wooded country

woodlouse NOUN a small crawling creature with seven pairs of legs, living in rotten wood or damp soil

woodpecker NOUN a bird that taps tree trunks with its beak to find insects

woodwind NOUN wind instruments that are usually made of wood, e.g. the clarinet and oboe

woodwork NOUN **①** making things out of wood **②** things made out of wood

woodworm NOUN the larva of a kind of beetle that bores into wooden furniture; the damage done to wood by this

woody ADJECTIVE **①** like wood; consisting of wood **②** full of trees

woof NOUN the gruff bark of a dog

wool NOUN **①** the thick soft hair of sheep and goats **②** thread or cloth made from this

woollen ADJECTIVE made of wool

woollens PLURAL NOUN clothes made of wool

woolly ADJECTIVE **①** covered with wool or wool-like hair **②** like wool or made of wool **③** not thinking clearly; vague or confused

word NOUN **①** a set of sounds or

letters that has a meaning and when written or printed has no spaces between the letters **②** a brief conversation **③** a promise **④** a command or spoken signal **⑤** a message or piece of news

word VERB to express something in words

word class NOUN any of the groups into which words are divided in grammar (noun, pronoun, determiner, adjective, verb, adverb, preposition, conjunction, exclamation)

wording NOUN the way something is worded

word of honour NOUN a solemn promise

word-perfect ADJECTIVE having memorized every word perfectly

word processor NOUN a type of computer or program used for editing and printing letters and documents

wore past tense of **wear**

work NOUN **①** something you have to do that needs effort or energy **②** a job; employment **③** something you write or produce at school **④** (in science) the result of applying a force to move an object **⑤** a piece of writing, painting, music, etc.

work VERB **①** to spend time doing something that needs effort or energy **②** to have a job or be employed **③** to act or operate correctly or successfully **④** to make something function or operate **⑤** to shape or press something **⑥** to gradually move into a particular position

workable *ADJECTIVE* that can be used or will work

worker *NOUN* ❶ a person who works in the working class ❷ a member of the working class ❸ a bee or ant that does the work in a hive or colony but does not produce eggs

workforce *NOUN* the number of people who work in a particular factory, industry, country, etc.

working class *NOUN* people who work for wages, especially in manual or industrial work

workman *NOUN* a man who works with his hands, especially at building or making things

workmanship *NOUN* a person's skill in making or producing something

work of art *NOUN* something produced by an artist, especially a painting or sculpture

workout *NOUN* a session of physical exercise or training

works *PLURAL NOUN* ❶ the moving parts of a machine ❷ a factory or industrial site

worksheet *NOUN* a sheet of paper with a set of questions about a subject for students, often used with a textbook

workshop *NOUN* a place where things are made or mended

world *NOUN* ❶ the earth with all its countries and peoples ❷ all the people on the earth; everyone ❸ a planet ❹ everything to do with a certain subject or activity

worldly *ADJECTIVE* ❶ to do with life on earth, not spiritual ❷ interested only in money, possessions and pleasure ❸ experienced about people and life

worldwide *ADJECTIVE & ADVERB* over the whole world

World Wide Web *NOUN* (*in computing*) a vast extensive information system that connects related sites and documents which can be accessed using the Internet

worm *NOUN* ❶ an animal with a long small soft rounded or flat body and no backbone or limbs ❷ (*informal*) an unimportant or unpleasant person

worm *VERB* to move along by wriggling or crawling

worn *past participle of* **wear**

worn *ADJECTIVE* damaged because it has been rubbed or used too much

worn-out *ADJECTIVE* ❶ tired and exhausted ❷ damaged by too much use

worried *ADJECTIVE* feeling or showing worry

worry *VERB* ❶ to feel anxious or troubled about something ❷ to make someone feel anxious or troubled about something ❸ an animal worries its prey when it holds it in its teeth and shakes it

worry *NOUN* ❶ worrying or being anxious ❷ something that makes a person worry

worse *ADJECTIVE & ADVERB* more bad or more badly; less good or less well

worsen *VERB* to become worse or to make something worse

worship *VERB* ❶ to give praise or respect to God or a god ❷ to love or respect a person or thing greatly

worship NOUN ❶ worshipping; religious ceremonies ❷ a title of respect for a mayor or certain magistrates

worst ADJECTIVE & ADVERB most bad or most badly; least good or least well

worsted NOUN a kind of woollen material

worth ADJECTIVE ❶ having a certain value ❷ deserving something; good or important enough for something

worth NOUN ❶ a person's or thing's value or usefulness ❷ the amount that a certain sum will buy

worthless ADJECTIVE having no value; useless

worthwhile ADJECTIVE important or good enough to deserve the time or effort needed

worthy ADJECTIVE deserving respect or support

would AUXILIARY VERB ❶ as the past tense of will ❷ used in questions and polite requests ❸ used with I and we and the verbs *like*, *prefer*, *be glad*, etc. ❹ used of something to be expected

would-be ADJECTIVE wanting or pretending to be something

wound (say woond) NOUN ❶ an injury done to someone's body, especially one in which the skin is cut ❷ a hurt to a person's feelings

wound (say woond) VERB ❶ to cause a wound to a person or animal ❷ to hurt a person's feelings

wound (say wownd) VERB past tense of wind VERB

wraith NOUN a ghost

wrangle VERB to have a noisy argument or quarrel

wrangle NOUN a noisy argument or quarrel

wrap VERB to put paper or some other covering round something

wrap NOUN ❶ a shawl or cloak worn to keep you warm ❷ a flour tortilla rolled around a filling and eaten as a sandwich

wrapper NOUN a piece of paper or plastic wrapped round something

wrapping NOUN material used to wrap something, especially a present

wrath (rhymes with *cloth*) NOUN extreme anger

wreak (say reek) VERB to cause great damage or harm

wreath (say reeth) NOUN ❶ flowers or leaves fastened into a circle ❷ a curving line of mist or smoke

wreathe (say reeth) VERB ❶ to surround or decorate something with a wreath ❷ to cover something ❸ to move in a curve

wreck VERB to damage or ruin something so badly that it cannot be used again

wreck NOUN ❶ a ship that has sunk or been very badly damaged ❷ the remains of a badly damaged vehicle or building ❸ a person who is in a bad mental or physical state

wreckage NOUN the pieces of a wreck

wren NOUN a very small brown bird

wrench VERB to twist or pull something violently

wrench NOUN ❶ a wrenching movement ❷ pain caused by parting ❸ an adjustable tool rather like a spanner, used for gripping and turning nuts or bolts

wrest VERB to take something away using force or effort

wrestle VERB ❶ to fight someone by grasping them and trying to throw them to the ground ❷ to struggle with a problem or difficulty

wrestle NOUN ❶ a wrestling match ❷ a hard struggle

wrestler NOUN a person who wrestles for sport

wretch NOUN ❶ a person who is very unhappy or who you pity ❷ a person who is disliked

wretched ADJECTIVE ❶ miserable or unhappy ❷ of bad quality ❸ not satisfactory; causing a nuisance

wriggle VERB to move with short twisting movements

wriggle NOUN a wriggling movement

wring VERB wrings, wringing, wrung ❶ to twist and squeeze a wet thing to get water out of it ❷ to squeeze something firmly or forcibly ❸ to get something by a great effort

wringer NOUN a device with a pair of rollers for squeezing water out of washed clothes

wrinkle NOUN ❶ wrinkles are the small lines and creases that appear in your skin as you get older ❷ a small crease in something

wrinkle VERB ❶ to make wrinkles in something ❷ to form wrinkles

wrist NOUN the joint that connects your hand to your arm

wristwatch NOUN a watch that you wear on your wrist

writ (say rit) NOUN a formal written command issued by a law court

write VERB writes, writing, wrote, written ❶ to put letters or words on paper or another surface ❷ to be the author or composer of something ❸ to send a letter to someone ❹ to enter data into a computer memory

writer NOUN a person who writes; an author

writhe VERB ❶ to twist your body about because of pain or discomfort ❷ to wriggle

writing NOUN ❶ something you write ❷ the way you write

wrong ADJECTIVE ❶ incorrect; not true ❷ not fair or morally right ❸ not working properly

wrong ADVERB wrongly

wrong NOUN something morally wrong; an injustice

wrong VERB to do wrong to someone; to treat a person unfairly

wrongdoer NOUN a person who does something dishonest or illegal

wrongful ADJECTIVE unfair or unjust; illegal

wrongly ADVERB in a way that is unfair or incorrect

wrought ADJECTIVE wrought iron or other metal is worked by being beaten out or shaped by hammering or rolling

wry ADJECTIVE slightly mocking or sarcastic

a
b
c
d
e
f
g
h
i
j
k
l
m
n
o
p
q
r
s
t
u
v
w
x
y
z

Xx

Xmas NOUN (*informal*) Christmas

X-ray NOUN a photograph or examination of the inside of something, especially a part of the body, made by a kind of radiation (called **X-rays**) that can penetrate solid things

X-ray VERB to make an X-ray of something

xylophone (say zy-lo-fohn) NOUN a musical instrument made of wooden bars of different lengths that you hit with small hammers

Yy

yacht (say yot) NOUN ❶ a sailing boat used for racing or cruising ❷ a private ship

yak NOUN an ox with long hair, found in central Asia

yam NOUN the edible root of a tropical plant, also known as a sweet potato

Yank NOUN (*informal*) a Yankee

yank (*informal*) VERB to pull something with a sudden sharp tug

yank NOUN a sudden sharp tug

Yankee NOUN an American, especially of the northern USA

yap VERB to bark in a noisy shrill way

yap NOUN a shrill bark

yard NOUN ❶ a measure of length, 36 inches or about 91 centimetres ❷ a long pole stretched out from a mast to support a sail ❸ an enclosed area beside a building or used for a certain kind of work

yarn NOUN ❶ thread spun by twisting fibres together, used in knitting, etc. ❷ (*informal*) a tale or story

yashmak NOUN a veil covering all of the face except for the eyes, worn by some Muslim women in public

yawn VERB ❶ to open your mouth wide and breathe in deeply because you feel sleepy or bored ❷ to form a wide opening

yawn NOUN an act of yawning

ye PRONOUN (*old use*) you (referring to two or more people)

yea (say yay) ADVERB (*old use*) yes

year NOUN ❶ the time the earth takes to go right round the sun, about 365¼ days ❷ the time from 1 January to 31 December ❸ any period of twelve months ❹ a group of students of roughly the same age

yearling NOUN an animal between one and two years old

yearly ADJECTIVE & ADVERB happening or done once a year

yearn VERB to long for something

yeast NOUN a substance that causes alcohol and carbon dioxide to form as it develops, used in making beer and wine and in baking bread

yell VERB to give a loud cry; to shout

yell NOUN a loud cry; a shout

yellow NOUN the colour of egg yolks and ripe lemons

yellow ADJECTIVE ❶ of yellow colour ❷ (*informal*) cowardly

yellow VERB to become yellow, especially with age

yelp VERB to give a shrill bark or cry, especially in pain

yelp NOUN a shrill bark or cry

yen NOUN ❶ a longing for something ❷ a unit of money in Japan

yeoman (say yoh-man) NOUN (old use) a man who owned and ran a small farm

yes EXCLAMATION used to agree to or accept something or as an answer meaning 'I am here'

yesterday NOUN & ADVERB the day before today

yet ADVERB ❶ up to this time; by this time ❷ eventually ❸ in addition; even

yet CONJUNCTION nevertheless

yeti NOUN a very large animal thought to live in the Himalayas, sometimes called the 'Abominable Snowman'

yew NOUN an evergreen tree with dark green needle-like leaves and red berries

yield VERB ❶ to give in or surrender ❷ to agree to do what is asked or ordered; to give way ❸ to produce a crop, profit or result

yield NOUN the amount yielded or produced

yodel VERB to sing or shout with your voice continually going from a low note to a high note and back again

yoga (say yoh-ga) NOUN a Hindu system of meditation and self-control; a system of physical exercises based on this

yoghurt, yogurt (say yog-ert) NOUN milk thickened by the action of certain bacteria, giving it a sharp taste

yoke NOUN ❶ a curved piece of wood put across the necks of animals pulling a cart or plough ❷ a shaped piece of wood fitted across a person's shoulders, with a pail or load hung at each end ❸ a close-fitting upper part of a piece of clothing, from which the rest hangs

yoke VERB to harness or join animals by means of a yoke

yokel (say yoh-kel) NOUN a simple country fellow

yolk (rhymes with coke) NOUN the round yellow part inside an egg

Yom Kippur (say yom kip-oor) NOUN the Day of Atonement, a solemn Jewish religious festival, a day of fasting and repentance

yon ADJECTIVE & ADVERB (dialect) over there; yonder

yonder ADJECTIVE & ADVERB (old use) over there

yore NOUN ➤ of yore of long ago

you PRONOUN ❶ the person or people being spoken to ❷ anyone or everyone; one

young ADJECTIVE having lived or existed for only a short time; not old

young PLURAL NOUN children or young animals or birds

youngster NOUN a child or young person

your DETERMINER belonging to you

you're (mainly spoken) you are

yours POSSESSIVE PRONOUN belonging to you

yourself PRONOUN you and nobody else. The word is used to refer back to the subject of a sentence

a b c d e f g h i j k l m n o p q r s t u v w x y z

(e.g. *Have you hurt yourself?*) or for emphasis (e.g. *You told me so yourself.*)

youth NOUN ❶ being young; the time when you are young ❷ a young man ❸ young people

youth club NOUN a club providing leisure activities for young people

youthful ADJECTIVE ❶ typical of young people ❷ young or looking young

youth hostel NOUN a place where young people can stay cheaply when they are hiking or on holiday

yo-yo NOUN a round wooden or plastic toy that moves up and down on a string that you hold

Yule NOUN (*old use*) the Christmas festival, also called **Yuletide**

yummy ADJECTIVE (*informal*) good to eat; delicious

Zz

zany ADJECTIVE funny in a weird or crazy way

zap VERB (*informal*) ❶ to attack or destroy something, especially in computer games ❷ to use a remote control to change television channels quickly

zeal NOUN enthusiasm or keenness

zealous (say zel-us) ADJECTIVE very keen or enthusiastic

zebra (say zeb-ra) NOUN an African animal of the horse family, with black and white stripes all over its body

zebra crossing NOUN (*British*) a place for pedestrians to cross a

road safely, marked with broad white stripes

zenith NOUN ❶ the part of the sky directly above you ❷ the highest point of something

zephyr (say zef-er) NOUN a soft gentle wind

zero NOUN zeros ❶ nought; the figure 0 ❷ the point marked 0 on a thermometer or other scale

zero VERB ➤ zero in on something to focus your aim or attention on something

zest NOUN ❶ great enjoyment or enthusiasm ❷ the coloured part of orange or lemon peel

zigzag NOUN a line or route that turns sharply from side to side

zigzag VERB to move in a series of sharp turns from one side to the other

zinc NOUN a white metal

zip NOUN ❶ a fastener consisting of two strips of material, each with rows of small teeth that fit together when a sliding tab brings them together ❷ liveliness or energy

zip VERB ❶ to fasten or close something with a zip ❷ to move quickly with a sharp sound ❸ (*in computing*) to compress a computer file in order to email it at a higher speed or for long-term storage

zodiac (say zoh-dee-ak) NOUN a strip of sky where the sun, moon and main planets are found, divided into twelve equal parts (called **signs of the zodiac**), each named after a constellation

zombie NOUN ❶ (*informal*) a person

who seems to be doing things without thinking, usually because they are very tired ❷ in voodoo and horror films, a corpse that has been brought back to life by witchcraft

zone NOUN an area of a special kind or for a particular purpose

zoo NOUN a place where wild animals are kept so that people can look at them or study them

zoology (say zoh-**ol**-o-jee) NOUN the scientific study of animals

zoom VERB ❶ to move or travel very quickly ❷ to rise or increase quickly ❸ to use a zoom lens to change from a distant view to a close-up

zoom lens NOUN a camera lens that can be adjusted to focus on things that are close up or far away

zucchini (say **zoo**-keen-ee) NOUN (North American) a courgette

Zulu NOUN a member of a South African people; the language spoken by this people

Vocabulary Toolkit

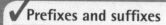

✓ Prefixes and suffixes

Common prefixes

A **prefix** is a group of letters joined to the beginning of a word to change its meaning, e.g.

| *re-* | **re**capture | = to capture again |
| *un-* | **un**known | = not known |

Some **prefixes** already form part of the word, e.g.

| *com-* | **com**municate | = to make contact with |

Once you know how **prefixes** work, you can use them to give existing words new meanings. Because there are so many possible combinations, not all words that begin with prefixes can be included in this dictionary.

Here are some examples of the more common English prefixes:

prefix	meaning	example
an-	not, without	anarchy
anti-	against	anti-British
arch-	chief	archbishop
auto-	self	automatic
co-	together	coeducation
com-, con-	together, with	communicate
contra-	against	contradict
cyber-	to do with electronic communication	cyberspace, cybercafe
de-	undoing or taking away	derail
dis-	not	dishonest
dis-	taking away	disconnect

prefix	meaning	example
eco-	to do with ecology and the environment	ecosystem
em-, en-	in, into	embark, entrust
ex-	that used to be, former	ex-president
extra-	beyond, outside	extraordinary, extraterrestrial
fore-	before, in front of	forefinger, foregoing
giga-	times 10^9 or (in ICT) 2^{30}	gigabyte
in-, il- im-, ir-	not	incorrect, illegal, impossible, irrelevant
inter-	between	international
mega-	times 10^6 or (in ICT) 2^{20}	megabyte
mis-	wrong	misbehave
mono-	one, single	monotone
multi-	many	multimedia
non-	not	non-existent
over-	too much	overdo
poly-	many	polygon
post-	after	post-war
pre-	before	prehistoric
pro-	supporting	pro-British
re-	again	recapture
semi-	half	semicircle
sub-	below	submarine
super-	over, beyond	superstore
tele-	at a distance	telecommunications
trans-	across	transport, transatlantic
ultra-	beyond	ultrasonic
un-	not, the opposite of	unknown, undo

Common suffixes

A **suffix** is a group of letters joined to the end of a word to change its meaning, e.g.

-able	eatable	= able to be eaten
-er	maker	= a person or machine that makes something
-ness	happiness	= the state of being happy

Suffixes often change the way that the word functions in the sentence, e.g.

| work – verb | worker – noun | workable – adjective |

Suffixes can be used to make many different combinations and not all of them are included in this dictionary. You can also make words with more than one suffix, e.g. *childishness* and *childishly*.

Here are some examples of the more common English suffixes:

suffix	meaning	example
-able, -ible -uble	able to be	eatable, accessible soluble
-dom	used to make nouns to do with condition or rank	martyrdom
-ee	someone who is affected	employee, refugee
-er	a person or thing that does something	maker, opener
-er	more	faster
-esque	in the style of	picturesque
-ess	a female person or animal	actress, lioness
-est	most	fastest
-ful	full (of)	beautiful, cupful
-hood	used to make nouns to do with state or condition	childhood, motherhood

suffix	meaning	example
-ic	belonging to, associated with	Islamic, terrific
-ish	rather like, somewhat	childish, greenish
-ism	used to make nouns to do with systems and beliefs	capitalism, Hinduism
-ist	someone who does something or believes something	dentist, Communist
-itis	used to make nouns for illnesses involving inflammation	appendicitis, tonsillitis
-ize	used to make verbs	criticize
-ise	used to make verbs	televise
-less	not having, without	senseless
-let	small	booklet
-like	like, resembling	childlike
-ling	a small person or thing	seedling
-ly	used to make adverbs and adjectives	bravely, leisurely
-ment	used to make nouns	amusement
-ness	used to make nouns	kindness, happiness
-oid	like or resembling	celluloid
-or	a person or thing that does something	sailor, escalator
-ous	used to make adjectives	dangerous
-ship	used to make nouns	friendship, citizenship
-some	full of	loathsome
-tion	used to make nouns	abbreviation, ignition, completion
-ty	used to make nouns	ability, anxiety
-ward,	in a particular direction	backward
-wards	in a particular direction	northwards

✓ Confusable words and phrases

Common errors

These words and phrases are easy to confuse. A dictionary will help you to choose the correct meaning for any words that you are unclear about.

all right / alright

➤ Are you **all right**? ➤ It's cold **all right**.

The correct spelling is as two words: **all right**.

advice / advise

Advice is a noun.

➤ She gave me one piece of **advice**: ignore the email.

Advise is a verb.

➤ She **advised** me to ignore the email.

affect / effect

Affect is a verb. It means 'to make a difference to something'. It can also mean 'to pretend'.

➤ My asthma **affects** my breathing.

➤ She **affected** ignorance about the test.

Effect is a noun. It means 'a result'. It can also be used as a verb meaning 'to bring about'.

➤ The weather has a big **effect** on my mood.

breath / breathe

Breath is a noun. It sounds similar to 'bread'.

➤ I am out of **breath**. ➤ Take a big **breath**.

Breathe (which sounds like 'breethe') is a verb.

➤ I can **breathe** underwater.

➤ Don't **breathe** a word of this to anyone.

past / passed

Past is a noun meaning 'the time gone by'.
> It happened in the **past**.

It is also a preposition meaning 'beyond a certain place' or 'after a certain time'.
> I walk **past** the bus stop everyday.
> It is **past** six now.

Passed is the past tense of the verb 'to pass'.
> She **passed** me a sweet. > I **passed** my exam!

stationery / stationary

Stationery is a noun meaning papers, pencils and envelopes.
> I got my pen in the **stationery** section.

The word 'envelope' begins with an 'e', so you can use it to remind you that stationery also has an 'e' in it.

Stationary is an adjective meaning 'not moving'.
> The car was **stationary** when it was hit by the van.

double negatives

You should never use **two negative words** together to make a **negative** statement:
> I **don't** want **no** more.
> They **never** said **nothing** about it.

The correct versions are:
> I **don't** want any more.
> They **never** said anything about it.

But you can use a **negative word** with a word beginning with a **negative prefix** like **in-** or **un-**. The two negatives cancel each other out and produce a **positive** meaning:
> The town is **not unattractive**.

This means that the town is fairly attractive.

I / me

You use *I* when it is the subject of a verb:
> ➤ *I want to see you.*

Strictly speaking you should use *I* also in sentences such as
It is I who saw you. This is because what comes after the verb
be should 'agree' with what comes before. I is the subject of the
verb *be* (here in the form *is*). But in informal conversation it is
acceptable to say *It is me* or *It was him.*

You use *me* when it is the object of a verb or comes after a
preposition such as *to* or *with*:
> ➤ *Give it to me.*
> ➤ *He came with me.*

You may be unsure whether to use *you and I* or *you and me*
when you have more than one pronoun together.

The rule is exactly the same: use *you and I* when it is the subject
of the verb 'be' in the sentence.
> ➤ *You and I were both there.*
> ➤ *This is a picture of you and me.*

it's / its

It is very important to remember the difference the apostrophe
makes.
It's (with an apostrophe) is short for 'it is' or 'it has':
> ➤ *It's (= it is) very late now.*
> ➤ *I think it's (= it has) been raining.*

Its (without an apostrophe) is a word like *his* and *their* (called a
possessive determiner) and means 'belonging to it':
> ➤ *The cat licked its paw.*
> ➤ *The class wrote its own dictionary.*

Homophones

These are words that sound the same but they have different meanings and spellings. Because they sound the same, they are easy to get confused. If you are not sure which word to use in a particular sentence, check both spellings in the dictionary.

new	—	knew	no	—	know
right	—	write	through	—	threw
hole	—	whole	great	—	grate
for	—	four, fore	heard	—	herd
see	—	sea	be	—	bee
blue	—	blew	bare	—	bear
one	—	won	cheap	—	cheep
night	—	knight	hear	—	here
vain	—	vein, vane	currant	—	current
dessert	—	desert	yolk	—	yoke

✔ Phrases from different languages

Sometimes foreign phrases are used to express an idea which is tricky to give in English.

ad infinitum (in-fi-ny-tum)
without limit; for ever
(Latin = to infinity)

à la carte
ordered and paid for as separate items from a menu
(French = from the menu)

alfresco
in the open air *an alfresco meal*
(from Italian al fresco = in the fresh air)

alter ego
another, very different, side of someone's personality
(Latin = other self)

angst
a strong feeling of anxiety or dread about something
(German = fear)

au fait (oh fay)
knowing a subject or procedure etc. well
(French = to the point)

au revoir (oh rev-wahr)
goodbye for the moment
(French = until seeing again)

avant-garde (av-ahn-gard)
people who use a modern style in art or literature etc.
(French = vanguard)

bona fide (boh-na fy-dee)
genuine; without fraud
(Latin = in good faith)

bon voyage (bawn vwah-yahzh)
(have a) pleasant journey!
(French)

carte blanche (kart blahnsh)
freedom to act as you think best
(French = blank paper)

c'est la vie (say la vee)
life is like that *(French = that is life)*

coup de grâce (koo der grahs)
a stroke or blow that puts an end to something
(French = mercy blow)

coup d'état (koo day-tah)
the sudden overthrow of a government
(French = blow of State)

crème de la crème (krem der la krem) the very best of something
(French = cream of the cream)

déjà vu (day-zha vew)
a feeling that you have already experienced what is happening now
(French = already seen)

dolce vita (dol-chay-vee-ta)
life of pleasure and luxury
(*Italian = sweet life*)

doppelgänger (doppel-geng-er) someone who looks exactly like someone else; a double
(*German = double-goer*)

en bloc (ahn blok)
all at the same time; in a block
(*French*)

en masse (ahn mass)
all together
(*French = in a mass*)

en route (ahn root)
on the way
(*French*)

entente (ahn-tahnt or on-tont)
a friendly understanding between nations
(*French*)

eureka (yoor-eek-a)
I have found it (i.e. the answer)!
(*Greek*)

faux pas (foh pah)
an embarrassing blunder
(*French = false step*)

gung-ho (gung-hoh)
eager to fight or take part in a war (*Chinese gonghe = work together, used as a slogan*)

hara-kiri (hara-kee-ri)
ritual suicide by cutting open the stomach with a sword
(*Japanese = belly cutting*)

Homo sapiens
human beings regarded as a species of animal
(*Latin = wise man*)

honcho
a leader
(*Japanese = group leader*)

hors-d'oeuvre (or-dervr)
food served as an appetizer at the start of a meal
(*French = outside the work*)

in memoriam
in memory (of) (*Latin*)

in situ (sit-yoo)
in its original place
(*Latin*)

joie de vivre (zhwah der veevr)
a feeling of great enjoyment of life (*French = joy of life*)

kowtow (rhymes with cow)
to obey someone slavishly
(*Chinese = knock the head, from the old practice of kneeling and touching the ground with the forehead as a sign of submission*)

laissez-faire (lay-say-fair)
not interfering
(*French = let (them) act*)

luau (loo-ow)
a party or feast
(*Hawaiian lu'au = feast*)

macho (mach-oh)
masculine in an aggressive way
(*Spanish = male*)

mano a mano (mah-noh a mah-noh)
(of a meeting, fight, etc.) between two people only; face to face *(Spanish = hand to hand)*

modus operandi (moh-dus op-er-and-ee)
❶ a person's way of working. ❷ the way a thing works *(Latin = way of working)*

nota bene (noh-ta ben-ee)
(usually shortened to NB) note carefully *(Latin = note well)*

par excellence (par eks-el-ahns)
more than all the others; to the greatest degree *(French = because of special excellence)*

per annum
for each year; yearly *(Latin)*

pièce de résistance (pee-ess der ray-zees-tahns)
the most important item *(French)*

quid pro quo
something given or done in return for something *(Latin = something for something)*

raison d'être (ray-zawn detr)
the purpose of a thing's existence *(French = reason for being)*

rigor mortis (ry-ger mor-tis)
stiffening of the body after death *(Latin = stiffness of death)*

RIP
may he or she (or they) rest in peace
(short for Latin *requiescat* (or *requiescant*) *in pace*)

sang-froid (sahn-frwah)
calmness in danger or difficulty *(French = cold blood)*

Schadenfreude (shah-den-froi-da)
pleasure at seeing someone else in trouble or difficulty *(German = harm joy)*

sotto voce (sot-oh voh-chee)
in a very quiet voice *(Italian = under the voice)*

status quo (stay-tus kwoh)
the state of affairs as it was before a change *(Latin = the state in which)*

terra firma
dry land; the ground *(Latin = firm land)*

tête-à-tête (tayt-ah-tayt)
a private conversation, especially between two people *(French = head to head)*

verboten (fer-boh-ten)
not allowed; forbidden *(German = forbidden)*

vis-à-vis (veez-ah-vee)
❶ in a position facing one another; opposite to. ❷ as compared with *(French = face to face)*

✓ Idioms

Idioms are groups of words that have a meaning that is often impossible to work out on your own. This is frequently because they refer to ideas or beliefs that are no longer current. In a dictionary an idiom will often be listed at the end of the entry of its key word. Below are some interesting examples.

an Achilles' heel

a weak or bad point in a person who is otherwise strong or good
(From the story of the Greek hero Achilles: his mother Thetis had dipped him in the River Styx because the water would prevent him from harm, but the water did not cover the heel by which she held him. So when the Trojan prince Paris killed Achilles he did it by throwing a spear into his heel.)

an albatross round someone's neck

something that is a constant worry or cause of feeling guilty
(An albatross was supposed to bring good luck to sailors at sea. In Coleridge's 1798 poem The Rime of the Ancient Mariner, the mariner (= sailor) shoots an albatross and this brings a curse on the ship. The crew force the mariner to wear the dead albatross round his neck as a punishment.)

in seventh heaven

blissfully happy
(In some religions, the seventh heaven is the last in a series of heavens that people's souls pass through after death.)

get out of bed on the wrong side

to be irritable all day
(The idea is that you are irritable from the moment you get up in the morning.)

a stiff upper lip

you are said to have a stiff upper lip when you are brave and self-controlled when life is difficult or dangerous
(Because the upper lip trembles when you are nervous or frightened. The phrase sounds British but in fact it occurs earliest in American writing.)

eat humble pie

to have to apologize or admit you were wrong about something
(A play on the words humble and umbles, which were the inner organs of deer or other animals used in pies.)

under the weather

feeling unwell or fed up
(A ship at sea was under the weather when a storm was overhead, making it uncomfortable for the people on board.)

the spitting image
a person who looks exactly like someone else
(From a strange old idea that a person could spit out an identical person from their mouth.)

have a chip on your shoulder
to feel jealous and resentful about life and the way you are treated compared with other people
(From an old American custom in which a person would place a chip of wood on their shoulder as a challenge to another person, who would accept the challenge by knocking the chip off.)

once in a blue moon
very rarely; hardly ever
(A blue moon is a second full moon in a month, which occurs rarely.)

out of the blue
without any warning; as a complete surprise
(Like something coming suddenly out of the blue of the sky.)

back to square one
back to the starting point after a failure or mistake
(Probably from the idea of going back to the first square as a penalty in a board game. Some people think the phrase is connected with early football commentaries, but this is unlikely.)

go hell for leather
at full speed
(From horse-riding, because the reins were made of leather, and people thought that going to hell must be very fast and reckless.)

break the ice
to make the first move in a conversation or undertaking
(From the idea of ships in very cold regions having to break through the ice to pass through.)

let the cat out of the bag
to reveal a secret by mistake
(Because cats do not like being confined, and it would be be hard to keep one in a bag in this way.)

full of beans
lively and energetic
(Horses used to be fed on beans to make them healthy.)

by hook or by crook
somehow or other; by any means possible
(From a practice in medieval times of allowing tenants to take as much firewood as they could from the trees by using these two tools.)

like water off a duck's back
having no effect on a person; making no impression
(Because water runs off the feathers of a duck without soaking through.)

from the horse's mouth
you get information straight from the horse's mouth when it comes from the person or people who originated it or who are most likely to know about it
(The idea is of someone wanting to make a bet asking the horses

themselves which one is likely to win the race.)

a wild goose chase
a pointless and hopeless search for something
(Originally a kind of horse race in which a leading horse had to run an erratic course which the other horses had to follow: wild geese run about in all directions.)

the lion's share
the largest share or part of something
(Because lions, being very strong and fierce, get the largest share of a killed animal's carcass; originally this expression meant 'all of something' as lions were not thought to share.)

have your cake and eat it
you say someone wants to have their cake and eat it when they seem to want to have or do two things when only one of them is possible
(Because if you eat your cake you cannot still 'have' it: have here means 'keep'.)

come up to scratch
to be good or strong enough for what is needed
(Scratch is the line marking the start of a race or other sports event.)

on the ball
alert and quick to act
(A player in a game is on the ball when they have possession of it and are playing it well.)

show somebody the ropes
to give someone basic instruction in a task or activity
(From the days of sailing ships, when ropes were used to control the ship's rigging.)

hit the nail on the head
to say something exactly right or suitable
(From the idea of hitting a nail squarely on the head with a hammer, so that it goes in well.)

pass the buck
to leave something you should take responsibility for for someone else to deal with
(In the game of poker the buck was a small piece placed in front of the dealer.)

rain cats and dogs
to rain very hard
(We cannot be sure where this phrase comes from and it may just be fanciful; originally it was the other way round: rain dogs and cats. One of the earliest uses is by Jonathan Swift, the author of Gulliver's Travels, in the 18th century.)

at sixes and sevens
with everything very confused and muddled
(The phrase is very old and is probably connected with throwing dice, because there is no 'seven' on a dice and so sixes and sevens would be impossible.)

✓ Proverbs

A proverb is a sentence that gives a piece of advice or says something wise or true.

all's well that ends well
If things succeed in the end then it doesn't matter so much about the troubles or difficulties experienced on the way.

an apple a day keeps the doctor away
If you eat well you will stay healthy and you won't need to see the doctor.

better late than never
Something done at the last moment is better than not doing it at all.

better safe than sorry
If in doubt it is better to be cautious than to take an unnecessary risk.

every cloud has a silver lining
Bad situations can often have some benefits.

once bitten, twice shy
Someone who has had a bad experience will avoid the same situation another time.

there's no time like the present
It is best to get on with a task straight away and not delay.

the proof of the pudding is in the eating
You can often only tell how good or useful something is by trying it.

a rolling stone gathers no moss
Someone who does not settle down in one place does not become important or wealthy. (Moss does not start to grow on stones that are moving.)

there's no smoke without fire
Rumours and reports usually have some truth about them. (If you can see smoke it usually means there is a fire near.)

a stitch in time saves nine
If you act promptly you will save yourself trouble later. (From the idea of mending clothes with stitches: *nine* is used because it makes a good rhyme with *time*.)

strike while the iron's hot
to act at the right moment (From metalwork, in which iron is shaped when hot by hitting it with a hammer.)